Operations Management

Operations Management

Fourth Edition
Jack R. Meredith
Scott M. Shafer
Wake Forest University

International Student Version

WILEY

John Wiley & Sons, Inc.

This book is dedicated to the Newest Generation:

Avery and Mitchell

J. R. M.

Brianna, Sammy, and Kacy

S. M. S.

Contents

Chapter 1:

Competitive Operations for the Global Arena/3

        Operations/7
        Customer Value/14
        Strategy and Competitiveness/25
        From Strategy to Structure/41

Chapter 2:

Designing the Transformation System/51

        Forms of Transformation Systems/55
        Selection of a Transformation System/77

Chapter 3:

Monitoring and Controlling the Transformation System/93

        Monitoring and Control/96
        Process Monitoring/97
        Process Control/104
        Controlling Service Quality/112

Chapter 4:

Six Sigma for Improving the Transformation System/123

        Approaches for Process Improvement/127
        Business Process Design (Reengineering)/128
        Six Sigma and the DMAIC Improvement Process/132
        Example Six Sigma Project/135
        The Define Phase/136
        The Measure Phase/142
        The Analyze Phase/152
        The Improve Phase/ 159
        The Control Phase /162
        Six Sigma In Practice/162

Chapter 5:

Lean Operations Improve Transformation System Value/171

History and Philosophy of Lean/175
Traditional Systems Compared with Lean/177
Specify Value/184
Identify the Value Stream/185
Make Value Flow/190
Pull Value Through the Value Stream/195
Pursue Perfection/198
Benefits of Lean/201
Lean Six Sigma/202

Chapter 6:

Project Management and the Transformation System/207

Defining a Project/210
Planning the Project/212
Scheduling the Project/221
Controlling the Project: Earned Value/236

Chapter 7:

Managing Supply Chain Logistics and Inventories/245

Defining Supply Chain Management/249
Supply Chain Strategy/252
Supply Chain Design/256
Outsourcing and Global Sourcing/261
Inventory Management/267
Role of Information Technology/272
Successful Supply Chain Management/277
The Beer Game/283
The Economic Order Quantity Model/289

Chapter 8:

Capacity Management through Location and Scheduling/295

Long-term Capacity Planning/299
Location Planning Strategies/305
Locating Pure Services/312
Effectively Utilizing Capacity Through Schedule Management/314

Short-term Capacity Planning/325
Forecasting/351
Forecasting Purposes and Methods/352
Time Series Analysis/355
Causal Forecasting with Regression/365

Cases/377

Index/419

Preface

The enthusiasm of the users of this MBA-oriented book has been greatly rewarding for us and we thank them for their comments, suggestions, criticism, and support. Although the book is not the massive seller that an undergraduate textbook can become, it is clear that there is, as we felt, a need for a solely MBA-level text. The book was originally written because of the express need we felt in our many MBA programs at Wake Forest University for an operations management textbook directed specifically to MBA students, and especially to those who had some real-world experience. We tried all of the current texts but found them either tomes that left no time for the cases and other materials we wanted to include or shorter but simplistic quantitative books. Moreover, all the books were so expensive they did not allow us to order all the cases, readings, and other supplements and class activities (such as the "Beer Game," see Chapter 7 Supplement) that we wanted to include in our course.

What we were looking for was a short, inexpensive book that would cover just the introductory, basic, and primarily conceptual material. This would allow us, as the professors, to tailor the course through supplementary cases and other materials for the unique class we would be teaching: executive, evening, full-time, short course, and so on. Although we wanted a brief, supplementary-type book so that we could add other material, we have colleagues who need a short book because they only have a half-semester module for the topic. Or they may have to include another course (e.g., management science or statistics) in the rest of the quarter or semester. In addition, we didn't need the depth of most texts that have two extensive chapters on supply chain management, two long chapters on scheduling, two chapters on quality, and so on; one chapter on each topic would be sufficient for our needs.

Changes in this Fourth Edition

The major changes in this edition are three. First, the book is now in two colors, as we hope you've noticed. We wanted to use the color to spruce up the figures and exhibits in particular, as well as facilitate easier and faster coverage of this basic material through color-coded sectioning and such. Second, we have added cases to the rear part of the book, some short and some long. Possible questions for the cases, as well as teaching notes, are included in the instructor's manual. Many of the cases can apply equally well to multiple chapters, and suggestions for doing this are also in the instructor's manual.

But the major change has been a complete reorganization of the material to emphasize the current thrusts of operations management: strategy, six sigma, lean, and supply chain management. The reviewers of the last edition were almost unanimous in suggesting this reorganization, some stating that we only really needed these four chapters and to either toss the rest or combine it with these topics. But other reviewers suggested perhaps five, or six chapters, but not always the same set of topics. We definitely agreed with their view, and set about to see how some reorganization along those lines might work. The result is eight chapters, not quite as succinct as some would have liked, but a major decrease from the previous eleven.

To capture the new direction of operations and also help clarify our new organization, we decided to divide the book into four parts: I: Operations Strategy, II: Operations Processes, III: Supply Chain Management, and IV: Cases. Part I includes just one chapter that combines our previous introduction/explanation of operations chapter with the strategy chapter. Part II focuses on processes, starting with a chapter on process planning and then followed by a chapter on process control (including quality). We then move into process improvement with two chapters, one on six sigma and another on lean. Finally, we cover implementing process improvement through project management. We have simplified some of the project management material by focusing only on activity-on-node networks, and combining previous examples; we then use a new six-sigma example for illustration. We have also added a bit more material on project management including managing project portfolios, constructing a project plan, creating a baseline schedule, and setting up a project responsibility matrix.

Part III includes only two chapters. The first covers the overall management of the supply chain, including logistics, inventory, and ERP material from other previous chapters. As well as the Beer Game supplement, we have added another supplement on the EOQ inventory model. The second chapter in this section covers capacity, scheduling, and location issues, with some of the material from the old scheduling chapter folded in here. To respond to frequent requests, the chapter has a supplement on forecasting.

In revising the book, we have kept the elements of our earlier philosophy. For example, we kept the other majors such as marketing and finance in mind—what did these students need to know about operations to help them in their careers? And we still minimize the heavier quantitative material, keeping only discussions and examples that illustrate a particular concept since finance and marketing majors would not be solving operations problems. Moreover, even operations managers probably wouldn't themselves be solving those problems; more likely, they would be assigned to an analyst. For those chapters in which exercises are included, they are intended only to help illustrate the concept we are trying to convey rather than make experts of the students.

We continued to add service examples throughout the text, since the great majority (over 80 percent these days!) of our students would be or are already employed in a service organization. And since these students will be working and competing in a highly global economy, we employ many international examples. We also kept the organization chart of the topics at the beginning of each chapter so the instructor and students can quickly and easily see what is coming and how it is organized. And we kept the textual flow of material in the chapters away from the current undergraduate trend of fracturing the material flow with sidebars, examples, applications, solved problems, and so forth, in an attempt to keep the students' interest and attention. Given the maturity of MBA students we instead worked these directly into the discussions to attain a smoother, clearer flow. We also added new examples for the chapter opener and wrote some new end-of-chapter caselettes that can form the basis of an interesting class discussion. As noted below, the Instructor's Manual includes suggestions for readings, cases, videos, and other course supplements that we have found to be particularly helpful for MBA classes since this book is intended to be only a small part of the MBA class.

Supplements

Our approach to supplementary MBA-level material here is to reference and annotate in the Instructor's Manual additional useful cases, books, video clips, and readings for each of the eight textbook chapters. The annotation is intended to help the instructors select the most appropriate materials for their unique course. Although, we have added some of our own and our colleagues' cases to the rear of this edition, we also rely on our favorite Harvard, Darden, Western Ontario, and European cases, plus *Harvard Business Review* readings to fully communicate the nature of the chapter topic we are covering. Although we didn't think that Test Bank Questions or PowerPoint slides would be used by most MBA instructors, these materials are available from the publisher also. For that matter, the publisher can also custom bind selected content from this text, our larger undergraduate (or any other) Web text, along with cases and articles, should this approach be of interest to the professor. Please contact your local Wiley representative for more details.

Your Inputs Appreciated

We would once again like to encourage users of this book to send us their comments and suggestions. Tell us if there is something we missed that you would like to see in the next edition (or the Instructor's Manual or web site) or if there is perhaps material that is unneeded for this audience. Also, please tell us about any errors you uncover, or if there are other elements of the book you like or don't like. We hope to continue keeping this a living, dynamic project that evolves to meet the needs of the MBA audience, an audience whose needs are also evolving as our economy and society evolve and change.

We want to thank the many reviewers of this book and its previous editions: Satya Chakravorty, Kennesaw State University; James A. Fitzsimmons, University of Texas; Lawrence D. Fredendall, Clemson University; William C. Giauque, Brigham Young University; Mike Godfrey, University of Wisconsin Oshkosh; Damodar Golhar, Western Michigan University; Suresh Kumar Goyal, Concordia University, Canada; Hector Guerrero, The College of William & Mary; Robert Handfield, North Carolina State University; Mark Gerard Haug, University of Kansas; Janelle Heineke, Boston University; David Hollingworth, Rensselaer Polytechnic Institute; James L. Hoyt, Troy State University; Mehdi Kaighobadi, Florida Atlantic University; Archie Lockamy III, Samford University; Manoj Malhotra, University of South Carolina; Gus Manoochehri, California State University, Fullerton; Robert F. Marsh, Sacred Heart; Ron McLachlin, University of Manitoba; Ivor P. Morgan, Babson College; Seungwook Park, California State University—Fullerton; Jaime S. Ribera, IESE-Universidad de Navarra, Spain; Gary D. Scudder, Vanderbilt University; Sue Perrott Siferd, Arizona State University; Donald E. Simmons, Ithaca College; William J. Tallon, Northern Illinois University; Asoo J. Vakharia, University of Florida; and Jerry C. Wei, University of Notre Dame.

For this edition we thank the following reviewers: Alexander Ansari, Seattle University; Okechi Geoffrey Egekwu, Michael H. Ensby, Clarkson University James Madison University; Michael R. Godfrey, University of Washington; Kendra Ingram, Texas A&M University-Commerce; Casey Kleindienst, California State University-Fullerton; Ranga V. Ramasesh, Texas Christian University; Samia Siha, Kennesaw State Unversity.

Jack Meredith
Babcock Graduate School of
  Management
Wake Forest University, P.O. Box 7659
Winston-Salem, NC 27109
jack.meredith@mba.wfu.edu
www.mba.wfu.edu/faculty/meredith
336.758.4467

Scott Shafer
Babcock Graduate School of
  Management
Wake Forest University, P.O. Box 7659
Winston-Salem, NC 27109
scott.shafer@mba.wfu.edu
www.mba.wfu.edu/faculty/shafer
336.758.368

PART I

Operations Strategy

We begin our discussion of the role of operations in the organization by examining how global competition drives organizations to define a strategy for survival and then execute on that strategy through efficient and effective operations. Chapter 1 describes the global competitive scene, what customers value, the evolution of strategy and supporting functional strategies, some strategic frameworks used in operations, and the organization's production system that executes that operations strategy. The chapter ends with a description of how the remaining chapters in the text all derive from the operations strategy.

Competitive Operations for the Global Arena

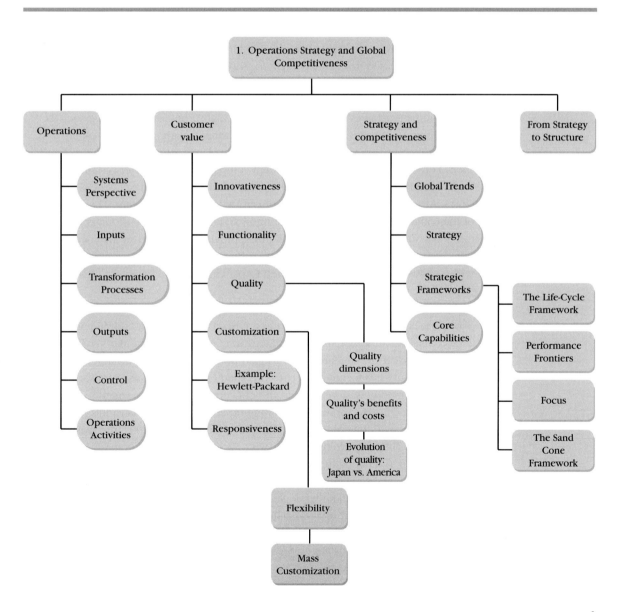

INTRODUCTION

- It is not well known that the Kmart and Wal-Mart chains both date back to 1962. By 1987 Kmart was clearly dominating the discount chain race, with almost twice as many stores and sales of $25.63 billion to Wal-Mart's $15.96 billion. However, for the retail year that ended in January 1991, Wal-Mart had overtaken Kmart, with sales of $32.6 billion to Kmart's sales of $29.7 billion. Interestingly, although Wal-Mart had taken the lead in sales in 1991, it still had fewer stores—1721 to Kmart's 2330. By the 2000 retail year, Wal-Mart had clearly established itself as the dominant discount chain, with sales of $188.1 billion to Kmart's $36.4 billion. Perhaps equally telling is the shift in market share experienced by these two companies. For the period from 1987 to 1995, Kmart's market share declined from 34.5 percent to 22.7 percent, while Wal-Mart's increased from 20.1 percent to 41.6 percent.

  What accounts for this reversal in fortunes? Kmart's response to the competition from Wal-Mart was to build on its marketing and merchandising strengths and invest heavily in national television campaigns using high-profile spokespeople such as Jaclyn Smith (a former Charlie's Angel) and Martha Stewart. Wal-Mart took an entirely different approach and invested heavily in operations in an effort to lower costs. For example, Wal-Mart developed a companywide computer system to link cash registers to headquarters, thereby greatly facilitating inventory control at the stores. Also, Wal-Mart developed a sophisticated distribution system. The integration of the computer system and the distribution system meant that customers would rarely encounter out-of-stock items. Further, the use of scanners at the checkout stations eliminated the need for price checks. By Kmart's own admission, its employees were seriously lacking the skills needed to plan and control inventory effectively (Duff and Ortega 1995).

  Fast forward to 2004 and Kmart was still having problems with getting merchandise on its shelves (Turner 2003, Duff and Ortega 1995, Merrick and Zimmerman 2004). Thus, Kmart adopted a new strategy to compete with Wal-Mart—merging with Sears, Roebuck & Co. in March 2005 to gain potential synergies through cross-selling and other retail sales techniques. The combined entity, known as Sears Holdings Corporation, tried new store formats and concepts but nothing seemed to work. Sears then tried a new approach, acquiring other retailers such as Land's End, but this strategy also didn't seem to turn things around. In March 2007, the Washington Post reported (http://en.wikipedia.org/wiki/Sears_Holdings_Corporation) that Sears was being run as a hedge fund, making a substantial portion of its profits on non-retail financial investments. By year-end 2007, Wal-Mart rang up sales of $379 billion (an 8.6% increase over 2006) while Sears sales were $51 billion (a 4.4% decrease), with earnings at Wal-Mart of $12.7 billion, up 12.6 percent, and $0.8 billion at Sears, *down* 44.6 percent! In terms of total stores, Wal-Mart had 7262 (up 7.1%) while Sears stayed at 3800 (0%). According to SAP's July 2008 Top 100 Retailers special report: "Sears hasn't turned the corner yet but not for lack of trying different things; the national economy hasn't helped, but many of the company's maneuvers have yet to pay off" (SAP 2008).

● In the early 2000s, GM's Chairman and CEO, Richard Wagoner Jr., relied on the strategy of using rebates to help generate cash and reverse GM's long, downward decline in market share from about 45 percent in 1980 to about 30 percent. In the highly competitive auto industry, maintaining market share is critical. For example, analysts estimate the impact of each percentage point of market share at GM is $1 billion in profits. Unfortunately for GM, as its market share continues to erode, it is becoming increasingly clear that the rebate strategy it pursued over the last several years is not working. A recent indication of this was that in the first two months of 2005, GM's market share declined by over two percentage points to just under 25 percent. Based on this decline, GM projected a loss for the first quarter of 2005 of over $800 million.

A closer examination of GM's situation suggests more fundamental problems. In particular, some analysts have suggested that GM's reliance on rebates is simply a reflection of weaknesses in its product offerings. For example, in 2005 GM had eight brands compared with Toyota's two. Aside from the issue of whether a company with less than 25 percent of the market needed so many brands, one result of having so many brands was a proliferation of similar vehicles across the brands: six similar front-wheel-drive midsize family sedans and four similar minivans. Furthermore, the problem with offering so many models created another problem for GM, namely, that it was unable to redesign its cars as frequently as its competitors. For example, it took GM 9 years to replace its Chevrolet Cavalier with the Cobalt. Honda, on the other hand, completely redesigns its Civic every five years (Welch 2005).

While GM's market share continued to drop to about 20 percent, the entire automotive industry got hit with a powerful one-two punch in 2008, throwing the weakened American automobile producers into chaos. First in early 2008 were extreme gasoline prices which killed the truck and SUV market and then the sudden credit crisis and recession killed the rest of the automobile market. The high cost of debt, unionized labor, and unfunded liabilities (pensions and healthcare) forced GM and Chrysler to go begging to the government for bailouts. By late 2008, they were burning through billions of dollars of cash every month. One industry analyst calculated that GM's obligations in March of 2009 amounted to $62 billion, 35 times its market capitalization (Denning 2009, p. C10)! At this time, it appears that Chrysler may be too far gone to save, and GM will need to go through at least some form of bankruptcy to emerge as a viable company. Although Ford has not asked for government monies, it is also in difficult straits. The future looks tumultuous for the automakers.

● Having rung up combined profits of $8 billion in 2004, manufacturers of flat-panel TVs appeared to be especially optimistic about the profit potential for the TV market in the years ahead. Indeed, a battle of epic proportions was brewing in the consumer electronics industry. On one side was a group of Asian manufacturers that spent $35 billion adding flat-panel capacity in 2004 and 2005. Among the Asian players were a joint venture between LG Electronics and Royal Philips Electronics that invested $5.1 billion to build the world's largest liquid-crystal display factory, a

$2 billion joint venture between Sony and Samsung to produce LCDs, and Matsushita Electronics' new $1.3 billion plant for producing chips for thin TVs. On the other side, North America's Dell was attempting to leverage its streamlined supply chain and direct-sales model and thereby shift the basis of competition from features to price. For example, in the fall of 2004 Dell introduced a high-definition 42-inch plasma TV for under $3,000 while the similar offerings of its Asian competitors were still priced above $4,000. As a result, Dell was able to capture 10 percent of the market in a span of only a couple of months. So, would the Asian strategy based on product innovation and appealing designs win out over Dell's strategy that seeks to commoditize the market and thereby shift the basis of competition to price? (Einhorn 2005)

Fast forward to 2007 and the flat-panel sets have now overtaken the CRT sets, with LCD sets taking a commanding lead of 58 percent of the market by the fourth quarter of 2008, CRTs with a 34 percent share, and Plasma with an 8 percent share. In addition, the market has jumped from an $11 billion industry in 1998 to $102 billion in 2007, just ten years! And the winners are: Samsung and Sony, each with about a 13 percent share of the market. Vizio is a close runner-up with 11 percent, and then Sharp with 8 percent. However, the future does not look quite as rosy as it did in 2004. Most of the consumers who wanted a flat-panel set now have one, multiple low-end producers have entered the market and kept prices low, and now the recession has resulted in a 3 percent drop in sales as of January 2009 (http://news.cnet.com/8301-10784_3-9891583-7.html).

These brief examples highlight the diversity and importance of operations while providing a glimpse of two themes that are central to operations: *customer satisfaction* and *competitiveness*. They also illustrate a more subtle point—that improvements made in operations can simultaneously increase customer satisfaction and lower costs. The Wal-Mart example demonstrates how a company obtained a substantial competitive advantage by improving basic operational activities such as controlling its supply chain. And the automobile industry example shows how losing an operations focus can drive a firm into bankruptcy. And also, we see that the field of operations is as applicable to service organizations such as Wal-Mart and Sears' retail services as it is to manufacturing.

Today, in our international marketplace, consumers purchase their products from the provider that offers them the most "value" for their money. To illustrate, you may be doing your course assignments on a Japanese notebook computer, driving in a German automobile, or watching a sitcom on a television made in Taiwan while cooking your food in a Korean microwave. However, most of your services—banking, insurance, personal care—are probably domestic, although some of these may also be owned by, or outsourced to, foreign corporations. There is a reason why most services are produced by domestic firms while products may be produced in part, or wholly, by foreign firms, and it concerns an area of business known as operations.

A great many societal changes that are occurring today intimately involve activities associated with operations. For example, there is great pressure among competing nations to increase their exports. And businesses are intent on building efficient and effective supply chains, improving their processes through "six-sigma," and successfully applying the precepts of "lean management" and other operations-based programs.

Another characteristic of our modern society is the explosion of new technology, an important aspect of operations. Technologies such as cell phones, e-mail, notebook computers, personal digital assistants, and the Web, to name a few, are profoundly affecting business and are fundamentally changing the nature of work. For example, many banks are shifting their focus from building new branch locations to using the Web as a way to establish and develop new customer relationships. Banks rely on technology to carry out more routine activities as well, such as transferring funds instantly across cities, states, and oceans. Our industries also rely increasingly on technology: robots carry and weld parts together, and workerless, dark "factories of the future" turn out a continuing stream of products. And soft operations technologies, such as "supply chain management" and "lean production" (Feld 2000; Womack and Jones 2003) have transformed world markets and the global economy.

This exciting, competitive world of operations is at the heart of every organization and, more than anything else, determines whether the organization survives in the international marketplace or disappears into bankruptcy or a takeover. It is this world that we will be covering in the following chapters.

 PERATIONS

Why do we argue that operations be considered the heart of every organization? Fundamentally, organizations exist to create value, and operations involves tasks that create value. Michael Hammer (2004) maintains that operational innovation can provide organizations with long-term strategic advantages over their competitors. Regardless of whether the organization is for-profit or not-for-profit, primarily service or manufacturer, public or private, it exists to create value. Thus, even nonprofit organizations like the Red Cross strive to create value for the recipients of their services in excess of their costs. Moreover, this has always been true, from the earliest days of bartering to the modern-day corporations.

Consider McDonald's as an example. This firm uses a number of inputs, including ingredients, labor, equipment, and facilities; transforms them in a way that adds value to them (e.g., by frying); and obtains an output, such as a chicken sandwich, that can be sold at a profit. This conversion process, termed a *production system*, is illustrated in Figure 1.1. The elements of the figure represent what is known as a ***system***[1]: ***a purposeful collection of people, objects, and procedures for operating within an environment***.

Note the word *purposeful;* systems are not merely arbitrary groupings but goal-directed or purposeful collections. Managing and running a production system efficiently and effectively is at the heart of the operations activities that will be discussed in this text. Since we will be using this term throughout the text, let us formally define it. ***Operations*** is concerned with transforming inputs into useful outputs according to the agreed-upon strategy and thereby adding value to some entity; this constitutes the primary activity of virtually every organization.

---

[1]Note the word *system* is being used here in a broad sense and should not be confused with more narrow usages such as information systems, planning and control systems, or performance evaluation systems.

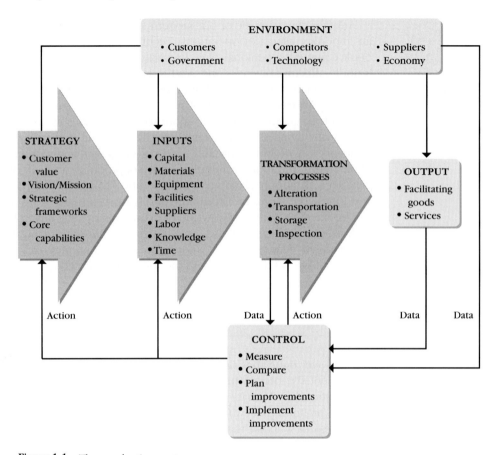

Figure 1.1   The production system.

Not only is operations central to organizations, it is also central to people's personal and professional activities, regardless of their position. People, too, must operate productively, adding value to inputs and producing quality outputs, whether those outputs are information, reports, services, products, or even personal accomplishments. Thus, operations should be of major interest to every reader, not just professionally but also personally.

Systems Perspective

As Figure 1.1 illustrates, a production system is defined in terms of the environment, a strategy, a set of inputs, the transformation process, the outputs, and some mechanism for controlling the overall system. The strategy includes such elements as what customers value, the vision and mission of the organization, an appropriate framework to execute this vision, and the core capabilities of the organization. We discuss the strategy in detail a bit later. The environment includes those things that are outside the actual production system but that influence it in some way. Because of its influence, we need to consider the environment, even though it is beyond the control of decision makers within the system.

For example, a large portion of the inputs to a production system are acquired from the environment. Also, government regulations related to pollution control and workplace safety affect the transformation system. Think about how changes in customers' needs, a competitor's new product, or a new advance in technology can influence the level of satisfaction with a production system's current outputs. As these examples show, the environment exerts a great deal of influence on the production system.

Because the world around us is constantly changing, it is necessary to monitor the production system and take action when the system is not meeting its strategic goals. Of course, it may be that the current strategy is no longer appropriate, indicating a need to revise the strategy. On the other hand, it may be found that the strategy is fine but that the inputs or transformation processes, or both, should be modified in some way. In either case, it is important to continuously collect data from the environment, the transformation processes, and the outputs, compare that data to the strategic plan, and if substantial deviations exist, design and implement improvements to the system, or perhaps the strategy, so that results agree with the strategic goals.

Thinking in terms of systems provides decision makers with numerous advantages. To begin, the systems perspective focuses on how the individual components that make up a system interact. Thus, the systems perspective provides decision makers with a broad and complete picture of an entire situation. Furthermore, the systems perspective emphasizes the relationships between the various system components. Without considering these relationships, decision makers are prone to a problem called *suboptimization.* Suboptimization occurs when one part of the system is improved to the detriment of other parts of the system, and perhaps the organization as a whole. For example, if a retailer decides to broaden its product line in an effort to increase sales, this could actually end up hurting the retailer as a whole if it does not have sufficient shelf space or service personnel available to accommodate the broader product line. Thus, decisions need to be evaluated in terms of their effect on the *entire* system, not simply in terms of how they will affect one component of the system.

In the remainder of this section we elaborate on inputs, the transformation processes, and outputs. In later sections and chapters we will further discuss both strategy and elements of the control system in more detail.

Inputs

The set of inputs used in a production system is more complex than might be supposed and typically involves many other areas such as marketing, finance, engineering, and human resource management. Obvious inputs include facilities, labor, capital, equipment, raw materials, and supplies. Supplies are distinguished from raw materials by the fact that they are not usually a part of the final output. Oil, paper clips, pens, tape, and other such items are commonly classified as supplies because they only aid in producing the output.

Another very important but perhaps less obvious input is knowledge of how to transform the inputs into outputs. The employees of the organization hold this knowledge. Finally, having sufficient time to accomplish the operations is always critical. Indeed, the operations function quite frequently fails in its task because it cannot complete the ***transformation activities*** within the required time limit.

Transformation Processes

The transformation processes are the part of the system that adds value to the inputs. Value can be added to an entity in a number of ways. Four major ways are described here.

1. *Alter:* Something can be changed structurally. That would be a *physical* change, and this approach is basic to our manufacturing industries where goods are cut, stamped, formed, assembled, and so on. We then go out and buy the shirt, or computer, or whatever the good is. But it need not be a separate object or entity; for example, what is altered may be *us.* We might get our hair cut, or we might have our appendix removed.

   Other, more subtle, alterations may also have value. *Sensual* alterations, such as heat when we are cold, or music, or beauty may be highly valued on certain occasions. Beyond this, even *psychological* alterations can have value, such as the feeling of worth from obtaining a college degree or the feeling of friendship from a long-distance phone call.

2. *Transport:* An entity, again including ourselves, may have more value if it is located somewhere other than where it currently is. We may appreciate having things brought to us, such as flowers, or removed from us, such as garbage.

3. *Store:* The value of an entity may be enhanced for us if it is kept in a protected environment for some period of time. Some examples are stock certificates kept in a safe-deposit box, our pet boarded at a kennel while we go on vacation, or ourselves staying in a hotel.

4. *Inspect:* Last, an entity may be more valued because we better understand its properties. This may apply to something we own, plan to use, or are considering purchasing, or, again, even to ourselves. Medical exams, elevator certifications, and jewelry appraisals fall into this category.

Thus, we see that value may be added to an entity in a number of different ways. The entity may be changed directly, in space, in time, or even just in our mind. Additionally, value may be added using a combination of these methods. To illustrate, an appliance store may create value by both storing merchandise and transporting (delivering) it. There are other, less frequent, ways of adding value as well, such as by "guaranteeing" something. These many varieties of transformations, and how they are managed, constitute some of the major issues to be discussed in this text.

Outputs

Two types of outputs commonly result from a production process: services and products. Generally, products are physical goods, such as a personal computer, and services are abstract or nonphysical. More specifically, we can consider the characteristics in Table 1.1 to help us distinguish between the two.

However, this classification may be more confusing than helpful. For example, consider a pizza delivery chain. Does this organization produce a product or provide

$\mathscr{T}_{ABLE}$ 1.1 • Characteristics of Products and Services

Products	Services
Tangible	Intangible
Minimal contact with customer	Extensive contact with customer
Minimal participation by customer in the delivery	Extensive participation by customer in the delivery
Delayed consumption	Immediate consumption
Equipment-intense production	Labor-intense production
Quality easily measured	Quality difficult to measure

a service? If you answered "a service," suppose that instead of delivering its pizzas to the actual consumer, it made the pizzas in a factory and sold them in the frozen-food section of grocery stores. Clearly the actual process of making pizzas for immediate consumption or to be frozen involves basically the same tasks, although one may be done on a larger scale and use more automated equipment. The point is, however, that both organizations produce a pizza, and defining one organization as a service and the other as a manufacturer seems to be a little arbitrary. In addition, both products and services can be produced as commodities or individually customized.

We avoid this ambiguity by adopting the point of view that *any physical entity accompanying a transformation that adds value is a **facilitating good*** (e.g., the pizza). In many cases, of course, there may be no facilitating good; we refer to these cases as *pure services.*

The advantage of this interpretation is that every transformation that adds value is simply a service, either with or without facilitating goods! If you buy a piece of lumber, you have not purchased a product. Rather, you have purchased a bundle of services, many of them embodied in a facilitating good: a tree-cutting service, a saw mill service, a transportation service, a storage service, and perhaps even an advertising service that told you where lumber was on sale. We refer to these services as a bundle of "benefits," of which some are tangible (the sawed length of lumber, the type of tree) and others are intangible (courteous salesclerks, a convenient location, payment by charge card). Some services may, of course, even be negative, such as an audit of your tax return. In summary, ***services* are bundles of benefits, some of which may be tangible and others intangible, and they may be accompanied by a facilitating good or goods.**

Firms often run into major difficulties when they ignore this aspect of their operations. They may think of, and even market themselves as, a "lumberyard" and not as providing a bundle of services. They may recognize that they have to include certain tangible services (such as cutting lumber to the length desired by the customer) but ignore the intangible services (charge sales, having a sufficient number of clerks). Another reason for not making a distinction between manufacturing and services is that when a company thinks of itself as a manufacturer, it tends to focus on measures of internal performance such as efficiency and utilization. But when companies consider themselves as providing services they tend to focus externally and ask questions such as "How can we serve our customers better?" This is not to imply that improving internal performance measures is not desirable. Rather, it suggests that improved customer service should be the primary impetus for all improvement efforts. It is generally not advisable to seek internal improvements if these improvements do not ultimately lead to corresponding improvements in customer service and customer satisfaction.

In this text we will adopt the point of view that all value-adding transformations (i.e., operations) are services, and there may or may not be a set of accompanying facilitating goods. Figure 1.2 illustrates how the tangible product (or facilitating good) portion and the intangible service portion for a variety of outputs contribute to the total value provided by each output. The outputs shown range from virtually pure services to what would be known as products. For example, the Plush restaurant appears to be about 75 percent service and 25 percent product. Although we work with "products" as extensively as with services throughout the chapters in this

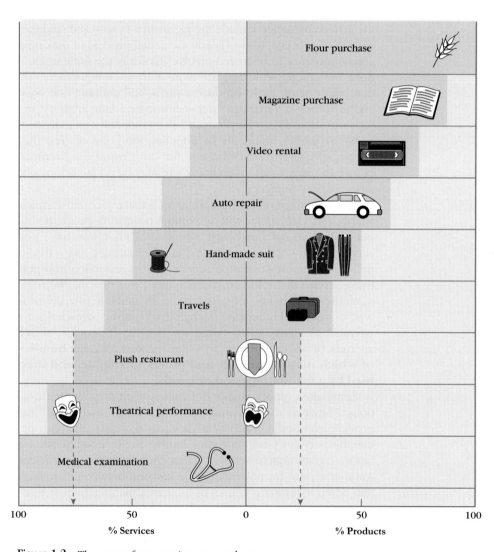

Figure 1.2   The range from services to products.

book, bear in mind that in these cases we are working with only a *portion* of the total service, the facilitating good. In general, we will use the nonspecific term *outputs* to mean either products or services.

One particular type of output that is substantially different from products and many other types of services is that of knowledge or information. These outputs often have the characteristic that the more they are used, the more valuable they become. For example, in a network the more entities that belong to the network, the more useful it may be. If you are on Facebook® or use email, the more other people that are also there, the more valuable it is to you. And when you share this output, you don't lose anything, you gain. Some other characteristics of information or knowledge that differ from normal goods and services are listed below.

- giving or selling the information/knowledge to someone doesn't mean you can't give or sell it to someone else;
- the information/knowledge doesn't wear out;
- the information/knowledge isn't subject to the law of diminishing returns;
- the information/knowledge can be replicated at minimal cost and trouble; and
- the more the knowledge is used, the more valuable it becomes.

Control

Suppose that in our production system we make a mistake. We must be able to observe this through, for example, accounting records (measurement data), compare it to standard to see how serious the error is, and then, if needed, plan and implement (usually via a project) some improvements. If the changes are not significantly affecting the outputs, then no control actions are needed. But if they are, management must intercede and apply corrective control to alter the inputs or the transformation processes and, thereby, the outputs. The control activities illustrated in Figure 1.1 are used extensively in systems, including management systems, and will be encountered throughout this text.

Table 1.2 lists a few examples of some components of the production system for a variety of common organizations.

Operations Activities

Operations include not only those activities associated specifically with the production system but also a variety of other activities. For example, purchasing or procurement activities are concerned with obtaining many of the inputs needed in the production system. Similarly, shipping and distribution are sometimes considered marketing activities and sometimes considered operations activities. Because of the important interdependencies of these activities, many organizations are attempting to manage these activities as one process commonly referred to as *supply chain management.*

As organizations begin to adopt new organizational structures based on business processes and abandon the traditional functional organization, it is becoming less important to classify activities as operations or nonoperations (e.g., sales, marketing, purchasing). However, to understand the tasks more easily, we divide the field of

$\mathcal{T}$ABLE 1.2 • Examples of Production System Components

Organization	Strategy	Inputs	Transformation Process	Outputs	Control	Environment
Post office	Regular Consistent Dependable	Labor Equipment Trucks	Transportation Printing	Mail deliveries Stamps	Weather Mail volumes Sorting/loss errors	Transportation network Weather Civil service
Bank	Secure Trustworthy Responsive Informative	Checks Deposits Vault ATMs	Safekeeping Investment Statement preparations	Interest Electronic transfer Loans Statements	Interest rates Wage rates Loan default rates	Federal Reserve Economy
Cinema	Enjoyable Variety Timely	Films Food People Theater	Film projection Food preparation	Entertainment Snacks	Film popularity Disposable incomes	Economy Entertainment industry
Manufacturer	Reliable Affordable Quality Variety	Materials Equipment Labor Technology	Cutting Forming Joining Mixing	Machines Chemicals Consumer goods Scrap	Material flows Production volumes	Economy Commodity prices Consumer market
School	Knowledge Safe Trustworthy Friendly	Books Teachers Facility Students	Learning Counseling Motivating	Educated students Skills Research	Demographics Grievances	State and county boards Tax system

operations into a series of subject areas as shown in Table 1.3. These areas are quite interdependent, but to make their workings more understandable we discuss them as though they were easily separable from each other. In some areas, a full-fledged department may be responsible for the activities, such as quality control or scheduling, but in other areas the activities (such as facility location) may be infrequent and simply assigned to a particular group or project team. Moreover, some of the subareas such as supply chain management or maintenance are critically important because they are a part of a larger business process or because other areas depend on them. Finally, since we consider all operations to be services, these subject areas are equally applicable to organizations that have traditionally been classified as manufacturers and services.

$\mathcal{C}$USTOMER VALUE

In the Introduction to this chapter we mentioned that customers support the provider of goods and services who offers them the most "value." In this section we elaborate on this concept. The equation for value is conceptually clear:

Value = perceived benefits/costs

$\mathscr{T}_{ABLE}$ 1.3 • Major Subject Areas in Operations

Chapter	Subject Area
1	*Strategy:* Determining the critical operations tasks to support the organization's overall mission.
1	*Output planning:* Selecting and designing the services and products the organization will offer to customers, patrons, or recipients.
1	*Reliability and maintenance:* Determining how the proper performance of both the output and the transformation process itself is to be maintained.
2	*Transformation process design:* Determining the physical transformation aspects of the production activities.
2	*Facility layout:* Devising an appropriate material flow and equipment layout within the facility to efficiently and effectively accommodate the transformation activities.
3	*Quality control:* Determining how quality standards are to be developed and maintained.
4,5	*Process improvement:* Applying process design techniques to improve the flow and efficiency of production systems.
5	*Lean management:* Using techniques from the Toyota Production System and JIT to eliminate waste and nonvalue-added activities.
6	*Project management:* Learning how to plan and control project activities to meet specifications for performance, schedule, and cost.
7	*Supply chain management:* Organizing the activities from the customer's order through final delivery for speed, efficiency, and quality.
7	*Inventory management:* Deciding what amounts of raw materials, work-in-process, and finished goods to hold.
7	*Enterprise and material requirements planning:* Using information management systems to coordinate enterprise-wide activities, especially for ordering or producing materials to meet a master delivery schedule.
8	*Capacity planning:* Determining when to have facilities, equipment, and labor available and in what amounts.
8	*Facility location:* Deciding where to locate production, storage, and other major facilities.
8	*Schedule planning:* Anticipating the yearly needs for labor, materials, and facilities by month, week, or day within the year.

The perceived benefits can take a wide variety of forms, but the costs are usually more straightforward:

- the upfront monetary investment;
- other monetary lifecycle costs for maintenance and such; and
- the hassles involved in obtaining the product or service such as travel distance, financing for the upfront investment, friendliness of service, and so on.

In contrast, the benefits can be multiple. We will consider five of these in detail: innovativeness, functionality, quality, customization, and responsiveness.

Innovativeness

Many people (called "early adopters" in marketing) will buy products and services simply because they are so innovative, or major improvements over what has been available formerly. It is the field of Research and Development (known as R&D) that

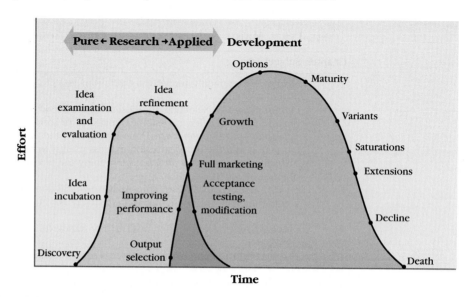

Figure 1.3   The development effort.

is primarily responsible for developing innovative new product and service ideas. R&D activities focus on creating and developing (but not producing) the organization's outputs. On occasion, R&D also creates new production methods by which outputs, either new or old, may be produced.

Research itself is typically divided into two types: pure and applied. Pure research is simply working with basic technology to develop new knowledge. Applied research is attempting to develop new knowledge along particular lines. For example, pure research might focus on developing a material that conducts electricity with zero resistance, whereas applied research could focus on further developing this material to be used in products for customers. *Development* is the attempt to utilize the findings of research and expand the possible applications, often consisting of modifications or extensions to existing outputs to meet customers' interests. Figure 1.3 illustrates the range of applicability of development as the output becomes more clearly defined. In the early years of a new output, development is oriented toward removing "bugs," increasing performance, improving quality, and so on. In the middle years, options and variants of the output are developed. In the later years, development is oriented toward extensions of the output that will prolong its life.

Unfortunately, the returns from R&D are frequently meager, whereas the costs are great. Figure 1.4 illustrates the ***mortality curve*** (fallout rate) associated with the concurrent design, evaluation, and selection for a hypothetical group of 50 potential chemical products, assuming that the 50 candidate products are available for consideration in year 3. (The first three years, on the average, are required for the necessary research preceding each candidate product.) Initial evaluation and screening reduce the 50 to about 22, and economic analysis further reduces the number to about 9. Development reduces this number even more, to about 5, and design and testing reduce it to perhaps 3. By the time construction (for production), market development, and a year's commercialization are completed, there is only one

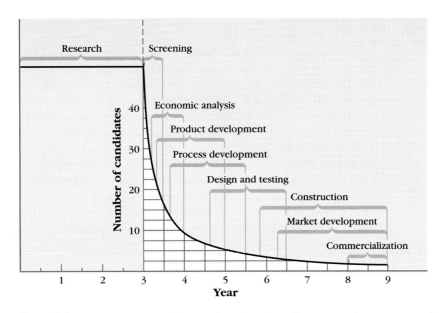

Figure 1.4 Mortality curve of chemical product ideas from research to commercialization.
Source: Adapted from *This is Dupont 30.* Wilmington, DE by permission of DuPont de Nemours and Co.

successful product left. (Sometimes there are none!) One study found that, beyond this, only 64 percent of the new products brought to market were successful, or about two out of three.

Two alternatives to research frequently used by organizations are *imitation* of a proven new idea (i.e., employing a second-to-market strategy) or outright *purchase* of someone else's invention. The outright purchase strategy is becoming extremely popular in those industries where bringing a new product to market can cost huge sums, such as pharmaceuticals and high technology. It is also employed in those industries where technology advances so rapidly that there isn't enough time to employ a second-to-market strategy. Although imitation does not put the organization first in the market with the new product or service, it does give an opportunity to study any possible defects in the original product or service and rapidly develop a better design, frequently at a better price. The second approach—purchasing an invention or the inventing company itself—eliminates the risks inherent in research, but it still requires the company to develop and market the product or service before knowing whether it will be successful. Either route spares the organization the risk and tremendous cost of conducting the actual research leading up to a new invention or improvement.

In addition to *product research* (as it is generally known), there is also *process research*, which involves the generation of new knowledge concerning *how to produce* outputs. Currently, the production of many familiar products out of plastic (toys, pipe, furniture, etc.) is an outstanding example of successful process research. Motorola, to take another example, extensively uses project teams that conduct process development at the same time as product development.

Functionality

Many people confuse *functionality* with quality (discussed next). But functionality involves the activities the product or service is intended to perform, thereby providing the benefits to the customer. A contemporary example is the ubiquitous "cell phone." These days it is probably rare to find a cell phone which is only a phone; many phones include a camera and a way to send its picture to another person, or provide access to the internet, as well as a myriad of other functions.

However, many products, especially electronics, but also some services, may be advertised to provide purchasers with a new, unique function and they may do so, but it *may not work well*, or *for long*. The former involves performance and the latter has to do with reliability. Clearly, these are different attributes of the output, and one can be well addressed while other attributes disappoint. Our discussion of quality, next, elaborates a bit more on the distinction between these attributes.

Quality

Quality is a relative term, meaning different things to different people at different times. Moreover, quality is not an absolute but, rather, is based on customers' perceptions. Customers' impressions can be influenced by a number of factors, including brand loyalty and an organization's reputation.

Quality dimensions

Richard J. Schonberger has compiled a list of multiple quality dimensions that customers often associate with products and services:

1. *Conformance to specifications.* Conformance to specifications is the extent to which the actual product matches the design specifications, such as a pizza delivery shop that consistently meets its advertised delivery time of 30 minutes.

2. *Performance.* Customers frequently equate the quality of products and services with their performance. (Note, however, that this dimension may in some cases actually refer to functionality.) Examples of performance include how quickly a sports car accelerates or the battery life of a cell phone.

3. *Features.* Features are the options that a product or service offers, such as side impact airbags in automobiles and leather seats. (Again, however, this dimension may also be confused with functionality.)

4. *Quick response.* Quick response is associated with the amount of time required to react to customers' demands. However, we consider this to be a separate benefit, discussed further below.

5. *Reliability.* Reliability is the probability that a product or service will perform as intended on any given trial or for some period of time, such as the probability that a car will start on any given morning.

6. *Durability.* Durability refers to how tough a product is, such as a notebook computer that still functions after being dropped, or a knife that can cut through steel and not need sharpening.

7. ***Serviceability.*** Serviceability refers to the ease with which maintenance or a repair can be performed.

8. ***Aesthetics.*** Aesthetics are factors that appeal to human senses, such as the taste of a steak or the sound of a sports car's engine.

9. ***Humanity.*** Humanity has to do with how the customer is treated, such as a private university that maintains small classes so students are not treated like numbers by its professors.

It is worth noting that not all the dimensions of quality are relevant to all products and services. Thus, organizations need to identify the dimensions of quality that are relevant to the products and services they offer. Market research about customers' needs is the primary input for determining which dimensions are important. Of course, measuring the quality of a service can often be more difficult than measuring the quality of a product or facilitating good. However, the dimensions of quality described above apply to both.

Quality's benefits and costs

Many benefits are associated with providing products and services that have high quality. Obviously, customers are more pleased with a high-quality product or service. They are more apt to encourage their friends to patronize the firm, as well as giving the firm their own repeat business. Top quality also establishes a reputation for the firm that is very difficult to obtain in any other manner, and it allows the firm to charge a premium price. And typically, high-quality products and services are not only the most profitable but also garner the largest market shares. High quality also tends to protect the firm from competitors, who may have to offer competing outputs at an especially low price (and low margins). It also enhances the attractiveness of follow-up products or services so that their chances of success are much improved. And, of course, high quality minimizes risks to safety and health and reduces liability for the firm.

Traditionally, it was thought that making products and services of excellent quality would translate into higher costs. Of course this view neglects the negative consequences of gaining a reputation for producing shoddy outputs. Also, the Japanese have demonstrated that it is often possible to improve quality and lower costs at the same time. One explanation for this phenomenon is that it is simply cheaper to do a job right the first time than to try to fix it or rework it later. And if quality is built into the production system, it improves workers' morale, reduces scrap and waste, smoothes work flows, improves control, and reduces a wide variety of other costs. As a result, Philip Crosby, a well-known quality consultant, maintains that "quality is free," as in the title of his book, *Quality Is Free* (1979), which sold approximately 1 million copies. Crosby estimates that firms can lose up to 25 percent of the amount of their sales because of poor quality.

Two primary sets of costs are involved in quality: control costs and failure costs. The aggregate of these costs runs between 15 and 35 percent of sales for many U.S. firms. Traditionally, these costs are broken down into four categories: prevention costs (including planning, training, product design, maintenance); appraisal costs (measuring, testing, test equipment, inspectors, reports); internal costs of defects (extra labor and materials to repair, scrap, rework interruptions, expediting); and external costs of defects (ill-will, complaints, quick response to correct, warranties, insurance, recalls, lawsuits). The first two costs are incurred in attempting to control quality, and the last two are the costs of failing to control quality. Costs of defects (or nonconformance) can run from 50 to 90 percent of the total cost of quality.

Evolution of quality: Japan vs. America

Although you might think that "made in Japan" signifies a product of superior quality, it may surprise you to learn that many of the techniques and philosophies Japanese companies employ today were actually developed in the United States, often around the end of World War II. Unfortunately, the sentiment among U.S. manufacturers at the end of World War II was that they already produced the highest-quality products in the world at the lowest cost. Thus, they were not particularly interested in or concerned with improving quality.

Japan was an entirely different story. Its products had a reputation for poor quality, and after it lost the war its economy was a shambles. As a result, Japanese manufacturers were eager for help related to quality improvement. In 1950 the Japanese government invited W. Edwards Deming (then a professor at New York University) to give a series of lectures on quality control to help Japanese engineers reindustrialize the country. But Deming insisted that the heads of the companies attend the talks too. As a result, the top Japanese managers were also invited, and they all showed up.

According to Deming (1986), the major cause of poor quality is *variation*. Thus, a key tenet of Deming's approach is to reduce variability in the process. (This topic is discussed further in Chapter 4: Process Improvement—Reducing Variation through Six Sigma.) Deming stressed that improving quality was the responsibility of top management. However, he also believed that all employees should be trained in the use of problem-solving tools and especially statistical techniques. Deming believed that improvements in quality created a chain reaction where improved quality leads to lower costs, which then translate into higher productivity. In contrast to Deming, Crosby focused more on management, organizational processes, and changing corporate culture than on the use of statistical techniques.

Deming promised the Japanese that if they followed his advice, they would be able to compete with the West within just a few years. They did! Now the most prestigious industrial quality award given in Japan each year is named the Deming Prize. But the Japanese did not stop there. They tied the concept of quality control directly into their production system—and now they have even tied it into their entire economy through inspections to guarantee the quality of exports. The natural inclinations of Japanese culture and traditions were exploited in this quality crusade. After nearly two decades of a national emphasis on quality, Japan's reputation for producing shoddy goods was totally reversed. And, when high quality is combined with competitive pricing—another strength of the Japanese system—the result is extremely strong competition for existing producers.

DILBERT: ©Scott Adams/Dist. by United Feature Syndicate, Inc.

A more recent concept (similar to zero defects) that the Japanese and some American firms have embraced is called *total quality management* (TQM) or *total quality control* (TQC). The basic idea of TQM is that it is extremely expensive to "inspect" quality into a company's outputs and much more efficient and effective to produce them right in the first place. As a result, responsibility for quality has been taken away from the quality control department and placed where it belongs—with the workers who produce the parts or provide the service in the first place. This is called *quality at the source*. It is the heart of *statistical quality control* (SQC), sometimes called *statistical process control* (SPC), which we discuss further in Chapter 3.

Customization

Customization refers to offering a product or service exactly suited to a customer's desires or needs. However, there is a range of accommodation to the customer's needs, as illustrated in Figure 1.5. At the left, there is the completely standard, world-class (excellence suitable for all markets) product or service. Moving to the right is the standard with options, continuing on to variants and alternative models, and ending at the right with made-to-order customization. In general, the more customization the better, if it can be provided quickly, with acceptable quality and cost.

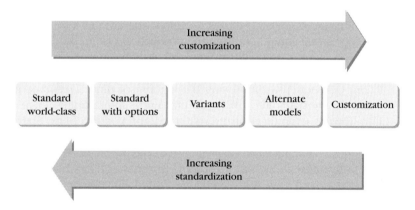

Figure 1.5   Continuum of customization.

Flexibility

However, to offer customization demands flexibility on the part of the firm. Professor David Upton (1994, p. 73), formerly of the Harvard Business School, defines flexibility as "the ability to change or react with little penalty in time, effort, cost, or performance." There are more than a dozen different types of flexibility that we will not pursue here—design, volume, routing through the production system, product mix, and many others. But having the right types of flexibility can offer the following major competitive advantages:

- Faster matches to customers' needs because changeover time from one product or service to another is quicker.
- Closer matches to customers' needs.

- Ability to supply the needed items in the volumes required for the markets as they develop.
- Faster design-to-market time to meet new customer needs.
- Lower cost of changing production to meet needs.
- Ability to offer a full line of products or services without the attendant cost of stocking large inventories.
- Ability to meet market demands even if delays develop in the production or distribution process.

Mass Customization

Until recently, it was widely believed that producing low-cost standard products (at the far left in Figure 1.5) required one type of transformation process and producing higher-cost customized products (far right) required another type of process. However, in addition to vast improvements in operating efficiency, an unexpected byproduct of the continuous improvement programs of the 1980s was substantial improvement in flexibility. Indeed, prior to this, efficiency and flexibility were thought to be tradeoffs. Increasing efficiency meant that flexibility had to be sacrificed, and vice versa.

Thus, with the emphasis on continuous improvement came the realization that increasing operating efficiency could also enhance flexibility. For example, many manufacturers initiated efforts to reduce the amount of time required to set up (or change over) equipment from the production of one product to another. Obviously, all time spent setting up equipment is wasteful, since the equipment is not being used during this time to produce outputs that ultimately create revenues for the organization. Consequently, improving the amount of time a resource is used productively directly translates into improved efficiency. Interestingly, these same reductions in equipment setup times also resulted in improved flexibility. Specifically, with shorter equipment setup times, manufacturers could produce economically in smaller-size batches, making it easier to switch from the production of one product to another.

In response to the discovery that efficiency and flexibility can be improved simultaneously and may not have to be traded off, the strategy of mass customization emerged (see Pine 1993 and Gilmore and Pine 1997). Organizations pursuing **mass customization** seek to produce low-cost, high-quality outputs in high variety. Of course, not all products and services lend themselves to being customized. This is particularly true of commodities such as sugar, gas, electricity, and flour. On the other hand, mass customization is often quite applicable to products characterized by short life cycles, rapidly advancing technology, or changing customer requirements. However, recent research suggests that successfully employing mass customization requires an organization to first develop a transformation process that can consistently deliver high-quality outputs at a low cost. With this foundation in place, the organization can then seek ways to increase the variety of its offerings while at the same time ensuring that quality and cost are not compromised.

In an article published in *Harvard Business Review*, Gilmore and Pine (1997) identified four mass customization strategies:

1. ***Collaborative customizers.*** These organizations establish a dialogue to help customers articulate their needs and then develop customized outputs to meet these needs. For example, one Japanese eyewear retailer developed

a computerized system to help customers select eyewear. The system combines a digital image of the customer's face and then various styles of eyware are displayed on the digital image. Once the customer is satisfied, the customized glasses are produced at the retail store within an hour.

2. ***Adaptive customizers.*** These organizations offer a standard product that customers can modify themselves, such as fast-food hamburgers (ketchup, etc.) and closet organizers. Each closet-organizer package is the same, but includes instructions and tools to cut the shelving and clothes rods so that the unit can fit a wide variety of closet sizes.

3. ***Cosmetic customizers.*** These organizations produce a standard product but present it differently to different customers. For example, Planters packages its peanuts and mixed nuts in a variety of containers on the basis of specific needs of its retailing customers such as Wal-Mart, 7-Eleven, and Safeway.

4. ***Transparent customizers.*** These organizations provide custom products without the customers knowing that a product has been customized for them. For example, Amazon.com provides book recommendations based on information about past purchases.

Example: Hewlett-Packard

Faced with increasing pressure from its customers for quicker order fulfillment and for more highly customized products, Hewlett-Packard (HP) wondered whether it was really possible to deliver mass-customized products rapidly, while at the same time continuing to reduce costs (Feitzinger and Lee 1997). HP's approach to mass customization can be summarized as effectively delaying tasks that customize a product as long as possible in the product supply process. It is based on the following three principles:

- Products should be designed around a number of independent modules that can be easily combined in a variety of ways.
- Manufacturing tasks should also be designed and performed as independent modules that can be relocated or rearranged to support new production requirements.
- The product supply process must perform two functions. First, it must cost-effectively supply the basic product to the locations that complete the customization activities. Second, it must have the requisite flexibility to process individual customers' orders.

HP has discovered that modular design provides three primary benefits. First, components that differentiate the product can be added during the later stages of production. This method of mass customization is generally called ***postponement***, and is one form of the assemble-to-order production process, discussed in more detail in Chapter 3. For example, the company designed its printers so that country-specific power supplies are combined with the printers at local distribution centers and actually plugged in by the customer when the printer is set up. Second, production time can be significantly reduced by simultaneously producing the required modules. Third, producing in modules facilitates the identification of production and quality problems.

Responsiveness

The competitive advantages of faster, dependable response to new markets or to the individual customer's needs have occasionally been noted in the business media (Vessey 1991, Eisenhardt and Brown 1998, and Stalk 1988). For example, in a study of the U.S. and Japanese robotics industry, the National Science Foundation found that the Japanese tend to be about 25 percent faster than Americans, and to spend 10 percent less, in developing and marketing new robots. The major difference is that the Americans spend more time and money on marketing, whereas the Japanese spend five times more than the Americans on developing more efficient production methods.

Table 1.4 identifies a number of prerequisites for and advantages of fast, dependable response. These include higher quality, faster revenue generation, and lower costs through elimination of overhead, reduction of inventories, greater efficiency, and fewer errors and scrap. One of the most important but least recognized advantages for managers is that by responding faster, they can allow a customer to delay an order until the exact need is known. Thus, the customer does not have to change the order—a perennial headache for most operations managers.

$\mathcal{T}$ABLE 1.4 • Prerequisites for and Advantages of Rapid Response

1	*Sharper focus on the customer.* Faster response for both standard and custom-designed items places the customer at the center of attention.
2	*Better management.* Attention shifts to management's real job, improving the firm's infrastructure and systems.
3	*Efficient processing.* Efficient processing reduces inventories, eliminates non-value-added processing steps, smoothes flows, and eliminates bottlenecks.
4	*Higher quality.* Since there is no time for rework, the production system must be sufficiently improved to make parts accurately, reliably, consistently, and correctly.
5	*Elimination of overhead.* More efficient, faster flows through fewer steps eliminate the overhead needed to support the remaining steps, processes, and systems.
6	*Improved focus.* A customer-based focus is provided for strategy, investment, and general attention (instead of an internal focus on surrogate measures such as utilization).
7	*Reduced changes.* With less time to delivery, there is less time for changes in product mix, engineering changes, and especially changes to the order by the customer who just wanted to get in the queue in the first place.
8	*Faster revenue generation.* With faster deliveries, orders can be billed faster, thereby improving cash flows and reducing the need for working capital.
9	*Better communication.* More direct communication lines result in fewer mistakes, oversights, and lost orders.
10	*Improved morale.* The reduced processing steps and overhead allow workers to see the results of their efforts, giving a feeling of working for a smaller firm, with its greater visibility and responsibility.

Faster response to a customer also can, up to a point, reduce the unit costs of the product or service, sometimes significantly. On the basis of empirical studies reported by Meredith et al. (1994) and illustrated in Figure 1.6, it seems that there is about a 2:1 (i.e., 0.50) relationship between response time and unit cost. That is, starting from typical values, an 80 percent reduction in response time results in a corresponding

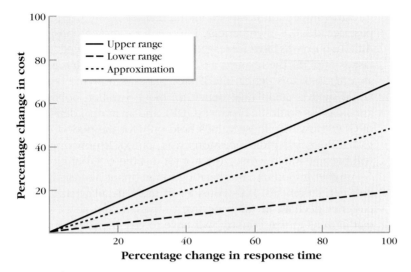

Figure 1.6 Cost reductions with decreases in response time.

40 percent reduction in unit cost. The actual empirical data indicated a range between about 0.60 and 0.20, so for an 80 percent reduction in response time there could be a cost reduction from a high of .60 × 80 percent = 48 percent to a low of 16 percent.

This is an overwhelming benefit because if corresponding price reductions are made, it improves the value delivered to the customer through both higher responsiveness and lower price. The result for the producer is a much higher market share. If the producer chooses not to reduce the price, then the result is both higher margins and higher sales, for significantly increased profitability.

$\mathscr{S}$TRATEGY AND COMPETITIVENESS _____

Competitiveness can be defined in a number of ways. We may think of it as the long-term viability of a firm or organization; or we may define it in a short-term context such as the current success of a firm in the marketplace as measured by its market share or its profitability. We can also talk about the competitiveness of a nation, in the sense of its aggregate competitive success in all markets. The U.S. President's Council on Industrial Competitiveness gave this definition in 1985:

> Competitiveness for a nation is the degree to which it can, under free and fair market conditions, produce goods and services that meet the test of international markets while simultaneously maintaining and expanding the real incomes of its citizens.

Global Trends

The United States provides a graphic example of global trade trends. The trend in merchandise trade for the United States is startling. Although some might think that foreign competition has been taking markets away from U.S. producers only in the past decade, U.S. merchandise imports have grown considerably for over 30 years. Although *exports* have increased over this period as well, they have not increased as fast as imports; the result is an exploding trade deficit with foreign countries. Partly as a result of this deficit, the United States is now the biggest debtor nation in the world, with a cumulative deficit of about 5 trillion dollars, nearly half of the U.S. annual gross domestic product (GDP), and an annual deficit running about 6 percent of GDP. However, these values hold only for the period up to mid-2008, when the global financial/credit/recession crisis started. It now appears that all these figures will become much worse, and not for just the U.S. but globally.

Another important issue relating to the financial crisis involves the exchange rate between currencies. Let's consider in more detail what it means when a country's currency declines in value relative to foreign currencies. A weaker currency means that citizens in that country will have to pay more for products imported from foreign countries. Meanwhile, the prices for products produced in that country and exported to foreign countries will decline, making them more desirable. Thus, a decline in the value of a country's currency is a double-edged sword. Such a decline makes imported goods more expensive for citizens to purchase but at the same time makes exports less expensive for foreign consumers, increasing the demand for domestic products.

As an example, let's consider the American dollar. In the financial crisis of 2008, the dollar grew stronger as Americans sold foreign assets and foreigners rushed to hold assets in the dollar, the world's strongest currency, as well as a "reserve" (commodities are priced in dollars) currency. However, given the massive amount of dollars the U.S. government borrowed and created to overcome the financial crisis, there is widespread concern that the dollar may weaken or even collapse in the future.

According to economic theory, a stronger dollar should make American products less desirable (or competitive) in foreign markets, and imports more desirable in American markets. However, some market actions that governments and businesses often take to keep from losing customers can alter this perfect economic relationship. For instance, in the 1990s, when the price of Japanese products in the United States started increasing in terms of dollars, Japanese firms initiated huge cost-cutting drives to reduce the cost (and thereby the dollar price) of their products, to keep from losing American customers, which was largely successful. Similarly, China controls the exchange rate of its currency, the renminbi, to stay at about 7 to the dollar (though they have been letting it strengthen recently) so it always sells its goods at a competitive price.

In the last decade, particularly with the economic rise of China and India, global markets, manufacturers, and service producers have evolved in a dramatic fashion. With the changes occurring in the World Trade Organization (WTO), international competition has grown very complex in the last two decades. Previously, firms were domestic, exporters, or international. A domestic firm produced and sold in the same country. An exporter sold goods, often someone else's, abroad. An international firm sold domestically produced as well as foreign-produced goods both domestically and in foreign countries. However, domestic sales were usually produced domestically, and foreign sales were made either in the home country or in a plant in the foreign country, typically altered to suit national regulations, needs, and tastes.

Now, however, there are global firms, joint ventures, partial ownerships, foreign subsidiaries, and other types of international producers. For example, Canon is a global producer that sells a standard "world-class" camera with options and add-ons available through the local dealer. And automobile producers frequently own stock in foreign automobile companies. Mazak, a fast-growing machine tool company, is the U.S. subsidiary of Yamazaki Machinery Company of Japan. Part of the reason for cross-ownerships and cross-endeavors is the spiraling cost of bringing out new products. New drugs and memory chips run in the hundreds of millions to billions of dollars to bring to market. By using joint ventures and other such approaches to share costs (and thereby lower risks), firms can remain competitive.

Whether to build offshore, assemble offshore, use foreign parts, employ a joint venture, and so on is a complex decision for any firm and depends on a multitude of factors. For example, the Japanese have many of their automobile manufacturing plants in foreign countries. The reasons are many and include: to circumvent foreign governmental regulation of importers, to avoid the high yen cost of Japanese-produced products, to avoid import fees and quotas, and to placate foreign consumers. Of course, other considerations are involved in producing in foreign countries: culture (e.g., if women are part of the labor force), political stability, laws, taxes, regulations, and image.

Other complex arrangements of suppliers can result in hidden international competition. For example, many products that bear an American nameplate have been totally produced and assembled in a foreign country and are simply imported under a U.S. manufacturer's or retailer's nameplate, such as Nike shoes. Even more confusing, many products contain a significant proportion of foreign parts, or may be composed entirely of foreign parts and only assembled in the United States (e.g., toasters, mixers, hand tools). This recent strategic approach of finding the best mix of producers and assemblers to deliver a product or service to a customer has come to be known as "supply chain management," a topic we discuss in detail in Chapter 7.

Strategy

The organization's business strategy is a set of objectives, plans, and policies for the organization to compete successfully in its markets. In effect, the business strategy specifies what an organization's competitive advantage will be and how this advantage will be achieved and sustained. As we will see, a key aspect of the business strategy is defining the organization's core competencies and focus. The actual strategic plan that details the business strategy is typically formulated at the executive committee level (CEO, president, vice presidents). It is usually long range, in the neighborhood of three to five years.

In fact, however, the decisions that are made over time *are* the long-range strategy. In too many firms, these decisions show no pattern at all, reflecting the truth that they have no active business strategy, even if they have gone through a process of strategic planning. In other cases these decisions bear little or no relationship to the organization's stated or official business strategy. The point is that an organization's actions often tell more about its true business strategy than its public statements.

The general process of formulating a business strategy is illustrated in Figure 1.7. Relevant inputs to the strategic planning process include the organization's vision/ mission statement, a variety of factors external to the organization, and a range of factors internal to the organization. One school of thought—the ***Resource Based View***—considers the set of resources (an internal factor in Figure 1.7) available to

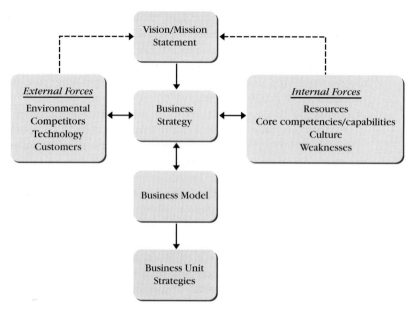

Figure 1.7   Strategy formulation.

the organization as the primary driver of the business strategy. For further discussion of this topic and its impact on the development of corporate strategy, consult Barney and Clark (2007) or Collis and Montgomery (2005).

After collectively considering these inputs, strategic planning is often initiated by developing a vision statement, a mission statement, or both. ***Vision statements*** are used to express the organization's values and aspirations. ***Mission statements*** express the organization's purpose or reason for existence. In some cases, organizations may choose to combine the vision and mission statements into a single statement. Regardless of whether separate statements or combined statements are developed, the intent is to communicate the organization's values, aspirations, and purpose so that employees can make decisions that are consistent with and support these objectives.

Effective vision and mission statements tend to be written using language that inspires employees to high levels of performance. Further, to foster employees' commitment, it is advisable to include a wide variety of employees in the development of the vision or mission statement, rather than enforcing top management's view by edict. Once the vision and mission statements are developed for the organization as a whole, divisions, departments, process teams, project teams, work groups, and so on can develop individual vision-mission statements that support the organization's overall statement. For example, after a university develops its overall vision-mission statement, each college could develop its own unique statements specifying the role that it will play in supporting the overall mission of the university. Likewise, once each school develops its own vision-mission statement, the departments within the school can develop unique statements. Having each organizational unit develop its own unique statements promotes wider participation in the process, helps employees think in terms of how their work supports the overall mission, and results

THE CENTRAL INTELLIGENCE AGENCY

Vision

One Agency. One Community. An Agency unmatched in its core capabilities, functioning as one team, fully integrated into the Intelligence Community.

Mission

We are the nation's first line of defense. We accomplish what others cannot accomplish and go where others cannot go. We carry out our mission by:

- Collecting information that reveals the plans, intentions, and capabilities of our adversaries and provides the basis for decision and action.

- Producing timely analysis that provided insight, warning, and opportunity to the President and decision makers charged with protecting and advancing America's interests.

- Conducting covert action at the direction of the President to preempt threats or achieve U.S. policy objectives.

Figure 1.8 An example of a vision and mission statement.

in statements that are more meaningful to a select group of employees. An example of an actual vision and mission statement are given in Figure 1.8.

In addition to the vision/mission statement, other important inputs in the formulation of the business strategy are categorized as forces external and forces internal to the organization in Figure 1.7. Although both sets of forces are considered to some extent in formulating the vision/mission statement (as shown by the dotted lines in the figure), they are considered at a more detailed level and more directly when developing the business strategy. Important external forces include the environment (e.g., the economy, government regulations, climate), competitors (e.g., new product introductions, industry consolidation, new entrants from outside the industry), the technology available, and customer requirements. Relevant internal forces include organizational resources, the organization's core competencies/capabilities, its culture, and its weaknesses. As shown, there is a bidirectional relationship between the organization's business strategy and both the internal and external forces. For example, an action by a key competitor may impact the organization's strategy just as its business strategy may force a reaction by a key competitor.

Overall, as seen in Figure 1.7, strategy is primarily concerned with making sets of choices that result in a "business model" which provides the tools to help further develop and communicate the strategy. In particular, the business model can help an organization verify that the elements of the strategy are consistent with one another, that they are logical, and that they are mutually reinforcing. Business models typically including expanded verbal discussions of key elements of the strategy as well as quantitative projections for important operational, marketing, and financial aspects of the business.

To help further understand the distinction between strategy and a business model, consider the construction of a custom home. Initially, the architect consults with the future homeowners to understand how they envision the home and their life within it. The architect then creates a design to fulfill this vision. This corresponds to strategy. Next, the architect prepares a detailed floor plan and elevation based on the choices made during the design process. These correspond to the business model. Just as a business model can be used to help analyze and communicate strategic choices, the floor plan can be used to help understand, analyze, and communicate the design choices that were made.

Once the business strategy has been developed and the resulting business model analyzed, the final step in strategy formulation is the development of business unit strategies. At this stage, each business unit develops its own strategy to guide its activities so that they are consistent and support the organization's overall business strategy. Although formulating the business strategy is displayed as rather straightforward in Figure 1.7, in reality it is very iterative.

Strategic Frameworks

We now move to a discussion of the Business Unit Strategies box in Figure 1.7. Clearly, there will be a Marketing Strategy, a Financial Strategy, an R&D Strategy, and so on. Here, of course, we are interested in the Operations Strategy. As it happens, there are a number of fairly well defined such strategies. One that is common to many of the functional areas is related to the life cycle of the organization's products or services.

The Life Cycle

A number of functional strategies are tied to the stages in the standard ***life cycle*** of products and services, shown in Figure 1.9. Studies of the introduction of new products indicate that the life cycle (or *stretched-S growth curve*, as it is also known)

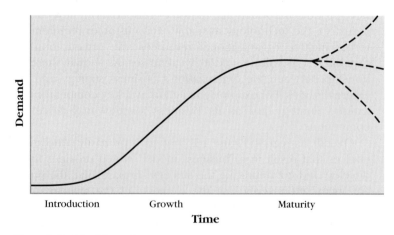

Figure 1.9   The life-cycle curve.

provides a good pattern for the growth of demand for a new output. The curve can be divided into three major segments: (1) introduction and early adoption, (2) acceptance and growth of the market, and (3) maturity with market saturation. After market saturation, demand may remain high or decline; or the output may be improved and possibly start on a new growth curve.

The length of product and service life cycles has been shrinking significantly in the last decade or so. In the past, a life cycle might have been five years, but it is now six months. This places a tremendous burden on the firm to constantly monitor its strategy and quickly change a strategy that becomes inappropriate to the market.

The life cycle begins with an *innovation*—a new output or process for the market, as discussed earlier. The innovation may be a patented product or process, a new combination of existing elements that has created a unique product or process, or some service that was previously unavailable. Initial versions of the product or service may change relatively frequently; production volumes are small, since the output has not caught on yet; and margins are high. As volume increases, the design of the output stabilizes and more competitors enter the market, frequently with more capital-intensive equipment. In the mature phase, the now high-volume output is a virtual commodity, and the firm that can produce an acceptable version at the lowest cost usually controls the market.

Clearly, a firm's business strategy should match the life-cycle stages of its products and services. If a firm such as Hewlett-Packard is good at innovation, it may choose to focus only on the introduction and acceptance phases of the product's life cycle and then sell or license production to others as the product moves beyond the introduction stage. If its strength is in high-volume, low-cost production, the company should stick with proven products that are in the maturity stage. Most common, perhaps, are firms that attempt to stick with products throughout their life cycle, changing their strategy with each stage.

One approach to categorizing an organization's business strategy is based on its timing of introductions of new outputs. Two researchers, Maidique and Patch (1979), suggest the following four product development strategies:

1. **First-to-market.** Organizations that use this strategy attempt to have their products available before the competition. To achieve this, strong applied research is needed. If a company is first to market, it has to decide if it wants to price its products high and thus skim the market to achieve large short-term profits or set a lower initial price to obtain a higher market share and perhaps larger long-term profits.

2. **Second-to-market.** Organizations that use this strategy try to quickly imitate successful outputs offered by first-to-market organizations. This strategy requires less emphasis on applied research and more emphasis on fast development. Often, firms that use the second-to-market strategy attempt to learn from the mistakes of the first-to-market firm and offer improved or enhanced versions of the original products.

3. **Cost minimization** or **late-to-market.** Organizations that use this strategy wait until a product becomes fairly standardized and is demanded in large volumes. They then attempt to compete on the basis of costs as opposed to

features of the product. These organizations focus most of their research and development on improving the production system, as opposed to focusing on product development.

4. ***Market segmentation.*** This strategy focuses on serving niche markets with specific needs. Applied engineering skills and flexible manufacturing systems are often needed for the market-segmentation strategy.

Be aware that a number of implicit tradeoffs are involved in developing a strategy. Let us use the first-to-market strategy to demonstrate. A first-to-market strategy requires large investments in product development in an effort to stay ahead of the competition. Typically, organizations that pursue this strategy expect to achieve relatively higher profit margins, larger market shares, or both as a result of initially having the market to themselves. The strategy is somewhat risky because a competitor may end up beating them to the market. Also, even if a company succeeds in getting to the market first, it may end up simply creating an opportunity for the competition to learn from its mistakes and overtake it in the market. To illustrate, although Sony introduced its Betamax format for VCRs in 1975, JVC's VHS format—introduced the following year— is the standard that ultimately gained widespread market acceptance.

Such tradeoffs are basic to the concept of selecting a business strategy. Although specific tasks must be done well to execute the selected strategy, not everything needs to be particularly outstanding—only a few things. And of course, strategies based on anything else—acquisitions, mergers, tax loss carry-forwards, even streams of high-technology products—will not be successful if the customer is ignored in the process.

Performance Frontiers

As we know from the earlier Customer Value section, there is a wide range of benefits and costs that organizations can compete on and various groups of customers value. If, say, n of these factors are important for an organization to consider, we might then conceive of a graph or space with n dimensions on it showing the organization's measures on each of the n factors as well as their competitor's measures. The curve connecting all these measures would then be called the organization's ***performance frontier*** (Clark 1996). For simplicity, let us use just two factors, say cost and variety, as shown in Figure 1.10 with the performance frontier curve labeled 1.

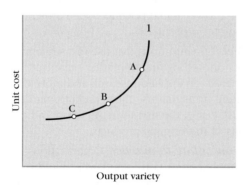

Figure 1.10   Example performance frontier.

As illustrated by the points A, B, and C, improving on one dimension can usually only be attained by sacrificing performance on another dimension. For example, as shown in Figure 1.10, increasing output variety may result in higher unit costs. In effect, this curve represents the level of performance that organizations in an industry can achieve across two dimensions given the technology available. According to the figure, company A is apparently pursuing more of a variety strategy than the two other competitors shown, offering a wider variety of outputs but incurring greater cost. We might think of J.C. Penney as perhaps fitting point A. Company C, perhaps Kmart, seems to be pursuing a standardization strategy, offering a smaller range of outputs but incurring lower unit costs.

An interesting use of this framework is to investigate and evaluate the impact of a change in technology or operational innovation (Hammer 2004). For example, in Figure 1.11, assume a new innovation such as "cross-docking" has been developed by company B, perhaps represented by Wal-Mart, shifting its performance frontier to curve 2. In this case, company B could hold its unit price constant and offer higher output variety than company A and at lower unit cost (position B1). Alternatively, company B could maintain its current level of output variety and lower its unit cost to levels below company C's (position B2), or perhaps choose a position somewhere between points B1 and B2.

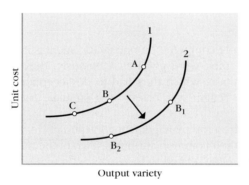

Figure 1.11   Development of new technology results in shift in the performance frontier.

Suppose you were employed at company A and company B chose to operate at point B1. In effect, company B can now offer a wider variety of outputs and at lower unit costs. What are your options? As it turns out, there are two generic options or ***improvement trajectories*** company A could try to follow. One improvement trajectory would be for company A to streamline its operations and make cost-variety tradeoffs, moving down curve 1 toward company C. Upon streamlining its operations, company A could then attempt to adopt the new technology and choose a position on the new frontier. A second improvement trajectory would be for company A to attempt to directly adopt the new technology and move to the new frontier without streamlining its current operations.

There are advantages and disadvantages associated with both trajectories. An advantage of streamlining operations first is that this may provide a better understanding of current processes. In turn, this better understanding may increase company A's options in choosing a location on the new frontier and may even better position it to adopt the new technology. One drawback of streamlining its current operations first is that the knowledge gained may be irrelevant when the new technology is eventually adopted, and delaying the adoption of the new technology may mean reduced market share and profits. Another important factor is the amount of time required to execute the improvement trajectory and get to the new position on the new performance frontier. However, although it might appear that streamlining the current operation first before adopting the new technology should take more time than immediately adopting the technology, when ease of implementation is considered, the former approach may in fact be more expedient.

On a more practical note, Kmart some years ago tried to challenge Wal-Mart on low prices but was unsuccessful. Then Sears and Kmart merged instead; but at this time, that didn't seem to work well either and now both seem to be in trouble.

One final point. In Figure 1.11 it was assumed that the result of the new technology/innovation was simply a shift in the performance frontier. It is also important to be aware of the possibility that a new technology can change the shape as well as the location of the performance frontier. Such a change in shape can have important implications regarding choosing a location on the new frontier as well as the nature of the tradeoff facing the industry. In either case, the way to beat your competition is through developing or using new technology to move to a new frontier.

Focus

In the past, firms primarily competed on one factor, such as low cost, or innovation, because that was what they were good at. Obviously, they could not ignore the other factors of competition, which they had to do acceptably on, but their heavy attention to their one strength was based on a strategic framework called *focus* (Skinner 1974).

McKinsey & Company, a top management consulting firm, studied 27 outstanding successful firms to find their common attributes. Two of the major attributes reported in *Business Week* are directly related to focus:

1. ***Stressing one key business value.*** At Hewlett-Packard, the key value is developing new products; at Dana Corporation, it is improving productivity.
2. ***Sticking to what they know best.*** All the outstanding firms define their core capabilities (or strengths) and then build on them. They resist the temptation to move into new areas or diversify.

When an organization chooses to stress one or two key areas of strength, it is referred to as a *focused organization*. For example, IBM is known for its customer service, General Electric for its technology, and Procter & Gamble for its consumer marketing. In general, most but not all areas of focus relate to operations. Some firms, such as those in the insurance industry, focus on financial strength and others focus on marketing strengths. For example, Harley-Davidson considers its strength to be in building relationships with its dealers and motorcycle owners. And many health care organizations are achieving significant operational efficiencies by focusing on a narrow range of ailments. For example, by treating only long-term acute cases, Intensiva HealthCare has been able to reduce its costs to 50 percent of those of a traditional intensive-care ward. Clearly, adapting a focus strategy means knowing not only what customers to concentrate on but also knowing what customers you do *not* want.

Table 1.5 identifies several areas of focus that organizations commonly choose when forming their competitive strategy; all are various forms of differentiation. Recent competitive behavior among firms seems to be dividing most of the factors in Table 1.5 into two sets that Terry Hill (2000), an operations strategist and researcher in England, calls *order qualifiers* and *order winners*. An **order qualifier** is a characteristic of the product or service that is required if the product is even to be considered or in the running. In other words, it is a prerequisite for entering the market. An **order winner** is a characteristic that will win the bid or the purchase. These qualifiers and winners vary with the market, of course, but some general commonalties exist across markets. For example, response time, performance, customization, innovation, and price seem to be frequent order winners, and the other factors (e.g., quality, reliability, and flexibility) tend to be order qualifiers. Working with marketing and sales to properly identify which factors are which is clearly of major strategic importance.

𝒯ABLE 1.5 • Common Areas of Organizational Focus

- *Innovation:* Bringing a range of new products and services to market quickly
- *Customization:* Being able to quickly redesign and produce a product or service to meet customers' unique needs
- *Flexibility of products and services:* Switching between different models or variants quickly to satisfy a customer or market
- *Flexibility of volume:* Changing quickly and economically from low-volume production to high volumes and vice versa
- *Performance:* Offering products and services with unique, valuable features
- *Quality:* Having better craftsmanship or consistency
- *Reliability of the product or service:* Always working acceptably, enabling customers to count on the performance
- *Reliability of delivery:* Always fulfilling promises with a product or service that is never late
- *Response:* Offering very short lead times to obtain products and services
- *After-sale service:* Making available extensive, continuing help
- *Price:* Having the lowest price

In addition to the advantages of being focused, there are also some dangers. A narrowly focused firm can easily become uncompetitive in the market if the customers' requirements change. In addition to being focused, a firm must also be flexible enough to alter its focus when the need changes and to spot the change in time. Frequently, a focus in one area can be used to an advantage in another way, if there is enough time to adapt—for example, to move into a new product line or alter the application of the focus. Moreover, as products go through their life cycle, the task of operations often changes, as shown in Figure 1.12, from being flexible enough to accept changes in design, to meeting the growing demand in the marketplace, to

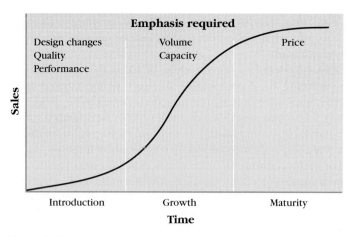

Figure 1.12   Product life cycle: stages and emphasis.

cutting costs. Throughout this life cycle, the focus of the organization has to change, if it stays with the same output. Many firms, however, choose to compete at only one stage of the life cycle and abandon other stages, so that they can keep the strength of their original focus.

An organization can also easily lose its focus. For example, in the traditional functional organization, purchasing may buy the cheapest materials it can. This requires buying large quantities with advance notice. Scheduling, however, is trying to reduce inventories so it orders materials on short notice and in small quantities. Quality control is trying to improve the output, so it carefully inspects every item, creating delays and extensive rework. In this example, each functional department is pursuing its own objectives but is not focusing on how it can support the organization's overall business strategy.

However, the most common reason a firm loses its focus is simply that the focus was never clearly identified in the first place. Never having been well defined, it could not be communicated to the employees, could therefore not gain their support, and thus was lost. Sometimes a focus is identified but not communicated throughout the organization, because management thinks that lower-level employees don't need to know the strategic focus of the firm in order to do their jobs.

The Sand Cone

For many organizations that relied on the focus framework of strategy, the traditional view was that competing on one competitive dimension required trading off performance on one or more other dimensions (e.g., higher quality results in higher costs). However, research suggests that, at least in some cases, building strengths along alternative competitive dimensions may in fact be cumulative and that building a strength on one dimension may facilitate building strengths on other dimensions (Ferdows and De Meyer 1990).

Furthermore, according to this research there is a preferred order in developing strengths on various competitive dimensions. According to the Sand Cone Model (as it is called) shown in Figure 1.13, organizations should first develop the capability to

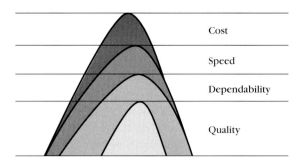

Figure 1.13   The Sand Cone Model. (Adapted from Ferdows and De Meyer 1990, p. 175.)

produce quality outputs. Once an organization has developed this proficiency, it is next appropriate to address the issue of delivery dependability. Next, according to the model, the competitive dimensions of speed and cost should be addressed, respectively.

In addition to providing guidance to organizations regarding the order in which to focus their attention and initiatives, the model has intuitive appeal. For example, it makes little sense to focus on improving delivery dependability before an organization can provide a consistent level of quality. In today's competitive marketplace, providing defective outputs in a timely fashion is not a recipe for long-term success. Likewise, organizations should achieve consistent quality levels and delivery dependability before attempting to reduce lead times. Of course, the model is not set in stone (remember it is called the Sand Cone) and organizations facing different circumstances may choose to address the competitive dimensions in a different order. We will return to these critical competitive factors in the final section of this chapter.

Core Capabilities

One important result of developing a business strategy is identifying the organization's core competencies and capabilities that provide those product/service dimensions important to customers and hence the source of customer value. **Core competencies** (Prahalad and Hamel 1990) are the collective knowledge and skills an organization has that distinguish it from the competition. In effect, these core competencies become the building blocks for organizational practices and business processes, referred to as **core capabilities** (Stalk et al. 1992). (Hereafter we will refer to both of these simply as "core capabilities.") The importance of these core capabilities derives from their strong relationship to an organization's ability to integrate a variety of technologies and skills in the development of new products and services. Clearly, then, one of top management's most important activities is the identification and development of the core capabilities the organization will need to successfully execute the business strategy.

In effect, core capabilities provide the basis for developing new products and services and are a primary factor in determining an organization's long-term competitiveness. Hammer (2004) points out the importance of "operational innovation" in the organization as one basis for sustained competitive advantage, the clear result of a core capability. Therefore, two important parts of strategic planning are identifying and predicting the core capabilities that will be critical to sustaining and enhancing the organization's competitive position. On this basis, an organization can also assess its suppliers' and competitors' capabilities. If the organization finds that it is not the leader, it must determine the cost and risks of catching up with the best versus the cost and risks of losing that core capability.

Hayes and Pisano (1994) stress the importance of a firm not looking for "the" solution to a current competitive problem but rather the "paths" to building one or two core capabilities to provide the source of customer value for the indefinite future. Moreover, the firm should not think in terms of "tradeoffs" between core capabilities (e.g., moving from flexibility as a strength to low cost), but rather "building" one capability on top of others, and which *set* will provide the most customer value.

Often, it is more useful to think of an organization in terms of its portfolio of core capabilities, rather than its portfolio of businesses or products. For instance, Sony is known for its expertise in miniaturization; 3M for its knowledge of substrates, coatings, and adhesives; Black and Decker for small electrical motors and industrial design; Boeing for its ability to integrate large-scale complex systems; and Honda for engines and power trains. Had Sony initially viewed itself as primarily a manufacturer of Walkmans, rather than as a company with expertise in miniaturization, it might have overlooked several profitable opportunities, such as entering the camcorder business. As another example, Boeing has successfully leveraged its core capability related to integrating large-scale systems in its production of commercial jetliners, space stations, fighter-bombers, and missiles.

As these examples illustrate, core capabilities are often used to gain access to a wide variety of markets. Cannon used its core capabilities in optics, imaging, and electronic controls to enter the markets for copiers, laser printers, cameras, and image scanners. In a similar fashion, Honda's core capabilities in engines and power trains comprise the basis for its entry into other businesses: automobiles, motorcycles, lawn mowers, and generators.

In addition to providing access to a variety of markets, a core capability should be strongly related to the benefits provided by the product or service that customers value. In Sony's case, its expertise in miniaturization translates directly into important product features such as portability and aesthetic designs. Alternatively, suppose Sony developed a core competence in writing understandable user manuals. Since people who purchase a Walkman or camcorder rarely base their purchase decision on the quality of the user manual (when was the last time you read a user manual?), this core capability would provide little if any competitive advantage.

Another characteristic of core capabilities is that they should be difficult to imitate. Clearly, no sustainable competitive advantage is provided by a core capability that is easily imitated. For example, Sony's expertise in miniaturization would mean little if other electronics manufacturers could match it simply by purchasing and taking apart Sony's products (this is called *reverse engineering*). Bartmess and Cerny (1996) identify three elements of a core capability that hinders imitation:

- It is complex and requires organizational learning over a long period of time
- It is based on multiple functional areas, both internal and external to the organization
- It is a result of *how the functions interact* rather than the skills/knowledge within the functions themselves.

The topic of core capabilities is also strongly related to the recent surge in out-sourcing and offshoring. **_Outsourcing_**—an approach increasingly common—involves subcontracting out certain activities or services. For example, a manufacturer might outsource the production of certain components, the management and main-tenance of its computer resources, employee recruitment, or the processing of its payroll.

When we consider the concept of core capability, it is important to recognize that not all parts, services, or activities are equal. Rather, these activities and parts can be thought of as falling on a continuum ranging from strategically important to unim-portant. Parts and activities are considered strategically important when:

- They are strongly related to what customers perceive to be the key character-istics of the product or service.

- They require highly specialized knowledge and skill, a core capability.

- They require highly specialized physical assets, and few other suppliers pos-sess these assets.

- The organization has a technological lead or is likely to obtain one.

Activities that are not strategic or core are candidates for outsourcing. These parts or activities are not strongly linked to key product characteristics, do not require highly specialized knowledge, do not need special physical assets, and the organization does not have the technological lead in this area. Thus, if it is beneficial to outsource these parts or activities—perhaps because of lower cost or higher quality—no loss in competitiveness should result. On the other hand, when a firm's strategic parts and activ-ities have been outsourced, particularly to a foreign supplier, called **_offshoring_**, the firm has become _hollow_ (Jonas 1986). As we have stated, the wise firm will outsource only nonstrategic, simple, relatively standard parts and processes such as screws or types of processes that are not worth the time for the firm to produce itself; the complex, proprietary parts and processes that give their products an edge in the marketplace are produced internally. If the firm outsources these parts and processes as well, it soon finds that the engineering design talent follows the production of the part out-side the firm, too, and its core capabilities have been lost. Then, the firm has been **_hollowed out_**, becoming merely a distributor of its supplier's products.

Given the huge potential effects of outsourcing, both positive and negative, a firm should consider such a move _very_ carefully. They need to think about the long-term and short-term effects. And they also need to consider the impact of this decision on their core capabilities, and everything else they do within the company. Such a major decision as outsourcing will affect other decisions as well, such as sourcing materials, hiring/releasing labor and management, marketing, finance, and a wide range of other areas.

So what is the problem? If a supplier can deliver the parts at lower cost and better quality when they are needed, why not use them? The problem is that the supplier gains the expertise (and core capabilities) to produce the critical parts you need, and as Hayes and Pisano (1994), among others, note: organizations quickly forget how they produced those critical parts. After a while, when the supplier has improved on the process and you have forgotten how to make the parts, it is likely to start com-peting with you, producing the products you have been selling and dropping you as a customer. This is even more dangerous if, as already noted, the product and transformation system has also been hollowed out, following the production activities to the supplier. This happened extensively in the television industry, where the Japanese learned first how to produce, and then how to engineer black-and-white and, later, color television sets. They then started tentatively introducing their own brands, to see if U.S. customers would buy them. Their products were inexpensive, of high quality, and caught on quickly in the free-enterprise American markets. The Japanese now virtually control this industry, as illustrated in one of our opening examples.

Outsourcing is a growing trend among U.S. manufacturers. The Big Three U.S. automakers are well-known examples of manufacturers that extensively outsourced for years. As other examples, Deere & Co. puts its name on midrange utility tractors produced by a Japanese company, and Agco Corp. outsources the production of almost all of the transmissions and engines used in its farm equipment. Of course, not all manufacturers are jumping on the outsourcing bandwagon. New Balance Athletic Shoes, for example, invested $25 million in its manufacturing facilities as part of an overall strategy to do more assembly in-house.

Kodak's Business Imaging Systems Division (BIS) is one firm that looked into off-shoring and decided against it (Bartmess and Cerny 1996). Initially they took the "traditional" perspective and discovered that overseas wage rates were 75 percent cheaper than domestic rates. [*Note*: Recent research reveals that wages in China are now commonly 96 percent cheaper than domestic U.S. wages!] The traditional perspective is one dominated by considering only current conditions with no thought about the future, a short-term response to a competitive threat, a heavy emphasis on cost (primarily labor), and a singular focus on one function, typically operations, to the exclusion of other functions such as engineering, marketing, and design.

But then BIS considered a capabilities perspective and discovered that:

- Offshore productivity was also low, negating the benefit of low wage rates.
- Large overhead costs were primarily fixed and would not shrink with overseas labor.
- Engineering would also have to accompany manufacturing overseas, but offshore engineering wages were almost equal to domestic wages. Moreover, BIS did not want to lose their domestic engineering competence.
- Over time, foreign wages would be increasing: ". . . once trained and experienced, labor does not stay cheap very long."
- Cost advantages almost equal to the benefit of low offshore wages were available through product redesigns.

BIS hence decided not to move their operation overseas, though they did decide to start an offshore plant for a low-end product for the foreign market, mainly to educate themselves in the advantages and disadvantages of offshore production as well as to learn ways to improve their internal low-cost manufacturing capabilities. (For another view on offshoring, see Markides and Berg 1988.)

Regarding the purpose for outsourcing, it is also important to be aware of another danger of outsourcing activities or parts primarily on the basis of "cost." To illustrate, assume a manufacturer produces four product lines each with an annual volume of 100,000 units. Further assume that the company's overhead is £1.2 million (British pounds). Allocating this overhead evenly across the four product lines would result in each unit being allocated £3 in overhead charges. Now suppose that in the interest of lowering its cost and increasing its competitiveness, the manufacturer investigates outsourcing products that can be produced at lower unit costs by external suppliers. In fact, suppose that a supplier is found for one of its product lines. What is the impact of outsourcing this product line? Clearly on one hand, the company obtains the product at a lower unit cost. But what is the impact on the remaining product lines and the organization's overhead?

More than likely, outsourcing one product line will not have a dramatic impact on total overhead; however, the amount of overhead each unit must now absorb increases from £3/unit to £4/unit. In effect, each unit now appears to be more expensive to produce internally. Thus, outsourcing other product lines now appears to be warranted and likely will be investigated. As you can see, this logic results in a vicious cycle commonly referred to as the ***creeping breakeven phenomenon.*** As outputs are outsourced, the remaining outputs appear to be more expensive to produce in-house. This creates an incentive to outsource even more outputs. The logical conclusion of this process is that the organization ends up producing no outputs and going bankrupt.

$\mathcal{F}$ROM STRATEGY TO STRUCTURE _____

Now that the subject of operations strategy has been described, we are ready to tackle the operations concepts that reflect this strategy in the remainder of the book. In general, there are two main sets of concepts that need to be discussed. One set is the major functions of operations that impact strategy, and the other is the three integrated thrusts we see occurring in organizations today: supply chain management, six sigma for improving processes, and lean for improving processes.

The book is divided into three parts: I: Operations Strategy, II: Operations Processes, and III: Supply Chain Management. We have just finished the first part, consisting solely of Chapter 1: Operations Strategy and Global Competitiveness. The others are discussed below.

Part II: OPERATIONS PROCESSES

Chapter 2: Designing the Transformation System—this chapter describes the various ways of organizing the transformation processes and each of their advantages and disadvantages. Such processes represent one of the major functions of operations.

Chapter 3: Monitoring and Controlling the Transformation System—in this chapter, we describe the control element of the production system, with special attention to quality control as our primary example.

Chapter 4: Six Sigma for Improving the Transformation System—we devote two chapters to the major thrusts in industry today to improve their processes. This chapter focuses on the use of the six sigma approach to follow up on the control element in Chapter 3, where the production processes have been found to need improvement in terms of reducing their variation.

Chapter 5: Lean Operations Improve Transformation System Value—here we investigate techniques to further improve the production processes by eliminating waste in processes, thereby saving cost, effort, and time.

Chapter 6: Project Management and the Transformation System—having decided on our production processes, or ways to improve them, we now need to execute on our plan. This is done through the procedures of project management. We illustrate the procedures with a process improvement example, but project management can be applied to many other activities that organizations undertake, and especially activities involving change.

Part III: SUPPLY CHAIN MANAGEMENT

Chapter 7: Managing Supply Chain Logistics and Inventories—in this chapter we cover a range of topics that involve the supply chain such as inventory, material requirements planning and enterprise requirements planning, logistics, purchasing, and many others.

Chapter 8: Capacity Management through Location and Scheduling—this chapter completes the description of the major functions of operations.

EXPAND YOUR UNDERSTANDING

1. Why is it so hard to increase productivity in the service sector?

2. Identify other major differences between services and products in addition to those listed in Table 1.1.

3. Many foreign firms have been successful in the following areas: steel, autos, cameras, radios, and televisions. Are services more protected from foreign competition? How?

4. It is commonly said that Japanese firms employ 10 times as many engineers per operations worker as U.S. firms and 10 times fewer accountants. What effect would you expect this to have on their competitiveness? Why?

5. How might the concept of a "facilitating good" alter the way we perceive a product? A service?

6. Is it wise for a firm to stick to what it knows best, or should it expand its market by moving into adjoining products or services? How can it avoid losing its focus?

7. What do you think the result will be of the continuing escalation of the U.S. trade deficit? Will a gradual devaluation of the dollar solve the "problem?" If it does, what do you think will be the resulting effect on the United States?

8. Can you think of any other areas of possible focus for a firm besides those identified in Table 1.5?

9. What core capabilities do you think China possesses? India? Japan? The United States?

10. According to K. Blanchard and N. V. Peale (*The Power of Ethical Management,* New York: Morrow, 1988), the following three ethical tests may be useful: (1) Is it legal or within company policy? (2) Is it balanced and fair in the short and long term? (3) Would you be proud if the public or your family knew about it? Apply these tests to the following situations:

   a. A foreign firm subsidizes its sales in another country.

   b. A foreign firm dumps its products (sells them for less than cost) in another country.

   c. A country imports products that, had they been made domestically, would have violated domestic laws (e.g., laws against pollution).

11. In responding faster to customers' needs, where might the cost savings come from? What benefits would result?

12. Can you think of companies that have moved the performance frontier of their industries?

13. Why do Americans invest more in marketing new products while the Japanese invest more in engineering? What advantages accrue to each investment?

14. Using new technologies, it is not uncommon for firms to cut their response times by a factor of ten. What effect would you expect this to have on their unit costs?

15. With the increasing trend of offshoring in the United States, although companies may get richer, what will happen to their workers? What will the future hold?

16. What are the order winners and order qualifiers for Wal-Mart? Toyota? BMW? Sony?

17. Given the recent trends in products and services, does the focus strategy or sand cone strategy seem most applicable these days?

18. Why don't we see more mass customization in products and services?

APPLY YOUR UNDERSTANDING
Incident 1: Taracare, Inc.

Taracare, Inc. operates a single factory in Ensenada, Mexico, where it fabricates and assembles a wide range of outdoor furniture for the USA market, including chairs, tables, and matching accessories. Taracare's primary production activities include extruding the aluminum furniture parts, bending and shaping the extruded parts, finishing and painting the parts, and then assembling the parts into completed furniture. Upholstery, glass tabletops, and all hardware are purchased from outside suppliers.

Jorge Gonzalez purchased Taracare in 2001. Before that, Jorge had distinguished himself as a top sales rep of outdoor furniture for the western region of one of the leading national manufacturers. However, after spending 10 years on the road, Jorge wanted to settle down and spend more time with his family back in Mexico. After searching for a couple of months, he came across what he believed to be an ideal opportunity. Not only was it in an industry that he had a great deal of knowledge about, but he would be his own boss. Unfortunately, the asking price was well beyond Jorge's means. However, after a month of negotiation, Jorge convinced Jesus Garza, Taracare's founder, to maintain a 25 percent stake in the business. Although Jesus had originally intended to sell out completely, he was impressed with Jorge's knowledge of the business, his extensive contacts, and his enthusiasm. He therefore agreed to sell Jorge 75 percent of Taracare and retain 25 percent as an investment.

Jorge's ambition for Taracare was to expand it from a small regional manufacturer to one that sold to major national retailers. To accomplish this objective, Jorge's first initiative was to triple Taracare's sales force in 2002. As sales began to increase, Jorge increased the support staff by hiring an accountant, a comptroller, two new designers, and a purchasing agent.

By mid-2005, Taracare's line was carried by several national retailers on a trial basis. However, Taracare was having difficulty both in meeting the deliveries its sales reps were promising and in satisfying the national retailers' standards for quality. To respond to this problem, Jorge hired Alfredo Diaz as the new manufacturing manager. Before accepting Jorge's offer, Alfredo was the plant manager of a factory that manufactured replacement windows sold by large regional and national retailers.

After several months on the job—and after making little progress toward improving on-time delivery and quality—Alfredo scheduled a meeting with Jorge to discuss his major concerns. Alfredo began:

> I requested this meeting with you, Jorge, because I am not satisfied with the progress we are making toward improving our delivery performance and quality. The bottom line is that I feel I'm getting very little cooperation from the other department heads. For example, last month purchasing switched to a new supplier for paint; and although it is true that the new paint costs

less per gallon, we have to apply a thicker coat to give the furniture the same protection. I haven't actually run the numbers, but I know it is actually costing us more, in both materials and labor.

Another problem is that we typically run a special promotion to coincide with launching new product lines. I understand that the sales guys want to get the product into the stores as quickly as possible, but they are making promises about delivery that we can't meet. It takes time to work out the bugs and get things running smoothly. Then there is the problem with the designers. They are constantly adding features to the product that make it almost impossible for us to produce. At the very least, they make it much more expensive for us to produce. For example, on the new "Destiny" line, they designed table legs that required a new die at a cost of 250,000 pesos. Why couldn't they have left the legs alone so that we could have used one of our existing dies? On top of this, we have the accounting department telling us that our equipment utilization is too low. Then, when we increase our equipment utilization and make more products, the finance guys tell us we have too much capital tied up in inventory. To be honest, I really don't feel that I'm getting very much support.

Rising from his chair, Jorge commented:

You have raised some important issues, Alfredo. Unfortunately, I have to run to another meeting right now. Why don't you send me a memo outlining these issues and your recommendations? Then perhaps I will call a meeting and we can discuss these issues with the other department heads. At least our production problems are really no worse than that of our competitors, and we don't expect you to solve all of our problems overnight. Keep up the good work and send me that memo at your earliest convenience.

Questions

1. Does Alfredo's previous experience running a plant that made replacement windows qualify him to run a plant that makes outdoor furniture?
2. What recommendations would you make if you were Alfredo?
3. Given Jorge's background and apparent priorities, how is he likely to respond to Alfredo's recommendations? On the basis of this likely response, is it possible to rephrase Alfredo's recommendations so they are more appealing to Jorge?

Incident 2: Izmir National University

Izmir National University (INU) was chartered in 2000 to facilitate Turkey's expected eventual entry into the economy of Europe, via the EU. To foster growth and development in the European economy, engineering, science, and business were deemed to be the institution's primary areas of intellectual endeavor. The university grew rapidly during its first three years. By 2005, the enrollment reached just over 9300 students. However, with this rapid growth came a number of problems. For example, because the faculty had to be hired so quickly, there was little real organization, and curriculum seemed to be decided on the basis of which adviser a student happened to consult. The administrative offices were often reshuffled, with vague responsibilities and short tenures.

The faculty of the new Business School was typical of the confusion that gripped the entire university. The 26 faculty members were mostly recent graduates of doctoral programs at major European and Turkish universities. There were 21 Assistant Docents and Lecturers, 3 Docents, and 2 full Professors, spread fairly evenly over the four Departments, each overseen by a Kürsü professor (department head). In addition, funds were available to hire 3 additional faculty members, either assistant or regular Docents. The background of the newly recruited Dekan (administrative head, dean) of the Business School included five years of teaching at a primarily Muslim university in Turkey and two years of departmental administration at a large southern European university.

Upon arriving at the Business School, the Dekan asked the faculty to e-mail their concerns to her so that she could begin to get a handle on the major issues confronting the school. Her office assistant selected the following comments as representative of the sentiments expressed.

- "Our student-teacher ratio is much higher than what it was at my former university. We need to fill those open slots as quickly as possible and ask the university to fund at least two more faculty positions."
- "If we don't get the quality of enrollments up in the MBA program, the Graduate School will never approve our application for a doctoral program. We need the doctoral program to attract the best faculty, and we need the doctoral students to help cover our courses."
- "Given that research is our primary mission, we need to fund more graduate research assistants."
- "The travel budget isn't sufficient to allow me to attend the meetings I'm interested in. How can we improve and maintain our visibility if we get funding for only one meeting per year?"
- "We need better staff support. Faculty members are required to submit their exams for copying five days before they are needed. However, doing this makes it difficult to test the students on the material covered in class right before the exam, since it's difficult to know ahead of time exactly how much material we will cover."
- "I think far too much emphasis is placed on research. We are here to teach."
- "Being limited in our consulting is far too restrictive. In Europe we were allowed one day a week. How are we supposed to stay current without consulting?"
- "We need a voice mail system. I never get my important messages."

Questions

1. What do the comments by the faculty tell you about INU's strategy?
2. What would you recommend the Dekan do regarding the Business School's strategic planning process? What role would you recommend the Dekan play in this process?
3. Productivity is defined as the ratio of output (including both goods and services) to the input used to produce it. How could the productivity of the Business School be measured? What would the effect be on productivity if the faculty all received a 10 percent raise but continued to teach the same number of classes and students?

BIBLIOGRAPHY

Barney, J. B. and D. N. Clark. Resource-Based Theory: *Creating and Sustaining Competitive Advantage*, Oxford, UK: Oxford University Press, 2007.

Bartlett, C. A. and S. Ghoshal. "Going Global: Lessons from Late Movers." *Harvard Business Review* (March–April 2000): 132–142.

Bartmess, A. and K. Cerny. "Building Competitive Advantage through a Global Network of Capabilities." Chapter 7 in R. A. Hayes, G. P. Pisano, and D. M. Upton: *Strategic Operations: Competing through Capabilities.* New York: The Free Press, 1996.

Bernstein, A. "Backlash: Behind the Anxiety of Globalization." *Business Week*, April 24, 2000: 38–44.

Bowen, D. E., R. E. Chase, and T. G. Cummings & Associates. *Service Management Effectiveness.* San Francisco: Jossey-Bass, 1990.

Bower, J. L., and C. M. Christensen. "Disruptive Technologies: Catching the Wave." *Harvard Business Review* (January–February 1995): 43–53.

Clark, K. "Competing Through Manufacturing and the New Manufacturing Paradigm: Is Manufacturing Strategy

Passé?" *Production and Operations Management*, 5 (1996): 42–58.

Collis, D. J., and C. A. Montgomery. *Corporate Strategy: A Resource Based Approach*, 2nd ed.. NY: McGraw-Hill/Irwin, 2005.

Crosby, P. B. *Quality is Free: The Art of Making Quality Certain*. New York: McGraw-Hill, 1979.

Deming, W. E. *Out of Crisis*. Cambridge, MA: MIT Press, 1986.

Denning, L. "The End of the Road is Nigh." *The Wall Street Journal*, 31 March 2009.

Duff, C., and B. Ortega. "How Wal-Mart Outdid a Once-Touted Kmart in Discount-Store Race." *Wall Street Journal* (March 24, 1995): A1, A4.

Einhorn, B. "Your Next TV." *Business Week* (April 4, 2005): 33–36.

Eisenhardt, K., and S. Brown. "Time-Pacing: Competing in Markets that Won't Stand Still." *Harvard Business Review* (March–April 1998): 59–69.

Evans, P., and T. S. Wurster. *Blown to Bits*. Boston: HBS Press, 2000.

Feitzinger, E., and H. L. Lee. "Mass Customization at Hewlett-Packard: The Power of Postponement." *Harvard Business Review* (January–February 1997): 116–121.

Feld, W. M. *Lean Manufacturing: Tools, Techniques, and How to Use Them*. Boca Raton, FL: CRC Press, 2000.

Ferdows, K., ed. *Managing International Manufacturing*. New York: North-Holland, 1989.

Ferdows, K., and A. DeMeyer. "Lasting Improvements in Manufacturing Performance: In Search of a New Theory." *Journal of Operations Management*, 9 (1990): 168–184.

Fitzsimmons, J. A., and M. J. Fitzsimmons. *Service Management for Competitive Advantage*, 5th ed.. New York: McGraw-Hill, 2006.

Gilmore, J. H., and B. J. Pine II. "The Four Faces of Mass Customization." *Harvard Business Review* (January–February 1997): 91–101.

Goldstein, S. M., R. Johnson, J. Duffy, and J. Rao. "The Service Concept: The Missing Link in Service Design Research?" *Journal of Operations Management*, Vol. 20 (2002): 121-134.

Goetsch, D. L., and S. B. Davis. *Quality Management: Introduction to Total Quality Management for Production, Processing, and Services*, 3rd ed. Upper Saddle River, NJ: Prentice Hall, 2000.

Hammer, M. "Deep Change: How Operational Innovation Can Transform Your Company." *Harvard Business Review*, April 2004: 85–93.

Hammer, M. and S. Stanton. "How Process Enterprises Really Work." *Harvard Business Review*, November–December 1999: 108–120.

Handfield, R. B., and E. L. Nichols, Jr. *Introduction to Supply Chain Management*. Upper Saddle River, NJ: Prentice-Hall, 1999.

Hayes, R. H., and G. P. Pisano. "Beyond World-Class: The New Manufacturing Strategy." *Harvard Business Review* (January–February 1994): 77–86.

Hayes, R. H., G. P. Pisano, D. M. Upton, and S. C. Wheelwright. *Operations, Strategy, and Technology: Pursuing the Competitive Edge*. New York: John Wiley, 2004.

Hill, T. *Manufacturing Strategy: Text and Cases*, 3rd ed., Homewood, IL: Irwin, 2000.

Jonas, N. "The Hollow Corporation." *Business Week* (March 3, 1986): 57–85.

Kaplan, R. S., and D. P. Norton. *The Strategy Focused Organization*. Boston: Harvard Business School Press, 2001.

Kaplan, R. S., and D. P. Norton. "Having Trouble with Your Strategy? Then Map It." *Harvard Business Review* (September–October 2000), pp. 167–176.

Maidique, M. A., and P. Patch. Corporate Strategy and Technological Policy. *Harvard Business School Case 9-679-033*, Boston, 1979.

Markides, C. C. and N. Berg. "Manufacturing Offshore is Bad Business." *Harvard Business Review* (September–October 1988): 113–120.

Meredith, J. R., D. M. McCutcheon, and J. Hartley. "Enhancing Competitiveness Through the New Market Value Equation." *International Journal of Operations and Production Management*, 14 (November 11, 1994): 7–21.

Merrick, A. and Zimmerman, A., "Can Sears and Kmart Take On a Goliath Named Wal-Mart?" *Wall Street Journal* (November 19, 2004): B1, B2.

Pande, P. S., R. P. Neuman, and R. R. Cavanagh. *The Six Sigma Way*. New York: McGraw-Hill, 2000.

Pine, B. J., II. *Mass Customization: The New Frontier in Business Competition*. Boston: Harvard Business School Press, 1993.

Porter, M. "What is Strategy?" *Harvard Business Review* (November–December 1996): 61–78.

Porter, M. E. *Competitive Advantage*. New York: Free Press, 1985.

Prahalad, C. K., and G. Hamel. "The Core Competence of the Corporation." *Harvard Business Review* (May–June 1990): 79–91.

SAP. *Top 100 Retailers.* SAP Special Report, July 2008. www.stores.org/pdf/08TOP100.pdf

Skinner, W. "The Focused Factory." *Harvard Business Review* (May–June 1974): 113–122.

Shafer, S. M., H. J. Smith, and J. C. Linder, "The Power of Business Models." *Business Horizons*, 48 (May–June 2005): 199–207.

Slack, N., and M. Lewis. *Operations Strategy.* New York: Financial Times Prentice-Hall, 2001.

Stalk, G. "Time—The Next Source of Competitive Advantage." *Harvard Business Review* (July–August 1988): 41–51.

Stalk, G., P. Evans, and L. E. Shulman. "Competing on Capabilities: The New Rules of Corporate Strategy." *Harvard Business Review* (March–April 1992): 57–69.

Turner, M. L. *Kmart's Ten Deadly Sins: How Incompetence Tainted an American Icon.* Hoboken, NJ: Wiley, 2003.

Upton, D. M. "The Management of Manufacturing Flexibility." *California Management Review* (Winter 1994): 72–89.

Vessey, J. T. "The New Competitors: They Think in Terms of 'Speed-to-Market.'" *Academy of Management Review,* 5 (April 1991): 23–33.

Welch, D., "Running Out of Gas." *Business Week* (March 28, 2005): 29–31.

Womack, J. P., and D. T. Jones. *Lean Thinking: Banish Waste and Create Wealth in you corporation,* rev. ed.. New York: Free Press, 2003.

PART II

Operations Processes

We next discuss the operations processes that will execute the strategy designed on the basis of the discussion presented in Chapter 1. No subject is probably more central to operations management than the design and implementation of transformation processes, to which we devote five chapters here. We start in Chapter 2 with a description of the various processes that are commonly used for producing the organization's outputs of goods and services. The design of the most appropriate processes depends substantially, of course, on the operations strategy we are attempting to execute. And not only must we design the operations processes but we must also design a procedure for monitoring and controlling them in case they become ineffective, or need to be changed to reflect changes in the market, environment, or the organization's strategy. This is addressed in Chapter 3, where we use the control of quality as an example of the entire procedure.

Over time, we know we will have to improve our processes, both in terms of their variability (covered in Chapter 4), to make the outputs more consistent or less costly, and in terms of reducing waste in all forms (including time and human effort), covered in Chapter 5. The contemporary concepts of *six sigma* and *lean* are used for reducing variation and for reducing waste, respectively. These two concepts are of major interest to all organizations today.

Last in this part of the text, we address in Chapter 6 the process of implementation through project management, focusing on using project management to implement process improvement projects. Planning is of course essential, but without successful implementation it is worthless, and organizations these days are using project management to implement almost every action they have planned.

Operations Processes

Designing the
Transformation System

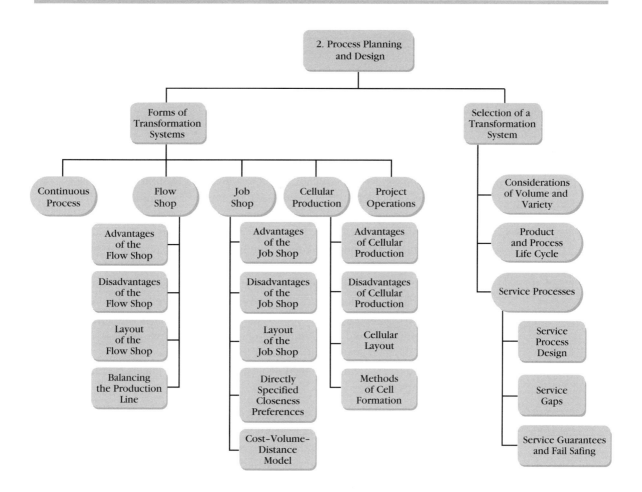

Chapter 1 identified the critical factors in providing value to the customer. This chapter discusses the selection and design of the transformation process that can deliver those factors—low cost, high quality, enhanced functionality, speed, and so on—in an efficient and effective manner. If an organization is using the wrong transformation process, either because the organization has changed or the market has changed, the organization will not be competitive on these critical value factors. The chapter begins with an overview of the five types of transformation processes, their layouts, and their respective advantages and disadvantages. Next, issues related to the selection of an appropriate transformation process such as considerations of volume, variety, and product life cycles are discussed. Last, explicit attention is given to the unique requirements of designing service operations.

INTRODUCTION

- Fender's Custom Shop has produced guitars for many famous and gifted guitarists, including Eric Clapton, John Deacon (Queen), David Gilmour (Pink Floyd), Yngwie Malmsteen, and Stevie Ray Vaughan, to name a few. The Custom Shop uses relatively new equipment and in some cases, prototypical equipment. To produce guitars, computer-controlled routers and lathes are first used to shape the bodies and necks to precise tolerances. Also, Fender has a state-of-the-art machine called a neck duplicator, which can produce a copy of the neck of any existing guitar. After the necks and bodies are fabricated, they are hand- and machine-sanded. Next, detailed inlay work is done with a Hegner precision scroll saw. Following this, paint and finishing operations are done in a special room where air is recirculated 10 times per minute to keep dust and impurities out of the finishes. After paint and finishing, the guitar parts are buffed and then hung up to be seasoned for two weeks. Next, they are moved to the final assembly area, where necks are attached to bodies, and the electronics and hardware are installed. Final assembly of the guitars is done by actual musicians (Bradley 1988).

- The assembly line at IBM's plant in Charlotte, North Carolina, was unlike any other in the world. What made it unique is that it was designed to produce 27 significantly different products. Indeed, the variety of products produced by the team of 40 workers who operated this line is astounding; these products included hand-held barcode scanners, portable medical computers, fiber-optic connectors, and satellite communications devices. The assembly line operated by delivering to each worker a "kit" of parts based on the production schedule. Since each product required different assembly procedures, each worker had a computer screen at his or her station that displayed updated assembly instructions for the current product (Bylinsky 1994).

- Rickard Associates, an editorial production company that produces magazines and marketing materials, was a pioneer in the mid-1990s of a new type of organization structure, the virtual organization. If we traveled back to that time, we would have found only two of its employees actually working at its headquarters in New Jersey: the art director worked in Arizona; the editors were located in Florida, Georgia, Michigan, and the District of Columbia; and the freelancers were even more scattered. To coordinate work, the Internet and America Online were used. For example, art directors were able to submit electronic files of finished pages to headquarters in a matter of minutes using these computer networks (Verity 1994).

- Martin Marietta's aerospace electronics manufacturing facility in Denver, Colorado, was initially set up as a job shop with numerous functional departments. As is typical of most job shops, the Marietta plant had high levels of work-in-process and long lead times, and parts had to travel long distances throughout the plant to complete their processing. Also, as is typical of functional organizations, departmental divisions created barriers to communication and often resulted in conflicting goals. To address these problems, Martin Marietta organized its plant into three focused factories. Each focused factory was completely responsible and accountable for building electronic assemblies for a particular application (e.g., flight, space, or ground use). The intent was to make each focused factory a separate business enterprise.

  A factory manager was assigned to each focused factory. The factory managers then engaged in a sort of "NFL draft" to select employees for their teams. Workers not drafted had to find other positions either inside or outside the company. Within the focused factories, product families were identified; these were based on the technology and processing requirements of the products. Next, standardized routings and sequences were identified for each product family. The plant realized a number of improvements as a result of these and other changes, including seven consecutive months of production with no scrap, a 50 percent reduction in work-in-process inventory, a 21 percent average reduction in lead times, and a 90 percent reduction in overtime (Ferras 1994).

These examples illustrate several transformation systems. The Fender Custom Shop is a job shop that has specialized departments for routing, lathe operations, inlaying, paint and finishing, and final assembly. Likewise, because work is organized by the task performed, Rickard Associates is also a job shop—even though the work is not performed in one location. Actually, and as mentioned in the example, companies like Rickard that rely on information technology to bring separated workers together are referred to as *virtual organizations*. Martin Marietta converted into *focused factories*. And assembly lines like the one IBM uses are referred to as flow shops.

As we noted in Chapter 1, the Sand Cone Model of additive and complementary competitive strengths emphasizes operations that can deliver quality, delivery dependability, speed, and low cost. The most important ingredient in achieving these strengths is selecting the most appropriate transformation process design and layout for the organization's operations. There are various basic forms of transformation process designs, each with their own layout, as well as myriad combinations and hybrids of them. This chapter describes these transformation systems, how the operations are laid out for each of them, and how to select the most appropriate one for maximum competitiveness.

The five basic forms of transformation systems are (1) continuous process, (2) flow shop, (3) job shop, (4) cellular, and (5) project. The continuous process industries are in many ways the most advanced, moving fluid material continuously through vats and pipes until a final product is obtained. Flow shops produce discrete, usually standardized outputs on a continuous basis by means of assembly lines or mass production, often using automated equipment. Cellular shops produce "families" of outputs within a variety of flow cells, but numerous cells within the plant can offer a range of families of outputs. Job shops offer a wide range of possible outputs, usually in batches, by individualized processing into and out of a number of functionally specialized departments. These departments typically consist of a set of largely identical equipment, as well as highly skilled workers. (Potentially, job shops could also produce unique—that is, one-of-a-kind—customized outputs, but job shops that do this are commonly called *model shops* or, in Europe, *jobbers*.) Finally, projects are temporary endeavors to achieve a unique outcome. The most commonly known projects are those performed on a massive scale when the labor and equipment are brought to each site rather than to a fixed production facility, such as dams, buildings, roadways, space launches, and so on.

The general procedure for selecting a transformation system is to consider all alternative forms and combinations to devise the best strategy for obtaining the desired outputs. The major considerations in designing the transformation system—*efficiency, effectiveness, volume, capacity, lead time, flexibility*, and so on—are so interdependent that changing the system to alter one will change the others as well. And the layout of the operations is another aspect that must be considered in the selection of the transformation system. The main purpose of *layout analysis* is to maximize the efficiency (cost-orientation) or effectiveness (e.g., quality, lead time, flexibility) of operations. Other purposes also exist, such as reducing safety or health hazards, minimizing interference or noise between different operational areas (e.g., separating painting from sanding), facilitating crucial staff interactions, or maximizing customers' exposure to products or services.

In laying out service operations, the emphasis may instead be on accommodating the customer rather than on operations per se. Moreover, capacity and layout analyses are frequently conducted simultaneously by analyzing service operations and the wait that the customer must endure. Thus, *waiting line* (or *queuing*) *theory*, a topic discussed in Chapter 8, is often used in the design of a service delivery system. The layouts of parking lots, entry zones, reception rooms, waiting areas, service facilities, and other points of customer contact are of top priority in service-oriented organizations such as clinics, stores, nightclubs, restaurants, and banks.

In a frequently changing environment, the transformation system and its layout will have to be constantly monitored and occasionally redesigned to cope with new demands, new products and services, new government regulations, and new technology. Technology, increasing global competition, and shortages of materials and energy are only a few examples of changes in the past decade that have forced organizations to recognize the necessity of adapting their operations.

FORMS OF TRANSFORMATION SYSTEMS _____

Continuous Process

The ***continuous transformation process*** is commonly used to produce highly standardized outputs, usually fluidic products, in extremely large volumes. In some cases these outputs have become so standardized that there are virtually no real differences between the outputs of different firms. Examples of such *commodities* include water, gases, chemicals, electricity, ores, rubber, flour, spirits, cements, petroleum, and milk. The name *continuous process* reflects the typical practice of running these operations 24 hours a day, seven days a week. One reason for running these systems continuously is to spread their enormous fixed cost over as large a volume as possible, thereby reducing unit costs. This is particularly important in commodity markets, where price can be the single most important factor in competing successfully. Another reason for operating these processes continuously is that stopping and starting them can be prohibitively expensive.

The continuous process industries constitute about half of the manufacturing industry in the United States. Although not all of this industry produces commodities, those are what is typically envisioned. The operations in these commodity industries are highly automated, with very specialized equipment and controls, often electronic and computerized. Such automation and the expense it entails are necessary because of strict processing requirements. Because of the highly specialized and automated nature of the equipment, changing the rate of output can be quite difficult. The facility is typically a maze of pipes, conveyors, tanks, valves, vats, and bins. The layout follows the processing stages of the product, and the output rate is controlled through equipment capacity and flow and mixture rates. Labor requirements are low and are devoted primarily to monitoring and maintaining the equipment.

Research (Dennis and Meredith 2000), however, has shown that there is a much wider range of continuous process industries than just commodity manufacturers. In fact, these industries range all the way from intermittent forms akin to *job shops* to rigidly continuous *flow shops* (both described next). In fact, there appear to be at least seven clearly differentiable forms of continuous processes. Some run for a short time making one product and then switch over to make another product, largely on demand and by the specification of individual customers, which is almost the opposite of commodity production. In addition to these two extremes, there are also blending types of continuous processes as well as unusual hybrids of both job and flow shops.

The major characteristic of processing industries, especially commodities, is that there is often one primary, "fluid"-type input material (gas, wood, wheat, milk, etc.). This input is then often converted to multiple outputs, although sometimes there may be only one output (e.g., clean, chlorinated water). In contrast, in discrete production many types of materials are made or purchased and combined to form the output.

Although human variation in continuous processing firms does not usually create the problems it creates in discrete manufacturing, the demands of processing are usually more critical. For example, chemical reactions must be accurately timed. The result is that the initial setup of equipment and procedures is even more complex and critical than it is for flow shops. Fixed costs are extremely high; the major variable cost is materials. Variable labor (excluding distribution) is usually insignificant.

Flow Shop

The *flow shop* is a transformation system similar to the continuous process, the major difference being that in the flow shop there is a discrete product or service, whereas in continuous processes the end product is not naturally divisible. Thus, in continuous processes an additional step, such as bottling or canning, might be needed to get the product into discrete units. Like the continuous process, the flow shop treats all the outputs as basically the same, and the flow of work is thus relatively continuous. Organizations that use this form are heavily automated, with large, special-purpose equipment. The characteristics of the flow shop are a fixed set of inputs, constant throughput times, and a fixed set of outputs. Examples of the flow form for discrete products are pencil manufacturing, steelmaking, and automobile assembly, whereas for services, some examples include the car wash, processing insurance claims, and the perennial fast food restaurant.

An organization that produces, or plans to produce, a high volume of a small variety of outputs will thus probably organize its operations as a flow shop. In doing so, the organization will take advantage of the simplicity and the savings in variable costs that such an approach offers. Because outputs and operations are standardized, specialized equipment can be used to perform the necessary operations at low per-unit costs, and the relatively large fixed costs of the equipment are distributed over a large volume of outputs.

Continuous types of materials-handling equipment, such as conveyors—again operating at low per-unit costs—can be used because the operations are standardized and, typically, all outputs follow the same path from one operation to the next. This standardization of treatment provides for a known, fixed throughput time, giving managers easier control of the system and more reliable delivery dates. The flow shop is easier to manage for other reasons as well: routing, scheduling, and control are all facilitated because each output does not have to be individually monitored and controlled. Standardization of operations means that fewer skilled workers can be used and each manager's span of control can increase.

The general form of the flow shop is illustrated in Figure 2.1, which shows a *production line*. (If only assembly operations were being performed, as in many automotive plants, the line would be called an *assembly line*.) This production line could represent new military inductees taking their physical exams, small appliances being assembled, or double-decker hamburgers being prepared.

Note that both services and products can be organized as flow shops and can capitalize on the many advantages of this form of processing.

Advantages of the Flow Shop

The primary advantage of a flow shop is the low per-unit cost that is attainable owing to specialized high-volume equipment, bulk purchasing, lower labor rates, efficient utilization of the facility, low in-process inventories, and simplified managerial control. In addition, with everyone working on all the required tasks simultaneously, referred to as **overlapping**, product or service outputs are produced very quickly and fast response to changing markets is possible.

Because of the high rate of output, materials can often be bought in large quantities at a significant savings. Also, because operations are standardized, processing times

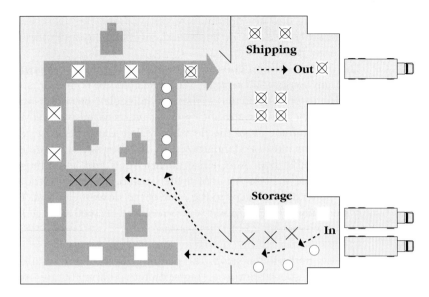

Figure 2.1 A generalized flow shop operation.

tend to remain constant so that large in-process inventories are not required to queue up for processing. This minimizes investment in in-process inventory and queue (*buffer*) space. Furthermore, because a standardized product is produced, inventory control and purchasing decisions are routine.

Because the machines are specialized, less-skilled operators are needed, and therefore, lower wages can be paid. In addition, fewer supervisors are needed, further reducing costs. Since the flow shop is generally continuous, with materials handling often built into the system itself, the operations can be designed to perform compactly and efficiently with narrow aisles, thereby making maximum use of space.

The simplification in managerial control of a well-designed flow shop should not be overlooked. Constant operations problems requiring unending managerial attention penalize the organization by distracting managers from their normal duties of planning and decision making.

Disadvantages of the Flow Shop

Despite the important cost advantage of the flow shop, it can have some serious drawbacks. Not only is a variety of output difficult to obtain, even changes in the rate of output are hard to make. Changing the *rate* of output may require using overtime, laying off workers, adding additional shifts, or temporarily closing the plant. Also, because the equipment is so specialized, minor changes in the design of the product often require substantial changes in the equipment. Thus, important changes in product design are infrequent, and this could weaken the organization's marketing position.

A well-known problem in flow shops is boredom and absenteeism among the labor force. Since the equipment performs the skilled tasks, there is no challenge for the workers. And, of course, the constant, unending, repetitive nature of the manufacturing line can dehumanize the workers. Because the rate of work flow is generally set (*paced*) by the line speed, incentive pay and other output-based incentives are not possible.

The flow production line form has another important drawback. If the line should stop for any reason—a breakdown of a machine or conveyor, a shortage of supplies, and so forth—production may come to an immediate halt unless work-in-process (WIP) is stored at key points in the line. Such occurrences are prohibitively expensive.

Other requirements of the flow shop also add to its cost and its problems. For example, parts must be standardized so that they will fit together easily and quickly on the assembly line. And, since all machines and labor must work at the same repetitive pace in order to coordinate operations, the work loads along the entire line are generally *balanced* to the pace of the slowest element. To keep the line running smoothly, a large support staff is required, as well as large stocks of raw materials, all of which also add to the expense.

Last, in the flow shop, simplicity in *ongoing operation* is achieved at the cost of complexity in the initial *setup.* The planning, design, and installation of the typically complicated, special-purpose, high-volume equipment are mammoth tasks. The equipment is costly not only to set up originally but also to maintain and service. Furthermore, such special-purpose equipment is very susceptible to obsolescence and is difficult to dispose of or to modify for other purposes.

Layout of the Flow Shop

The crux of the problem of realizing the advantages of a flow shop is whether the work flow can be subdivided sufficiently so that labor and equipment are utilized smoothly throughout the processing operations. If, for example, one operation takes longer than all the others, this single operation (perhaps a machine) will become a bottleneck, delaying all the operations following it and restricting the output rate of the entire process.

Obtaining smooth utilization of workers and equipment across all operations involves assigning to groups tasks that take about the same amount of time to complete. This balancing applies to production lines where parts or outputs are produced, as well as to assembly lines where parts are assembled into final products.

Final assembly operations usually have more labor input and fewer fixed-equipment cycles and can therefore be subdivided more easily for smooth flow. Either of two types of lines can then be used. A ***paced line*** uses some sort of conveyor and moves the output along at a continuous rate, and operators do their work as the output passes by them. For longer operations the worker may walk or ride alongside the conveyor and then have to walk back to the starting workstation. The many disadvantages of this arrangement, such as boredom and monotony, are, of course, well known. An automobile assembly line is a common example of a paced line. Workers install doors, engines, hoods, and the like as the conveyor moves past them.

In unpaced lines, the workers build up queues between workstations and can then vary their pace to meet the needs of the job or their personal desires; however, average daily output must remain the same. The advantage of an unpaced line is that a worker can spend longer on the more difficult outputs and balance this with the easier outputs. Similarly, workers can vary their pace to add variety to a boring task. For example, a worker may work fast to get ahead of the pace for a few seconds before returning to the task.

There are some disadvantages to unpaced lines, however. For one thing, they cannot be used with large, bulky products because too much in-process storage space is required. More important, minimum output rates are difficult to maintain because short durations in one operation usually do not dovetail with long durations in the next operation. When long durations coincide, operators downstream from these operations may run out of in-process inventory to work on and may thus be forced to sit idle.

For operations that can be smoothed to obtain the benefits of a production line, there are two main elements in designing the most efficient line. The first is formulating the situation by determining the necessary output rate, the available work time per day, the times for operational tasks, and the order of precedence of the operations. The second element is actually to solve the balancing problem by subdividing and grouping the operations into balanced jobs. To more clearly communicate the concept of a balanced production line, we will give an example that addresses both of these main elements. In reality, of course, one of a variety of computer packages would be employed.

Balancing the Production Line

We illustrate the formulation of the ***line balancing*** situation with an example. Longform Credit receives 1200 credit applications a day, on the average. Longform competes on the basis of its ability to process applications within hours. Daily application processing tasks, average times, and required preceding tasks (tasks that must be completed before the next task) are listed in Table 2.1.

The *precedence graph* for these tasks is shown in Figure 2.2; it is constructed directly from Table 2.1. This graph is simply a picture of the operations (boxed) with arrows indicating which tasks must precede others. The number or letter of the operation is shown above the box, with its time inside.

$\mathcal{T}$ABLE 2.1 ● Tasks in Credit Application Processing

Task	Average Time (minutes)	Immediately Preceding Tasks
a Open and stack applications	0.20	none
b Process enclosed letter; make note of and handle any special requirements	0.37	*a*
c Check off form 1 for page 1 of application	0.21	*a*
d Check off form 2 for page 2 of application; file original copy of application	0.18	*a*
e Calculate credit limit from standardized tables according to forms 1 and 2	0.19	*c, d*
f Supervisor checks quotation in light of special processing of letter, notes type of form letter, address, and credit limit to return to applicant	0.39	*b, e*
g Secretary types in details on form letter and mails	0.36	*f*
Total	**1.90**	

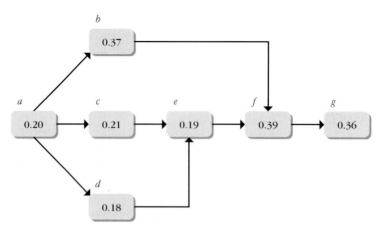

Figure 2.2   Precedence graph for credit applications.

In balancing a line, the intent is to find a *cycle time* in which each workstation can complete its tasks. A workstation is usually a single person, but it may include any number of people responsible for completing all the tasks associated with the job for that station. Conceptually, at the end of this time every workstation passes its part on to the next station, and of course, one item comes off the end of the line fully complete. (Industry now refers to the cycle time (based on the demand required) as *takt time*, since so many firms have erroneously used the term "cycle time" to refer instead to the time it takes to complete all the work to produce a finished item (i.e., its total throughput time).) Task elements are thus grouped for each workstation so as to utilize as much of this cycle time as possible but not to exceed it. Each workstation will have a slightly different *idle time* within the cycle time.

$$\text{Cycle time} = \text{available work time/demand}$$
$$= \frac{8 \text{ hr} \times 60 \text{ min/hr}}{1200 \text{ applications}} = (0.4 \text{ min/application})$$

The cycle time is determined from the required output rate. In this case, the average daily output rate must equal the average daily input rate, 1200. If it is less than this figure, a backlog of applications will accumulate. If it is more than this, unnecessary idle time will result. Assuming an eight-hour day, 1200 applications per eight hours means completing 150 every hour or one every 0.4 minute—this, then, is the cycle time.

Adding up the task times in Table 2.1, we can see that the total is 1.9 minutes. Since every workstation will do no more than 0.4 minute's work during each cycle, it is clear that a minimum of 1.9/0.4 = 4.75 workstations are needed—or, always rounding *up*, five workstations.

$$\text{Number of theoretical workstations, } N_T = \sum \text{task times/cycle time}$$
$$= \frac{1.9}{0.4} = 4.75 \, (\text{i.e., } 5)$$

It may be, however, that the work cannot be divided and balanced in five stations—that six, or even seven, may be needed. For example, precedence relationships may interfere with assigning two tasks to the same workstation. This is why we referred to N_T as the *theoretical* number of workstations needed. If more workstations are actually needed than the theoretical number, the production line will be less efficient. The *efficiency* of the line with N_A actual stations may be computed from

$$\text{Efficiency} = \frac{\text{output}}{\text{input}} = \frac{\text{total task time}}{(N_A \text{ stations}) \times \text{cycle time}}$$

$$\frac{1.9}{5 \times 0.4} = 95 \text{ percent if the line can be balanced with 5 stations}$$

$$\frac{1.9}{6 \times 0.4} = 79 \text{ percent if 6 stations are required}$$

In the formula for efficiency, input is represented by the amount of work required to produce one unit, and output is represented by the amount of work that actually goes into producing one unit.

Now that the problem has been formulated, we can attempt to balance the line by assigning tasks to stations. We begin by assuming that all workers can do any of the tasks and check back on this later. There are many heuristic rules for deciding which task to assign to a station next. We will use the LOT rule; select the task with the *longest operation time* next. The general procedure for line balancing is:

- Construct a list of the tasks whose predecessor tasks have already been completed.
- Consider each of these tasks, one at a time, in LOT order and place them within the station.
- As a task is tentatively placed in a station, new follower tasks can now be added to the list.
- Consider adding to the station any tasks in this list whose time fits within the remaining time for that station.
- Continue in this manner until as little idle time as possible remains for the station.

We will now demonstrate this procedure with reference to Longform, using the information in Table 2.1 and Figure 2.2. The first tasks to consider are those with no preceding tasks. Thus, task *a*, taking 0.2 of the 0.4 minute available, is assigned to station 1. This, then, makes tasks *b* (0.37 minute), *c* (0.21 minute), and *d* (0.18 minute) eligible for assignment. Trying the longest first, *b*, then *c*, and last *d*, we find that only *d* can be assigned to station 1 without exceeding the 0.4-minute cycle time; thus, station 1 will include tasks *a* and *d*. Since only 0.02 minute remains unassigned in station 1 and no task is that short, we then consider assignments to station 2.

Only *b* and *c* are eligible for assignment (since *e* requires that *c* be completed first), and *b* (0.37 minute) will clearly require a station by itself; *b* is, therefore, assigned to station 2. Only *c* is now eligible for assignment, since *f* requires that both *e* and *b* be completed and *e* is not yet completed. But when we assign *c* (0.21 minute) to station 3, task *e* (0.19 minute) becomes available and can also be just accommodated in station 3. Task *f* (0.39 minute), the next eligible task, requires its own station; this leaves *g* (0.36 minute) to station 5. These assignments are illustrated in Figure 2.3 and Table 2.2.

$\mathscr{T}$ABLE 2.2 • Station Task Assignments

Station	Time Available	Eligible Tasks	Task Assigned	Idle Time
1	.40	a	a	
	.20	b, c, d	d	
	.02	b, c	none will fit	.02
2	.40	b, c	b	
	.03	c	c will not fit	.03
3	.40	c	c	
	.19	e	e	.00
4	.40	f	f	
	.01	g	g will not fit	.01
5	.40	g	g	.04

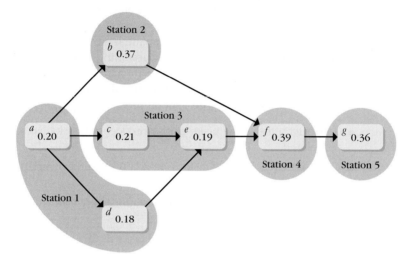

Figure 2.3   Station assignments.

We now check the feasibility of these assignments. In many cases, several aspects must be considered in this check (as discussed later), but here our only concern is that the clerk or the secretary does not do task *f* and that the supervisor does not do task *g* (or, we hope, much of *a* through *e*). As it happens, task *f* is a station by itself, so there is no problem.

As we saw, short tasks are often combined to reach the cycle time. However, long tasks may have to be split up to meet the cycle time requirements. If a task cannot be split, we can "clone" the station as many times as needed to effectively reduce its cycle time, with each station alternating in its output to match, in essence, the required cycle time.

Job Shop

The ***job shop*** gets its name because unique jobs must be produced. In this form of transformation system each output, or each small batch of outputs, is processed differently. Therefore, the flow of work through the facility tends to be intermittent.

The general characteristics of a job shop are *grouping* of staff and equipment according to function; a large *variety* of inputs; a considerable amount of *transport* of staff, materials, or recipients; and large *variations* in system flow times (the time it takes for a complete "job"). In general, each output takes a different route through the organization, requires different operations, uses different inputs, and takes a different amount of time.

This transformation system is common when the outputs differ significantly in form, structure, materials, or processing required. For example, an organization that has a wide variety of outputs or does custom work (e.g., custom guitars) would probably be a job shop. Specific examples of product and service organizations of this form are tailor shops, general offices, machine shops, public parks, hospitals, universities, automobile repair shops, criminal justice systems, and department stores. By and large, the job shop is especially appropriate for service organizations because services are often customized, and hence, each service requires different operations.

Clearly, the efficient management of a job shop is a difficult task, since every output must be treated differently. In addition, the resources available for processing are limited. Furthermore, not only is it management's task to ensure the performance of the proper functions of each output, where considerations of quality and deadlines may vary, but management must also be sure that the available resources (staff, equipment, materials, supplies, capital) are being efficiently utilized. Often there is a difficult tradeoff between efficiency and flexibility of operations. Job-based processes tend to emphasize flexibility over efficiency.

Figure 2.4 represents the flow through a job shop. This facility might be a library, an auto repair shop, or an office. Each particular "job" travels from one area to another, and so on, according to its unique routing, until it is fully processed. Temporary in-process storage may occur between various operations while jobs are waiting for subsequent processing (standing in line for the coffee machine).

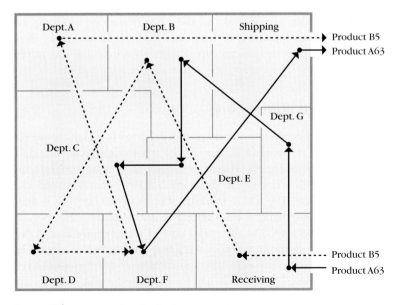

Figure 2.4 A generalized job shop operation.

Advantages of the Job Shop

The widespread use of the job shop form is due to its many advantages. The job shop is usually selected to provide the organization with the flexibility needed to respond to individual, small-volume demands (or even custom demands). The ability to produce a wide variety of outputs at reasonable cost is thus the primary advantage of this form. General-purpose equipment is used, and this is in greater demand and is usually available from more suppliers at a lower price than special-purpose equipment. In addition, used equipment is more likely to be available, further reducing the necessary investment. There is a larger base of experience with general-purpose equipment; therefore, problems with installation and maintenance are more predictable, and replacement parts are more widely available. Last, because general-purpose equipment is easier to modify or use elsewhere and disposal is much easier, the expense of obsolescence is minimized.

Because of the functional arrangement of the equipment, there are also other advantages. Resources for a function requiring special staff, materials, or facilities (e.g., painting or audiovisual equipment) may be centralized at the location of that function, and the organization can thus save expense through high utilization rates. Distracting or dangerous equipment, supplies, or activities may also be segregated from other operations in facilities that are soundproof, airtight, explosion-proof, and so forth.

One advantage to the staff is that with more highly skilled work involving constantly varying jobs, responsibility and pride in one's work are increased, and boredom is reduced. Other advantages to the staff are that concentrations of experience and expertise are available and morale increases when people with similar skills work together in centralized locations (all market researchers together). Because all workers who perform similar activities are grouped together, each worker has the opportunity to learn from others, and the workers can easily collaborate to solve difficult problems. Furthermore, because the pace of the work is not dictated by a moving "line," incentive arrangements may be set up. Last, because no line exists that must forever keep moving, the entire set of organizational operations does not halt whenever any one part of the operation stops working; other functional areas can continue operating, at least until in-process inventory is depleted. Also, other general-purpose resources can usually substitute for the nonfunctioning resource: one machine for another, one staff member for another, one material for another.

Disadvantages of the Job Shop

The general-purpose equipment of job shops is usually slower than special-purpose equipment, resulting in higher variable (per-unit) costs. In addition, the cost of direct labor for the experienced staff necessary to operate general-purpose equipment further increases unit costs of production above what semiskilled or unskilled workers would require. The result, in terms of costs of the outputs, is that the variable costs of production are higher for the general-purpose than for the special-purpose equipment, facilities, and staff, but the initial cost of the equipment and facilities is significantly less. For small-output volumes the job shop results in a lower total cost. As volume of output increases, however, the high variable costs begin to outweigh the savings in initial investment. The result is that, for high-production volumes, the job shop is not the most economic approach (although its use may still be dictated by other considerations, as when particular equipment threatens workers' health or safety).

Inventories are also frequently a disadvantage in the job shop, especially in product organizations. Not only do many types of raw materials, parts, and supplies have to be kept for the wide variety of outputs anticipated, but *in-process inventories*, that is, jobs waiting for processing, typically become very large and thereby represent a sizable capital investment for the organization. It is not unusual for batches of parts in these environments to spend 90–95 percent of the time they are in the shop either waiting to be moved or waiting to be processed. Furthermore, because there are so many inventory items that must travel between operating departments in order to be processed, the cost of handling materials is also typically high. Because job routings between operations are not identical, inexpensive fixed materials-handling mechanisms like conveyor belts cannot be used. Instead, larger and more costly equipment is used; therefore, corridors and aisles must be large enough to accommodate it. This necessitates allocating even more space, beyond the extra space needed to store additional inventories.

Finally, managerial control of the job shop is extremely difficult, as mentioned earlier. Because the output varies in terms of function, processing, quality, and timing, the managerial tasks of routing, scheduling, cost accounting, and such become nearly impossible when demand for the output is high. Expediters must track down lost jobs and reorder priorities. In addition to watching the progress of individual jobs, management must continually strive to achieve the proper balance of materials, staff, and equipment; otherwise, highly expensive resources will sit idle while bottlenecks occur elsewhere.

Layout of the Job Shop

Because of its relative permanence, the layout of the operations is probably one of the most crucial elements affecting the efficiency of a job shop. In general, the problem of laying out operations in a job shop is quite complex. The difficulty stems from the variety of outputs and the constant changes in outputs that are characteristic of organizations with an intermittent transformation system. The optimal layout for the existing set of outputs may be relatively inefficient for the outputs to be produced six months from now. This is particularly true of job shops where there is no proprietary product and only for-contract work is performed. One week such a shop might produce 1000 wheels, and the next week it might produce an 8000-gallon vat. Therefore, a job-shop layout is based on the historically stable output pattern of the organization and expected changes in that pattern, rather than on current operations or outputs.

A variety of factors can be important in the interrelations among the operations of a job shop. If all the qualitative and quantitative factors can be analyzed and combined, the relative importance of locating each department close to or far from each of the other departments may be used to determine a layout. This approach is particularly useful for service operations where movements of materials are not particularly significant. To illustrate how this concept might be achieved in practice, we next present a simplified example. Following this, we illustrate how a purely cost-based layout could be achieved.

Directly Specified Closeness Preferences

As a simplified example, consider Table 2.3, where six departments have been analyzed for the desirability of closeness to each other. Assume we are given the organization's

$\mathscr{T}_{ABLE}$ 2.3 • Directly Specified Closeness Preferences*

	Department					
Department	1	2	3	4	5	6
1		E	A	U	U	U
2			U	I	I	U
3				U	U	A
4					I	U
5						I
6						

*Note:

A = Absolutely necessary   O = Ordinary closeness OK

E = Especially important   U = Unimportant

I = Important   X = Undesirable

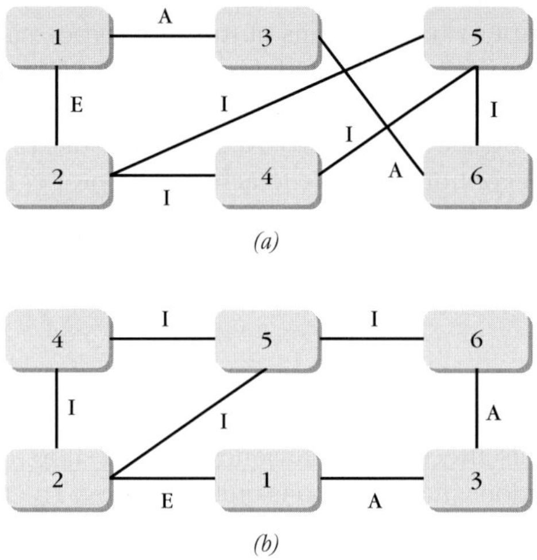

Figure 2.5 Closeness preferences layout: (*a*) Initial layout. (*b*) Final layout.

closeness preferences, indicated by the letters A, E, I, O, U, and X, with the meanings given in the table. In general, the desirability of closeness decreases along the alphabet until U, which is "unimportant," and then jumps to "undesirable" with X; there is no range of undesirability in this case, although there could be, of course.

One way of starting the layout process is simply to draw boxes representing the departments in the order given in the table and show closeness preferences on the arcs (line segments) joining them. Figure 2.5*a* illustrates this for Table 2.3. The next step is to shift the departments with A on their arcs nearer each other and those with X away from each other. When these have been shifted as much as possible, the E arcs, then the I arcs, and finally the O arcs will be considered for relocation, resulting in an improved layout, such as in Figure 2.5*b*.

Cost–Volume–Distance Model

In the cost–volume–distance (CVD) approach, the desirability of closeness is based on the total cost of moving materials or people between departments. Clearly, a layout can never be completely reduced to just one such objective, but where the cost of movement is significant, this approach produces reasonable first approximations. The objective is to minimize the costs of interrelations among operations by locating those operations that interrelate extensively close to one another. If we label one of the departments i and another department j, then the cost of moving materials between departments i and j depends on the distance between i and j, D_{ij}. In addition, the cost will usually depend on the amount or volume moving from i to j, such as trips, cases, volume, weight, or some other such measure, which we will denote by V_{ij}. Then, if the cost of the flow from i to j per-unit amount per-unit distance is C_{ij}, the total cost of i relating with j is $C_{ij}V_{ij}D_{ij}$. Note that C, V, and D may have different values for different types of flows and that they need not have the same values from j to i as from i to j, since the flow in opposite directions may be of an entirely different nature. For example, information may be flowing from i to j, following a certain paperwork path; but sheet steel may flow from j to i, following a lift truck or conveyor belt path.

Adding the flows from i to every one of N possible departments, we find that the total cost of department i interrelating with all other departments is

$$\sum_{j=1}^{n} C_{ij}V_{ij}D_{ij}$$

(It is normally assumed that $C_{ii}V_{ii}D_{ii} = 0$, because the distance from i to itself is zero.) Adding together the costs for all the departments results in the total cost.

$$TC = \sum_{i=1}^{N} \sum_{j=1}^{N} C_{ij}V_{ij}D_{ij}$$

Our goal is to find the layout that minimizes this total cost. This may be done by evaluating the cost of promising layouts or, as in the following simplified example, by evaluating *all possible* layouts.

The section of a business school containing the administrative offices of the operations management department is illustrated in Figure 2.6. Each office is approximately 10 feet by 10 feet, so the walking distance (D) between adjacent offices (i.e., offices 1 and 2, and offices 2 and 3) is 10 feet, whereas the distance between diagonal offices (offices 1 and 3) is approximately 15 feet.

The average number of interpersonal trips made each day is given in a travel or load matrix (Table 2.4). According to Table 2.4, each day the assistant makes five trips to the chairperson's office and 17 trips to the secretary's office. Thus, the assistant would travel 305 feet (10 feet × 5 trips + 15 feet × 17 trips) each day.

Assuming that the chairperson is paid approximately twice as much as the secretary and the junior administrative assistant, determine if the current arrangement is best (i.e., least costly) in terms of transit time and, if not, what arrangement would be better.

For convenience, the offices are numbered in Figure 2.6. Before calculating total costs of all possible arrangements, some preliminary analysis is worthwhile. First, because of special utility connections, restrooms are usually not considered relocatable. In addition, the relocation of the restrooms in this example would not achieve any result that could not be achieved by moving the other offices instead.

Second, many arrangements are mirror images of other arrangements and thus need not be evaluated, since their cost will be the same. For example, interchanging

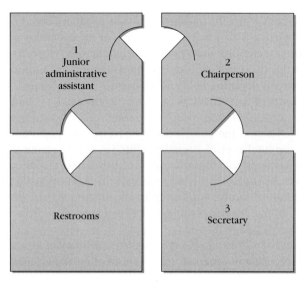

Figure 2.6 Office layout.

offices 1 and 3 will result in the same costs as the current layout. The essence of the problem, then, is to *determine which office should be located diagonally across from the restrooms.* There are three alternatives: chairperson, assistant, or secretary.

$\mathscr{T}_{ABLE}$ 2.4 ● Load Matrix, V_{ij} (trips)

	To		
From	1 Assistant	2 Chair	3 Secretary
1 Assistant	—	5	17
2 Chair	10	—	5
3 Secretary	13	25	—

Now, let us evaluate each of the three possibilities as the "diagonal office"—first the chairperson, then the assistant, and last the secretary. The costs will simply be denoted as 1 for the assistant and the secretary or 2 for the chairperson (who earns twice as much as the others). As noted, the V_{ij} "volumes" will be the number of trips from i to j taken from the load matrix, and the distances will depend on who has the diagonal office across from the restrooms. The calculations for each arrangement are shown here.

1. Chairperson: $TC = 1(5)10 + 1(17)15 + 2(10)10 + 2(5)10 + 1(13)15 + 1(25)10 = 1050$

2. Assistant: $TC = 1(5)10 + 1(17)10 + 2(10)10 + 2(5)15 + 1(13)10 + 1(25)15 = 1075$

3. Secretary: $TC = 1(5)15 + 1(17)10 + 2(10)15 + 2(5)10 + 1(13)10 + 1(25)10 = 1025$ (lowest)

To better understand these calculations, consider the current arrangement in which the chair has the office diagonal to the restrooms. In this case, the assistant must travel 305 feet each day, as was explained earlier. Each day the chairperson would have to travel 150 feet: (10 feet × 10 trips to the assistant) + (10 feet × 5 trips to the secretary). Finally, the secretary would have to travel 445 feet each day: (15 feet × 13 trips to the assistant) + (10 feet × 25 trips to the chair). Because the chairperson is paid twice as much as the secretary and assistant, we weight the chairperson's travel distance as twice that of the other two workers. Using this weighting scheme provides a total cost of the current office arrangement of 1050: that is, 305 + (2 × 150) + 445. The best arrangement is to put the secretary in the office diagonal to the restrooms for a relative cost of 1025. Again, if faced with an actual layout task, a computer package could be used.

DILBERT: © Scott Adams/Dist. by United Feature Syndicate, Inc.

Cellular Production

Cellular production is a relatively new type of transformation system that many firms have recently been adopting. It combines the advantages of the job shop and flow shop to obtain the high variety possible with the job form and the reduced costs and short response times available with the flow form. Figure 2.7 contrasts the job shop with cellular production for a manufacturing firm. The job shop in Figure 2.7*a* has separate departments for welding, turning, heat treat, milling, and forming. This type of layout provides flexibility to produce a wide range of products simply by varying the sequence in which the products visit the five processing departments. Also, flexibility is enhanced, as machines are easily substituted for one another should a specified machine be busy or nonoperational.

Figure 2.7*b* shows a reorganization of the plant for cellular production. The cellular form is based on **group technology**, which seeks to achieve efficiency by exploiting similarities inherent in parts. In production, this is accomplished by identifying groups of parts that have similar processing requirements. Parts with similar processing requirements are called *part families*. Figure 2.8 provides an example of how a variety of parts can be organized into part families.

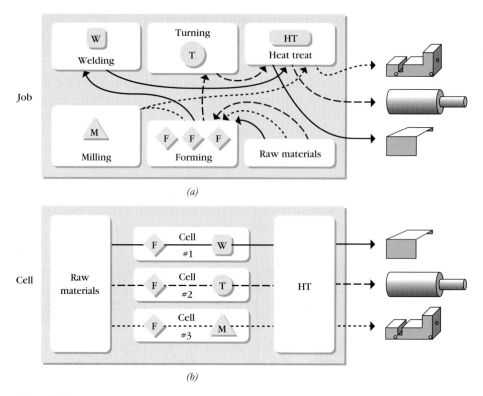

(a)

Job

Cell

(b)

Figure 2.7   Conversion of (*a*) a job shop layout into (*b*) a cellular layout for part families.

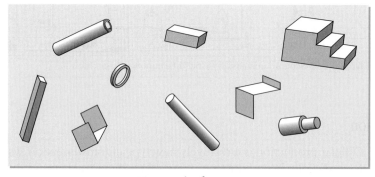

Unorganized parts

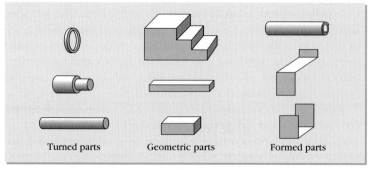

Turned parts   Geometric parts   Formed parts

Parts organized by families

Figure 2.8   Organization of miscellaneous parts into families.

After the parts are divided into families, a *cell* is created that includes the human skills and all the equipment required to produce a family. Since the outputs are all similar, the equipment can be set up in one pattern to produce the entire family and does not need to be set up again for another type of output (as is necessary in a job shop). Some cells consist of just one machine producing a complete product or service. Other cells may have as many as 50 people working with dozens of machines.

A facility using cells is generally organized on the basis of *teams*. That is, a team is completely responsible for conducting the work within its cell. The team members usually schedule and inspect the work themselves, once they know when it is due. Occasionally, work must be taken outside a cell for a special treatment or process that is unavailable within the cell, but these operations are minimized whenever possible.

The families are derived from one of a number of different approaches. Sometimes the basis is the machines that are needed to produce the output, or the families may be based on the size of the equipment, the quality required, the skills needed, or any other overriding consideration. This is called the *classification* stage. Items are classified into families—sometimes by simple inspection and other times by complex analysis of their routing requirements, production requirements, part geometry, and the like. It is generally not feasible to classify all the outputs into one of a limited number of families, so at some point all the miscellaneous outputs are placed in a "remainder" cell, which is operated as a minijob shop.

Advantages of Cellular Production

Organizations adopt the cellular form to achieve many of the efficiencies associated with products and servicees that are mass-produced using flow transformation systems in less repetitive job shop environments. However, not all the advantages of a full flow shop or a full job shop can be obtained, because not enough high-volume equipment can be purchased to obtain the economies of scale that flow shops enjoy. And because the equipment is dedicated to part families, some of the variety afforded by job shops is lost.

One of the most important advantages of the cellular form is reduced machine setup times. In the job shop, when a worker completes the processing of one batch, the machine is set up for the next batch. Because a wide variety of parts typically flow through each department in a job shop, the next batch of parts processed by the worker will likely be different from the one just completed. This means that the worker may have to spend several hours or more simply setting up and preparing the machine for the next batch of parts. In cellular production, machine setup times are minimized because each cell processes only parts that have similar (or identical) setup and processing requirements. It is extremely desirable to minimize machine set-up times, because setup time takes away from the amount of time machines can be used to produce the outputs.

Decreasing machine setup times provides several benefits. First, as we have just noted, when setup times decrease, the amount of time equipment is available to process parts increases. Second, increased capacity means that the company can produce at a given level with fewer machines. Reducing the number of machines used not only reduces the costs of equipment and maintenance, but also reduces the amount of floor space needed. Third, shorter setup times make it more economical to produce smaller batches. For instance, if the setup time is four hours, it would not be efficient to produce a small number of parts using a particular machine, only to spend another four hours to set it up for the next batch. However, if the machine required only a few minutes of setup time, it might be practical to produce a few parts on the machine.

There are numerous benefits associated with producing parts in small batches. To begin, producing small batches enhances an organization's flexibility in responding to changes in product mix. Also, reducing the size of batches leads to reductions in work-in-process inventory. Less inventory means that less space is needed to store it and less capital is tied up in it. Also, product lead times are shorter, and throughput times are faster due to overlapping the tasks. Shorter lead times and faster throughput facilitate more accurate forecasting, faster response to market changes, faster revenue generation, and perhaps the most important advantage of all—less time for engineers to change the output or customers to change (or cancel) the order!

Another major advantage of the cellular form is that parts are produced in one cell. Processing the parts in one cell simplifies control of the shop floor. To illustrate this, compare the amount of effort required to coordinate the production activities in the job shop and the cellular layout shown in Figure 2.7. Producing parts in a single cell also reduces the amount of labor and equipment needed to move materials because travel distances between successive operations are shorter. Additionally, producing the parts in one cell provides an opportunity to increase the workers' accountability, responsibility, and autonomy. Finally, reducing material handling and increasing the workers' accountability typically translate into reduced defects. In a job shop, it is difficult to hold the workers accountable for quality because the product is processed in several different departments and the workers in one department can always blame problems on another department.

A unique advantage of the cell form is that it maximizes the inherent benefits of the team approach. In a flow shop, there is little teamwork because the equipment does most of the work; the labor primarily involves oversight and maintenance. Job shops are organized by department, and this allows for some teamwork—but not in terms of specific jobs, because everyone is working on a different job. In a cell, all the workers are totally responsible for completing every job. Thus, the effect is to enrich the work, provide challenges, encourage communication and teamwork, meet due dates, and maintain quality.

An additional advantage for manufacturers is the minimal cost required to move to cellular production. Although some cells may be highly automated, with expensive special-purpose equipment, it is not necessary to invest any additional capital in order to adopt the cellular form. It requires only the movement of equipment and labor into cells. Or, with even less trouble—though with some loss of efficiency—the firm can simply designate certain pieces of equipment as dedicated to a single part family, but not relocate them. The term used in this case is ***virtual cell*** or *logical cell* (also known as *nominal*), because the equipment is not physically adjoining but is still reserved for production of only one part family.

Another form of cellular production is called a miniplant. Here, the cell not only does the manufacturing but also has its own industrial engineer, quality manager, accountant, marketing representative, and salesperson, and almost all the other support services that a regular plant has. Only far-removed services, such as R&D and human resources, are not dedicated to the miniplant. The entire facility of the firm is thus broken down into a number of miniplants, each with its own general manager, production workers, and support services so that it can operate as an independent profit center.

Disadvantages of Cellular Production

Some disadvantages of the cellular form are those of the flow shop and the job shop, but they are not as serious. As in a flow shop, if a piece of equipment should break down, it can stop production in the cell; but in a cell form—unlike a flow shop, where that might be the only piece of equipment in the facility—work might, if permissible, temporarily be shifted to other cells to get a job out.

However, obtaining balance among the cells when demands for a product or service family keep changing is a problem that is less in both flow and job shops. Flow shops are relatively fixed in capacity and they produce a standard output, so there is no question of balance. Job shops simply draw from a pool of skilled labor for whatever job comes in. With cells, by contrast, if demand for a family dries up, it may be necessary to break up that cell and redistribute the equipment, or reform the families. In the short run, though, labor can generally be assigned to whatever cell needs it, including the remainder cell.

Of course, volumes are too small in cellular production to allow the purchase of the high-volume, efficient equipment that flow shops use. The cellular form also does not allow for the extent of customization usually found in job shops, since the labor pool has largely been disbursed to independent cells (although the remainder cell may be able to do the work). Moreover, the fostering of specialized knowledge associated with various operational activities is reduced because the workers who perform these activities are spread out and therefore have limited opportunities to collaborate.

Cellular Layout

Cellular production creates teams of workers and equipment to produce families of outputs. The workers are cross-trained so that they can operate any of the equipment in their cell, and they take full responsibility for the proper performance or result of the outputs. Whenever feasible, these outputs are final products or services. At other times, particularly in manufacturing, the outputs are parts that go into a final product. If the latter is the case, it is common to group the cells closely around the main production or assembly line so that they feed their output directly into the line as it is needed.

In some cases, a *virtual cell* is formed by identifying certain equipment and dedicating it to the production of families of outputs, but without moving the equipment into an actual, physical cell. In that case, no "layout" analysis is required at all; the organization simply keeps the layout it had. The essence of the problem, then, is the identification of the output families and the equipment to dedicate to each of them.

It is more common for an organization to actually form physical cells. When physical cells are created, the layout of the cell may resemble a sort of miniflow shop, a job shop, or a mix of these, depending on the situation. Thus, we will direct our attention here to the formation of the part or product families and their associated equipment, leaving the issues of physical layout to be addressed in the discussions of the flow shop and job shop.

In practice, organizations often use the term cell to include a wide range of very different situations: a functional department consisting of identical machines, a single machine that automatically performs a variety of operations, or even a dedicated assembly line. Earlier, we also referred to the portion of a shop that is not associated with a specific part family as a cell: a *remainder cell*. Nevertheless, we do not consider all these groups as part of what we are calling cellular production.

Organizations that formally plan their shop layouts typically choose to group their equipment on the basis of either the function it performs (i.e., job shops) or the processing requirements of a product or group of products (i.e., flow shops). As we discussed, the purpose of grouping equipment on the basis of its function is to maximize flexibility, whereas the purpose of grouping it on the basis of processing requirements is to maximize efficiency.

Companies that adopt cellular manufacturing typically create a *pilot cell* initially to experiment with the cellular approach, and therefore most of the equipment in the shop remains in functional departments at this stage. As these firms gain experience with the cell and become convinced that it is beneficial, they begin a phase of implementing additional cells. This can be referred to as the *hybrid stage* because as the shop is incrementally converted to cells, a significant portion of the facilities are still arranged in functional departments. At some point, the formation of additional cells is terminated and the firm may or may not have the majority of its equipment arranged in cells. Often companies stop creating new cells when the volume of the remaining parts is insufficient to justify forming additional cells. To clarify the concept of a cellular layout based on product families and machine cells, we present a detailed example based on one of the more common approaches to cell formation in the next subsection.

Methods of Cell Formation

There are a variety of ways to determine what outputs should constitute a family and be produced in the same cell. Sometimes a family is dictated by the size or weight of the output; for example, huge pieces of steel may require an overhead crane to lift them onto the machines for processing. Sometimes electronic parts have special requirements for quality, such as being produced in a "clean room" or being welded in an inert gas environment. Sometimes it is obvious what family a part belongs in simply by looking at it and seeing how it was made (i.e., by what machines).

Most commonly, some form of manual determination based on human judgment is used. One relatively simple approach involves taking photographs of a sample of the parts and then manually sorting these photographs into families based on the geometry, size, or other visual characteristics of the parts. Another approach is to sort the parts based on the drawing name.

A more sophisticated manual procedure is called ***production flow analysis*** (PFA). In this approach, families are determined by evaluating the resource requirements for producing the outputs. Outputs that have the same complete set of resource needs are grouped into a single family. It should then be possible to cluster a set of the necessary resources together in a cell to produce that family. However, this is not always the case because there may not be enough of all resources to place each one in each of the cells that needs it or low levels of usage may not justify placing each resource in each cell. In these cases the resources can be shared between cells or additional resources acquired. For example, maternity wings at many hospitals are set up as cells having their own dedicated doctors, nurses, and even operating rooms. However, typically the amount of time the anesthesiologists are needed in the maternity wing does not justify dedicating anesthesiologists to the unit. Thus, the anesthesiologists split their time supporting several hospital units. At other times, even if there are sufficient quantities of the resources to assign each to the appropriate cells, two or three such resources may be needed in one cell to handle its capacity requirements while half a resource or less is needed in another cell. These difficulties are handled case by case.

The essence of PFA is to determine the *resource-output matrix* and then identify the outputs (parts or services) with common resource requirements. In manufacturing operations, the matrix is based on information contained in the part routings and is formed by listing all the outputs (parts, patients, services) across the top and all the resources (workers, machines, nurses) down the side. Then 1's are written in the matrix wherever, say, a part uses a machine. For example, Table 2.5 shows a matrix with seven parts that together require six machines. The objective is to reorder the parts and machines so that "blocks" of 1's that identify the cells are formed along the diagonal, as shown in Table 2.6. Similar resource-output matrices could be developed for service organizations. For example, a hospital might identify type of treatment as the output (e.g., maternity, cardiac, oncology) and the resources as the equipment required (X-ray, respirator, defibrillator, heart monitor). Once the treatment-equipment matrix was developed, it could be reordered to identify the resources needed to set up dedicated treatment cells.

$\mathcal{T}$ABLE 2.5 • Original Machine-Part Matrix

Machines	Parts						
	1	2	3	4	5	6	7
1		1			1		
2	1			1			1
3	1		1			1	
4		1					
5			1			1	
6	1						1

$\mathcal{T}$ABLE 2.6 • Reordered Matrix

Machines	Parts						
	7	4	1	3	6	2	5
6	1						
2	1	1	1	Cell 1			
3				1	1	Cell 2	
5					1	1	
1						1	1
4				Cell 3		1	

Note that it is acceptable for an output not to use every resource in a cell and for a resource not to process every output. However, no output should interact with a resource *outside* of its cell. Thus, in Table 2.6, part 1 is listed as needing machine 3, but this is problematic. In this case, if we could duplicate machine 3, we could put it in both cell 1 and cell 2. Or we might consider putting machine 3 in cell 2 and sending component 1 to cell 2 after it is finished in cell 1 (but this violates our desire to produce cell-complete parts). Or we could remove part 1 from the families and put it in a remainder cell (if there are other components and machines not listed in Table 2.5 within the facility).

The general guidelines for reordering the matrix by PFA are as follows:

- Incompatible resources should be in separate cells.
- Each output should be produced in only one cell.
- Any investment in duplicate resources should be minimized.
- The cells should be limited to a reasonable size.

Another, less common method of cell formation is *classification and coding*. With classification and coding, an alphanumeric code is assigned to each part on the basis of design characteristics, processing requirements, or both. Parts with similar codes can be identified and grouped into families.

Project Operations

Project operations are of large scale and finite duration; also, they are nonrepetitive, consisting of multiple, and often simultaneous, tasks that are highly interdependent. However, the primary characteristics of the tasks are their limited duration and, if the output is a physical product, their immobility during processing. Generally, staff, materials, and equipment are brought to the output and located in a nearby *staging area* until needed. Projects have particularly limited lives. Resources are brought together for the duration of the project: Some are consumed, and others, such as equipment and personnel, are deployed to other uses at the conclusion of the project. Typically, the output is unique (a dam, product development, a presidential campaign, a trial).

In designing a processing system, a number of considerations may indicate that the project form is appropriate. One of these is the rate of change in the organization's outputs. If one department must keep current on a number of markets that are rapidly changing, the typical organization would quickly fall behind its competition. The project form offers extremely short reaction times to environmental or internal changes and would thus be called for. In addition, if the tasks are for a limited duration only, the project form is indicated. Finally, the project form is chosen when the output is of a very large scale with multiple, interdependent activities requiring close coordination. During the project, coordination is achieved through frequent meetings of the representatives of the various functional areas on the project team.

One of the advantages of the project form, as noted earlier, is its ability to perform under time and cost constraints. Therefore, if meeting a due date or staying within budget is crucial, the project form is most appropriate. However, a disadvantage of the project form with its mixed personnel from different functional areas (an engineer, a scientist, a businessperson, a technician, etc.), is that it has less depth in any one technical area compared to functional organization by technical specialty. In that case, a number of specialists can be brought together to solve a problem. In addition, specialized resources (e.g. technical equipment) often cannot be justified for a project because of its low utilization; hence, generalized resources must be used instead. The project form of transformation processes is discussed in more detail in Chapter 6.

$\mathscr{S}$ELECTION OF A TRANSFORMATION SYSTEM _____

This section addresses the issue of selecting the appropriate transformation system, or mix of systems, to produce an output. From the preceding discussion, it should be clear that the five transformation systems are somewhat simplified extremes of what is likely to be observed in practice. Few organizations use one of the five forms in a pure sense; most combine two or more forms in what we call a **hybrid** shop. For example, in manufacturing computer keyboards, some parts and sub-assemblies are produced in job shops or cells but then feed into a flow shop at the final assembly line, where a batch of one model is produced. Then the line is modified to produce a batch of another model. Even in "custom" work, jobs are often handled in groups of generally common items throughout most of their processing, leaving minor finishing details such as the fabric on a couch or the facade of a house to give the impression of customizing.

Although services typically take the form of a job shop, the emphasis has recently been on trying to mass-produce them (using cells or flow shops) so as to increase volume and reduce unit costs. Some examples are fast-food outlets, multiphasic medical screening, and group life insurance. Even with services, we often find combined forms of process design: McDonald's prepares batches of Big Macs but will accept individual custom orders. Burger King uses a conveyor assembly line for its Whoppers but advertises its ability to customize its burgers to suit any taste.

The problem for the operations manager is to decide what processing form(s) is most appropriate for the organization, considering long-run efficiency, effectiveness, lead time, capacity, quality, and flexibility. Selection may be even more difficult because, as mentioned previously, it is possible to combine processing forms to attain efficiency in some portions of the production process and flexibility in other portions. It is clear that the tradeoffs must be well understood by the manager, and the expected benefits and costs must be well known.

Unfortunately, most plants do not have the luxury of time for completely reorganizing their processes. As a result, they often grow into a hodge-podge of machines and processes scattered somewhat randomly around the plant, barely resembling any of the above five forms, even if they started out with one of them.

Considerations of Volume and Variety

One of the most important factors in the design of a transformation system is establishing the volume and variety of outputs the organization will produce. High volumes tend to indicate that highly automated mass production will be necessary. High variety, on the other hand, implies the use of skilled labor and general-purpose tools and facilities.

A related consideration here is whether the output will be make-to-stock or make-to-order. A **make-to-stock** item is produced in batches of some size that is economical (for the firm) and then stocked (in a warehouse, on shelves, etc.). As customers purchase them, the items are withdrawn from stock. A ***make-to-order*** item is usu-ally produced in a batch of a size set by the customer (sometimes just one) and is delivered to the customer upon its completion. Generally, make-to-stock items are produced in large volumes with low variety, whereas make-to-order items are pro-duced in low volumes with high variety. (Quite often, *every* item is different.)

Clearly, services will not normally be of a type that can be stocked, even if every service is identical (e.g., a physical examination). Also, exceptions to these generali-zations are abundant. Automobiles, for example, are made to order, but are produced in high volume and with high variety. (However, autos are really *assembled* to order; the assembly components are produced to stock.) And general-purpose machine shops often produce high volumes of low-variety items for specific customers.

Figure 2.9*a*, based on the *product-process matrix* developed by Hayes and Wheelwright (1979), illustrates these points as they relate to the various transforma-tion systems. The horizontal axis shows volume, as measured by the batch size, and the left vertical axis shows the variety of outputs. Organizations making a single unit of output that varies each time (such as dams and custom-built machines) use the project form or sometimes the job shop. Some services also fall into this region, as indicated by the upper left tip of the oval. Job shop and cellular systems, however, are mainly used when a considerable variety of outputs are required in relatively small batches. This is particularly characteristic of services. When the size of a batch increases significantly, with a corresponding decrease in variety, then a flow shop is appropriate. Some services also fall into this category. Last, when all the output is the same and the batch is extremely large (or essentially infinite, as in the ore, petro-chemical, and food and drink industries), the continuous process is appropriate. Very few services exist here.

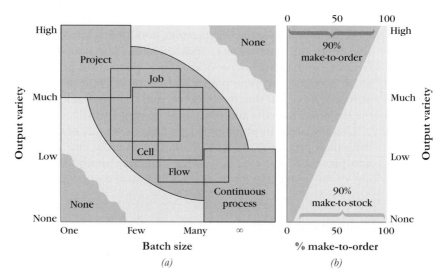

(a)   *(b)*

Figure 2.9   Effect of output characteristics on transformation systems—the product-process matrix.

Note that the standard, viable transformation forms lie on the diagonal of the product-process matrix. Operating at some point off this diagonal can be dangerous for the organization unless done carefully as a well-planned strategy. Essentially, no organizations operate in the upper right or lower left segments of this grid. The lower left does, however, represent manufacturing 200 years ago. If you wanted four identical dressers, say, for your four children, they were made one at a time by hand (whether identical or all different, for that matter). Today, however, it is simply too expensive to produce items this way; if the items are all identical, they are made in a large batch and then sold separately. In some cases, it is almost impossible to buy a single unit of some items, such as common ten-penny nails—you have to buy a blister-pack of ten or so. Similarly, the upper right may represent manufacturing in the future, when advanced technology can turn out great masses of completely customized products as cheaply as standard items. Currently, however, we have trouble doing this (in spite of such popular concepts as "mass customization"). Some products, however, lend themselves to approximations to this goal through such specialized techniques as assembly-to-order: fast food, Internet-purchased based computers, and so on. These firms have developed strategies, and the production techniques to accompany them, for successfully using "off-diagonal" transformation processes.

Note the overlap in the different forms. This means, for example, that on occasion some organizations will use a flow shop for outputs with smaller batches or larger variety, or both, than the outputs of organizations using a job shop. There are many possible reasons for this, including economic and historical factors. The organization may also simply be using an inappropriate transformation system. The point is that the categories are not rigid, and many variations do occur. Many organizations also use hybrids or combinations of systems, such as producing components to stock but assembling finished products to order, as in the auto industry.

Note in Figure 2.9*b* the general breakdown of make-to-order and make-to-stock with output variety and size of batch. Project forms (high variety, unit batch size) are almost always make-to-order, and continuous processing forms (no variety, infinite batch size) are almost always make-to-stock, though exceptions occasionally occur.

Product and Process Life Cycle

In Chapter 1 we described the life cycle of an output: how long it takes to develop, bring to market, and catch on; how quickly it grows in popularity; how different versions are developed for different market segments; how the output reaches market saturation; how price competition emerges. A similar life cycle occurs in the production system for an output. As a result, a project form of transformation system may be used for the development of a new output, may evolve into a job shop or cellular layout as a market develops, and finally may evolve into a flow shop as full standardization and high volumes develop. (We assume here that a continuous process is not appropriate for the output.) We briefly elaborate on this production life cycle.

In the R&D stage, many variations are investigated during the development of a product. As the output is being developed, prototypes are made in small volumes in a relatively inefficient, uncoordinated manner typically in a job shop. As demand grows and competitors enter the market, price competition begins and a cellular or flow system, with its high volume and low variable costs, becomes preferred. At the peak of the cycle, demand may increase to the point where such a system is justified.

This progress is illustrated in Figure 2.10, which presents a breakeven analysis for each of four transformation systems. The dark bold line illustrates the lowest-cost system for each stage of the life cycle. At the stage of project development and

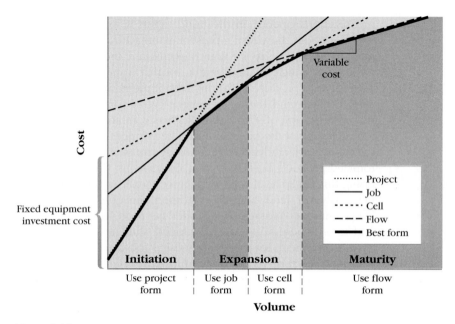

Figure 2.10 Selection of transformation systems by stage of life cycle.

initiation (R&D and initial production), the cost of fixed equipment is nil, and labor is the predominant contributor to high variable costs. In the expansion stage, the job shop allows some tradeoff of equipment for labor with a corresponding reduction in variable unit costs, thus leading, at these volumes, to a reduction in overall unit costs. Finally, at high volumes characterizing maturity, a nearly complete replacement of expensive labor with equipment is possible, using cellular form and the flow shop.

Be advised, however, that not all outputs can or should follow this sequence. The point is that the transformation system should evolve as the market and output evolve. But many organizations see their strength in operating a particular transformation system, such as R&D or low-cost production of large volumes. If their outputs evolve into another stage of the life cycle in which a different transformation system form is preferable, they drop the output (or license it to someone else) and switch to another output more appropriate to their strengths.

Failing to maintain this focus in the organization's production system can quickly result in a "white elephant"—a facility built to be efficient at one task but being inefficiently used for something else. This can also happen if the organization, in an attempt to please every customer, mixes the production of outputs that require different transformation systems. Japanese plants are very carefully planned to maintain one strong focus in each plant. If an output requiring a different process is to be produced, a new plant is acquired or built.

From the previous discussion it is clear that there is a close relationship between the design of a product or service and the design of the production system. Actually, the link is even closer than it seems. Figure 2.11 illustrates the relationship between the innovations throughout the life cycle of a product or service and innovations throughout the life cycle of its production system. At the left, when the product or service is introduced, innovations and changes in its design are frequent. At this point, the production system is more of the project or modeling/job shop form since the design is still changing (the number of *product* innovations is high). Toward the middle, the product design has largely stabilized, and cost competition is forcing innovations in the production process, particularly the substitution of cellular or flow shop machinery for labor (the number of *process* innovations is high). At the right, this phenomenon has subsided and innovations in production methods are primarily the result of competitors' actions, government regulations, and other external factors.

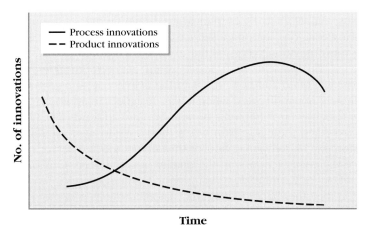

Figure 2.11   Product-process innovations over time.

Although not typically involved on the research side of such innovations in production methods (a laboratory engineering function), the operations manager is intimately involved in *applying* these developments in day-to-day production. The possible tradeoffs in such applications are many and complex. The new production system might be more expensive but might produce a higher-quality output (and thus, the repeat volume may be higher, or perhaps the price can be increased). Or the new production system might be more expensive and might produce a lower-quality output but be simpler and easier to maintain, resulting in a lower total cost and, ultimately, higher profits. Clearly, many considerations—labor, maintenance, quality, materials, capital investment, and so on—are involved in the successful application of research to operations.

Service Processes

As with the design of transformation systems for products, the design of transformation systems for services depends heavily on knowing exactly what characteristics of the service need to be emphasized: its explicit and implicit benefits, its cost, its time duration, its location, and accessibility. Knowing the importance of each of these allows the designer to make the necessary tradeoffs in costs and benefits to offer an effective yet reasonably priced service.

Unfortunately, service transformation systems are frequently implemented with little development or pretesting, which is also a major reason why so many of them fail.

Consider the extensive development and testing of the McDonald's fast-food production system, of airline reservations systems, and of many life insurance policies. Each of these also illustrate the many hours of training required to use equipment and procedures properly and efficiently. Yet most new service firms frequently fail to train their personnel adequately, again inviting failure.

In most cases, the various forms and layouts of manufacturing transformation processes apply equally well to services. Flow shops are seen in fast food restaurants, job shops are seen in banks and hospitals, and projects are seen in individual services such as salons and house construction. Chapter 8 includes an example of a *service blueprint* that is commonly used for process flow and capacity analysis purposes, but also may be helpful when designing the service up front.

However, one important service element that is usually missing from manufacturing transformation design is the extensive customer contact during delivery of the service. This presents both problems and also opportunities. For one thing, the customer will often add new inputs to the delivery system or make new demands on it that were not anticipated when it was designed. In addition, customers do not arrive at smooth, even increments of time but instead tend to bunch up, as during lunch periods, and then complain when they have to wait for service. Furthermore, the customers' biased perception of the server, and the server's skills, can often influence their satisfaction with the quality of the service. Obviously, this can either be beneficial or harmful, depending on the circumstances.

On the other hand, having the customer involved in the delivery of a service can also present opportunities to improve it. Since customers know their own needs best, it is wise to let them aid in the preparation or delivery of the service—as with automatic teller machines, salad bars, and pay-at-pump gas stations. In addition to improving the quality of the service, this can save the firm money by making it unnecessary to hire additional servers. However, the customer can also negligently—and quickly—ruin a machine or a tool, and may even sue if injured by it, so the service firm must carefully consider how much self-service it is willing to let the customer perform.

Chase and Tansik (1983) devised a helpful way to view this customer contact when designing service delivery systems. Chase's suggestion is to evaluate whether the service is, in general, high contact or low contact, and what portions of the service, in particular, are each. The value of this analysis is that the service can be made both more efficient and more effective by separating these two portions and designing them differently. For example, the high-contact portions of the service should be handled by workers who are skilled at social interaction, whereas the low-contact portion should employ more technical workers and take advantage of labor-saving equipment. For example, a bank might have a back office where checks are encoded separately from the front office, where customers deposit them. In this back office, equipment and efficiency are the critical job elements, whereas in the front office, interpersonal skills and friendliness are critical.

Whenever possible, the low-contact portion of a service should be decoupled from the high-contact portion so that it may be conducted with efficiency, whereas the high-contact portion is conducted with grace and friendliness. Close analysis of the service tasks may also reveal opportunities for decreasing contact with the customer—through, for example, automated teller machines, phone service, self-service, or the Web, if this is appropriate—with a concomitant opportunity for improving both the efficiency and level of service. In particular, allowing customers to use the Web to obtain service (e.g., obtain account information, place orders) offers them convenient access, 24 hours per day, 365 days per year, and immediate attention (i.e., no longer being placed on hold for the next available representative).

Similarly, there may be some opportunities for increasing the amount of customer contact, such as phone or mail follow-ups after service, which should be exploited to improve the overall service and its image. The service provider should thoroughly investigate these opportunities.

Service Process Design

Like the product-process matrix for manufacturing, Schmenner (1986) has developed a similar matrix for services that not only classifies four major and quite different types of services but gives some insights on how to design the best service system. The service matrix is shown in Figure 2.12. Service systems are divided into those with high versus low contact intensity customization (similar to Chase), and whether they are capital intensive or labor intensive. Schmenner names each of the quadrants with an easily understood identifier that captures the essence of that quadrant: service factory, service shop, mass service, and professional service.

	Customer contact intensity	
	Low	**High**
Capital Intensive	**Service factory** Airlines Package/postal services Hotels Recreation	**Service shop** Hospitals Computer dating Repair services Travel agencies
Labor Intensive	**Mass service** Sporting events School classes Retailing Fast food	**Professional service** Legal services Physicians Interior decorators Tax preparers

Figure 2.12   The service matrix.

Each of the quadrants represents a unique service transformation process, with unique managerial challenges and having unique characteristics. Those services at the high contact side of the matrix have low volumes with high customization and must attain their profitability through high prices. Those on the other side with low contact and customization attain profitability through high volumes. The investment axis identifies whether the service provider puts their resources into expensive equipment or into labor. Thus, one axis is a combination of customer variety and volume (like the product-process matrix) and the other axis is based on the inputs to conduct the service. Examples of typical services in each quadrant are given in the figure.

The matrix is also useful in identifying the managerial challenges for each of the quadrants. In the low contact left end, the managerial challenge is making the service appear warm and friendly so as to attract high volumes. If the level of contact is high, the managerial challenge is trying to be optimally efficient in using capital and labor resources, while keeping prices high. If the service is equipment intensive, the challenge is to keep capital investment costs low. If instead the service is labor intensive, the challenge is to minimize wages and time spent on each customer.

The matrix is also useful in redesigning a service. For example, a firm may decide to move from one quadrant to another to better use their resources or environment. For example, a tax preparation service may start as a high-priced professional service but then move either toward a more automated service shop through computer preparation of the forms, or a less-personalized mass service using less skilled tax preparers.

Service Gaps

For designing services, it can be useful to inspect the service design and delivery for potential "gaps" between what the customer/client needs and what the service provider is offering (Parasuraman et al. 1988). By identifying the possible gaps in the service process, a service provider can better control the quality, productivity, cost, and performance of their service offering, thereby resulting in greater profit and market share. It can also help identify service industries where better service may offer a competitive advantage.

Figure 2.13 illustrates the concept. Essentially, there is commonly a gap between what the customer/client actually needs and what is delivered that involves gaps throughout the selection, design, and delivery process. We start with gap 1, the reasonable difference between the ideal service that the customer actually needs and what the customer expects. This gap is often influenced heavily by advertising and other communications from the service provider. Gap 2 is the imbalance between what the customer expected and his/her perception of what was actually received. Gap 3 is the final gap on the customer's side; it represents the difference between what was actually delivered and the customer's perception of that reality.

The seven remaining gaps are all on the provider's side. Gap 4 is the misperception by the service provider of what the customer truly needs. Gap 5 is the difference between that misperception and what the provider chooses to offer (the selected service). Gap 6 is the discrepancy between the service that was selected and the service that was designed. Gap 7 concerns marketing and sales and is the disparity between the designed service and what these functions understand it to be. Continuing this path, gap 8 concerns the difference between what the provider is attempting to communicate to the customer and what the customer actually understands. Then returning to the service delivery process, the last two gaps concern the contrast between what was designed and: what was perceived as delivered (gap 9), and what was actually delivered (gap 10).

Clearly, with nine possible opportunities for the service provider to not meet the customer's expectations, not to mention the customer's needs (gap 1), there are a lot

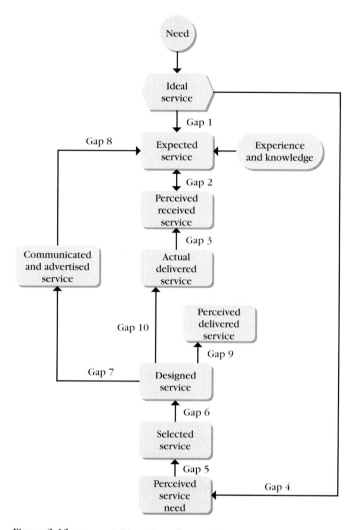

Figure 2.13 Potential locations for service gaps.

of ways to fail in the service provision process. It behooves every service (and product) provider to carefully examine each of these potential failure points in their own business to see if they can improve their service provision process, especially before someone else discovers the opportunity and moves to close the gaps.

Service Guarantees and Fail Safing

Service guarantees are increasingly common among service providers who have confidence they can meet them, and who desire a competitive advantage in their industry. Package transportation companies were among the first to use them, and since then have been adopted by hotels, restaurants, and others in those service businesses that have extensive contact with the public but a reputation for poor service.

There are four major elements of a service guarantee:

1. It must be meaningful to the customer in the sense that it in fact repays the customer for the failure of the service to meet his or her expectations. A guarantee with a trivial payoff that does not satisfy the customer will just increase the customer's dissatisfaction and negate the purpose of the guarantee program in the first place.

2. The guarantee must be unconditional. Again, if there are "exceptions" that exclude the common reasons why the service might fail, the customer will only be more dissatisfied.

3. The guarantee must be easy to communicate and for the customer (and employees) to understand. If the guarantee is complex or complicated to explain, it will not serve to attract customers to the service provider. And employees who are charged with making good on the guarantee also need to fully understand it and be able to execute the guarantee provisions.

4. The guarantee must be easy to "use" in the sense of immediately invoking it when a service failure occurs. If the customer has to return home, mail in a coupon, and wait for satisfaction, the guarantee program will not achieve its purpose.

The information technology field is a leader in the development and use of formalized service guarantees, referring to them as service level agreements (SLAs). Here, a SLA is a written contract between an information technology provider and the user of the technology specifying the level of service that will be provided, typically in measurable terms. In addition to using SLAs to specify the levels of service that will be provided by external organizations, it is also becoming increasingly common for internal information system departments to develop SLAs for the other departments they support within the enterprise. Representative SLA metrics for information technology providers include the percentage of uptime, help desk response times, and the timely reporting of usage statistics.

One approach organizations use to help guarantee their service is a concept called *fail safing* (Chase and Stewart 1994), which anticipates where a service failure might occur and installs preventive measures. The service blueprint in Chapter 8, mentioned earlier, includes potential failure points in the service process that should be considered for fail safing. As an example of fail safing, fast-food playgrounds are ubiquitous these days, but children who are too large can be a danger on the equipment for smaller children (or to themselves), hence the "maximum height" signs at their entrance. And outpatient health clinics give vibrating beepers to patients who sign in so they aren't "lost" in the system.

But it is not only the customer who needs fail safing; the service providers also need their systems designed to force them into doing the service correctly. A familiar example to both service providers and customers is computer screens that disallow entries in on-line forms that don't match the protocol, or when required fields are inadvertently left empty. Another is McDonald's now-famous french-fry scoop that picks up, straightens, and optimally sizes the amount of fries for the bag, all without human contact. And when using dangerous equipment, it can't be activated unless the operator's hands and body are sensed to be out of danger.

In large part, the emergence of the concepts of service guarantees and fail safing reflect the tremendous growth and availability of services in our economy, and the increasingly poor record of satisfactory service being provided by so many of these new services. Examples abound: telephone answering systems with unending menus that keep customers from reaching a real person who can fix their problem, airline cancellations/delays/lost baggage, and so on. Although technology is often helpful in solving our problems, it can also multiply them.

EXPAND YOUR UNDERSTANDING

1. When a line cannot be perfectly balanced, some people will have more work time than others within each cycle. What might be a solution for this situation?

2. A current sociological trend is to move away from paced lines. Yet increasing automation is pushing workers to match their work pace to that of machines and computers. How can both of these trends be happening at the same time?

3. If a job shop was being laid out in a third-world country, how might the procedure be different? What other factors might enter in that would not exist in an industrialized country? Might the layout also differ among industrialized countries such as Europe and Japan? How about a flow shop?

4. In highly automated facilities, firms frequently increase the job responsibilities of the skilled workers who remain after automation has replaced the manual laborers, although there is less potential for applying their skills. Workers complain that they are under increased pressure to perform but have less control over the automated equipment. Is this ethical on the part of the companies involved? What approach would be better?

5. Cellular production is often conducted in a U-shaped (horseshoe-shaped) cell, rather than the rectangular cells shown in Figure 2.7b. What might be the advantages of this U shape?

6. What benefits would a virtual cell obtain, and not obtain, compared with a physical cell?

7. A number of firms are moving toward mini-factories. What advantages might this offer over straight cellular production?

8. If efficiency, variety, and so on are the important measures of the low-contact, or no-contact portion of a service, what are the important measures of the high-contact portion?

9. As the process life cycle changes with the product life cycle, should a firm change along with it or move into new products more appropriate to its existing process? What factors must be considered in this decision?

10. In Figure 2.9, showing the five transformation systems, why don't firms operate in the regions marked "none"?

11. Identify the similarities in Figures 2.9 and 2.12. Also, the differences.

APPLY YOUR UNDERSTANDING

Paradise State University

Paradise State University (PSU) is a medium-sized private university offering both undergraduate and graduate degrees. Students typically choose Paradise State because of its emphasis on high levels of interaction and relatively small classes. University policy prohibits classes with more than 75 students (unless special permission is obtained from the provost), and the target class size is 25 students. All courses are taught by tenure-track faculty members with appropriate terminal degrees. Faculty members teach two courses each semester.

The Business School at PSU offers only an MBA degree in one of six areas of concentration: accounting, finance, general management, management information systems (MIS), marketing, and operations management (OM). The MBA program is a one-year (two-semester) lockstep program. Since the Business School does not offer undergraduate business courses, students entering the program are required to have completed all the undergraduate business prerequisites from an accredited university. The faculty is organized into six functional departments. The table below lists the number of faculty members in each department and the average number of students each year who choose a particular concentration. Students are not permitted to have double concentrations, and PSU does not offer minors at the graduate level.

Department	Faculty	Number of Students per Year
Accounting	8	100
Finance	6	40
General Management	7	70
MIS	10	150
Marketing	6	50
OM	10	30

The number of courses required by each concentration in each department are listed in the table below. For example, a student concentrating in accounting is required to take four accounting classes, one finance class, one management class, one MIS course, one marketing class, and two OM classes.

Concentration	Accounting	Finance	Management	MIS	Marketing	OM
Accounting	4	1	1	1	1	2
Finance	1	4	1	1	1	2
General Management	1	1	4	1	1	2
MIS	1	1	1	4	1	2
Marketing	1	1	1	1	4	2
OM	1	1	1	1	1	5

Number of Courses Taken in Respective Departments

Questions

1. How many student semesters must each department teach each semester? Given the target class size—25 students—are there enough faculty members?
2. Conceptually, how could the cellular production approach be applied to the Business School?
3. What would be the advantages and disadvantages of adopting a cellular approach at the Business School? As a student, would you prefer a functional organization or a cellular organization? As a faculty member, what would you prefer?
4. On the basis of the information given, develop a rough plan detailing how the Business School faculty might be assigned to cells.

X-Opoly, Inc.

X-Opoly, Inc., was founded by two first-year college students to produce a knockoff real estate board game similar to the popular Parker Brothers' game Monopoly®. Initially, the partners started the company just to produce a board game based on popular local landmarks in their small college town, as a way to help pay for their college expenses. However, the game was a big success and because they enjoyed running their own business, they decided to pursue the business full-time after graduation.

X-Opoly has grown rapidly over the last couple of years, designing and producing custom real estate trading games for universities, municipalities, chambers of commerce, and lately even some businesses. Orders range from a couple of hundred games to an occasional order for several thousand. This year X-Opoly expects to sell 50,000 units and projects that its sales will grow 25 percent annually for the next five years.

X-Opoly's orders are either for a new game board that has not been produced before, or repeat orders for a game that was previously produced. If the order is for a new game, the client first meets with a graphic designer from X-Opoly's art department and the actual game board is designed. The design of the board can take anywhere from a few hours to several weeks, depending on how much the client has thought about the game before the meeting. All design work is done on personal computers.

After the design is approved by the client, a copy of the computer file containing the design is transferred electronically to the printing department. Workers in the printing department load the file onto their own personal computers and print out the board design on special decals, 19.25 inches by 19.25 inches, using high-quality color inkjet printers. The side of the decal that is printed on is usually light gray, and the other side contains an adhesive that is covered by a removable backing.

The printing department is also responsible for printing the property cards, game cards, and money. The money is printed on colored paper using standard laser printers. Ten copies of a particular denomination are printed on each 8.5-inch by 11-inch piece of paper. The money is then moved to the cutting department, where it is cut into individual bills. The property cards and game cards are produced similarly, the major difference being that they are printed on material resembling posterboard.

In addition to cutting the money, game cards, and property cards, the cutting department also cuts the cardboard that serves as the substrate for the actual game board. The game board consists of two boards created by cutting a single 19-inch by 19.25-inch piece of cardboard in half, yielding two boards each measuring 19.25 inches by 9.5 inches. After being cut, game boards, money, and cards are stored in totes in a work-in-process area and delivered to the appropriate station on the assembly line as needed.

Because of its explosive growth, X-Opoly's assembly line was never formally planned. It simply evolved into the 19 stations shown in the following table.

Station Number	Task(s) Performed at Station	Time to Perform Task
1	Get box bottom and place plastic money tray in box bottom. Take two dice from bin and place in box bottom in area not taken up by tray.	10 seconds
2	Count out 35 plastic houses and place in box bottom.	35 seconds
3	Count out 15 plastic hotels and place in box bottom.	15 seconds
4	Take one game piece from each of eight bins and place them in box bottom.	15 seconds
5	Take one property card from each of 28 bins. Place rubber band around property cards and place cards in box bottom.	40 seconds
6	Take one orange card from each of 15 bins. Place rubber band around cards and place cards in box bottom.	20 seconds
7	Take one yellow card from each of 15 bins. Take orange cards from box and remove rubber band. Place yellow cards on top of orange cards. Place rubber band around yellow and orange cards and place cards in box bottom.	35 seconds
8	Count out 25 $500 bills and attach to cardboard strip with rubber band. Place money in box bottom.	30 seconds
9	Count out 25 $100 bills. Take $500 bills from box bottom and remove rubber band. Place $100 bills on top of $500 bills. Attach rubber band around money and place in box bottom.	40 seconds
10	Count out 25 $50 bills. Take $500 and $100 bills from box bottom and remove rubber band. Place $50 bills on top. Attach rubber band around money and place in box bottom.	40 seconds
11	Count out 50 $20 bills. Take money in box and remove rubber band. Place $20 bills on top. Attach rubber band around money and place in box bottom.	55 seconds

(Continued)

Station Number	Task(s) Performed at Station	Time to Perform Task
12	Count out 40 $10 bills. Take money in box and remove rubber band. Place $10 bills on top. Attach rubber band around money and place in box bottom.	45 seconds
13	Count out 40 $5 bills. Take money in box and remove rubber band. Place $5 bills on top. Attach rubber band around money and place in box bottom.	45 seconds
14	Count out 40 $1 bills. Take money in box and remove rubber band. Place $1 bills on top. Attach rubber band around money and place in box bottom.	45 seconds
15	Take money and remove rubber band. Shrink wrap money and place back in box bottom.	20 seconds
16	Take houses, hotels, dice, and game pieces and place in bag. Seal bag and place bag in box.	30 seconds
17	Place two cardboard game board halves in fixture so that they are separated by ¼ in. Peel backing off of printed game board decal. Align decal over board halves and lower it down. Remove board from fixture and flip it over. Attach solid blue backing decal. Flip game board over again and fold blue backing over front of game board, creating a ¼-in. border. Fold game board in half and place in box covering money tray, game pieces, and cards.	90 seconds
18	Place game instructions in box. Place box top on box bottom. Shrink wrap entire box.	30 seconds
19	Place completed box in carton.	10 seconds

Questions

1. What kind(s) of transformation system(s) does X-Opoly use?
2. What would be involved in switching the assembly line over from the production of one game to the production of another?
3. What is the cycle time of the 19-station line? What is its efficiency?
4. What is the line's maximum capacity per day, assuming that it is operated for one 8-hour shift less two 15-minute breaks? Assuming that X-Opoly operates 200 days per year, what is its annual capacity? How does its capacity compare with its projected demand?
5. On the basis of the task descriptions, develop a precedence graph for the assembly tasks. (Assume that tasks performed in the 19 stations cannot be further divided.) Using these precedence relationships, develop a list of recommendations for rebalancing the line in order to improve its performance.
6. What would be the impact on the line's capacity and efficiency if your recommendations were implemented?

EXERCISES

1. Given the following machine-component matrix, form cells using PFA.

	Components						
Machines	1	2	3	4	5	6	7
1	1				1		
2			1		1		
3			1	1			
4		1			1		1
5	1					1	

2. a. Given the following load matrix of a DVD player factory in Nagoya, Japan, find the best layout and its cost based on rectangular distances.

	Department					
Department	1	2	3	4	5	6
1	—	4	6	2	0	7
2		—	3	5	1	3
3				2	6	5
4				—	5	2
5					—	3

b. Resolve part a if the rates are ¥4 from odd to even departments, ¥5 from even to odd, ¥6 from odd to odd, and ¥7 from even to even.

3. An insurance office in London is laid out as in the following table. The office manager is considering switching departments 2 and 6 to reduce transport costs. Should this be done? [Use rectangular (rather than shortest) distances. Assume that offices are 10 feet on a side.] What is the difference in annual cost, assuming a 250-day work year?

1	2	3
4	5	6

Daily Trip Matrix

	To					
From	1	2	3	4	5	6
1	x	40	x	x	x	40
2	30	x	20	30	60	0
3	x	70	x	x	x	20
4	x	0	x	x	x	30
5	x	10	x	x	x	0
6	40	50	20	0	10	x

Trip Cost (to any department) per foot from

1	2	3	4	5	6
£0.02	£0.03	£0.01	£0.03	£0.02	£0.02

4. Re-layout the office in Exercise 3 given the following desired closeness ratings.

Department	1	2	3	4	5	6
1		I	A	X	O	U
2			X	E	I	O
3				O	X	I
4					I	E
5						A
6						

5. Demand for a certain subassembly in a toy manufacturing facility at the North Pole is 96 items per 8-hour shift of elves. The following six tasks are required to produce one subassembly.

Task	Time Required (minutes)	Predecessor Tasks
a	4	—
b	5	a
c	3	a
d	2	b
e	1	b,c
f	5	d,e

What is the required cycle time? Theoretically, how many stations will be required? Balance the line. What is the line's efficiency?

6. An assembly line has the following tasks (times shown in minutes).

a. Six assemblies are required per hour. Balance the line.

b. What is the efficiency of the line?

c. Rebalance the line if task e has a time of 1 minute instead of 3.

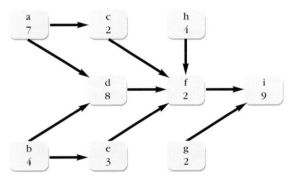

7. Given the following machine-component matrix, form cells using PFA.

	Components				
Machines	1	2	3	4	5
1				1	1
2			1		
3	1	1			
4				1	1
5				1	1
6					1
7		1			
8		1			

8. Kobenhavn Fine Products wishes to balance its line to meet a daily demand of 240 units. Kobenhavn works an 8-hour day on the following tasks:

Task	Time (mins)	Preceding Tasks
1	0.4	none
2	0.3	1
3	1.1	1
4	0.2	3
5	0.5	2
6	0.3	3
7	0.6	5
8	0.6	4, 6, 7

a. Find the cycle time, efficiency, and minimum number of stations. Balance the line.

b. Rebalance the line if task 8 requires 0.7 minutes.

9. If the times in Problem 8 were normally distributed, how might Crystal Ball be useful in solving the problem?

BIBLIOGRAPHY

Anupindi, R., S. Chopra, S. D. Deshmukh, J. A. van Mieghem, and E. Zemel. *Managing Business Process Flows*, Upper Saddle River, NJ: Prentice Hall, 1999.

Bradley, T. "Fender Blenders." *1988–1989 Guitar Buyers' Guide*. 129–133.

Bylinski, G. "The Digital Factory." *Fortune* (November 14, 1994): 92–107.

Chase, R. B., and S. Dasu. "Want to Perfect Your Company's Service? Use Behavioral Science." *Harvard Business Review* (June 2001): 78–84.

Chase, R. B., and D. M. Stewart. "Make Your Service Fail-Safe." *Sloan Management Review* (Spring 1994): 35–44.

Chase, R. B., and D. A. Tansik. "The Customer Contact Model for Organization Design." *Management Science*, 29 (September 1983): 1037–1050.

Dennis, D., and J. Meredith. "An Empirical Analysis of Process Industry Transformation Systems." *Management Science*, 46 (August 2000): 1085–1099.

Ferras, L. "Continuous Improvements in Electronics Manufacturing." *Production and Inventory Management Journal* (Second Quarter 1994): 1–5.

Firnstahl, T. W. "My Employees Are My Service Guarantee." *Harvard Business Review* (July–August 1999): 28–32.

Fitzsimmons, J. A., and M. J. Fitzsimmons. *Service Management: Operations, Strategy, and Information Technology*, 5th ed. New York: Irwin/McGraw-Hill, 2006.

Francis, R. L., L. F. McGinnis, Jr., and J. A. White. *Facility Layout and Location: An Analytical Approach*, 2nd ed. Englewood Cliffs, N.J.: Prentice-Hall, 1998.

Hayes, R. H., and S. C. Wheelwright. "Link Manufacturing Process and Product Life Cycles." *Harvard Business Review* (January–February 1979): 133–140.

Heskett, J. L., W. E. Sasser, Jr., and L. A. Schlesinger. *The Service Profit Chain*. New York: Free Press, 1997.

Hyer, N.L. and Brown, K.A. Work Cells with Staying Power: Lessons for Process Complete Operations. *California Management Review*, 46:1 (2003), 27–52.

Metters, R., K. King-Metters, and M. Pullman. *Successful Service Operations Management*. Mason, OH: SouthWestern, 2003.

Parasuraman, A., V. A. Zeithaml, and L. L. Berry. "SERVQUAL: A Multiple-Item Scale for Measuring Consumer Perceptions of Service Quality." *Journal of Retailing*, 64 (1988): 12–40.

Schmenner, R. W. How can service businesses survive and prosper? Sloan Management Review, 28:3 (1986), 21–32.

Spear, S., and H. K. Bowen. "Decoding the DNA of the Toyota Production System." *Harvard Business Review* (September–October 1999): 95–106.

Verity, J. W. "A Company That's 100% Virtual." *Business Week* (November 21, 1994): 85.

CHAPTER 3

Monitoring and Controlling the Transformation System

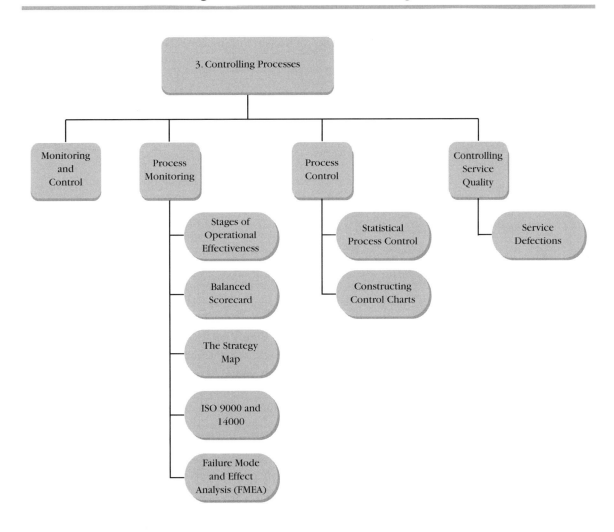

Once the organization's processes have been designed, they must be implemented, of course. However, this is not a one-time task because every time a process is implemented, changes occur in the environment, both independently and also due to the new process itself, that require further changes in the process. Hence, every process must be monitored and controlled to be sure it continues to achieve its objectives, as noted in Chapter 1, and we must thus plan ahead for how we will execute this monitoring and controlling activity. This chapter discusses the task of monitoring and control. It includes some discussion of the measures that will be monitored and ways to then exercise control to correct the process. We illustrate the control process with the example of controlling quality through the use of quality control charts. Other topics include such well-popularized subjects as the balanced scorecard, strategy maps, ISO 9000/14000, benchmarking, process capability, and service defections. After completing our discussion of how to plan for process monitoring and control, the next two chapters will then delve into ways to improve these processes.

INTRODUCTION

- When Texas Instruments, Inc. wanted to add several leading-edge technologies to their Accounts Receivable (AR) system, they turned to ViewStar Corporation to design the new AR system. To monitor and control their costs, ViewStar identified a variety of measures to track, including actual versus projected spending. However, a problem immediately arose—the planned budget exceeded the contract funds available! Because top management was especially interested in winning this particular contract, they decided to arbitrarily reduce the budget for selected early-on tasks so that the overall budget matched the funds available. Their strategy was to then carefully monitor the actual expenses to put pressure on the design team to keep costs to a minimum and thereby bring their total funds spent back into budgetary control. As the contract progressed, the underbudgeted items showed up quickly in the measures of actual versus projected spending. To bring the spending back into control, the team manager was instructed to pay special attention to meeting only *key* requirements for later system design tasks. As a result, expenses began to fall back toward the projected spending. Near the very end of the project, the client asked for additional technology, which Viewstar easily provided in trade for the client completing some of the more expensive tasks themselves, thereby completing the system at only 1 percent over budget. (Ingram 1995)

- The Automotive Systems Group of Johnson Controls was having trouble controlling their product development (PD) process because each manager used a different process, the workers didn't know who was responsible for what, developments were failing because of rapid company growth, and new employees were having trouble fitting into the culture. To achieve control over this critically important process, top management interviewed their most experienced and successful PD managers and then condensed their PD tactics into four detailed procedures for everyone managing PD. The first procedure is approval for authorizing the expenditure of funds and use of resources. Thus, each PD is now scrutinized much more closely before work is started and money spent; when more questions are asked and more people are involved, better decisions tend to be made. The second procedure is identifying agreements and assumptions for each PD. Here, both the customer and top management must sign off before product design work begins, thereby reducing misunderstandings. The third procedure is breaking the work into nine specific life-cycle phases running from definition through production, with each phase including the specification of the tasks, their timing, the responsible individuals, and the due dates. The last procedure is a set of milestone management reviews, each one crucial to successful completion. Both the content and timing of these reviews are specified in advance, and progression to the next phase cannot occur until senior management has approved the prespecified requirements, objectives, and quality criteria for that phase. The procedure also specifies questions that must be answered and work that *must* be reviewed by senior management. Through the use of these procedures, which are updated and improved on a regular basis, the Automotive Systems Group has brought their critical product development process back under control (Reith and Kandt 1991).

- North Shore—Long Island Jewish Health System (LIJ), located in Great Neck, NY, found its "accessioning" registration process was out of control. Accessioning occurs when the information in the paper requisition for obtaining specimen samples is entered into the lab's information system and a label is generated and placed on a sample tube. LIJ performs more than 3.5 million tests annually for all 18 of the system's hospitals as well as all the microbiology, molecular diagnostics, complex reference tests, long-term care facilities, clinical trials, and physician offices in the network. Accessioning errors had been measured historically for years and had been a chronic problem. However, when the rate of incomplete or inaccurate specimens reached 5 percent (i.e., 175,000!), LIJ decided to step in and exercise control. A multidisciplinary team was formed to investigate and correct the problem. Before the study began, the team assumed the handwriting of the physicians would be the culprit, but it was found that half the errors were due to incorrect entering of the patients' social security numbers. This was due to the difficulty in reading an addressograph label, which was then replaced with a bar code reader. In addition, it was found that a small percentage of the staff made the majority of errors, indicating additional training was desirable. Further investigation showed that a lack of established best practices in the laboratory was another major source of errors, and discussion with the staff led to the creation of a "lead accessioner" position to set standard practices for the lab. As a result of these changes, the lab increased its accuracy rate to 99 percent, and its handling capacity by 43 percent, resulting in a positive financial impact of about $339,000 a year (Riebling 2004).

As these examples illustrate, monitoring and control are central to achieving the purposes for which processes were initially designed. It doesn't matter if the process needing control is cost, quality, time, progress or something else; to properly obtain the objectives we desire, we need to identify measures to track and, when needed, exercise control to bring results into agreement with our plans.

We begin the chapter with a general overview of the topics of monitoring and control. We then discuss the task of identifying appropriate measures to monitor, or track, as the processes get underway and describe a variety of tracking and control mechanisms that are available. Next, we illustrate one of the most fully developed control systems, statistical process control, using the control of quality as an example. Finally, we discuss a special case of control, that of service quality.

MONITORING AND CONTROL

As we noted in Figure 1.1 back in Chapter 1 when we described the production system, we will want to monitor not only our processes, but our output and even the environment to make sure that our strategy, inputs, and transformation processes are appropriate to achieve our goals. To do this we will first need to identify the key factors to be controlled, which in turn depend upon our goals for the production system. That is, in designing the system, we work backwards from our goals for the production system, but in operation the various elements work forward meaning that monitoring precedes control, which is the order we will discuss them here.

The monitoring system is a direct connection between planning and control. But if it does not collect and report information on some significant element of the production system, control can be faulty. Unfortunately, it is common to focus monitoring activities on data that are easily gathered—rather than important—or to concentrate on "objective" measures that are easily defended at the expense of softer, more subjective data that may be more valuable for control. When monitoring output performance, we should concentrate primarily on measuring various facets of output rather than intensity of activity. It is crucial to remember that effective managers are not primarily interested in how hard their employees work—they are interested in the results achieved.

Although we will be monitoring the environment and our processes as well as our outputs, the measurement of output performance usually poses the most difficult data gathering problem. There is a strong tendency, particularly in service operations, to let inputs serve as surrogate measures for output. If we have spent 50 percent of the budget (or of the scheduled time), we assume we have also completed 50 percent of the work or reached 50 percent of our goal.

Given all this, performance criteria, standards, and data collection procedures must be established for each of the factors to be measured. However, more often than not, standards and criteria change because of factors that are not under the control of management. For example, the market, our competitors, or government regulations, may change. Standards may also be changed by the community as a response to some shift in public policy—witness the changes in the performance standards imposed on nuclear power installations or automotive exhaust systems. Shifts in the prime rate of interest or in unemployment levels often alter the standards that management must use for making decisions. The monitoring process is based on the criteria and standards because they dictate, or at least constrain, the set of relevant measures.

Next, the information to be collected must be identified. This may consist of accounting data, operating data, engineering test data, customer reactions, regulations, competitors' prices, specification changes, and the like. The fundamental problem is to determine precisely which of all the available data should be collected. It is worth repeating that the typical determinant for collecting data too often seems to be simply the ease with which they can be gathered. Again, the nature of the required data is dictated by the organization's objectives or goals.

Perhaps the most common error made when monitoring data is to gather information that is clearly related to performance but has little or no probability of changing significantly from one collection period to the next. Prior to its breakup, the American Telephone and Telegraph Company used to collect monthly statistics on a very large number of indicators of operating efficiency. The extent of the collection was such that it filled a telephone-book-sized volume known as "Ma Bell's Green Book." For a great many of the indicators, the likelihood of a significant change from one month to the next was extremely small. When asked about the matter, one official remarked that the mere collection of the data kept the operating companies "on their toes." We feel that there are other, more positive and less expensive ways of motivating personnel. Certainly, "collect everything" is inappropriate as a monitoring policy.

Therefore, the first task is to identify the objectives desired from the production system. Data must be identified that measure achievement against these goals, and mechanisms designed that will gather and store such data. Next, we must examine the purposes of the various processes and find measures that provide us with insight into how these processes are performing. As an aside, if at least some of the data do not relate to the individual work level, no useful action is apt to be taken. In the end, it is the detailed work of the processes that must be altered if any aspect of performance is to be changed. A reading of the fascinating book *The Soul of a New Machine* (Kidder, 1981) reveals the crucial roles that organizational factors, interpersonal relationships, and managerial style play in determining process success.

There is a range of ways to determine what measures to monitor and then, if necessary, take action to control. We describe some of the more important ways in the next section.

$\mathscr{P}$ROCESS MONITORING

From the above discussion, it is clear that there is a wide variety of elements of the production system and environment that we may wish to monitor, but too much data can be worse than too little data since it obscures the information that may be most important in the various measures we are watching. Most importantly, we need to monitor to make sure that we are effective in an overall competitive sense, and our next topic on stages of operational effectiveness discusses some measures for this crucial objective. We next want to monitor our various processes, and we can make use of the balanced scorecard and strategy maps to guide us here. We also need to monitor the environment, including community standards, levels of risk, and other such elements. Since every situation faces unique environmental effects, we give only two examples of monitoring the environment, using ISO standards to illustrate the international environment and FMEA to illustrate one approach to monitoring for risk.

Stages of Operational Effectiveness

Wheelwright and Hayes (1985) suggest that organizations can progress through four stages of effectiveness in terms of the role their operations play in supporting and achieving the overall strategic objectives of a business's production system. As a diagnostic tool, this framework helps determine the extent to which an organization is utilizing its operations to support and possibly attain a sustainable competitive advantage. As a prescriptive tool, the framework helps focus an organization on appropriate future courses of action because it is argued that stages cannot be skipped. Important managerial challenges are also identified for each stage of effectiveness.

Organizations in stage 1 of the model are labeled ***internally neutral***. These organizations tend to view operations as having little impact on the organization's competitive success. In fact, these organizations often consider the operations area as primarily a source of problems (e.g., quality problems, late shipments, too much capital tied up in inventory). Thus, believing that operations have little strategic importance, the emphasis in these organizations is on minimizing the negative impact of operations.

Stage 2 is labeled ***externally neutral***. As the name suggests, organizations at this stage attempt to match the operational practices of the industry. Thus, organizations in this stage still tend to view operations as having little strategic importance, but they at least attempt to follow standard industry practices. Because these organizations follow industry practice, they tend to be more reactive than proactive in the operations area. Furthermore, operational investments and improvements tend to be tied to reducing costs.

Stage 3 is called ***internally supportive***. In this stage of development the organization expects its operations to support the overall business strategy and competitive position. In many cases this is stated as a formal operations strategy. Thus, operational decisions are evaluated based on their consistency with and the extent to which they support the organization's overall mission. Internally supportive organizations tend to be more proactive in terms of identifying opportunities to support the organization's overall competitiveness. It is important to point out, however, that while stage 3 organizations expect operations to support the overall business strategy, operations is typically not involved in actually formulating it.

Stage 4 organizations depend on their operations to achieve a competitive advantage and are referred to as ***externally supportive***. In effect, these organizations use core capabilities residing in the operations area to obtain a sustainable competitive advantage.

Because different parts of an organization may evolve at different rates, determining an organization's stage of effectiveness may require making a judgment about where the balance of the organization is positioned. Thus, it is possible that some departments or areas of a stage 2 organization exhibit characteristics of a stage 3 organization. However, if the majority of the organization is most appropriately characterized as being in stage 2, then the organization should be categorized as being in stage 2.

Thus, evaluating an organization's evolution is based not on its most evolved area, but rather on the balance of its organizational practices.

Using the definitions of the four operational effectiveness stages above, Dangayach and Deshmukh (2006) developed perceptual measures for each of these stages, some of which are given in Table 3.1. By asking managers how closely their company followed each of these policy measures (on a 1–5 scale), they were able to classify firms into one of the four stages and relate them to the firms' overall performance. Thus, these measures would be excellent items for monitoring the evolving competitive strength of manufacturing firms and taking control actions when they showed competitive slippage.

*T*ABLE 3.1 • Measures for Operational Effectiveness

Stage	Measures
Internally Neutral	Minimize manufacturing's negative potential
	Fire fighting is common
	Outside experts are called in for strategic decisions
	Manufacturing is primarily reactive
Externally Neutral	Industry practice is followed
	Aim is to achieve competitive parity
Internally Supportive	Manufacturing investments support the business strategy
	A manufacturing strategy is formulated and pursued
Externally Supportive	Manufacturing is involved up front in major strategic decisions
	Aim is to achieve a competitive advantage through manufacturing
	Goal is to achieve competitive superiority

Balanced Scorecard

The balanced scorecard approach (Kaplan and Norton 1996) is becoming increasingly recognized for helping organizations translate their strategy into appropriate performance measures to monitor their success. In the past, it was not uncommon for managers to rely primarily on financial performance measures. However, when the inadequacies of these measures were discovered, managers often responded by either trying to improve them or by abandoning them in favor of operational performance measures such as cycle time and defect rates. Many organizations now realize that no single type of measure can provide insight into all the critical areas of the business. Thus, the purpose of the balanced scorecard is to develop a set of measures that provides a comprehensive view of the organization.

Organizations that have developed a balanced scorecard report numerous benefits, including:

- An effective way to clarify and gain consensus of the strategy.

- A mechanism for communicating the strategy throughout the entire organization.

- A mechanism for aligning departmental and personal goals to the strategy.
- A way to ensure that strategic objectives are linked to annual budgets.
- Timely feedback related to improving the strategy.

One problem with traditional performance measurement systems based primarily on financial measures is that they often encourage short-sighted decisions such as reducing investments in product development, employee training, and information technology. The balanced scorecard approach corrects this problem by measuring performance in four major areas: (1) financial performance, (2) customer performance, (3) internal business process performance, and (4) organizational learning and growth.

The financial performance measures included in the balanced scorecard are typically related to profitability, such as return on equity, return on capital, and economic value added. Customer performance measures focus on customer satisfaction, customer retention, customer profitability, market share, and customer acquisition. The internal business process dimension addresses the issue of what the organization must excel at to achieve its financial and customer objectives. Examples of performance measures for internal business processes include quality, response time, cost, new-product launch time, and the ratio of processing time to total throughput time. Finally, the learning and growth dimension focuses on the infrastructure the organization must build to sustain its competitive advantage. Learning and growth performance measures include employee satisfaction, employee retention, worker productivity, and the availability of timely and accurate information.

The process of developing a balanced scorecard begins with top management translating the mission and strategy into specific customer and financial objectives. Based on the customer and financial objectives, related measures for the internal business processes are identified. Finally, investments in employee training and information technology are linked to the customer, financial, and internal business process objectives. Note that a properly constructed balanced scorecard contains an appropriate mix of outcome measures related to the actual results achieved and measures that drive future performance.

The balanced scorecard is based on the premise that a strategy is a set of hypotheses about cause-and-effect relationships that can be stated as if–then statements. For example, management of a department store might hypothesize that increasing the training that sales associates receive will lead to improved selling skills. These managers might further hypothesize that better selling skills will translate into higher commissions for the sales associates and will therefore result in less turnover. Happier and more experienced sales associates would likely lead to increased sales per store, which ultimately translates into an increase in return on investment. Since a properly developed balanced scorecard tells a story about the cause-and-effect relationships underlying the strategy, all measures included in the scorecard should be an element in the chain of cause-and-effect relationships.

One aspect of monitoring we have not yet addressed in detail is the role of our competitors in the environment. Obviously, being able to attain our mission and goals is not completely up to us, and our competitors have a strong impact on our success. Fortunately, there are again some well-formulated concepts for monitoring how our competitors are doing and whether or not they are threatening our success. One such approach is called "benchmarking," essentially documenting the level of competence of either competitors or even noncompetitor "best-in-class" organizations.

This can show how our competitors are doing on those measures of importance to our customers or clients, as well as on other measures of interest to us such as those included in the balanced scorecard.

But benchmarking can also be used simply to find out how well some aspects of production can be done, known as "state-of-the-art," "worldclass," or "best-in-class." These leaders, often in another industry from our own, can help us to improve our own operations even if our competitors are not at that level, giving us a potential competitive advantage. Hence, the topic of benchmarking will be described later in Chapter 4 on Improving Processes.

The Strategy Map

In extending their earlier work on the Balanced Scorecard, Kaplan and Norton (2000) proposed the development of Strategy Maps (see also Scholey, 2005) as a way to illustrate and monitor the cause-and-effect relationships identified through the development of a Balanced Scorecard. In particular, Strategy Maps provide organizations with a tool that helps them better monitor important details about their strategic business processes, thereby enhancing their employees' understanding of the strategy interactions which in turn facilitates implementing the business strategy.

Like the Balanced Scorecard, Strategy Maps address four perspectives: the financial perspective, the customer perspective, the internal business process perspective, and the learning and growing perspective. An example Strategy Map for a department store that desires to improve its performance is shown in Figure 3.1.

At the top of the Strategy Map the goal is specified, which in our example is to improve the store's ROI. Management has determined that the goal of improving the store's ROI can be accomplished by increasing revenue and/or improving the store's productivity. The remainder of the Strategy Map explicitly shows the chain of cause-and-effect relationships management has hypothesized about how the store's ROI can be improved. For example, it is believed that providing the sales associates with additional training will lead to improved selling skills, which should then result in increased sales per square foot of retail space and happier associates. Happier associates in turn should result in both friendly and courteous sales associates and less turnover among the associates. Ultimately, the Strategy Map hypothesizes that increased sales per square foot will help the store increase its revenue and its inventory turns, which then leads to revenue growth and productivity improvements.

ISO 9000 and 14000

ISO 9000 was developed as a guideline for designing, manufacturing, selling, and servicing products; in a sense, it is a sort of "checklist" of good business practices. Thus, the intent of the ISO 9000 standard is that, if an organization selects a supplier that is ISO 9000-certified, it has some assurance that the supplier follows accepted business practices in the areas specified in the standard. However, one criticism of ISO 9000 is that it does not require any specific actions, and therefore each organization determines how it can best meet the requirements of the standard.

ISO 9000 was developed by the International Organization for Standardization and first issued in March 1987. A major revision to ISO 9000 was completed in

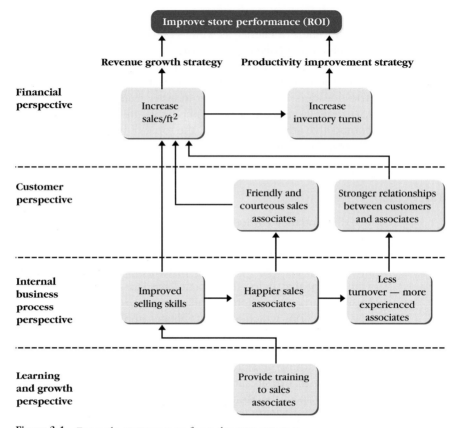

Figure 3.1   Example strategy map for a department store.

December 2008, and the new standard is commonly referred to as ISO 9000:2008. Since its introduction, ISO 9000 has become the most widely recognized standard in the world. To illustrate its importance, in 1993 the European Community required that companies in several industries become certified as a condition of conducting business in Europe. In fact, over 630,000 organizations in 152 countries have implemented ISO 9000 and/or ISO 14000.

ISO 14000 is a series of standards covering environmental management systems, environmental auditing, evaluation of environmental performance, environmental labeling, and life-cycle assessment. Like ISO 9000, ISO 14001 (a subset of the ISO 14000 series) is a standard in which organizations can become certified. The focus of ISO 14001 is on an organization's environmental management system. However, like ISO 9000, ISO 14001 does not prescribe specific standards for performance or levels of improvement. Rather, its intent is to help organizations improve their environmental performance through documentation control, operational control, control of records, training, statistical techniques, and corrective and preventive actions.

Clearly, this set of international standards for both production and environmental maintenance certification will lead to a range of measures that should be considered for monitoring the proper functioning of the production system. But more focused measures specific to the production system at hand can also be developed, such as through Failure Mode and Effect Analysis (FMEA) as described next.

Failure Mode and Effect Analysis (FMEA)

FMEA was developed by the space program in the 1960s (Stamatis, 2003) as a structured approach to help identify and prioritize for close monitoring and control those elements of a system that might give rise to failure. It employs a scoring model approach set up in a series of six straightforward steps, as follows.

1. List the possible ways a production system might fail.
2. Evaluate the severity (**S**) of the consequences of each type of failure on a 10-point scale where "1" is "no effect" and "10" is "very severe."
3. For each cause of failure, estimate the likelihood (**L**) of its occurrence on a 10-point scale where "1" is "remote" and 10 is "almost certain."
4. Estimate the ability to detect (**D**) a failure associated with each cause. Using a 10 point scale, "1" means detectability is almost certain using normal monitoring/control systems and "10" means it is practically certain that failure will not be detected in time to avoid or mitigate it.
5. Find the ***Risk Priority Number*** (**RPN**) where **RPN = S × L × D**.
6. Consider ways to reduce the **S**, **L**, and **D** for each cause of failure with a significantly high RPN.

Table 3.2 illustrates the application of FMEA to a new concept fast food restaurant. Here we primarily are illustrating how to apply the approach but in a real situation our items of failure would be much more specific and narrow: a particular machine, a particularly difficult process, a unique government regulation, and other such items that clearly could result in missing our goals for the new concept. In the table, we have identified training and marketing as the elements with the highest RPNs and thus those we particularly want to monitor and control very carefully. We might invest additional time and effort in training our employees to offset the first threat but since L is low already, it might be more productive to find ways to detect this inadequacy faster, such as surveying our customers to monitor their perceptions of our service. This might then reduce D to 3 instead of 5 and thereby mitigate the threat. As well, we could include a question on the survey to help determine what marketing approaches are having the greatest results, reducing D from 8 to perhaps 5.

$\mathcal{T}$ABLE 3.2 ● FMEA for a New Fast Food Concept

Potential Ways to Fail	S	L	D	RPN
Inadequate training	8	4	5	160
Weak marketing	6	3	8	144
Poor location	7	5	3	105
Defective concept	9	3	3	81
Local restaurant regulation change	3	5	8	120
Competitors' reactions (e.g., price, ads)	4	6	4	96

It was noted above that more specific items might be included in the FMEA list, such as a particular machine or difficult process. One way to identify such items for inclusion in the FMEA list, or for monitoring in general, is by evaluating their "process capability," a topic we explain in detail in Chapter 4 when we talk about Process Improvement. In essence, however, if the specifications for a machine (or process) are relatively tight compared to the natural variation in the machine, we have to carefully monitor the machine's process capability to satisfy the requirements of the production system. For example, in our new concept fast food example above, if the concept required a difficult and time-consuming step in the preparation of a particular menu item, we might fail because our customers got tired of waiting for their food. Hence, we would want to monitor the time this process required very carefully and take controlling steps if it started to exceed the required specifications of our production system.

$\mathscr{P}$ROCESS CONTROL

Process control is the act of reducing differences between plan and reality for each process. Monitoring and comparing activities with plan, and then reporting these findings is to no avail if actions are not taken when reality deviates significantly from what was planned. In fact, the simple act of noting and reporting discrepancies may motivate the actions required to correct the deviations. When it does not, however, active control is needed to bring performance back in line with plan. Control has the primary purpose of ensuring that the process is in compliance with its objectives. In large production systems particularly, early control is crucial since the longer we wait, the more difficult to correct the deviation.

Control is one of the manager's most difficult tasks, invariably involving both mechanistic and human elements. As well, control can be difficult because problems are rarely clear cut and hence the need for change and redirection may be fuzzy. Determining what to control raises further difficulties—did someone take an incorrect action or is the system to blame, or perhaps simply Mother Nature?

A good control system should also possess some specific characteristics:

- The system should be flexible. Where possible, it should be able to react to unforeseen changes in system performance.
- The system should be cost effective and the cost of control should never exceed the value of control. For example, bear in mind that control is not always less expensive than scrap.
- The system should be as simple as possible to operate.
- The system must operate in a timely manner. Problems must be reported while there is still time to do something about them.
- Sensors and monitors should be sufficiently precise to control the project within limits that are truly functional for the organization.
- The control system should be easy to maintain.
- The system should signal the manager if it goes out of order.
- The system should be capable of being extended or otherwise altered.

- Control systems should be fully documented when installed, and the documentation should include a complete training program in system operation.
- The system must operate in an ethical manner.

Next, we turn to a common tool for controlling processes, the Control Chart, and illustrate it with the case of controlling quality. However, it can also be used for controlling many other measures such as scrap, turnover, revenues, progress (see, for example, Meredith et al., 2009, pp. 490–493), costs, and so on.

Statistical Process Control

One of management's most difficult decisions in quality control centers on whether an activity needs adjustment. This requires some form of inspection, and in quality control there are two major types of inspection, either (1) *measuring* something or (2) simply determining the *existence* of a *characteristic*.

1) Type 1, inspection by measuring, is called *inspection for variables*, and usually relates to weight, length, temperature, diameter, or some other variable that can be *scaled*.

2) Type 2, inspection by identifying a *characteristic*, is called *inspection of attributes* and can also examine scaled variables but usually considers *dichotomous* variables such as right–wrong, acceptable–defective, black–white, timely–late, and other such characteristics that either cannot be measured or do not *need* to be measured with any more precision than yes–no.

Walter A. Shewhart developed the concept of statistical *control charts* in the 1920s to distinguish between *chance variation* in a system that is still in control and variation caused by the system's being out of control, which he called *assignable variation*. Should a process go out of control, that must first be detected, then the assignable cause must be identified, and finally the appropriate control action or adjustment must be performed. The "control chart" is used to detect when a process has gone out of control.

A repetitive operation will seldom produce *exactly* the same quality, size, and so on; rather, with each repetition the operation will generate variation around some average. This variation is particularly characteristic of a sampling process where random samples are taken and a sample mean is calculated. Because this variation usually has a large number of small, uncontrollable sources, the pattern of variability is often well described by a standard frequency distribution such as the *normal distribution*, shown plotted against the vertical scale in Figure 3.2.

The succession of measures that results from the continued repetition of some process can thus be thought of as a *population* of numbers, normally distributed, with some mean and standard deviation. As long as the distribution remains the same, the process is considered to be in control and simply exhibiting chance variation. One way to determine if the distribution is staying the same is to keep checking the mean of the distribution—if it changes to some other value, the operation may be considered out of control. The problem, however, is that it is too expensive for organizations to keep constantly checking operations. Therefore, *samples* of the output are checked instead.

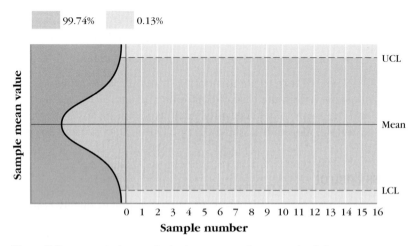

Figure 3.2   Control chart with the limits set at three standard deviations.

In sampling the output for inspection, it is imperative that the sample fully *represent* the population being checked; therefore, a *rational subgroup* of data should be used. But when checks are made only of sample averages, rather than 100 percent of the output, there is always a chance of selecting a sample with an unusually high or low mean. The problem facing the operations manager is thus to decide what is *too high* or *too low* and therefore should be considered out of control. Also, the manager must consider the fact that the more samples eventually taken, the higher the likelihood of accidentally selecting a sample with too high (or too low) a mean *when the process is actually still under control*.

The values of the sample mean that are too high or low are called the ***upper control limit*** (UCL) and the ***lower control limit*** (LCL), respectively. These limits generally allow an approach to control that is known as ***management by exception***, because, theoretically, the manager need take no action unless a ***sample mean*** exceeds the control limits. The control limits most commonly used in organizations are plus and minus ***three standard deviations***. We know from statistics that the chance that a sample mean will exceed three standard deviations, in either direction, due simply to chance variation, is less than 0.3 percent (i.e., 3 times per 1000 samples). Thus, the chance that a sample will fall above the UCL or below the LCL because of natural random causes is so small that this occurrence is strong evidence of assignable variation. Figure 3.2 illustrates the use of control limits set at three standard deviations. Of course, using the higher limit values (3 or more) increases the risk of not detecting a process that is only slightly out of control.

An even better approach is to use control charts to predict when an out-of-control situation is likely to occur rather than waiting for a process to actually go out of control. If only chance variation is present in the process, the points plotted on a control chart will not typically exhibit any pattern. On the other hand, if the points exhibit some systematic pattern, this is an indication that assignable variation may be present and corrective action should be taken.

The control chart, though originally developed for quality control in manufacturing, is applicable to all sorts of repetitive activities in any kind of organization. Thus, it can be used for services as well as products, for people or machines, for cost or quality, and so on.

For the control of *variables*—that is, *measured characteristics*—two control charts are required:

1. Chart of the *sample means* ($\bar{X}$).

2. Chart of the *range* (*R*) of values in each sample (largest value in sample minus smallest value in sample).

It is important to use two control charts for variables because of the way in which control of process quality can be lost. To illustrate this phenomenon, we will use the data supplied in Table 3.3, which correspond to the minutes to process a form at an insurance company. Three samples are taken each day: one in the morning, one near noon, and one just before closing. Each sample consists of three forms randomly selected from the staff working on these forms in the Processing Dept.

$\mathcal{T}_{ABLE}$ 3.3 • Sample Data of Process Times (minutes)

Sample	Scenario 1	Scenario 2
1	4, 5, 6	5, 4, 6
2	6, 7, 8	3, 5, 7
3	7, 9, 8	8, 2, 5

Referring to scenario 1, we can easily determine that the average of sample 1 is 5 minutes and the range is 2 minutes ($\bar{X}_1 = 5$, $R_1 = 2$). Similarly, $\bar{X}_2 = 7$, $R_2 = 2$, $\bar{X}_3 = 8$, and $R_3 = 2$. If we consider only the ranges of the samples, no problem is indicated, because all three samples have a range of 2 (assuming that a range of 2 minutes is acceptable to management). On the other hand, the behavior of the process means shows evidence of a problem. Specifically, the process means (minutes) have increased throughout the day from an average of 5 minutes to an average of 8 minutes. Thus, for the data listed in scenario 1, the sample ranges indicate acceptable process performance while the sample means indicate unacceptable process performance.

The sample statistics can be calculated in the same way for scenario 2: $\bar{X}_1 = 5$, $R_1 = 2$, $\bar{X}_2 = 5$, $R_2 = 4$, $\bar{X}_3 = 5$, and $R_3 = 6$. In contrast to scenario 1, the sample means show acceptable performance while the sample ranges show possibly unacceptable performance. Thus, we see the necessity of monitoring both the mean and the variability of a process.

Figure 3.3 illustrates these two patterns of change in the distribution of process values more formally. These changes might be due to boredom, tool wear, improper training, the weather, fatigue, or any other such influence. In Figure 3.3*a* the variability in the process remains the same but the mean changes (scenario 1); this effect would be seen in the means ($\bar{X}$) chart but not in the range (*R*) chart. In Figure 3.3*b* the mean remains the same, but the variability tends to increase (as in scenario 2 above); this would be seen in the range (*R*) chart but not the means ($\bar{X}$) chart.

In terms of quality of the output, either type of change could result in lower quality, depending on the situation. Regarding control limits, the lower control limit

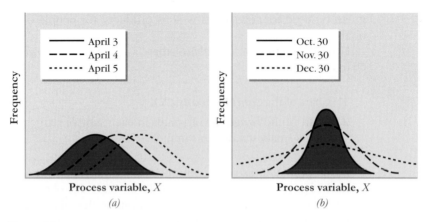

Figure 3.3   Patterns of change in process distributions.

(LCL) for the means chart may be negative, depending on the variable being measured. For example, variables such as profit and temperature can be negative, but variables such as time, length, diameter, and weight cannot. Since (by definition) the range can **never** be negative, if calculations indicate a negative LCL for the range chart, it should simply be set to zero.

As indicated earlier, control limits for the means chart are usually set at plus and minus three standard deviations. But if a range chart is also being used, these limits for the means chart can be found by using the average range, which is directly related to the standard deviation, in the following equations (where $\overline{\overline{X}}$ is the average of the sample means):

$$\text{UCL}_{\overline{x}} = \overline{\overline{X}} + A_2 \overline{R}$$
$$\text{LCL}_{\overline{x}} = \overline{\overline{X}} - A_2 \overline{R}$$

Similarly, control limits for the range chart are found from

$$\text{UCL}_R = D_4 \overline{R}$$
$$\text{LCR}_R = D_3 \overline{R}$$

The factors A_2, D_3, and D_4 vary with the sample size and are tabulated in Table 3.4.

Constructing Control Charts

The best way to illustrate the construction of control charts is by example. Assume that a bank with 10 branches is interested in monitoring the age of the applications for home mortgages being processed at its branches. To maintain a continuing check on this measure of customer responsiveness, one could select branches at random each day and note the ages of the applications. To set up the control charts, initial samples need to be taken. These data will, if considered representative by management, be used to set standards (i.e., control limits) for future applications. For our

$\mathcal{T}$ABLE 3.4 • Control Chart Factors to Determine Control Limits

Sample Size, n	A_2	D_3	D_4
2	1.880	0	3.267
3	1.023	0	2.575
4	0.729	0	2.282
5	0.577	0	2.115
6	0.483	0	2.004
7	0.419	0.076	1.924
8	0.373	0.136	1.864
9	0.337	0.184	1.816
10	0.308	0.223	1.777
12	0.266	0.284	1.716
14	0.235	0.329	1.671
16	0.212	0.364	1.636
18	0.194	0.392	1.608
20	0.180	0.414	1.586
22	0.167	0.434	1.566
24	0.157	0.452	1.548

example, we assume that a sample of $n = 4$ of the 10 branches each day will give the best control for the trouble involved. The mean age and range in ages for the initial samples were entered into the spreadsheet shown in Table 3.5. Note that each sample mean and sample range shown in Table 3.5 is based on data collected by randomly visiting four branches. The grand mean $\overline{\overline{X}}_1$, and the average range ($\overline{R}$) were also calculated (cells B23 and C23, respectively). The grand mean is then simply the average of all the daily means:

$$\overline{\overline{X}} = \frac{\sum \overline{X}}{N}$$

where N is 20 days of samples and the average range is

$$\overline{R} = \frac{\sum R}{N}$$

The data in Table 3.5 can now be used to construct control charts that will indicate to management any sudden change, for better or worse, in the ages of the mortgage applications. Both a chart of means, to check the age of the applications, and a chart of ranges, to check consistency among branches should be used.

The grand mean and average range will give the center line on these charts, respectively. The values of A_2, D_3, and D_4 are obtained from Table 3.4 for $n = 4$,

$\mathcal{T}_{ABLE}$ 3.5 • Mean and Range of Ages of Mortgage Applications

	A	B	C
		Sample	Sample
1		Sample	Sample
2	Date	Mean	Range
3	June 1	10	18
4	June 2	13	13
5	June 3	11	15
6	June 4	14	14
7	June 5	9	14
8	June 6	11	10
9	June 7	8	15
10	June 8	12	17
11	June 9	13	9
12	June 10	10	16
13	June 11	13	12
14	June 12	12	14
15	June 13	8	13
16	June 14	11	15
17	June 15	11	11
18	June 16	9	14
19	June 17	10	13
20	June 18	9	19
21	June 19	12	14
22	June 20	14	14
23	**Average**	**11**	**14**

resulting in the following control limits:

$$\text{UCL}_{\bar{x}} = 11 + 0.729(14) = 21.206$$
$$\text{LCL}_{\bar{x}} = 11 - 0.729(14) = 0.794$$
$$\text{UCL}_{R} = 2.282(14) = 31.948$$
$$\text{LCL}_{R} = 0(14) = 0$$

The control charts for this example were developed using a spreadsheet and are shown in Figures 3.4 and 3.5. In addition, the data in Table 3.5 are graphed on the charts. As seen in Figure 3.4, no pattern is apparent from the data; the points appear to fall randomly around the grand mean (centerline) and thus are considered by management to be representative.

The range chart, Figure 3.5, again shows no apparent pattern and is also acceptable to management. Each day, as a new sample is taken, $\bar{X}$ and R will be calculated and plotted on the two charts. If either $\bar{X}$ or R is outside the LCL or UCL, management must then undertake to find the assignable cause for the variation.

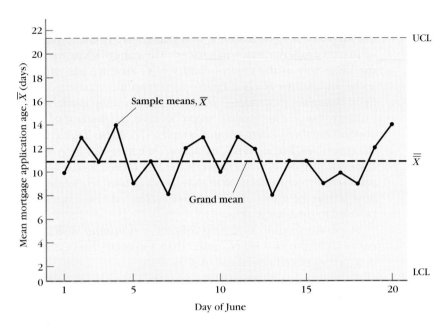

Figure 3.4 Mean mortgage application age.

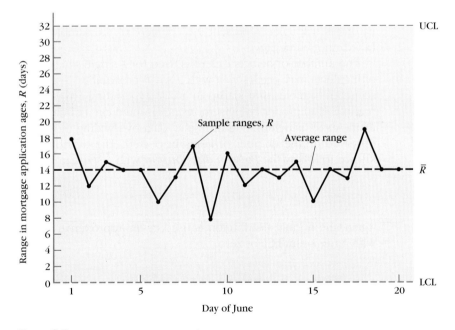

Figure 3.5 Range in mortgage application age.

Control charts can also be used for controlling attributes of the output, the second type of inspection we described earlier. The most common of these charts are the **fraction-defective p chart** and the **number-of-defects c chart**. As with the range chart, the lower control limit for attribute charts can never be negative.

The fraction-defective *p* chart can be used for any two-state (**dichotomous**) process such as heavy versus light, acceptable versus unacceptable, on-time versus late, or placed properly versus misplaced. The control chart for *p* is constructed in much the same way as the control chart for $\bar{X}$. First, a large sample of historical data is gathered, and the fraction (percent) having the characteristic in question (e.g., too light, defective, misplaced), $\bar{p}$, is computed on the entire set of data as a whole.

Large samples are usually taken because the fraction of interest is typically small and the number of items in the samples should be large enough to include some of the defectives. For example, a fraction defective may be 3 percent or less. Therefore, a sample size of 33 would have to be taken (i.e., 1/0.03 = 33) to expect to include **even one** defective item. Note that the data used to **derive** the control chart do not have to use the same size sample as is collected to use the chart. **Any** set of data can be used to determine $\bar{p}$.

Since the fraction defective follows a **binomial** distribution (bi means "two": either an item is or it is not) rather than a normal distribution, the standard deviation may be calculated directly from $\bar{p}$ as

$$\sigma_p = \sqrt{\frac{\bar{p}(1 - \bar{p})}{n}}$$

where *n* is the uniform sample size to be used for controlling quality. Although the fraction defective follows the binomial distribution, if $n\bar{p}$ and $n(1-\bar{p})$ are both greater than 5, the normal distribution is a good approximation and the control limits of $3\sigma_p$ will again represent 99.7 percent of the sample observations. Again, the LCL cannot be negative.

The number-of-defects *c* chart is used for a single situation in which any number of incidents may occur, each with a small probability. Typical of such incidents are scratches in tables, fire alarms in a city, typesetting errors in a newspaper, and the number of improper autoinsertions per printed circuit board. An average number of incidents, $\bar{c}$, is determined from past data by dividing the total number of incidents observed by the number of items inspected. The distribution of such incidents is known to follow the **Poisson distribution** with a standard deviation of

$$\sigma_c = \sqrt{\bar{c}}$$

Again, the normal distribution is used as an approximation to derive control limits with a minimum LCL of zero.

$\mathcal{C}$ONTROLLING SERVICE QUALITY

For process control, strategy maps and control charts can also be used for controlling the quality of services, assuming the right measures are being monitored. However, measuring the quality of the service portion of an output is often more difficult than measuring the quality of the facilitating good for a variety of reasons—including the service portion being abstract rather than concrete, transient rather than permanent, and psychological rather than physical. One way to cope with these difficulties, as indicated earlier, is to use customer satisfaction surveys. For example, J.D. Power and Associates (www.jdpower.com) makes extensive use of customer satisfaction surveys to rate airlines, hotel chains, and rental car companies. For example, its ratings of airlines in 2008 were based on almost 20,000 flight evaluations supplied by a national survey of frequent flyers. According to these travelers, there was a substantial decline in overall satisfaction from 2007, primarily due to poorer customer service, which was twice the amount of decline in satisfaction with price. In 2008, Alaska Airlines received the highest ranking among the traditional airlines and JetBlue had the highest ranking in the low-cost airlines category.

J.D. Power ranks hotel chains and rental car companies in a similar fashion. For example, in 2008, J. D. Power ranked the overall satisfaction of five categories of hotels (luxury, upscale, economy, etc.) on the basis of over 53,000 individual evaluations of hotels. According to J. D. Power, the primary factors impacting upscale hotel customer satisfaction are satisfaction with the guest room, the reservation process, the check-in/check-out process, the facilities, their service, the food and beverages, and the cost. In 2008, Embassy Suites Hotels was the highest ranked upscale hotel for the second year in a row.

A common approach to improving the quality of services is to methodically train the employees in standard procedures and to use equipment that reinforces this training. The ultimate example is McDonald's Hamburger University, where managers are intensively trained in the McDonald's system of food preparation and delivery. Not only is training intensive, but follow-up checkups are continuous, and incentives and rewards are given for continuing to pay attention to quality. Furthermore, the equipment is designed to reinforce the quality process taught to the employee, and to discourage sloppy habits that lead to lesser quality.

Financial services can also benefit from better quality. Several years ago, a major bank noticed that its requests for letters of credit were handled by nine different employees who conducted dozens of steps, a process that consumed four days. By retraining its employees so that each would be able to process a customer's request through all the steps, the bank was able to let each customer deal with only one employee, who could complete the process within a day. Now each time a letter of credit is ordered, the customer is placed back with the same employee. As a result, the department involved has been able to double its output of letters of credit using the services of 49 percent fewer employees.

By paying attention to the quality delivered to customers, American Express was able to cut the processing time for new credit applications from 22 days to 11 days, thereby more than doubling the revenue per employee in its credit card division. It had previously tracked errors and processing time internally but had ignored the impacts on the customer. When it began focusing on the customer, it suddenly found that speed in the credit department was often immaterial in shortening the customer's waiting time for credit approval, because four more departments still had to process every new application.

Service Defections

When a tangible product is produced, quality is often measured in terms of defects. In services, the analogy to a product defect is a defecting customer—that is, a customer who takes his or her business elsewhere. Thus, service defections can be measured in a variety of ways, such as the percent of customers that do not renew their membership (health clubs), percent of sales from new versus repeat customers (office supply store), and the number of customers that cancel their service (long-distance phone companies). Of course, the concept of a defecting customer is equally applicable to organizations that produce tangible outputs.

Organizations should monitor their defecting customers for a number of reasons. First, research suggests that long-time customers offer organizations a number of benefits. For example, the longer a customer has a relationship with an organization, the more likely that customer is to purchase additional products and services and the less price-sensitive they are. In addition, no advertising is necessary to get the business of long-term customers. In fact, long-term customers may actually be a source of free advertising for the company. One study published in the *Harvard Business Review* concluded that cutting defections in half more than doubles the average company's rate of growth. Likewise, improving customer retention rates by 5 percent can double profits.

Defections by customers can provide a variety of useful information. First, feedback obtained from defecting customers can be used to identify areas that need improvement. Also, the feedback can be used to determine what can be done to win these customers back. Finally, monitoring for increases in the defection rate can be used as an early warning signal that control actions are immediately needed.

EXPAND YOUR UNDERSTANDING

1. We often divide "control" into two categories: preventive and corrective. Would you classify FMEA as a tool for monitoring, preventive control, or corrective control? Explain.

2. Does the balanced scorecard monitor all the elements of the production system of Figure 1.1? If not, what does it miss? Does it include anything not in Figure 1.1? If so, why, and why isn't it in Figure 1.1?

3. Since service defections are analogous to defects in products, could they be controlled with control charts in the same way? Would they use charts based on inspection of variables or attributes? Give an example(s).

4. Under what kinds of circumstances might an organization wish to use control limits of two standard deviations or even one standard deviation? What should it bear in mind when using these lower limits?

5. Why are two control charts not necessary in controlling for attributes? Might not the variability of the fraction defective or the number of defects also be going out of control?

6. It is generally not appropriate to apply control charts to the same data that were used to derive the mean and limits. Why? What are the two possible outcomes if this is done, how likely is each, and what are the appropriate interpretations?

7. In deriving the p chart, why can the sample size vary? What must be remembered if the p chart is applied to a different sample size each time?

8. Firms regularly employ a taster for drinkable food products. What is the purpose of this taster?

9. How is quality handled differently in service firms and product firms? Does quality mean something different in a service firm?

10. For many years, the Balanced Scorecard was seen to be more appropriate for "implementing" strategy than for planning it. Now that Strategy Maps have been conceived, does this replace the Balanced Scorecard or does each do something different, and if so, which one is concerned with "implementing" strategy?

APPLY YOUR UNDERSTANDING
Paint Tint

Late last month, Jim Runnels, a sales representative for the Paint Tint Corporation, was called to the plant of Townhouse Paint Company, one of his largest accounts. The purchasing agent for Townhouse Paint was complaining that the tubes of paint tint it had received over the last couple of weeks were not within the specified range of 4.9 to 5.1 ounces.

The off-weight tubes had not been detected by Townhouse's receiving clerks and had not been weighed or otherwise checked by their quality control staff. The problem arose when Townhouse began to use the tubes of tinting agent and found that the paint colors were not matching the specifications. The mixing charts used by the salespeople in Townhouse's retail stores were based on 5-ounce tubes of tinting agent. Overfilled or underfilled tubes would result in improper paint mixes, and therefore in colors that did not meet customers' expectations.

In consequence, Townhouse had to issue special instructions to all of its retail people that would allow them to compensate for the off-weight tubes. The Townhouse purchasing agent made it clear that a new supplier would be sought if this problem recurred. Paint Tint's quality control department was immediately summoned to assist in determining the cause of the problem.

Paint Tint's quality manager, Ronald Wilson, speculated that the cause of the problem was with the second shift. To analyze the problem, he entered into a spreadsheet the data from all the previous samples taken over the last two months. As it turned out, 15 random samples had been taken over the two-month period for both the first and the second shifts. Samples always consisted of 10 randomly selected tubes of paint tint. Also, separate sampling schedules were used for the first and second shifts so that the second shift would not automatically assume that it would be subject to a random sample just because the first shift had been earlier in the day.

After entering the sample weight data of the tubes into the following spreadsheet and calculating the sample means, Ronald was quite puzzled. There did not seem to be any noticeable difference in the average weights across the two shifts. Furthermore, although the lines were running at less than full capacity during the first six samples, there still did not seem to be any change in either line after reaching full production.

	A	B	C	D	E	F	G	H	I	J	K	L	M	N	O	P
1	**First Shift**															
2							**Sample Number**									
3	**Observation**	**1**	**2**	**3**	**4**	**5**	**6**	**7**	**8**	**9**	**10**	**11**	**12**	**13**	**14**	**15**
4	**1**	4.90	5.05	4.96	4.92	4.96	5.03	4.99	5.00	5.02	5.03	5.01	4.95	5.02	4.96	5.06
5	**2**	5.03	5.04	4.96	5.00	5.00	4.99	5.03	5.01	5.05	4.90	4.94	4.95	4.95	4.97	4.97
6	**3**	5.00	5.00	4.92	5.05	5.03	4.98	5.01	4.95	5.00	4.95	5.00	5.06	5.00	4.93	5.00
7	**4**	5.03	5.11	5.01	5.03	4.98	4.99	5.02	5.01	5.01	5.01	5.00	5.02	4.98	5.01	5.00
8	**5**	5.02	4.94	4.98	5.01	5.00	4.98	5.01	4.99	5.03	5.01	4.96	4.94	5.04	5.00	5.03
9	**6**	4.92	5.02	5.00	5.02	5.02	5.01	4.99	4.98	5.00	4.94	4.98	4.99	5.02	5.04	5.08
10	**7**	5.04	5.03	4.98	5.02	5.00	4.99	5.06	4.96	5.01	4.98	5.01	4.97	4.99	4.98	4.97
11	**8**	4.92	5.00	5.00	4.96	5.01	5.01	5.05	5.00	4.97	4.98	4.97	4.97	5.05	5.08	4.98
12	**9**	4.95	4.95	4.94	5.02	4.95	4.98	4.97	4.94	5.07	5.00	5.00	4.96	5.02	4.94	5.00
13	**10**	5.02	4.99	5.08	4.94	5.00	4.95	5.04	4.98	5.02	5.01	4.98	5.02	5.06	5.02	4.97
14	**Average**	**4.98**	**5.01**	**4.98**	**5.00**	**5.00**	**4.99**	**5.02**	**4.98**	**5.02**	**4.98**	**4.99**	**4.98**	**5.01**	**4.99**	**5.01**
15																
16																

(*Continued*)

	A	B	C	D	E	F	G	H	I	J	K	L	M	N	O	P
17	**Second Shift**															
18							**Sample Number**									
19	**Observation**	**1**	**2**	**3**	**4**	**5**	**6**	**7**	**8**	**9**	**10**	**11**	**12**	**13**	**14**	**15**
20	1	5.03	5.02	4.99	4.96	5.03	5.02	5.08	5.10	5.16	5.00	4.97	5.11	5.11	4.90	5.02
21	2	4.90	4.95	4.97	4.97	4.98	5.03	4.97	4.93	4.92	4.97	4.91	5.05	4.98	4.92	4.98
22	3	5.02	4.94	5.04	4.98	5.00	4.98	4.93	4.92	4.99	5.08	5.15	4.93	5.13	4.97	4.86
23	4	4.98	5.05	5.02	5.00	4.97	5.06	4.84	4.93	5.00	5.07	4.96	5.15	5.15	4.92	4.94
24	5	5.01	4.95	5.02	5.02	4.98	5.04	5.07	5.03	4.98	4.94	4.91	4.98	5.10	5.04	4.93
25	6	4.99	4.99	4.99	5.03	5.00	5.04	4.95	4.96	4.99	4.96	5.07	4.88	5.12	5.03	4.97
26	7	4.99	4.97	5.00	4.98	4.99	4.99	4.93	4.86	5.01	5.13	5.15	4.74	5.01	4.91	5.05
27	8	5.02	5.00	5.00	4.96	4.98	4.98	4.99	5.08	5.07	4.93	4.95	4.90	4.93	4.95	4.97
28	9	5.01	5.00	5.05	5.02	5.03	4.97	4.82	4.96	4.93	4.96	4.91	5.03	5.04	4.98	5.03
29	10	4.97	4.99	4.95	5.03	5.00	4.99	5.05	5.14	5.03	4.91	5.11	5.04	5.03	5.08	4.92
30	**Average**	**4.99**	**4.99**	**5.00**	**5.00**	**5.00**	**5.01**	**4.96**	**4.99**	**5.01**	**5.00**	**5.01**	**4.98**	**5.06**	**4.97**	**4.97**

Questions

1. Can you identify any difference between the first and second shifts that explains the weight problem? If so, when is this difference first detectable?
2. Do you think Paint Tint's production process can meet Townhouse Paint's requirements? Why (or why not)?

KoalaTech, Ltd.

KoalaTech, Ltd., of Sydney, Australia, produces office equipment for small businesses and home offices. Several months ago it launched its PFS 1000, a single unit that functions as a color printer, color scanner, color copier, and fax machine. The PFS 1000 won rave reviews for its functionality, affordable price, and innovative design. This, coupled with KoalaTech's reputation for producing highly reliable products, quickly led to a severe backlog. Koala-Tech's plant simply could not keep up with demand.

Initially, KoalaTech's President, Nancy Samuelson, was extremely concerned about the backlog and put a great deal of pressure on the plant manager, George Johnson, to increase production. However, Nancy abruptly shifted gears when a new report indicated that returns and complaints for the PFS 1000 were running four times higher than the usual industry rate. Because KoalaTech's reputation was on the line, Nancy decided that the problem required immediate attention. She also decided that the quickest way to diagnose the problem and to avoid the usual mentality of "blaming it on the other department" would be to bring in an outside consultant with expertise in these matters.

Nancy hired Ken Cathey to investigate the problem. Nancy and Ken agreed that Ken should spend his first week interviewing key personnel in an effort to learn as much about the problem as possible. Because of the urgency of the problem, Nancy promised Ken that he would have complete access to—and the cooperation of—all employees. Nancy would send out a memo immediately informing all employees that they were expected to cooperate and assist Ken in any way they could.

The next morning, Ken decided to begin his investigation by discussing the quality problem with several of the production supervisors. He began with the supervisor of the final assembly area, Todd Allision. Todd commented:

> I received Nancy's memo yesterday, and frankly, the problem with the PFS 1000 does not surprise me. One of the problems we've had in final assembly is with the casing. Basically, the case is composed of a top and a bottom. The problem that we are having is that these pieces rarely fit together, so we typically have to force them together. I'm sure this is adding a lot of extra stress on the cases. I haven't seen a breakdown on what the problems with quality are, but it wouldn't surprise me if one of the problems was cracked cases or cases that are coming apart. I should also mention that we never had this problem with our old supplier. However, when purchasing determined that we could save over $A1 per unit, we switched to a new supplier for the cases.

The meeting with Todd lasted for about 1 1/2 hours, and Ken decided that rather than meet with someone else, he would be better off reviewing the notes he had taken and filling in any gaps while the conversation was still fresh in his mind. Then he would break for lunch and meet with one or two additional people in the afternoon.

After returning from lunch, Ken stopped by to talk with Steve Morgan, the production supervisor for the printed circuit boards. Ken found Steve and an equipment operator staring at one of the auto-insertion machines used to place components such as integrated circuits, capacitors, and resistors on the printed circuit board before wave soldering. Arriving, Ken introduced himself to Steve and asked, "What's up?" Steve responded:

> We are having an extremely difficult time making the printed circuit boards for the PFS 1000. The designers placed the components closer together than this generation of equipment was designed to handle. As a result, the leads of the components are constantly being bent. I doubt that more than 25 percent of the boards have all their components installed properly. As a result, we are spending a great deal of time inspecting all the boards and reworking the ones with problems. Also, because of the huge backlog for these boards and the large number that must be reworked, we have been trying to operate the equipment 20 percent faster than its normal operating rate. This has caused the machine to break down much more frequently. I estimate that on a given eight-hour shift, the machine is down one to two hours.
>
> In terms of your job—to determine the cause of the problems with quality—faulty circuit boards are very likely a key contributor. We are doing our best to find and correct all the defects, but inspecting and reworking the boards is a very tedious process, and the employees are putting in a lot of extra hours. In addition, we are under enormous pressure to get the boards to final assembly. My biggest regret is that I didn't have more input when they were building the prototypes of the PFS 1000. The prototypes are all built by highly trained technicians using primarily a manual process. Unfortunately, the prototypes are built only to give the engineers feedback on their designs. Had they shown some people in production the prototypes, we could have made suggestions on changes that would have made the design easier to produce.

Ken decided to end the day by talking to the plant manager, Harvey Michaels. Harvey was in complete agreement with Todd and Steve and discussed at length the enormous pressure he was under to get product out the door: "The bottom line is that no one cooperates. Purchasing changes suppliers to save a few bucks, and we end up with components that can't be used. Then our own engineers design products that we can't produce. We need to work together."

On his second day, Ken decided to follow up on the information he had gathered the day before. He first visited the director of purchasing, Marilyn Reagan. When asked about the problem of the cases that did not fit together, Marilyn responded:

> The fact of the matter is that switching suppliers for the cases saved $A1.04 per unit. That may not sound like a lot, but multiply that by the 125,000 units we are expecting to sell this year, and it turns out to be pretty significant. Those guys in production think the world revolves around them. I am, however, sympathetic to their problems, and I plan on discussing the problem with the supplier the next time we meet. That should be some time next month.

After wrapping up the meeting with Marilyn, Ken decided he would next talk to the director of engineering. On the way, he recognized a person at a vending machine as the worker who had been standing next to Steve at the auto-insertion machine. Ken introduced himself and decided to talk with the worker for a few minutes. The worker introduced himself as Jim and discussed how he had been working in the shipping department just two weeks ago. The operator before Jim had quit because of the pressure. Jim hadn't received any formal training in operating the new equipment, but he said that Steve tried to check on him a couple of times a day to see how things were going. Jim appreciated Steve's efforts, but the quality inspectors made him nervous and he felt that they were always looking over his shoulder.

Ken thanked Jim for his input and then headed off to meet with the director of engineering, Jack Carel. After introducing himself, Ken took a seat in front of Jack's desk. Jack began:

> So you are here to investigate our little quality snafu. The pressure that we are under here in engineering is the need to shrink things down. Two years ago fax machines, printers, scanners, and copiers were all separate pieces of equipment. Now, with the introduction of the PFS 1000, all this functionality is included in one piece of equipment not much larger than the original printer. That means design tolerances are going to be a lot tighter and the product is going to be more difficult to manufacture. But the fact of the matter is that manufacturing is going to have to get its act together if we are going to survive. The engineering department did its job. We designed a state-of-the-art piece of office equipment, and the prototypes we built proved that the design works. It's now up to the manufacturing guys to figure out how to produce it. We have done all that we can and should be expected to do.

To end his second day, Ken decided to meet with the director of quality assurance, Debbie Lynn. Debbie commented:

> My biggest challenge as director of quality assurance is trying to convince the rest of the organization the importance quality plays. Sure everyone gives lip-service to the importance of quality, but as the end of the month approaches, getting the product out the door is always the highest priority. Also, while I am officially held accountable for quality, I have no formal authority over the production workers. The quality inspectors that report to me do little more than inspect product and tag it if it doesn't meet the specifications so that it is sent to the rework area. In all honesty, I am quite optimistic about Nancy's current concern for quality and very much welcome the opportunity to work closely with you to improve KoalaTech's quality initiatives.

Questions

1. Which departments at KoalaTech have the most impact on quality? What role should each department play in helping KoalaTech improve overall quality?
2. What recommendations would you make to Nancy concerning KoalaTech's problem with quality? What role should the quality assurance department play?

EXERCISES

1. The city government is planning a "career fair" weekend in two months and wishes to use a FMEA table to identify risk elements to monitor and possible actions to take in controlling the risks. They believe that there are 4 major risks to the fair:

   1. Insufficient employer turnout—The severity if this happens they rate as an 8, the likelihood as a 4, and the detectability as a 5.
   2. Insufficient job seeker turnout—For this they rate the severity as a 6, likelihood as 7, and detectability as a 5.
   3. Inclement weather—Severity 4, likelihood 5, detectability 4.
   4. Economy—Severity 7, likelihood 5, detectability 6.

   Determine the most important risk elements and suggest ways to control them.

2. Pick two different processes to run a FMEA analysis of, such as running an end-of-semester party and passing an upcoming advanced finance course. Identify the major risks for success with each one and give each a severity, likelihood, and detectability

rating to calculate the RPN for each risk. How would you monitor each of these risk elements for impending failure and what steps might you take to control them?

3. Top management of the Royal Scottish Bank monitors the volume of activity at 38 branch banks with control charts. If deposit volume (or any of perhaps a dozen other volume indicators) at a branch falls below the LCL, there is apparently some problem with the branch's market share. If, on the other hand, the volume exceeds the UCL, it means the branch should be considered for expansion or that a new branch might be opened in an adjacent neighborhood.

    Given the 10-day samples for each of the six months below, prepare an $\overline{X}$ chart for the deposit volume (in hundreds of thousands of pounds) for the Kilmarnock branch. Use control limits of $\pm 3\sigma$. The average range of the six samples was found to be £85,260.

	Average of 10 Days of Deposits (£100,000)
June	0.93
July	1.05
August	1.21
September	0.91
October	0.89
November	1.13

4. Using the following weekly demand data for a new soft drink, determine the upper and lower control limits that can be used in recognizing a change in demand patterns. Use $\pm 3\sigma$ control limits.

Week	Demand (6-packs)
1	3500
2	4100
3	3750
4	4300
5	4000
6	3650

5. A control chart has a mean of 50 and two-sigma control limits of 40 and 60. The following data are plotted on the chart: 38, 55, 58, 42, 64, 49, 51, 58, 61, 46, 44, 50. Should action be taken?

6. Given the following data, construct a 3σ range control chart.

Day of Sample	Sample Values
Saturday	22, 19, 20
Sunday	21, 20, 17
Monday	16, 17, 18
Tuesday	20, 16, 21
Wednesday	23. 20, 20
Thursday	19, 16, 21

   a. If Friday's results are 15, 14, and 21, is the process in control?

   b. Construct a 3σ means control chart and determine if the process is still in control on Friday.

7. a. Using the following data, prepare a p chart for the control of picking accuracy in a wholesale food warehouse. Sample size is expected to be 100 cases.

Day	Number of Cases Picked	Number of Incorrect Picks
1	4700	38
2	5100	49
3	3800	27
4	4100	31
5	4500	42
6	5200	48

   b. Determine if days 7, 8, and 9 are under control.

Day	Number of Cases Picked	Number of Incorrect Picks
7	100	1
8	100	2
9	100	4

8. A new machine for making nails produced 25 defective nails on Monday, 36 on Tuesday, 17 on Wednesday, and 47 on Thursday. Construct an $\overline{X}$ chart, p chart, and c chart based on the results for Monday through Wednesday and determine if Thursday's production was in control. The machine produces 1 million or so nails a day. Which is the proper chart to use?

9. Construct a p chart using 2σ limits based on the results of 20 samples of size 400 in Table A.

Table A

Sample Number	Number of Defects
1	2
2	0
3	8
4	5
5	8
6	4
7	4
8	2
9	9
10	2
11	3
12	0
13	5
14	6
15	7
16	1
17	5
18	8
19	2
20	1

10. Twenty samples of 100 were taken, with the following number of defectives: 8, 5, 3, 9, 4, 5, 8, 5, 3, 6, 4, 3, 5, 6, 2, 5, 0, 3, 4, 2. Construct a 3σ p chart.

11. Sheets of Styrofoam are being inspected for flaws. The first day's results from a new machine that produced five sheets are 17, 28, 9, 21, 14. Design a control chart for future production.

BIBLIOGRAPHY

Alwan, L. *Statistical Process Analysis*. New York: Irwin/McGraw-Hill, 2000.

Besterfield, D. H. *Quality Control*, 6th ed. Upper Saddle River, NJ: Prentice Hall, 2001.

Dangayach, G. S., and S. G. Deshmukh. "An Exploratory study of Manufacturing Strategy Practices of Machinery Manufacturing Companies in India." *OMEGA: The International Journal of Management Science*, 34 (2006): 254–273.

Fitzsimmons, J. A., and M. J. Fitzsimmons. *Service Management for Competitive Advantage*, 5th ed. New York: McGraw-Hill, 2006.

Evans, J. R., and W. M. Lindsay. *The Management and Control of Quality*. Cincinnati: South-Western, 1999.

Goetsch, D. L., and S. B. Davis. *Quality Management: Introduction to Total Quality Management for Production, Processing, and Services*, 3rd ed. Upper Saddle River, NJ: Prentice Hall, 2000.

Gupta, V. K., and D. J. Graham. "A Customer Driven Quality Improvement and Management Project at Diamond Offshore Drilling." *Project Management Journal*, September 1997.

Harvey, J. "Service Quality: A Tutorial." *Journal of Operations Management*, 16 (1998): 583–597.

Ingram, T. "Client/Server, Imaging and Earned Value: A Success Story," *PM Network*, December 1995: 21–25.

Ibbs, C. W., and Y.-H. Kwak, "Benchmarking Project Management Organizations." *PM Network*, February 1998.

Jones, T. O., and W. E. Sasser, Jr. "Why Satisfied Customers Defect." *Harvard Business Review* (November–December 1995): 89–99.

Juran, J. M., and F. M. Gryna, Jr. *Quality Planning and Analysis*, 3rd ed. New York: McGraw-Hill, 1993.

Kaplan, R. S., and D. P. Norton. *The Balanced Scorecard*. Boston: Harvard Business School Press, 1996.

Kaplan, R. S., and D. P. Norton. "Having Trouble with Your Strategy? Then Map It." *Harvard Business Review* (September–October 2000), pp. 167–176.

Kidder, T. *The Soul of a New Machine*. Boston: Little, Brown, 1981.

Ledolter, J., and C. Burrill. *Statistical Quality Control: Strategies and Tools for Continual Improvement*. New York: John Wiley and Sons, 1999.

Livingston, J. L., and R. Ronen. "Motivation and Management Control Systems." *Decision Sciences,* April 1975.

Meredith, J. R., and S. J. Mantel, Jr. *Project Management: A Managerial Process,* 7th ed. Hoboken, NJ: Wiley, 2009.

McGrath, R. G., and I. MacMillan, "Discovery-Driven Planning." *Harvard Business Review,* July–August 1995.

Montgomery, D. C. *Introduction to Statistical Quality Control,* 4th ed. New York: Wiley, 2001.

Nixon, T. R. "Project Management at the New Parliament House, Canberra," *Project Management Journal,* September 1987.

Ott, E., E. G. Schilling, and D. Neubauer. *Process Quality Control.* New York: McGraw-Hill, 2000.

Reichheld, F. F. "Learning from Customer Defections." *Harvard Business Review* (March–April 1996): 56–69.

Reith, W. D., and D. B. Kandt, "Project Management at a Major Automotive Seating Supplier," *Project Management Journal,* September 1991.

Riebling, N. B., S. Condon, and D. Gopen. "Toward Error Free Lab Work," *Six Sigma Forum Magazine,* November 2004, p. 23–29.

Schoderbek, C. G., P. P. Schoderbek, and A. G. Kefalas. *Management Systems,* 4th ed. Homewood, IL: Irwin, 1989.

Scholey, C. "A Step-by-Step Guide to Measuring, Managing, and Communicating the Plan." *Journal of Business Strategy,* 26 (3, 2005): 12–19.

Stamatis, D. H. *Failure Mode and Effect Analysis: FMEA from Theory to Execution,* 2nd ed. ASQ Quality Press, 2003.

Summers, D. *Quality,* 2nd ed. Upper Saddle River, NJ: Prentice Hall, 2000.

Thamhain, H. J. "Best Practices for Controlling Technology-Based Projects." *Project Management Journal,* December 1996.

Wheelwright, S. C., and R. H. Hayes. "Competing Through Manufacturing." *Harvard Business Review* (January–February 1985): 99–109.

CHAPTER 4

Six Sigma for Improving the Transformation System

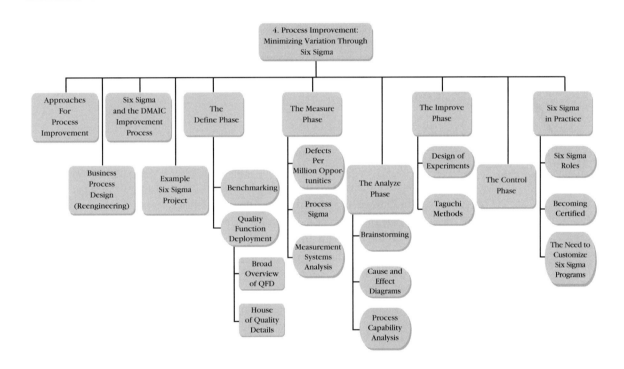

This chapter discusses ways operational activities support the business strategy and enhance competitiveness: the redesign and continuous improvement of business processes. To put our discussion in perspective, we begin with an overview of three alternative approaches for process improvement. We then turn our attention to the first process improvement strategy, Business Process Design.

This is then followed by a detailed discussion of the second process improvement strategy, Six Sigma. Next, each phase in Six Sigma's DMAIC approach is discussed in more detail including illustrating the use of representative Six Sigma tools in each phase. The chapter conludes with a discussion of Six Sigma in practice. Here we discuss the various roles associated with Six Sigma, becoming certified, and the need for organizations to customize their approach to Six Sigma training and implementation. In the next chapter we continue our discussion of process improvement strategies and address the third process improvement strategy, namely lean. The trend toward integrating Six Sigma and lean will also be discussed in the next chapter.

*I*NTRODUCTION

- In the early 1990s, Nynex released Robert Thrasher from his duties as chief operating officer and assigned him to lead an effort aiming to reinvent the company. From the very beginning, Thrasher chose not to examine the company in the traditional way in terms of its divisions, departments, and functions. Rather, he opted to analyze the company in terms of four core processes that cut across the entire organization. Thrasher defined these processes as customer operations, customer support, customer contact, and customer provisioning. With the processes defined, Thrasher decided to obtain the services of the Boston Consulting Group (BCG) to help reengineer the process. Teams were then formed from 80 Nynex employees and 20 BCG consultants with the charge of reducing operating expenses by 35 to 40 percent.

  To stimulate their thinking and to learn from the best, team members visited 152 "best practice" companies, thereby identifying a number of major inefficiencies at Nynex. For example, the teams learned that Nynex purchased 83 different brands of personal computers, that $500 per truck was being spent painting newly purchased trucks a different shade of white, and that $4.5 million was spent to identify and pursue $900,000 in unpaid bills. After identifying these problems, the teams developed a list of 85 "quick wins." For instance, Nynex will save $7 million a year in postage costs by printing on both sides of customers' bills and will save $25 million by standardizing on two personal computer models. Companywide, the teams' suggestions reduced Nynex's $6 billion operating expenses by $1.5 to $1.7 billion in 1997. Doing this was expected to provide Nynex with an internal rate of return of 1025 percent and pay back its investment in two years (*Business Week* 1994).

- Error prone and inefficient, Bank of America (B of A) was paying a price in terms of both money and customer dissatisfaction. As one example, on a ten-point scale, only 40 percent of B of A's customers rated their experience with the company at the top, that is, a nine or ten. Internally, hundreds of thousands of defects were being created per million opportunities.

  Ken Lewis, the company's CEO, decided in 2001 that a change in strategy was needed. This entailed a shift from fueling growth by mergers and acquisitions toward more organic growth based on retaining and deepening the relationship with existing customers. Thus, in 2001 the company embarked on its quality journey. Based on his belief that the company needed a more disciplined and comprehensive approach to process improvement, Lewis turned to Six Sigma. A new senior manager reporting directly to Lewis was hired to oversee Quality and Productivity.

  Being a financial services organization, it was to be expected that many in the organization would be skeptical of the applicability of an approach that was developed for factories. One way CEO Lewis addressed this concern was by being among the first to personally complete a Green Belt project and further requiring all of his direct reports to complete projects as well. Each of these projects was a success, providing benefits such as improved customer satisfaction with problem resolution, significantly reduced travel expenses, and increased employee retention.

  If you ask executives at B of A, they will tell you Six Sigma is not a fad but the way we conduct business. To get its Six Sigma initiative off the ground, B of A recruited Black Belts and Master Black Belts from leading Six Sigma organizations such as General Electric, Motorola, and Honeywell. By 2004 B of A estimated that there were over 100 open senior leadership positions requiring a background in Six Sigma. One senior executive at B of A had gone so far as to speculate that Black Belt certification will be a mandatory qualification for leadership roles at B of A. By early 2004, B of A had trained in excess of 10,000 employees in the use of Six Sigma tools to support the DMAIC methodology. But perhaps the most compelling statistics relate to the overall benefits B of A has received as a result of its Six Sigma initiatives. In particular, B of A estimates that it has obtained benefits in excess of $2 billion in less than three years while at the same time increasing its customer delight by 25% (Jones 2004).

- In 2002, the nuclear medicine department of Southside Hospital, a not-for-profit community hospital located in Bayshore, NY, was receiving numerous complaints regarding the turnaround times for stress tests. The turnaround time for a stress test is measured as the elapsed time from when the stress test was ordered by a physician until the results were signed off by a radiologist in the nuclear medicine department. Delays in receiving the results from stress tests impacted the timeliness of treating the patients, which in turn could affect the length of time a patient was required to stay in the hospital. To address the problem associated with excessive turnaround times, hospital administrators decided to test Six Sigma's define, measure, analyze, improve, and control (DMAIC) approach to assess its applicability to healthcare operations. To execute the project, a team consisting of one Black Belt and three Green Belts was created. In the course of completing the project, the team utilized many traditional Six Sigma tools including voice of the customer, "critical to quality" trees, process mapping, stakeholder analysis, defects per million opportunities, cause and effect diagrams, regression analysis, and Pareto analysis. In the end, the team was able to reduce the turnaround times for stress tests by over 50 percent, from 68 hours to 32 hours (the standard deviation was also reduced from 32 hours to nine hours). In addition, the team was able to increase the process sigma level (discussed later in this chapter) from less than 0.1 to 2. Finally, the project resulted in an overall increase in capacity with no additional cost. In fact, costs actually decreased by $34,000 stemming from savings in salaries. In the end, hospital administrators acknowledged the extent to which such a data-driven approach enhanced the ultimate success of the project (Godin, Raven, Sweetapple, and Del Giudice 2004).

- One of the tasks performed by TRW's corporate law department is the registration of trademarks. The company estimates that it costs an average of $1,200 (not including processing costs) to renew a trademark worldwide. To evaluate the trademark renewal process, a team utilized many traditional Six Sigma tools including voice of the customer, determining the critical to quality characteristics, logistic regression analysis, and value-added process mapping to evaluate the process. One finding from the project was that in numerous cases trademarks were being renewed more out of a sense of history and nostalgia as opposed to providing value to the business. In the end, the project produced hard savings of $1.8 million by eliminating the renewal of entire classes of trademarks. Numerous process improvements in the trademark renewal process were also identified, producing additional soft savings. Finally, by clearly defining defects in the trademark renewal process, the project team was able to establish a baseline process sigma level of 2.18, which can be used to assess the impact of future process improvements (Das, Colello, and Davidson 2004).

As some of these later examples illustrate, Six Sigma has become a particularly timely topic in business. As a result, people with a background in Six Sigma are presently in high demand. In fact, at 3M, 25 percent of the 1000 employees who completed Six Sigma training have been promoted two levels or more! To further illustrate the point, a search in early 2009 at Monster.com using the keyword "six sigma" yielded over 1900 hits across virtually all industries, including manufacturing, consulting, technology, financial services, insurance, healthcare, and retail.

As further evidence of the value industry is placing on individuals with Six Sigma experience, consider the following quote taken from the letter to shareholders in GE's 2000 annual report whose co-authors included Chairman and CEO Jack Welch and President and Chairman-Elect Jeffrey Immelt (p. 6):

> It is reasonable to guess that the next CEO of this Company, decades down the road, is probably a Six Sigma Black Belt or Master Black Belt somewhere in GE right now, or on the verge of being offered—as all our early-career (3–5 years) top 20% perform-ers will be—a two- to three-year Black Belt assignment. The generic nature of a Black Belt assignment, in addition to its rigorous process discipline and relentless customer focus, makes Six Sigma the perfect training for growing 21st century GE leadership.

A question that naturally arises is what is driving industry's interest in Six Sigma? Perhaps the primary reason for the current popularity of Six Sigma is that it works, as exemplified by the significant benefits several high profile organizations have reported from their Six Sigma initiatives. To illustrate this, Table 4.1 summarizes the financial benefits obtained by organizations across a variety of industries. The table also provides summary information related to the number of employees that were trained at various Six Sigma levels.

$\mathcal{T}$ABLE 4.1 • Examples of Six Sigma Training and Benefits

Company	Time Period	Number of Master Black Belts Trained	Number of Black Belts Trained	Number of Green Belts Trained	Monetary Benefits from Six Sigma ($M)
Air Canada	2002–2005	11	51	1,200	$450
American Express	2002				$200
American Standard	2000–2004	44	673	4,302	$170
Cummins	2000–2005	65	500		$1,000
Merrill Lynch	2001–2005	20	406	874	
Sun Microsystems	2000–2005	6	122	207	$1,170
Tyco International	2002–2005		263	870	$800

As you can see from this introduction, Six Sigma is among the most timely topics in business today. Furthermore, Six Sigma is equally applicable to organizations that produce a tangible output (e.g., Cummins and Sun Microsystems) or deliver an intangible service (e.g., Air Canada and American Express) as well as to organizations that exist to make a profit (e.g., B of A, American Standard, and Tyco International) or are nonprofit organizations such as Southside Hospital.

To put our discussion into perspective, we begin with a brief overview of alternative approaches to process improvement. Based on this overview, we then turn our attention to the first process improvement strategy, Business Process Design. This is then followed by a detailed discussion of the second process improvement approach—Six Sigma's DMAIC improvement process. Following this overview of the DMAIC approach, each of its phases is discussed in more detail and representative Six Sigma tools are overviewed. The chapter concludes with a discussion of Six Sigma in practice. In the next chapter we continue our discussion of process improvement and address a third process improvement approach, namely, the lean approach to process improvement. The trend toward integrating Six Sigma and lean will also be discussed in the next chapter.

$\mathcal{A}$PPROACHES FOR PROCESS IMPROVEMENT

The appropriate process improvement strategy to employ depends on the nature of the challenge to be addressed. Figure 4.1 provides a roadmap for selecting the appropriate process improvement strategy. As is shown in the figure, Business

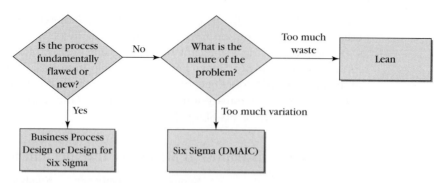

Figure 4.1   Alternative process design and improvement strategies.

Process Design or Design for Six Sigma is the appropriate process improvement strategy to employ in situations where it is determined that the process is fundamentally flawed, or when a brand new process must be created. In cases where the process is fundamentally flawed, it is best to start with a clean slate and redesign the process from scratch. In cases where the process is not fundamentally flawed but there are opportunities to improve it, we must consider the nature of the problem to determine the appropriate process improvement strategy. In cases where it is determined that there is too much variation in the process, the Six Sigma methodology is appropriate. In cases where it is determined that the efficiency of the process needs to be improved, lean is the appropriate process improvement strategy. Of course, it is also common for a process to suffer from both too much variation and waste in which case a combination of Six Sigma and lean tools can be applied to the process improvement initiative. This is often referred to as Lean Sigma. We now turn our attention to discussing Business Process Design and Six Sigma in more detail. Lean is the topic of the next chapter.

BUSINESS PROCESS DESIGN (REENGINEERING)

Business Process Design (BPD) is the appropriate strategy for processes that require improvements beyond what can be done via incremental enhancements or in situations where a new process that does not currently exist must be developed. BPD is often needed when there is a major advance in technology and/or a major shift in customer requirements. It may also be needed in cases where a process has not been improved over a long period of time. BPD is perhaps most commonly referred to as **reengineering**, but a wide variety of other names are also frequently used, such as *business process reengineering, business process engineering, business process innovation,* and *business process design* (BPD) or *redesign.* To compound the confusion, often managers incorrectly use terms such as *downsizing* and *restructuring* interchangeably with BPD.

To help put BPD in perspective, consider that the roots of the functional organization date back to the late 1700s, when Adam Smith proposed his concept of the division of labor in *An Inquiry into the Nature and Causes of the Wealth of Nations* (1776). Referring to the 17 operations required to produce a pin, Smith argued that assigning one task to each of 17 workers would be more efficient and would produce more pins than having 17 workers each autonomously perform all 17 tasks.

Although there have been dramatic advances in technology and significant shifts in customer requirements since Smith first proposed the division of labor concept, it is only recently that organizations have begun to challenge the concept and look for better ways to organize and integrate work. Indeed, if you were to compare how companies are organized today and how they were organized 20 or 30 years ago, you would find that little has changed in their organizational structures. This is true despite technological advances such as personal computers, fax machines, cellular phones, laser printers, the Web, spreadsheets, word processors, client–server computing, e-mail, and Wi-Fi, to name a few.

Initially, when these technologies were first adopted by organizations, the dramatic improvements in performance that were expected did not materialize. One popular explanation for this is that organizations were not taking advantage of the capabilities the new technologies offered. Rather, companies were simply using technology to speed up and automate existing practices. Clearly, if an activity or a set of activities is not effective to begin with, performing it faster and with less human intervention does not automatically make it effective.

For instance, one major financial institution reported that more than 90 steps were required for an office worker to get office supplies. These steps mostly involved filling out forms and getting the required signatures. Given the capabilities of information technology, it is certainly true that these steps could be automated and speeded up. For example, an information system could be developed to generate all the forms automatically and then automatically email them to the appropriate person for authorization. However, is automating all these steps the best solution? Might it not make more sense to eliminate most of them? Consider that even if the forms are generated and dispatched faster, valuable managerial time is still being used to examine and approve these requests every time an employee needs a pad of paper or ballpoint pen. Indeed, when the cost of the controls is weighed against the benefits, it might be much more effective to give employees access to the supply cabinet to retrieve their own supplies as needed. Dr. Michael Hammer uses the term *paving cow paths* to describe organizations that simply implement a new technology without considering the capabilities it offers to perform work in entirely new and better ways.

The Nynex example at the beginning of the chapter provides a glimpse of several major themes associated with BPD. First, BPD's primary objective is improved customer service. This was clearly illustrated by Nynex's four core processes as each began with the word *customer.* This brings us to a second theme associated with BPD, a concern with making *quantum* improvements in performance rather than small, *incremental* improvements. Nynex's goal to lower its operating expenses by 35 to 40 percent certainly represents a quantum improvement, as does its expected 1025 percent internal rate of return.

A third important theme of BPD is the central role of technology. When many of the new information technologies were initially adopted by companies, the expected improvements in organizational efficiency and effectiveness often did not materialize. On closer examination, it was discovered that many companies were adapting new technology to fit current business practices rather than attempting to take advantage of the capabilities offered by the technology to perform activities in perhaps entirely different and better ways. The early 1990s marked the beginning of the reengineering movement—companies started to consider the capabilities that technology offered in relationship to the way work was performed and organized.

Michael Hammer and Steven Stanton, in their book *The Reengineering Revolution* (New York: Harper Business, 1995), define reengineering as "the fundamental rethinking and **radical redesign** of business **processes** to bring about **dramatic** improvements in performance" (p. 3). The keywords *radical, redesign, process,* and *dramatic* are particularly important to understanding the concept of reengineering or BPD. The word **radical** is used to signify that the purpose of BPD is to *profoundly* change the way work is performed, not to make *superficial* changes. It has to do with understanding the foundation upon which work is based and eliminating old ways that no longer make sense. In other words, it refers to *reinventing* the way work is performed and organized, not simply improving it. Radically changing work is often best accomplished by starting with a clean slate and making no assumptions about how work activities are performed.

The second keyword, **redesign**, denotes the fact that BPD is concerned with the design of work. Typically people think of design as being primarily applicable to products. However, the way work is accomplished can also be designed. In fact, Hammer and Stanton point out that having intelligent, capable, well-trained, motivated employees is of little value if work is badly designed to begin with.

The third keyword is **process**. Although all organizations perform processes, it was not until recently that they began organizing work on the basis of these processes. Partly as a result of total quality management (TQM, discussed in Chapter 1), companies began to focus more on meeting customers' needs. As they did this, they soon realized that customers are not particularly interested in the individual activities that are performed to create a product or service. Rather, they are more concerned about the final result of these activities. Of course, because companies were not organized on the basis of their processes, they were not managed on the basis of processes either. Therefore, no one was assigned responsibility for the entire process that created the results of interest to the customer. Using the scenario of product design, a typical company would have departmental managers to oversee market research, manufacturing, and customer service. However, there was no manager responsible for ensuring that the results of all these activities were meeting customers' requirements. We use the term **process-centered** to refer to companies that have organized their work activities on the basis of specific value-creating processes.

The last keyword is **dramatic**. BPD is concerned with making quantum improvements in performance, not small or incremental improvements. Thus, BPD focuses on achieving breakthroughs in performance. A company that lowers its lead time by 10 percent from the previous year does not exemplify a dramatic improvement. On the other hand, a company that reduces its lead time from three weeks to three days does.

To illustrate these concepts, consider the experiences of IBM Credit Corporation. IBM Credit is in the business of financing purchases of IBM office equipment. Numerous companies—including General Motors, Ford, Chrysler, and General Electric—are in the lending business. These companies have found that operating financial units can be extremely profitable in addition to offering customers a higher level of service.

Originally, IBM Credit was organized into functional departments. The steps involved in processing a credit request are shown in Figure 4.2. The process began when an IBM sales rep closed a deal and the customer wanted to finance the

Figure 4.2   Processing credit requests at IBM credit.

purchase through IBM Credit. In this case the sales rep would relay the pertinent information to one of 14 order loggers at IBM Credit. The order loggers sat in a conference room and manually wrote down on pieces of paper the information supplied by the sales reps. Periodically during the day, the pieces of paper were carted upstairs to the credit department. Employees in the credit department entered the pertinent information into a computer to check the borrower's creditworthiness. The results of this check were then recorded on another piece of paper.

Next, the documents would be transferred to the business practices department. This department would modify the standard loan covenant in response to specific requests by customers. The business practices department used its own computer system. After being processed in the business practices department, the documents were transported to the pricing department, where pricers entered the data into a program running on a personal computer to determine the appropriate interest rate. Finally, the entire dossier was transported to an administrator, who converted all the information into a "quote letter." The quote letter was then sent by Federal Express to the field sales rep.

The sales reps were extremely dissatisfied with this process. First of all, the entire process took an average of 6 days and sometimes as long as two weeks. What salesperson wants to give his or her customers two weeks to think over a purchase? On top of this, when a sales rep called to check on the status of a customer's credit request, often the request could not even be located.

As a result of complaints from the sales reps, a manager at IBM Credit decided to investigate the problem. The first thing this manager wanted to determine was how much work time actually went into processing a credit request. To determine this, the manager employed the strategy of "becoming the part" or in this case "becoming the loan request" by walking an actual request through the entire process. First, he recorded the time it took to log an actual order. Then, he took the order that was just called in and personally carried it to the credit department. Arriving at the credit department, he selected a worker at random and told the worker to stop what he or she was currently working on and perform the credit check. After repeating this in the other departments, the manager determined that the actual processing time of a credit request was about 90 minutes. Thus, out of an average of six days, each application was being processed only about 90 minutes, indicating a significant opportunity for improvement.

IBM Credit's approach to improving this process was to combine all these activities into one job called a *deal structurer*. Thus, one worker handled all the activities required to process a credit request, from logging the information to writing the quote letter. As a result of using deal structurers, turnaround times were reduced to an average of four hours. Furthermore, with a small reduction in head count, the number of deals processed by IBM Credit increased 100 times (not 100 percent). Do these results qualify as dramatic?

Given these results, you may wonder why IBM Credit had ever adopted a functional organizational structure in the first place. To answer this, let's put ourselves in the shoes of a manager at IBM Credit. Suppose we were asked to develop an organization to process credit requests. One requirement that might occur to us is that the process should be able to handle any possible type of credit request. Given this requirement, if you look again at Figure 4.2, you will see that IBM Credit's original functional arrangement accomplishes this objective. For example, no matter how difficult checking a particular borrower's creditworthiness might be, the process could handle it, because everyone in the credit department was a highly trained specialist. The same is true of all the other departments. However, another important question is: How often will this specialized knowledge be needed? In other words, what percent of the credit requests are relatively routine and what percent require deep, specialized knowledge? As IBM found out, the vast majority of credit requests could be handled relatively routinely.

Another explanation for why IBM Credit originally created a functional organization relates to the technology that was available at the time. A key ingredient that allowed IBM Credit to move to the deal-structurer model was advances in technology. For example, spreadsheets, databases, and other decision support tools were adopted so that the deal structurers could quickly check interest rates, access standard clauses, and check the creditworthiness of the borrowers. In effect, the new technology allowed the deal structurers, who had only general knowledge, to function as though they had the specialized knowledge of an expert in a particular discipline.

Six Sigma and the DMAIC Improvement Process

The Six Sigma concept was developed by Bill Smith, a senior engineer at Motorola, in 1986 as a way to standardize the way defects were tallied. As you probably already know, sigma is the Greek symbol used in statistics to refer to standard deviation which is a measure of variation. Adding "six" to "sigma" combines a measure of process performance (*sigma*) with the goal of nearly perfect quality (*six*). More specifically, to some the term Six Sigma literally translates into making no more than 3.4 mistakes (defects) per 1 million opportunities to make a mistake (defect).

While Six Sigma's original definition of 3.4 defects per million opportunities is a rather narrow measure of quality, Six Sigma itself has evolved and now encompasses a broad methodology for designing and improving business processes. In fact, many organizations (e.g., B of A and GE) view Six Sigma as an integral part of their overall business strategy. In the popular book *The Six Sigma Way*, Six Sigma is defined as:

> a comprehensive and flexible system for achieving, sustaining and maximizing business success. Six Sigma is uniquely driven by close understanding of customer needs, disciplined use of facts, data, and statistical analysis, and diligent attention to managing, improving, and reinventing business processes. (p. xi)

At Motorola, Six Sigma is defined as "a business improvement process that focuses an organization on customer requirements, process alignment, analytical rigor, and timely execution".[1] While numerous additional definitions of Six Sigma could be cited, we remark that common themes tend to emerge across the range of suggested definitions, including rigorous (often statistical) analysis, customer focus, data driven, and improving overall business performance. Likewise, a number of benefits are commonly associated with Six Sigma initiatives, including increased profitability, improved quality, improved employee morale, lower costs, higher productivity, market share growth, improved levels of customer retention and satisfaction, and shorter lead times. Interestingly, Motorola became the first company to win the Malcolm Baldrige National Quality Award in 1988. Furthermore, Motorola estimates that in the 18 years Six Sigma has been deployed, it has saved in excess of over $16 billion—which translates into almost $1 billion per year!

Arguably, one reason for the success of Six Sigma programs where others have failed is that Six Sigma provides a structured, logical, and disciplined approach to problem solving. More specifically, as shown in Figure 4.3, Six Sigma projects generally follow a well-defined process consisting of five phases. The phases are **d**efine, **m**easure, **a**nalyze, **i**mprove, and **c**ontrol which are collectively referred to as ***DMAIC*** (pronounced dey-MAY-ihk). As the names of the phases suggest, the DMAIC improvement process can be thought of as an adaptation of the scientific method to process improvement.

Before discussing the DMAIC phases in more detail, a couple of comments are in order. First, as shown in Figure 4.3, the phases in a DMAIC project often serve as project milestones and thus used as gateways to the next phase in the project. In particular, the progress and outcomes associated with the project are evaluated at the end of each phase to assess the merits of permitting the project to move on

---

[1] www.motorola.com/content/0,2409-4904,00.html, September 20, 2004.

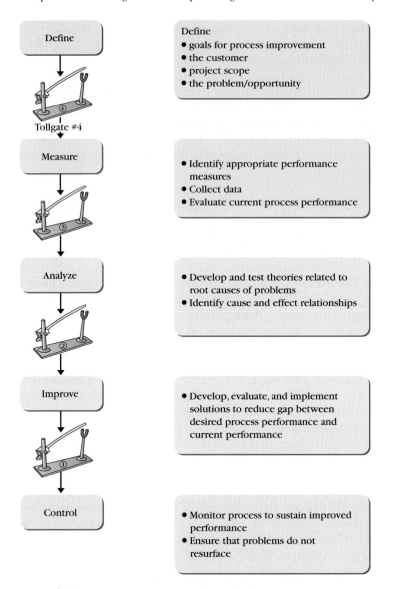

Figure 4.3 The Six Sigma DMAIC approach for process improvement.

to the next phase. The extent to which organizational resources will continue to be allocated to the project is typically assessed at these milestones as well.

Second, there are large numbers of standard Six Sigma tools and methodologies that are used at various phases in a DMAIC project. Table 4.2 summarizes some frequently used Six Sigma tools and methodologies and lists the DMAIC phases where these tools/methodologies are most commonly used. Before turning our attention to discussing each DMAIC phase in more detail, we first provide a detailed example of an actual Six Sigma project.

$\mathcal{T}_{ABLE}$ 4.2 • Common Tools and Methodologies in the Six Sigma Toolset

Six Sigma Tool/Methodology	DMAIC Phase(s) Most Commonly Used in
Affinity diagram	D, A
Benchmarking	D, M
Brainstorming	A, I
Business case	D
Cause and effect diagrams	M, A
Control charts	M, A, I, C
Critical to quality tree	D
Data collection forms	M, A, I, C
Data mining	M
Design for Six Sigma (DFSS)	An entire collection of tools/methodologies that can be used across all phases
Design of experiments (DOE)	A, I
Defects per million opportunities (DPMO)	M
Failure modes and effects analysis (FMEA)	M, I, C
Gantt chart	Tool used to manage entire DMAIC project
Kano model	D, M
Lean tools	An entire collection of tools/methodologies that can be used across all phases
Measurement systems analysis (gage R&R)	M
Nominal group technique	D, M
Pareto analysis	D, M, A, I
Process capability	M, A, I
Process maps	D, M, A, I, C
Process sigma	M, I
Project charter	D
Quality function deployment (QFD)	D, M
Regression	A
Rolled throughput yield (RTY)	D, M, A
Simulation	A, I
SIPOC	D
Stakeholder analysis	D, I
Theory of constraints (TOC)	One of the lean tools
Voice of customer (VOC)	D

$\mathcal{E}$XAMPLE SIX SIGMA PROJECT

With increasing patient volumes, the Northshore University Hospital located in Manhasset, NY initiated a Six Sigma project in 2004 to reduce the bed assignment turnaround time. The bed turnaround time is the elapsed time from when the discharge instructions are given to a patient to the time the admission nurse is notified that a clean bed is ready. Within six months, the Six Sigma team was able to reduce the average bed turnaround time by over two hours.

The Six Sigma team began the Define Phase by developing a process map that identified all the steps in the process from the time the patient received the discharge instructions to the time the admission nurse was notified that a clean bed was ready. The team also defined the admissions nurses as the customer of the process and surveyed these nurses to collect voice of the customer data. Based on the voice of the customer data collected, the team established a target bed turnaround time of two hours and an upper specification limit of 2.5 hours.

In the Measure Phase, the team developed the operational definition of a defect as any case where more than 2.5 hours were required to turnaround a bed. The team also conducted a measurement systems analysis to verify the effectiveness of its measurement system and hence the data collected to study the process. In addition, the team calculated the defects per million opportunities (DPMO) of the current process. The team discovered that the average bed turnaround time was over 3.75 hours and that the DPMO was 672,725. Finally, the team created a cause and effect diagram to identify the variables that influenced the bed turnaround times.

In the Analyze Phase the team performed hypothesis tests and used analysis of variance to identify variables that were statistically significant. As the team analyzed the data they discovered communication and technical problems in two key steps. To address these problems the team developed four recommendations in the Improve Phase. For example, one recommendation related to revising the discharge assessment sticker to include additional information. Another recommendation was to better utilize the admission RN beepers so they would be immediately notified of when a clean bed was ready.

In the Control Phase, control charts were created to monitor bed turnaround times. The control charts helped ensure the improvements made to the process continued and also served as an early detection system should performance begin to deteriorate.

This example illustrates another characteristic of Six Sigma projects. Namely, with Six Sigma, we let the story naturally unfold as we objectively analyze the data. This means that, as difficult as it is to do at times, we resist the tendency to try to solve the problem as soon as it is defined. Rather, we engage in a process of progressively gaining additional insight into the root causes of the problem by sequentially answering new questions as they arise. Thus, as the insights we gain from investigating a particular issue often naturally lead to new questions, we utilize the tools in the Six Sigma toolkit to help find answers to these new questions. Through this process of applying the Six Sigma methodology and tools, we ultimately gain a clear understanding of the root causes of the problem which in turn well positions us to address it.

It is also worth pointing out that often the hardest part of solving a problem is simply figuring out where to start. The DMAIC approach not only provides a disciplined approach for solving problems, but also adds structure to what otherwise might appear to be an unstructured problem. Of course it is possible that what we learn in one phase of a Six Sigma project requires that we revisit an earlier phase. We now turn attention to discussing each of the phases of a Six Sigma project in more detail.

THE DEFINE PHASE

The define phase of a DMAIC project focuses on clearly specifying the problem or opportunity, what the goals are for the process improvement project, and identifying the scope of the project. Identifying who the customers are and their requirements is also critical given that the overarching goal for all Six Sigma projects is improving the organization's ability to meet the needs of its customers. In this section we overview two tools commonly used in the Define phase of a DMAIC project: Benchmarking and Quality Function Deployment (QFD).

Benchmarking

In conjunction with their efforts to improve their products and processes, many organizations are engaging in an activity called ***benchmarking***. Essentially, benchmarking involves comparing an organization's processes with the best practices to be found. Benchmarking is used for a variety of purposes, including:

- Comparing an organization's processes with the best organization's processes. When used in this way, benchmarking activities should not be restricted to other organizations in the same industry. Rather, the companies that are best in the world at performing a particular activity, *regardless of industry*, should be studied. For example, Xerox used L.L. Bean to benchmark the order fulfillment process.
- Comparing an organization's products and services with those of other organizations.
- Identifying the best practices to emulate.
- Projecting trends in order to be able to respond proactively to future challenges and opportunities.

Benchmarking generally involves three steps. The first step is concerned with preparing for the benchmarking study. In this phase it is important to get the support of senior management and its input on what should be benchmarked. Problem areas, activities related to serving the customer better, and activities related to the mission of the organization are all appropriate candidates for inclusion in the benchmarking study.

The second phase of benchmarking consists of collecting data. There are two general sources of benchmarking data. One source is *published data*. These are often available from universities, financial filings (e.g., 10k reports), consultants, periodicals, trade journals, and books. The other source of data is *original research* conducted by the organization itself. If this approach is employed, a list of organizations to benchmark might include companies that have recently received quality awards or other business awards, are top-rated by industry analysts, have been the subject of recent business articles, or have a track record of superior financial performance. Once the companies have been identified, data can be collected in a variety of ways including interviews, site visits, and surveys.

The third and final phase of benchmarking involves using what has been learned to improve organizational performance. Once the second phase has been completed, identified gaps in performance can be used to set challenging but realistic goals (often called *stretch goals*). Also, the results of the benchmarking study can be used to overcome and eliminate complacency within the organization.

Quality Function Deployment

Arguably, two key drivers of an organization's long-term competitive success are the extent to which its new products or services meet customers' needs, and having the organizational capabilities to develop and deliver such new products and services. Clearly, no amount of clever advertising and no degree of production efficiency will entice customers to continue to purchase products or services that do not meet their needs. Likewise, it serves no purpose for an organization to design new products or services that it does not have the capability to produce or deliver. To illustrate, it would make little sense for a local phone company to market a new service that offers *voice over the Internet (VoIP)* calling if the firm did not have the infrastructure to deliver this type of service. Even if the phone company was able to work out the bugs for such calling, it could still take years to install the hardware that is necessary to deliver this type of service on a large scale. Of course, the desire to offer new products and services can serve as the impetus for acquiring additional process capabilities; however, organizations typically seek to develop new products and services that capitalize on their existing capabilities.

Quality function deployment (QFD) is a powerful tool for helping translate customer requirements into process capabilities. In effect, the use of QFD ensures that newly designed or improved products and services satisfy market requirements and are ultimately producible by the firm. As Figure 4.4 illustrates, the QFD methodology utilizes a series of tables to maintain links between customer requirements, technical requirements, component requirements, process requirements, and ultimately specific process activities. Because of their shape, these tables are often referred to as the *houses of quality*. Before discussing the contents of a house of quality in detail, we first broadly overview the QFD process and discuss the links between the four houses of quality.

Broad Overview of QFD

QFD begins by using *voice of the customer (VOC)* data to specify the customer requirements in the rows of the first house, the Output Planning Matrix, shown in Figure 4.4. The name VOC stems from the fact that the customer's own language is used to capture these requirements. As examples, a sample of mountain bike riders might offer responses regarding their preferences for a new bike such as "the bike should shift effortlessly," "there should be no bob on climbs," "the bike should climb, descend, and handle great," "the bike should suck up the bumps," and "I like a bike that is well balanced with a low center of gravity."

Next, based on the customer requirements listed in the rows, the technical requirements for the product or service are generated and listed in the columns of this house.

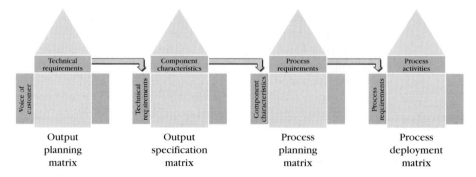

Figure 4.4 Quality Function Deployment process.

While the customer requirements are expressed in the customer's own language, the technical requirements are often expressed in a more specialized language such as that used by engineers. Thus, technical requirements for a product might be expressed in terms of dimensions, weights, performance, tensile strength, and compression.

Once the rows and columns are generated for the Output Planning Matrix, the relationship matrix in the middle of the house is completed. The cells in the relationship matrix correspond to the intersection of a particular customer requirement and technical requirement. In each cell the strength of the relationship between the corresponding customer requirement and technical requirement is evaluated. An important use of the relationship matrix is to ensure that each customer requirement is addressed by one or more technical requirements. Likewise, the relationship matrix can be used to ensure that designers do not add technical requirements to the product or service that do not address specific customer requirements. Designers who do not specifically consider customers' requirements run the risk of adding a number of "bells and whistles" that the customer may not be interested in. In these cases the designers are simply adding to the cost of the final product or service without proportionally increasing its value. For example, it might be an interesting challenge for an engineer to design a five-speed motor for garage doors. However, since customers would most likely operate it at only its fastest speed, adding the extra controls for additional speeds would not add value for the typical customer.

In the next house of quality, referred to as the Output Specification Matrix in Figure 4.4, the technical requirements which were the columns in the previous house of quality now become the rows. Thus, in the Output Specification Matrix the task now becomes generating a list of the elemental or component characteristics for the product or service which will become the columns in this house of quality. Then, once the columns are specified, the relationship matrix is completed to ensure that: (1) each technical requirement is addressed by one or more component pieces of the product or service, and (2) component requirements that are not related to specific technical requirements are not added.

In the third house shown in Figure 4.4, the Process Planning Matrix, component requirements listed in the columns of the previous house now become the rows of the new house. Next, process requirements are generated based on the component requirements listed in the rows and entered in the columns of the new house. Following this, the relationship matrix is completed for this house to ensure that each component requirement is matched to specific process requirements, and that each process requirement is linked to specific component requirements. The former result ensures that the organization has the capability to produce or deliver the components; the latter result ensures that the organization does not attempt to develop process capabilities that are not related to the component requirements.

Finally, in the Process Deployment Matrix, the process requirements from the columns of the previous house become the rows and specific process activities are generated for each process requirement. Then in a similar fashion to the other houses, the relationship matrix is completed and checks are performed to ensure that all process requirements are addressed by one or more process activities and that no process activities are added that do not address at least one process requirement.

Thus, we see that QFD provides a logical and straightforward approach for ensuring that designs for new or improved products and services meet customers' requirements and are ultimately producible. This is accomplished by first translating the voice of the customer into the technical language of engineers and other specialists.

Next, these technical requirements are translated into specific requirements for the components of the new product or service. The component requirements are subsequently translated into specific process requirements, which in turn are translated into specific process activities. In the end, however, it is the customer requirements that drive the entire QFD process.

House of Quality Details

With this general overview of QFD and its four houses of quality, we now turn our attention to the specific information listed in each house of quality. A summary of the general structure of a house of quality is shown in Figure 4.5. Constructing a house of quality begins by listing what it is we are trying to accomplish in the rows at the far left of the house. In the first house, these "Whats," as they are generally called, are the customer requirements or the voice of the customer. After specifying what it is we would like to accomplish, the next task is to think about how to meet these requirements. Thus, the "Hows," as they are called, are listed in the columns of the house. In the case of the first house of quality, the Hows are the technical requirements of the product or service given the customer requirements listed in the rows. The intersection of each What (row) and How (column) is a cell in the relationship matrix. In this relationship matrix, the strength of the relationship between each What and How is evaluated. Likewise, the roof of the house corresponds to a triangular correlation table where the correlations between the technical requirements are assessed. This assessment helps identify those technical requirements that

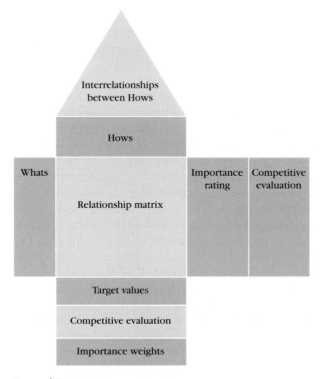

Figure 4.5 The House of Quality.

are synergistic with each other and which conflict with one another and therefore where a tradeoff may exist. At the far right of the house, customer importance ratings and the results of a competitive evaluation are summarized. Finally, at the bottom of the house, target values, a competitive evaluation, and importance weights are summarized for each How.

To illustrate the QFD process, consider a fast-food restaurant chain that is interested in improving its offerings. Figure 4.6 provides the completed Output Planning Matrix for the chain. At the far left of the house, the voice of the customer data is listed and includes customer statements such as "food that tastes good" and "get what I ordered." Based on these customer requirements, a list of technical requirements was generated and listed in the columns. In the relationship matrix, the relationship between each customer requirement and technical requirement was assessed. Thus we see that that there is a strong relationship between the taste of the food and the use of fresh ingredients, while there is only a moderate relationship between the taste of the food and the time it takes to make and deliver it to the

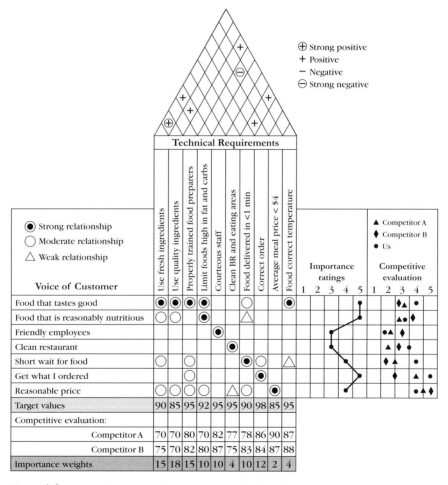

Figure 4.6   Example Output Planning matrix for fast-food restaurant chain.

customer. In the roof of the house the correlations between each of the technical requirements are evaluated and listed. In our example we note that the requirements of "fresh ingredients" and "quality ingredients" are consistent with one another while a tradeoff exists between "limiting the fat and carbohydrate content of the food" and "keeping meal price down." At the far right, customer importance ratings and a competitive evaluation are summarized. Thus we see that good taste, nutrition, and accuracy of the order are the most important aspects of the service to the customers surveyed. On these three dimensions we see that the organization in question has the best tasting food, has the second most nutritional offerings, and has the highest order accuracy. At the bottom of the house, target values and a competitive evaluation are listed for each How. For example, in terms of using fresh ingredients, the chain in question has set a goal of achieving a score of 90 on this dimension and estimates that Competitors A and B score 70 and 75, respectively, on this dimension. Finally, the importance weight or priority for each How is listed at the very bottom of the house. This can help in making tradeoffs when conflicts are discovered in the roof of the house. In the present case the most important technical requirement is the use of quality ingredients.

The other houses of quality are completed in a similar fashion. The process begins with the columns of the current house becoming the rows of the subsequent house. Then columns and the other information is determined for the new house.

One key advantage of QFD is that it is a visual tool. Through the use of QFD a firm can analyze its outputs in terms of customers' desires, compare its outputs with competitors' outputs, determine what it takes to better meet each customer's requirements, and figure out how to do it. In addition, it provides a means of linking these customer requirements through the entire planning process, ending with the specification of detailed process activities. A number of firms such as Toyota and Hewlett-Packard have adopted QFD and found that it cut their product development time by one-third to one-half and their costs by up to 60 percent (while improving quality).

THE MEASURE PHASE

Typically the measure phase begins with the identification of the key process performance metrics. Correctly choosing process performance metrics is critical in order to have an accurate picture of how the process is actually performing in terms of meeting customer requirements. Unfortunately, it is not uncommon for analysts to select performance metrics based on their ease of measurement and/or the availability of data, and not on their ability to provide insights into how the process is meeting customer requirements. For example, some organizations use machine utilization to assess the performance of their manufacturing processes. In reality, machine utilization has at best an indirect relationship to what really matters to customers—shorter lead times, higher quality, the percent of orders shipped on time, and so on. As a service example, consider a call center. In this case, performance measures such as the percent of calls answered by the third ring, the percent of calls processed without having to be escalated, and the average hold time are all better indicators of how well the process is performing than, for example, labor utilization.

Once the key process performance metrics have been specified, related process and customer data are collected. One early use of these data is to evaluate the process's current performance, which can then be used as a baseline to evaluate the benefits of potential process improvements that are identified later in the project.

As shown in Table 4.2, there are a variety of tools in the Six Sigma toolkit that are useful during the Measure Phase. We begin our discussion of the Measure Phase with two commonly used process performance measures, namely, *Defects per Million Opportunities (DPMO)* and *Process Sigma.* We then conclude our discussion of the Measure Phase with a brief overview of Measurement Systems Analysis.

Defects Per Million Opportunities

Earlier it was noted that a literal interpretation of Six Sigma is 3.4 defects per million opportunities (DPMO). This may have caused some confusion for more statistically inclined readers, which we shall now attempt to reconcile. To reconcile this difference, we need to discuss an important assumption Motorola made when it originally developed the Six Sigma concept. Specifically, Motorola assumed that the mean of a process can shift (or drift) over time by as much as 1.5 standard deviations, as is illustrated in Figure 4.7. In Figure 4.7, the bold normal curve in the middle corresponds to the process mean when it is perfectly aligned with the target value while the other two normal curves correspond to shifts in the process mean of 1.5 standard deviations both up and down. Note also that it is assumed that the shifts in the process mean do not affect the process standard deviation or customer requirements.

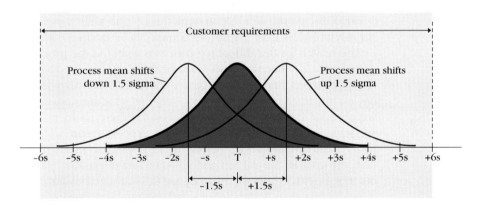

Figure 4.7 Motorola's assumption that the process mean can shift by as much as 1.5 standard deviations.

To understand the implications associated with a shift in the process mean, consider a restaurant that buys frozen hamburger patties with a target weight of 4 ounces. The supplier has provided data that the average weight of its hamburger patties are 4.0 ounces and the process standard deviation is 0.1 ounces. According to Motorola's assumption, the average weight of a hamburger could change over time. More specifically, as shown in Figure 4.8, the average weight of a hamburger could drop to as low as 3.85 ounces or increase to 4.15 ounces. Note that we are referring to the average weight of all hamburgers produced by the process at a particular point in time, not to the weight of individual hamburgers. Also, recall that we

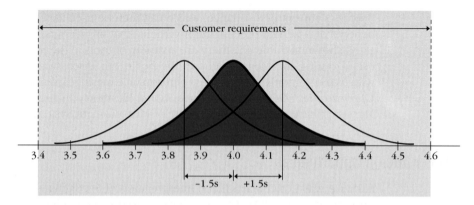

Figure 4.8   Shift in distribution of hamburger weights (after cooking) at a restaurant.

assume that the process standard deviation and restaurant's requirements are not affected by a shift in the process mean.

To see the impact that results from a shift in the process mean, let's assume that the restaurant's requirements for hamburgers are right at plus or minus six standard deviations from the target weight of 4 ounces, or at six sigma, as shown in Figure 4.8. In this case the restaurant would consider a hamburger acceptable as long as it weighed between 3.4 and 4.6 ounces. It can be easily verified that the area in one tail beyond six standard deviations is 0.0000001%, which yields a combined area of 0.0000002% in both tails. Multiplying this by one million yields .002 DPMO, which is considerably less than 3.4 DPMO commonly associated with Six Sigma.

The reason for this difference concerns a shift in the process mean. For example, what happens when the process mean shifts up by 1.5 standard deviations such that the hamburgers have an average weight of 4.15 ounces while the process standard deviation and the restaurant's requirements stay the same? Referring to Figure 4.7, we observe that now the upper tail beyond the customers' requirements would be 4.5 standard deviations above the new process mean while the lower tail would be 7.5 standard deviations below the new process mean. For the normal distribution, the area in the tail beyond 4.5 standard deviations is 0.00034%, which works out to 3.4 DPMO while the area beyond 7.5 standard deviations is 0.0000000000032%, which is less than 1 in a trillion and for practical purposes is zero. Therefore we observe that when the process mean shifts by 1.5 standard deviations, the combined area in the tails is approximately 0.00034%, which is equivalent to 3.4 DPMO. Because the normal distribution is symmetrical, the same results are obtained in cases where the process mean shifts down by 1.5 standard deviations. The only difference is that the areas in the two tails are reversed. Finally, note that the 3.4 DPMO represents the worst possible performance because it corresponds to the largest shift in the process mean. Smaller shifts in the process mean yield lower DPMO values.

An important advantage of using DPMO as a measure of process performance is that it provides a standard measure of process performance. As such, it provides a mechanism for comparing the performance across a range of processes that otherwise would be difficult to compare. In fact, as we now illustrate, DPMO makes such comparisons possible across varying processes by incorporating an adjustment for the complexity of each process.

To illustrate the calculation of the DPMO and how it adjusts for process complexity, consider a bank that processes two types of loans. Process A is used to process relatively simple loans such as for a car and consists of five steps, while Process B is used to process more complex loans such as mortgages and requires the completion of 25 steps. Let's further assume that of the last 10,000 loans processed by each process, a total of 100 errors were made in each process. In this case the number of *defects per unit (DPU)* is the same for both methods and is calculated as follows (note that here a loan represents a unit):

$$\text{DPU} = \frac{\text{Number of defects}}{\text{Number of units}} = \frac{100}{10,000} = 0.01$$

This result suggests that each process is averaging 0.01 errors (or defects) per loan, or one error per 100 loans. Is it then reasonable to conclude that both processes are performing at the same level? Because this comparison has not accounted for the differences between the methods in terms of their complexity, the answer is no. Thinking about this situation intuitively, we would generally expect the number of errors or defects to increase as the complexity of the process increases. Unfortunately, the DPU measure does not reflect this logic.

To account for the differences in the complexity of the processes, an adjustment is needed. Up to this point we have counted each loan (unit) processed as representing one opportunity for a defect. In reality, there are typically multiple opportunities to create a defect (error). To illustrate, Figure 4.9 displays 33 specific defects organized into seven categories associated with staying at a hotel. As this figure illustrates, for virtually all products and services there are numerous opportunities for introducing defects or making errors. Thus, rather than treating each unit or customer as a single opportunity for a defect, an alternative approach is to develop a preliminary list of all the opportunities for creating a defect for a given product or service. Then, the *number of defects per opportunity (DPO)* can be calculated as follows:

$$\text{DPO} = \frac{\text{Number of Defects}}{\text{Number of Units (Customers)} \times \text{Number of Opportunities}}$$

An important issue that must be addressed in using the DPO measure relates to developing the list of opportunities. In particular, it is possible to make it appear that performance is better than it actually is by padding the list with additional opportunities. To illustrate, in Figure 4.9 there are 33 specific opportunities for defects listed in seven categories. Let's assume that a survey of 100 customers revealed 200 occurrences of the 33 items listed in the figure. Based on this, if we consider each of these 33 items as a valid opportunity for a defect, then the DPO works out to be

$$\frac{200}{100 \times 33} = 0.06$$

Alternatively, if we consider each stage in the service delivery process (i.e., the seven categories listed in Figure 4.9) as an opportunity for a defect, then the DPO increases to

$$\frac{200}{100 \times 7} = 0.29$$

Hotel reservation	<ul><li>Name entered incorrectly</li><li>Wrong date of arrival entered</li><li>Wrong departure date entered</li><li>Error entering credit card number or expiration date</li><li>Wrong address entered</li><li>Incorrect number of people staying in room entered</li><li>Wrong room reserved (e.g., smoking versus nonsmoking, number of beds)</li><li>Incorrect number of baby cribs reserved</li><li>Wrong room rate entered</li></ul>
Check-in	<ul><li>Lost reservation</li><li>Excessive wait</li><li>Defective or wrong room key</li><li>Desk staff not courteous</li><li>No baggage carts available</li></ul>
Room cleaning	<ul><li>Dirty shower</li><li>Dirty linens</li><li>Dirty sink</li><li>Carpet not vacuumed</li><li>Trash cans not emptied</li></ul>
Room supplies	<ul><li>No clean towels</li><li>No toilet paper</li><li>No shampoo/hand soap</li></ul>
TV	<ul><li>Cable out</li><li>No remote control/remote control defective</li></ul>
Room Service	<ul><li>Late food order</li><li>Missing items</li><li>Billed incorrectly</li><li>Food not prepared properly</li><li>Food is cold</li></ul>
Checkout	<ul><li>Incorrect charge for room service</li><li>Incorrect telephone charges</li><li>Excessive wait for desk clerk</li><li>Excessive wait for bell captain</li></ul>

Figure 4.9   Defect opportunities associated with a stay at a hotel.

Thus we see that increasing the number of opportunities considered can make the performance look better. Along these lines then, a less than honest manager or supplier could inflate the list of opportunities for defects by including some opportunities that in reality never occur. Besides being unethical, pursuing this strategy greatly undermines the value of using DPO as a standardized measure of process performance. In the end, there are no firm rules for what to include and what not to include. As a general rule of thumb, however, it is suggested that only those defects that are meaningful to the customer be included. One strategy for determining the list of opportunities is to simply treat each stage as representing one opportunity for a defect. Based on this approach, there would be seven opportunities for a defect per hotel customer (of course some of these defects could be repeated over a multiple-day stay). Thus, a hotel customer whose reservation was lost and who experienced an excessive wait for check-in would count as one check-in defect as opposed to two defects.

Based on this logic and returning to our original objective of comparing loan Processes A and B, we determine that Process A has five opportunities to create a defect while Process B has 25. Then, based on the data collected indicating that 100 errors were made in both processes out of the last 10,000 loans processed, we can calculate the DPO for both processes as follows:

$$DPO_A = \frac{100}{10,000 \times 5} = 0.002$$

$$DPO_B = \frac{100}{10,000 \times 25} = 0.0004$$

In contrast to our earlier analysis based on the DPU measure, we now observe a significant difference in the performance of the two processes. This difference is now observable because we have adjusted the performance measure to account for the complexity of the processes. In particular we see that Process A produces an average of 0.002 defect per opportunity while Process B only produces an average of 0.0004 defect per opportunity. Because it is somewhat cumbersome to deal with such small numbers, it is common to multiply the DPO measure by 1 million to yield the DPMO measure discussed earlier. In this case, the DPMOs for Processes A and B are 2000 and 400, respectively. Thus, it is expected that Process A would make 2000 mistakes per 1 million opportunities to make a mistake while Process B would make only 400 mistakes per million opportunities.

Process Sigma

Regarding the term Six Sigma, it was noted earlier that *sigma* corresponds to a measure of process performance. Having clarified why Six Sigma translates into 3.4 DPMO positions us to now examine how *sigma* itself can be used to measure the performance of a process. We now know that when customers consider an output to be of acceptable quality as long as it is within plus or minus six standard deviations from the target value and the process mean can shift by as much as 1.5 standard deviations, the process itself will produce 3.4 DPMO. In effect then, the inherent variability of the process itself relative to the customer requirements provides a measure of the capability of the process to meet the customers' requirements. In other words, one way to measure the performance of a process is to calculate the number of standard deviations the customer requirements are from the process mean or target value. According to this measure, called ***process sigma***, a higher value corresponds to higher process performance. In the examples at the beginning of the chapter, it was noted that Southside Hospital was able to increase its process sigma from 0.1 to 2 while TRW's legal department established a baseline process sigma level of 2.18.

To see why a higher process sigma corresponds to higher process performance, refer to Figure 4.10. In particular, two levels of process sigma are shown in the

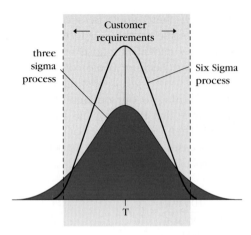

Figure 4.10   Comparison of three sigma process and Six Sigma process.

figure. The normal curve drawn with the thin line corresponds to a process where the customer requirements are at plus or minus three of the process's standard deviations (3 sigma) from the target value (T) and the normal curve drawn with the thick, bold line corresponds to a process where customer requirements are at plus or minus six of the process's standard deviations (6 sigma) from the target value. From this figure we observe that the 3 sigma process exhibits more variation and therefore has more area in its tails beyond the customer requirements. This greater amount of area in the tails corresponds to a higher probability of producing an outcome that is not acceptable to the customer.

Table 4.3 examines the impact on process performance for a range of process sigma values for two levels of process drift. Referring back to Figure 4.10, we see from the middle column in Table 4.3, which assumes the process mean can shift by as much as 1.5 standard deviations, that a 3 sigma process produces 66,811 DPMO while a 6 sigma process produces 3.4 DPMO. Note that we are defining a defect rather broadly here in terms of the entire unit of output being either defective or not defective.

$\mathcal{T}$ABLE 4.3 • DPMO for Alternative Process Sigma Levels

Process Sigma	DPMO (Based on Process Mean Shifting by up to 1.5 Standard Deviations)	DPMO (Based on Process Mean Shifting by up to 1.0 Standard Deviations)
1.0	697,672	522,751
1.5	501,350	314,747
2.0	308,770	160,005
2.5	158,687	67,040
3.0	66,811	22,782
3.5	22,750	6,213
4.0	6,210	1,350
4.5	1,350	233
5.0	233	32
5.5	32	3.4
6.0	3.4	0.3

The last column of Table 4.3 examines the impact of process stability on process performance. Specifically, while the DPMO values listed in the middle column of the table are based on Motorola's original assumption of shifts in the process mean of as much as 1.5 standard deviations, the last column is based on a process shift of no more than one standard deviation. As can be seen in comparing these two columns, the number of defects produced by a process can be significantly reduced by increasing the stability of the process. For example, at three sigma, a process produces 66,811 DPMO when the process mean shifts by as much as 1.5 standard deviations. If the process's stability is increased so that the process mean shifts by no more than one standard deviation, the DPMO drops by 66 percent to 22,782 DPMO. Based on the results shown in the table, we point out that another way to achieve the target value of 3.4 DPMO is to operate a process at 5.5 sigma while ensuring that the process mean shifts by no more than one standard deviation.

As another example, 3.4 DPMO would be achieved in cases where the process operated at 5 sigma and the process mean shifted by no more than half a standard deviation. This discussion illustrates that there are three drivers of process sigma: the actual customer requirements, the variation in the process as measured by the process standard deviation, and the stability of the process as measured by how much it can shift over time. Thus, the sigma of a process can be increased by widening the customer requirements surrounding the target value, reducing the variation of the process, and/or increasing the stability of the process.

Measurement Systems Analysis

Whenever we deal with data that were collected via measurement, measures of variation like the standard deviation and variance may not accurately reflect the true variation in the sample or population of interest. In particular, measurement errors may introduce another source of variation. For example, measuring a person's blood pressure manually requires both good eyesight and hearing. It also requires that the dial gauges be properly recalibrated over time.

As an example, consider the 10 systolic blood pressure values shown in Table 4.4 for a random sample of male diabetic patients. In particular we note that the average systolic blood pressure for this sample of patients was 130.5 with a standard deviation of 21 and variance of 442.9. As you may recall from an earlier statistics course, the purpose for measures like the standard deviation and variance is to provide a sense of how much variation or dispersion there is across the population of interest or, in the present case, how much variation there is across male diabetics' systolic blood pressure.

Figure 4.11 illustrates that the measurement system contributes to the total variance that is actually calculated. More specifically, we note that a calculated or observed value of variation can be broken down into two major components: the actual variation in the process and the variation introduced by the measurement system itself. Based on this insight and referring back to our blood pressure example, we observe that the total calculated variance of 442.9 is the result of the actual differences in the patients' blood pressure (process variation) and perhaps errors made in measuring the patients' blood pressure (measurement system variation). Mathematically this can be expressed as follows:

$$\sigma_T^2 = \sigma_p^2 + \sigma_m^2$$

$\mathcal{T}_{ABLE}$ 4.4 • Systolic Blood Pressure Values
for Sample of Male Diabetic Patients

Patient	Systolic Blood Pressure
S. Jones	123
K. Smith	106
T. Carter	136
F. Lance	145
J. Porter	153
L. Davis	157
H. Johnson	101
R. Jones	124
G. Scott	152
B. Regan	108
Average	130.5
Std. Dev.	21.0
Variance	442.9

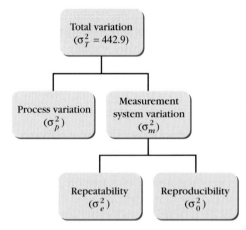

Figure 4.11   Components of total process variation.

where:

σ_T^2 = the total observed or calculated variation,

σ_p^2 = the actual variation inherent in the process and commonly referred to as the part-to-part variation (or, in our example, patient-to-patient variation)

σ_m^2 = variation introduced by the measurement system.

Recall from basic statistics that calculating the total variation arising from multiple sources requires summing the variances from each source, not their standard deviations. Therefore, the total observed standard deviation, σ_T, is calculated as

$$\sigma_T = \sqrt{\sigma_p^2 + \sigma_m^2}$$

The variance introduced by the measurement system can be further broken down into two sources: repeatability and reproducibility. Repeatability corresponds to the ability of the same person doing the measuring to get consistent measurement results when measuring a given item. Ideally, a person would obtain the same measurement results when the same item is measured using the same measurement instrument at different points in time. In our blood pressure example, repeatability corresponds to the ability of a given technician to get the same blood pressure reading for a given patient (assuming the patient's blood pressure has not changed) using the same sphygmomanometer. In contrast, reproducibility corresponds to the consistency in the measurement readings when different people measure a particular item using the same measurement instrument. Ideally, different people would obtain the same measurement result when the same item is measured using a common measurement instrument. In the blood pressure example, reproducibility corresponds to the extent to which different technicians get the same blood pressure reading when they take the blood pressure of a given patient (again assuming the patient's blood pressure has not changed) using a common sphygmomanometer. Mathematically, the variation introduced by the measurement system can be expressed as

$$\sigma_m^2 = \sigma_e^2 + \sigma_o^2$$

where:

σ_e^2 = repeatability or the variation introduced when the same person measures the same item *at different points in time* using the same measuring instrument and obtains different results across the trials

σ_o^2 = reproducibility or the variation introduced when *different people* measure the same item using the same measuring instrument

The measurement standard deviation is calculated as:

$$\sigma_m = \sqrt{\sigma_e^2 + \sigma_o^2}$$

To assess the variation introduced by the measurement system, a **Measurement Systems Analysis** study (or a Gage R&R, for repeatability and reproducibility, study as it is commonly called) is conducted. The purpose of a Measurement Systems Analysis study is to assess what percent of the observed variation is being introduced by the measurement system itself and what percent represents the actual underlying variation in the process. The smaller the percentage of variation introduced by the measurement system, the better.

Performing a Measurement Systems Analysis requires having two or more workers take repeated measurements of multiple test units with known standard values. For example, a Measurement Systems Analysis for taking blood pressure could be done by selecting two or more nurses and having the nurses rotate across multiple patients, taking a patient's blood pressure one time and then moving on to the next patient. Once a nurse finished taking the blood pressure of all patients, the process would be repeated one or more times so that each nurse took each patient's blood pressure two or more times. Prior to the study, the patients could be required to lie down in order to stabilize their blood pressure and remain lying down throughout the study in order to maintain a constant blood pressure. Furthermore, each patient's blood pressure would need to be taken both at the beginning of the study and the end of the study using a digital blood pressure monitor to establish the patient's true blood pressure and ensure that the patient's blood pressure did not change during the study. If it were discovered that one or more of the patients' blood pressures changed during the study, the study would need to be repeated for these patients. Once the data are collected from a Measurement Systems Analysis study, they are analyzed and the total observed variation is partitioned into its constituent parts using analysis of variance (ANOVA) or other similar techniques.

Both the repeatability and reproducibility of a measurement system relate to the impact the measurement system has on the observed variation. In addition to considering the impact the measurement system has on the variation of observed values, it is also important to consider the impact the measurement system has on the mean (or location) of the observed values. To access the impact the measurement system has on the mean of observed values, three additional measurement system metrics are employed:

1. ***Bias*** represents the difference between the average of a number of observations and the true value. For example, assume a nurse takes the systolic blood pressure of a patient three times and observes the following blood pressures: 126, 128, and 127. Further, assume that it was known at the time the patient's blood pressure was taken that the patient had an actual blood pressure of 125. In this case we can average the three nurse readings and calculate an average blood pressure value of 127. Based on this, the bias would be 2 (i.e., 127 − 125), suggesting that the nurse tends to overestimate a patient's blood pressure by 2. Thus, bias is a measure of the tendency of the measurement system to under- or overestimate the measurement value of interest, perhaps due to a defective instrument, such as the sphygmomanometer. While there may be errors made in taking individual measurements, ideally these errors should cancel out over time and the average should be close to the true value, which would in turn yield a bias of approximately zero.

2. ***Linearity*** of a measurement system corresponds to the accuracy of the measurement system across the entire range of possible entities to be measured. Ideally, a measurement system's accuracy should not be impacted by an entity's position in the range of possible values. Thus, a blood pressure measuring system that is more accurate for people with a blood pressure of 115 than for people with a blood pressure of 155 does not possess the characteristic of linearity.

3. ***Stability*** of a measurement system corresponds to the ability of the measurement system to get consistent results over time. For example, assuming a patient's blood pressure remains constant over time, the results of taking the patient's blood pressure at his or her annual physical should yield similar results.

THE ANALYZE PHASE

Having first defined the problem/opportunity, the customer, and the goals for the Six Sigma project and then subsequently considered appropriate performance measures, collected the relevant data, and evaluated the process' current perform-ance, we are now ready to begin the Analyze Phase. In this phase of the project, our objective is to utilize the data that have been collected to develop and test theories related to the root causes of existing gaps between the process's current and desired performance. Ultimately, our goal is to identify key cause and effect relationships that can be leveraged to improve the overall performance of the process.

Referring to Table 4.2 again, there are a number of tools in the Six Sigma toolset that are useful in the Analyze Phase. In this section we will overview three of these tools: (1) brainstorming, (2) cause and effect diagrams, and (3) process capability analysis. Because design of experiments is equally applicable to the improve phase, we defer our discussion of it until the next section.

Brainstorming

Brainstorming is among the most, if not the most, widely used techniques in busi-ness to stimulate and foster creativity. It is widely used to facilitate the identification of ways to improve business processes. Brainstorming was originally developed by Alex Osborn, an advertising executive, in the 1950s. The basis for brainstorming was Osborn's belief that while on the one hand there can be a synergistic effect associ-ated with having people work in teams (i.e., two heads are better than one), the team's overall creativity and effectiveness is often limited by a tendency to prema-turely evaluate ideas as they are being generated. In an effort to capitalize on the strengths of working in teams while at the same time eliminating the drawbacks, Osborn developed the brainstorming approach which includes the following four guidelines:

1. Do not criticize ideas during the brainstorming session.
2. Express all ideas no matter how radical, bizarre, unconventional, ridiculous, or impractical they may seem.
3. Generate as many ideas as possible.
4. Combine, extend, and/or improve on one another's ideas.

As you can see, brainstorming focuses more on the quantity of ideas generated rather than the quality. This is intentional, the point being that there will be ample opportunity to critically evaluate the ideas after the brainstorming session has ended. Therefore, the temptation to criticize or judge ideas early in the process should be avoided so as to not stifle the creativity of the participants during the brainstorming session.

It is interesting to note that despite the wide acceptance and use of brainstorming in industry, much of the research in the area questions its effectiveness. As one example, Diehl and Stroebe (1987) compared both the quantity and quality of ideas generated by people working in teams and individually. In this study, they found that the teams generated an average number of 28 ideas while the same number of people working individually generated an average of 74.5 ideas. Furthermore, when the ideas were evaluated by experts, only 8.9% of the ideas generated by the teams on average were considered "good ideas" compared with 12.7% of the ideas generated by the people working independently. Based on these results and the results of other studies, Professor Leigh Thompson identified four threats to team creativity:

1. **Social loafing.** When working in teams, people may feel they will not get credit for their ideas and therefore may not work as hard in groups compared with the amount of effort they would invest if working individually.

2. **Conformity.** When working in teams, people may be overly conservative with what they are willing to share with the team because of concerns they may have about the reaction of others.

3. **Production blocking.** There are physical limitations that can restrict the productivity of a team. For example, only one person can speak at a time. Likewise, people cannot listen and concentrate on what others are saying and simultaneously generate their own new ideas. When working alone, there are likely to be fewer distractions interrupting a person's train of thought.

4. **Downward norm setting.** Research on teams suggests that individuals working in a team environment tend to match the productivity of the least productive team member.

Fortunately, in addition to identifying these threats to team creativity, Professor Thompson also identified a number of specific actions that can be used to mitigate the threats and actually enhance team creativity. These actions include:

- *Create diversified teams.* Teams consisting of members with a variety of different skills, experiences, training, and so on will position the team to view a problem from multiple perspectives.

- *Use analogical reasoning.* With analogical reasoning, concepts from one discipline or area are applied to other areas. For example, Dr. Eliyahu Goldratt originally developed the Theory of Constraints (discussed in the next chapter) as a way to improve the efficiency of a factory. More recently, his theory has been extended and applied to the field of project management.

- *Use brainwriting.* Brainwriting involves having the participants in a brainstorming session take periodic breaks to write down their own ideas silently. A key benefit of brainwriting is that it can greatly eliminate production blocking.

- *Use the Nominal Group Technique.* The Nominal Group Technique (NGT) is often included as part of the Six Sigma toolkit as shown in Table 4.3. With the NGT, team members first work independently for perhaps five to ten minutes generating a list of ideas. The team members then share their ideas with the team, often in a round-robin fashion, and the ideas are listed. After all the ideas are listed, the team moves on to discussing, clarifying, and extending them. At the end of the discussion, team members individually rank order the ideas. Depending on the number of ideas, the team may rank order each idea or alternatively select their five or ten favorite ideas and then rank order this subset. The team then evaluates the results, perhaps considering the scores of the ideas or the frequency with which an idea was selected.

- *Record team ideas.* Recording ideas can help a team utilize its time together more effectively by eliminating repetitive discussions and ensuring that ideas are not forgotten.

- *Use trained facilitators to run the brainstorming session.* As experts in brainstorming, trained facilitators can ensure the rules are followed and that the discussion stays on task.

- *Set high standards.* In some cases, a team's lack of performance may be the result of misunderstandings of what is expected or even possible. For example, feedback regarding how many ideas the team has generated in comparison to the number of ideas other teams have generated after similar durations may help increase the quantity of ideas generated.

- *Change the composition of the team.* Research supports that periodically replacing team members helps increase both the quantity of ideas generated by the team as well as the number of different types of ideas generated.

- *Use electronic brainstorming.* With electronic brainstorming, team members are seated in a room with individual computer workstations for each team member. The team members work individually and enter their ideas into the computer. A computer screen located at the front of the room anonymously displays all ideas generated. Thus, the participants are able to build off of one another's ideas without the constraint that only one person can speak at a time or without the interruptions of having to listen to someone else while trying to think independently.

- *Make the workplace a playground.* Creativity can be fostered by making simple changes to the work environment. While the possibilities are endless, the common denominator is to make the environment fun. Some ideas include placing toys that foster creativity at each seat (e.g., Play-Doh, Legos, building blocks), painting a conference room in nontraditional colors, and changing the name of the room from "the conference room" to "the innovation zone."

Cause and Effect Diagrams

Cause and effect diagrams are another widely used Six Sigma tool. In fact, developing a cause and effect diagram often goes hand-in-hand with brainstorming. For example, a cause and effect diagram provides an effective way to organize the ideas that are generated in a brainstorming session addressing the causes of a particular problem. Alternatively, a brainstorming session may be held to develop the cause and effect diagram.

As an example, Figure 4.12 provides a simplified version of the cause and effect diagram developed at the West Babylon School District in Long Island, NY. In particular, there was a common perception by the teachers that insufficient time was being spent covering the curriculum. To better help understand the problem and analyze it, a cause and effect diagram was developed.

Creating cause and effect diagrams is a fairly straightforward process. First, a box summarizing the problem is drawn at the far right of the workspace and a horizontal line with an arrow terminating at the box is added. Next, the major causes of the problem are identified and connected to the original horizontal line. Referring to Figure 4.12, four major causes were identified regarding the problem associated with a lack of teaching time in the fifth grade: (1) scheduling, (2) staffing, (3) no priority given for classroom instruction time, and (4) state mandates. The process of creating a cause and effect diagram continues by attempting to break down each major cause into more detailed causes and then possibly breaking down these detailed

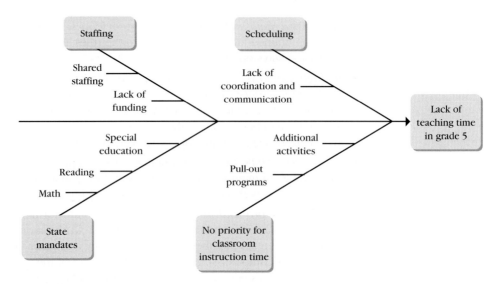

Figure 4.12   Fishbone diagram to analyze the problem of insufficent time being spent covering the curriculum. *Source:* Adapted from R. Manley and J. Manley. "Sharing the Wealth: TQM Spreads from Business to Education." *Quality Progress* (June 1996), pp. 51–55.

causes even further. For example, according to Figure 4.12, we observe that issues related to shared staffing and lack of funding contribute to the staffing problem.

Not only can cause and effect diagrams be developed quickly, they provide an intuitive approach for better understanding problems. Furthermore, important insights are often obtained through the process of creating the diagram, as well as from the diagram itself. However, it should also be noted that, while the cause and effect diagram is well structured, the process of creating one is usually not. It is typical to bounce around from the detailed analysis of a particular cause to adding one or more additional major causes. Furthermore, as additional ideas are generated, it may be decided to eliminate, move, combine, and/or rename the major causes or the more detailed causes. Finally, note that because of its appearance, cause and effect diagrams are often referred to as "fishbone" diagrams.

Process Capability Analysis

With the advent of total quality management programs and their emphasis on "making it right the first time," organizations are becoming increasingly concerned with the ability of their production processes and service delivery processes to meet customer requirements. Process Capability Analysis allows an organization to measure the extent to which its processes can meet its customer requirements or the design specifications for the product or service. As shown in Figure 4.13, process capability depends on:

1. Location of the process mean.
2. Natural variability inherent in the process.
3. Stability of the process.
4. Product's design requirements.

In Figure 4.13*a* the natural variation inherent in the process and the product's design specifications are well matched, resulting in a production system that is consistently capable of meeting the design requirements. However, in Figure 4.13*b* the natural variation in the production process is greater than the product's design requirements. This will lead to the production of a large amount of product that does not meet the requirements: The production process simply does not have the necessary ability. Options in this situation include improving the production process, relaxing the design requirements, or producing a large quantity of product that is unfit for use.

In Figure 4.13*c* the situation is reversed: The product has wider design specifications than the natural variation inherent in the production system. In this case the production process is easily able to meet the design specifications, and the organization may choose to investigate more economical production process in order to lower costs. Finally, although the widths of design specifications and process variation are equal in Figure 4.13*d*, their means are out of sync. Thus, this process will produce a fair amount of output above the upper specification limit (USL). In this situation the solution would be to shift the process mean to the left so that it is better aligned with the design specifications.

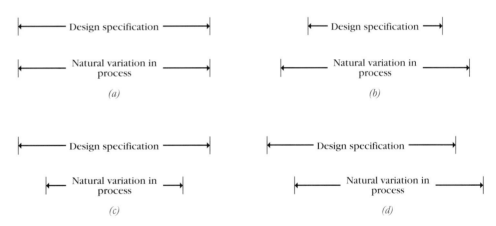

Figure 4.13   Natural variation in a production system versus product design specifications.

More formally, the relationship between the natural variation in the production system and the product's design specifications can be quantified using a ***process capability index***. The process capability index (C_p) is typically defined as the ratio of the width of the product's design specification to six standard deviations of the production system. Six standard deviations for the production process is used because three standard deviations above and below the production process' mean will include 99.7 percent of the possible production outcomes, assuming that the output of the production system can be approximated with a normal distribution. Mathematically, the process capability index is calculated as

$$C_P = \frac{\text{product's design specification range}}{6 \text{ standard deviations of the production system}} = \frac{\text{USL} - \text{LSL}}{6\sigma}$$

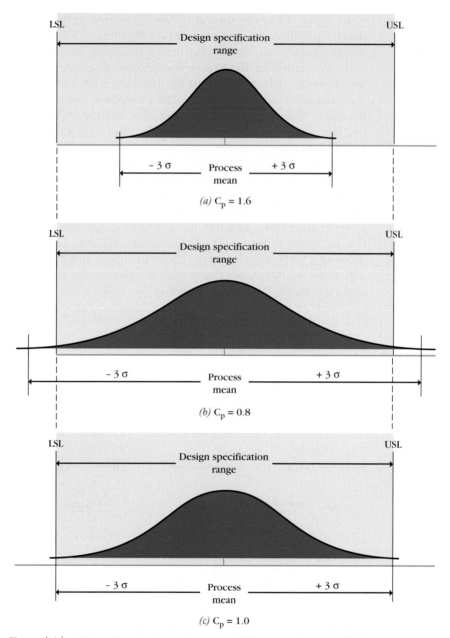

Figure 4.14 Effect of production system variability on process capability index.
(*a*) $C_p = 1.6$; (*b*) $C_p = 0.8$; (*c*) $C_p = 1.0$.

where LSL and USL are a product's lower and upper design specification limits, respectively, and σ is the standard deviation of the production system.

According to this index, a C_p of less than 1 indicates that a particular process is not capable of consistently meeting design specifications; a C_p greater than 1 indicates that the production process is capable of consistently meeting the requirements. As a rule of thumb, many organizations desire a C_p index of at least 1.5

(Evans and Lindsay 1999). Achieving *Six Sigma quality* with no more than 3.4 defective parts per million provides a C_p index of 2.0 (assuming the process mean can shift by as much as 1.5 standard deviations).

Figure 4.14 illustrates the effect that changes in the natural variation of the production system have on the C_p index for fixed product design specifications. In Figure 4.14*a* the natural variation in the process is much less than the product's design specification range, yielding a C_p index greater than 1. In contrast, in Figure 4.14*b* the natural variation in the process is larger than the product's design specifications, yielding a C_p index less than 1. Finally, in Figure 4.14*c* the natural process variation and the design specifications are equal, yielding a C_p index equal to 1.

One limitation of the process capability index is that it only compares the magnitudes of the product's design specification range and the process's natural variation. It does not consider the degree to which these ranges are actually aligned. For example, the situations shown in Figure 4.13*a* and Figure 4.13*d* both yield a C_p index of 1. However, as was pointed out earlier, a considerable amount of defective product would be produced in the situation shown in Figure 4.13*d*, owing to the lack of alignment between the design specifications and the process mean. The most common way to evaluate the extent to which the process mean is centered within the product's design specification range is to calculate a one-sided process capability index C_{pk}, as follows:

$$C_{pu} = \frac{\text{USL} - \text{process mean}}{3\sigma}$$

$$C_{pl} = \frac{\text{process mean} - \text{LSL}}{3\sigma}$$

$$C_{pk} = \min(C_{pl},\ C_{pu})$$

Typically, the data collected to construct the control charts (see Chapter 3) for the process is used to calculate the process standard deviation used in the Capability Index formulas.

THE IMPROVE PHASE

Having defined the problem, measured the process's current performance, and analyzed the process, we are now in a position to identify and test options for improving the process. In the remainder of this section, our focus will be on the use of Design of Experiments (DOE) as a process improvement tool.

Design of Experiments

Perhaps the most common approach to analyzing problems is to investigate one factor at a time (aka OFAT or 1FAT). Unfortunately, the one factor at a time approach suffers from several important shortcomings. To illustrate these shortcomings, consider the operation of a financial institution's call center for its credit cards.

A representative performance measure would be the time it takes the call center's customer service reps (CSRs) to process an incoming call. Factors or variables that might initially be identified as having an impact on the time to process a call include the nature of the call, the time of day, and the CSR that handles the call.

The first shortcoming with OFAT is that it is not typically possible to test one factor at a time and hold all the other factors constant. For example, assume that processing time data were collected for two CSRs over some period of time and it was determined that CSR A averaged five minutes per call while CSR B averaged seven minutes per call. Based on these data, can we conclude that CSR A is more efficient than CSR B? The answer is no because the impact of other variables has not been accounted for. In this case it could be that CSR B's calls were of a more difficult nature to handle. Or perhaps the data for CSR A were collected around lunch time when there was a high volume of calls and numerous callers on hold while the data from CSR B were collected early in the morning when the call volume was lower and there were virtually no callers on hold. The point is that when one variable is studied at a time and the values of other variables are not controlled or otherwise accounted for, it is difficult, if not impossible, to draw valid conclusions about the impact of a single variable.

One approach to overcoming the shortcomings associated with the OFAT approach is to use design of experiments (DOE) techniques. DOE techniques utilize the principles of statistics to design experiments to investigate multiple process variables simultaneously. With DOE techniques, multiple factors are varied and therefore studied simultaneously, and repeated measurements are typically taken for each combination of factor level settings.

Some major considerations associated with DOE include:

- *Determining which factors to include in the experiment.* Interviewing subject matter experts (SME) is one way to identify relevant factors. Work in the previous phases of the Six Sigma project may also provide important insights into relevant factors. Along these lines, cause and effect diagrams are often particularly helpful for identifying relevant factors.

- *Specifying the levels for each factor.* Once the factors are identified, the levels of each factor must be specified. For example, referring to the Southside Hospital example from the beginning of the chapter, Table 4.5 summarizes an experiment that investigates four factors that are hypothesized to have an impact on the lead time for stress tests. For the first factor, method used to order the stress test, two levels have been specified—using either a fax

$\mathcal{T}$ABLE   4.5 • Representative Factors and Their Levels for a Stress Test Study

Factor	Levels
Method used to order stress test	Fax, Web
Method used to schedule patient appointments	Fixed time appointments; patients given a time window
Method used to educate patients about stress test	Information sheet; phone call from nurse; in-person meeting with nurse
Dictation technology	Tape recorder and transcriber; speech recognition

machine or the Web to order the test. Thus, the study will investigate the impact these two alternative methods for ordering stress tests has on the overall stress test lead time. Notice that the factor related to the method used to educate the patients about the stress test has three levels, while each of the other factors has two levels.

- *Determining how much data to collect.* In the experimental design listed in Table 4.5 there are a total of 24 treatment combinations (2 levels of the method used to order the stress test × 2 levels of the patient scheduling method × 3 levels of the patient education method × 2 levels of the dictation technology). Therefore, 24 patients are needed in order to obtain one observation for each possible treatment combination. Of course, to have confidence in the results of a study, it is necessary to collect more than one observation. In DOE terminology, we refer to multiple observations for a treatment combination as replication. If historical data are available, preliminary calculations may be performed to determine how many replications are needed in order to obtain a specified level of statistical confidence. In other cases, limitations such as the time available to complete the study, personnel, or money may dictate the number of replications possible.

- *Determining the type of experimental design.* Fundamentally, there are two types of experimental designs. A full factorial experiment corresponds to a study where data are collected for all possible treatment combinations. A fractional factorial experiment corresponds to a study where data are collected for only a subset of all possible treatment combinations. Fractional factorial experiments are used when the number of treatment combinations is so large that it is not practical to collect data for each treatment combination. For example, a study with seven factors, each with three levels, would have 2187 treatment combinations (3^7). In many cases, investigating 2187 treatment combinations is not practical. Fortunately, in these cases fractional factorial designs can be developed that reduce the number of treatment combinations while at the same time still providing the most relevant information. In effect, DOE techniques utilize statistical principles to maximize the amount of information that can be obtained from a given number of treatment combinations. Because the calculations are quite complex, the design of fractional factorial experiments is typically done with the aid of specialized computer software or published experimental design catalogues.

Taguchi Methods

Among the more popular approaches used to design experiments are Taguchi methods, named after Genichi Taguchi. According to Taguchi, most of the quality of products and services are determined at the design stage, and therefore the production system can affect quality only slightly. Taguchi focused on this fact to develop an approach to designing quality into outputs. Rather than trying to constantly control equipment and workers to stay within specifications—sizes, finishes, times—he has devised a procedure for statistical testing to determine the best combination of product and process design to make the output relatively independent of normal fluctuations in the production system. To do this, statistical experimentation is conducted to determine what product and process designs produce outputs with the highest uniformity at lowest cost.

The Control Phase

As the Six Sigma project nears completion, the focus in the final phase shifts to the development of procedures to again monitor the process. Here our purpose is to ensure that the process's new higher level of performance is maintained and that previous problems do not resurface. We discussed the use of control charts—the most commonly used control tool—in Chapter 3 and will describe the use of "earned value" to control projects in Chapter 6.

Six Sigma in Practice

To conclude our introduction to Six Sigma, we now turn our attention to issues related to employing Six Sigma to improve business processes and performance. Here our focus will be on the various roles played in Six Sigma initiatives, becoming certified in Six Sigma, and the need for each organization to customize its Six Sigma program to its unique needs.

Six Sigma Roles

One aspect that differentiates Six Sigma from other earlier process improvement programs including total quality management and reengineering is that with Six Sigma, specific roles and titles for these roles have been defined and generally accepted. The central roles to Six Sigma include:

- *Master Black Belts.* Master Black Belts combine an advanced knowledge of the Six Sigma toolkit with a deep understanding of the business. The primary roles of Master Black Belts are to develop and execute Six Sigma training programs and to work with senior management to ensure that Six Sigma initiatives are being best leveraged to help the organization achieve its strategic goals.

- *Black Belts.* With a solid background in the Six Sigma toolkit, the two primary roles of Black Belts are conducting Six Sigma training and leading Six Sigma projects. Both Black Belt and Master Black Belt positions tend to be full-time positions.

- *Green Belts.* Green belts have broad knowledge of the Six Sigma toolkit, but not nearly as much depth in the tools as Black Belts and Master Black Belts. The majority of the work of Six Sigma projects is typically completed by Green Belts under the guidance and direction of Black Belts and, on occasion, Master Black Belts. Usually, Green Belts split their time between their work on Six Sigma projects and other work responsibilities.

- *Yellow Belts.* Although not as common as Master Black Belts, Black Belts, and Green Belts, some organizations have added the Yellow Belt rank as a designation for those employees that have completed Six Sigma awareness training.

In addition to these central roles, there are also a number of important supporting roles including:

- *Champions/Sponsors.* Champions are senior managers that support and promote Six Sigma projects. The employees working on a Six Sigma project rely on the champion's senior position within the organization to help them obtain the needed resources to successfully complete the project as well as to remove hurdles that might otherwise derail the successful completion of the project.

- *Process owners.* Although process owners are the managers with end-to-end responsibility for a particular business process, typically they do not direct Six Sigma projects. Rather, they are best viewed as being the customers of Six Sigma projects.

Becoming Certified

In addition to having well-defined roles, another aspect that differentiates Six Sigma from earlier programs is that accompanying each of the central Six Sigma roles is a certification process. Along these lines, it is a common practice for organizations to make a distinction between employees who are Six Sigma trained at a certain level and those who are certified at the level. In these organizations, becoming certified at a given level entails meeting additional requirements beyond receiving the training, such as passing an examination and/or successfully completing one or more Six Sigma projects.

Generally speaking, there are four alternative ways of obtaining Black Belt certification. Perhaps the most common approach is for employees to be trained and certified internally by their current employer. In fact, based on their success with Six Sigma, some organizations actually open their training programs to people outside their organizations. One notable example is Motorola University (www.motorola.com/motorolauniversity).

A second approach for obtaining certification is through numerous consulting organizations that offer both training and certification programs. These organizations can be easily found by doing a search of the Web using a search string such as "six sigma certification." Third, a number of universities have begun offering training and in some cases certification programs. Several universities even offer this training and certification through online distance education programs. Finally, individuals can obtain certification through professional societies, perhaps most commonly through ASQ (www.asq.org).

Given the wide range of options for becoming certified, it is somewhat surprising to observe the extent to which these varied certification programs are standardized both in terms of duration and content. For example, it appears that the standard for Black Belt training is a four-month program during which students receive one week of formal in-class training each month and use the time between training sessions to work on a Black Belt project.

The Need to Customize Six Sigma Programs

Although there is a fair amount of consensus related to the roles, body of knowledge, and training practices surrounding Six Sigma programs, organizations that have succeeded with their Six Sigma programs also recognize the need to tailor their Six Sigma approach to their unique needs. ScottishPower, an electric and gas provider to more than 5 million customers in the United States and United Kingdom, serves as an excellent example of this. In May 2001, ScottishPower brought in an external consultant to begin training its first wave of 20 full-time Black Belts. Because of the limited data that were available and the relatively generic nature of the external consultant's training program, ScottishPower emphasized the use of the more simple tools in its early Six Sigma projects including process mapping, Pareto analysis, cause and effect diagrams, and stakeholder analysis. Six months after the first wave of Black Belt training, a second group of 20 employees was selected for full-time Black Belt training. Based on their experience from the first round, ScottishPower identified the need to better use statistical analysis to identify the root causes of problems. Thus the second wave of training, which was performed by ScottishPower's own Black Belts that were trained in the first wave, emphasized statistical techniques such as the use of t-tests, ANOVA, correlation, regression, and DOE. Based on a desire to gain additional value from the data that were being collected, Scottish-Power began emphasizing additional techniques in subsequent waves including chi-square tests, nonparametric tests such as Mann-Whitney and Kruskall-Wallis, and Box-Cox transformations. ScottishPower's experience and success with Six Sigma highlights the importance of customizing a Six Sigma program to the organization's unique needs and adopting the training as the organization becomes more sophisticated in both its ability to collect and analyze data.

EXPAND YOUR UNDERSTANDING

1. Contrast Six Sigma and Business Process Design.
2. Is there any relationship between process sigma, DPMO, and process capability?
3. Measurement Systems Analysis focuses primarily on the variation introduced into the measurement system by human operators. Can you think of other sources of variation introduced by the measurement system beyond the human operators?
4. Is the DMAIC approach more applicable to projects focusing on incremental change or radical change? Why?

5. Are there any limitations you see associated with QFD? Benchmarking?
6. What phase of DMAIC do you imagine is the most important phase? What phase do you imagine takes the longest?
7. In the example given in the discussion of DPMO, it was stated that the restaurant's requirements for the hamburger patties that it purchased from its supplier should be between 3.4 and 4.6 ounces. Why would the restaurant be concerned about hamburgers weighing too much?

APPLY YOUR UNDERSTANDING

Three Dot Four Capital Management

John Galt was recently promoted to Senior Vice President of Consumer Lending at Three Dot Four Capital Management. Three Dot Four is a large financial services organization ranked among the top 20 financial institutions in terms of total assets. A key consideration in John's promotion was his past success leading the bank's quality and productivity group. In particular, there appears to be a significant amount of dissatisfaction among both the bank's customers and the bank's loan officers with its online mortgage application process.

The online mortgage application process is initiated when a customer clicks on the **Apply for a Home Mortgage Now** link located on Three Dot Four's homepage. This link takes the user to an **Instruction** page that overviews the application process and provides a checklist of the information the applicant will be asked to supply on subsequent web pages. Clicking on the **Continue** button at the bottom of the **Instruction** page takes the user to the first of four web pages, each containing a web-based form to collect the required data.

The first web page, **Personal Information**, solicits information regarding the applicant and requires entering information in 33 fields. Information collected on this page includes the applicant's and co-applicant's names, full addresses, previous addresses, dates of birth, social security numbers, phone numbers, email addresses, and so on. To continue on to the next page, the user selects the **Continue** button located at the bottom of the **Personal Information** page. When the **Continue** button is selected on a given page, a check is made to ensure that none of the required fields has been left blank. If the validation check is passed, the next web page in the application process is displayed. In cases were the validation check fails, the blank fields are highlighted and the user is asked to enter the information in these fields.

Once information has been entered for all required fields on the **Personal Information** page, the second page – **Property, Loan, and Expenses** – is displayed. This page is used to collect information about the property the loan will be used to purchase, the type of loan the applicant desires, and information about the applicant's monthly expenses. In total, the **Property, Loan, and Expenses** page contains 10 data fields.

Once the information has been entered for all required fields on the **Property, Loan, and Expenses** page, the **Employment** page is displayed. This page captures information about the applicant and co-applicant's employment history including salary and other income information. The **Employment** page contains 16 user fields. Finally, the last web page in the application process captures information about the applicant's **Assets and Liabilities**. In particular, the user is asked to supply information about checking accounts, savings accounts, credit card accounts, investment accounts, car loans, and so on. In total, this page contains 22 data fields.

When the applicant clicks on the **Submit Application** button at the bottom of the **Assets and Liabilities** page, a final validation check is performed and the information is transferred to one of the bank's loan officers. The loan officers subsequently print out the information and then add the application to their backlog of other in-process applications. To even out the work across the loan officers, all loan officers process loan applications submitted via the web, as well as applications received via the mail and applications completed at one of the bank's branch offices.

Initially, John identified two areas in need of improvement: the fairness of loan approval decisions and the information accuracy of loan applications submitted online. In terms of the fairness of loan approval decisions, over the last couple of years the company has received numerous complaints from applicants questioning the organization's fairness in making loan approval decisions. To begin understanding this problem, John initiated a study where 25 loan applications were randomly selected. These loan applications were then evaluated by a panel of three experts to determine whether the loan should be approved or rejected. Next, three loan officers were selected and asked to evaluate each of the 25 loans two times. The data collected from this study is summarized in Table 1.

To investigate the issue related to the accuracy of online mortgage application submissions, John formed a process improvement team. The team began by collecting data on the total number of hits each page in the web submission application process received as well as the number of times the page was actually completed during the month of January. In addition, the team performed a detailed audit of all the information that was submitted during January and tallied the number of fields that contained errors across all submitted information. A summary of the team's preliminary results is given in Table 2.

$\mathcal{T}$ABLE 1 • Summary of loan approval fairness study

Loan	Expert Panel	Loan Officer 1 01/01/2005	Loan Officer 1 02/01/2005	Loan Officer 2 01/01/2005	Loan Officer 2 02/01/2005	Loan Officer 3 01/01/2005	Loan Officer 3 02/01/2005
1	A	A	A	A	A	A	A
2	R	R	R	R	R	R	A
3	A	A	A	A	A	A	A
4	A	R	R	R	R	R	R
5	R	R	R	R	R	R	R
6	R	R	R	A	A	R	R
7	A	A	A	A	R	A	A
8	R	R	R	R	R	R	R
9	A	A	R	R	R	A	R
10	R	R	R	R	R	R	R
11	R	R	R	R	R	R	R
12	A	A	A	A	A	A	A
13	A	A	A	A	R	A	A
14	R	R	R	R	R	R	R
15	R	R	R	A	R	R	R
16	A	A	A	A	A	A	A
17	A	A	A	R	A	A	A
18	A	A	A	A	A	A	A
19	R	R	R	R	R	R	R
20	R	R	R	R	A	R	R
21	R	R	A	R	A	R	A
22	A	A	A	A	A	A	A
23	A	R	R	R	R	R	R
24	A	A	R	A	R	R	R
25	A	A	A	A	A	R	A

A = Loan approved

R = Loan not approved

$\mathcal{T}$ABLE 2 • Online mortgage application submissions, January 2005

Web Page	Number of Hits	Number Submitted	Number of Errors
Personal Information	108,571	68,400	45,144
Property, Loan, and Expense Information	68,400	62,928	22,025
Employment Information	62,928	59,781	28,695
Asset and Liability Information	59,781	52,009	51,489

Questions

1. What is the DPMO for the loan applications submitted via the web?
2. What could be done to improve the DPMO?
3. Approximately, what is the process sigma of the loan application process?
4. Develop intuitive measures of repeatability and reproducibility for the loan approval process. What do the results of this analysis tell you about the fairness of the loan approval process?
5. Regarding the fairness of the loan approval process, what recommendations would you make?

Valley County Medical Clinic

Valley County operates a walk-in medical clinic (VCMC) to meet the nonacute medical needs of its approximately 15,000 citizens. Patients arriving at the clinic are served on a first-come, first-served basis.

As part of a new total quality management program, VCMC conducted an in-depth, four-month study of its current operations. A key component of the study was a survey, distributed to all county citizens. The purpose of the survey was to identify and prioritize areas most in need of improvement. An impressive 44 percent of the surveys were returned and deemed usable. Follow-up analysis indicated that the people who responded were representative of the population served by the clinic. After the results were tabulated, it was determined that the walk-in medical clinic was located near the bottom of the rankings, indicating a great deal of dissatisfaction with the clinic. Preliminary analysis of the respondents' comments indicated that people were reasonably satisfied with the treatment they received at the clinic but were very dissatisfied with the amount of time they had to wait to see a caregiver.

Upon arriving at the clinic, patients receive a form from the receptionist requesting basic biographical information and the nature of the medical condition for which treatment is being sought. Completing the form typically requires two to three minutes. After the form is returned to the receptionist, it is time-stamped and placed in a tray. Clerks collect the forms and retrieve the corresponding patients' files from the basement. The forms typically remain in the tray for about five minutes before being picked up, and it takes the clerk approximately 12 minutes to retrieve the files. After a patient's file is retrieved, the form describing the medical problem is attached to it with a paper clip, and it is placed in a stack with other files. The stack of files is ordered according to the time stamps on the forms.

When the nurse practitioners finish with their current patient, they select the next file from the stack and escort that patient to one of the treatment rooms. On average, files remain in the stack for ten minutes, but this varies considerably depending on the time of day and the day of the week. On Monday mornings, for example, it is common for files to remain in the stack for 30 minutes or more.

Once in the treatment room, the nurse practitioner reads over the form describing the patient's ailment. Next, the nurse discusses the problem with the patient while taking some standard measurements such as blood pressure and temperature. The nurse practitioner then makes a rough diagnosis, based on the measurements and symptoms, to determine if the ailment is one of the 20 that state law permits nurse practitioners to treat. If the condition is treatable by the nurse practitioner, a more thorough diagnosis is undertaken and treatment is prescribed. It typically takes about five minutes for the nurse practitioners to make the rough diagnosis and another 20 minutes to complete the detailed diagnosis and discuss the treatment with the patient. If the condition (as roughly diagnosed) is not treatable by the nurse practitioner, the patient's file is placed in the stack for the on-duty MD. Because of the higher cost of MDs versus nurse practitioners, there is typically only one MD on duty at any time. Thus, patients wait an average of 25 minutes for the MD. On the other hand, because of their higher training and skill, the MDs are able to diagnose and treat the patients in 15 minutes, despite the fact that they deal with the more difficult and less routine cases. Incidentally, an expert system for nurse practitioners is being tested at another clinic that—if shown to be effective—would initially double the number of ailments treatable by nurse practitioners and over time would probably increase the list even more, as the tool continued to be improved.

Questions

1. Develop a process map for the medical clinic that shows the times of the various activities. Is the patients' dissatisfaction with the clinic justified?
2. What do you imagine are the patients' key requirements for the clinic?

3. What assumptions are being made about the way work is performed and treatment administered at the clinic?

4. Redesign the process of treating patients at the clinic using technologies you are familiar with, to better meet the patients' needs as listed in question 2.

EXERCISES

1. A call center has determined there are five types of defects that can occur in processing customer calls: the customer spends too long on hold, the customer is given the wrong information, the customer rep handles the call in an unprofessional way, the customer is transferred to the wrong destination, and the customer is disconnected. A total of 468 calls were subject to a quality audit last month and the results obtained from the audit are summarized in the list below. What is the DPMO for the call center?

Number of Defects/Call	Frequency
1	73
2	13
3	3
4	1
5	0

2. Over the last quarter, 742 shots were administered at a walk-in clinic. To be treated properly, patients must be given the correct dosage of the correct medication. During the quarter in question, it was determined that one patient received the incorrect dosage of the correct medication, another patient received the wrong medication, and a third patient received both the wrong medication and the wrong dosage given her age and weight. What is the DPMO and process sigma level for the clinic?

3. A silk screening company prints 6000 decals per month. A random sample of 150 decals is taken every week and inspected based on four characteristics. The data for the last four weeks is summarized in the table below. Assuming the data in the table are representative of the process, what is the DPMO and process sigma level for the silk screening process?

Decal Characteristic	Number of Defects Observed
Color accuracy	10
Image alignment	7
Color consistency	8
Image sharpness	3

4. A hospital made 225 medication errors last year. Of these errors, 30 percent were the result of an error with the prescription while 70 percent were from errors made while dispensing the medication. The hospital admitted 8465 patients last year, and the patients received an average of 4.8 prescriptions per hospital stay. Medications are dispensed at the time they are needed and each medication is dispensed four times per day on average. The average patient stay at the hospital is 3.5 days. Compute the DPMO and process sigma level for the patient medicine process. What assumptions, if any, were needed to calculate the DPMO?

5. In the chapter it was noted that when the process mean can shift by as much as 1.5 standard deviations, a C_p of 2.0 is needed in order to achieve 3.4 defective parts per million. What C_p is needed in order to achieve the same 3.4 defective parts per million assuming the process is perfectly stable and its mean does not shift?

6. Customers of Dough Boy Ltd. have specified that pizza crusts they order should be 28–32 centimeters in diameter. Sample data recently collected indicate that Dough Boy's crusts average 30 centimeters in diameter, with a standard deviation of 1.1 centimeters. Is Dough Boy's pizza crust production system capable of meeting its customers' requirements? If not, what options does Dough Boy have to rectify this situation?

7. Design specifications for a bottled product are that it should contain 350–363 milliliters. Sample data indicate that the bottles contain an average of 355 milliliters, with a standard deviation of 2 milliliters. Is the filling operation capable of meeting the design specifications? Why or why not?

BIBLIOGRAPHY

Alwan, L. *Statistical Process Analysis*. New York: Irwin/McGraw-Hill, 2000.

Arndt, M. "Quality Isn't Just for Widgets; Six Sigma, the Quality-Control and Cost-Cutting Power Tool, Is Proving Its Worth on the Service Side," *Business Week*, (July 22, 2002): 72.

Breyfogel III, F. W., *Implementing Six Sigma*, 2nd ed. New York: Wiley, 2003.

Business Week. "He's Gutsy, Brilliant, and Carries an Ax." (May 9, 1994): 62–66.

Das, R., S. Colello, and H. Davidson, "Six Sigma in Corporate Law." *Six Sigma Forum* (November 2004): 30–36.

Diehl, M., and W. Stroebe, "Productivity Loss in Brainstorming Groups: Towards a Solution of a Riddle," *Journal of Personality and Social Psychology*, 53 (1987): 497–509.

Godin, E., D. Raven, C. Sweetapple, and F. R. Del Giudice, "Faster Test Results," *Quality Progress* (January 2004): 33–39.

Hammer, M. *Beyond Reengineering*. New York: Harper Business, 1996.

Harrington, H. J., and J. S. Harrington. *High Performance Benchmarking*. New York: McGraw-Hill, 1996.

Jones Jr., M. H., "Six Sigma . . . at a Bank?" *Six Sigma Forum Magazine* (February 2004): 13–17.

Pande, P. S., R. P. Neuman, and R. R. Cavanagh. *The Six Sigma Way*. New York: McGraw-Hill, 2000.

Peace, G. S. *Taguchi Methods: A Hands-On Approach*. Reading, MA: Addison-Wesley, 1993.

Pellicone, A, and M. Martocci. "Faster Turnaround Time," *Quality Progress* (March 2006): 31—36.

Pyzdek, T. *The Six Sigma Handbook,* rev. ed. New York: McGraw Hill, 2003.

Rath & Strong. *Rath & Strong's Six Sigma Pocket Guide*. Rath & Strong, Inc., 2000.

Rohleder, T. R., and E. A. Silver. "A Tutorial on Business Process Improvement." *Journal of Operations Management*, 15 (May 1997): 139–154.

Sester, D. "Motorola: A Tradition of Quality." *Quality* (October 2001): 30–34.

Shafer, S. M. "Karate in Business School? This is Not Your Father's Black Belt," *Quality Management Journal*, 12 (No. 2, 2005): 47–56.

Thompson, L., "Improving the Creativity of Organizational Work Groups," *Academy of Management Executive*, 17 (2003): 96–111.

Wortman, B., W. R. Richardson, G. Gee, M. Williams, T. Pearson, F. Bensley, J. P. Patel, J. DeSimone, and D. R. Carlson, *CSSBB Primer*. West Terre Haute, IN: Quality Council of Indiana, 2001.

CHAPTER 5

Lean Operations Improve Transformation System Value

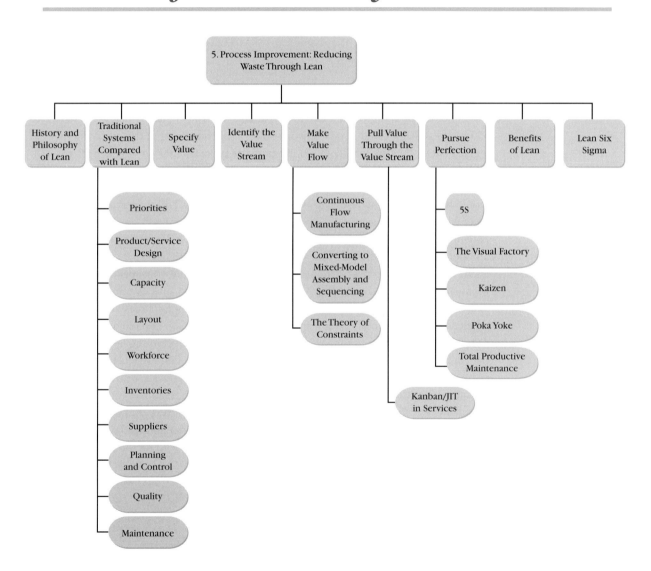

In this chapter, we continue our discussion of process improvement and focus on the management approach for minimizing waste and maximizing value. Lean management has taken on the aura of a global competitive philosophy because so many firms that embrace it have been so successful: Toyota, Deere, and numerous others. We first address the history and philosophy of lean and then make a comparison between traditional production systems and lean enterprises. Following this, we continue with a discussion of five lean principles: (1) specify value from the customer's point of view, (2) identify the value stream, (3) make value flow, (4) have the customer pull value, and (5) pursue perfection. The chapter concludes with a discussion of the benefits associated with lean.

INTRODUCTION

- It was not uncommon for chemotherapy patients at Virginia Mason Medical Center, a 350-bed hospital located in downtown Seattle, to spend an entire day receiving their weekly chemotherapy treatment. To illustrate the process, after arriving at 8:00 A.M. and checking in on the first floor, the patient would be asked to go to the laboratory for blood testing located on the sixth floor. After having the blood drawn, the patient would then wait for the results to be sent to the oncologist and then eventually meet with the oncologist on the second floor. If things progressed smoothly, the patient would begin receiving the intravenous chemotherapy treatment by noon in an open and noisy room that was shared with six other patients.

  To improve this process, Virginia Mason has turned to the concepts of lean pioneered by Toyota shortly after World War II. Virginia Mason's overarching goal was to improve the patient experience while at the same time increasing the overall efficiency of the process. Using lean concepts, Virginia Mason completely redesigned the process for chemotherapy patients so that everything flows to the patient as opposed to the patient flowing through the process. For example, instead of being located on separate floors, the labs and doctors' offices are now adjacent to private patient treatment rooms. Furthermore, each private treatment room has a flat-screen TV, a computer, nursing supplies, and toilet facilities. A dedicated pharmacy was also added to the cancer treatment center, thereby eliminating delays for patients of up to two hours. Other improvements have reduced the preparation time for chemotherapy treatments from three hours to less than one hour. Across the entire medical center, hospital administrators estimate that its lean initiatives have resulted in savings of $6 million in capital spending, freed up 13,000 square feet, reduced inventory costs by $360,000, and reduced the distance hospital staff walk each day by 34 miles. In addition to these tangible results, the hospital achieved a number of other benefits including improved patient satisfaction, shorter bill collection times, and lower infection rates. To achieve these benefits, the hospital spent approximately $1.5 million, primarily for consultants, travel, and training (Connolly 2005).

- Although Xerox often gets more publicity for its financial difficulties, it does have a long track record in the area of quality management. Xerox's journey began in the early 1980s when it established its Leadership Through Quality Initiative which focused on improving business processes in order to improve customer satisfaction, quality, and productivity. Fast forward to the late 1990s and we see Six Sigma and Lean being adopted by Xerox's manufacturing and supply chain functions. While limited in scope, the Lean and Six Sigma programs help Xerox improve its operating efficiency and effectiveness. Perhaps in part due to the success of these limited initiatives, in mid-2002 Xerox's leadership decided to integrate its Lean and Six Sigma programs across the entire enterprise, naming the initiative Xerox Lean Six Sigma. To support this initiative, Xerox kicked off an intense Black Belt training program in January 2003 which included employees from all functional areas. By August 2004, 400 Black Belts had been trained, 2500 employees had completed or were in the process of completing Green Belt training, 2000 leaders had completed a two-day workshop, and 10,000 employees had completed Yellow Belt awareness training. Furthermore, a total of 700 Lean Six Sigma projects have been completed across all areas of Xerox including product design, supply chain, marketing and sales, customer service, and strategy deployment. Xerox estimates that it achieved an initial $6 million return in 2003 based on a $14 million investment in Lean Six Sigma and expects even bigger gains in the years ahead (Fornari and Maszle 2004).

- Honeywell International, a diversified technology company with 2004 sales in excess of $25 billion, is another company that has successfully integrated its Six Sigma initiatives with its lean initiatives. In particular, Honeywell has combined Six Sigma's traditional emphasis on variation reduction with lean's emphasis on waste reduction to create its Six Sigma Plus program.

  Honeywell competes in four major industry segments: (1) Aerospace, (2) Automation and Control Solutions, (3) Specialty Materials, and (4) Transportation Systems. The business unit for each of these industry segments is headed by a group president. Reporting to each group president is a Six Sigma Plus Leader (SSPL) that is responsible for developing the strategic plans and deploying these plans for Six Sigma Plus initiatives within the group. Reporting to the SSPL is a team composed of Master Black Belts (MBBs), Lean Masters (LMs), Black Belts (BBs), and Lean Experts (LEs). MBBs and LMs, also referred to as Honeywell Masters (HMs), work on projects that have more than a $1 million financial impact and are also responsible for training, mentoring, and certifying BBs and LEs. BBs and LEs work on projects that have a financial impact in the range of $200,000 to $250,000 and train, mentor, and certify Green Belts. In 2002, two HM training waves, five LE waves, 15 BB waves, and 15 BBL training waves, each with 20 to 30 employees, were conducted in North America and additional waves were conducted in Europe and Asia. The HM waves consist of five weeks of training while the BB and LE waves consist of four weeks of training. The BBL training supplements the core BB training with additional lean topics.

In addition to the SSPLs in each business unit, Honeywell has a Vice President of Six Sigma that reports directly to the CEO. This VP chairs the Six Sigma Plus Executive Council which in turn oversees all training and ensures a common curriculum is used company wide. In 2002, Honeywell reported productivity improvement gains of $1.2 billion. Looking to the future, Honeywell's 2004 Annual Report announced the introduction of the Honeywell Operating System (HOS). The HOS is based on the Toyota Production System and will be used to provide a roadmap to further integrate Six Sigma and lean tools (Hill and Kearney 2003).

- The hospital patient discharge process is often associated with substantial patient dissatisfaction. However, in addition to frustrating patients, delays in the discharge process can create problems in other areas of the hospital such as admitting and the emergency department, as these areas must wait for the rooms vacated by discharged patients. To address the inefficiencies often associated with the patient discharge process, Valley Baptist Hospital in Harlingen, Texas utilized Lean, Six Sigma, and change management techniques. One specific goal of this project was to substantially reduce the time from when a patient discharge order was entered into the computer until the time the patient was transported from the room.

  The process improvement team began by mapping the current patient discharge process. In mapping the process, the team discovered that the there was little consistency across the nurses in terms of their approaches to discharging patients. Further analysis of the process map was undertaken to identify the activities in the discharge process that were not adding value or, in this case, helping discharge patients faster. In the end, all activities were classified as either value-added, nonvalue-added, or value enabler. The team further enhanced the process map to show rework loops, communication flows among the staff, and physical movements. Key performance metrics were also added to the process map which highlighted a substantial amount of nonvalue-added time.

  As the team further embellished and analyzed the process map, it was able to identify several primary drivers of waste in the patient discharge process. For example, the team discovered that in 21 percent of the cases, nurses required clarification from a doctor before the discharge order could be entered into the computer. The need to clarify an order added an average of 33 minutes to the discharge process. As another example, the team discovered that in some cases the primary nurse took the patient's vital signs while in other cases a second nurse took the vital signs, which were then reported to the primary nurse. Having the primary nurse take the vital signs himself or herself reduced the elapsed time by an average of 64 minutes.

  Based on these insights and others, the process improvement team developed a new standard operating procedure consisting of six steps for the patient discharge process. After adopting the new process, the mean time to discharge a patient was reduced by 74 percent, from 185 minutes to 48 minutes. Furthermore, the standard deviation of discharge times also decreased by 71 percent, from 128.7 minutes to 37.2 minutes. Finally, the percentage of discharged patients that vacated their rooms in 45 minutes or less increased from 6.9 percent to 61.7 percent (DeBusk and Rangel 2005).

As these examples illustrate, *lean* is a philosophy that seeks to eliminate all types of waste whether it be excessive delays in treating patients, excessive lead times, carrying excessive levels of inventory, workers or parts traveling excessive distances, spending too much time setting up equipment, unneeded space, reworking defective products, clarifying patient orders, idle facilities, and scrap. The examples also illustrate several other important themes associated with lean. First, since waste can be thought of as those activities and outcomes that do not add value for the customer, a strong customer orientation is central to lean. This was illustrated in the Virginia Mason example where the chemotherapy process was redesigned so that the treatment process flowed to the patient as opposed to the patient flowing through the process. In fact, Virginia Mason made additional changes not mentioned in the example to improve the customer experience, including allocating the best rooms with windows to patients, adding a waterfall and meditation room to help ease patient stress, and adding an Internet café. A second theme relates to the large payoff that can be achieved through lean initiatives. This is exemplified by Honeywell's $1.2 billion in productivity gains, Virginia Mason's cost, space, and travel savings, and Valley Baptist's 74 percent reduction in patient discharge time. Finally, a third theme that emerges from the examples is the trend for organizations to merge their Six Sigma (discussed in Chapter 4) programs with their Lean programs. This trend reflects the complementary nature of these two programs: Six Sigma's focus on variation reduction and lean's focus on eliminating waste. Clearly, a process with little variation but lots of waste would not be desirable and vice versa.

In essence, the goal of lean is to accomplish more with fewer resources; less workers, inventory, space, equipment, time, scrap, and so on. To accomplish this goal, Womack and Jones, in their book *Lean Thinking*, identify five lean principles:

1. Specify value from the customer's point of view.
2. Identify the value stream, the complete set of activities required to create the output valued by the customer.
3. Make value flow through the value stream by eliminating nonvalue added activities and streamlining the remaining value-added steps.
4. Have the customer pull value through the value stream.
5. Pursue perfection.

Lean cannot be reduced to a "formula," and therefore every firm must apply the philosophy differently. In the remainder of this chapter, we discuss these five lean principles in more detail. However, before discussing these principles in detail, we begin our discussion with an overview of the lean philosophy to put it in proper context.

HISTORY AND PHILOSOPHY OF LEAN

Lean production (also known as *synchronous manufacturing* or simply *lean*) is the name given to the Toyota Production System. Toyota began developing its approach to manufacturing shortly after World War II. The Toyota system is known for its minimal use of resources and elimination of all forms of waste, including time.

Thus, for example, just-in-time (JIT) is a substantial portion of the Toyota system. Similarly, lean production is an integral element of supply chain management as it is currently envisioned. As such, it requires identifying and eliminating all forms of nonvalue-added activities throughout the entire supply chain. Teams of multiskilled workers are employed at all levels of the organization to root out inefficiency and waste. To understand why lean was developed, it is important to understand a little about the history and culture of Japan.

Japan is a small country with minimal resources and a large population. Thus, the Japanese have always been careful not to waste resources, including space (especially land), as well as time and labor. Waste is abhorrent because the country has so little space and so few natural resources to begin with. Therefore, the Japanese have been motivated to maximize the gain or yield from the few resources available. It has also been necessary for them to maintain their respect for each other in order to work and live together smoothly and effectively in such a densely populated space. As a result, their work systems tend to be based on three primary tenets:

1. Minimizing waste in all forms
2. Continually improving processes and systems
3. Maintaining respect for all workers

During production, the Japanese studiously avoid waste of materials, space, and labor. They therefore pay significant attention to identifying and correcting problems that could potentially lead to such waste. Moreover, operations and procedures are constantly being improved and fine-tuned to increase productivity and yield, further eliminating waste. Equal respect is paid to all workers, and the trappings of status are minimized so that respect among all can be maintained.

Although low cost and consistent quality are important goals when a firm adopts lean, many other benefits also have accrued in those firms where it has been implemented. Examples include reduced inventories of all types (and thus less need for the space they require), greater productivity among both labor and staff, shorter lead times, improved processes, increased equipment productivity and utilization, better quality, fewer errors, and higher morale among the workforce and managers. Because of its broad nature and wide range of benefits, lean has become for many companies a major element in their competitive strategy as the Xerox example at the beginning of the chapter illustrated.

The second tenet of Japanese work systems is continuous improvement which corresponds to the lean principle of pursuing perfection. Accordingly, lean is not considered simply a one-time event to streamline the transformation system from a sloppy, wasteful form to an efficient, competitive form. Rather it is an ongoing journey that seeks to make continuing improvements throughout the system to keep the firm competitive and profitable in the future.

Perhaps the most important of the three tenets is the third, maintaining respect for all workers. Unfortunately, U.S. industry seems to be moving more slowly in this direction, and U.S. firms seem far behind the Japanese in obtaining respect and loyalty from their workers. This is probably because these firms and industries do not show respect for and loyalty to their employees in the first place.

Initially, in the early 1980s, the Japanese approach to production was greeted with a great deal of ambivalence in the United States. Typical of the sentiment at this time was, "It will never work here." However, this view abruptly changed when a number of domestic companies such as Hewlett-Packard and Harley-Davidson began demonstrating the significant benefits of JIT, an important component of lean.

Next, we describe the most common characteristics of lean systems and compare them with the more traditional systems.

TRADITIONAL SYSTEMS COMPARED WITH LEAN

Table 5.1 presents a dozen characteristics of lean systems that tend to distinguish them from the more traditional systems historically used in U.S. industry. These characteristics

TABLE 5.1 • Comparison of Traditional Systems and Lean

Characteristic	Traditional	Lean
Priorities	Accept all orders	Limited market
	Many options	Few options
		Low cost, high quality
Product/Service design	Customized outputs	Standardized outputs
	Design from scratch	Incremental design
		Simplify, design for manufacturing
Capacity	Highly utilized	Moderately utilized
	Inflexible	Flexible
Transformation system	Job shop	Flow shops, cellular manufacturing
Layout	Large space	Small space
	Materials handling equipment	Close, manual transfer
Work force	Narrow skills	Broad skills
	Specialized	Flexible
	Individualized	Work teams
	Competitive attitude	Cooperative attitude
	Change by edict	Change by consensus
	Easy pace	Hard pace
	Status: symbols, pay, privilege	No status differentials
Scheduling	Long setups	Quick changeovers
	Long runs	Mixed-model runs
Inventories	Large WIP buffers	Small WIP buffers
	Stores, cribs, stockrooms	Floor stock
Suppliers	Many	Few or single-sourced
	Competitive	Cooperative, network
	Deliveries to central receiving area	Deliveries directly to assembly line
	Independent forecasts	Shared forecasts
Planning and control	Planning-oriented	Control-oriented
	Complex	Simple
	Computerized	Visual
Quality	Via inspection	At the source
	Critical points	Continuous
	Acceptance sampling	Statistical process control
Maintenance	Corrective	Preventive
	By experts	By operator
	Run equipment fast	Run equipment slowly
	Run one shift	Run 24 hours

range from philosophy and culture to standard operating procedures. Several of the contrasts summarized in Table 5.1 are elaborated on in the remainder of this section.

Priorities

Traditionally, most firms want to accept all customer orders, or at least provide a large number of options from which customers may order. However, this confuses the production task, increases the chance of errors, and increases costs. With lean, the target market is usually limited and the options are also limited. A wise lean firm knows which customers it does *not* want.

Thus, we see that right from the start the overall priorities of lean firms are different from those of the traditional firm. This perspective is reflected in the approach lean firms take to each of the other characteristics as well. In one sense, their "strategy" for competing is different from that of the traditional firm, and this strategy permeates their production system.

Product/Service Design

In line with the priorities, engineering in the lean firm designs standard outputs and incrementally improves each design. The parts and subassemblies that make up each output are also standardized; over time they are further simplified and improved. More traditionally, engineers attempt to design custom outputs to satisfy unique customers, starting from scratch each time and designing new parts and subassemblies. The reason for the new parts and subassemblies is often that the engineers change and do not know what their predecessors have already designed. Yet even if the same engineers are doing the design work, they often design new parts when a previously designed, tested, and proven part would do—because they cannot afford the time to find the previous design.

Furthermore, designers in lean organizations usually include considerations about the manufacturability of the part or product. This is called ***design for manufacturability*** (DFM) or ***design for assembly*** (DFA). Too often, the traditional firm whips up an engineering design as quickly as it can (since it has had to start from scratch) and then passes the design on to manufacturing without giving a thought to how it can be made (sometimes it cannot). With this approach, poor quality and high costs often result and cannot be improved on the shop floor, since they were designed in from the start. If the product or part absolutely cannot be made, or perhaps cannot be assembled, then the design is sent back to engineering to modify, taking more time and costing more in engineering hours.

Capacity

In terms of capacity, traditional firms tend to design extra capacities of all kinds into the system ***just-in-case*** a problem arises and they are needed. These capacities may consist of extra equipment, overtime, partial shifts, and frequently, large work-in-process (WIP) inventories. All of them cost extra money to acquire and maintain, which eventually increases the cost of the product.

In lean organizations, excess capacities are kept to a minimum to avoid inherent waste, particularly the WIP inventories, as will be discussed in more detail later. In place of the excess capacities, tighter control is exerted over the production system so that conditions do not arise where significant additional capacity is needed in the first place.

Layout

The traditional method of layout follows the job-shop approach of using widely spread-out equipment with space for stockrooms, tool cribs, and work-in-process inventories between the equipment. To handle and move all this inventory, automated or semiautomated equipment such as conveyors, carousels, and forklifts is also required, which takes even more space.

With lean, equipment is moved as close together as possible so that parts can be actually handed from one worker or machine to the next. The use of cells and flow lines permits the production of parts in small lots with minimal work-in-process and material moving equipment. The cells are often U-shaped so that one worker can easily access all the machines without moving very far, and finished products will exit at the same point where raw materials enter the cell.

It is not unusual for the work flows in a traditional job shop to look like a plate of spaghetti when traced on a diagram of the shop. In fact, creating such a diagram where the physical flows of the parts are mapped onto the shop floor is referred to as a ***spaghetti chart*** and is a commonly used lean tool. In particular, spaghetti charts can be used to identify excessive travel distances, backtracking, and other sources of waste. Based on the insights gained from creating and analyzing a spaghetti chart, ideas for shortening work flows and making them more direct with fewer major part-family flow streams can be identified and implemented. In service-oriented and transactional processes, spaghetti charts can be created by having a person assume the role of the part and actually walking through the process as would a patient or invoice.

Workforce

A key element of lean is the role of the work force as a means of uncovering and solving problems. Rather than considering the workers as the traditional cogs in the great plant machine, each with its own tasks, skills, and narrow responsibilities, lean strives for a broadly skilled, flexible worker who will look for and solve production problems wherever they appear.

In the traditional shop, much of the employees' time is nonworking time: looking for parts, moving materials, setting up machines, getting instructions, and so on. Thus, when actually working, the employees tend to work fast, producing parts at a rapid pace whether or not the parts are needed. (This, of course, results in errors, scrap, and machine breakdowns, which again provide a reason to stop working.) The outcome is a stop-and-go situation that, overall, results in a relatively inefficient, ineffective pace for most workers.

Conversely, with lean, the workers produce only when the next worker is ready. The pace is steady and fast, although never frantic. In spite of the built-in rule that workers should be idle if work is not needed, the focus on smooth flows, short set-ups, and other such simplifications means that workers are rarely idle. (Of course, if they *are* idle; that is an immediate signal to the system designers that work is not progressing smoothly through the plant and adjustments need to be made.)

Inventories

In Japan, inventory is seen as an evil in itself. It is a resource sitting idle, wasting money. But, more important, inventory tends to hide problems. In the traditional plant, inventories are used to buffer operations so that problems at one stage don't affect the next stage. However, inventories also hide problems, such as defective parts, until the inventory is needed and then is found to be defective. For example, in a plant with lots of work-in-process inventory, a worker who discovers a batch of defective parts can simply put them aside and work on something else. By the time the worker returns to the defective batch, if ever, so much time has elapsed since the batch was processed upstream that the cause of the problem is unlikely to be discovered and corrected to prevent a recurrence. In contrast, in an environment where there is little or no buffer inventory, a worker who discovers a defective batch has no choice but to work on the batch. Furthermore, the worker can then notify upstream operations of the problem so they can correct it and ensure that it does not occur in the future.

The Japanese liken inventory, and the money it represents, to the water in a lake. They see problems as boulders and obstacles under the water, as shown in Figure 5.1. To expose the problems, they reduce the inventories, also shown in Figure 5.1, and then solve the problems. Then they lower the inventory more, exposing more problems, and solve those, too. They continue this until all the problems are solved and the inventory investment is practically gone. The result is a greatly improved and smoother production system.

Figure 5.1   Lowering inventory investment to expose problems.

In the traditional plant, almost the opposite happens. Because managers know that their plant produces, say, 15 percent defective products, they produce 15 percent extra, which goes into inventory. That's the wrong way to handle the problem—they should fix the problem in the first place, not cover it up with expensive inventory.

All types of inventories are considered liabilities: work-in-process, raw materials, finished goods, component parts, and so on. By eliminating storage space, not only do we save space, but we also disallow inventories where defectives can be hidden until no one knows who made them. And by eliminating queues of work waiting for machines, we facilitate automatic inspection by workers of hand-passed parts, thereby identifying problems when they begin rather than after 1000 units have been made incorrectly.

If the space saved when operations are moved closer to each other—frequently 33 percent of the original space—is immediately used for something else, then inventory can't be dumped there. This facilitates reducing simultaneously the lead time, smoothing the workload, and reducing the inventory.

Last, with minimal or no inventory, control of materials is much easier and less expensive. Parts don't get lost, don't have to be moved, don't have to be labeled, and don't have to be held in computer memory or inventory records. Basically, discipline and quality are much improved and cost is reduced, simultaneously.

In Chapter 8, the economic order quantity (EOQ) will be presented as the optimal order quantity, given the tradeoff between inventory carrying cost and setup or ordering cost. The EOQ model also demonstrates the relationship between setup cost and average inventory levels: order quantities, and consequently average inventory levels, increase as setup time and cost increase. Knowing that the EOQ minimized total costs, managers in the United States simply plugged values into the EOQ formula to determine optimal order quantities. However, use of the EOQ model assumes that its inputs are fixed. In contrast to their American counterparts, managers in Japan did not assume that these inputs were fixed. In fact, they invested significant amounts of time and other resources in finding ways to reduce equipment setup times. These efforts led to substantial reductions in setup times and therefore in setup costs, and ultimately to much smaller batch sizes, which became the basis of the JIT system.

As discussed in Chapter 2, one approach to reducing setup times is to adopt cellular manufacturing. Another approach, if the equipment is available and utilization rates are not a problem, is to use multiple machines that have already been set up for the new task. Alternatively, some of the more advanced and automated equipment will automatically reset itself. In the remaining cases, the setup task can be made much more efficient through a number of techniques that have been largely identified and catalogued by the Japanese. Some of these are described next.

One lean tool used to reduce setup times is SMED, which stands for single minute exchange of die. SMED was developed by Shigeo Shingo, and is an important component of the Toyota Production System. While SMED literally translates to a single minute for practical purposes, the goal is to reduce setup times to under 10 minutes (i.e., a single digit, not a single minute). An excellent example of SMED is provided by the CMI factory that is jointly operated by GM and Suzuki, where machine setup times were reduced from 36 hours to 6 minutes.

A key element of SMED is distinguishing between internal setup time, which requires that the machine be turned off, and external setup time, which can be conducted while the machine is still working on the previous part. First, a major effort is directed toward converting internal to external setup time, which is easier to reduce. This is largely done by identifying all the previously internal setup tasks that can either be conducted just as easily as external setup work or, with some changes in the operation, be done externally. Then, the external task times are reduced by such techniques as staging dies, using duplicate fixtures, employing shuttles, and installing roller supports. Last, internal time is reduced by such creative approaches as using hinged bolts, folding brackets, guide pins, or Lazy Susans.

Once the setup times are reduced, the firm gains not only in smoother work flows and shorter lead times, but also in flexibility to any changes in production schedules stemming from accidents, unexpected breakages, customers' problems, and so on. Clearly, this flexibility is immensely valuable.

Suppliers

Traditional practice has been to treat suppliers as adversaries and play them off against each other. Multiple sourcing purportedly keeps prices down and ensures a wide supply of parts. However, multiple sourcing also means that no supplier is getting an important fraction of the order; thus, there is no incentive to work with the firm to meet specifications for quality and delivery.

With lean, the desire is for frequent, smooth deliveries of small lots, with the supplier considered part of the team. As part of the team, the supplier is even expected to help plan and design the purchased parts to be supplied. Schedules must be closely coordinated, and many small deliveries are expected every day. Thus, it is in the supplier's interest to locate a plant or warehouse close to the customer. Clearly then, the supplier must have a large enough order to make this trouble worthwhile; thus, **single-sourcing** for 100 percent of the requirements is common. But with such large orders, the customer can expect the supplier to become more efficient in producing the larger quantities of items, so quantity discounts become available. Moreover, having just one source is also more convenient for a firm that must interact and coordinate closely with the supplier. Companies that develop single-sourcing relationships recognize the mutual dependency of the supplier–customer relationship. Specifically, for the customer to prosper in the marketplace, the supplier must supply high-quality items in the right quantities on time. On the other hand, the more successful the customer, the more business is generated for the supplier.

Perhaps equally significant, there is no incoming inspection of the materials to check their quality—all parts must be of specified quality and guaranteed by the supplier. Again, this requires a cooperative rather than an adversarial approach, with the supplier working with the team. Many lean firms are now establishing a list of "certified" suppliers that they can count on to deliver perfect quality and thus become members of their production teams. In fact, many organizations implementing such programs will purchase products only from suppliers that pass their certification criteria. Often, companies that set up certification programs work with their suppliers to help them become certified.

Single-sourcing also has some disadvantages, however. The largest, of course, is the risk of being totally dependent on one supplier. If the supplier, perhaps through no fault on its part, cannot deliver as needed, the firm is stuck. With the minimal buffers typical of a lean organization, this could mean expensive idled production and large shortages. There is also some question about the supplier's incentive to become more creative in terms of producing higher quality or less expensive parts, because it already has the single-source contract. Yet the Japanese constantly pressure their suppliers to continue reducing prices, expecting that, at the least, the effect of increased learning with higher volumes will result in lower prices.

Planning and Control

In the traditional firm, planning is the focus, and it is typically complex and computerized. Materials Requirements Planning (MRP, discussed in Chapter 7) is a good example of the level of planning and analysis that goes into the traditional production system. Unfortunately, plans often go astray, but since the firm is focused on planning rather than control, the result is to try to improve planning the next time, and this, in turn, results in ever more complex plans. Thus, these firms spend most of their time planning and replanning and very little time actually executing the plans.

In the lean approach, the focus is on control. Thus, procedures are kept simple, visual, and made as routine as possible. Rather than planning and forecasting for an uncertain future, the firm attempts to respond to what actually happens in real time with flexible, quick operations. Some planning is certainly conducted, but to be even more effective and efficient in responding to actual events, the planning is directed to simple expectations and improvements in the control system.

But is there any way to combine the advantages of the lean JIT approach and MRP? Yes, there is a way. It consists of using MRP to pull the long-lead-time items and purchases *into* the shop, and it then employs JIT once the parts and raw materials have entered the shop. Dover's OPW Division used this approach, for example. It employed MRP's explosion and lead-time offsetting to identify and order the external parts and raw materials and used JIT's procedures to run a smooth, efficient plant once the parts and materials arrived. In other cases MRP is used as a planning tool for order releases and final assembly schedules, while JIT is used to execute and implement the plan.

Quality

The traditional approach to quality is to inspect the goods at critical points in the production system to weed out bad items and correct the system. At the least, final inspection on a sample should be conducted before a lot is sent to a customer. If too many defectives are found, the entire lot is inspected and the bad items are replaced with good ones. Scrap rates are tracked so that the firm knows how many to initiate through the production system in order to yield the number of good items desired by the customer.

With lean, the goal is zero defects and perfect quality. A number of approaches are used for this purpose, as described in Chapters 1 and 3. But the most important elements are the workers themselves—who check the parts as they hand them to the next worker—and the small lot sizes produced, as described earlier. If a part is bad, it is caught at the time of production, and the error in the production system is corrected immediately.

Maintenance

In the traditional approach to production, maintenance has been what is termed **corrective maintenance**, although **preventive maintenance** is also common. Corrective maintenance is repairing a machine when it breaks down, whereas preventive maintenance is conducting maintenance before the machine is expected to fail, or at regular intervals. Corrective maintenance is more acceptable in the traditional firm, because there are queues of material sitting in front of the machines to be worked on so that production can continue undisturbed, at least until the queues are gone.

But in the lean enterprise, if a machine breaks down it will eventually stop all the following *downstream* equipment for lack of work. (It will almost immediately stop all *upstream* equipment as well, through the pull system.) Therefore, in lean organizations, the maintenance function assumes greater responsibility and has greater visibility. To reflect its expanded role, lean organizations refer to the maintenance function as total productive maintenance (TPM). One key aspect of TPM is that instead of employing a "crew" of experts who do nothing but repair broken equipment, the lean enterprise relies much more heavily on the operator for many of the maintenance tasks, especially simple preventive maintenance. We will return to the topic of TPM later in the chapter.

With our comparison of traditional and lean organizations complete, we now turn our attention to the five principles of lean and discuss each in more detail. This discussion will include an overview of representative tools and methodologies commonly used to support each principle.

$\mathscr{S}$PECIFY VALUE

At the heart of lean is the concept of value. While producers and service providers seek to create value for their customers, it is important to recognize that value is ultimately defined by the customer. Thus, one way to define value is to consider what and how much a customer is willing to pay for a particular product or service. Of course, related to how much a customer is willing to pay for a product or service is the strength of the customer's desires and needs, and the variety of options available to satisfy these needs.

Alternatively, another common definition of value is that it is the opposite of waste or **muda**. Waste can be defined as those activities that consume resources but from the customer's perspective create no value. From this perspective, waste is often classified into one of the following seven categories:

1. *Overproduction.* Creating more of an output than is needed at a particular point in time. Producing more than is needed creates the need for additional space to store the surplus, requires purchasing more raw materials than were needed, and often has a detrimental effect on profit margins as the surplus may need to be disposed of at distressed prices.

2. *Inventory.* Inventory takes a variety of forms, including raw materials, work-in-process, and finished goods. It requires space for its storage, leading to lease and utility expenses. Furthermore, the inventory must be insured, handled, financed, and tracked, further increasing the cost of holding it. However, despite all these efforts, some portion of inventory will tend to get damaged, some may become obsolete, and some may even be stolen. Unfortunately, most, if not all, of the work related to maintaining inventory is not value added in the eyes of the customer.

3. *Waiting.* Waiting relates to delays or events that prevent a worker from performing his or her work. A worker with nothing to work on because of a delay in an upstream activity, a worker who is idle because a piece of equipment broke down, or a worker who is idle while waiting for a piece of equipment to be set up all exemplify the waste of waiting.

4. *Unnecessary transport.* Any time a worker or a part must be moved, it is considered waste. One goal of lean is to seek ways to reduce the distance people or work must travel, as was illustrated by the Virginia Mason Medical Center example at the beginning of the chapter.

5. *Unnecessary processing.* Unnecessary processing relates to extra steps in a process. Examples of unnecessary processing include removing burrs from machined parts, reworking defective parts, and entering the same information into multiple databases. Also, from the lean perspective, inspections are generally considered unnecessary processing.

6. *Unnecessary human motions.* Using the human body efficiently and effectively is not only vital to the health of the workers, but also to the productivity of the organization. Time and motion studies as well as ergonomic studies are used to help design work environments that increase the efficiency, safety, and effectiveness of workers.

7. *Defects.* Parts that must be reworked, or in more extreme cases scrapped, represent the final category of waste. Having to perform rework requires repeating steps that were already performed, while scrapping parts results in extra material and processing charges with no corresponding output to offset these charges. The key to providing outputs that are valued by the customer is developing a solid understanding of customer needs. Establishing the voice of the customer, perhaps through a quality function deployment initiative (see Chapter 4), is one approach commonly used to help identify and better understand customer needs.

Based on a better understanding of how the customer defines value, the next logical task is to define a target cost. Generally speaking, the low-cost producer in an industry has more options available to it than other organizations in the industry. For example, the low-cost producer has the option of matching its competitors' prices and thereby maintaining a higher profit margin. Alternatively, the low-cost provider can offer its products and services at a lower price than the competition in an effort to increase its market share.

IDENTIFY THE VALUE STREAM

Once value has been defined from the customer's perspective and a target cost established, the next step is to identify the set of activities or value stream required to create the customer-valued output. Broadly speaking, the value stream includes all activities (value added and nonvalue added) from the creation of the raw materials to the final delivery of the output to the end consumer. Within the organization, the value stream includes the design of the output, continues through the operations function where raw materials are transformed into finished goods, and ends with the delivery of its output to the customer. However, it should also be pointed out that a properly crafted value stream map should transcend organizational boundaries. Thus, a complete value stream map would include an organization's suppliers, the suppliers to its suppliers, and any distributors, retailers, and so on between the organization and the end consumer.

The activities within a value stream map are often broadly categorized as:

- Value-added (e.g., patient diagnosis)
- Nonvalue-added but necessary (e.g., requiring patients to sign a HIPAA form)
- Nonvalue-added and not necessary (e.g., waiting for the doctor)

The challenge associated with value-added activities is to identify ways to perform these activities in such a way that more value is created and/or less resources consumed. Likewise, the challenge for both types of nonvalue-added activities is to identify opportunities to eliminate them or perhaps transform the activity into something that is valued by the customer.

An example value stream map for a service firm, in this case a contract manufacturer of metal cases for servers, is shown in Figure 5.2. In this example, the contract manufacturer provides the service of fabricating the metal cases for the servers that their customer, Allied Computer, Inc (shown in the upper right-hand corner of the figure) assembles for *its* customers. The most frequently used value stream symbols are summarized in Table 5.2.

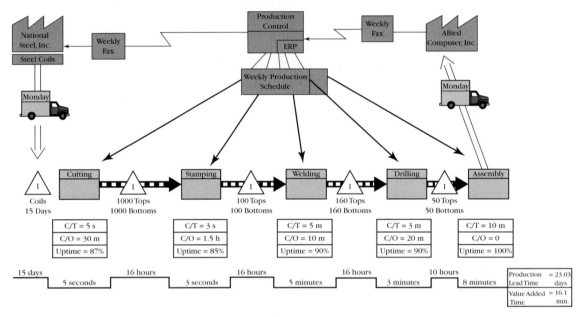

Figure 5.2   As-Is value stream map for metal case contract manufacturer. *Source:* Adapted from www.mamtc.com/lean/building_vsm.asp

A value stream map shows the flow of materials and information with suppliers shown on the left of the diagram and customers on the right. In studying the value stream map shown in Figure 5.2, we see that our contract manufacturer gets a shipment of steel coils from its supplier National Steel Coils, Inc. every Monday. Also shown in the value stream map are the quantities of inventory held at each stage of the value stream and the details of the operational activities at each stage in the process. Inventory is represented by triangles and processing activities by rectangles in the value stream map. In the case of our contract manufacturer, a 15-day supply of coils is maintained in front of the cutting operation. Also, additional details about the processing steps are included in Data Boxes near each operational activity.

$\mathcal{T}$ABLE 5.2 • Commonly Used Value Stream Symbols

Value Stream Map Symbol	Description	Use
Customer/ Supplier	Customer/Supplier	When in upper left represents a supplier. When in upper right represents a customer. Supplier or customer name entered inside symbol.
Frequency	External Shipment	Used to represent shipments from a supplier or to a customer. The frequency of the shipment is often entered inside the symbol.
	Shipments	Block arrows used to show the movement of raw materials and finished goods.
	Inventory	Used to show inventory between stages in the process. The amount of inventory and a description of what is being stored is often entered below the symbol.
Process	Process	This symbol represents a process, operation, machine, or department that material flows through.
C/T = C/O = Avail =	Data Box	Data Boxes are used with other symbols to provide additional information. They most frequently are used with Process symbols. Information frequently captured about a process includes its cycle time (C/T), changeover time (C/O), uptime, available capacity, batch size, and scrap rate.
NVA NVA VA VA VA	Timeline	A timeline is often placed at the bottom of the Value Stream Map to show value added (VA) and non-value added (NVA) time.
Production Control	Production Control	The Production Control symbol is used to capture how production is scheduled and controlled.

(Continued)

*T*ABLE 5.2 • *(Continued)*

→	Manual Information	A straight thin arrow is used to show the flow of information that is conveyed manually such as memos, reports, and meetings. The frequency with which the information is conveyed can also be added.
(wiggle arrow)	Electronic Information	A wiggle arrow represents information that is conveyed electronically such as via the web or faxes. The frequency with which the information is conveyed can also be added.
(starburst symbol)	Kaizen Blitz	This symbol is used to document specific process improvement projects that are expected to be executed.
(workcell symbol)	Workcell	This symbol represents the production of part families in cells.
(striped push arrow)	Push Arrow	This symbol is used when the output of one process stage is pushed to the next stage in the process.
P — W	Production and Withdrawal Kanbans	Production kanbans are used to trigger production. Withdrawal kanbans are used authorize the material movement to down-stream processes.
(supermarket symbol)	Supermarket	A supermarket is a small amount of inventory that is stored at the point of usage.

Information often captured in Data Boxes includes the cycle time[1] of the activity, how long it takes to change over the equipment, the capacity of the processing stage, and other relevant details about the activity or operation. We also see that a weekly production schedule is generated by an ERP system and that each stage in the process works at its own pace and pushes its product on to the next operation. We contrast push and pull systems later in this chapter. Along the bottom of the value stream

---

[1]Note that usage of the term cycle time has a slightly different meaning compared to its usage in the context of assembly line balancing. Here our usage of cycle time refers to the amount of time it takes the particular stage to complete its operation which may vary across the different processing stages. In assembly line balancing, cycle time refers to the amount of time each station has to complete its activities where the cycle time is constant across all processing stations.

map is a timeline that tracks value added and nonvalue added time. In our example we see that out of the total lead time of just over 23 days, only 16.1 minutes are considered to be adding value. Finally, at the far right, we observe that the contract manufacturer makes weekly shipments on Monday to its customer Allied Computer, Inc. Also note that information from the contract manufacturer's ERP system is used to generate orders for raw materials which are faxed to its supplier, National Steel, weekly. Likewise, the contract manufacturer receives a weekly fax from its customer, Allied Computer, which is input into its ERP system.

The value stream map shown in Figure 5.2 is referred to as the "As-Is" value stream map since it describes the current value stream. After the As-Is map is created, it is carefully studied to identify opportunities for improving the process and a "To-Be" value stream map is crafted. Following this, a transition plan from the As-Is process to the To-Be process is developed.

Figure 5.3 provides the To-Be value stream map for the contract manufacturer. The To-Be map calls for the following process improvements:

- Reducing the quantity of steel coils held in inventory from 15 day's worth to 1 day's worth. This reduction is made possible in part by getting daily shipments from National Steel as opposed to weekly shipments.

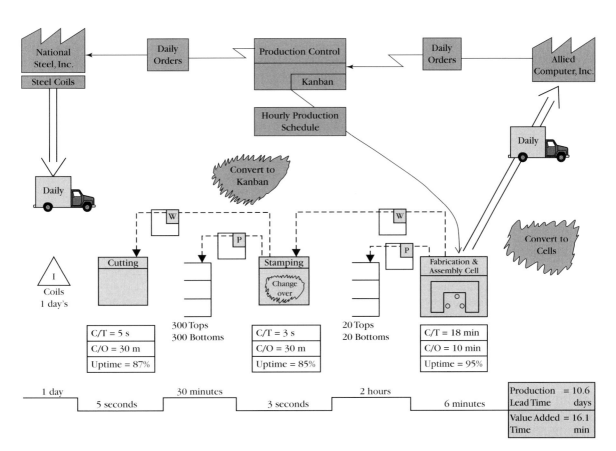

Figure 5.3 To-Be value stream map for metal case contract manufacturer. *Source:* Adapted from www.mamtc.com/lean/building_vsm.asp

- Reductions in work-process inventory levels made possible by eliminating the old push system and adopting a kanban pull system (discussed later in the chapter).

- Kaizen events (discussed later in the chapter) to reduce the changeover time of the stamping machine, convert to the kanban system, and convert from the functional layout to a cellular layout (as discussed in Chapter 2).

- Communicating electronically and daily with its suppliers and customers.

- Reducing the production lead time from 23 days to 10.6 days.

MAKE VALUE FLOW

Erratic flows in one part of the value stream often become magnified in other parts of the system, not only further down the stream but, because of scheduling, further *up* the line as well. This is due to the formation of queues in the production system, the batching of parts for processing on machines, the lot-sizing rules we use to initiate production, and many other similar policies. These disruptions to the smooth flow of goods are costly to the production system and waste time, materials, and human energy. Thus, having identified the value stream, the next step is to transform it from the traditional batch and wait approach to one where the flow is continuous. This is accomplished by eliminating nonvalue-added activities and streamlining the remaining value-added steps. In fact, many lean organizations make the analogy that goods should "flow like water." A key aspect to achieving such a smooth flow is to master-schedule small lots of final products.

Another obstacle to smooth flows is the traditional functional organization structure. In the functional organization, work is organized based on the similarity of the work performed. Thus, you have accounting departments, marketing departments, radiology units, quality assurance departments, and so on. The problem with organizing work on the basis of the type of work performed is that work must then be handed off from department to department. Such hand-offs inevitably create delays in the process and introduce opportunities for making errors. Therefore, lean organizations have a bias toward organizing work based on the value creating process the work supports, as opposed to organizing work functionally.

It should also be pointed out that early production or delivery is just as inappropriate as late delivery. The goal is *perfect* adherence to schedule—without this, erratic flows are introduced throughout the value stream. With continuous, smooth flows of parts come continuous, level flows of work so there are no peak demands on workers, machines, or other resources. Then, once adequate capacity has been attained it will always be sufficient.

Continuous Flow Manufacturing

An important tenet to making value flow in lean enterprises is continuous flow manufacturing (CFM). According to this tenet, work should flow through the process without interruption, one unit at a time based on the customer's demand rate. Thus, once the processing of a unit has begun, the work should continue uninterrupted until the unit is completed. This is reflected by the phrase, "Don't let the parts touch the floor." To accomplish this, delays associated with setting up equipment, moving work between departments, storing work because a needed resource is unavailable, equipment breakdowns, and so on must be eliminated.

To synchronize the flow of work with the customer's demand rate, the ***takt time*** is calculated (the same as the cycle time, as noted in Chapter 2). The term takt time, German for the baton used by orchestra conductors, was coined by Toyota and translates the customer demand rate into time. In effect, the takt time defines the rhythm or pace that work must be completed at in order to meet the customer demand rate. More specifically, takt time is calculated as:

$$\text{Takt time} = \frac{\text{Available work time}}{\text{Customer required volume}}$$

To illustrate the concept of takt time, consider an insurance company that operates nine hours per day processing claims. Assume that the employees get two 15-minute breaks and one hour for lunch. Further assume that the company receives 6000 claims per month and that there are 20 working days per month. In this case, the takt time would be calculated as:

$$\text{Takt time} = \frac{540 \text{ min} - 30 \text{ min} - 60 \text{ min}}{\dfrac{6000}{20}} = \frac{450}{300} = 1.5 \text{ minutes/claim}$$

In this case, the insurance company must process a claim every 1.5 minutes. But suppose the processing of an application requires 15 minutes of work. Then in this case, 10 employees working in parallel would be needed. In other words, processing 10 applications every 15 minutes is equivalent to processing one application every 1.5 minutes.

Converting to Mixed-Model Assembly and Sequencing

Another approach for enhancing the flow of work is mixed-model assembly and sequencing. With mixed-model assembly, items are produced smoothly throughout the day rather than in large batches of one item, followed by long shutdowns and setups and then by another large batch of another item. Let us demonstrate with an example.

Suppose three different models are being produced in a plant that operates two shifts, and the monthly demands are as given in Table 5.3. Dividing the monthly demand by 20 working days per month and then again by two shifts per day gives the daily production requirements per shift. A common divisor of the required production per shift of 20 A's, 15 B's, and 10 C's is 5. Using 5 as the common divisor means that we would produce five batches of each of these models each shift. Dividing the required production per shift of each model by five batches indicates that on each production cycle, 4 units of A, 3 units of B, and 2 units of C will be produced. Assuming two 15-minute breaks per 8-hour shift (480 minutes), the production rate must be 45 units per 450 minute shift (480 − 15 − 15 = 450), or 10 minutes per unit (450 minutes per shift/45 units per shift). Because one cycle consists of 9 units (4 A's, 3 B's, and 2 C's), the entire cycle will take 90 minutes. Thus, each

$\mathcal{T}$ABLE 5.3 • Mixed-Model Assembly Cycle

Model	Monthly Demand	Required/Shift	Units/Cycle
A	800	$800/(20 \times 2) = 20$	4
B	600	15	3
C	400	10	2
Total	1800	45	9

production cycle of 4 A's, 3 B's, and 2 C's will be repeated five times each shift to produce the required 45 units.

One possible production cycle would be to produce the three models in batches using a sequence such as A-A-A-A-B-B-B-C-C. Alternatively, to smooth the production of the nine units throughout the production cycle, a sequence such as A-B-A-B-C-A-B-A-C might be used. Clearly, numerous other sequences are also possible. With daily production of all models, no erratic changes are introduced into the plant through customer demand, because some of every product is always available. When models are produced in traditional batches (such as producing 1000 A's, then 750 B's, followed by 500 C's), one or more batches may well be depleted before the other batches are finished. This then necessitates putting a "rush" order through the plant (in order not to lose a customer for the models that are out of stock), disrupting ongoing work, and adding to the cost of all products—not to mention the frustration involved.

The Theory of Constraints

The **theory of constraints** (Goldratt 1990), offers a systematic way to view and analyze process flows. Key aspects of the theory of constraints (TOC) include identifying the bottlenecks in the process and balancing the work flows in the system. Other names for the same concept are drum-buffer-rope (DBR), goal system, and synchronous manufacturing. TOC is often compared to kanban (discussed later in this chapter) and MRP (Chapter 7) as another way to plan production and schedule operations. Studies comparing these systems seem to show that each has different strengths—MRP to generate time-phased requirements, TOC to plan medium-time-horizon bottleneck facilities, and JIT to maximize throughput—and manufacturers should employ a combination of the three.

The theory of constraints was originally implemented through a proprietary package primarily used in the make-to-order and automotive industries called *optimized production technology* (OPT), which is based on an alternative approach to capacity planning. The basic procedure is first to identify bottleneck workstations in the shop, schedule them to keep them fully utilized, and then schedule the non–bottleneck workstations to keep the bottlenecks busy so that they are never waiting for work. The following ten guidelines capture the essence of the theory:

1. *Flows rather than capacities should be balanced throughout the shop.* The objective is to move material quickly and smoothly through the production system, not to balance capacities or utilization of equipment or human resources.

2. *Fluctuations in a tightly connected, sequence-dependent system add to each other rather than averaging out.*

3. *Utilization of a non–bottleneck is determined by other constraints in the system, such as bottlenecks.* Nonbottleneck resources do not restrict the amount of output that a production system can create. Thus, these resources should be managed to support the operations of those resources (i.e., the bottlenecks) that do constrain the amount of output. Clearly, operating a nonbottleneck resource at a higher rate of output than the bottleneck resource does nothing to increase the output produced by the entire production system.

4. *Utilizing a workstation (producing when material is not yet needed) is not the same as activation.* Traditionally, managers have not made a distinction between "using" a resource and "activating" it. However, according to the theory of constraints, a resource is considered *utilized* only if it is helping the entire system create more output. If a machine is independently producing more output than the rest of the system, the time the machine is operated to produce outputs over and above what the overall system is producing is considered activation, not utilization.

5. *An hour lost at a bottleneck is an hour lost for the whole shop.* Since the bottleneck resource limits the amount of output the entire system can create, time when this resource is not producing output is a loss to the entire system that cannot be made up. Lost time at a bottleneck resource can result because of down time for maintenance or because the resource was starved for work. For example, if a hair stylist is idle for an hour because no customers arrive, this hour of lost haircuts cannot be made up, even if twice as many customers as usual arrive in the next hour.

6. *An hour saved at a non–bottleneck is a mirage.* Since non–bottlenecks have plenty of capacity and do not limit the output of the production system, saving time at these resources does not increase total output. The implication for managers is that time-saving improvements to the system should be directed at bottleneck resources.

7. *Bottlenecks govern shop throughput and work-in-process inventories.*

8. *The transfer batch need not be the same size as the process batch.* The size of the *process batch* is the size of the batch produced each time a job is run. Often, this size is determined by trading off various costs, as is done with the economic order quantity (EOQ) model discussed in Chapter 8. On the other hand, the size of the *transfer batch* is the size of the batch of parts moved from one work center to another work center. Clearly, parts can be moved in smaller batches than the process batch. Indeed, considerable reductions in batch flow times can often be obtained by using a transfer batch that is smaller than the process batch. For example, assume that a manufacturer produces a part in batches of 10. This part requires three operations, each performed on a different machine. The operation time is 5 minutes per part per operation. Figure 5.4*a* demonstrates the effect on flow time when a process batch of 10 units is reduced to a transfer batch of one unit. Specifically, in Figure 5.4*a* the transfer batch is the same size as the process batch, and a flow time of 150 minutes results. In Figure 5.4*b*, the one-unit transfer batch reduces flow time to 60 minutes. The reason for long flow time with a large

Time	5	10	15	20	25	30	35	40	45	50	55	60	65	70	75	80	85	90	95	100	105	110	115	120	125	130	135	140	145	150
Opn 1	P1	P2	P3	P4	P5	P6	P7	P8	P9	P10																				
Opn 2											P1	P2	P3	P4	P5	P6	P7	P8	P9	P10										
Opn 3																					P1	P2	P3	P4	P5	P6	P7	P8	P9	P10

(a)

Time	5	10	15	20	25	30	35	40	45	50	55	60
Opn 1	P1	P2	P3	P4	P5	P6	P7	P8	P9	P10		
Opn 2		P1	P2	P3	P4	P5	P6	P7	P8	P9	P10	
Opn 3			P1	P2	P3	P4	P5	P6	P7	P8	P9	P10

(b)

Figure 5.4 Transfer batch size and its effects on flow time. (*a*) Transfer batch size equals process batch size. (*b*) Transfer batch size equals one part.

transfer batch is that in any batch, the first part must always wait for all the other parts to complete their processing before it is started on the next machine. In Figure 5.4*a*, the first part in the batch has to wait 45 minutes for the other nine parts. When the transfer batch is reduced to one unit, the parts in the batch do not have to wait for the other parts in the process batch.

9. *The size of the process batch should be variable, not fixed.* Because the economics of different resources can vary, the process batch does not need to be the same size at all stages of production. For example, consider an item that is produced on an injection molding machine and then visits a trimming department. Because the time and cost to set up injection molding equipment are likely to be very different from the time and cost to set up the trimming equipment, there is no reason why the batch size should be the same at each of these stages. Thus, batch size at each stage should be determined by the specific economics of that stage.

10. *A shop schedule should be set by examining all the shop constraints simultaneously.* Traditionally, schedules are determined sequentially. First, the batch size is determined. Next, lead times are calculated and priorities set.

Finally, schedules are adjusted on the basis of capacity constraints. The theory of constraints advocates considering all constraints simultaneously in developing schedules. The theory also argues that lead times are the result of the schedules and therefore cannot be determined beforehand.

The critical aspect of these guidelines is the focus on bottleneck workstations, not overloading the workstations, and the splitting of batches in order to move items along to the next workstation when desirable. A five-step process is recommended for implementing the theory of constraints:

1. *Identify the system's constraint(s).* Usually the process-flow diagram will help identify the constraints, but the ultimate constraint may in fact be sales representatives' time, capital available for investment, mandated policies such as a single shift, or even demand in the marketplace.

2. *Exploit the constraint.* Find ways to maximize the return per unit of the constraint. An example here would be to use the scarce resource to produce as much of the highest profit item as possible.

3. *Subordinate all else to the constraint.* The objective here is to make sure the constraint is always productive and that something else isn't drawing resources away from the constraint. For example, perhaps inventories should be built in front of a scarce machine or worker.

4. *Elevate the constraint.* Again, find ways to make the constraint as productive as possible, such as extra maintenance; saving time on the constraint by using other, perhaps less-efficient machines more intensively; or even obtaining more of the constraint.

5. *If the constraint is no longer a bottleneck, find the next constraint and repeat the steps.* Once a bottleneck has been eliminated, something else becomes the bottleneck—perhaps another machine or storage facility, or perhaps the demand in the marketplace.

PULL VALUE THROUGH THE VALUE STREAM

In the traditional firm, long lead times are often thought to allow more time to make decisions and get work performed. But in the lean enterprise, short lead times mean easier, more accurate forecasting and planning. Moreover, a way to capitalize on the increasing strategic importance of fast response to the customer is to minimize all the lead times. If lead times are reduced, there is less time for things to go awry, to get lost, or to be changed. For example, it is quite common for an order placed two months ago to be changed every three weeks until it is delivered: change an option, change the quantity ordered, and so on. However, if the delivery time is one week or less, the customers can place the order when they know exactly what they need and can therefore delay ordering until the week before they need it.

As opposed to the MRP approach of "pushing" materials through a plant, lean enterprises rely on **pull systems** whereby actual customer demand drives the production process. Push systems are planning-based systems that determine when workstations will probably need parts if everything goes according to plan. However, operations rarely go according to plan, and as a result, materials may be either too late or too early. To safeguard against being too late and to make sure that people always have enough work to keep busy, safety stocks are used, even with MRP; these may not even be needed, but they further increase the stocks of materials in the plant. Thus, in a push system we see workers always busy making items and lots of material in the plant.

In comparison, a pull system is a control-based system that signals the requirement for parts as they are needed in reality. The result is that workers may occasionally (and sometimes frequently) be idle because more materials are not needed. This keeps material from being produced when it is not needed (waste). The appearance of a plant using a pull system is quiet and slow, with minimal material around.

To further contrast the differences between push and pull systems, consider the production system shown in Figure 5.5. The system consists of one machine of type A and one machine of type B. Machine A has the capacity to produce 75 units per day, and machine B has the capacity to produce 50 units per day. All products are first produced on machine A and then processed on machine B. Daily demand for the organization is 50 units.

Figure 5.5   Sequential production system with two machines.

In a push system, each work center would work as fast as it could and *push* the product on to work centers downstream, regardless of whether they needed additional materials. In Figure 5.5, after the first day of operation, machine A would produce 75 units, machine B would process 50 of the 75 units it received from machine A, and 25 units would be added to work-in-process inventory. Each day the system operates in this fashion, 25 more units will be added to the work-in-process inventory in front of machine B. This might seem irrational to you, but the only way for inventory not to be built up is for machine A to produce less than it is capable of producing. In this example, we could idle machine A 33 percent of the day and produce and transport only 50 units to machine B. However, if you were the plant manager and you noticed that the worker assigned to machine A was working only 67 percent of the time, what would you think? You might think the worker was goofing off and order him or her to run the machine. Of course, doing this only increases the amount of money tied up in inventory and does nothing to increase the amount of product completed and shipped to the customer.

In a pull system, the worker at machine A would produce only in response to requests for more materials made by the worker at machine B. Furthermore, the worker at machine B is authorized to make additional product only to replenish product that is used to meet actual customer demand. If there is no customer demand, machine B will sit idle. And if machine B sits idle, machine A will be idle. In this way, the production of the entire operation is matched to actual demand.

The signals used in a pull system to authorize production may be of various kinds. Dover Corporation's OPW Division makes gasoline nozzles for gas pumps and uses wire bins as signals. Each bin holds 500 nozzles, and two are used at any time. Raw material is taken out of one bin until it is empty, and then material is drawn from the second bin. A bin collector constantly scouts the plant, looking for empty bins, and returns them to the stockroom where they are refilled and returned to the workstations. In this manner, no more than two bins' worth of material (1000 units) is ever in process.

Hewlett-Packard uses yellow tape to make squares about 1 foot on a side as the signals for its assembly lines. One square lies between every two workers. When workers finish an item, they draw the next unit to work on from the square between them and the previous worker. When the square is empty, this is the signal that another item is needed from the previous worker. Thus there are never more than two items in process per worker.

These two examples are actually modifications of Toyota's original JIT system. Toyota's materials management system is known as ***kanban***, which means "card" in Japanese. The idea behind this system is to authorize materials for production only if there is a need for them. Through the use of kanban authorization cards, production is "pulled" through the system, instead of pushed out before it is needed and then stored. Thus, the MPS authorizes final assembly, which in turn authorizes subassembly production, which in its turn authorizes parts assembly, and so on. If production stops at some point in the system, immediately all downstream production also stops, and soon thereafter all upstream production as well.

Typically, two cards are used—a withdrawal kanban and a production kanban. The cards are very simple, showing only the part number and name, the work centers involved, a storage location, and the container capacity. The approach is illustrated in Figure 5.6.

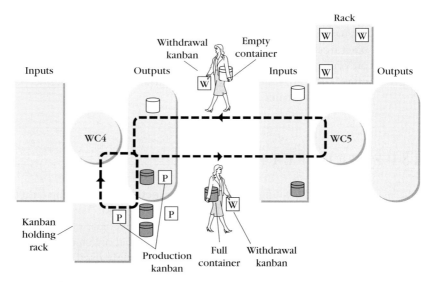

Figure 5.6   Kanban process.

Assume that work flows from work center (WC) 4 to WC5, and containers are used to transport the output from WC4 to WC5, where they are used as inputs. When WC5 sees that it will be needing more input parts, it takes an empty container and a withdrawal kanban back to WC4. There it leaves the empty container and locates a full one, which has a production kanban with it. WC5's withdrawal kanban authorizes it to remove the full container and put the production kanban in a rack at WC4, thereby authorizing the production of another container of parts. Back at WC5, the withdrawal kanban is placed back in its rack. WC4 cannot initiate production and fill an empty container until it has a production kanban on the rack authorizing additional production. Thus, withdrawal kanbans authorize the acquisition of additional materials from a supplying work center and production kanbans authorize a work center to make additional product.

The advantage of such a system is its simplicity. Being entirely visual in nature, it facilitates smooth production flow, quality inspection, minimization of inventory, and clear control of the production system.

Kanban/JIT in Services

Of course many services, and especially pure services, have no choice but to provide their service exactly when it is demanded. For example, a hair stylist cannot build up inventories of cuts and styles before the actual customers arrive. Now JIT is being adopted in other services that use materials rather extensively. For example, professors can choose materials from a wide variety of sources and let a "just-in-time" publisher compile the material into a custom-made book as quickly and cheaply as a standard book. Supermarkets replenish their shelves on a JIT basis as customers withdraw purchases. And everyone is familiar with fast-turnaround operations such as cleaners, automobile oil changes, photo processing, and eyeglass lenses, not to mention fast food.

Many, if not most, of the techniques used in manufacturing to become lean are equally applicable to services such as close supplier ties (food spoils), maintaining a flexible workforce (customization), and using reservation systems and off-peak pricing to keep level loads on the system. In addition, the general advantages that manufacturers accrue through defect-free operations, flexible layouts, minimal inventories, preventive maintenance, advanced technologies, standardized work methods, and other such approaches provide equal advantages to service organizations, and in some cases greater advantages.

$\mathcal{P}$URSUE PERFECTION

At the risk of stating the obvious, competition is a moving target. By the same token, opportunities to improve processes never end. Therefore, it is common for lean enterprises to focus less on meeting the immediate challenges posed by the competition and to focus more on the long-term goal of achieving perfection. In the remainder of this section, we overview five commonly used tools lean organizations turn to in their pursuit of perfection: 5S, the visual factory, kaizen, poka yoke, and total productive maintenance.

5S

A widely used approach for increasing the efficiency of individual work activities is 5S. The approach consists of the following five steps:

1. *Sort.* Distinguish what work must be performed to complete a task from what does not need to be done. Eliminate the unnecessary steps.

2. *Straighten (Set in order).* A common phrase in industrial engineering is "A place for everything and everything in its place."

3. *Scrub (Shine).* Maintain a workplace that is clean and free of clutter.

4. *Systemize.* Develop and implement standardized procedures for maintaining an orderly work environment.

5. *Standardize (Sustain).* Make the previous four steps a habit.

The Visual Factory

With little or no slack to absorb disruptions, successful execution in a lean environment requires that workers and decision makers are constantly up to date with the conditions in the work environment. One way lean organizations accomplish this is through an approach called the visual factory. The objectives of the visual factory are to help make problems visible, help employees stay up to date on current operating conditions, and to communicate process improvement goals. With the visual factory, problems can be made visible through the use of charts displayed throughout the workplace that plot trends related to quality, on time delivery performance, safety, machine downtime, productivity, and so on. Likewise, visual factories make use of production and schedule boards to help employees stay up to date on current conditions. It should be noted that the concept of a visual factory is equally applicable to services. For example, a call center one of the authors recently visited had a board that displayed updated information on the percent of calls that were answered within the desired time frame.

Kaizen

The Japanese word "kaizen" literally translates into continuous improvement. The lean journey in the pursuit of perfection requires a continuous series of incremental improvements. In some cases, a continuous improvement initiative may take a year or longer to implement. However, recently a short-term approach to continuous improvement called the ***kaizen blitz*** (a.k.a. kaizen workshops, kaizen events) is becoming increasingly popular. In a kaizen blitz, a cross-functional team completes a continuous improvement project in under a week. Often the kaizen blitz begins with a day or two of formal training in lean concepts. The training is then followed by the team completing a continuous improvement project. The project requires the team to collect any needed data, analyze the data, and then immediately implement the proposed improvements. Typical goals for a kaizen blitz include one or more of the following: reducing the amount of floor space needed, increasing process flexibility, improving work flows, improving quality, enhancing the safety of the working environment, and reducing or eliminating nonvalue-added activities.

Poka Yoke

The goal of poka yoke is to mistake-proof work activities in a way that prevents errors from being committed in the first place. Examples of poka yoke include supplementing electronic forms with computer code or scripts that check the validity of information entered into fields as it is being entered, designing a machine that requires the operator to press two buttons simultaneously to cycle the machine so that neither hand can be caught in the machine when it is operating, and placing parts in kits based on their assembly sequence.

Total Productive Maintenance

A key driver of waste and therefore an important component of lean is the effective use of equipment. In particular, equipment impacts waste in a number of ways including:

- *Breakdowns*. When a piece of equipment fails, it is no longer creating valued outputs, which can lead to customer dissatisfaction as well as economic repercussions for the firm. Furthermore, workers may be made idle during the breakdown, further adding to the firm's cost without corresponding increases in sales.

- *Setups*. Like breakdowns, a piece of equipment undergoing a setup or changeover is not creating valued outputs. Moreover, during the setup, workers are being paid to make the changeover and if a specialized group performs the setup, the machine operators may be idled during the setup period.

- *Stoppages*. At times, production on a piece of equipment may need to be halted because its output is unacceptable.

- *Reduced speed*. Another potential loss occurs when a piece of equipment is operated at a lower production rate than the rate it was designed to operate at.

- *Yields*. Yield relates to the percent of the total output produced that is acceptable. Lower yields correspond to greater amounts of waste in the form of scrap and rework.

Total productive maintenance (TPM) focuses broadly on the cost of equipment over its entire life cycle and encompasses a variety of tools and techniques to improve equipment maintenance practices as well as to help prevent and predict equipment failures. Key components of a TPM program include:

- Identifying ways to maximize equipment effectiveness.

- Developing a productive maintenance system for maintaining equipment over its entire life cycle.

- Coordinating the work of engineering, operations, and maintenance employees.

- Giving employees the responsibility to maintain the equipment they operate.

A measure of ***overall equipment effectiveness*** is calculated as the product of equipment availability, equipment efficiency, and the rate of quality output. Equipment availability represents the percent of time a piece of equipment is available to produce output. Equipment efficiency is a function of the theoretical cycle time, the actual cycle time, actual processing time, and equipment operating time. The rate of quality output corresponds to the yield on the piece of equipment. An overall effectiveness rating of 85 percent is considered excellent.

$\mathcal{B}$ENEFITS OF LEAN

In summary, it appears that lean is not one of the annual fads of American management but rather a philosophy for efficiently and effectively using the resources an organization already has at its disposal. As such, it will not disappear from the scene, though its tenets are increasingly being merged with other programs such as Six Sigma and supply chain management. And in spite of the concerns about the timely physical transportation of goods, a major challenge for the future will be the effective utilization of the many information technologies available to managers, such as the Internet. In too many cases, organizations are relying too much on internal forecasts rather than using the Internet and other information and communications technologies to access their customer's real-time production schedules. In the future, lean organizations will increasingly make use of satellite tracking systems, wireless communication, scanning technology, global positioning systems, two-dimensional bar codes and RFID tags, and paperless documentation across the entire value chain.

As we have seen, lean offers a variety of possible benefits: reduced inventories and space, faster response to customers due to shorter lead times, less scrap, higher quality, increased communication and teamwork, and greater emphasis on identifying and solving problems. In general, there are five primary types of benefits: (1) cost savings, (2) revenue increases, (3) investment savings, (4) workforce improvements, and (5) uncovering problems.

1. *Cost savings.* Costs are saved a number of ways: inventory reductions, reduced scrap, fewer defects, fewer changes due to both customers and engineering, less space, decreased labor hours, less rework, reduced overhead, and other such effects.

2. *Revenue increases.* Revenues are increased primarily through better service and quality to the customer. Short lead times and faster response to customers' needs result in better margins and higher sales. In addition, revenues will be coming in faster on newer products and services.

3. *Investment savings.* Investment is saved through three primary effects. First, less space (about a third) is needed for the same capacity. Second, inventory is reduced to the point that turns run about 50 to 100 a year (compared with 3 or 4, historically). Third, the volume of work produced in the same facility is significantly increased, frequently by as much as 100 percent.

4. *Workforce improvements.* The employees of lean firms are much more satisfied with their work. They prefer the teamwork it demands, and they like the fact that fewer problems arise. They are also better trained for the flexibility and skills needed with lean (e.g., problem solving, maintenance), and they enjoy the growth they experience in their jobs. All this translates into better, more productive work.

5. *Uncovering problems.* One of the unexpected benefits is the greater visibility to problems that lean allows, if management is willing to capitalize on the opportunity to fix these problems. In trying to speed up a process, all types of difficulties are uncovered and most of them are various forms of waste, so not only is response time improved but cost is also.

LEAN SIX SIGMA

Earlier in the chapter it was mentioned that a current trend is for organizations to merge their lean and Six Sigma initiatives. Xerox calls its merged program Lean Six Sigma while Honeywell refers to its program as Six Sigma Plus. Merging Six Sigma and lean makes sense because being competitive in today's environment requires processes that are both efficient and consistent. An organization that only focuses on the elimination of waste through lean and does not also address the consistency of its processes will be missing significant opportunities to enhance the effectiveness of its processes. Likewise, focusing only on reducing the variation inherent in an inconsistent process and not simultaneously addressing ways to make it more efficient also limits the overall effectiveness of the process.

However, beyond simply addressing different aspects of process effectiveness, Six Sigma and lean have proven to be excellent complements to one another. For example, most of the tools associated with lean are more applicable to the improve and control phases of DMAIC. Thus, merging lean with Six Sigma provides lean practitioners with the disciplined and structured DMAIC approach and a richer set of tools, particularly those associated with the define, measure, and analyze phases. Likewise, the lean tools nicely complement the traditional Six Sigma tools and methodologies.

A project completed at one of Honeywell's European chemical plants provides an excellent illustration of the complementary nature of lean and Six Sigma. The impetus for the project was the fact that the operation was losing almost 1 million dollars per year. To turn around the operation it was determined that capacity needed to be doubled while prices needed to be reduced by 50 percent.

The project team began by analyzing a detailed process map and categorizing the steps in the process as value adding or nonvalue adding activities. Through this analysis the team also discovered that each stage in the process was a bottleneck. Using the detailed process map, the team determined whether a quality requirement or an issue related to process flow was the cause of the bottleneck. As it turned out, one bottleneck was the result of a quality issue and the bottlenecks at the other four stages were caused by issues related to process flow.

To resolve the bottleneck caused by quality issues, the team relied on traditional Six Sigma tools including Measurement Systems Analysis, process mapping, FMEA, cause and effect matrices, and design of experiments (see Chapter 4 for a discussion of these tools). To address the bottlenecks that resulted from process flow issues, lean tools were used to eliminate the nonvalue-adding steps such as unnecessary product movements and material handling. By utilizing both lean and Six Sigma tools, the team was able to meet the goal of doubling capacity and reducing costs by 50 percent. And the profit of the operation increased from losing almost 1 million dollars annually to generating a profit of 3.4 million dollars annually. Of course the similarity between the 3.4 million dollars in annual profit is just a coincidence with Six Sigma's goal of achieving no more than 3.4 defects per million opportunities. Or is it?

EXPAND YOUR UNDERSTANDING

1. In your opinion, does it make more sense for an organization to merge its lean and Six Sigma programs or keep them separate?

2. Describe how trying to please every customer turns into a "trap" for traditional production. Aren't customization and multiple options the way of the future, particularly for differing national tastes and preferences?

3. The Japanese say that "a defect is a treasure." What way do they mean, and how does this relate to lean?

4. How smooth is a production flow where every item requires a setup? Wouldn't flows be smoother with long runs where no setups were required for days?

5. Does the theory of constraints apply to services as well as to products?

6. One JIT consultant suggests that managers implement JIT by just removing inventories from the floor. What is likely to happen if they do this? What would the Japanese do?

7. With single-sourcing, how does the firm protect itself from price gouging? From strikes or interruptions to supply?

8. How might lean apply to a service like an airline? A retailer? A university?

9. American managers hate to see high-paid workers sitting idle, even maintenance employees. What is the alternative?

10. The theory of constraints distinguishes between process batches and transfer batches. It also recommends that process batches vary according to the economics of efficiency at each stage of production. Considering the effects of order size and size of the preceding process batch, how then should transfer batches be determined?

11. Consider a service you are familiar with. List examples for each of the seven categories of waste for the service.

12. In identifying the value stream, why is it important to go beyond the boundaries of the organization of interest?

APPLY YOUR UNDERSTANDING
J. Galt Lock Ltd.

J. Galt Lock Ltd., located in Sydney, Australia, produces a line of door locksets and hardware for the residential, light commercial, and retail markets. The company's single plant is just over 200,000 square feet and is organized into the following functional departments: screw machines, presses, machining, maintenance, tool and dies, latches, plating, buffing, subassembly, and final assembly. The company employs approximately 375 people, 290 of whom are hourly workers. The largest category of employees—assemblers—accounts for two-thirds of the workforce.

The company uses a proprietary planning and scheduling system that uses both an AS/400 minicomputer and spreadsheet analysis performed on a microcomputer to determine production and purchasing requirements. At any given time, there are 1500 to 3000 open work orders on the shop floor. The average lot size is 50,000 parts, but for some products the size is as high as 250,000 parts.

The planning system creates work orders for each part number in the bills of materials, which are delivered to the various departments. Department supervisors determine the order in which to process the jobs, since the system does not prioritize the work orders. A variety of scheduling methods are used throughout the plant, including kanbans, work orders, and expediters; however, the use of these different methods often creates problems. For example, one production manager commented that although a "kanban pull scheduling system is being used between subassembly and final assembly, frequently the right card is not used at the right time, the correct quantity is not always produced, and there are no predetermined schedules and paths for the pickup and delivery of parts." In fact, it was discovered that work orders were often being superseded by expediters and supervisors, large lag times existed between the decision to produce a batch and the start of actual production, and suppliers were not being included in the "information pipeline." One production supervisor commented:

We routinely abort the plans generated by our formal planning system because we figure out other ways of pushing product. Although we use Kanban systems in two areas of the plant, in reality everything here is a push system. Everything is based on inventory levels and/or incoming customer orders. We push not just the customer order but all the raw materials and everything that is associated with the product being assembled.

In an effort to improve its operations, Galt Lock hired a consulting company. The consultant determined that 36 percent of the floor space was being used to hold inventory, 25 percent was for work centers, 14 percent for aisles, 7 percent for offices, and 18 percent for nonvalue-adding activities. The production manager commented:

We have an entire department that is dedicated to inventory storage consisting of 10 to 11 aisles of parts. What is bad is that we have all these parts, and none of them are the right ones. Lots of parts, and we still can't build.

The consultant also determined that the upstream "supplying" work centers were often far from the downstream "using" work centers, material flows were discontinuous as the parts were picked up and set down numerous times, and workers and supervisors often spent a considerable amount of time hunting for parts. The production manager commented:

Work-in-process is everywhere. You can find work-in-process at every one of the stations on the shop floor. It is extremely difficult to find materials on the shop floor because of the tremendous amount of inventory on the shop floor. It is also very difficult to tell at what state a customer order is in or the material necessary to make that customer order, because we have such long runs of components and subassemblies.

The plant manager commented:

My biggest concern is consistent delivery to customers. We just started monitoring on-time delivery performance, and it was the first time that measurement had ever been used at this operation. We found out how poorly we are actually doing. It is a matter of routinely trying to chase things down in the factory that will complete customer orders. The challenge of more consistent delivery is compounded by the fact that we have to respond much faster. Our customers used to give us three to six weeks of lead time, but now the big retailers we are starting to deal with give us only two or three days. And if we don't get it out in that short period of time, we lose the customer.

Questions

1. Evaluate and critique the existing operation and the management of J. Galt Lock.
2. How applicable is JIT to a situation like this? Would converting from a functional layout to a cellular layout facilitate the implementation of JIT?
3. Where could the principles of lean production be of value to J. Galt Lock?

EXERCISES

1. The time between patient arrivals to the blood drawing unit of a medical lab averages 2 minutes. The lab is staffed with two nurses that actually draw the patients' blood. The nurses work from 9:00 A.M. to 5:30 P.M. and get two 10-minute breaks and a half-hour for lunch. What is the takt time for drawing patient blood?

2. Referring to Exercise 1, assume that additional analysis was performed and it was determined that an average of 255 patients (with a standard deviation of 30) requiring blood work come to the lab each day. It was further determined that the duration of the nurses' breaks ranged between 9 to 13.5 minutes, with all times in the range equally likely and that the time taken for lunch ranged between 28 minutes and 34 minutes, again with all times in the range equally likely. Using Crystal Ball or another simulation package, develop a

distribution for the takt time assuming that the number of patients that arrive on a given day is normally distributed. What are the managerial implications of your analysis?

3. The high-speed copier of a printing and document services firm is available 95% of the operating hours. The copier is operated at a rate of three copies per second, although it was designed to make four copies per second. Data suggest that about 3 percent of the copied pages must be scrapped and recopied. What is the overall equipment effectiveness of the high-speed copier?

4. Referring to Exercise 3, assume that the copier availability follows a triangular distribution and that sometimes the copier is available for as few as 2 hours in a 12-hour day, is typically available 10 hours a day, and occasionally is available all 12 hours. Further assume that the rate the copier operates varies based on the type of job, from two copies per second to four copies per second with all rates in this range equally likely. Finally, assume that the scrap rate is normally distributed with a mean of 3 percent and standard deviation of 0.7 percent. Using Crystal Ball or another simulation package, develop the distribution for the copier's overall equipment effectiveness. What are the managerial implications of your analysis?

BIBLIOGRAPHY

Connolly, C. "Hospital takes Page from Toyota," *The Washington Post,* (January 3, 2005): www.msnbc.msn.com/id/8079313/.

DeBusk, C., and A. Rangel Jr. "Creating a Lean Six Sigma Hospital Process," healthcare.isixsigma.com, (May 30, 2005).

Fornari, A., and S. Maszle "Lean Six Sigma Leads Xerox," *Six Sigma Forum Magazine* (August 2004): pp. 11–16.

George, M. *Lean Six Sigma: Combining Six Sigma Quality with Lean Production Speed.* New York: McGraw Hill, 2002.

Goldratt, E. M. *Theory of Constraints,* 2nd rev. ed. Croton-on-Hudson: North River Press, 1990.

Hill, W. J., and W. Kearney "The Honeywell Experience," *Six Sigma Forum Magazine* (February 2003): pp. 34–37.

Mascitelli, R. "Lean Thinking: It's about Efficient Value Creation." *Target* (Second Quarter 2000): 22–26.

Monden, Y. *Toyota Production System: An Integrated Approach to Just-in-Time.* Atlanta, GA: Institute of Industrial Engineers, 1998.

Pyzdek, T. *The Six Sigma Handbook.* New York: McGraw-Hill, 2003.

Schniederjans, M. *Topics in Just-in-Time Management.* Boston: Allyn & Bacon, 1993.

Schonberger, R. *World Class Manufacturing: The Next Decade: Building Power, Strength, and Value.* New York: Free Press, 1996.

Snee, R. D., When Worlds Collide: Lean and Six Sigma," *Quality Progress,* September 2005: 63–66.

Tonkin, L. "System Sensor's Lean Journey." *Target* (Second Quarter 2002): 44–47.

White, R. E., J. N. Pearson, and J. R. Wilson. "JIT Manufacturing: A Survey of Implementations in Small and Large U.S. Manufacturers." *Management Science,* 45 (January 1999): 1–15.

Womack, J. "Lean Thinking for Process Management," Presented at the Decision Sciences Institute Annual Meeting, November 22, 2004.

Womack, J., and D. Jones. *Lean Thinking: Banish Waste and Create Wealth in Your Corporation.* New York: Simon & Schuster, 2003.

Wortman, B., W. R. Richardson, G. Gee, M. Williams, T. Pearson, F. Bensley, J. P. Patel, J. DeSimone, and D. R. Carlson, CSSBB Primer (West Terre Haute, IN: Quality Council of Indiana, 2001).

Zipkin, P. H., *Foundations of Inventory Management.* New York: Irwin/McGraw-Hill, 2000.

CHAPTER 6

Project Management and the Transformation System

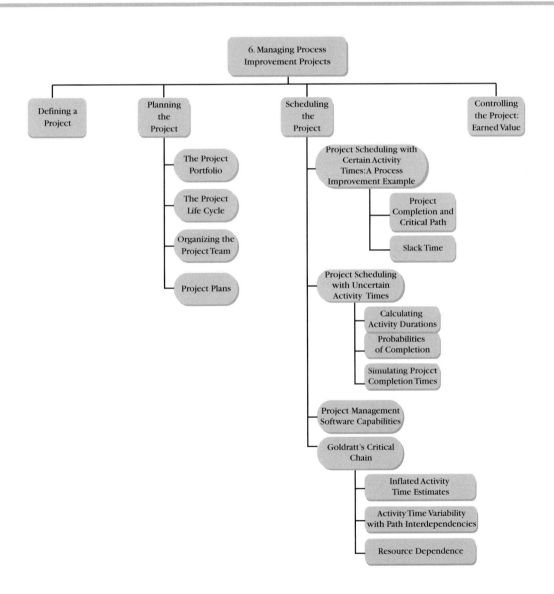

CHAPTER IN PERSPECTIVE

In this chapter, we shift our attention to the management of projects. We use a process improvement project as an example, but projects are used in all kinds of organizations for every conceivable purpose. They range from simple combinations of tactical tasks to strategic organizational change, and from setting up a party to putting a person on the moon. The chapter begins with a discussion of the crucial topics of project selection, project planning, and organizing the project team. We then move on to an explanation of some project-scheduling techniques, showing some typical project management software printouts that are available to project managers. The chapter continues with a discussion of controlling project cost and performance, primarily through the use of "earned value," and then concludes with a brief description of Goldratt's "critical chain."

INTRODUCTION

- Hewlett-Packard found itself in the common position of having more ongoing projects than it could effectively control and came up with a process dubbed the HP Project Management Initiative. The goal of the "Initiative" was to develop an "aggregate project plan," or map, to help them distinguish between projects that contributed to their strategic goals and the great mass of others that did not. This map illustrated on a grid the various types of projects that were ongoing, the degree of change each involved in terms of products and processes, the resource requirements of each project, and the history of the projects. At one extreme were the R&D or "blue sky" projects that could pay off in the distant future, and at the other extreme were the incremental variants on existing projects. By intensely scrutinizing all the projects and taking into consideration the gaps and excesses on their aggregate project plan, HP was able to prioritize the projects and concentrate on those that made the greatest contribution to their strategic goals for the least resource use. The Initiative helped one organization systematically reduce 120 projects down to 30, and another organization from 50 to 17, thereby increasing the chances of success for the most important projects (Englund and Graham 1999).

- One day, Melvin Wilson was simply a marketing manager for little 1250-employee Mississippi Power in Gulfport, Mississippi. But the next day, after Hurricane Katrina hit New Orleans and Gulfport, he was the firm's "Director of Storm Logistics," responsible for 11,000 repairmen with a goal of restoring power to 195,000 customers within 12 days. Although Mississippi Power's primary storm center at headquarters was knocked out, they had a backup storm center 5 miles inland. However, when Wilson got there, the cars were floating in the parking lot, so he moved his group in charge to a third location, an old service office without electricity or running water. In spite of the phone lines being down, the group managed to get word of their needs to the outside world and within days, 11,000 repairmen from 24 states and Canada came to help. To support the 11,000 workers, the group needed housing, beds, food, clean water, showers, laundry, bulldozers, 5000 trucks, 140,000 gallons of fuel each day, 8000 tetanus shots, and hundreds of other such items. Directing such a massive project as the restoration of power was far beyond the experience of little Mississippi Power's group, but they succeeded, and the power was restored to every customer who could handle it within 12 days (Cauchon 2005).

- In March 2003, the United Kingdom's Child Support Agency (CSA) started using their new $860 million software system for receiving and disbursing child support payments. However, by the end of 2004, only about 12 percent of all applications had received payments, and even those took about three times longer to process than they were supposed to take. CSA thus threatened to scrap the entire system and withhold $2 million/month in service payments to the software vendor. The problem was thought to be due to both scope creep and the lack of a risk management strategy. The vendor claimed that the project was disrupted constantly by CSA's 2500 change requests, while CSA maintained there were only 50, but the contract did not include a scope management plan to help define what constituted a scope change request. And the lack of a risk management strategy resulted in no contingency or fallback plans in case of trouble, so when project delays surfaced and inadequate training became apparent, there was no way to recover (Project Management Institute 2005).

- To speed passengers to Shanghai's new international airport, China built a magnetic levitation (maglev) train that runs every 10 minutes from Shanghai's business center to the Pudong International Airport. Reaching speeds over 300 miles an hour, it whisks people to the airport 20 miles away in less than 8 minutes. However, according to the vice-director of the train company, "We are not lucky with ticket sales." since the trains are virtually empty. The reason is because to meet the project's time deadline and budget, the train station was located 6 miles outside the city center, requiring lengthy public transportation to get there. So in spite of the technical, budget, and timing success of the project, it failed to meet the needs of the passengers. China is currently investigating extending the line to the downtown area, but that will be a much more expensive and time-consuming project (Project Management Institute 2004a).

- Boston's "Big Dig" highway/tunnel project is considered one of the largest, most complex, and technologically challenging highway projects in U.S. history. In early 2003, Boston's "Big Dig," originally expected to cost less than $3 billion, was declared complete, after two decades and over $14 billion for planning and construction. This project was clearly one that offered little value to the city if it wasn't completed, so it continued far past what planners thought was a worthwhile investment, primarily because the federal government was paying 85 percent of its cost. With an estimated benefit of $500 million per year in reduced congestion, pollution, accidents, fuel costs, and lateness, but a total investment cost of $14.6 billion (a 470 percent cost overrun), it is expected to take 78 years to pay its costs back. The overrun is attributed to two major factors (1) A major underestimate of the initial project scope, typical of government projects; and (2) lack of control, particularly costs, including conflicts of interest between the public and private sectors. One clear lesson from the project has been that unless the state and local governments are required to pay at least half the cost of these megaprojects, there won't be serious local deliberation of their pros and cons (Abrams 2003, Project Management Institute 2004b).

From the above examples, we see the ubiquitous role of project management in all types of organizations and in all countries. And we see how some tools can help in the management and control of projects, and what can go wrong when such management is missing. Project management is concerned with managing organizational activities that result in some particular, desired output. Although we have titled this chapter Managing Process Improvement Projects, it should be clear that this is only one use among many for project management. For example, in the traditional functional organization, a product development team with representatives from production, finance, marketing, and engineering can be assembled to ensure that new product designs simultaneously meet the requirements of each area. Ensuring that each area's requirements are being met as the new design is developed reduces the likelihood that costly changes will have to be made later in the process. The result is that new products can be developed faster and less expensively, thereby enhancing the firm's overall responsiveness. Perhaps a better product is developed as well, owing to the synergy of including a variety of different perspectives earlier in the design process.

In this chapter, we describe the many activities required in the successful management of projects. We start with the definition of a project and why project management is different from managing functional activities. We then move into the project life cycle activities starting with planning the project, which includes an understanding of the role of the project in the organization's strategy. We next describe the two major types of project life cycles and why it is important to be able to tell which is applicable for the project at hand. This is then followed by a discussion about organizing the project team and the various techniques available to the project manager for planning the project activities. Following this, we discuss the major topics of scheduling the project and determining the probability of completing it by its due date. In the process, we describe the capabilities and outputs of some project management software packages. Moving along the project life cycle, we then address the topics of controlling the project's cost and performance. The chapter concludes with a discussion of the "critical chain" concept of project management.

DEFINING A PROJECT

Up to this point, you might not have realized that projects are actually a special type of process. As described in Chapter 2, the term *process* refers to a set of activities that, taken together, creates something of value to customers. Typically, the term process is used to refer to a set of activities that are routinely repeated, such as processing insurance forms, handling customers' complaints, and assembling an

MP3 player. The term *project* also refers to a set of activities that, taken together, produces a valued output. However, unlike a typical process, each project is unique and has a clear beginning and end. Therefore, projects are processes that are performed infrequently and ad hoc, with a clear specification of the desired objective.

There are two other typical characteristics of projects which are less obvious. One is that there is a limited budget to attain the unique desired objective. The second is that the objective is extremely important to the organization. If neither of these two characteristics were true, it would be foolish to designate a *special* project team to accomplish the project since, with an unlimited budget, it could be done by regular functional departmental employees doing their routine work.

In Chapter 2, the project form of the transformation process was briefly described. The choice of the project form usually indicates the importance of the project objective to the organization, and the many other *stakeholders* such as the client, subcontractors, consultants, the project team, the project management office, the government (sometimes), the community, and possibly others. Thus, top-grade resources, including staff, are often made available for project operations. As a result, project organizations become professionalized and are often managed on that basis. That is, minimal supervision is exercised, administrative routine is minimized, and the project team professionals are charged with solving the problem and obtaining the required results (cost, performance, deadline). The project team is then given the privacy and freedom to decide *how* to solve the problem.

Projects frequently require different emphases during their life cycle. For example, technical performance may be crucial at the beginning, cost overruns in the middle, and on-time completion at the end. The flexibility of making spur-of-the-moment changes in emphasis by trading off one criterion for another is basic to the project design form. This ability results from the close contact of the project manager with the technical staff—there are few, if any, "middle managers."

Following are some examples of projects:

- Constructing highways, bridges, tunnels, and dams
- Building ships, planes, and rockets, or a doghouse
- Erecting skyscrapers, steel mills, homes, and processing plants
- Locating and laying out amusement parks, camping grounds, and refuges
- Organizing conferences, banquets, conventions, and weddings
- Managing R&D projects such as the Manhattan Project (which developed the atomic bomb)
- Running political campaigns, war operations, advertising campaigns, or fire-fighting operations
- Chairing ad hoc task forces, overseeing planning for government agencies, or conducting corporate audits
- Converting from one computer system to another

As may be noticed in this list, the number of project operations is growing in our economy, probably at about the same rate as services (which many of them are). Some of the reasons for this growth in project operations are as follows:

1. *More sophisticated technology.* An outgrowth of our information age, and its technology, has been increased public awareness of project operations (e.g., Project Apollo) and interest in using the project form to achieve society's goals (Project Head Start).

2. *Better-educated citizens.* People are more aware of the world around them, and of techniques (such as project management) for achieving their objectives.

3. *More leisure time.* People have the time available to follow, and even participate in, projects.

4. *Increased accountability.* Society as a whole has increased its emphasis on the attainment of objectives (affirmative action, environmental protection, better fuel economy) and the evaluation of activities leading toward those objectives.

5. *Higher productivity.* People and organizations are involved in more activities, and are more productive in those activities, than ever before.

6. *Faster response to clients.* Today's intense competition has escalated the importance of quick response to clients' needs, and projects are often more responsive and flexible than bureaucracies or functionally organized firms.

7. *Greater customization for clients.* Intense competition has also increased the importance of better meeting the client's unique needs in terms of both the service and the facilitating good. The project form of organizing is more likely to meet this need.

In physical project operations, such as bridge construction, most of the *production* per se is completed elsewhere and brought to the project area at the proper time. As a result, a great many project activities are *assembly* operations. The project design form concentrates resources on the achievement of specific objectives primarily through proper *scheduling* and *control* of activities, many of which are simultaneous. Some of the scheduling considerations in project management are knowing what activities must be completed and in what order, how long they will take, when to increase and decrease the labor force, and when to order materials so that they will not arrive too early (thus requiring storage and being in the way) or too late (thus delaying the project). The control activities include anticipating what can and might go wrong, knowing what resources can be shifted among activities to keep the project on schedule, and so forth.

𝒫LANNING THE PROJECT

In this section, we focus in detail on the planning of projects. In the area of project management, planning is probably the single most important element in the success of the project and considerable research has been done on the topic. We start with the role of the organization's many projects in achieving its strategy, known as the organization's **project portfolio**. This portfolio evolves over time since projects have a finite life cycle, as discussed in the next subsection. Following this, we discuss the project team and its tie to the parent organization. Last, we describe the actual project planning tools.

The Project Portfolio

The long-term purpose of projects in the organization is to ultimately achieve the organization's goals. This tie is accomplished through the project portfolio, also known as the organization's **aggregate project plan**. In making project selection decisions, it is vital to consider the interactions among various projects and to manage the projects as a set. This is in stark contrast to the common practice of simply setting a project budget and specified return on investment (ROI) hurdle rate, then funding projects until either the budget or supply of acceptable projects is exhausted. Organizations that fund all projects that meet their ROI criterion typically end up with significantly more ongoing projects than they can competently manage and thus their contribution to the organization's long-term goals can be lost. Because ROI is an insufficient selection criterion, the set of projects chosen may not be close to an optimal portfolio for achieving their purpose.

In an attempt to better tie the firm's product development projects to their strategic objectives, Professors Wheelwright and Clark (1992) of the Harvard Business School developed a framework for categorizing projects that they call the Aggregate Project Plan. The purpose of the framework is to illustrate the *distribution* of all the organization's product/service design projects across a variety of measures such as resource demands, innovativeness, product lines, time, and project type. It is important to point out, however, that it is typically not a single project that determines the organization's long-run success, but rather the set of research projects pursued by the organization, or its **project portfolio**. Therefore, in making project selection decisions, it is vital to consider the interactions among various projects and to manage the projects as a set in order to achieve the organization's strategic objectives.

Using this framework, output development projects are categorized along two dimensions: (1) the extent of changes made to the output and (2) the degree of process change. Based on these two dimensions, projects can then be categorized into the following four categories as shown in Figure 6.1:

1. **Derivative projects.** Derivative projects seek to make incremental improvements in the output and/or process. Projects that seek to reduce the output's cost or make minor product line extensions exemplify these types of projects. Developing a stripped down version of a notebook computer or adding a new menu item at a fast-food restaurant would qualify as derivative projects. This category accounts for a large majority of all innovations.

2. **Breakthrough projects.** These projects are at the opposite end of the continuum from derivative projects and typically seek the development of a new generation of outputs. A computer that operated by voice recognition as opposed to a keyboard and mouse, or an entirely online grocery store is an example of a breakthrough project.

3. **Platform projects.** Platform projects fall between derivative and breakthrough projects. In general, the result of these projects is an output that can serve as the *platform* for an entire line of new outputs. A key difference between platform projects and breakthrough projects is that platform projects stick with existing technology. As an example, the development of an ultrathin netbook computer would qualify as a platform project. If this computer succeeds, it could serve as the basis for a number of derivative

projects focusing on cost improvement and the development of other computer models with different features.

4. *R&D projects.* R&D projects entail working with basic technology to develop new knowledge. Depending on its focus, an R&D project might lead to breakthrough, platform, or derivative innovations.

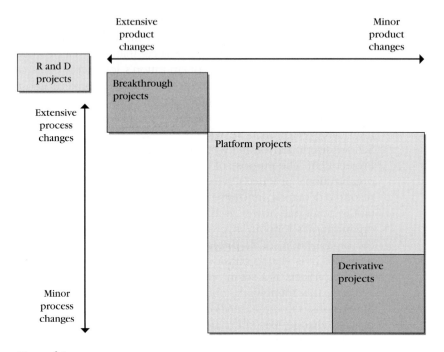

Figure 6.1   The aggregate project plan.

Use of the aggregate project plan requires that all projects be identified and plotted. The size of the points plotted for each project should be proportional to the amount of resources the project will require. In Figure 6.2, we have used different shapes to indicate different types of projects. Internal projects are plotted using circles while projects pursued as part of a strategic alliance with other firms are plotted using squares.

There are a number of ways the aggregate project plan can be used. The identification of gaps in the types of projects being undertaken is probably most important. For example, are the types of projects undertaken too heavily skewed toward derivative type projects? This might indicate an inadequate consideration of the firm's long-run competitive position. Also, the aggregate project plan facilitates evaluation of the resource commitments of the ongoing as well as proposed projects. Finally, this framework can serve as a model for employee development. New employees can be initially assigned to a team working on a derivative project. After gaining experience, employees can be assigned to a platform project, then assigned to *manage* a derivative project. As managerial skill accumulates, the employee will qualify for larger and more valuable projects. Of course, we must remember that the

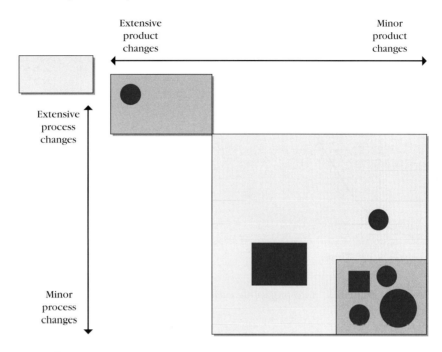

Figure 6.2 An example aggregate project plan.

fundamental purpose of this entire process is to ensure that the set of projects accurately reflects the organization's strategic goals and objectives.

The Project Life Cycle

It has been found, for example, that progress in a project is rarely uniform, but instead often follows one of two common forms, as shown in Figure 6.3. In the stretched-S life cycle form, illustrated in Figure 6.3*a*, when the project is initiated, progress is slow as responsibilities are assigned and organization takes place. But the project gathers speed during the implementation stage, and much progress is made. As the end of the project draws near, the more difficult tasks that were postponed earlier must now be completed, yet people are being drawn off the project and activity is "winding down," so the end keeps slipping out of reach.

In the exponential form, illustrated in Figure 6.3*b*, after the project is initiated there is continuous activity on numerous aspects of the project, but until all the elemental parts come together at the end, there is no final output. This is typical of projects that require final assembly of components to produce the whole (like a car), or goods (like a cake, which is only glop until it is baked in the oven). It is especially typical of office and other such service work where the final output is a life insurance policy, or ad piece, or perhaps even an MBA degree. Without that last signature, or piece of paper, or earned credit, there is virtually no product. (However, if a student is auditing courses with the goal of understanding rather than getting a degree, the progress toward their goal may indeed be linear with every day they spend in class.)

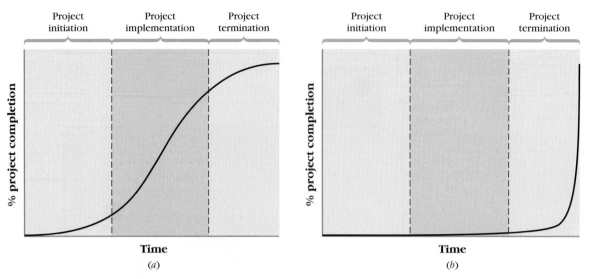

Figure 6.3 Two project life cycles. (*a*) Stretched-S. (*b*) Exponential.

The reason it is important to contrast these two forms, besides pointing out their difference in managerial needs, is that during the budgeting stage, if there is a flat across-the-board budget cut of, say, 10 percent and the project is of the stretched-S form, then not being able to spend that last 10 percent of the budget is of no urgent matter, since probably 97 percent of the benefits will be achieved anyway. However, if the project is of the exponential form, then missing the last 10 percent is catastrophic because this is where all the value is attained. Another perspective on the same issue is the effect of early termination of the project. Terminating the stretched-S form early will have negligible impact, but terminating the exponential form will be a complete disaster. It is imperative the project manager and top management know which type of project they are working with before taking such actions.

Organizing the Project Team

Projects can be organized in any of a number of ways. There is the ad hoc project form in a functional organization that reports to a senior executive. And there are projects that are just another activity in a project organization that is completely organized in terms of projects. Management consulting firms typify project organizations. There are matrix organizations where projects have both a functional and a program superior. Combinations of these forms are also common, such as the "weak" or functional matrix, and the "strong" or project matrix. Each of these has its own advantages and disadvantages, and what works the best depends largely on the circumstances of the organization and the reason it started a project.

Regardless of the form of the project, a team will be required to run the project. Some members of the team may be directly assigned to the project manager for the duration, while others may have only partial responsibilities for the project and still report to their functional superior. There are three types of team members who should report directly to the project manager (PM), however:

- Those who will be having a long-term relationship with the project
- Those with whom the PM will need to communicate closely or continuously
- Those with rare skills necessary to project success

Yet, even if these people report to the PM, it is still not common for the PM to have the authority to reward these people with pay bonuses, extra vacation, or other such personnel matters—that authority normally still resides with the functional manager. Thus, there are not a lot of incentives the PM can give people for working hard on the project. The main ones are the fun and excitement of the challenge, and doing something that will be important to the organization.

With the pressures that tend to gravitate toward such important and high-profile projects, it may be assumed that there is also a lot of opportunity for conflict to arise. This is true, and not only between the PM and other organizational units, but even between members of the project team. According to Thamhain and Wilemon (1975), at project formation the main sources of conflict were priorities and procedures. As the project got under way, priorities and schedules became the main points of conflict. During the main implementation stage, conflict shifted to technical issues and schedules. But toward the end of the project when timing was becoming crucial, only schedules were the source of conflict. Knowing when to expect trouble, and what kinds, throughout the project can help the PM keep peace within the project team and facilitate smooth project progress.

Project Plans

The initiation of a project should in most cases include the development of some level of **project charter** (also known as the *project plan*), unless the project is highly routine. The elements that constitute the project plan and form the basis for more detailed planning of the budgets, schedules, work plan, and general management of the project are described below. It should be noted that the process of developing the project charter varies from organization to organization, but any project charter should contain some level of information regarding the following elements.

- **Overview** This is a short summary of what the client expects from the project. It is directed to top management and contains a statement of the goals of the project, a brief explanation of their relationship to the firm's objectives, a description of the managerial structure that will be used for the project, and a list of the major milestones in the project schedule.

- **Goals, or Scope** This contains a more detailed statement of the general goals noted in the overview section and the specific requirements of the stakeholders, sponsor, and client that must be satisfactorily completed.

- **Business Case** This describes the justification for the project in terms of the benefits to the project organization. It includes the expected profits and ROI (return on investment) of course, but also other gains such as experience, establishing a strong track record, working with an important client, and so on, which may be more important than profits.

- **General Approach** This describes both the managerial and the technical approaches to the work, such as whether the project is an extension of work done by the company for an earlier project and whether there are any deviations from routine procedure—for instance, the use of subcontractors for some parts of the work.

- **Contractual Aspects** This includes a complete list and description of all reporting requirements, customer-supplied resources, liaison arrangements, etc., as well as the technical deliverables and their specifications, delivery schedules, and the procedures for changing any of the above.

- **Schedule and Milestones** This outlines the schedule and lists milestone events. Each task is listed, and the estimated time for each task should be obtained from those who will do the work. The project master schedule is constructed from these inputs.

- **Resources** There are two primary aspects to be considered here. The first is the *project budget*. Both capital and expense requirements are detailed by task. Second, cost monitoring and control procedures should be described.

- **Personnel** This lists both who must be involved in the review and approval process as well as the time-phased personnel requirements of the project, that is, the *team* and other involved departments. If known, the name and authority level of the project manager should also be included here. Special skills, types of training needed, possible recruiting problems, legal or policy restrictions on work force composition, and any other special requirements, such as security clearances, should be noted. Time-phasing the personnel needs makes clear to management and other departments when the various types of contributors are needed and in what numbers.

- **Risk Management Plan** This covers potential problems that could affect the project. One or more issues such as subcontractor default, unexpected technical breakthroughs, strikes, hurricanes, new markets for our technology, tight deadlines and budgets, and sudden moves by a competitor are certain to occur—the only uncertainties are which, when, and their impact. Plans to deal with unfavorable (or favorable) contingencies should be developed early in the project's life.

- **Evaluation Method** Every project should be evaluated against standards and by methods established at the project's inception. This includes a brief description of the procedures to be followed in monitoring, collecting, storing, and evaluating the history of the project.

Almost by definition, a project is an attempt to meet specified performance or "scope" requirements by a specific deadline within a limited budget. These objectives are generally illustrated in Figure 6.4. The Project Plan described above lays out these three objectives in detail but the task for the manager is to "make it happen."

To achieve these three project objectives, one of the project manager's first responsibilities is to define all the tasks in as much detail as possible so that they can be scheduled and costed out, and responsibility can be assigned. This set of task descriptions is called the **work breakdown structure** (WBS), and it provides the inputs for the **project schedule** (usually put into a format known as the *project Gantt chart*) and the linear responsibility chart that depicts the tasks of those outside the project team but with responsibilities related to the project. The linear responsibility chart is similar to a RACI matrix, which stands for the four main project responsibilities: Responsible (for a task), Approval, Consult (or coordinate for support), and Inform (notify). The main difference is that the letters R, A, C, and I are put in

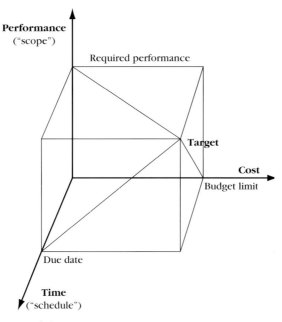

Figure 6.4   Three project objectives. Reprinted with permission from J. Meredith and S. J. Mantel, Jr., *Project Management: A Managerial Approach*, 7th ed. New York: Wiley 2009.

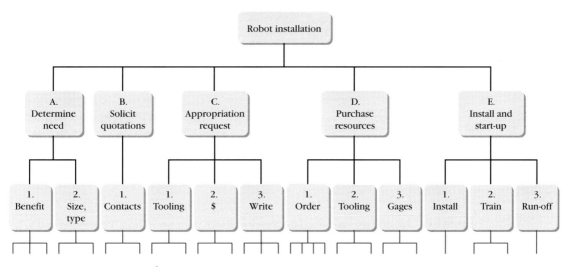

Figure 6.5   Work breakdown structure.

place of the symbols in a RACI matrix, and a linear responsibility chart may have other personnel involvement included as well such as "initiate" or "supervise."

A typical WBS and project schedule are illustrated in Figures 6.5 and 6.6 for a project installing robots on a manufacturing assembly line. Milestone, commitment, and completion points are shown, and actual progress is graphed. The last status update shows that the project is a month behind schedule. Figure 6.7 illustrates the linear responsibility chart or RACI matrix for the robot project.

The scheduling of project activities is highly complex because of (1) the number of activities required, (2) the precedence relationships among the activities, and

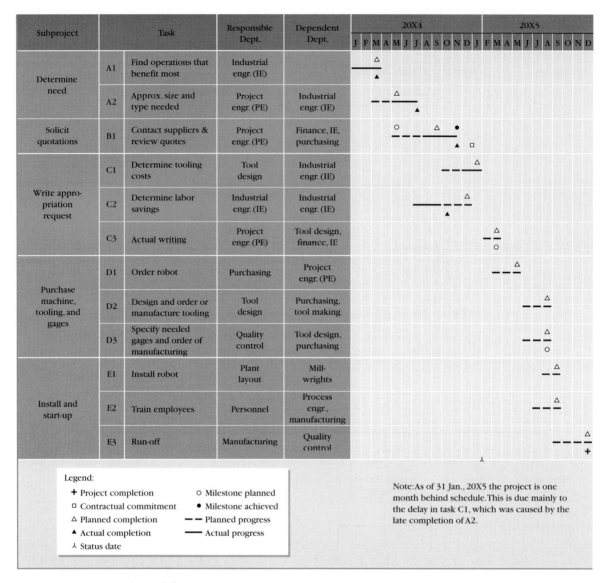

Figure 6.6   Project baseline schedule. Reprinted with permission from J. Meredith and S. J. Mantel, Jr., *Project Management: A Managerial Approach*, 7th ed. Hoboken, NJ: Wiley 2009.

(3) the limited time of the project. Project scheduling is similar to the scheduling discussed earlier in some ways but still differs significantly. For example, the basic network approaches—***program evaluation and review technique*** (PERT) and ***critical path method*** (CPM)—are based on variations of the Gantt chart. Figure 6.6 is a project Gantt chart but is inadequate for scheduling the multitude of subtasks that compose, for example, task A1. That is, a project schedule has to handle an enormous number of different activities, which must be coordinated in such a way that the subsequent activities can take place and the entire project (job) can be completed by the due date.

WBS		Responsiblity				Field Oper.	
Subproject	Task	Project Office				Field Manager	
		Project Manager	Contract Admin.	Project Eng.	Inductrial Eng.		
Determine need	A1	A		C	R		
	A2	I	A	R	C		
Solicit quotations	B1	A	I	R		C	
Writ approp. request.	C1	I	R	A	C		
	C2		C	A	R		
	C3	C	I	R		I	
"	"						
"	"						
"	"						

Legend:
R Responsible
A Approval
C Consult
I Inform

Figure 6.7 Linear responsibility chart or RACI matrix. Reprinted with permission from J. Meredith and S. J. Mantel, Jr., *Project Management: A Managerial Approach*, 7th ed. Hoboken, NJ: Wiley 2009.

The scheduling procedure for project operations must be able not only to identify and handle the variety of tasks that must be done, but also to handle their time sequencing. In addition, it must be able to integrate the performance and timing of all the tasks with the project as a whole so that control can be exercised, for example, by shifting resources from operations with slack (permissible slippage) to other operations whose delay might threaten the project's timely completion. The tasks involved in planning and scheduling project operations are:

- *Planning.* Determining what must be done and which tasks must *precede* others
- *Scheduling.* Determining *when* the tasks must be completed; when they *can* and when they *must* be started; which tasks are *critical* to the timely completion of the project; and which tasks have *slack* in their timing and how much

SCHEDULING THE PROJECT

The project scheduling process is based on the activities that must be conducted to achieve the project's goals, the length of time each requires, and the order in which they must be completed. If a number of similar projects must be conducted, sometimes these activities can be structured generically to apply equally well to all the projects.

Two primary techniques have been developed to plan projects consisting of ordered activities: PERT and CPM. Although PERT and CPM originally had some differences in the way activities were determined and laid out, many current approaches to project scheduling minimize these differences and present an integrated view, as we will see here. It will be helpful to define some terms first.

- *Activity.* One of the project operations, or tasks; an activity requires resources and takes some amount of time to complete.
- *Event.* Completion of an activity, or series of activities, at a particular point in time.
- *Network.* The set of all project activities graphically interrelated through precedence relationships. In this text, boxes (called *nodes*) represent activities and arrows between the boxes represent precedence. (This is typical of the CPM approach; in PERT the arrows represent activities.)
- *Path.* A series of connected activities from the start to the finish of the project.
- *Critical path.* Any path that if delayed will delay the completion of the entire project.
- *Critical activities.* The activities on the critical path or paths.

We next illustrate the process of scheduling with a Six Sigma process improvement project example. We use the DMAIC approach (see Chapter 4) to improve a bank's process for handling mortgage refinancing applications.

Project Scheduling with Certain Activity Times: A Process Improvement Example

The primary inputs to project planning are a list of the activities that must be completed, the *activity completion times* (also called activity *durations*), and precedence relationships among the activities (i.e., what activities must be completed before another activity can be started). In this section, we assume that activity completion times are known with certainty. Later, we relax this assumption and consider situations in which activity completion times are uncertain.

Important outputs of project scheduling include:

- Graphical representation of the entire project, showing all precedence relationships among the activities
- Time it will take to complete the project
- Identification of critical path or paths
- Identification of critical activities
- Slack times for all activities and paths
- Earliest and latest time each activity can be started
- Earliest and latest time each activity can be completed

$\mathcal{T}_{\text{ABLE}}$ 6.1 • Data for a Mortgage Refinancing Project

Activity	Expected Time, t_e	Preceding Activities
A: Identify all stakeholders	10	—
B: Develop the project charter	10	—
C: Uncover all relevant regulations	5	—
D: Set up project procedures	7	A
E: Determine total refinancing time	5	B, C
F: Use accounting data for total cost	7	B, C
G: Interview to determine unknown risks	2	B, C
H: Redesign so as to reduce tasks times	5	C
I: Determine cost reductions of new design	8	G, H
J: Uncover any new constraints on design	4	D, E

Project Completion and Critical Paths

Table 6.1 shows the activity times and precedence for the ten activities that must all be finished to complete a bank's process improvement project. According to the table, activities A, B, and C can be started at any time. Activity D can be started once activity A is completed. Activities E, F, and G cannot be started until both activities B and C are finished, and so on. The network diagram for this project is shown in Figure 6.8, in which ellipses show the start and end of the project, arrows represent the required precedence, and rectangular nodes represent the activities A-J in Table 6.1. The rectangular nodes list the activity by letter, followed by its expected time (in days). This way of depicting a project is known as "activity-on-node" (AON) and is typical of CPM; the PERT alternative, activity-on-arrow (AOA), is also common however (see Meredith and Mantel 2009 for examples).

To determine the expected completion time of each of the nodes on the network and thus the entire project, *early start times* T_{ES} and *early finish times* T_{EF} are calculated for each activity, as shown in Figure 6.8. The values of T_{ES} and T_{EF} are calculated moving left to right through the network. Thus, we begin with the Start node and work our way to the End node. To illustrate, the project starts at time zero (sometimes this is not the case), then activities A, B, and C can also be started as early as time zero, since none of them is preceded by another activity. Since activity A requires 10 days, if it is started at time zero (T_{ES}), it can be completed (T_{EF}) as early as day 10. Likewise, if activity B is started at time zero, it can be completed as early as day 10 and activity C can be completed by day 5. Continuing on, since activity A can be finished as early as day 10, activity D can start as early as day 10 and, since it takes seven days, can finish as early as day 17. The same logic applies to activities E through H.

Now consider activity J. Activity J cannot be started until activities D and E are *both* completed. Since activity D can be finished as early as day 17 and E can be finished as early as day 15, activity J can be started only as early as day 17, the *latest* of its preceding activities (remember, J cannot start until both activities D and E are completed). Since J takes four days, then it can be finished as early as 21 days. The same logic applies to activity I. It cannot start until the latest of its predecessors is

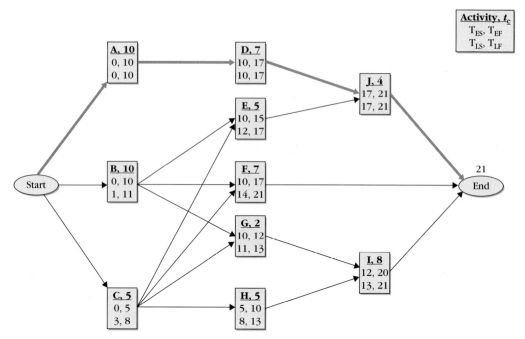

Figure 6.8 Network diagram for process improvement project.

completed, 12 for G and 10 for H, and hence 12. Since it takes eight days, it can be completed by day 20. Now that T_{ES} and T_{EF} have been calculated for all the activities, we can determine the earliest time that the project can be completed. Since the project "End" cannot be completed until all its predecessors are completed, the earliest it could be completed is day 21, based on activity J.

We can now find the critical path and critical activities for the project. Since the End of the project depended on activity J, we bold the arrow from J to End. Similarly, J's start time depended on activity D, rather than E, so we bold the arrow from D to J. And D depended on the completion of A, so we bold that arrow, and then the arrow from the Start node to A, resulting in the critical path A-D-J and the critical activities A, D, and J.

Once T_{ES} and T_{EF} have been calculated for each activity, the *latest* times each activity can be started and finished without delaying the completion of the project can be determined. In contrast to T_{ES} and T_{EF}, the *latest start time* (T_{LS}) and *latest finish time* (T_{LF}) are calculated by moving *backward* through the network, from right to left. These T_{LS} and T_{LF} times are also shown in Figure 6.8.

In calculating T_{ES} and T_{EF}, we determined that the project could be completed by day 21. If the project is to be completed by day 21, then activities J, F, and I can be completed as late as day 21 without delaying completion of the project. Thus, the latest finish time for activities J, F, and I is 21. Since activity J requires four days, it can start as late as $21 - 4$ or 17 and still finish by day 21. Likewise, activity I can start as late as $21 - 8$ or 13 and still finish by day 21 and activity F can start as late as $21 - 7 = 14$. Continuing on, since activity J can start as late as day 17, activity D can finish as late as day 17. Since activity D requires seven days, it can start as late as day $17 - 7 = 10$ without delaying the entire project. Activities G and H are handled similarly, resulting in the late start and finish times for activities G and H.

Now let's look at activity B, which precedes activities E, F, and G. The latest it can finish is the *earliest* late start date of activities E, F, and G since if it doesn't start by then, that activity will be late and will delay the entire project. Since the late start dates of these three activities are 12 (for E), 14, and 11, activity B's latest finish date must be 11 because if it doesn't finish by 11, activity G can't start and will delay activity I which will delay the project. The latest dates for activity C are found in the same manner.

Note in Figure 6.8 that the latest dates for the critical activities (A, D, and J) are identical to the earliest dates. That is, the latest dates cannot be delayed from the earliest dates at all, or else the entire project will be delayed! This will always be the case since this represents the critical path of the project.

Slack Time

The times T_{ES}, T_{EF}, T_{LS}, and T_{LF} can be used by the project manager to help plan and develop schedules for the project. For example, if an activity requires a key resource or individual, its earliest and latest start times provide a window during which that resource can be acquired or assigned to the project. Alternatively, if an activity falls behind schedule, the latest completion time provides an indication of whether the slippage will delay the entire project or can simply be absorbed.

Notice in Figure 6.8 that for some activities, T_{ES} is less than its T_{LS} and its T_{EF} is less than its T_{LF}. In these cases the project manager can exercise some discretion in terms of when the activity is started and when it is completed. The amount of flexibility the project manager has in terms of starting and completing an activity is referred to as its **slack** (or **float**) and is calculated as

$$\text{Activity slack} = T_{LS} - T_{ES} = T_{LF} - T_{EF}$$

All activities on the critical path have zero slack—that is, there is no room for delay in any activity on the critical path without delaying the entire project. But activities off the critical path may delay up to a point where further delay would delay the entire project. For example, activity H has a late start time of 8 and an early start time of 5, leaving three days of possible slack. If resources for activity H are sitting idle and could be used to expedite activity A, for example, the project manager may choose to do this, perhaps reducing the duration of activity A by one day and bringing the project in at day 20 instead of 21, for an early completion!

In addition to calculating slack times for individual activities, slack times can be calculated for entire paths. Since all paths must be finished to complete the project, the time to complete the project is the time to complete the path with the longest duration. Thus, the path with the longest duration is critical in the sense that any delay in completing it will delay the completion of the entire project. Path slacks are calculated as

$$\text{Path slack} = \text{duration of critical path} - \text{path duration}$$

If we consider path C-H-I, it has a duration of 18 so its path slack is $21 - 18 = 3$ days. but path B-G-I has a path slack of only 1 day. Since activity I is on both paths, its slack is always the lesser of the two paths, one day in this case.

Before leaving the topic of slack, it is important to point out that the slack times computed for individual activities are not additive over a path. To illustrate, both activities C and H have slacks of three days, but if we use those three days for activity C, starting it at day 3 instead of 0, there is then no slack for activities H or I. The point is that slack times for individual activities are computed on the assumption that only one particular activity is delayed.

Project Scheduling with Uncertain Activity Times

The previous section discussed project planning in situations where the activity completion times were known with certainty before the project was actually started. In reality, however, project activity times are frequently not known with certainty beforehand. In these cases, project managers often develop three estimates for each activity: an optimistic time t_o, a pessimistic time t_p, and a most likely time t_m. The *optimistic time* is the amount of time the project manager estimates it will take to complete the activity under ideal conditions; that is, only one time in a hundred would it take less time than this. The *pessimistic time* refers to how long the activity will take to complete under the worst-case scenario; again, there is only a 1 percent chance it would ever take longer than this. The *most likely time* is the project manager's best estimate of how long the activity will actually take to complete. In addition to these three time estimates, the precedence relationships among the activities are also needed as inputs to the project planning process.

The primary outputs of project planning when activity times are not known with certainty include:

- Graphical representation of the entire project, showing all precedence relationships among the activities
- Expected activity and path completion times
- Variance of activity and path completion times
- Probability that the project will be completed by a specified time
- That time corresponding to certain probability of the project being complete

In Table 6.2 we present the three activity times that gave rise to the expected times in previous Table 6.1. Table 6.2 also includes the variance of the expected time, whose calculation, as well as the calculation of the expected time, we describe next.

Calculating Activity Durations

The estimates of the three activity times in Table 6.2 are based on the assumption that the activities are independent of one another. Therefore, an activity whose duration is changed will not necessarily affect the duration of the other activities. Additionally, it is assumed that the difference between t_o and t_m need *not* be the same as the difference between t_p and t_m. For example, a critical piece of equipment may be wearing out. If it is working particularly well, this equipment can do a task in two hours that normally takes three hours; but if the equipment is performing poorly, the task may require 10 hours. Thus, we may see nonsymmetrical optimistic and pessimistic task times for project activities, as for activities E and H in Table 6.2. Note also that for some activities, such as B, the durations are known with certainty.

$\mathscr{T}$ABLE 6.2 • Six Sigma Activity Times (days)

Project Activity	Optimistic Time t_o	Most Likely Time t_m	Pessimistic Time t_p	Expected Time t_e, and Variance σ^2
A	5	11	11	10, 1
B	10	10	10	10, 0
C	2	5	8	5, 1
D	1	7	13	7, 4
E	4	4	10	5, 1
F	4	7	10	7, 1
G	2	2	2	2, 0
H	0	6	6	5, 1
I	2	8	14	8, 4
J	1	4	7	4, 1

The general form of nonsymmetrical or skewed distribution used in approximating PERT activity times is called the beta distribution and has a mean (expected completion time t_e) and a variance, or uncertainty in this time, σ^2, as given below. The beta distribution is used because it is flexible enough to allow one tail of the distribution to be longer than the other (more things will typically go worse than expected than will go better than expected in a project) and is thus a more appropriate distribution for activity completion times.

$$t_e = \frac{t_o + 4t_m + t_p}{6}$$

$$\sigma^2 = \left(\frac{t_p - t_o}{6}\right)^2$$

The above equation for the expected completion time is simply a weighted average of the three time estimates, with weights of 1, 4, and 1, and the denominator of 6 is, of course, the sum of the weights. The value of 6 in the estimate of the variance, however, comes from a different source, the assumption that the optimistic and pessimistic times are each three standard deviations (3) from the mean. This only applies, however, to estimates made at the 99 percent sure level. If a manager is reluctant to make estimates at that level and feels that a 95 percent, or 90 percent, level is easier to estimate, then the equations for the standard deviation change (the approximation for the mean is still acceptable, however) to:

95% level: $\sigma = (t_p - t_o)/3.3$

90% level: $\sigma = (t_p - t_o)/2.6$

The results of these calculations (at the 99 percent level) are listed in Table 6.2.

The discussion of project management with known activity times included critical paths, critical activities, and slack. These concepts are not quite as useful in situations where activity times are not known with certainty. Without knowing the activity times with certainty, any of the paths may have the potential to be the longest path. Furthermore, we will not know which of the paths will take longest to complete until the project is actually completed. And since we cannot determine with certainty before the start of the project which path will be critical, we cannot determine how much slack the other paths have. We can, however, use probability estimates and simulation to help us gain more confidence, as described in the next two subsections.

Probabilities of Completion

When activity times are not known with certainty, we cannot determine how long it will actually take to complete the project. However, using the variance of each activity (the variances in Table 6.2), we can compute the likelihood or probability of completing the project in a given time period, assuming that the activity durations are independent of each other. The distribution of a path's completion time will be approximately normally distributed if the path has a large number of activities on it. (Recall from the central limit theorem in statistics that this is true regardless of the distribution of the activities themselves, beta in our case.) For example, the mean time along path A−D−J was found to be 21 days. The variance is found by summing the variances of each of the activities on the path. In our example, this would be

$$V_{\text{path A}-\text{D}-\text{J}} = \sigma^2_A + \sigma^2_D + \sigma^2_J$$
$$= 1 + 4 + 1$$
$$= 6$$

The probability of completing this path in, say, 23 days is then found by calculating the standard normal deviate of the desired completion time less the expected completion time, and using the table of the standard normal probability distribution (inside rear cover) to find the corresponding probability:

$$Z = \frac{\text{Desired completion time} - \text{expected completion time}}{\sqrt{V}}$$
$$= \frac{23 - 21}{\sqrt{6}}$$
$$= 0.818$$

which results in a probability (see Figure 6.9) of 79 percent. This can also be found in Excel® using the NORMDIST function with the syntax =NORMDIST(D,t_e,σ,TRUE) where D is the desired time of interest, 23 days in our case. Similarly, we can calculate that completion time by which we would be, say, 90% sure the project would be completed. From Appendix A, we find the standard normal deviate corresponding to 90% as about 1.28, so $21 + (1.28\sqrt{\sigma}) = 24.14$ days. Again, this could also be found in Excel® from the NORMINV function with syntax =NORMINV(probability, t_e,σ), which in our case would be =NORMINV(.90,21,2.449) = 24.14 days.

So far, we have determined only that there is a 79 percent chance that path A−D−J will be completed in 23 days or less. If we were interested in calculating the probability that the entire project will be completed in 23 days, we would need to

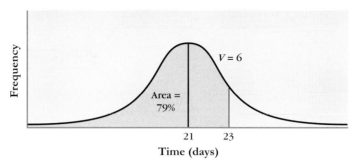

Figure 6.9 Probability distribution of path completion time.

calculate the probability that all paths will be finished within 23 days. To calculate the probability that all paths will be finished in 23 days or less, we first calculate the probability that each path will be finished in 23 days or less, as we just did for path A−D−J. Then we multiply these probabilities together to determine the probability that all paths will be completed by the specified time. The reason we multiply these probabilities together is that we are assuming that path completion times are independent of one another. Of course, if the paths have activities in common, they are not truly independent of one another and a more complex analysis or simulation, illustrated next, is necessary.

To simplify the number of calculations required to compute the probability that a project will be completed by some specified time, for practical purposes it is reasonable to include only those paths whose expected time plus 2.33 standard deviations is more than the specified time. The reason for doing this is that if the sum of a path's expected time and 2.33 of its standard deviations is less than the specified time, then the probability that this path will take longer than the specified time is very small (i.e., less than 1 percent), and therefore we assume that the probability that it will be completed by the specified time is 100 percent. Finally, note that to calculate the probability that a project will take longer than some specified time, we first calculate the probability that it will take less than the specified time and then subtract this value from 1.

Simulating Project Completion Times

When activity times are uncertain, it is usually not possible to know which path will be the critical path before the project is actually completed. In these situations, simulation analysis can provide some insights into the range and distribution of project completion times. To illustrate this, we use the network diagram in Figure 6.10 consisting of six activities labeled A through F.

Based on historical data, it has been determined that all the activity times are approximately normally distributed with the means and standard deviations given in the nodes of Figure 6.10 following the letter of the activity. Inspection of the network diagram reveals three paths: A−C−F, B−D−F, and B−E.

To simulate the completion of this project using Crystal Ball® (see www.oracle.com/crystalball/index.html for details on Crystal Ball®), the spreadsheet in Figure 6.11 was developed. In the spreadsheet, completing the project is simulated by generating random numbers for the six activities and then adding up the activity times

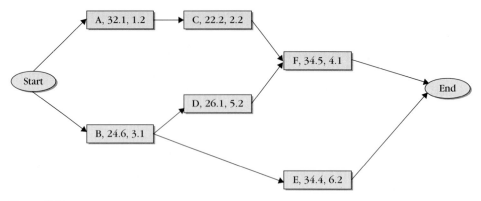

Figure 6.10   Network for simulating.

	A	B	C	D	E	F	G	H	I	J
1	**Activity**	**Activity**	**Activity**	**Activity**	**Activity**	**Activity**	**Path**	**Path**	**Path**	**Completion**
2	**A**	**B**	**C**	**D**	**E**	**F**	**ACF**	**BDF**	**BE**	**Time**
3	**32.1**	**24.6**	**22.2**	**26.1**	**34.4**	**34.5**	88.8	85.2	59	88.8
4										
5										
6							Assumption Cells		Forecast Cell	
7										
8										
9	**Formulae:**									
10	Cell G3	= A3 + C3 + F3								
11	Cell H3	= B3 + D3 + F3								
12	Cell I3	= B3 + E3								
13	Cell J3	= MAX (G3:I3)								

Figure 6.11   Spreadsheet for simulating the network.

that make up each path to determine how long the paths take to complete. The longest path determines the project completion time.

In the spreadsheet, randomly generated activity times from a normal distribution for each activity are generated in cells A3:F3 by defining these cells as assumption cells. For example, cell A3 was defined as an assumption cell with a normal distribution and mean and standard deviation of 32.1 and 1.2, respectively. In column G the time to complete path A−C−F is calculated based on the activity times generated in cells A3:F3. For example, in cell G3, the formula = A3 + C3 + F3 was entered. In a similar fashion, cells H3 and I3 are used to calculate the time to complete paths B−D−F and B−E, respectively. Cell J3 keeps track of when the project is actually completed on a given replication. Since the longest path determines the time when the project is completed, = MAX(G3:I3) was entered in cell J3.

The results of simulating the project are summarized in Figure 6.12. The results indicate that, on the average, the project required 90.28 days to complete. Furthermore, across the 1000 replications of the project, the fastest project completion time was 75.77 days and the longest was 109.77 days. The simulation package can also show the probabilities of completing the project before any given date, or after any given date, or even between any two dates.

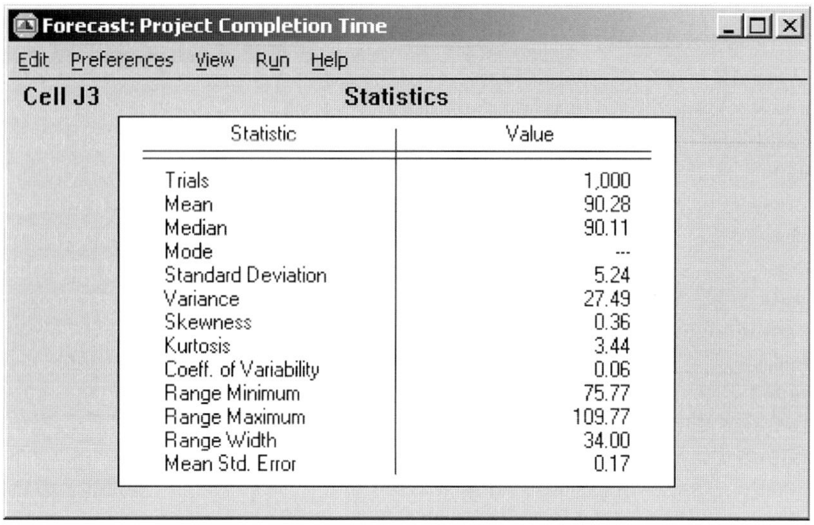

Statistic	Value
Trials	1,000
Mean	90.28
Median	90.11
Mode	---
Standard Deviation	5.24
Variance	27.49
Skewness	0.36
Kurtosis	3.44
Coeff. of Variability	0.06
Range Minimum	75.77
Range Maximum	109.77
Range Width	34.00
Mean Std. Error	0.17

Figure 6.12 Simulation results.

Project Management Software Capabilities

There is a wide range of project management software packages and capabilities available, depending on the project need and the funds available. The main aspects to consider when selecting a package are the capabilities required and the time and money available to invest in a package. If the project is very large and complex, or one that interacts with a number of other projects that must also be managed with the software, then some of the more sophisticated packages are appropriate. However, not only do these cost more, they also take longer to learn and greater computer power to run. On the other hand, if the project is simpler, a less elaborate package that is easier to learn and use may be the best choice.

A yearly survey and analysis of such packages is conducted by the Project Management Institute. These surveys give details on the friendliness of each package, their capabilities (schedules, calendars, budgets, resource diagrams and tables, graphics, their migration capabilities, report generation, tracking capability, etc.), their computer requirements, and their cost.

Probably the most commonly used package these days is Microsoft's Project. This package is fairly sophisticated for the cost and is extremely easy to learn and use. Examples of some of its report capabilities are given in Figures 6.13, 6.14, and 6.15.

Goldratt's Critical Chain*

In the *Critical Chain*, Eliyahu Goldratt (1997) applies his Theory of Constraints (described in Chapter 5) to the field of project management. In this theory he primarily focuses on three phenomena that tend to bias the expected completion time of projects, based on the network techniques we described above, toward shorter times

* Adapted from S. J. Mantel, Jr., J. R. Meredith, S. M. Shafer, and M. M. Sutton, *Project Management in Practice*, 3rd ed., Hoboken, NJ: Wiley, 2008.

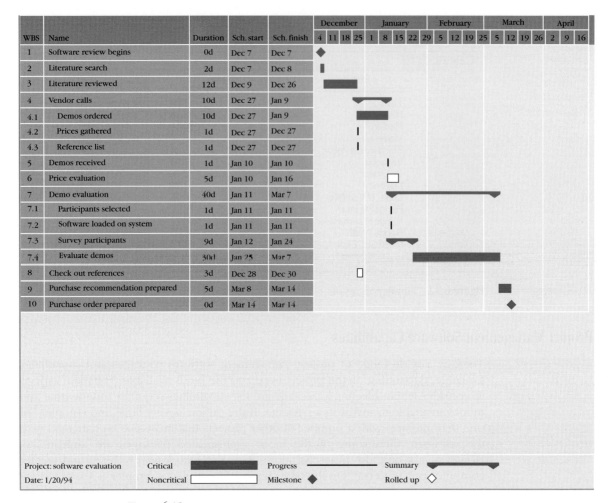

WBS	Name	Duration	Sch. start	Sch. finish
1	Software review begins	0d	Dec 7	Dec 7
2	Literature search	2d	Dec 7	Dec 8
3	Literature reviewed	12d	Dec 9	Dec 26
4	Vendor calls	10d	Dec 27	Jan 9
4.1	Demos ordered	10d	Dec 27	Jan 9
4.2	Prices gathered	1d	Dec 27	Dec 27
4.3	Reference list	1d	Dec 27	Dec 27
5	Demos received	1d	Jan 10	Jan 10
6	Price evaluation	5d	Jan 10	Jan 16
7	Demo evaluation	40d	Jan 11	Mar 7
7.1	Participants selected	1d	Jan 11	Jan 11
7.2	Software loaded on system	1d	Jan 11	Jan 11
7.3	Survey participants	9d	Jan 12	Jan 24
7.4	Evaluate demos	30d	Jan 25	Mar 7
8	Check out references	3d	Dec 28	Dec 30
9	Purchase recommendation prepared	5d	Mar 8	Mar 14
10	Purchase order prepared	0d	Mar 14	Mar 14

Project: software evaluation   Date: 1/20/94

Critical   Noncritical   Progress   Milestone   Summary   Rolled up

Figure 6.13   Microsoft Project's Gantt chart.

than occur in reality. These three phenomena are inflated activity time estimates, activity time variability with path interdependencies, and resource dependence.

Inflated Activity Time Estimates

Assuming that project workers have a general desire to be recognized for good performance, what do you imagine project workers do when they are asked to provide time estimates for tasks they will be responsible for? Do you think they give an estimate that they believe provides them with only a 50 percent chance of being met? Or, more likely, do you imagine they inflate or *pad* their estimate to increase the likelihood of successfully completing the task on time? What would you do?

We suspect that if you are like most people, you would tend to somewhat inflate your time estimate. Unfortunately, inflated time estimates tend to create even more problems. First, inflating the time estimate has no impact on the actual probability distribution of completing the activity. Second, what do you imagine happens in cases

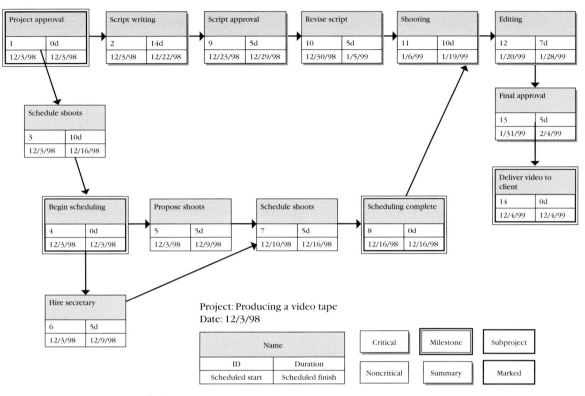

Figure 6.14 PERT chart generated by Microsoft Project.

where a project team member finishes early? More than likely, the team member believes that it is in his or her best interest to remain silent about completing activities in less than the allotted time so that future time estimates are not automatically discounted by management based on a track record of early task completions. Moreover, there are sometimes penalties for completing early, such as storage of materials.

Third, just as things tend to fill the available closet and storage space in your home, work tends to fill the available time. Thus, the scope of the task may be expanded to fill the available time. Perhaps even more dangerous than the inflated estimate becoming a self-fulfilling prophecy is that, after receiving approval for a task based on an inflated time estimate, workers may perceive that they now have plenty of time to complete the task and therefore *delay starting the task*. Goldratt refers to this as the *student syndrome*, likening it to the way students often delay writing a term paper until the last minute. The problem of delaying the start of a task is that obstacles are frequently not discovered until the task has been underway for some time. By delaying the start of the task, the opportunity to effectively deal with these obstacles and complete the task on time is greatly diminished.

Activity Time Variability with Path Interdependencies

Another factor that tends to favorably bias the expected project completion time is the effect of variability in the activity times when there are multiple and interconnecting

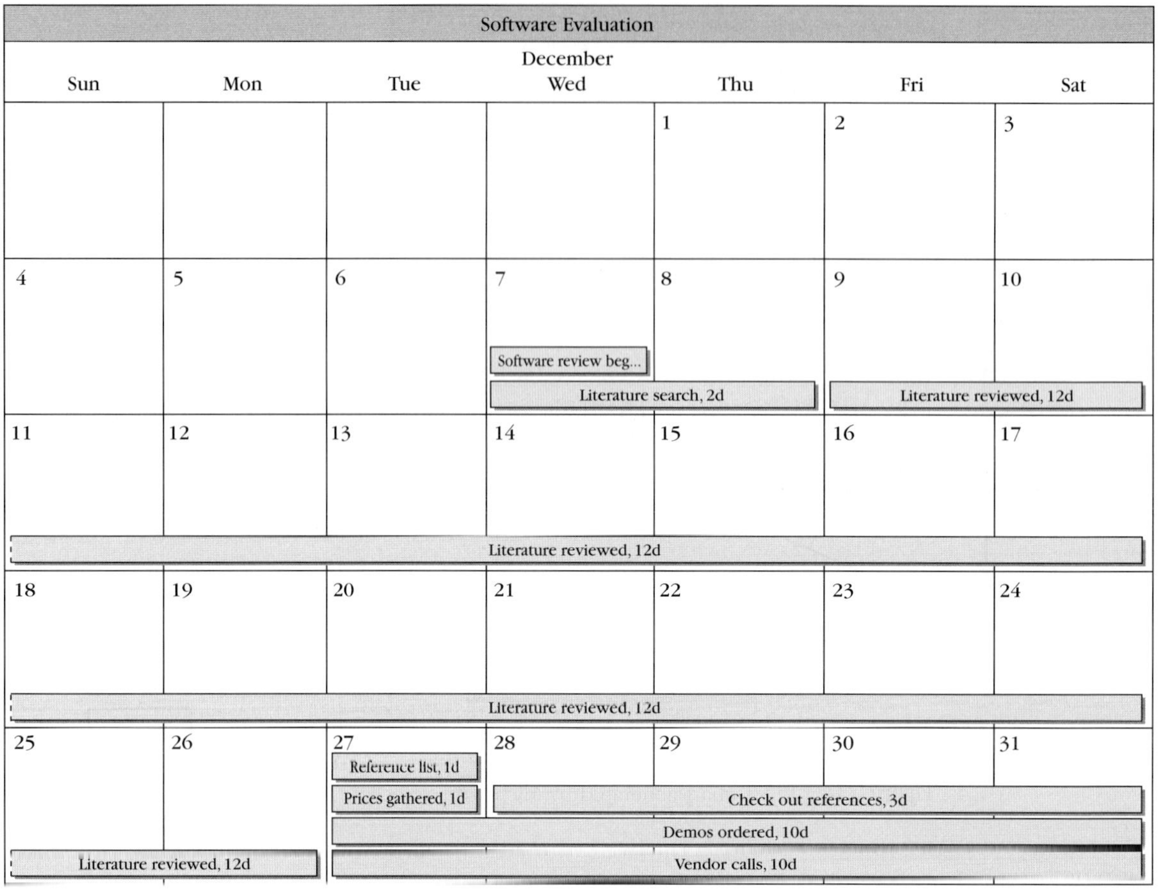

Software Evaluation						
			December			
Sun	Mon	Tue	Wed	Thu	Fri	Sat
				1	2	3
4	5	6	7	8	9	10

Software review beg...
Literature search, 2d
Literature reviewed, 12d

| 11 | 12 | 13 | 14 | 15 | 16 | 17 |

Literature reviewed, 12d

| 18 | 19 | 20 | 21 | 22 | 23 | 24 |

Literature reviewed, 12d

| 25 | 26 | 27 | 28 | 29 | 30 | 31 |

Reference list, 1d
Prices gathered, 1d
Check out references, 3d
Demos ordered, 10d
Literature reviewed, 12d
Vendor calls, 10d

Figure 6.15   Calendar of activities created by Microsoft Project.

paths in a network. First consider a project with say ten activities all in a line (i.e., in series), each of the same expected duration and variability. It seems clear that if random events affect the activities, some will finish early and others late, but the general overall effect will be that the early completions will largely offset the late completions and the project will finish about when expected. However, suppose now that another project also has ten activities, but they are all in parallel, and all must be completed to complete the project. Since the project will not be done until every activity is completed, the slowest activity of the ten—that is, the one whose random events delay the activity the most—will be the one that determines when the project is actually completed.

Most projects are not like either of the above two examples, but instead have many activities in series and many in parallel. As we saw above, the activities in series tend to cancel out their random effects but not so with the parallel activities which tend to delay the project. Eventually, all the interacting paths of activities throughout the network act like our parallel activities and have a delaying effect on the project due to their random variations. In particular, if there is another path(s) through the network that is close to the length of the critical path and has substantial variability, it is quite likely that this path may determine when the project is completed rather than the supposedly "critical path."

Resource Dependence

Last, it frequently happens that some activities need the same (scarce) resource (perhaps a machine, or a particularly skilled person) at the same time. If this happens, then there is no alternative but for one activity to wait until the other activity has finished with the resource, unless of course the organization is willing to spend extra funds to acquire or rent another resource, but this will then negatively affect the budget. As a result, resource dependence within a project can also seriously delay a project beyond its expected completion time based on the critical path.

Goldratt's approach for addressing these three issues is based on elementary statistics. It is easily shown that the amount of safety time needed to protect a particular path in a project is less than the sum of the safety times required to protect the individual activities making up the path. The same approach is commonly used in inventory management, where it can be shown that less safety stock is needed at a central warehouse to provide a certain service level to customers than the amount of safety stock that would be required to provide this same service level if carried at multiple distributed (e.g., retail) locations.

Based on this intuition, Goldratt suggests reducing the amount of safety time added to individual tasks and adding some fraction of the safety time reduced back to be used as a bank of safety buffer for the entire project, called the *project buffer*. The amount of time each task is reduced depends on how much of a reduction is needed to get project team members to change their behavior. For example, the allotted time for tasks should be reduced to the point that the student syndrome is eliminated. To motivate the project team members, Goldratt suggests using activity durations where in fact there is a high probability that the task will *not* be finished on time.

To address the need to consider both precedence relationships and resource dependencies, Goldratt proposes thinking in terms of the longest chain of consecutively dependent tasks where such dependencies can arise from a variety of sources, including precedence relationships among the tasks and resource dependencies. Goldratt coined the term *critical chain* to refer to the longest chain of consecutively dependent activities.

Based on this definition of the critical chain, there are two potential sources that can delay the completion of a project. In a similar fashion to the critical path concept, one source of delay is the tasks that make up the critical chain. The project buffer discussed earlier is used to protect against these delays (see Figure 6.16). But as noted above, tasks external to the critical chain can also delay the completion of the project if these delays end up delaying one or more of the tasks on the critical chain. As shown in Figure 6.16, safety time can be added to these paths as well to ensure that they do not delay tasks on the critical chain. The safety time added to chains other than the critical chain is called a *feeding buffer* since these paths often feed into the critical chain. Thus, the objective of feeding buffers is to ensure that non-critical chains are completed so that they do not delay tasks on the critical chain.

Clearly, activities on the critical chain should be given the highest priority. Likewise, to ensure that resources are available when needed, they should be contacted at the

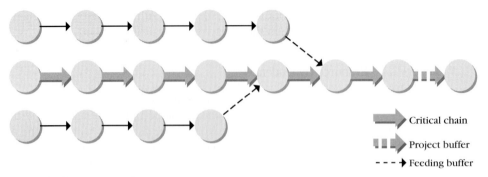

Figure 6.16   Project and feeding buffers.

start of the project. It is also wise to keep these resources updated on the status of the project and to remind them periodically of when their input will be needed. Goldratt suggests reminding these resources two weeks before the start of their work, then three days prior to their start, and finally the day before they start. Since any delay of an activity on the critical chain can cause a delay of the entire project, it is important that a resource immediately switch to the task on the critical chain when needed.

$\mathscr{C}$ONTROLLING THE PROJECT: EARNED VALUE

One of the control systems most widely used in projects is the cost variance report. Cost standards are determined through engineering estimates or through analysis of past performance. They become the target costs for the project. The actual costs are then monitored by the organization's cost-accounting system and are compared with the cost standard. Feedback is provided to the project manager, who can exert any necessary control if the difference between standard and actual (called a variance) is considered significant.

As an example, consider the cost-schedule charts in Figure 6.17. In Figure 6.17a, actual progress is plotted alongside planned progress, and the "effective" progress time (TE) is noted. Because progress is less than planned, TE is less than the actual time (TA). On the cost chart (Figure 6.17b) we see that the apparent variance between the planned value and actual cost at this time (PV − AC) is quite small, despite the lack of progress (earned value, EV). But this is misleading; the variance should be much more given the lack of progress.

These two graphs are combined for project managers into an ***earned value*** chart—Figure 6.18—where the planned value (PV), actual cost (AC), and earned value completed (actual earned dollars of progress, EV) are plotted. Here we see that the actual cost variance is now substantial, given the poor progress and large schedule variance. Plotted in this manner, one chart will serve to monitor both progress and cost. We can then define three variances: (1) a *cost variance* equal to the value completed less the actual cost (EV − AC), where a cost overrun is negative; (2) a *schedule variance* equal to the value completed less the planned value (EV − PV), where "behind" is negative; and (3) a *time variance* equal to the effective time less the actual time (TE − TA), where a delay is negative.

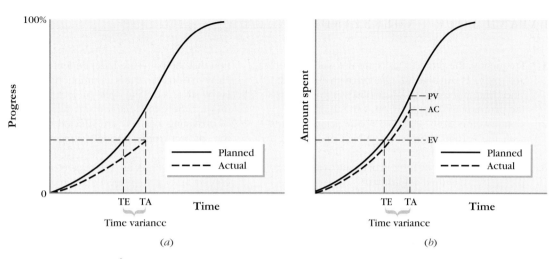

Figure 6.17 Cost–schedule reconciliation charts.

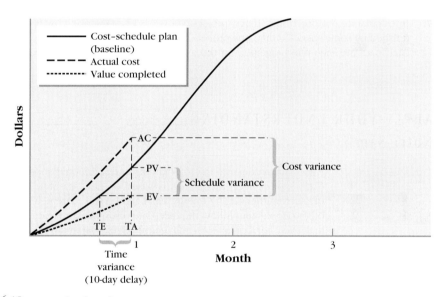

Figure 6.18 Earned value chart.

When these variances are significant, the project manager must identify (or at least attempt to identify) an *assignable cause* for the variance. That is, he or she must study the project to determine why the variance occurred. This is so that the proper remedy can be used to keep the variance from recurring. A corrective action is called for if some inefficiency or change in the prescribed process caused the variance.

Variances can be both favorable and unfavorable. A significant *favorable variance* (e.g., a variance resulting from a large quantity discount on material) will usually not require corrective action, though investigation is still worthwhile so that this better-than-expected performance can be repeated.

EXPAND YOUR UNDERSTANDING

1. Frequently, the project's tasks are not well defined, and there is an urge to "get on with the work," since time is critical. How serious is it to minimize the planning effort and get on with the project?

2. Contrast the cost–schedule reconciliation charts with the earned value chart. Which one would a project manager prefer?

3. How would a manager calculate the value completed for an earned value chart?

4. Do you think people's estimates are more accurate for optimistic or pessimistic activity times?

5. Of the reasons discussed for the growth in project operations, which do you think are contributing most?

6. Why doesn't it make sense to think in terms of a critical path when activity times are not known with certainty?

7. In calculating the probability that a project will be finished by some specified time, the probabilities of each path are multiplied together, on the assumption that the paths are independent of one another. How reasonable is this assumption?

8. Is the stretched-S life cycle project form more common or the exponential form? What other aspects of managing a project are affected by the nature of the project form besides budgeting and early termination?

9. What do you think are the reasons for the topics of conflict among the project team in each stage of the project?

10. Given the powerful nature of project management software packages today, why should a project manager have to know how to construct a PERT chart or work breakdown structure?

11. Given the ease of use of simulation software such as Crystal Ball®, what other data used in project management should probably be simulated?

12. Describe how to actually calculate earned value.

13. What does the project portfolio illustrate? How might it be useful to management?

APPLY YOUR UNDERSTANDING

Nutri-Sam

Nutri-Sam produces a line of vitamins and nutritional supplements. It recently introduced its Nutri-Sports Energy Bar, which is based on new scientific findings about the proper balance of macronutrients. The energy bar has become extremely popular among elite athletes and other people who follow the diet. One distinguishing feature of the Nutri-Sports Energy Bar is that each bar contains 50 milligrams of eicosapentaenoic acid (EPA), a substance strongly linked to reducing the risk of cancer but found in only a few foods, such as salmon. Nutri-Sam was able to include EPA in its sports bars because it had previously developed and patented a process to refine EPA for its line of fish-oil capsules.

Because of the success of the Nutri-Sports Energy Bar in the United States, Nutri-Sam is considering offering it in Latin America. With its domestic facility currently operating at capacity, the president of Nutri-Sam has decided to investigate the option of adding approximately 10,000 square feet of production space to its facility in Latin America at a cost of $5 million.

The project to expand the Latin American facility involves four major phases: (1) concept development, (2) definition of the plan, (3) design and construction, and (4) start-up and turnover. During the concept development phase, a program manager is chosen who will oversee all four phases of the project and the manager is given a budget to develop a plan. The outcome of the concept development phase is a rough plan, feasibility estimates for the project, and a rough schedule. Also, a justification for the project and a budget for the next phase are developed.

In the plan definition phase, the program manager selects a project manager to oversee the activities associated with this phase. Plan definition consists of four major activities that are completed more or less concurrently: defining the project scope, developing a broad schedule of activities, developing detailed cost estimates, and developing a plan for staffing.

The output of this phase is a detailed plan and proposal for management specifying how much the project will cost, how long it will take, and what the deliverables are.

If the project gets management's approval and management provides the appropriations, the project progresses to the third phase, design and construction. This phase consists of four major activities: detailed engineering, mobilization of the construction employees, procurement of production equipment, and construction of the facility. Typically, the detailed engineering and the mobilization of the construction employees are done concurrently. Once these activities are completed, construction of the facility and procurement of the production equipment are done concurrently. The outcome of this phase is the physical construction of the facility.

The final phase, start-up and turnover, consists of four major activities: pre-start-up inspection of the facility, recruiting and training the workforce, solving start-up problems, and determining optimal operating parameters (called centerlining). Once the pre-start-up inspection is completed, the workforce is recruited and trained at the same time that startup problems are solved. Centerlining is initiated upon the completion of these activities. The desired outcome of this phase is a facility operating at design requirements.

The next table provides optimistic, most likely, and pessimistic time estimates for the major activities.

Activity	Optimistic Time (months)	Most Likely Time (months)	Pessimistic Time (months)
A: Concept Development	3	12	24
Plan Definition			
B: Define project scope	1	2	12
C: Develop broad schedule	0.25	0.5	1
D: Detailed cost estimates	0.2	0.3	0.5
E: Develop staffing Plan	0.2	0.3	0.6
Design and Construction			
F: Detailed engineering	2	3	6
G: Facility construction	8	12	24
H: Mobilization of employees	0.5	2	4
I: Procurement of equipment	1	3	12
Start-up and Turnover			
J: Pre-start-up inspection	0.25	0.5	1
K: Recruiting and training	0.25	0.5	1
L: Solving start-up problems	0	1	2
M: Centerlining	0	1	4

Questions

1. Draw a network diagram for this project. Identify the four "near-critical" paths through the network diagram.
2. Find the probability that the project can be completed within 30 months. What is the probability that the project will take longer than 40 months? What is the probability that the project will take between 30 and 40 months?
3. ** Use Crystal Ball® (or other simulation package) to simulate the completion of this project 1000 times assuming that activity times follow a triangular distribution. Estimate the mean and standard deviation of the project completion time. Answer Question 2 and compare your results.

EXERCISES

1. The following AON chart was prepared at the beginning of a small construction project. The duration, in days, follows the letter of each activity. What is the critical path? Which activities should be monitored most closely?

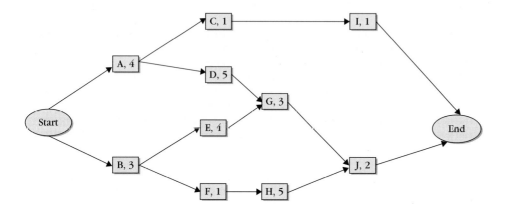

At the end of the first week of construction, it was noted that activity A was completed in 2.5 days, but activity B required 4.5 days. What impact does this have on the project? Are the same activities critical?

2. Refer to Exercise 1. Compute the earliest start and finish times, the latest start and finish times, and the slack times for each activity. Also, calculate the slack for each path.

3. Given the following German autobahn repair project, find the probability of completion by 17 weeks; by 24 weeks.

	Times (weeks)			Required
Activity	Optimistic	Most Likely	Pessimistic	Precedence
A	5	11	11	—
B	10	10	10	—
C	2	5	8	—
D	1	7	13	A
E	4	4	10	B
F	4	7	10	B
G	2	2	2	B
H	0	6	6	C
I	2	8	14	G, H
J	1	4	7	D, E

If the firm can complete the project within 18 weeks, it will receive a bonus of €10,000. But if the project is delayed beyond 22 weeks, it must pay a penalty of €5000. If the firm can choose whether or not to bid on this project, what should its decision be if this is normally only a breakeven project?

4. Construct a network for the project below and find its expected completion time.

Activity	t_e (weeks)	Preceding Activities
a	3	None
b	5	a
c	3	a
d	1	c
e	3	b
f	4	b, d
g	2	c
h	3	g, f
i	1	e, h

5. Given the estimated activity times and precedences below:

		Times (days)		Required
Activity	Optimistic	Most Likely	Pessimistic	Precedence
A	6	7	14	—
B	8	10	12	—
C	2	3	4	—
D	6	7	8	A
E	5	5.5	9	B, C
F	5	7	9	B, C
G	4	6	8	D, E
H	2.7	3	3.5	F

What is the probability that the project will be completed within:

a. 21 days? b. 22 days? c. 25 days?

6. Pusan Iron and Steel, located on the eastern coast of South Korea, is a major supplier of both girder and rolled steel to the emerging construction, appliance, and automobile companies of China. Due to growing sales volumes and the need for faster delivery, Pusan is converting its current single weigh station to a larger, multiple drive-through station. The new drive-through weigh station will consist of a heated, air-conditioned building with a large floor and a small office. The large room will have the scales, a 15-foot counter, and several display cases for its equipment.

Before erection of the building, the project manager evaluated the project using CPM analysis. The following activities with their corresponding times were recorded.

#	Activity	Times Optimistic	Most Likely	Pessimistic	Preceding Tasks
1	Lay foundation	8	10	13	—
2	Dig hole for scale	5	6	8	—
3	Insert scale bases	13	15	21	2
4	Erect frame	10	12	14	1, 3
5	Complete building	11	20	30	4
6	Insert scales	4	5	8	5
7	Insert display cases	2	3	4	5
8	Put in office equipment	4	6	10	7
9	Give finishing touches	2	3	4	8, 6

Using CPM analysis, find the expected completion time.

7. As in the situation illustrated in Figure 6.18, an Irish Web-design project at day 70 exhibits only 35 percent progress when 40 percent was planned, for an effective date of 55. Planned value was €17,000 at day 55 and €24,000 at day 70, and actual cost was €20,000 at day 55 and €30,000 at day 70. Find the time variance, cost variance, and schedule variance at day 70.

8. As in the situation shown in Figure 6.18, a project at month 2 exhibited an actual cost of $78,000, a planned value of $84,000, and a value completed of $81,000. Find the cost and schedule variances. Estimate the time variance.

9. A project at month 5 had an actual cost of $34,000, a planned value of $42,000, and an earned value of $39,000. Find the cost and schedule variances.

10. Given a network:

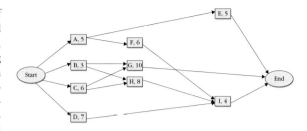

Note that four activities can start immediately. Find:

a. Critical path.

b. Earliest time to complete the project.

c. Slack on activities E, F, and H.

11. Given the activities data in the table below:

a. Draw the network.

b. Find the critical path.

c. Find the slacks on all activities.

Activity	Times (weeks)	Preceding Activities
A	3	—
B	6	—
C	8	—
D	7	A
E	5	B
F	10	C
G	4	C
H	5	D, E, F
I	6	G

12.

Activity	Duration	Preceding Activities
1	1	—
2	2	—
3	3	—
4	4	3
5	3	2,4
6	8	3
7	2	2,4
8	4	1,5
9	2	17
10	6	2,4
11	5	6,10
12	10	7,8,11
13	11	7,8,11
14	1	6,10
15	9	12
16	3	6,10
17	8	12
18	6	13,14,15

a. Draw the diagram.

b. Find the critical path.

c. Find the completion time.

13. In the project network shown in the following figure, the number alongside each activity designates its known duration in weeks. Determine:

a. Earliest and latest start and finish times for each activity.

b. Earliest time that the project can be completed.

c. Slack for activities.

d. Critical activities.

e. Critical path.

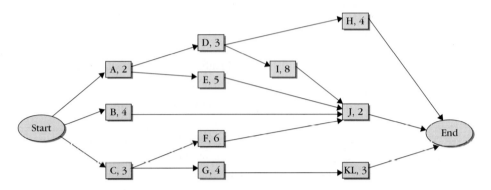

BIBLIOGRAPHY

Abrams, S. "The Big Dig," Kennedy School Bulletin, Spring 2003, p. 30–35.

Angus, R. B., N. A. Gundersen, and T. P. Cullinane. *Planning, Performing, and Controlling Projects: Principles and Applications,* 3rd ed. Upper Saddle River, NJ: Prentice Hall, 2003.

Cauchon, D. "The Little Company that Could," *USA Today,* October 9, 2005.

Cleland, D. I. *Project Managers' Portable Handbook,* 2nd ed. New York: McGraw-Hill, 2004.

Englund, R. L., and R. J. Graham. "From Experience: Linking Projects to Strategy." *Journal of Product Innovation Management,* Vol. 16, No. 1, 1999.

Gido, J., and J. P. Clements. *Successful Project Management (with Microsoft Project CD-ROM),* Cincinnati: Thompson/South-Western, 2008.

Goldratt, E. M. *Critical Chain.* Great Barrington, MA: North River Press, 1997.

Gray, C. F., and E. W. Larson. *Project Management: The Managerial Process,* 4th ed. New York: McGraw-Hill/Irwin, 2008.

Ibbs, C. W., and Y.-H. Kwak. "Assessing Project Management Maturity." *Project Management Journal,* March 2000.

Kerzner, H. *Project Management: A Systems Approach to Planning, Scheduling, and Controlling,* 9th ed. New York: Wiley, 2006.

Kerzner, H. *Advanced Project Management: Best Practices on Implementation.* New York: Wiley, 2004.

Kolisch, R. "Resource Allocation Capabilities of Commercial Project Management Software Packages," *Interfaces,* 29 (July–August 1999): 19–31.

Meredith, J. R., and S. J. Mantel, Jr. *Project Management: A Managerial Approach,* 7th ed. New York: Wiley, 2009.

Mantel, S. J., Jr., J. R. Meredith, S. M. Shafer, and M. M. Sutton. *Project Management in Practice,* 3rd ed. New York: Wiley, 2008.

Nicholas, J. M. and H. Steyn. *Project Management for Business, Engineering, and Technology.* Englewood Cliffs, NJ: Prentice Hall, 2008.

Project Management Institute. *A Guide to the Project Management Body of Knowledge,* 4th ed. Newtown Square, PA: Project Management Institute, 2009.

Project Management Institute. "Digging Deep," *PM Network,* August 2004b, p. 1.

Project Management Institute. "A Derailed Vision," PM Network, April 2004a, p. 1.

Project Management Institute. "Lack of Support," PM Network, Jan. 2005, p. 1.

Thamhain, H. J., and D. L. Wilemon. "Conflict Management in Project Life Cycles." *Sloan Management Review* (Summer 1975).

PART III

Supply Chain Management

Finally, we discuss what many consider to be perhaps the main task of operations in these days of outsourcing and global competition, supply chain management. In the past, operations used to consist of a great range of independent topics such as inventory control, capacity, scheduling, purchasing, logistics, distribution, materials planning, facility location, and so on. Today however, all these topics are being lumped into one integrated concept referred to as the *supply chain*. And indeed, all these topics are intimately related so to achieve the most efficient and effective operations, they must be considered together. In Chapter 7 we focus our attention on managing the active elements of the supply chain itself, such as materials planning, sourcing, logistics, inventories, and other such aspects. Chapter 8 then picks up some of the ancillary upfront issues including forecasting, capacity planning, facility location, and scheduling.

Managing Supply Chain Logistics and Inventories

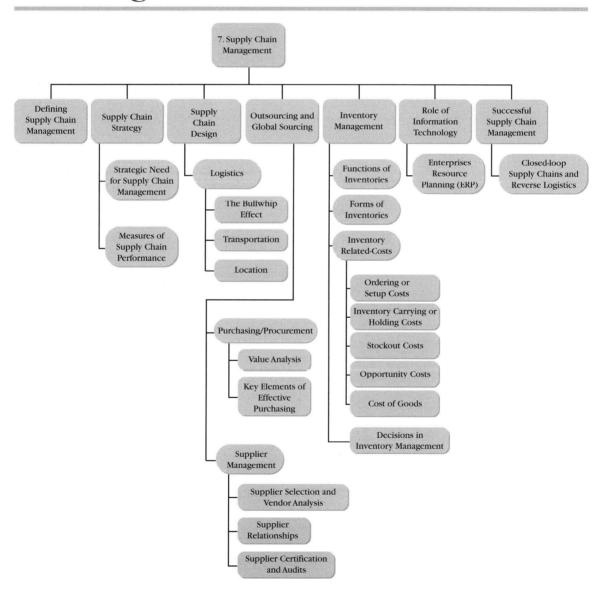

In this chapter we address issues related to supply chain management, a strategic consideration involving topics such as designing and restructuring the value chain, outsourcing, and e-commerce. Competent management of the supply chain has major impacts on all the strategic sand cone factors described in Chapter 1: quality, dependability, speed, and cost. We first define the concept of supply chains and discuss their strategic importance. We then describe the many elements involved in their design, such as logistics, global sourcing, and supplier management. From this we move to the role of information technology and provide guidelines for successful supply chain management. We conclude the chapter with a discussion of closed-loop supply chains.

INTRODUCTION

- During the year 2000, Palm Inc. was selling every PDA (computerized Personal Digital Assistant) they could make but their sourcing processes were largely tactical: How soon could they receive the components they needed? Recognizing the limitations of their tactical approach, Palm developed a strategic supply chain management function, including a Strategic Sourcing organization. As a result, they have gone from doing business with hundreds of suppliers to developing deep relationships with only a few suppliers. For example, in 2001 about 150 suppliers accounted for about 80 percent of Palm's purchasing expenditures. By 2003, they had 50. Furthermore, its strategic sourcing strategy helped Palm reduce its overall costs by 27 percent, increase inventory turns from 3 to 22, and achieve a 30 percent increase in profit margins.

  One example of the advantages of developing such deep relationships with suppliers has been the success of their Zire PDA, introduced with the surprisingly low price of $99 when most new PDAs cost over $400. The secret to driving the cost so low was working closely with their suppliers to hit tight cost targets for the display, the processor, the memory, the battery, and the mechanicals. As a result, the Zire became Palm's fastest selling PDA in their history, with 90 percent of the buyers being first-time PDA users (Carbone 2003).

- Liz Claiborne used to have 250 suppliers in 35 countries spread around the globe, from Mexico to Cambodia. With the expiration of 30-year-old international apparel quotas on January 1, 2005, Liz Claiborne is considering how much of their clothing production to consolidate at Luen Thai Holdings Ltd. in Dongguan, southern China. This is where a new "supply chain city" is being created that includes a 2-million square foot factory, dormitories for 4000 workers, and all the supporting infrastructure required to consolidate design, production, and shipment of clothing across the globe. Liz Claiborne estimates they will be able to eliminate 40 percent of some clothing labor costs through this consolidation, and cut their concept-to-shipment time from 90 to 60 days (Kahn 2004).

- Even with the lean inventories that have resulted from the prevalence of just-in-time inventory systems, shifts in economic cycles can still wreak havoc for industry-wide supply chains. The electronics industry during the global recession of 2008–2009 illustrates this well.

  At one end of the electronics supply chain are the retailers that sell electronic products to end consumers. With the financial crisis rapidly escalating in fall 2008, Minnesota based retailer Best Buy experienced a significant decline in sales. Best Buy orders electronic products such as DVD players six weeks prior to when they are needed. With the 2008 Thanksgiving shopping season approaching, Best Buy revised its prior forecast and dramatically reduced its orders to its suppliers such as Japan's Toshiba and Korea's Samsung Electronics in early October 2008. As the financial crisis was uncharted territory, Best Buy's merchandising chief had to make his best guess in deciding how to modify the forecast.

  Lacking a direct relationship with the final consumers, Best Buy's suppliers were caught off guard by its revised forecast and reduced orders. As expected, these suppliers in turn reduced orders from their suppliers. As an example, Zoran Corp, a designer of specialty chips used in electronic products such as TVs, cameras, cell phones, DVD players and digital picture frames, saw its revenue decline in the fourth quarter of 2008 by 42 percent. Zoran, which only designs chips, relies on companies like Taiwan Semiconductor Manufacturing Company (TSMC) to produce its chips. Faced with decreased orders for its chips, Zoran slashed its orders to TSMC. In January and February of 2009, TSMC saw its revenue decrease by 58 percent compared to the prior year and was only utilizing 35 percent of its plant capacity.

  With decreased demand for its chips, TSMC in turn reduced its orders for chip making equipment by 20 percent. Applied Materials is one company that makes the equipment used in chip making factories. With the downturn in demand for chip making equipment, Applied Materials was forced to lay off 2,000 workers and require another 12,000 workers to take an unpaid leave.

  With the downturn in its business, Applied Materials reduced orders to its suppliers. For example, D&H Manufacturing Company, which makes aluminum parts for chip making equipment, reduced its employment from 600 workers to 150 workers in 18 months because of the drop-off in business. It also found itself sitting on a one year supply of inventory versus its usual three months of inventory.

  This example illustrates how the effects and decisions made at one end of the supply chain are often amplified as they cascade to the other end. And because the players at different stages in the supply chain are often caught off-guard, it is not surprising that they frequently overreact to the situation. In the present example, in the early part of 2009 Best Buy was actually having trouble keeping its shelves stocked despite the decline in demand. In fact, Best Buy estimated in March 2009 that it could have sold more in the preceding three months had its suppliers made less-drastic reductions to their production plans (Dvorak 2009).

- To many, the mere mention of inventory management conjures up images of detailed calculations and analysis. However, while inventory management is often considered to be a rather bland and narrow topic, there are a number of areas related to inventory management that are generating significant interest. One such area is radio frequency identification (RFID). With RFID, conventional bar codes are replaced with computer chips or smart tags. These smart tags use wireless technology to track inventory. In addition to labor savings, RFID allows organizations to manage their inventory more effectively. In 2005, spending on RFID had already reached $1 billion and was projected to increase to $4.6 billion by 2007.

One early adopter of RFID was Wal-Mart, a company well known for its investments in supply chain technology. By January 2005, 53 of its top 100 suppliers were sending RFID-tagged goods to its three distribution centers in the Dallas, Texas area. Wal-Mart's goal was to have all top-100 suppliers shipping RFID-tagged goods by the end of February 2005 in addition to 37 other suppliers. In subsequent waves, Wal-Mart planned to have the next 200 suppliers onboard by January 2006 and its entire supplier base onboard by the end of 2006. Wal-Mart itself has installed RFID readers in 104 of its Wal-Mart stores and 36 Sam's Clubs.

The impetus for Wal-Mart's investment in RFID was the lack of visibility it had into its backroom storage areas. Better visibility would translate into better information with which to base replenishment orders which in turn would provide a better overall customer experience by helping it get inventory onto the store shelves in a more timely manner.

The major drawback to RFID is its cost. In 2005, the cost of smart tags was $0.25 each if purchased in volume, and $0.75 if purchased in smaller quantities. For many organizations, this translates into a payback period of more than two years. However, the stated goal in the industry is to get the price of smart tags down to $.05, which would make adopting RFID more appealing and economical for many organizations (Lacy 2004; Blanchard 2005).

- Vendor-managed inventory (VMI) is another inventory management topic that is generating a significant amount of interest. With VMI, suppliers are given responsibility for managing the inventory carried by their retail or wholesale customers. The customers still own the inventory; however, the suppliers are given the responsibility for managing it. Using point-of-sale data, suppliers determine the timing and quantity of inventory replenishment orders.

Rich Products, a $2 billion family-owned food company headquartered in Buffalo, has a partnership with IBM to provide VMI services to the grocery industry for its frozen food items. With this service, grocery stores provide information daily to IBM electronically about inventory withdrawals and inventory balances. Rich accesses this information and then uses its customers' own purchasing systems to generate replenishment orders based on service performance agreements. These purchase orders are then sent to Rich electronically. Through the use of VMI, retailers hope to increase their inventory turnover while at the same time reducing the occurrence of stockouts. (Richardson 2004).

The concept of supply chain management has taken on the nature of a crusade in U.S. industry, in part because of the tremendous benefits that accrue to firms participating in a well-managed supply chain. It is worth noting that, although the benefits of superior supply chain management are clear for manufacturing and distribution firms, even service organizations benefit from good supply chain management. This is because services not only use supplies and facilitating goods in the delivery of their service (as noted in Chapter 1), but also because they, too, outsource many of their internal functions, such as information technology, accounting, and human resource management, just like manufacturers do. Thus, the provision of these services becomes part of another supply chain, a chain of services rather than goods, but nonetheless one requiring the same attention to strategy, purchasing, logistics, and management oversight, just like for goods.

We begin the chapter with some definitions of the supply chain and supply chain management. As with any new concept, not everyone envisions supply chain management in the same way. We then discuss some of the important strategic advantages that accrue to wise management of the supply chain. From this overview, we then consider the elements of the supply chain in depth, including purchasing/procurement, logistics, transportation, global sourcing, and supplier management. An important element of supply chain management is the critical role of information technology as a major catalyst in the supply chain movement. Next, we provide some guidelines for successful supply chain management. We conclude with a discussion of closed-loop supply chains.

DEFINING SUPPLY CHAIN MANAGEMENT

The term **supply chain** generally refers to all the activities involved in supplying an end user with a product or service. The perception of each organization that is involved—the ore refiners, the transporters, the component producers, the manufacturer, the wholesaler, the retailer, and the customer—being a link in the process makes the analogy of a chain quite appropriate. In Figure 7.1, we show the position of a typical company (A) in the chain, with its suppliers to the left of it, all the way "upstream" (as it is often called) to the raw materials, and its customers to the right, all the way "downstream" to the ultimate consumer. However, company C in the

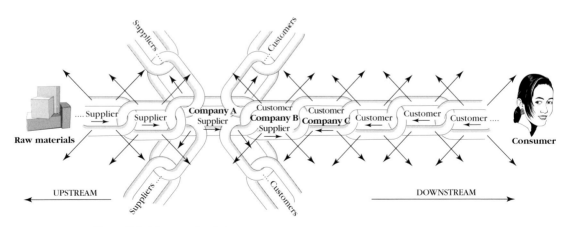

Figure 7.1 The supply chain.

chain (a downstream "customer" as far as company A is considered) sees the same thing as company A, with its suppliers (including upstream supplier company A) to its left and its customers to its right. And as is seen, company B in the middle is the customer of one firm and the supplier to another firm, as is the situation of almost all the companies in the chain.

Of course, all these companies need multiple materials and services, typically, to serve their immediate customer in the chain, so there is really a bunch of upstream supplier company links connected on the left side of each link in the chain (only shown with links for company A, arrows for all others). And most firms typically sell to more than one customer, so there are also multiple downstream customer links connected on the right side of each link in the chain (again shown only for company A). Clearly, managing all these links, that is, suppliers and customers, even if only those directly connected to your company, is a major task!

Given such a lengthy process, it may behoove companies to store inventories of their outputs (if feasible) for immediate delivery. Moreover, it must be remembered that it is not just goods that are flowing along the chain but also information, funds, paper, people, and other such items, and they are flowing in *both* directions along the chain. In addition, the green revolution encourages recycling, recovery, and reuse of products so even the used product may be flowing back up the chain. (We will return to the topic of closed-loop supply chains later in this chapter.) In addition, the supply chain also involves other functional areas and activities such as product/service design, finance, accounting, marketing, human resources, and engineering. Thus, instead of a chain, we should probably think of the supply process as more of a network, with everyone communicating with, and passing monies and items between, everyone else.

Supply chain management (SCM) then concerns the process of trying to manage this entire chain from initial receipt of the ultimate consumer's order all the way back to the raw materials providers and then ultimate delivery back to the consumer. Note that SCM is not restricted to managing only the links that connect with your company's position in the chain, but *all* the links along the chain, so that savings (or increased value) in any part of the chain can be shared or leveraged by other companies along the chain. For example, Toyota is famous for teaching their suppliers how to install and operate their famed Toyota Production System (also known as **lean manufacturing**). But the teaching doesn't stop there, since Toyota's first tier suppliers can gain additional improvements by teaching their suppliers, the second tier, and so on up the supply chain. Supply chain management has exploded in interest primarily because of the development of new information technologies such as intranets, e-mail, EDI (electronic data interchange), and of course, the Internet. These technologies, in conjunction with greater global competition, have fostered an interest and ability in improving processes along the entire supply chain, resulting in better performance at reduced cost.

SCM also can be considered to include a number of other managerial thrusts, such as quality management (Chapters 1 and 3), inventory management (discussed later), enterprise resource planning (ERP, also discussed later), and lean production (including just-in-time, Chapter 5). But it is even more comprehensive than that. For example, it includes marketing aspects in terms of communication with the customer, engineering issues involved in product/service design, financial aspects in terms of payments and float, purchasing elements such as sole-sourcing, and of course, technological initiatives such as the omnipresent Internet. To a large extent, this breakthrough in conceptualizing the potential for improvement in customer value by including all elements of the value chain is due to the development of advanced information technologies, such as the Internet.

Other definitions of SCM include the following points (Walker and Alber 1999):

- SCM coordinates and integrates all the supply chain activities into a seamless process and links all of the partners in the chain, including departments within an organization as well as the external suppliers, carriers, third-party companies, and information system providers.

- SCM enables manufacturers to actively plan and collaborate across a distributed supply chain, to ensure all parties are aware of commitments, schedules, and expedites. By actively collaborating as a virtual corporation, manufacturers and their suppliers can source, produce, and deliver products with minimal lead time and expense.

- The goal of SCM is to optimally deliver the right product to the right place at the right time, while yielding the greatest possible profit.

The SCM objective of attempting to manage activities that lie outside a manager's normal realm of internal responsibility (that is, managing 2nd- or 3rd-tier suppliers, or downstream customers) is to reduce the costs of delivering a product or service to a user and improve its value. Sometimes a distinction is made between a "value" chain, a "demand" chain, and a narrowly defined supply chain that simply manages suppliers to obtain the lowest cost. The conceptualization of the **value chain** is that it considers other important aspects of customer value besides cost such as timeliness, quality, and functionality. That is, where the supply chain tends to focus on efficiency, the value chain focuses on effectiveness. These important issues will be discussed in more detail in the next section.

Also, as many are now pointing out (e.g., Lummus and Vokurka 1999), the current conceptualization of the supply chain still has many elements of the old "push" system of production. The newer "pull" systems, consisting of just-in-time deliveries (JIT), lean manufacturing, and so on, dictate a different view of the value chain, called a **demand chain**. In this conceptualization, a customer order *pulls* the product through the chain on demand, thereby further improving costs and benefits. Of course, acting after the fact rather than anticipating demand will put even further stress on the ability of the value chain to respond in a timely manner.

Another layer of complexity is often added when managing service supply chains as the customers of the service can also serve as suppliers. For example, you supply the yard to your landscaping service. Likewise, your lifestyle and budget are important inputs to the architect you hire to design your dream house. Because the customers of a service may also be a supplier, it is likely that these customer-suppliers need to be handled differently than suppliers that are not customers. For example, suppliers that are not customers need to be selected but customer-suppliers need to be attracted.

The dual nature of the customer–supplier role further compounds the complexity of the service supply chain. With a more manufacturing oriented supply chain the goods tend to flow in one direction downstream. In service supply chains and the dual customer-supplier role, services flow in both directions with the customer both upstream and downstream from the service provider. Finally, service providers may require additional flexibility to deal with the added variation that is associated with customer supplied inputs compared to other situations where the inputs are supplied by a more limited set of suppliers.

Attempts to reduce the costs of supply (previously considered as "purchasing" or "procurement") have been ongoing for decades, of course. However, management has also realized that there are costs other than strict materials and production costs in the supply chain that can be reduced with better information sharing and tighter management, and these costs are at the forefront of attention in supply chain management. For example, costs of multiple shipments, costs of inappropriate functionality, costs of low quality, costs of late delivery—these are all costs that can be eliminated with better information sharing and managerial oversight.

Supply Chain Strategy

The concept of the value chain was mentioned earlier, and it should be emphasized that an organization's supply chain strategy needs to be tailored to meet the needs of its customers, which isn't always the lowest cost. In fashion goods, for example, fast response to short fashion seasons is much more important than lowest cost. And in high technology, new functionality (or reliability, or security) may be more important than cost. Thus, the strategy for building an organization's supply chain should focus on maximizing the value to their customers, where value can be considered to be benefits received for the price paid, or benefits/cost.

In situations where the goods are basic commodities with standard benefits (food, home supplies, standard clothing), then cost reduction will be the focus. But in fashion goods, timeliness should be the focus of the supply chain, meaning quick deliveries, stockpiling of long lead time items, and so on. In new notebook computers, the focus might be on identifying firms that offer new functionality; in telecom the focus might be on reliability; in music the focus might be on flexibility to meet quickly changing tastes or talent. Thus, the supply chain needs to be carefully matched to the firm's market and needs. Where the firm operates in multiple markets, or appeals to multiple needs within the same market, it may find it necessary to operate different supply chains for each focus. Although most of the remaining discussion in this chapter is directed toward the traditional supply chain strategy of minimizing costs, which is always an important consideration and probably the major focus of most supply chains today, the other possible strategic purposes should be kept in mind also.

It is also important to point out that many organizations choose to outsource portions of the supply chain management function to so-called third-party logistics (3PL) companies. These 3PL companies provide a range of services including handling the distribution of the organization's products, receiving incoming materials, managing the organization's warehouses, managing the purchasing function, and handling product returns. The balance of activities kept in-house and those outsourced vary by company and should be driven by the organization's strategy and competencies.

There a number of reasons why organizations choose to outsource portions of or the entire supply chain function to a 3PL. First, assuming that supply chain management is not the organization's core competency, shifting these activities to a 3PL allows the organization to focus more directly on its core competencies. Second, outsourcing these activities reduces the capital investments in the infrastructure needed to support these activities. In effect, the use of a 3PL converts a significant portion of what was a fixed cost into a variable cost. Finally, by utilizing a 3PL, the organization gains access to the best practices and technologies that it might not be able to afford or develop if the function was kept in-house. 3PLs are able to make the investment to develop these best practices and technologies because these development costs are spread across multiple organizations served by the 3PL.

Strategic Need for Supply Chain Management

To understand the potential for obtaining strategic advantage from better management of the supply chain, whether it is kept in-house or outsourced to a 3PL, it is useful to realize that total supply chain costs represent better than half, and in some cases three-quarters, of the total operating expenses for most organizations (Quinn 1997). To understand these values, bear in mind that the broader concept of the supply chain includes the supply, storage, and movement of materials, information, personnel, equipment, and finished goods within the organization and between it and its environment. The objective of supply chain management is to integrate the entire process of satisfying the customer's needs all along the supply chain. This includes procuring different groups of raw materials from multiple sources (often through purchasing or recycling or recovery), transporting them to various processing and assembly facilities, and distributing them through appropriate distributors or retailers to the final consumer. Within this process are a great variety of activities such as packaging, schedule coordination, credit establishment, inventory management, warehousing, maintenance, purchasing, order processing, and supplier selection and management.

As organizations have continued to adopt more efficient production techniques such as lean manufacturing, total quality management, inventory reduction techniques to reduce costs and improve the quality, functionality, and speed of delivery of their products and services to customers, the costs and delays of *procuring* the requisite inputs and *distributing* the resulting goods and services are taking a greater and greater fraction of the total cost and time. For example, the cost of just physical distribution itself is now up to 30 percent of sales in the food industry. To achieve quick response with quality goods that accurately satisfy the need at the lowest possible cost requires taking a broad, long-range, integrated perspective of the entire customer fulfillment process instead of focusing on the little segments and pieces of the chain.

For instance, if each segment of the supply chain is acting in a way to optimize its own value, there will be discontinuities at the interfaces and unnecessary costs will result. If an integrated view is taken instead, there may be opportunities in the supply chain where additional expense or time in one segment can save tremendous expense or time in another segment. If a broad enough view is then taken, the savings in the one segment could be shared with the losing segment, so everyone would be further ahead. This broad, integrated view of the supply chain is more feasible these days due to the recent capabilities of advanced information technology and computer processing (e.g., bar codes, computerized manufacturing, the Internet, enterprise resource planning systems, electronic funds transfer).

Other factors are also driving the need to better manage the supply chain:

- **Increasing global competition.** In addition to increased pressure on cost from global competitors who have lower labor rates, they also frequently offer better quality, functionality, and customer responsiveness. This is pressuring firms to look globally for better or cheaper suppliers, resulting in increased outsourcing and off-shoring.

- **Outsourcing.** Since more organizations are outsourcing and thereby increasing the need for transportation, this has pushed up transportation costs.

- **E-commerce.** The advent of e-commerce and other electronic technologies has made it easier and cheaper to outsource, either domestically or even globally.

- **Shorter life cycles.** Customers are demanding greater variety, faster response, higher quality, and cheaper prices. One result of these demands is shorter product life cycles, which means constantly changing supply chains, and more chains over the same period of time.

- **Greater supply chain complexity.** Finally, simply the increased complexity of the supply chains requires much more attention and better management of these chains. For example, in early 2001 when the bottom fell out of the telecom market, Solectron Corp., the world's biggest electronics contract manufacturer, was holding $4.7 billion of inventory from its 4000 suppliers to fill firm orders from Cisco, Ericsson, Lucent, and other telecoms. But when the telecoms cancelled their orders, no one knew who owned all that inventory (Engardio 2001)!

Implementing supply chain management has brought significant documented benefits to many companies. Ferguson (2000) reports, for example, that compared to their competitors, such firms enjoy a 45 percent supply chain cost advantage, an order-cycle time and inventory days of supply 50 percent lower, and finished product delivery 17 percent faster. Lummus et al. (1998) note that these firms operate with 36 percent lower logistics costs which, by itself, translates into a 4 percent increase in net profit margins. One firm reported a 25–50 percent reduction in finished product inventories, a 10 percent reduction in cost, and a 10–25 percent improvement in production process reliability.

Of course, these are primarily the cost aspects of the SCM process, which are more easily measured than the qualitative benefits such as more loyal customers and a larger market share. There are also significant effects on other important aspects of an organization, such as its ability to learn new procedures and ways of operating, the morale of its employees, and the ability to change direction quickly.

Measures of Supply Chain Performance

Better supply chain performance will show up in a number of standard financial measures of a company's health. Lower inventories, normally considered an asset, will be reflected in less need for *working capital* (WC) and a higher *return on asset* (ROA) ratio (since assets are reduced). And the lower cost to carry these inventories (as well as other reduced costs in the supply chain) will be seen in a reduced *cost of goods sold* (CGS), and thus a higher *contribution margin, return on sales* (ROS), and *operating income*. Moreover, if the supply chain is also better managed to provide other benefits to the consumer, as mentioned earlier, the effect should be seen in higher *total revenue* since the consumer will be willing to pay more. Lower costs, if used to reduce prices, will also result in higher volumes, which will further increase revenues.

One performance measure that provides managers with a broad view of the supply chain is the cash conversion cycle. This financial performance metric helps a company assess how well it is managing its capital. In effect the cash conversion cycle is the amount of time the organization's cash is tied up in working capital before being returned by customers as they pay for delivered products or services. The key inputs needed to calculate the cash conversion cycle are inventory (I), accounts receivable (AR), and accounts payable (AP). These inputs are readily available from the organization's financial statements. Before calculating the cash conversion cycle (CCC), the inputs are standardized into days as follows:

$$I = \frac{Inventory}{Annual\ Cost\ of\ Goods\ Sold} \times 365$$

$$AR = \frac{Accounts\ Receivable}{Annual\ Net\ Sales} \times 365$$

$$AP = \frac{Accounts\ Payable}{Annual\ Cost\ of\ Goods\ Sold} \times 365$$

These standardized inputs are used to calculate the cash conversion cycle as follows:

$$Cash\ Conversion\ Cycle = I + AR - AP$$

A positive cash conversion cycle represents the number of days the organization's capital is tied up waiting for the customer to pay for the products or services. A negative cash conversion cycle represents the number of days the organization is able to receive cash from its sales before it pays its suppliers. Thus, the smaller the cash conversion cycle including negative numbers, the better the organization is performing.

Dell has reduced their supply time so much that they actually receive payment from the customer *before* (known as *float*, another financial term) they have to pay their suppliers for the parts that make up the customer's product! In 1998 Dell's CCC was −9 days. By 2005 it had improved to −30 days, and by 2009 it was −44 days (Dignan 2002; Magretta 1998).

Beyond these standard financial measures, however, we can also look at some more operations-oriented measures that we typically use to see how well operations is performing, such as defect rates, lead times, inventory turns, productivity ratios, and so on. Since one of the major cost savings in SCM is the cost of inventories, it is worthwhile to examine some performance measures related to inventory reduction. One such measure to track is the percent of the firm's assets represented by inventory. First we calculate the aggregate inventory value (at cost) on average for the year (AAIV):

$$AAIV = raw\ materials + work\text{-}in\text{-}process + finished\ goods$$

$$\%\ Assets\ in\ Inventories = AAIV/total\ assets$$

Another inventory measure is the inventory turnover (or "turns," as it is sometimes called):

$$\text{Inventory turnover ("turns")} = \text{annual cost of goods sold/AAIV}$$

Note that the inventory turnover is based on the same items that make up total annual revenues, but is based on their cost instead of their price. Turnover essentially represents how often the inventory is replenished to obtain the total sales for the year. Like ROA, the more the inventory and assets can be reduced and still maintain the same sales, the better! Inverting the equation for turns gives us the same information but through a measure of the proportion of the year's sales we are holding in inventory. This is usually expressed in daily (or weekly) periods:

$$\text{Days of supply} = \text{AAIV/daily CGS}$$

In some firms that have achieved supply chain excellence, they measure their supply in *hours* instead of days. Dell Computer is one of these firms (Dignan 2002; Magretta 1998) due to the outstanding job they have done on fine-honing their supply chains.

$\mathscr{S}$UPPLY CHAIN DESIGN

As shown in Figure 7.2, the supply chain consists of the network of organizations that supply inputs to the business unit, the business unit itself, and the customer network. Note that the supplier network can include both internal suppliers (i.e., other operating divisions of the same organization) and external suppliers (i.e., operating divisions of separate organizations). Also, note how design activities cut across the supplier network and the business unit, and how distribution activities cut across the business unit and the customer network. This broader view of the entire process of serving customer needs provides numerous benefits. For example, it focuses management attention on the entire process that creates value for the customer, not the individual activities. When viewed in this way, information is more freely shared up and down the supply chain, keeping all parties informed of one another's needs. Furthermore, activities can be performed at the point in the supply chain where they make the most sense. To illustrate, instead of providing Johnson Controls with detailed specifications for car seats, car manufacturers provide broad specifications and rely on Johnson Controls' expertise to design and manufacture their car seats.

In this section we will look at each of the major logistical elements of the supply chain to better understand how they operate and interact to deliver value to the final customer: the "bull-whip" effect, transportation, and location. Outsourcing, purchasing, supplier management, and the role of information technology are discussed later in the chapter.

Logistics

Logistics can be defined as planning and controlling efficient, effective flows of goods, services, and information from one point to another. As such, it consists of inventories, distribution networks, storage and warehousing, transportation, information

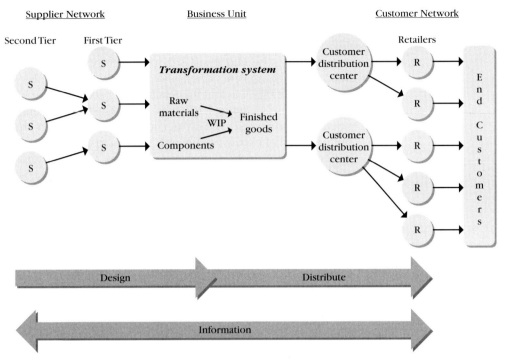

Figure 7.2 Simplified supply chain.

processing, and even production—a rather all-enveloping term. Here we will deal with logistics in general, and in terms of its tradeoffs with transportation. In later subsections we deal with the subcomponents concerning transportation, distribution, and production.

In these days of intense worldwide competition, international production in supply chains, and global distribution, logistics is taking on tremendous importance. Labor cost is dropping as a proportion of total output cost, as are manufacturing costs in general, but the costs of acquisition and distribution have remained about the same and now account, as noted above, for up to 30 percent of sales. Moreover, as quality and functionality become more standardized, speed of response and cost are becoming particularly important in the final selection of a supplier.

The Bullwhip Effect

An important logistical effect that is now better understood is known as the ***bullwhip effect***, named after the action of a whip where each segment further down the whip goes faster than that above it. The same effect occurs in a supply chain, but in reverse order, and has been well documented. More specifically, in supply chains the bullwhip effect results when the variability of demand increases from the customer stage upstream to the factory stage. This is often the result of different parties in the supply chain being overly reactive in their ordering practices, as in the Best Buy example at the beginning of the chapter. For example, this happens when a small percentage increase in a retailer's orders results in the wholesaler increasing its orders by an amount greater than that of the retailer—a safety stock—just to be covered in case demand is increasing. Then the distribution center sees this greater demand from its wholesalers and increases its orders by some safety percentage, also to be safe. The end result is that the factory sees a huge jump in demand. As it orders more equipment, labor, and materials to satisfy this big increase, too much is fed into the pipeline and the retailer cuts back, with the wholesaler and distribution center likewise cutting back even more. The factory then sees a tremendous drop in demand and reverses the cycle, cutting excessively into production and initiating another round of excessive demand. This boom-bust cycle is particularly prevalent in some industries, such as commercial building. Obviously, both overproduction and underproduction are expensive and drive up supply chain costs.

The bullwhip effect can occur whenever any one of three conditions is extreme enough to cause the boom–bust cycle. The first condition is simply long lead times between the stages of the supply chain, so that changes in demand requirements are slow moving up and down the chain, thereby allowing excessive changes to occur in the other stages of the chain. The second condition is large lot sizes with infrequent orders, resulting again in lags in information. And the third condition is the sole transmission of information occurring by handoffs from one link of the chain to the next.

The ways to eliminate the bullwhip effect are to reverse these three conditions. Reducing lead times through just-in-time programs, for example, will result in immediate deliveries of the ordered amounts so safety stocks are unnecessary. Reducing lot sizes means smaller, more frequent deliveries, which again eliminates the need for large safety stocks. And finally, the sharing of information from the retailer throughout the supply chain gives the factory, as well as the other supply chain partners, accurate information so appropriate amounts of items are produced and delivered.

In addition to these three conditions, there are a number of business practices that also contribute to the bullwhip effect. One business practice is the tendency for customers to have a preference for placing all their orders either at the beginning or the end of the week (or month) rather than spacing orders out evenly. This leads to a situation where incoming orders will be bunched up around the beginning and end of the week (or month) thereby increasing the variability of the supplier's daily demand beyond that of the variability of the customers' daily demand. Furthermore, this problem tends to be amplified as the orders cascade upstream.

Another business practice that contributes to the bullwhip effect is the use of standard batch sizes. For example, if a particular product is packaged in cases of 24 units, then replenishment orders for this product will be done in multiples of 24. This practice further bunches up orders and again results in the supplier's daily demand being larger than that of the customers placing the orders.

Trade promotions are yet another practice that contributes to the bullwhip effect. Trade promotions are short-term discounts suppliers offer their customers. These discounts provide customers with an incentive to order more product than they need, called forward buying. Because customers will choose to place their orders when the trade promotion is offered and even delay orders in anticipation of a trade promotion, these trade promotions create another order bunching problem.

A final practice that contributes to the bullwhip effect is shortage gaming. This practice occurs in situations where a product is in short supply. Anticipating that the supplier will allocate its inventory to its customers, some suppliers inflate their orders fearing that they will be shipped less than what they order. Attempting to game the system in this fashion exacerbates the shortage problem as some customers end up with less than they can sell because they did not inflate their orders while others end up with more than they can sell. In some cases, the suppliers themselves further compound this problem by allowing their customers to return unsold inventory.

There are several actions suppliers can take to mitigate these practices. For example, suppliers can ask their customers to share information more frequently about actual demand. Likewise, suppliers can coordinate with their customers to eliminate the batching of orders. Alternatively, suppliers can encourage their customers to make greater use of technology such as the Web and electronic data interchange (EDI) to place smaller but more frequent orders. Furthermore, suppliers can eliminate the practice of offering trade promotions. Finally, suppliers can enhance the value proposition they provide their customers while at the same time helping smooth out incoming orders by taking over the management of their customers' inventory, referred to as "vendor-managed" inventory and illustrated by the Rich Products example in the introduction to this chapter.

Transportation

The four major **transportation modes** are, historically, water, rail, truck, and air. Water is the least expensive mode and is good for long trips with bulky, nonperishable items. But it is very slow and of limited accessibility. It handles the majority of ton-miles of traffic. However, railroads handle the most total tons of traffic and are thus used for shorter hauls than water. They have many advantages: ability to handle small as well as large items, good accessibility, specialized services (e.g., refrigeration, liquids, cattle), and still a relatively low cost.

Trucking holds more advantages for short hauls with small volumes to specialized locations. Truck transport has grown at the expense of rail for several reasons, such as growth of the national highway system, better equipment, and liberalized regulations.

Air transport is used for small, high-value, or perishable items such as electronic components, lobsters, optical instruments, and important paperwork. Its main advantage is speed of delivery over long distances. Thus, for the appropriate products, it can significantly reduce inventory and warehousing costs, with a corresponding improvement in customer service.

Taking all the pros and cons of each mode of transportation into consideration in planning is a complex task. Table 7.1 lists the major considerations that should be factored into the decision. Each particular situation may have additional factors to consider.

Independent of the specific mode of transport are additional transportation problems involving such considerations as the *number* of transporting vehicles, their capacities, and the *routes* that each vehicle will take. In general, these interrelated problems are frequently included as part of the *routing problem*. Solving the routing problem involves finding the best number of vehicles and their routes to deliver the organization's output to a group of geographically dispersed recipients. When only one vehicle is serving all the recipients, the problem is known as the *traveling salesman problem*. In this problem, a number of possible routes exist between the organization and all the recipients, but only a few or perhaps just one of these routes will minimize the total cost of delivery. In the routing and traveling salesman problems,

$\mathcal{T}$ABLE 7.1 ● Factors to Consider in Transportation Decisions

- Cost per unit shipped
- Ability to fill the transporting vehicle
- Total shipment cost
- Protection of contents from theft, weather, and the like
- Shipping time
- Availability of insurance on contents, delivery, and so forth
- Difficulty of arranging shipment (governmental regulations, transportation to shipment site, etc.)
- Delivery accommodations (to customer's site, transfer to another transportation mode, extra charges)
- Seasonal considerations: weather, holidays, and so on
- Consolidation possibilities (among multiple products)
- Risk (to contents, to delivery promises, to cost, etc.)
- Size of product being shipped
- Perishability of product during shipment

certain procedures are available to minimize either the distance traveled or the cost, but quite often there are other considerations, such as balancing workloads among vehicles or minimizing idle or delay time.

Location

Besides distributing outputs to customers by transporting them, if there is a facilitating good, we can also locate where our customers can easily obtain them. Since service outputs without a facilitating good are generally difficult, expensive, or even impossible to transport, service organizations distribute their output primarily by locating in the vicinity of their recipients. Examples of this approach include medical clinics, churches, playgrounds, restaurants, and beauty shops.

Advances in information and telecommunications technology have allowed some pure service organizations (i.e., those without a facilitating good) to reach their recipients through phone, cable, the Internet, or microwave links. Thus, stockbrokers, banks, and other such service providers may locate in areas removed from their customers or recipients but more economical in other respects, such as proximity to the stock exchange or the downtown business district.

Some pure service organizations, however, do attempt to transport their services, although frequently with a great deal of trouble. These instances occur when the nature of the service (a traveling carnival, a home show) makes it impractical to remain in one fixed location for an extended duration or, more commonly, when the service (mobile X-ray, blood donor vehicle, bookmobile) is deemed very important to the public but may otherwise be inaccessible.

Product organizations, on the other hand, can generally trade transportation costs for location costs more easily and, therefore, can usually minimize their logistics costs. This allows goods producers to locate in the best global locations for each stage in their supply chains. In some instances, however, even product organizations are forced into fixed locations. One of these instances concerns the nature of the firm's inputs, and the other concerns its outputs.

Processing Natural Resources   Organizations that process natural or basic resources as raw materials or other essential inputs to obtain their outputs will locate near their resource if one of the following conditions holds:

1. There is a large loss in size or weight during processing.

2. High economies of scale exist for the product. That is, the operating cost of one large plant with the same total capacity as two smaller plants is significantly less than the combined operating costs of the two small plants.

3. The raw material is perishable (as in fish processing and canning) and cannot be shipped long distances before being processed.

Examples of these types of industries include mining, canning, beer production, and lumber. In these cases the natural inputs (raw materials) are either voluminous or perishable, and the final product is much reduced in size, thus greatly reducing the cost of transportation to the recipients (either final users or further processors).

Immobile Outputs   The outputs of some organizations may be relatively immobile, such as dams, roads, buildings, and bridges. In these cases (referred to as projects) the organization locates itself at the construction site and transports all required inputs to that location. The home office is frequently little more than one room with a phone, secretary, files, and billing and record-keeping facilities.

Product organizations may also locate close to their market, not necessarily to minimize transportation costs of distribution, but to improve customer service. Being close to the market makes it easier for the recipient to contact the organization and also allows the organization to respond to changes in demand (involving both quantity and variety) from current and new recipients. As in war, the people on the front line are closest to the action and are able to respond to changing situations faster than those far away, simply because information about changes is available sooner and is generally more accurate.

OUTSOURCING AND GLOBAL SOURCING

Outsourcing is the process of contracting with external suppliers for goods and services that were formerly provided internally and offers an important benefit for SCM. Global sourcing is an important aspect of supply chain outsourcing strategy and we see it occurring more and more. In the news, we read and hear about the meetings of GATT (General Agreement on Tariffs and Trade), the latest accords of the G-7 major trading nations, the dangers of NAFTA (North American Free Trade Agreement), the job losses due to overseas outsourcing (furniture manufacturers closing U.S. plants and sourcing from Asia, call centers being relocated to India), and so on. When asked on the Lou Dobbs show for the reasons all this outsourcing is occurring now, the economist Paul Craig Roberts responded that two primary factors were responsible: (1) the fall of communism and the economic insulation it had maintained; and (2) the advent of telecommunications and computer technology that physically allowed work that previously had to be done locally or regionally to now be conducted overseas.

The classic example of global outsourcing has been Nike, where the shoes were designed in the United States but all the production was done overseas. The strategic appeal of this lean model of business to other manufacturing and consumer firms is multiple. First, overseas production offers the promise of much cheaper labor costs, clearly a strategic benefit. But equally attractive to many firms that are outsourcing, whether globally or domestically, is the ability to dump a large portion of their capital-intensive production assets and staff, thus giving a big boost to their balance sheets, especially their return on assets. In addition, not being burdened with fixed, unchangeable capital production assets allows the firm to be more flexible and responsive to their customers' changing needs.

There is a danger to outsourcing however, particularly overseas outsourcing, and that is the possibility of being *hollowed out*, as noted in Chapter 1. To summarize, this is the situation where the supplier has been trained to produce, and even sometimes design, the customer's product so well that they can simply sell the product under their own brand and compete successfully against their former customer. In many cases, the customer has gone so long without designing or producing their own product—simply slapping their logo on the foreign-produced item—that they have lost the knowledge and skills to even compete in the market. This happened in the 1980s when American manufacturers trained foreign firms in how to produce television sets and other electronic goods, and lost those entire industries. Clearly, decisions about outsourcing at this level are strategic ones for the organization, involving both great potential benefits but also great risks, and should be deliberated thoroughly.

A more recent phenomenon is the trend toward outsourcing the entire production process to third-party ***contract manufacturers***. In this case, the firms often conclude that their core competency is not in manufacturing, per se, but rather in system innovation or design. In the electronics industry, this is becoming a major element of SCM strategy for firms like Cisco, Dell, IBM, and many others. Cisco, for example, hardly makes any products itself. The big players in this growing industry are Jabil Circuit, Venture, Flextronics, and SCI Systems. In fact, in the electronics sector, contract manufacturing was growing faster than the rate of growth of electronics itself in the late 1990s. In spite of the provision of products, these contract manufacturers consider themselves manufacturing *service* providers, and indeed, this is a substantial service they offer their customers. However, in addition to the major impacts outsourcing involves for operations, it also has major impacts on other functional areas of the organization such as marketing, finance, R&D, and human resource management. Moreover, to use this approach successfully requires that the firm maintain a strong, perhaps even core, competence in outsourcing. Many failures have resulted when firms jumped into outsourcing but didn't have the skills to manage it properly.

Outsourcing in general is a strategic element of SCM these days, not just for production materials but for a wide range of services as well. For example, organizations are coming to realize that many of the activities they perform internally, such as accounting, human resources, R&D, and even product design and information systems, are not part of their *core competencies* and can be performed more efficiently and effectively by third-party providers, often at a fraction of the cost of in-house workers. There is thus a growing movement toward increasing the span of SCM to include the acquisition of these services.

Purchasing/Procurement

Organizations depend heavily on purchasing activities to help them achieve their supply chain strategy by obtaining quality materials and services at the right cost when they are needed. Purchasing is expected to be able to quickly identify and qualify suppliers, negotiate contracts for the best price, arrange for transportation, and then continue to oversee and manage these suppliers. Lately, purchasing has been given the added responsibility in many organizations for also supplying major services to the organization, such as information technology, accounting, human resources, and other previously internal functions.

Another common term for the purchasing function is **_procurement_**. Whereas "purchasing" implies a _monetary_ transaction, "procurement" is the responsibility for acquiring the goods and services the organization needs, by any means. Thus, it may include, for example, scrap and recycled, as well as purchased materials. Procurement thus allows the consideration of environmental aspects of obtaining and distributing products. For example, there is often the possibility of recovering certain materials through recycling, reuse, or scrap purchases. And remanufacturing of goods is an inexpensive alternative to virgin production. On the distribution side, the concept of _reverse logistics_ is being practiced in Germany, where packaging must reverse the logistics chain and flow back to the producer who originated it, for disposal or reuse.

The purchasing area has a major potential for lowering costs and increasing profits—perhaps the most powerful within the organization. Consider the following data concerning a simple manufacturing organization.

$$
\begin{aligned}
\text{Total sales} &= \$10,000,000 \\
\text{Purchased materials} &= 7,000,000 \\
\text{Labor and salaries} &= 2,000,000 \\
\text{Overhead} &= 500,000 \\
\text{Profit} &= 500,000
\end{aligned}
$$

To double profits to $1 million, one or a combination of the following five actions could be taken.

1. Increase sales by 100 percent
2. Increase selling price by 5 percent (same volume)
3. Decrease labor and salaries by 25 percent
4. Decrease overhead by 100 percent
5. Decrease purchase costs by 7.1 percent

Although action 2 may appear easiest, it may well be impossible, since competitors and the market often set prices. Moreover, raising prices almost always reduces the sales volume. In fact, raising prices often decreases the total profit (through lower volume). Alternative 5 is thus particularly appealing. Decreasing the cost of purchased material provides significant profit leverage. In the previous example, every 1 percent decrease in the cost of purchases results in a 14 percent increase in profits. This potential is often neglected in both business and public organizations.

Furthermore, this logic is also applicable to service organizations. For example, investment firms typically spend 15 percent of their revenues on purchases. However, manufacturing firms spend about 55 percent of their revenues for outside materials and services (Tully 1995)! And with factory automation and outsourcing increasing, the percentage of expenditures on purchases is increasing even more. In addition, with lean and JIT programs at so many firms (discussed in greater detail in Chapter 5), "just-in-time purchasing" is even further increasing the importance of the purchasing and procurement, since delays in the receipt of materials, or receiving the wrong materials, will stop a JIT program dead in its tracks.

SCM programs are putting ever greater emphasis on the purchasing function. Thus, we are seeing multiple new initiatives for cutting purchasing costs, including reverse auctions and joint venture websites by organizations who are normally competitors. Reverse auctions use a website to list the items a company wants to buy and bidders make proposals to supply them, the lowest qualified bidder typically winning the auction. Joint venture websites are typically for the same purpose but combine the purchasing power of multiple large players in an industry—automobile manufacturing, aerospace, health care, for example—in order to obtain even bigger cost savings. Such sites are virtual online bazaars, including all the goods and services the joint partners wish to outsource. But the range and volumes are massive, considering that the old big three U.S. auto companies each spent close to $80 billion a year on such purchases.

Value Analysis

A special responsibility of purchasing, or purchasing working jointly with engineering/design and operations (and sometimes even the supplier), is to regularly evaluate the *function* of purchased items or services, especially those that are expensive or used in high volumes. The goal is to either reduce the cost of the item or improve its performance. This is called "value analysis" because the task is to investigate the total value of the item to see if the item can be eliminated, redesigned for reduced cost, replaced with a less expensive or more beneficial item, or even if the specifications can be relaxed. Other aspects are investigated, too, such as the packaging, the lead time, the transportation mode, the materials the item is made from, whether the part can be combined with another part or parts, and so on.

Recent efforts in this area have extended the reach further up the supply chain to involve second and third tier suppliers, and even bringing them in before the product is designed in order to improve its value up front, called *early supplier involvement*. Value analysis should be a continuing effort to improve supply chain performance and increase its value to the ultimate consumer.

Key Elements of Effective Purchasing

Organizations that are highly effective in SCM purchasing seem to follow three practices:

1. ***They leverage their buying power.*** The advantages associated with decentralization are typically not achieved when it comes to purchasing. For example, Columbia/HCA combines the purchases of its 200-plus hospitals to increase its overall purchasing power. By combining all of its purchases for supplies ranging from cotton swabs to IV solution, for instance, it was able to reduce purchasing costs by $200 million and boost profits by 15 percent.

2. ***They commit to a small number of dependable suppliers.*** Leading suppliers are invited to compete for an organization's business on the basis of set requirements, such as state-of-the-art products, financial condition, reliable delivery, and commitment to continuous improvement. The best one-to-three suppliers are selected from the field of bidders on the basis of the specified requirements. Typically, 1- to 5-year contracts are awarded to the selected suppliers. These contracts provide the supplier with the opportunity to demonstrate its commitment to the partnership. The customer shares information and technology with the supplier, and the supplier responds in turn. If a supplier is able to consistently improve its performance, the organization reciprocates by increasing the volume of business awarded to that supplier and extending the contract.

3. ***They work with and help their suppliers reduce total cost.*** Often, organizations will send their own production people to a supplier's plant to help the supplier improve its operating efficiency, improve its quality, and reduce waste. Additionally, an organization may benchmark key aspects of a supplier's operation such as prices, costs, and technologies. If it is discovered that a supplier has slipped relative to the competition, the organization can try to help the supplier regain its lead. If the supplier is unable or unwilling to take the steps necessary to regain its leadership position, the organization may need to find a new partner.

Supplier Management

Our discussion of the management of an organization's suppliers will focus on three areas: (1) selecting the suppliers, (2) contemporary relationships with suppliers, and (3) certification and auditing of ongoing suppliers.

Supplier Selection and Vendor Analysis

The general characteristics of a good supplier are:

- Deliveries are made on time and are of the quality and in the quantity specified.
- Prices are fair, and efforts are made to hold or reduce the price.
- Supplier is able to react to unforeseen changes such as an increase or decrease in demand, quality, specifications, or delivery schedules—all frequent occurrences.
- Supplier continually improves products and services.
- Supplier is willing to share information and be an important link in the supply chain.

However, these are not the only factors considered in selecting a supplier. Additional considerations involve the supplier's reputation/reliability, having a nearby location (especially important for JIT delivery), their financial strength, the strength of their management, and even what other customers and suppliers are involved with the supplier. For example, if we are a relatively small customer, we might be more at risk of not getting a delivery if a larger customer experiences a problem and needs our supplier's immediate help. Or if our supplier has weak or unreliable second or third tier suppliers, we might encounter a problem getting our supplies through no fault of our direct supplier.

Supplier Relationships

In these days of intense global competition and supply chain management, the relationship between customers and suppliers has changed significantly. In the past, most customers purchased from the lowest bidders who could meet their quality and delivery needs, often maintaining at least two or three suppliers in case one was suddenly unable to meet their needs due to a wildcat strike or delivery problem. As pressure mounted to reduce costs, they often pressured their suppliers to cut costs by promising larger volumes to those who had the lowest costs and smaller amounts to the others.

To implement SCM, customers are seeking a closer, more cooperative relationship with their suppliers. They are cutting back the total number of their suppliers by a factor of 10 or 20 and combining their purchases, with those remaining getting the overwhelming volume of all their business. They are also asking suppliers to do a greater portion of assembly, such as with automobile seats and other automotive components, which can then simply be installed as a package rather than assembled first and then installed. Not only does the reduced assembly labor save them cost but in return for the higher volumes, they are expecting even further reductions in cost from their reduced number of suppliers.

DILBERT: ©Scott Adams/Dist. by United Feature Syndiate, Inc.

Supplier Certification and Audits

As can be seen, these **sole-sourcing** arrangements are becoming virtual partnerships, with the customer asking the supplier to become more involved even at the design stage, and asking for smaller, more frequent JIT deliveries of higher-quality items. This means longer-term relationships, help with each other's problems, joint planning, sharing of information, and so on. To do this, suppliers are being *certified* or *qualified* so that their shipments do not need to be inspected by the customer—the items go directly to the production line. This is often referred to as **stockless purchasing**, because the items do not sit in the stockroom costing capital for holding and securing them. To ensure that the contracted supplies will be available when needed, the customers periodically conduct **supplier audits** of their vendors, checking for potential production or delivery problems, quality assurance, design competence, process improvement procedures, and the management of corrective actions. Some customers rely on standard industry certifications such as ISO 9000 (see Chapter 3) rather than incurring the time and expense of conducting their own certification. Such certified suppliers are sometimes known as *world-class* suppliers.

Of course, most of the benefits of this partnership accrue to the customer rather than the supplier. The main immediate benefit to the supplier is that they stay in business, and even grow. If managed properly, they should even become more profitable. However, with the help of their customers, their production processes should improve substantially, both in quality and efficiency, resulting in cost reductions that are shared between the partners. Toyota is known for helping their suppliers, and even their second and third tier suppliers, in this kind of fashion.

In the not-too-distant past, when just-in-time (JIT) production was still novel, customers were using sole-sourcing as a way to put pressure on their suppliers, forcing the supplier to stock inventories of items for immediate delivery rather than holding the stock themselves. Singing the praises of JIT—and insisting that the supplier implement JIT so that its deliveries could be made in smaller, more frequent batches—was often just a ploy to accommodate the customers' own sloppy schedules, because they never knew from week to week what they were going to need the following week. Today, firms are moving to Lean/JIT (described in detail in Chapter 5) and bringing their suppliers along with them. In many cases, the customer, like Toyota, is teaching the supplier how to implement effective Lean/JIT programs in their own organizations.

*I*NVENTORY MANAGEMENT

A key aspect of supply chain management is the use of inventory. In this section we look at the use of inventory and the factors that help determine the best levels of inventories to hold. We describe the various functions of inventories, the forms of inventories, specific inventory-related costs, and the two fundamental inventory decisions all organizations must make. A supplement to the chapter provides additional details on using the economic order quantity model to determine how much inventory should be ordered.

Although inventory is inanimate, the topic of inventory and inventory control can arouse completely different sentiments in the minds of people in various departments within an organization. The salespeople generally prefer large quantities of inventory to be on hand. In this way they can meet customers' requests without having to wait. Customer service is their primary concern. The accounting and financial personnel see inventory in a different light. High inventories do not translate into high customer service in the accountant's language; rather, they translate into large amounts of tied-up capital that could otherwise be used to reduce debt or for other more economically advantageous purposes. From the viewpoint of the operations manager, inventories are a tool that can be used to promote efficient operation of the production facilities. Neither high inventories nor low inventories, per se, are desirable; inventories are simply allowed to fluctuate so that production can be adjusted to its most efficient level. And top management's concern is with the "bottom line"—what advantages the inventories are providing versus their costs.

Functions of Inventories

There are many purposes for holding inventory, but, in general, inventories have five basic functions. Be aware that inventories will not generally be identified and segregated within the organization by these functions and that not all functions will be represented in all organizations.

1. ***Transit inventories***. Transit inventories exist because materials must be moved from one location to another. (These are also known as ***pipeline inventories***.) A truckload of merchandise from a retailer's regional warehouse to one of its retail stores is an example of transit inventory. This inventory results because of the transportation time required.

2. ***Buffer inventories***. Another purpose of inventories is to protect against the uncertainties of supply and demand. Buffer inventories—or, as they are sometimes called, ***safety stocks***—serve to cushion the effect of unpredictable events. The amount of inventory over and above the average demand requirement is considered to be buffer stock held to meet any demand in excess of the average. The higher the level of inventory, the better the customer service—that is, the fewer the ***stockouts*** and ***backorders***. A stockout exists when a customer's order for an item cannot be filled because the inventory of that item has run out. If there is a stockout, the firm will usually backorder the item immediately, rather than wait until the next regular ordering period.

3. ***Anticipation inventories***. An anticipated future event such as a price increase, a strike, or a seasonal increase in demand is the reason for holding anticipation inventories. For example, rather than operating with excessive overtime in one period and then allowing the productive system to be idle or shut down because of insufficient demand in another period, inventories can be allowed to build up before an event to be consumed during or after the event. Manufacturers, wholesalers, and retailers build anticipation inventories before occasions such as Christmas and Halloween, when demand for specialized products will be high.

4. ***Decoupling inventories***. It would be a rare production system in which all equipment and personnel operated at exactly the same rate. Yet if you were to take an inspection tour through a production facility, you would notice that most of the equipment and people were producing. Products move smoothly even though one machine can process parts five times as fast as the one before or after it. An inventory of parts between machines, or fluid in a vat, known as decoupling inventory, acts to disengage the production system. That is, inventories act as shock absorbers, or cushions, increasing and decreasing in size as parts are added to and used up from the stock.

Even if a preceding machine were to break down, the following machines could still produce (at least for a while), since an in-process inventory of parts would be waiting for production. The more inventories management carries between stages in the manufacturing and distribution system, the less coordination is needed to keep the system running smoothly. Clearly, there is an optimum balance between inventory level and coordination in the operations system. Without decoupling inventories, each operation in the plant would have to produce at an identical rate (a paced line) to keep the production flowing smoothly, and when one operation broke down, the entire plant would come to a standstill.

5. **Cycle inventories**. Cycle inventories—or, as they are sometimes called, *lot-size* inventories—exist for a different reason from the others just discussed. Each of the previous types of inventories serves one of the major purposes for holding inventory. Cycle inventories, on the other hand, result from management's attempt to minimize the total cost of carrying and ordering inventory. If the annual demand for a particular part is 12,000 units, management could decide to place one order for 12,000 units and maintain a rather large inventory throughout the year or place 12 orders of 1000 each and maintain a lower level of inventory. But the costs associated with ordering and receiving would increase. Cycle inventories are the inventories that result from ordering in batches or "lots" rather than as needed.

Forms of Inventories

Inventories are usually classified into four forms, some of which correspond directly with the previous inventory functions but some of which do not.

1. *Raw materials*. Raw materials are objects, commodities, elements, and items that are received (usually purchased) from outside the organization to be used directly in the production of the final output. When we think of raw materials, we think of such things as sheet metal, flour, paint, structural steel, chemicals, and other basic materials. But nuts and bolts, hydraulic cylinders, pizza crusts, syringes, engines, frames, integrated circuits, and other assemblies purchased from outside the organization would also be considered part of the raw materials inventory.

2. *Maintenance, repair, and operating supplies*. Maintenance, repair, and operating (MRO) supplies are items used to support and maintain the operation, including spares, supplies, and stores. Spares are sometimes produced by the organization itself rather than purchased. These are usually machine parts or supplies that are crucial to production. The term *supplies* is often used synonymously with *inventories*. The general convention, and the one that we will adopt in this book, is that supplies are stocks of items used (consumed) in the production of goods or services but are not directly a part of the finished product. Examples are copier paper, staples, pencils, and packing material. Stores commonly include both supplies and raw materials that are kept in stock or on shelves in a special location.

3. *Work-in-process*. **Work-in-process** (WIP) inventory consists of all the materials, parts, and assemblies that are being worked on or are waiting to be processed within the operations system. Decoupling inventories are an example of work-in-process. That is, they are all the items that have left the

raw materials inventory but have not yet been converted or assembled into a final product.

4. *Finished goods.* The **finished goods** inventory is the stock of completed products. Goods, once completed, are transferred out of work-in-process inventory and into the finished goods inventory. From here they can be sent to distribution centers, sold to wholesalers, or sold directly to retailers or final customers.

As you can see from this discussion, the inventory system and the operations system within an organization are strongly interrelated. Inventories affect customer service, utilization of facilities and equipment, capacity, and efficiency of labor. Therefore, the plans concerning the acquisition and storage of materials, or "inventories," are vital to the production system.

The ultimate objective of any inventory system is to make decisions regarding the level of inventory that will result in a good balance between the purposes for holding inventories and the costs associated with them. Typically, we hear inventory management practitioners and researchers speaking of *total cost minimization* as the objective of an inventory system. If we were able to place dollar costs on interruptions in the smooth flow of goods through the operations system, on not meeting customers' demands, or on failures to provide the other purposes for which inventories exist, then minimization of total costs would be a reasonable objective. But since we are unable to assign costs to many of these subjective factors, we must be satisfied with obtaining a good balance between the costs and the functions of inventories.

Inventory-Related Costs

There are essentially five broad categories of costs associated with inventory systems: ordering or setup costs, inventory carrying or holding costs, stockout costs, opportunity costs, and cost of goods. This section looks at these costs in turn.

Ordering or Setup Costs

Ordering costs are costs associated with outside procurement of material, and **setup costs** are costs associated with internal procurement (i.e., internal manufacture) of parts of material. Ordering costs include writing the order, processing the order through the purchasing system, postage, processing invoices, processing accounts payable, and the work of the receiving department, such as handling, testing, inspection, and transporting. Setup costs also include writing orders and processing for the internal production system, setup labor, machine downtime due to a new setup (e.g., cost of an idle, nonproducing machine), parts damaged during setup (e.g., actual parts are often used for tests during setup), and costs associated with employees' learning curve (e.g., the cost of early production spoilage and low productivity immediately after a new production run is started).

Inventory Carrying or Holding Costs

Inventory **carrying** or **holding** costs have the following major components:

- Capital costs
- Storage costs
- Risk costs

Capital costs include interest on money invested in inventory and in the land, buildings, and equipment necessary to hold and maintain the inventory, an item of special interest to both financial and top management. These rates often exceed 20 percent of the cost of the goods. If these investments were not required, the organization could invest the capital in an alternative that would earn some return on investment.

Storage costs include rent, taxes, and insurance on buildings; depreciation of buildings; maintenance and repairs; heat, power, and light; salaries of security personnel; taxes on the inventory; labor costs for handling inventory; clerical costs for keeping records; taxes and insurance on equipment; depreciation of equipment; fuel and energy for equipment; and repairs and maintenance. Some of these costs are variable, some fixed, and some "semifixed."

Risk costs include the costs of obsolete inventory, insurance on inventory, physical deterioration of the inventory, and losses from pilferage.

Even though some of these costs are relatively small, the total costs of carrying items in inventory can be quite large. Studies have found that for a typical manufacturing firm, the cost is frequently as large as 35 percent of the cost of the inventoried items. A large portion of this is the cost of the invested capital.

Stockout Costs

If inventory is unavailable when customers request it, a situation that marketing detests, or when it is needed for production, a stockout occurs. Several costs are associated with each type of stockout. A stockout of an item demanded by a customer or client can result in lost sales or demand, lost goodwill (which is very difficult to estimate), and costs associated with processing back orders (such as extra paperwork, expediting, special handling, and higher shipping costs). A stockout of an item needed for production results in costs for rescheduling production, costs of down time and delays caused by the shortage, the cost of "rush" shipping of needed parts, and possibly the cost of substituting a more expensive part or material.

Opportunity Costs

Often capacity and inventory costs can be traded off for one another. For example, capacity costs can be incurred because a change in productive capacity is necessary or because there is a temporary shortage of or excess in capacity. Why would capacity be too great or too small? If, for example, a company tried to meet seasonal demand (or any fluctuations in demand) by changing the level of production rather than by allowing the level of inventory to rise or fall, capacity would have to be increased during high-demand periods and lie idle during low-demand periods. Also, capacity problems are often due to scheduling conflicts. These commonly arise when multiple products have to be produced on the same set of facilities.

Opportunity costs include the overtime required to increase capacity; the human resource management costs of hiring, training, and terminating employees; the cost of using less-skilled workers during peak periods; and the cost of idle time if capacity is *not* reduced during periods when demand decreases.

Cost of Goods

Last, the goods themselves must be paid for. Although they must be acquired sooner or later anyway, *when* they are acquired can influence their cost considerably, as through quantity discounts.

Decisions in Inventory Management

The objective of an inventory management system is to make decisions regarding the appropriate level of inventory and changes in the level of inventory. To maintain the appropriate level of inventory, decision rules are needed to answer two basic questions:

1. When should an order be placed to replenish the inventory?
2. How much should be ordered?

The decision rules guide the inventory manager or computerized materials management system in evaluating the current state of the inventory and deciding if some action, such as replenishment, is required. Various types of inventory management systems incorporate different rules to decide "when" and "how much." Some depend on time and others on the level of inventory, but the essential decisions are the same. Even when complexities, such as uncertainty in demand and delivery times, are introduced, deciding "how many" and "when to order" still remains the basis of sound inventory management (refer to supplement B in the back of this chapter).

$\mathcal{R}$OLE OF INFORMATION TECHNOLOGY

In the not-too-distant past, the primary means of communication between members of a supply chain was paper. Unfortunately, communicating via paper-based transactions is slow, often unreliable, and prone to errors. For example, Campbell Soup Company estimated that 60 percent of the fax and phone orders it received contained errors (Verity 1996). As a result, salespeople often spent 40 percent of their time correcting these errors rather than making additional sales. To correct this problem, Campbell invested $30 million in the electronic redesign of its order-processing system. The company expected the new system to increase the percentage of paperless orders it received to 80 percent. Managers estimated the system would reduce costs by $18 million annually while at the same time reducing delivery times.

Some problems with paper-based systems have been the time and money that are wasted rekeying the same information into different computer systems. And, of course, the more times the same information is entered, the more opportunities there are for making mistakes. Some analysts estimate that the use of information technology has reduced the cost of processing a purchase order from $150 to $25.

As Campbell Soup illustrates, electronic information technology is a key element and the primary enabler of effective supply chain management. In today's highly competitive environment, the effective use of information technology helps organizations reduce cycle times, adopt more responsive cross-functional organizational structures, capture more timely information, and reduce errors and costs. The ultimate goal of such information systems is to make available to all participants in the supply chain all the information needed at the time it is needed. Such information includes the status of orders, product availabilities, delivery schedules, and other such supply chain data.

Everyone knows that computers are everywhere these days, and embedded in all kinds of products that one would not have expected. But why is this, and why now? Professor Richard Chase of the University of Southern California believes that the answer lies in two esoteric laws—one about physical goods and the other about abstract information. The first is the better known of the two: Moore's law, which states that computing power doubles every 18–24 months. The unstated surprise about Moore's law is that this doubling of power comes at the same or lower cost as before the doubling. Clearly, with enough money our big computer companies could double computing power every 18 (or 12 or 6) months, but the size of the computers would grow enormously, as well as their costs. Yet this law implies that the cost and size does *not* increase. As a result, more and more computing power is becoming available for less and less money; hence it is becoming omnipresent, appearing everywhere we go and in everything we buy.

The second law is less familiar to the public but derives from the fact that information assets, like knowledge, tend to grow with use rather than dwindle, as with physical assets. This second law is called Metcalfe's law, which says that the value of a network increases with the square of the number of elements (or users) connected to the network. This is why Amazon and Microsoft and eBay have been so successful—with more people in a network, the value of the network to the user is enhanced, so more people join this network. And competing networks, with fewer users, are of less value and hence fade away.

As a result of these two laws, the growth of computers, which support networks, and networks that support people's needs (business transactions, communication, blogging, etc.), has exploded. This phenomenon has been particularly prevalent in business, where it has contributed to both increased value (and thus revenues) and reduced costs, thereby having a double impact on increased profits. Next we will look at some particular types of information technology that are commonly used in business, especially to support supply chain management.

Electronic business (*e-business*) is the use of electronic information technology to help various groups of business people communicate and conduct business transactions. Its three primary advantages are enhanced productivity and reduced costs, speed, and the creation of new value opportunities. The primary enablers of e-business have been electronic data interchange (EDI), e-commerce, intranets and extranets, groupware applications, customer relationship management (CRM) systems, and enterprise resource planning (ERP) systems (discussed in more detail at the end of this section).

One early approach to e-business was *electronic data interchange* (EDI)—the ability of one organization's computer to communicate with another's computer. With EDI, business documents such as purchase orders and invoices are transferred between the computers of different organizations in a standard format. The benefits of EDI include faster access to information, reduced paperwork, less redundancy, improved customer service, and better order tracing. And, of course, the costs of paper transactions, both physical (paper handling, mailing, printing, etc.) and quality (errors), are reduced substantially.

Electronic commerce (***e-commerce***) is the term used to describe the execution of business transactions in a paperless environment, primarily through the Internet. In essence, this consists of two major parts: an Internet portal, such as a website (discussed a bit later) for information and communication, and the fulfillment transactions to deliver the product or service. These, in turn, include the use of bar coding and scanning, radio frequency identification (RFID), databases, point of sale (POS) terminals, e-mail, electronic funds transfer, the Internet, and websites and hubs. ***Bar coding*** and ***scanning*** technologies permit the rapid collection and dissemination of information throughout the supply chain. For example, Wal-Mart is well known for making available the ***point-of-sale*** (***POS***) information it collects at its check-out terminals to its supply chain partners. Federal Express uses the same technology to provide its customers with up-to-date tracking information on their packages. Firms also use bar coding and scanning within their production facilities to correctly produce and process items, and to keep track of different stock-keeping units (SKUs).

Most people are familiar with bar codes and scanning, but the new ***RFID*** tags/transponders are much less familiar. As mentioned in the example at the beginning of the chapter, Wal-Mart has also become known for initiating the retail use of this new technology through their suppliers in order to better track their products. RFID tags provide much more information than bar codes and come in two versions, passive and active. The passive tags are as small as the head of a pin and as thin as a sheet of paper; readers can interrogate them as they pass by, typically within about 20 feet. Active tags broadcast their information and can be read from much greater distances. However, the main difficulty with employing these technologies has been the cost of the tags, running about $0.25/apiece as of 2005, but the industry goal is to get the price down to $0.05 in the years ahead.

Arguably the most significant information technology development for supply chain management is the ***Internet***, and more specifically, its graphical component known as the ***World Wide Web*** (Web). Without a doubt, the Web offers enormous opportunities for members of a supply chain to share information. Companies such as IBM, General Electric, Dun & Bradstreet, and Microsoft are rapidly developing products and services that will help make the Web the global infrastructure for electronic commerce (Verity 1996).

For example, as noted earlier in the purchasing discussion, the Web will allow various forms of purchasing fulfillment to take place, from placing electronic catalogues on a website to holding joint purchasing bazaars, exchanges, and auction marketplaces involving massive amounts of materials. Bazaars and reverse auctions (one buyer, multiple sellers) were discussed earlier, but exchanges are for information transfer (often hosted by third parties, such as mySAP.com), and auction marketplaces (one seller, multiple buyers) are primarily for selling commodities or near-commodities at low prices. Of course, the costs of initiating and executing these forms of purchasing will be almost trivial compared to their paper-based predecessors. For example, updating an electronic catalogue can be done instantaneously, rather than waiting until next year's printing. In addition, password-protected customized catalogues reflecting negotiated prices can also be placed on a firm's website for use by individual customers.

Intranets are web-based networks that allow all employees of a firm to intercommunicate. They are usually firewall protected and use existing Internet technologies to create portals for company-specific information and communication, such as newsletters, training, human resource information and forms, product information, and so on. ***Extranets*** are private networks to allow the organization to securely interact with external parties. They use Internet protocols and public telecommunication systems to work with external vendors, suppliers, dealers, customers, and so on. Clearly, the extranet would be a major element of a firm's supply chain information system.

Groupware simply refers to any of the various systems, either internal or commercial, that facilitate the work of groups or teams in the organization. Their purpose is for communication, collaboration, and coordination (of schedules, workflow, etc.). Most groupware systems these days are web based. The major commercial systems are Lotus Notes, Novell Groupwise, and Microsoft Exchange and Netmeeting.

Customer relationship management (***CRM***) systems are designed to collect and interpret customer-based data (Ragins and Greco 2003). This could be from internal sources such as marketing, sales, or customer support services or from external sources like market research or the customer. The aim is to develop a process for improving the firm's response to their customers' needs, especially the most profitable customers. CRM systems thus provide comprehensive customer data so the firm can provide better customer service and design and offer the most appropriate products and services for them.

Enterprise Resource Planning (ERP)

Enterprise resource planning (***ERP***) systems greatly facilitate communication throughout the supply chain and over the Internet. The ERP system embodies much more than just the supply chain, however; it also includes all the electronic information concerning the various parts of the firm. These massive systems can not only reduce costs and allow instant access to the entire firm's database but can also help increase revenues, by up to 25 percent in some cases (Mabert 2001, p. 50).

As the name suggests, the objective of these systems is to provide seamless, real-time information to all employees who need it, throughout the entire organization (or enterprise), and to those outside the organization. Figure 7.3 provides a broad overview of SAP's MySAP ERP system. MySAP, announced in 2003, represents the latest evolution of SAP's ERP system. SAP introduced its R/2 system in 1979, which was an ERP system that ran on mainframe computers and its R/3 system for client server computing environments in 1992. MySAP takes the evolution one step further and is based on service-oriented architecture (SOA) whereby organizations will be able to access the SAP software via the Internet and thereby have access to the full functionality of the software without having to actually install and deploy the software throughout the enterprise. With the introduction of MySAP, SAP has announced that they will no longer continue to develop R/3.

As shown in Figure 7.3, an ERP system consists of a number of modules that provide the functionality to support a variety of organizational processes. These modules all access data from the central database, and changes made via these modules update the central database. Using ERP, each area interacts with a centralized database and servers so suppliers can check on the latest demands and customers can determine the status of their order or available capacity for new orders. ERP can also

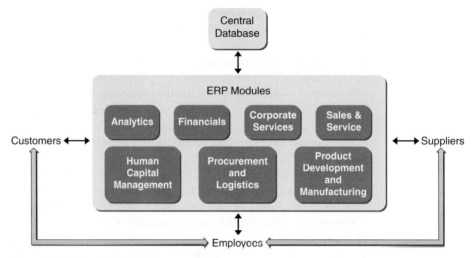

Figure 7.3 SAP's MySAP ERP system.

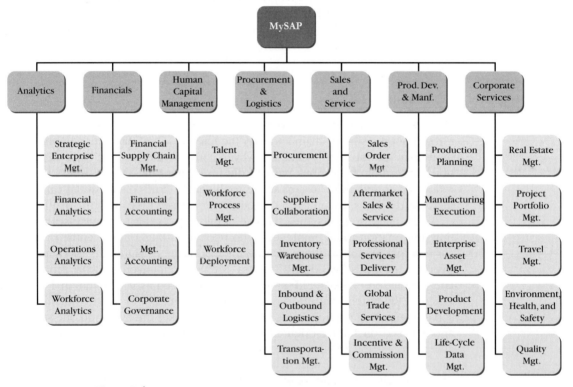

Figure 7.4 Detailed view of MySAP's modules.

handle international complications such as differences in taxes, currency, accounting rules, and language. Figure 7.4 provides additional details about the functionality offered by each MySAP module.

With the ERP approach, information is entered once at the source and made available to all stakeholders needing it. Clearly, this approach eliminates the incompatibility created when different functional departments use different systems, and it also eliminates the need for people in different parts of the organization to reenter the same information over and over again into separate computer systems. Although ERP ties all these areas together, the actual implementation of an ERP system in an organization may include only portions of these modules on an as-needed basis.

Davenport (1998) provides an example that illustrates the opportunity to automate tasks in a business process with an ERP system. In the example, a Paris-based sales rep of a U.S. manufacturer prepares a quote for a customer in Paris. After entering the customer information into a notebook computer, the ERP system creates the sales contract in French. Included in the sales contract are important details of the order such as the product's configuration, quantity ordered, price, delivery date, and payment terms. When the customer agrees to the terms of the quote, the sales rep submits the order electronically with a single keystroke. The system then automatically checks the customer's credit and accepts the order if it is within the customer's credit limit. Upon accepting the order, the ERP system then schedules the shipment of the completed order based on the agreed-upon delivery date, and then based on the delivery date and appropriate lead times reserves the required raw materials. The system also determines if the required materials will be available and, if not, automatically generates the orders for the needed materials from suppliers. Next, the ERP system schedules the actual assembly of the order in one of the organization's Asian facilities. In addition, sales and production forecasts are updated, the commission due the rep is calculated and credited to his or her account (in French francs), and the profitability of the order in U.S. dollars computed. Finally, the business units and corporate financial statements such as balance sheets, accounts-payable, accounts-receivable, cash flows, and so on are immediately updated.

As this example illustrates, the integration offered by ERP systems provides organizations with the potential to achieve dramatic improvements in the execution of their business processes. Owens Corning achieved this integration by replacing 211 legacy systems with one ERP system. Much of the benefit associated with this integration stems from having real-time access to operating and financial data. For example, after implementing an ERP system, Autodesk reduced the time it took to deliver an order from an average of two weeks to shipping 98% of its orders within 24 hours. Before implementing an ERP system, it took IBM's Storage Systems division 5 days to reprice all of its products. After implementing an ERP system it was able to accomplish the same task in 5 minutes. IBM also reduced the time required to ship replacement parts from 22 days to 3 days, and reduced the time to perform credit checks from 20 minutes to 3 seconds! Fujitsu Microelectronics achieved similar benefits, reducing its order fulfillment time from 18 days to less than two days and reducing the time required to close its financial books from eight days to four days.

$\mathscr{S}$UCCESSFUL SUPPLY CHAIN MANAGEMENT

The basic requirements for successful supply chain management are trustworthy partners, good communication, appropriate performance measures, and competent managers with vision. Innovation to suit the particular situation of the individual organization is particularly desirable. Some examples of visionary SCM innovations that have been developed are:

- Dell's "direct model" (Magretta 1998) and, as described earlier, Palm's "strategic sourcing."

- Wal-Mart's "***cross-docking***" technique of off-loading goods from incoming trucks at a warehouse directly into outbound distribution trucks instead of being placed into inventory.

- The relatively common approach used by Dell and many others of "***delayed differentiation***" where final modules are either inventoried for last-minute assembly to customer order, or differentiating features are added to the final product upon receipt of the customer's order.

- Sport Obermeyer's and Hewlett-Packard's "***postponement***" approach to delayed differentiation where variety and customization are delayed until as late in the production process as possible, sometimes even arranging with the carrier to perform the final customization (called ***channel assembly***). In Sport Obermeyer's (Fisher et al. 1994) version, those product lines where demand is better known are produced first, while customer demand volume information is being collected on less easily forecast lines whose production has thus been postponed. Similarly, Hewlett-Packard ships generic DeskJet printers to regional centers around the globe, where local workers add country-specific power supplies, power cords, and local language instructions. Another variant of postponement was mentioned in the Dell example cited earlier, where *drop shipping* arrangements are made with the carrier to deliver third-party supplied elements of the product (e.g., monitors) to the customer at the same time that the main product is being delivered.

Closed-Loop Supply Chains and Reverse Logistics

Guide and Van Wassenhove (2009, p. 10) define closed loop supply chain management as "the design, control, and operation of a system to maximize value creation over the entire life cycle of a product with dynamic recovery of value from different types and volumes of returns over time." An important aspect of closed loop supply chain management is recovering value from returned products. The potential for recovering value from returns is enormous as it is estimated that commercial returns exceed $100 billion annually (Stock et al. 2002). Large retailers like Home Depot can expect to have 10 percent or more of their sales returned while Hewlett Packard estimates that it incurs costs equivalent to 2 percent of its outbound sales in returned merchandise.

Product returns are categorized as commercial returns, end-of-use returns, end-of-life returns, and repair and warranty returns. Commercial returns are returns typically to the reseller and occur within 90 days of purchase. For example, many cell phone companies allow customers to return their cell phones for any reason within 30 days of purchase. End-of-use returns occur when a product is returned so that its functionality can be upgraded. For example, in the United States it is estimated that 80 percent of cell phone users upgrade their perfectly usable cell phones annually. End-of-life returns occur when the product still functions but is technologically obsolete. Finally, between commercial returns to end-of-life returns, customers return products to be repaired.

The type of product return has important implications for how the return is handled. For example, commercial returns have usually only been lightly used. Therefore they typically require minor processing such as cleaning and perhaps some minor repairs. End-of-use returns have been used more heavily and there is likely to be more variability in the quality of these returns. Given this, these returns will typically require more extensive processing. The focus on end-of-life returns is on parts recovery and recycling since these products are technologically obsolete. In summary then, commercial returns are repaired, end-of-use returns are remanufactured, and end-of-life returns are recycled.

In addition to significant environmental benefits, the goal of operating a closed-loop supply chain is to generate more value through the recovery activities than the cost of performing these activities. The steps involved in operating a closed-loop supply chain include acquiring the right quantities of the used-product with the right quality and at the right time; reverse logistics or moving the product back upstream from the customer to the repair/remanufacturing operations; sorting, testing and grading the returned products to determine their disposition; repairing/remanufacturing the returned products; and finally, remarketing the refurbished products. Some products such as consumer electronics and computers have short life cycles and therefore lose a significant portion of their value per week. In these cases a slow reverse supply chain can erode much if not all of the potential value that can be recovered.

EXPAND YOUR UNDERSTANDING

1. Why is supply chain management such a topic of interest lately, especially multifacility distribution? Why wasn't it previously?

2. Will all production eventually reside in China? What exceptions might exist?

3. What appears to be the primary "secret" of successful supply chain management?

4. Given that the current conceptualization of the supply chain includes JIT and lean manufacturing, what other elements of SCM need to be changed to move toward the idea of a *demand* chain?

5. In what way can contract manufacturers consider themselves service providers? Hasn't Nike been doing this for years? What's the difference?

6. To date it appears that purchasing has been the primary beneficiary of supply chain management. Why do you think this is so? What do you expect will happen in the future?

7. The bullwhip effect is often blamed for the boom and bust cycles in our national economy. Which of the remedies for eliminating this effect in a supply chain might also benefit the national economy?

8. How does postponement differ from assemble to order?

9. Why does the Internet rather than the older EDI now seem to be the information foundation for SCM?

10. Why do you think Wal-Mart has been the pioneer of RFID technology?

11. E-commerce has been supplanted by e-business. What is the basic difference between the two?

12. Contrast SCM systems with ERP systems. Which do you suspect are larger and more costly?

13. What additional information might a retailer such as Wal-Mart be interested in putting on an RFID tag, beyond the basic product identification that a bar code communicates?

14. Do any of the five functions and four forms of inventories exist in service firms? If so, which ones, and why? If not, how are the functions served?

15. Contrast the functions and forms of inventories. Does every form exist for each function and vice versa, or are some more common?

16. In many of today's firms, the customer's computer is tied to the supplier's computer so that purchase orders go directly into the supplier's planning system. What are the implications of this close relationship?

17. Discuss the pros and cons of relying on outside expertise in the selection and implementation of an ERP system.

APPLY YOUR UNDERSTANDING
Dart's Parts, Inc.

Z. "Dart" Mitchell leaned forward in his chair to read the e-mail that had just arrived from one of his major customers, Avery Machine Corp. It read as follows:

"To all our preferred suppliers—

Due to our commitments to our primary customer, Globus Enterprises, we will in the future be doing all of our supply chain business by way of the Internet, e-mail, and EDI. This includes order preparation, bidding, forecasting, production scheduling, delivery monitoring, cost control, accounts payable and receivable, credit and financing, market and advertising planning, human resource acquisition, engineering specifications, and so on. To maintain compatibility with our systems, you will have to invest in a specific set of EDI hardware and software, available from GoingBust.com on the Web. Although the hardware and software are expensive, we anticipate that the cost savings and increased business this will provide over the coming years can more than offset the additional cost. Please let us know if we can continue to count on you as one of our preferred suppliers as we move our supply chain into the information age.

J. R. Avery, Chairman
Avery Machine Corp."

Dart's Parts had been founded in 1974, when the country was coming out of the 1973–74 recession and the need for machine part fabricators was great. Over the years, Dart had built up the business to where it now had a solid base of major customers and a comfortable backlog of orders. Dart had increased the capacity of the plant substantially over the years, moving from a small rented facility to its own 200,000 square foot plant, with a separate 50,000 square foot warehouse located adjacent to the main plant. Although not a "first adopter" when it came to new technology, Dart's embraced proven advanced technologies both on the plant floor, such as robots and numerically controlled machine tools, as well as in the office with computers, digital copiers, and other such office equipment.

Dart Mitchell had been reading industry magazines about some of these new technologies and had to admit they sounded promising. However, he had read about some horror stories too, when the much-advertised features turned into a nightmare. In one case, a customer had forced its suppliers to obtain production schedules off their website. Initially responding to high growth in a new product line, the firm had put their component needs on their website but when a major order was cancelled, they were late changing the Web production schedule. As a result, the suppliers were stuck with hundreds of unneeded components and the company wouldn't reimburse them. In another case, a manufacturer had made a bid for electronic parts on a Web auction and won. However, when they received the parts, they were too large to fit in the standard-sized enclosure they were using and they all had to be scrapped.

Dart believed that this new technology was indeed the future of the industry, but was concerned about getting in too early and being stuck with the wrong equipment. Learning about the new supply chain technology would undoubtedly open avenues to increased business, and might also cut a number of costs. Of course, it would also save their reputation with Avery, a major customer. However, obtaining the EDI system would be a major financial investment for the firm, particularly if Avery later dropped this approach and went to an all-Internet ERP system like some customers had been talking about doing. At this point, Dart wasn't sure what to do.

Questions

1. Identify the trade-offs facing Dart's Parts.
2. What are the pros and cons of each alternative?
3. What additional information would be useful to have?
4. What recommendations would you make to Dart Mitchell?

BIBLIOGRAPHY

Ballou, R. H. *Business Logistics: Supply Chain Management,* 5th ed. Upper Saddle River, NJ: Prentice-Hall, 2003.

Bender, P. S. "Debunking 5 Supply Chain Myths." *Supply Chain Management Review* (March 2000): 52–58.

Bjurstrom, T. "How Outsourcing Supply Chain Services to 3PLs can Affect Your Company's Bottom Line." *Contract Management* (February 2008), pp. 52—55.

Blackwell, R. D., and K. Blackwell. "The Century of the Consumer: Converting Supply Chains into Demand Chains." *Supply Chain Management Review* (Fall 1999): 22–32.

Blanchard, D. "RFID is Off and Running at Wal-Mart." *Logistics Today*, 46 (February 2005): pp. 1–2.

Bowersox, D. J., D. J. Closs, and M. B. Cooper. *Supply Chain Logistics Management.* New York: Irwin/McGraw-Hill, 2002.

Burt, D. N., D. W. Dobler, and S. L. Starling. *World Class Supply Managment^{SM}: The Key to Supply Chain Management,* 7th ed. New York: McGraw-Hill/Irwin, 2003.

Cachon G. and C. Terwiesch. *Matching Supply with Demand,* second edition, New York: McGraw-Hill/Irwin, 2009.

Carbone, J. "Strategic Sourcing is Palm's Pilot." *Purchasing,* April 17, 2003.

Champion, D. "Mastering the Value Chain." *Harvard Business Review* (June 2001): 109–115.

Chopra, S., and P. Meindl. *Supply Chain Management: Strategy, Planning, and Operation.* Upper Saddle River, NJ: Prentice-Hall, 2001.

Coyle, J. J., E. J. Bardi, and R. A. Novack. *Transportation.* Cincinnati: South-Western, 2000.

Cross, G. J. "How E-Business is Transforming Supply Chain Management." *Engineering Management Review,* 28 (Third Quarter 2000): 17–19.

Davenport, T. "Putting the Enterprise into the Enterprise System." *Harvard Business Review* (July–August 1998): 121–131.

Davenport, T. *Mission Critical: Realizing the Promise of Enterprise Systems.* Boston: Harvard Business School Press, 2000.

Dignan, L. "Is Dell Hitting the Efficiency Wall?" MSNBC News.Com, July 29, 2002, pp. 1–5.

Dvorak, P. "Clarity Is Missing Link in Supply Chain," *Wall Street Journal* (May 18, 2009), A1, A14.

Ellram, L. M., and B. Liu. "The Financial Impact of Supply Management." *Supply Chain Management Review* (November–December 2002): 30–37.

Engardio, P. "Why the Supply Chain Broke Down." *Business Week* (March 19, 2001), p. 41.

Evans, P., and T. S. Wurster. "Getting Real about Virtual Commerce." *Harvard Business Review* (November–December 1999): 84–94.

Fisher, M. L., J. H. Hammond, W.R. Obermeyer, and A. Raman. "Making Supply Meet Demand in an Uncertain World." *Harvard Business Review* (May–June 1994): 83–93.

Fisher, M. L. "What Is the Right Supply Chain for Your Product?" *Harvard Business Review* (March–April 1997): 105–116.

Frohlich, M. T., and R. Westbrook. "Arcs of Integration: An International Study of Supply Chain Strategies." *Journal of Operations Management,* 19 (2001): 185–200.

Ferguson, B. R., "Implementing Supply Chain Management." *Production and Inventory Management Journal,* 40 (Second Quarter 2000): 64–67.

Guide Jr., V. D. R., and L. N. Van Wassenhove, "The Evolution of Closed-Loop Supply Chain Research," *Operations Research,* vol. 57, no. 1 (January-February 2009), pp. 10–18.

Hammer, M. "The Superefficient Company." *Harvard Business Review* (Sept. 2001): 82–91.

Handfield, R. B., and E. L. Nichols, Jr. *Introduction to Supply Chain Management.* Upper Saddle River, NJ: Prentice-Hall, 1999.

Hutchison, P. D., M. T. Farris II and S.B. Anders, "Cash-to-Cash Analysis and Management," The CPA Journal, August 2007.

Kahn, G. "Making Labels for Less: Supply-Chain City Transforms Apparel Industry." *Wall Street Journal* (August 13, 2004): B1, B3.

Kanakamedala, K., G. Ramsdell, and V. Srivatsan. "Getting Supply Chain Software Right." *The McKinsey Quarterly,* no. 1 (2003).

Kanet, J. J., and A. R. Cannon. "Implementing Supply Chain Management: Lessons Learned at Becton Dickinson." *Production and Inventory Management Journal,* 41 (Second Quarter 2000): 33–40.

Kaplan, S., and M. Sawhney. "E-Hubs: The New B2B Marketplaces." *Harvard Business Review* (May–June 2000): 97–103.

Lacy, S. "Inching Toward the RFID Revolution," *Business Week Online*, August 31, 2004.

Lee, H. L., and C. Billington. "Managing Supply Chain Inventory: Pitfalls and Opportunities." *Sloan Management Review*, 33 (Spring 1992): 65–73.

Lummus, R. R., and R. J. Vokurka. "Managing the Demand Chain Through Managing the Information Flow: Capturing 'Moments of Information'." *Production and Inventory Management Journal*, 40 (First Quarter 1999): 16–20.

Lummus, R. R., and R. J. Vokurka. "Strategic Supply Chain Planning." *Production and Inventory Management Journal*, 39 (Third Quarter 1998): 49–58.

Mabert, V. A., A. Soni, and M. A. Venkataramanan. "Enterprise Resource Planning: Measuring Value." *Production and Inventory Management Journal*, 42 (Third/Fourth Quarter 2001): 46–51.

Magretta, J. "The Power of Virtual Integration: An Interview with Dell Computer's Michael Dell." *Harvard Business Review* (March–April 1998): 72–84.

Quinn, F. J. "What's the Buzz? Supply Chain Management; Part 1." *Logistics Management*, 36 (February 1997), 43.

Ragins, E. J., and A. J. Greco. "Customer Relationship Management and E-Business: More Than a Software Solution." *Review of Business*, Winter, 2003, 25–30.

Richardson, H. L., "The Ins & Outs of VMI," *Logistics Today*, 45 (March 2004): 19–21.

Sampson, S. E. and C. M. Froehle, Foundations and Implications of a Proposed Unified Services Theory," *Production and Operations Management*, vol. 15, no. 2 (2006): 329–343.

SAP, "mySAP ERP Solution Overview." www.sap.com/solutions/business-suite/erp/pdf/ BWP_mySAP_ERP_Overview.pdf, June 26, 2005.

Simchi-Levi, D., P. Kaminsky, and E. Simchi-Levi. *Supply Chain Management,* 2nd ed. New York: McGraw-Hill, 2003.

Shapiro, C., and H. R. Varian. *Information Rules: A Strategic Guide to the Network Economy.* Boston: Harvard Business School Press, 1999.

Stock, J., T. Speh, and H. Shear, "Many Happy (Product) Returns," *Harvard Business Review*, vol. 80, no. 7 (2002): pp. 16–17.

Tully, S. "Purchasing's New Muscle." *Fortune* (February 20, 1995): 75–83.

Turban, E., J. Lee, D. King, and H. M. Chung. *Electronic Commerce: A Managerial Perspective.* Upper Saddle River, NJ: Prentice Hall, 2000.

Verity, J. W. "Invoice? What's an Invoice?" *Business Week* (June 10, 1996): 110–112.

Walker, W. T., and K. L. Alber. "Understanding Supply Chain Management." *APICS—The Performance Advantage,* 9 (January 1999), 38–43.

The Beer Game[1]

[1]Adapted from J. Sterman "Instructions for Running the Beer Distribution Game, Massachusetts Institute of Technology, October 1894; J. H. Hammond. "The Beer Game: Description of Exercise," Harvard Business School, 9-964-104.

The *Beer Game* has become a staple of the operations management course in MBA programs across the country. In effect, the game simulates material and information flows in a simplified supply chain. As shown in Figure 7SA.1, the supply chain consists of four stages. Moving from the factory downstream, the supply chain consists of a factory, wholesaler, distributor, and retailer. Accordingly, each stage in the supply chain is required to manage its inventory levels given the receipt of orders from its downstream customer through the placement of orders with its upstream supplier. The only exceptions to this are that the retailer's demand comes from the final consumer and the factory schedules production requests as opposed to placing an order from an upstream supplier.

There is a 2-week delay between the retailer, wholesaler, and distributor. Thus, orders from the retailer to the wholesaler in a given week arrive 2 weeks after the wholesaler ships them. Likewise, orders from the wholesaler to the distributor in a particular week arrive two weeks after the distributor ships it. Production orders at the factory are available to ship three weeks after the production requests.

Your objective in playing the game is to minimize the sum of your total weekly costs. Weekly costs consist of two components: an inventory cost and a backlog cost. More specifically, weekly inventory cost is calculated at the rate of $.50/keg of beer in inventory at the end of the week, while backlog costs are calculated at the rate of $1.00/keg on backlog at the end of the week. Obviously, only one of these costs can be positive in any given week (although it is possible that they both could be zero in a particular week).

Because a supply chain for the beer industry in reality would likely be characterized by multiple factories, dozens of distributors, hundreds of wholesalers, and tens of thousands of retailers, it is often the case that the only information shared between a supplier and its customer is order information. Therefore, in the game, the only communication you may have with your upstream supplier is the placement of your order.

In terms of the initial conditions, as it turns out, the demand at the retailer stage has been quite stable at four kegs per week for the last several weeks. Therefore, every order placed throughout the entire supply chain has been for four kegs over this period. Furthermore, each stage has maintained an inventory level of 12 kegs or the equivalent of three weeks of demand. However, as the weather turns warmer in the near future, demand is expected to increase. Also, it is expected that there will be one or more promotions over the coming months.

In playing the game, you will be assigned to one of the four stages in the supply chain. During each week of simulated time, you will be required to perform the following five tasks. It is important that these tasks be completed in the order listed below and that each stage in the supply chain complete the task simultaneously with the other stages. Note that only the final task requires you to make a decision.

1. Deliver your beer and advance shipments. Move the beer in the **Shipping Delay** box (on the right, adjacent to your **Current Inventory** box) into the **Current Inventory** box. Next, move beer in the other **Shipping Delay** box to the right to the now empty **Shipping Delay** box. [Factories move the inventory from the **Production Delay** box directly to the right of the **Current Inventory** box into the **Current Inventory** box. Then move inventory from the top **Production Delay** box to the bottom **Production Delay** box.]

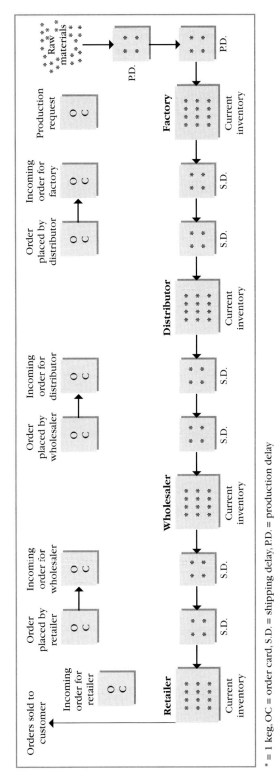

* = 1 keg, OC = order card, S.D. = shipping delay, P.D. = production delay

Figure 7SA.1 The beer game board and initial conditions.

2. Pick up the incoming order from your downstream customer in your **Incoming Order** box at your top left (retailers read incoming order from the consumer). Fill as much of the order as you can from your current inventory by placing the appropriate quantity of kegs in the **Shipping Delay** box directly to the left of your **Current Inventory** box. Quantities ordered above your current inventory level become part of your current backlog. More specifically, the amount to ship this week is calculated as follows:

$$\text{Quantity to Ship} = \text{Incoming Order This Week} + \text{Previous Week's Backlog}$$

3. Calculate and record in Figure 7SA.2 your ending inventory or backlog position (as a negative number.) Count the number of kegs remaining in your

Week	Inventory	Order Placed	Week	Inventory	Order Placed
1			26		
2			27		
3			28		
4			29		
5			30		
6			31		
7			32		
8			33		
9			34		
10			35		
11			36		
12			37		
13			38		
14			39		
15			40		
16			41		
17			42		
18			43		
19			44		
20			45		
21			46		
22			47		
23			48		
24			49		
25			50		

Figure 7SA.2 Data sheet.

current inventory after the shipment for the week has been made. If you get into a backlog situation, the backlog must be accumulated from week to week since quantities ordered but not shipped must be made up. The week's ending backlog position is calculated as follows:

$$\text{Current Week's Backlog} = \text{Previous Week's Backlog} \\ + \text{Incoming Order} - \text{Shipments Received this Week}$$

4. Advance your order cards. (Factories fill their production requests.) Advance the order from the **Order Placed** box to the **Incoming Order** box (or, for the factory, read the **Production Request** and fill the **Production Delay** box from the raw materials inventory). Make sure to keep the order cards face down as you move them.

5. Decide how much to order, write it down on your order card (and in Figure 7SA.2), and place the card face down in the **Orders Placed** box. Factories decide how much to schedule for production, write it down on your order, and place the card face down in the **Production Request** box.

6. Repeat steps 1–5.

Most likely, your instructor will have the class complete one or more practice runs or go through the first couple of weeks at a slow pace.

The Economic Order Quantity Model

The concept of ***economic order quantity*** (EOQ) applies to inventory items that are replenished in *batches* or *orders* and are not produced and delivered continuously. Although we have identified a number of costs associated with inventory decisions in the chapter, only two categories, carrying cost and ordering cost, are considered in the basic EOQ model. Shortage costs and opportunity costs are not relevant because shortages and changes in capacity should not occur if demand is constant, as we assume in this basic case. The cost of the goods is considered to be fixed and, hence, does not alter the decisions as to *when* inventory should be reordered or *how much* should be ordered.

More specifically, we assume the following in the basic EOQ model:

1. Rate of demand is constant (e.g., 50 units per day).
2. Shortages are not allowed.
3. Lead times are known with certainty, so stock replenishment can be scheduled to arrive exactly when the inventory drops to zero.
4. Purchase price, ordering cost, and per-unit holding cost are independent of quantity ordered.
5. Items are ordered independently of each other.

Let us consider a water distributor which sells 1000 5-gallon bottles per month (30 days) and purchases in quantities of 2000 per order. Lead time for the receipt of an order is six days. The cost accounting department has analyzed inventory costs and has determined that the cost of placing an order is $60 and the annual cost of holding one 5-gallon bottle in inventory is $10.[1]

Under its current policy of ordering 2000 per order, what is the water distributor's total annual inventory cost? Its inventory pattern is represented by the "saw-tooth" curve of Figure 7SB.1. For simplicity, let

$$Q = \text{order quantity}$$
$$U = \text{annual usage}$$
$$C_O = \text{cost to place one order}$$
$$C_H = \text{annual holding cost per unit}$$

To determine the total annual incremental cost of the distributor's current inventory policy, we must determine two separate annual costs: total annual holding cost and total annual ordering cost.

The *ordering* cost is determined by C_O, the cost to place one order ($60), and the number of orders placed per year. Since the distributor sells 12,000 5-gallon bottles per year and orders 2000 per order, it must place six (that is, 12,000/2000) orders per year, for a total ordering cost of $360 (6 orders per year × $60 per order). Using our notation, we write the annual ordering cost as

$$\text{annual ordering cost} = \frac{U}{Q} \times C_O$$

---

[1]Sometimes holding cost is given as a fixed value per year and other times as a percentage of the value of the inventory, especially when interest charges represent the major holding costs. Then holding cost $C_H = iC$, where C is the cost of the inventory item and i is the interest rate.

The annual holding cost is determined by C_H, the cost of holding one five-gallon bottle for one year ($10), and the number of bottles held as "cycle stock." Notice that the inventory level is constantly changing and that no single bottle ever remains in inventory for an entire year. On average, however, there are 1000 bottles in the inventory. Consider one cycle of the distributor's inventory graph, as shown in Figure 7SB.2. The inventory level begins at 2000 units and falls to 0 units before the next cycle begins. Since the rate of decline in inventory is constant (i.e., 1000 per month), the average level is 1000 units, or simply the arithmetic average of the two levels: $(2000 + 0)/2 = 1000$.

If, on the average, there are 1000 bottles in inventory over the entire year, then the annual inventory holding cost is $10,000 ($10 per unit $\times$ 1000 units). Or, in our general notation,

$$\text{annual holding cost} = \frac{Q}{2} \times C_H$$

Adding annual ordering cost and annual holding cost gives the following equation for total annual cost (TAC):

$$\text{TAC} = \left(\frac{U}{Q}\right)C_O + \left(\frac{Q}{2}\right)C_H$$

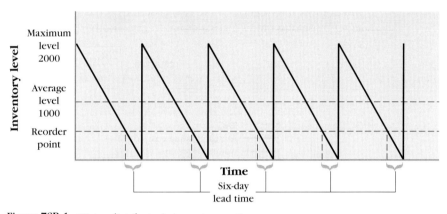

Figure 7SB.1 Water distributor's inventory pattern.

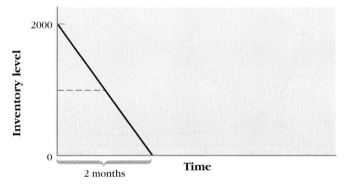

Figure 7SB.2 Water distributor's inventory graph.

For the water distributor, TAC is $360 + $10,000 = $10,360. Thus, its current inventory policy of ordering quantities of 2000 bottles is costing $10,360 per year. Is this the best policy, or can it be improved?

Finding an Optimal Policy

We can graph annual holding cost and annual ordering cost as a function of the order quantity, as shown in Figure 7SB.3. Since the annual holding cost is $(Q/2)C_H$, which can be written $(C_H/2)Q$, we see that holding cost is linear and increasing with respect to Q. Annual order cost is $(U/Q)C_O$, which can be rewritten as $(UC_O)/Q$. We can see that ordering cost is nonlinear with respect to Q and decreases as Q increases.

Now, if we add the two graphed quantities for all values of Q, we have the TAC curve shown in Figure 7SB.3. Note that TAC first decreases as ordering cost decreases but then starts to increase quickly. The point at which TAC is minimized is the optimal order quantity; that is, it gives the quantity Q that provides the least total annual inventory cost. This point is called the *economic order quantity* (EOQ), and for this inventory problem it happens to occur where the order cost curve intersects the holding cost curve. (The minimum point is not *always* where two curves intersect; it just happens to be so in the case of EOQ.) From Figure 7SB.3 we can see that EOQ is approximately 400 bottles per order.

We can compute an accurate value algebraically by noting that the value of Q at the point of intersection of the two cost lines is the EOQ. We can find an equation for EOQ by setting the two costs equal to one another and solving for the value of Q:

$$\text{EOQ} = \sqrt{\frac{2UC_O}{C_H}}$$

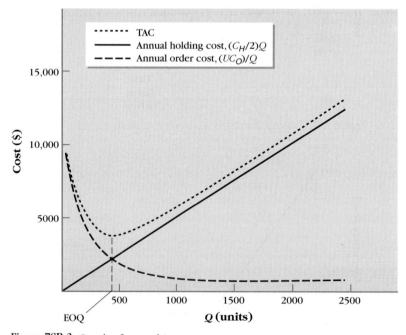

Figure 7SB.3 Graph of annual inventory costs.

For the water distributor, we can compute EOQ as

$$\text{EOQ} = \sqrt{\frac{2(12,000)60}{10}} = \sqrt{144,000} = 379.6$$

Obviously, since we cannot order a fraction of a bottle, the order quantity would be rounded to 380 units.

The total annual cost (TAC) of this policy would be

$$\text{TAC} = \left(\frac{12,000}{380}\right)60 + \frac{380}{2}10 = 1894.74 + 1900 = \$3794.74$$

Note that this is an improvement in total annual cost of $6,565.26 over the present policy of ordering 2000. Actual inventory situations often exhibit relative "insensitivity" to changes in quantity in the vicinity of EOQ. To the inventory manager, what this means is added flexibility in order quantities. If, for example, shipping and handling was more convenient or economical in quantities of 500 (perhaps the items are shipped on pallets in quantities of 250), the additional 120 units per order would cost the organization only an extra $145.26 per year.

Cautions Regarding EOQ

The EOQ is a computed minimum-cost order quantity. As with any model or formula, the GIGO rule (garbage in, garbage out) applies. If the values used in computing EOQ are inaccurate, then EOQ will be inaccurate—though, as mentioned previously, a slight error will not increase costs significantly. EOQ relies heavily on two variables that are subject to considerable misinterpretation. These are the two cost elements: holding cost (C_H) and order cost (C_O). In the derivation of EOQ, we assumed that by ordering fewer units per order, the cost of holding inventory would be reduced. Similarly, it was assumed that by reducing the number of orders placed each year the cost of ordering could be proportionately reduced. Both assumptions must be thoroughly questioned in looking at each cost element that is included in both C_H and C_O.

For example, if a single purchasing agent is employed by the firm, and orders are reduced from 3000 per year to 2000 per year, does it stand to reason that the purchasing expense will be reduced by one-third? Unless the person is paid on a piece-work basis, the answer is clearly no. Similarly, suppose we rent a warehouse that will hold 100,000 items and that we currently keep it full. If the order sizes are reduced so that the warehouse is only 65 percent occupied, can we persuade the owners to charge us only 65 percent of the rental price? Again, the answer is no. Clearly, then, when costs are determined for computations, only real, out-of-pocket costs should be used. Costs that are committed or "sunk," no matter what the inventory level or number of orders is, should be excluded.

Note also that C_H and C_O are *controllable* costs. That is, they can be reduced, if this is advantageous. This is exactly what the Japanese recognized. The problems they saw with holding inventory were:

- Product defects become hidden in the inventory, thereby increasing scrap and rework later in the production system, when defects are harder to repair. Just as important, the problem in the system that led to the defective part cannot be tracked down so easily later.

- Storage space takes up precious room and separates all the company's functions and equipment, thereby increasing problems with communication. Space itself is extremely expensive in Japan (directly increasing the variable C_H).

- More inventory in the plant means that more control is needed, more planning is required, larger systems are required to move all that stock, and in general more "hassle" is created, which leads to errors, defects, missed deliveries, long lead times, and more difficulty in product changeovers.

Rarely do U.S. firms consider these real costs in the EOQ formula. More typically, these costs are considered part of the indirect, overhead, or "burden" costs that are assumed to be uncontrollable. Again, the message is: Be very careful about the values used in the EOQ formula.

Also, it should be noted that very small EOQ values (e.g., 2) will not usually be valid, because the cost functions are questionable for such small orders. Last, EOQ reorder sizes should not be followed blindly. There may not be enough cash just now to pay for an EOQ, or storage space may be insufficient.

EXERCISES

1. Frame-Up, a self-service picture framing shop for tourists in Sevilla, Spain, orders 3000 meters of a certain molding every month. The order cost is €40 and the holding cost is €0.05 per meter per year. What is the current annual inventory cost? What is the maximum inventory level? What is the EOQ?

2. The Corner Convenient Store (CCS) in northern Chicago, USA receives orders from its distributor in three days from the time an order is placed. Light Cola sells at the rate of 860 cans per day. (It can sell 250 days of the year.) A six-pack of Light Cola costs CCS $1.20. Annual holding cost is 10 percent of the cost of the cola. Order cost is $25.00. What is CCS's EOQ?

3. A Liverpool, England camera supplies wholesaler purchases £1 million worth of camera equipment each year. It costs £100 to place and receive an order, and the annual holding cost per item is 20 percent of the item's value.
   a. What is the £ value of the EOQ?

   b. How many months' supply is the EOQ?
   c. How often should orders be placed?
   d. How much will the annual holding cost change if the company orders monthly? How much will the annual ordering cost change?
   e. What should the £ value of the EOQ be if the wholesaler doubles its annual purchases? What should it be if (instead) the ordering cost doubles? What should it be if the holding cost drops to 10 percent?

4. Wing Computer Corporation of Xiamen, China uses 15,000 keyboards each year in the production of computer terminals for major computer manufacturers headquartered in Taiwan. Order cost for the keyboards is 50 renminbi and the holding cost for one keyboard is 1.5 renminbi per unit per year. What is the EOQ? If Wing orders 1250 per month, what will be the total annual cost? What is the average inventory level?

BIBLIOGRAPHY

Greene, J. H. *Production and Inventory Control Handbook*, 3rd ed. New York: McGraw-Hill, 1997.

Landvater, D. V. *World Class Production and Inventory Management*. Newburg, NH: Oliver Wight Publications, 1997.

Silver, E. A., D. F. Pyke, and R. Peterson. *Inventory Management, Production Planning, and Scheduling*, 3rd ed. New York, Wiley, 1998.

Sipper, D., and R. Bulfin. *Production: Planning, Control, and Integration*. New York: McGraw-Hill (1997).

Vollmann, T. E., W. L. Berry, D. C. Whybark, and F. R. Jacobs *Manufacturing Planning and Control Systems for Supply Chain Management*, 5th ed. NY: McGraw-Hill 2004.

Waters, D., *Inventory Control and Management*, NJ: Wiley, 2003.

Zipkin, P. H. *Foundations of Inventory Management*. New York: Irwin/McGraw-Hill, 2000.

Chapter 8

Capacity Management through Location and Scheduling

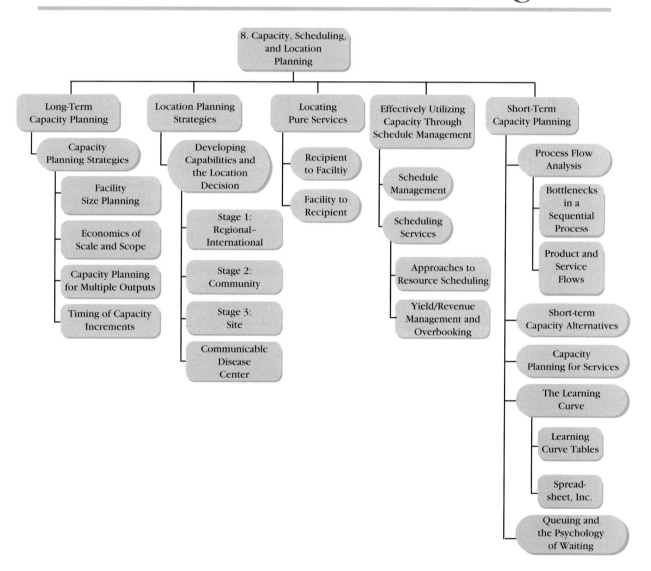

CHAPTER IN PERSPECTIVE

In this chapter our attention turns to determining the amount of capacity needed, where it should be located, and how to effectively schedule its use. Having adequate capacity and effectively utilizing it are critical for dependability and speed, while having excess capacity will impair costs, all strategic competitive factors. We begin the chapter with an overview of various measures of capacity and then discuss issues related to long-term capacity planning and location planning strategies.

In the next section we address the unique aspects of making location decisions for pure services. Following this, we consider issues related to efficiently using the available capacity through effective schedule management. The chapter concludes with a discussion of short-term capacity planning including process flow analysis, the relationship between capacity and scheduling, and how humans' ability to learn affects capacity planning.

INTRODUCTION

- You might be surprised to learn that the semiconductor industry is taking a lesson from the steel industry. After all, the semiconductor industry is on the leading edge of technology, whereas the steel industry is decidedly mature. However, these industries have an important characteristic in common: Both tend to require factories that are large and expensive (i.e., in excess of $1 billion). However, in the late 1980s steelmakers began to abandon economies of scale as a rationale for building large factories and began to develop smaller production facilities called minimills. Now chip makers are adopting a similar approach: they are constructing smaller and more automated wafer fabrication factories. One reason for this is that shorter product life cycles will make it virtually impossible to recoup the costs to build a conventional wafer fab. It takes 22 to 30 months to recapture the investment in a conventional wafer fabrication facility, but it is projected that it will take only 10 months to recoup the development costs of a so-called minifab. Another important benefit associated with the minifabs is that because equipment can be grouped in clusters, the time required to complete the 200 processing steps can be reduced from the current 60 to 90 days to 7 days. This is particularly important because studies indicate that getting a new chip to market a few months earlier can result in as much as $1 billion in added revenues (Port 1994).

- In the early 1990s, Mercedes-Benz began investigating the feasibility of producing a luxury sports-utility vehicle, referred to as the *Multi-Purpose Vehicle* (MPV). Faced with increasing international competition, Mercedes deviated from its established procedures and staffed the project team with young product planners, engineers, and marketers. The team was charged with finding a site outside of Germany to build the MPV (up to this time, all Mercedes automobiles had been built in Germany). The team initially narrowed the search for the new facility to North

America, because the combined costs of labor, shipping, and components would be lowest in this region. Costs were particularly important since the MPV was to be priced about the same as a fully loaded Jeep Grand Cherokee, yet Mercedes would operate its plant at a much lower volume than producers such as Chrysler.

After further analysis, the team decided to limit the search to sites in the United States in order to be close to the primary market and to avoid the penalties associated with currency fluctuations. The team identified 100 possible sites in 35 states. As it began analyzing the sites, its primary concern was the cost of transportation. Since the MPV was going to be built only in the United States and half of its output would be exported, the team focused on sites near Atlantic or Gulf seaports, major highways, and rail lines. Also, workers' ages and mix of skills were considered.

Eventually, the original list of sites was pared down to three sites in North Carolina, South Carolina, and Alabama. All three finalists were evaluated as relatively equal in terms of business climate, education levels, transportation, and long-term operating costs. According to the managing director, the decision to locate the new facility in Alabama came down to a perception on the part of Mercedes that Alabama was the most dedicated to the project (Woodruff and Templeman 1993).

- A *geographic information system* (GIS) is used to view and analyze data on digital maps as opposed to analyzing the same data printed out in massive tables that require reams of paper. One upscale clothing retailer with stores in Eau Claire and Green Bay, Wisconsin, analyzed its sales data on a map of the central part of the state. The map showed that each store drew the majority of its customers from a 20-mile radius.

  The map also highlighted an area between Eau Claire and Green Bay where only 15 percent of the potential customers had actually visited either store. Management's conclusion was that a new store in Wausau was needed to reach this untapped market. To take another example, at Super Valu (one of the nation's largest supermarket wholesalers), analysts would spread out paper maps and compare them with demographic data. Now, using a GIS, the same information is displayed on the screen of a personal computer, making it much easier to read and analyze (Tetzeli 1993).

- In industries such as fashion, which are characterized by highly volatile demand, the combined costs of stockouts and markdowns can be greater than total manufacturing costs. One approach to forecasting in these highly volatile industries is to determine what can and cannot be predicted well. Products in the "predictable" category are made farthest in advance, saving manufacturing capacity for the "unpredictable" products so that they can be produced closer to their actual selling season. Using this approach, Sport Obermeyer, a producer of fashionable skiwear, increased its profits between 50 percent and 100 percent over a three-year period in the early 1990s (Fisher, Hammond, Obermeyer, and Raman 1994).

- Package Products, in Pittsburgh, Pennsylvania, produces folding carton packing for the bakery and deli industries. A key aspect of Package Products' strategy is to be recognized by its customers for quality, reliability, and service. Significant growth during the 1990s greatly complicated the task of managing the company's operations. In addition, its customers were becoming more demanding, and the marketplace was becoming more competitive. To gain better control over its operations. Package Products implemented a finite capacity scheduling (FCS) software package. Before it acquired the FCS system, a Gantt chart was maintained manually to schedule jobs. Problems with the manual system included chronic capacity shortages and the fact that key data resided in the heads of people who were scattered throughout the organization. Two criteria used for selecting the FCS software package were that it should work with the company's existing business system and that it should not be a "black box," claiming to provide optimal schedules that no one could really understand. Through the use of the FCS program, overtime has been substantially reduced, on-time delivery has been improved by 32 percent, and backorders have been reduced by 53 percent. Additionally, customer service can now respond to customers' inquiries in an average of 22 seconds—versus taking overnight previously (Trail 1996).

As we will discuss in more detail throughout this chapter, **capacity** represents the rate at which a transformation system can create outputs. Capacity planning is as important to service organizations as it is to manufacturing organizations. For example, the transformation process at Burger King is designed so that capacity can be quickly adjusted to match a highly variable demand rate throughout the day. And in manufacturing, semiconductor firms incur enormous costs associated with expanding capacity. To further complicate matters for manufacturing businesses, shorter product life cycles mean that they have less time to recoup their investment, especially when the next generation of products makes their current products obsolete.

Clearly, capacity and location are important elements of a firm's competitive strategy, and in fact play a major role in the Sand Cone competitive dimensions described earlier in Chapter 1: quality, delivery dependability, speed, and cost. For example, if capacity is insufficient for demand peaks, then confusion and errors will result when attempting to meet excessive demand, lowering the quality of the firm's outputs. And without capacity and a convenient location, customers cannot depend on the availability of the output and may turn to competitors. In terms of speed, sufficient capacity and a convenient location allow the organization to meet demand quickly, whenever and wherever it arises. And finally, if the firm has insufficient capacity, it will cost considerably more to engage the extra resources to meet unexpected demand whether the resources are additional labor in the form of overtime or hiring, subcontracting out a portion of the demand, or storing inventory to meet demand peaks.

Capacity planning decisions are driven by projected demand estimates for the organization's outputs. (The role of forecasting is discussed in the supplement to this chapter). Over the long term, capacity and location are interwoven considerations, as will be described later in the chapter. Following the long-term discussion, we move into a description of efficiently utilizing the available capacity through schedule management and then into a description of short-term capacity alternatives, but here we are largely past the point of making a location decision.

ＬONG-TERM CAPACITY PLANNING

Capacity and location decisions are highly strategic because they are very expensive investments and, once made, are not easily changed or reversed. Hence, they must be carefully and thoroughly analyzed beforehand, using all available tools at management's disposal. **Capacity** is generally taken to mean the maximum *rate* at which a transformation system produces outputs or processes inputs, though the rate may be "all at once." Table 8.1 lists measures of capacity for a number of production systems. Notice that since capacity is defined as a rate, measures should be clear about the *time dimension.* For instance, how meaningful is it to know that a hospital can perform 25 surgeries? Without knowing whether this is simultaneously, per day, per week, or possibly per month, the number is relatively meaningless.

As illustrated in Table 8.1, airlines often measure their capacity in *available seat miles* (ASMs) per year. One ASM is one seat available for one passenger for 1 mile. Clearly, the number of planes an airline has, their size, how often they are flown, and the route structure of the airline all affect its ASMs, or capacity. However, we may also talk about the capacity of a single plane, such as a 550-seat jumbo, and here we clearly mean "all at once." Nevertheless, this capacity measure is not very useful without knowing to what use the plane may be put, such as constantly being in the air generating ASMs or used as an occasional backup. Similarly, an elementary measure of a hospital's capacity is often simply the number of beds it has (for the full year is implied). Thus, a 50-bed hospital is "small" and a 1000-bed hospital is "large." And a restaurant may measure its capacity in tables (per hour), a hotel in rooms (per night), and a public service agency in family contacts (per weekday).

Notice that these measures of capacity do not recognize the multiple types of outputs with which an organization may, in reality, be concerned. ASMs say nothing about the freight capacity of an airline, but freight may be a major contributor to profits. Similarly, number of beds says nothing about outpatient treatment, ambulance rescues, and other services provided by a hospital. Thus, capacity planning must often consider the capacity to produce multiple outputs. Unfortunately, some of the outputs may require the same organizational resources, as well as some very specialized resources.

ＴABLE 8.1 • Examples of Measures of Capacity

Production System	Measure of Capacity in Terms of Outputs Produced	Measure of Capacity in Terms of Inputs Processed
Airline	available seat miles per year	reservation calls handled per day
Hospital	babies delivered per month	patients admitted per week
Supermarket	customers checked out per hour	cartons unloaded per hour
Post Office	packages delivered per day	letters sorted per hour
University	graduates per year	students admitted per year
Automobile Assembly Plant	autos assembled per year	deliveries of parts per day

The provision of adequate capacity is clearly a generic problem, common to all types of organizations, but in pure service organizations capacity is a special problem because the output cannot normally be stored for later use. A utility, for example, must have capacity available to meet peak power demands, yet the *average* power demand may be much, much lower. Where the provision of the service is by human labor, low productivity is a danger when staffing is provided to meet the demand peaks.

Another characteristic of capacity is that, frequently, a variety of restrictions can limit it. For example, the capacity of a fast-food restaurant may be limited not only by the number of order-takers on duty but also by the number of cooks, the number of machines to prepare the food, the amount of food in stock, the space in the restaurant, and even the number of parking spaces outside. Any one of these factors can become a ***bottleneck*** (discussed in a later section of the chapter) that limits the restaurant's normal operating capacity to something less than its theoretical or design capacity.

In addition, during the production process there are often natural losses, waste (avoidable), scrap (unavoidable), defects, errors, and so on that again limit the capacity of a system. These losses are considered in a measure known as the ***yield*** of the process: the amount of output of acceptable quality emerging from a production system compared with the amount that entered it. ***Yield management***, also known as ***revenue management***, is a somewhat different topic but of high interest these days, particularly in services. We return to the topic or yield management later in the chapter.

In the process of trying to forecast the long-run capacity needs for the organization, the issue of location of the facility, or facilities, cannot be ignored because the demand may well be a function of *where* the facility is located. And if there are multiple facilities, the capacity needs for any one will certainly depend on how many others are serving the same geographic needs. Moreover, transportation may also be a factor if there is a facilitating good, or product, involved, as well as inventories, warehouses, and other such matters that concern ***supply chain management***. In these days of intense worldwide competition, supply chain management is taking on significantly more importance, as it accounts for a greater and greater proportion of the total cost of all outputs. Although we discuss the interplay between capacity and location in this chapter, and we covered supply chain management in Chapter 7.

Capacity Planning Strategies

Issues of capacity planning over the long run relate primarily to the strategic issues of initiating, expanding, and contracting the major facilities used in producing the output. Note the interdependence of the capacity decision with the location decision. Every capacity decision requires a corresponding location decision. For example, expanding an existing facility defines the location of the new capacity to be an existing facility. This section covers capacity planning strategies in terms of facility size, economies of scale and scope, timing of capacity increments, and capacity for multiple outputs. The following section covers the location aspects and relationships.

Facility Size Planning

Figure 8.1 illustrates the issue of facility size in terms of capacity and unit cost. Product cost curves are shown for five sizes of production facilities. When plants are operated

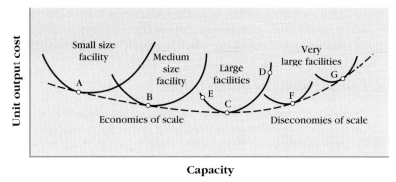

Figure 8.1   Envelope of lowest unit output costs with facility size.

at their lowest-cost production level (A, B, or C), the larger facilities will generally have the lowest costs, a phenomenon known as *economies of scale*. However, if production levels must be set at a value other than the lowest-cost level, the advantage of a larger facility may be lost. For example, point D is characterized by congestion and excessive overtime, and point E by idle labor and low equipment utilization. Points F and G illustrate some of the diseconomies of scale, as described next.

Economies of Scale and Scope

Obtaining lower unit costs through the use of larger facilities is known as ***economies of scale***. Primarily, the economy comes from spreading the required fixed costs—land, administration, sales force, facilities, and such other factors—over a larger volume of products or services, although there are also economies obtained through stronger purchasing power and learning curve effects (discussed in a later section). However, as illustrated by points F and G in Figure 8.1, there is a limit to the benefits that can be obtained, because the inherent inefficiencies of large facilities begin to counter their economic benefits. This occurs through increased bureaucracy, poor communication, long lines of responsibility and authority, and the like. Many manufacturers now have a corporate policy that no plant will be larger than 200 to 250 workers, often considered an optimum size.

Managers frequently think in terms of economies of scale when making decisions about where to produce new products or services, or whether or not to extend their line of products and services. However, the focus lost through adding these new production requirements can jeopardize the competitive strength of a firm. Managers would be well advised to examine more closely where the economies are expected to come from: sometimes it is from higher volumes, sometimes from the use of common technology, sometimes from availability of off-peak capacity. If the source of the economy results in offsetting diseconomies of scale, as a result of loss of focus or for other reasons, the firm should not proceed.

An allied concept related to the use of many of the advanced, flexible technologies such as programmable robots is called ***economies of scope***. The phrase implies that economies can also be obtained with flexibility by offering variety instead of volume. However, upon closer examination it is not clear why being flexible offers any particular economies. The real reason for economies of scope derives from the same economies as those of scale—spreading fixed costs among more products or services—but the scale is now obtained over many small batches of a wide variety of outputs, rather than large batches of only a few standard outputs.

Capacity Planning for Multiple Outputs

Realistically, organizations are not always expanding their capacity. We usually focus on this issue because we are studying firms in the process of growth, but even successful organizations often reduce their capacity. Major ways of contracting capacity are to divest the firm of operations, lay off workers, outsourcing, and sell or lease equipment and facilities. Most organizations, however, try to contract only capacity that is inefficient or inappropriate for their circumstances, owing in part to a felt responsibility to the community. If it appears that organizational resources are going to be excessively idle in the future, organizations often attempt to add new outputs to their current output mix rather than contracting capacity (the latter frequently being done at a loss). This entails an analysis of the candidate output's life and seasonal demand cycles.

It is traditional in fire departments to use the slack months for building inspections, conducting fire prevention programs, giving talks on safety, and other such activities. The large investment in labor and equipment is thus more effectively utilized throughout the year by adoption of an *anticyclic* output (an output counter to the fire cycle)—fire prevention. For many of the same reasons, many fire departments have been given the responsibility for the city or county's medical rescue service (although rescue alarms are not entirely anticyclic to fire alarms).

Clearly, many organizations, such as the makers of greeting cards, fur coats, swimming pool equipment, and fireworks, face this cyclic difficulty. A classic case of **seasonality** is that of furnace dealers. For the last 100 years all their business typically was in the late autumn and winter, as illustrated in Figure 8.2. With the rapid acceptance of air conditioning in the 1950s and 1960s, many furnace dealers eagerly added

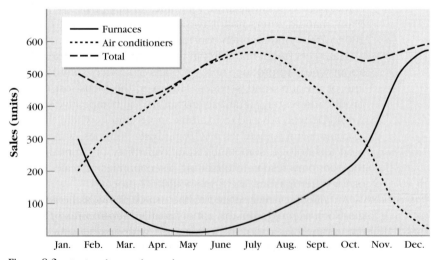

Figure 8.2   Anticyclic product sales.

this product to their output mix. Not only was it conceptually along the same lines (environmental comfort) and often physically interconnected with the home furnace but, most important, it was almost completely anticyclic to the seasonal heating cycle. As shown in Figure 8.2, the addition of air conditioning considerably leveled dealers' sales throughout the year in comparison with furnace sales alone.

In a similar manner, and for much the same reasons, organizations add to their mix outputs that are anticyclic to existing output *life cycles*. Figure 8.3 illustrates the expected life cycles of an organization's current and projected outputs. Total required capacity is found by adding together the separate capacities of each of the required outputs. Note the projected dip in required capacity five years in the future, and, of course, beyond the 8-year R&D planning horizon.

The message of Figure 8.3 should be clear to the organization—an output with a three-year life cycle (appearing similar to the shaded area) is needed between years 4 and 7 in order to maintain efficient utilization of the organization's available capacity. A priority output development program will have to be instituted immediately. At this point it is probably too late to develop something through R&D; a more effective strategy, especially in light of the relatively low volume and short life cycle, might be an extension of an existing output.

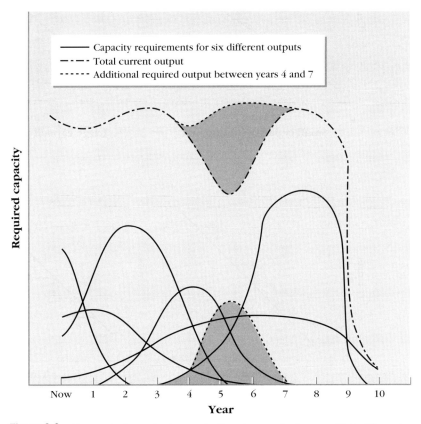

Figure 8.3   Forecast of required organizational capacity from multiple life cycles.

Timing of Capacity Increments

Once the best alternative for obtaining the desired capacity has been determined, the timing and manner must still be chosen. A number of approaches are illustrated in Figure 8.4. Sometimes there is an opportunity to add capacity in small increments (Figure 8.4a) rather than as one large chunk (Figure 8.4b), such as an entire plant.

Clearly, small increments are less risky, but they do not offer an opportunity to upgrade the entire production system at one time, as a single chunk does. Other choices are to add capacity before the demand has arisen (Figure 8.4c) or after (Figure 8.4d). Adding capacity before demand occurs upstages the competition and enhances customers' loyalty but risks the cost of the capacity if the expected demand never materializes. Adding capacity after demand arises will encourage the competition to move into the market and take away part of your share. Clearly, the most appropriate strategy must be carefully evaluated for the situation at hand.

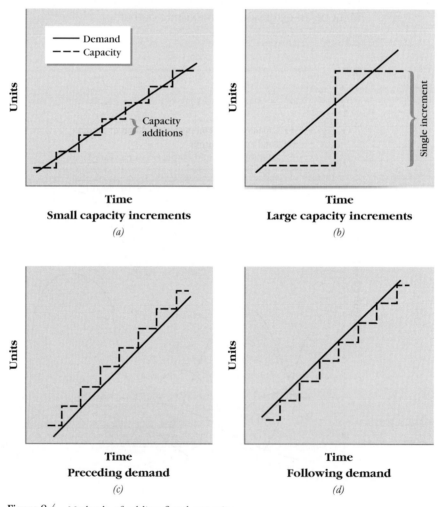

Figure 8.4 Methods of adding fixed capacity.

$\mathcal{L}$OCATION PLANNING STRATEGIES_____

Having determined capacity requirements, we next discuss the most economical way to obtain the inputs needed to produce and deliver the output to the customer. This includes determining the location of the facility relative to suppliers and potential customers. Although we are discussing capacity and location planning sequentially, as noted earlier, these decisions are typically considered simultaneously since every capacity decision requires a location decision (e.g., where to add the new capacity or which plant should be closed).

In general, the decision about location is divided into three stages: regional (including international), community, and site. Sources of information for these stages are chambers of commerce, realtors, utilities, banks, suppliers, transportation companies, savings and loan associations, government agencies, and management consultants who specialize in relocation. For some pure service organizations (e.g., physicians), only the site selection stage may be relevant because they are already focused on a specific region and community. Before discussing these stages in detail, however, we first highlight the relationship between the location decision and the development of core capabilities.

Developing Capabilities and the Location Decision

In examining the rationale offered by organizations regarding their decisions to relocate existing facilities or open new ones, it often appears that these decisions are being driven primarily by short-term considerations such as differentials in wage rates and fluctuations in exchange rates. In addition to having the appearance of being more band-aid solutions than addressing how to improve long term competitiveness, these decisions are often dominated by operational factors such as wage rates and transportation costs. The problem with such static and one-dimensional analyses is that conditions change. For example, if one competitor chooses a location based on low wage rates, there is very little to prevent its competitors from locating in the same region. Furthermore, the benefit of low wages is likely to be short-lived as the demand for labor will increase when more organizations locate in the region.

An alternative approach to the location decision is to consider the impact these decisions have on the development of key organizational capabilities. In Chapter 1 we defined core capabilities as the organizational practices and business processes that distinguish an organization from its competition. Clearly, the way various organizational units are located relative to one another can have a significant impact on interactions between these units, which in turn impacts the development of core capabilities.

In order to leverage the location decision to enhance the development of long-term capabilities, Bartmess and Cerny (1993) suggest the following six-step process:

1. Identify the sources of value the company will deliver to its customers. In effect, this translates into identifying the order winners discussed in Chapter 1.

2. Once the order winners have been defined, the organization needs to identify the key organizational capabilities needed in order to have a competitive advantage.

3. Based on the capabilities identified, implications for the location of organizational units should be assessed. For example, if the company determines that a rapid product development capability is needed, then it follows that design needs to be in close contact with manufacturing and leading edge customers. Alternatively, if operational flexibility is needed, then it follows that manufacturing needs to be in close proximity to design, customers, marketing, and management information systems.

4. Identify potential locations.

5. Evaluate the sites in terms of their impact on the development of capabilities, as well as on financial and operational criteria.

6. Develop a strategy for building an appropriate network of locations.

Having highlighted the relationship between choosing a location and the development of capabilities, we next turn our attention to the actual stages that location decisions typically progress through.

Stage 1: Regional–International

In the regional–international stage, an organization focuses on what part of the world (e.g., North America, Europe, Pacific rim) or perhaps in what region of a country (e.g., Southwest, Midwest, Northeast) it wants to locate its new facility. For example, when Mercedes-Benz needed a new facility to produce its new multi-purpose vehicle (MPV), it initially decided that its new facility should be located in North America and subsequently further narrowed the region to sites in the southeastern United States. There are four major considerations in selecting a national or overseas region for a facility: *proximity, labor supply, availability of inputs,* and *environment.*

To minimize transportation costs and provide acceptable service to customers, the facility should be located in a region in close *proximity* to customers and suppliers. Although methods of finding the location with the minimum transportation costs will be presented later in this chapter, a common rule of thumb within the United States is that the facility should be within 200 miles of major industrial and commercial customers and suppliers. Beyond this range, transportation costs begin to rise quickly.

The region should have the proper *supply of labor* available and in the correct proportions of required skills. One important reason for the past expansion of American firms abroad, particularly to Japan in the 1980s, was the availability of labor there at wage rates much lower than rates at home. Currently, this disparity has been eliminated because of Japan's increased wages. However, the real consideration should not be wage rates, but rather the productivity of domestic labor relative to productivity abroad. This comparison would thus involve level of skills, use of equipment, wage rates, and even work ethics (which differ even between regions within the United States) to determine the most favorable labor supply in terms of output per dollar of wages and capital investment. The organization of the labor pool should also be given consideration—that is, whether all the skills are unionized or whether there is an open shop. Some states have passed *right-to-work laws* that forbid any requirement that all employees join a union in order to work in an organization. Often, these laws result in significantly lower wage rates in these states.

The region selected for location of the facility should have the necessary *inputs* available. For example, supplies that are difficult, expensive, or time-consuming to ship and those that are necessary to the organization (i.e., no reasonable substitutes exist) should be readily available. The proper type (rail, water, highway, air) and supply of transportation; sufficient quantities of basic resources such as water, electricity, gas, coal, and oil; and appropriate communication facilities should also be available. Obviously, many American industries are located abroad in order to use raw materials (oil, copper, etc.) available there.

The regional *environment* should be conducive to the work of the organization. Not only should the weather be appropriate, but the political, legal, and social climate should also be favorable. The following matters should be considered:

1. Regional taxes
2. Regional regulations on operations (pollution, hiring, etc.)
3. Barriers to imports or exports
4. Political stability (nationalization policies, kidnappings)
5. Cultural and economic peculiarities (e.g., restrictions on working women)

These factors are especially critical in locating in a foreign country, particularly an underdeveloped country. Firms locating in such regions should not be surprised to find large differences in the way things are done. For example, in some countries governmental decisions tend to move slowly, with extreme centralization of authority. Very little planning seems to occur. Events appear to occur by "God's will" or by default. The pace of work is unhurried, and at times discipline, especially among managers, seems totally absent. Corruption and payoffs often seem to be normal ways of doing business, and accounting systems are highly suspect. Living conditions for the workers, especially in urbanized areas, are depressing. Transportation and communication systems (roads, ports, phone service) can be incomplete and notoriously unreliable. Attempting to achieve something under such conditions can, understandably, be very discouraging. When locating in such countries, a firm should allow for such difficulties and unexpected problems. In such an environment, Murphy's law thrives.

With the escalating use of outsourcing, and especially offshoring, the roles of location and capacity in the competitive elements of a firm's strategy take on increased importance. By subcontracting production to another firm, an organization can often save substantially on labor costs (especially when offshoring) and at the same time reduce their own asset base tremendously, thereby increasing both their profit margins and their return on assets (ROA). Contract manufacturers such as Flextronics, Selectron, and Jabil Circuit are quick to point out these advantages and others, such as leaving the organization free to concentrate on their strengths such as design, brand building, marketing, and strategy. There are, however, also disadvantages in both outsourcing and offshoring. One is the loss of control of the product. Another is a probable reduction in speed of response to customers. A third, which is especially sensitive in communities and is increasingly publicized by the media, is the loss of domestic jobs when the company outsources its work. And outsourcing production is always a dangerous action, first because engineering and then design typically must follow production overseas, meaning the additional loss of these capabilities within the organization. And second, there is the increased potential that the firm is simply training a powerful competitor (especially if engineering and design have also been outsourced), thereby "hollowing itself out." In the 1980s, many firms in the television and video cassette recording industries outsourced all their production overseas, simply slapping on their own logo to sell their product domestically. Then the foreign producers started introducing their own brands and all the formerly domestic producers went out of business, losing the entire industry to foreign competition.

A model to help make the regional–national location decision is the CVD model we described for helping with the job shop layout in Chapter 2. In this case, we are interested in the total of all the supply costs into the facility and all the distribution costs out to customers. The procedure is to select some initial site for the facility that appears to be good and then sum the products of the transportation rate (C), the volume or weights (V), and the distance (D) over all the locations. Then we can simply consider placing the facility in another site and see if the cost is less, and so on. If all the sites are prespecified, then the site with the lowest cost is deemed best (at least on this one measure).

Stage 2: Community

After the region of a new facility has been selected, candidate communities within the region are identified for further analysis. Many of the considerations made at the regional–international stage should also be considered at this next stage. For example, the availability of acceptable sites, attitudes of the local government, regulations, zoning, taxes, labor supply, the size and characteristics of the market, and the weather would again be considered. In addition, the availability of local financing, monetary inducements (such as tax incentives) for establishing operations there, and the community's attitude toward the organization itself would be additional factors of interest to the organization.

Last, the preferences of the organization's staff should play a role in selecting a community. These would probably be influenced by the amenities available in the community such as homes, religious congregations, shopping centers, schools and universities, medical care, fire and police protection, and entertainment, as well as local tax rates and other costs. Upper-level educational institutions may also be of interest to the organization in terms of opportunity for relevant research and development. For example, it was no coincidence that major IBM plants were located in Lexington, Kentucky, Denver, Colorado, and Austin, Texas, which are also sites of major state universities.

The standard "breakeven" or "cost-volume-profit" model can be helpful for this stage of the location decision, except that there is no revenue line and there are multiple costs lines, each representing a different community's costs. We assume that the problem is to choose from among a set of predetermined communities, on the basis of a range of fixed and variable costs rather than just distribution cost, as calculated by the CVD model just given. That is, distribution cost may be considered, but it is only one factor (perhaps fixed, perhaps variable with output volume) among many that need to be considered to make a decision. Although the relevant *factors* for comparison between the communities may be known (e.g., labor costs, taxes, utility charges), their values may be uncertain, particularly if they are a function of the output rate of the facility being located. The various alternatives for location are then

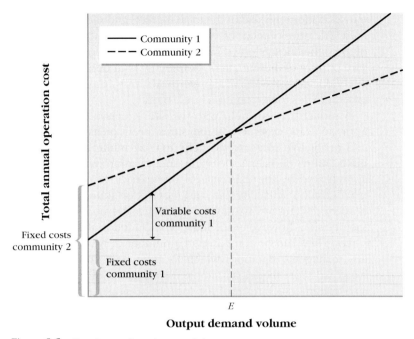

Figure 8.5   Breakeven location model.

compared by graphing total operating costs for each alternative at different levels of demand, as in Figure 8.5.

This is accomplished by dividing the total operating cost into two components—fixed costs that do not vary with the demand for the output (e.g., land, buildings, equipment, property taxes, insurance) and variable costs such as labor, materials, and transportation—and plotting them on the axes of a graph. At the demand point E (the intersection of the two lines) the costs for the two alternatives are the same; for demand levels in excess of E, community 2 is best, and for levels less than E, community 1 is best. Thus, if the range of uncertainty concerning the output volume is entirely *above* point E, the manager need not be concerned about which community to choose—community 2 is best. Similar reasoning holds for any uncertainty existing entirely *below* point E—community 1 is best.

If the range of uncertainty is closely restricted to point E, then either community may be selected because the costs will be approximately the same in either case. However, if the range of uncertainty is broad and varies considerably from point E in both directions, then the breakeven chart will indicate to the manager the extra costs that will be incurred by choosing the wrong community. Before selecting either community, the manager should probably attempt to gather more information, to reduce the range of uncertainty in demand.

Stage 3: Site

After a list of candidate communities is developed, specific sites within them are identified. The *site*—the actual location of the facility—should be appropriate to the nature of the operation. Such matters as size; adjoining land; zoning; community attitudes; drainage; soil; the availability of water, sewers, and utilities; waste disposal;

transportation; the size of the local market; and the costs of development are considered. The development of industrial parks in some communities has alleviated many of the difficulties involved in choosing a site, since the developer automatically takes care of most of these matters. Before any final decision is made, a cash-flow analysis is conducted for each of the candidate sites; this includes the cost of labor, land, taxes, utilities, transportation, and so on.

A model that can help with the site selection is the *weighted score model*. This approach can combine cost measures, profit measures, other quantitative measures, and qualitative measures to help analyze multiple locations (as well as any other multi-criteria decision). Deciding on a location, whether for products or services, is complicated by the existence of multiple criteria such as executives' preferences, maximization of facility use, and customers' attitudes. These and other criteria may be very difficult to quantify, or even measure qualitatively; if they are important to the decision, however, they must be included in the location analysis.

Locations can be compared in a number of ways. The most common is probably just managerial intuition: which location best satisfies the important criteria? The weighted score model is a simple formalization of this intuitive process that is useful as a rough screening tool for locating a single facility. In this model a weight is assigned to each factor (*criterion*), depending on its importance to the manager. The most important factors receive proportionately higher weights. Then a score is assigned to each of the alternative locations on each factor, again with higher scores representing better results. The product of the weights and the scores then gives a set of weighted scores, which are added up for each location. The location with the highest weighted score is considered best. In quantitative terms:

$$\text{Total weighted score} = \sum_i W_i S_i$$

where

i = index for factors
W_i = weight of factor i
S_i = score of the location being evaluated on factor i

The following example illustrates the method.

Communicable Disease Center

A province health department is investigating three possible locations for a specialized control clinic that will monitor acquired immune deficiency syndrome (AIDS) and other sexually transmitted diseases (STDs). The director of public health for the province is particularly concerned with four factors.

1. The most important consideration in the treatment of STDs is ease of access for those infected. Since they are generally disinclined to recognize and seek treatment, it is foolish to locate a clinic where it is not easily accessible to as many patients as possible. This aspect of location is probably as much as 50 percent more important than the lease cost of the building.

2. Still, the annual cost of the lease is not a minor consideration. Unfortunately, the health department is limited to a very tight budget, and any extra cost for the lease will mean that less equipment and staff are available to the clinic.

3. For some patients it is of the utmost importance that confidentiality be maintained. Thus, although the clinic must be easily accessible, it must also be relatively inconspicuous. This factor is probably just as important as the cost of the lease.

4. The director also wants to consider the convenience of the location for the staff, since many of the physicians will be donating their time to the clinic. This consideration is the least important of all, perhaps only half as important as the cost of the lease.

The three locations being considered are a relatively accessible building on Adams Avenue, an inconspicuous office complex near the downtown bus terminal, and a group of public offices in the Civic Center, which would be almost rent-free.

The director has decided to evaluate (score) each of these alternative locations on each of the four factors. He has decided to use a 4-point scale on which 1 represents "poor" and 4 represents "excellent." His scores and the weights (derived from the relative importance of the four factors) are shown in Table 8.2. The problem now is somehow to use this information to determine the best location for the clinic.

To determine the weighted score for each location, we multiply each score by the weight for that factor and then the sum over all factors for each location, as illustrated in Table 8.3. Since higher scores indicate better ratings, the location with the largest score—B, the office near the bus terminal—is best, followed by C, the Civic Center.

*T*ABLE 8.2 • Potential Clinic Sites

		Potential Locations		
W: Weight	F: Factor	A: Adams Avenue	B: Bus Terminal Complex	C: Civic Center
2	1. Annual lease cost	1	3	4
3	2. Accessibility for patients	3	3	2
2	3. Inconspicuousness	2	4	2
1	4. Accessibility for personnel	4	1	2

Note: Factor scoring scale: 1, poor; 2, acceptable; 3, good; 4, excellent.

*T*ABLE 8.3 • Comparison of Site Factors by the Weighted Score Method

		Sites:		
Factor	Weight	A	B	C
1	2	$2 \times 1 = 2$	$2 \times 3 = 6$	$2 \times 4 = 8$
2	3	$3 \times 3 = 9$	$3 \times 3 = 9$	$3 \times 2 = 6$
3	2	$2 \times 2 = 4$	$2 \times 4 = 8$	$2 \times 2 = 4$
4	1	$1 \times 4 = 4$	$1 \times 1 = 1$	$1 \times 2 = 2$
Total		19	24	20

Quebec City, Canada, provides a good example of almost exactly this process (Price and Turcotte 1986). The Red Cross Blood Donor Clinic and Transfusion Center of Quebec City in Canada was located in a confined spot in the downtown area and wanted to expand in another location. The center's main activities affecting the choice of a new location were receiving donors, delivering blood and blood products throughout the community and the province of Quebec, and holding blood donor clinics over the same region.

Accordingly, the criteria for a site were identified as

- Highway access for both clinics and blood deliveries
- Ability to attract more donors as a result of improved accessibility and visibility
- Convenience to both public and private transportation
- Ease of travel for employees
- Internal floor space
- Lot size
- Acceptability of the site to management and governmental authorities involved in the decision

The analysis of the problem was very complicated, owing to conflicting requirements and the unavailability of data. Nevertheless, five sites were finally identified and evaluated on the basis of four final criteria. The five sites were then ranked on each of these criteria, and a scoring model was constructed to help management determine the best location. The weights were to be determined by management, and they could be modified to determine if changing them would have any effect on the best location. The final scores and rankings, assuming equal weights across the four criteria, are shown in Table 8.4.

𝒯ABLE 8.4 • Comparison of Quebec City's Site Factors

Site	Road Access	Bus Access	Proximity	Availability	Rank
1	0.4	0.0	0.4	0.7	1
2	0.2	0.2	0.3	0.7	2
3	0.3	0.3	0.2	0.0	4
4	0.0	0.4	0.1	0.0	5
5	0.1	0.1	0.0	0.7	3

ℒOCATING PURE SERVICES

Although all the material presented so far applies equally to services and product firms, some situations unique to service organizations are worth noting. Two that we will look at in detail here involve the recipient coming to the facility, as in retailing, and the facility going to the recipient, as with "alarm" services.

Recipient to Facility

In recipient-to-facility situations, the facility draws customers or recipients from an area surrounding it, possibly in competition with other, similar facilities. Research has found that under these circumstances the drawing power of retail facilities is proportional to the size of the facility and inversely proportional to the square (or cube, in some cases) of the average recipient's travel time. This assumes that all other factors—such as price and quality—are equivalent or insignificant. This type of relationship is known as a *gravity* method because, like gravity, it operates by drawing nearby objects in.

Next, consider the situation of public services such as health clinics, libraries, and colleges. Apart from the difficulty of framing a location model is the probably more significant problem of choosing a measure, or measures, of service: number of recipients served (a "surrogate" measure), change in the recipient's condition (a direct measure of benefit), quantity of services offered (another surrogate), and so on. Some measures recommended in the literature on health clinics, which can be used for trial-and-error procedures, are:

1. ***Facility utilization.*** Maximize the number of visits to the facilities.
2. ***Travel distance per citizen.*** Minimize the average distance per person in the region to the nearest clinic.
3. ***Travel distance per visit.*** Minimize the average distance per visit to the nearest clinic. No one measure has been found to work best for all cases of deciding on a location.

Facility to Recipient

Facility-to-recipient situations are common among the urban "alarm" services: fire, police, and ambulance. Again, the problem of measuring a service appropriately involves such factors as number of recipients served, average waiting time for service, value of property saved, and number of service facilities. Two general cases are encountered in this problem, whether a single- or multiple-facility service is being located:

1. High-density demand for services where multiple vehicles are located in the same facility and vehicles are often dispatched from one alarm directly to another
2. Widely distributed demand for services where extreme travel distances require additional facilities

Typical of situation 1 are fire companies and ambulances. Results in these cases have been basically the same. There is a significant drop-off in the returns to scale as more units are added to the system. Typically, the first three or four will improve all measures by up to 80 percent of the maximum improvement. Each additional unit gains less. A second common finding is that optimally located facilities yield only about a 15 percent improvement over existing or evenly dispersed facilities. Last, incremental approaches to selecting additional locations provide slightly poorer service than a total relocation analysis of all the facilities.

EFFECTIVELY UTILIZING CAPACITY THROUGH SCHEDULE MANAGEMENT

An important aspect of capacity worth emphasizing is its close tie to scheduling. That is, poor scheduling may result in what appears to be a capacity problem, and a shortage of capacity may lead to constant scheduling difficulties. Thus, capacity planning is closely related to the scheduling function. The difference is that capacity is oriented primarily toward the *acquisition* of productive resources, whereas scheduling concerns the *timing* of their use. However, it is often difficult to separate the two, especially where human resources are involved, such as in the use of overtime or the overlapping of shifts.

As a simple example, suppose that an organization has to complete within 2 weeks the two customers' jobs shown in Table 8.5. The table shows the sequential processing operations still to be completed and the times required. (The operations resources may be of any form—a facility, a piece of equipment, or an especially skilled worker.) In total, 60 hours of resource A are needed, 45 hours of B, and 25 hours of C. It would appear that 2 weeks (80 hours) of capacity on each of these three resources would be sufficient, and additional capacity would, therefore, be unnecessary.

TABLE 8.5 • Sequential Operations Required for Two Jobs

Job	Operations Resource Needed	Time Required (hours)
1	A	10
	C	10
	A	30
	B	20
	C	5
2	B	15
	A	10
	C	10
	A	10
	B	10

Figure 8.6 shows the resource requirements of the two jobs plotted along a time scale. Such a chart is called a **Gantt chart** and can be used to show time schedules and capacities of facilities, workers, jobs, activities, machines, and so forth. In Figure 8.6a, each job was scheduled on the required resource as soon as it finished on the previous resource, whether or not the new resource was occupied with the other job. This infeasible schedule is called **infinite loading** because work is scheduled on the resource as if it had infinite capacity to handle any and all jobs. Note that in this way capacity conflicts and possible resolutions can be easily visualized. Shifting the jobs to avoid such conflicts—this is called **finite loading**—gives the longer but feasible schedule shown in Figure 8.6b.

The first resource conflict in Figure 8.6a occurs at 20 hours, when job 1 finishes on resource C and next requires resource A, which is still working on job 2. The second conflict, again at A, occurs at 35 hours, and the third, on B, at 50 hours. It is

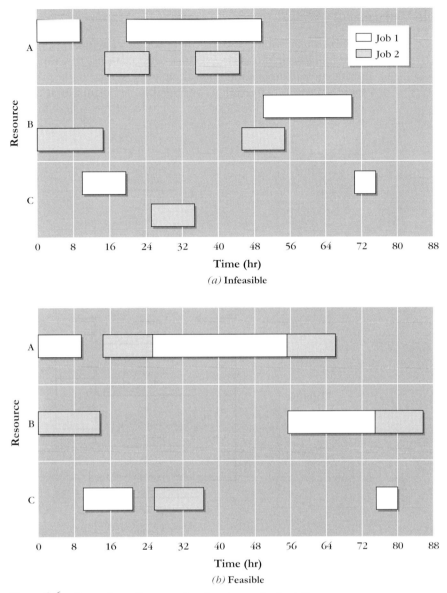

Figure 8.6 Gantt charts for capacity planning and scheduling.

quickly found that deferring one job for the other has drastic consequences for conflicts of resources later (sometimes adding conflicts and sometimes avoiding them)
as well as for job completion times. Another consideration, not specified here, is
whether an operation can be stopped for awhile and then restarted (called *operation
splitting*), for example to let another job pass through (called *preemption*), or, once
started, must be worked on until completion. If splitting were allowed for job 2, we
could have stopped work at resource A on job 2 at 20 hours to let job 1 begin and
then finished the work starting at time 50 when job 1 was finished on resource A.
Such operation splitting allows flexibility for rush work but hurts productivity
because machines must be taken down and set up multiple times for the same job.

Schedule Management

In most organizations a department (or an individual) is specifically responsible for scheduling operations. In product organizations, this function is frequently called production planning and control, or some similar name. The breadth of this department's responsibility varies considerably; for example, it may consist only of planning gross output levels or may include all the scheduling activities illustrated in Figure 8.7.

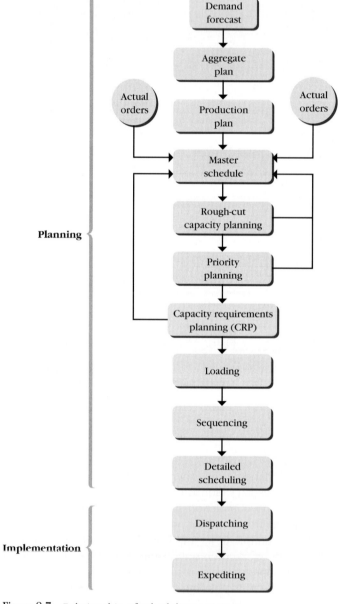

Figure 8.7   Relationship of scheduling activities.

This figure does not describe a *standardized* scheduling system, such as might exist in an available computer package; rather, it shows a complex set of activities and terms that are often grouped under *scheduling*. Many of these have become major activities only since the advent of computerized scheduling. Before that, they were simply a matter of individual judgment (as some of them still are).

The foundation that supports scheduling is, in most cases, the forecast of demand for the upcoming planning horizon. In some industries, however, only minimal forecasting is needed because customers place orders a year or more ahead of the time when the output will be needed. For example, in the airframe industry, airlines may place orders years ahead of time because of long lead times and backlogs of orders. In these situations, organizational operations are scheduled on the basis of actual orders instead of forecasted demand.

Most organizations do not operate in such a favorable environment, however, and their success often hinges on the accuracy of their forecasts of demand. In these cases the concepts and techniques of forecasting briefly overviewed in the chapter supplement are especially relevant for scheduling.

It might be noted that forecasts over different periods are used for different purposes. For example, long-range forecasts (i.e., 2–5 years) are used for facility and capacity planning.

The **aggregate plan** is a preliminary, approximate schedule of an organization's overall operations that will satisfy the demand forecast at minimum cost. The *planning horizon*, the period over which changes and demands are taken into consideration, is often one year or more and is broken into monthly or quarterly periods. This is because one of the purposes of aggregate planning is to minimize the effects of shortsighted, day-to-day scheduling, in which small amounts of material may be ordered from a supplier and workers laid off one week, only to be followed by reordering more material and rehiring the workers the next week. By taking a longer-term perspective on the use of resources, short-term changes in requirements can be minimized with a considerable saving in costs.

In minimizing short-term variations, the basic approach is to work only with "aggregate" units (i.e., units grouped or bunched together). Aggregate resources are used, such as total number of workers, hours of machine time, and tons of raw materials, as well as aggregate units of output—gallons of product, hours of service delivered, number of patients seen, and so on—totally ignoring the fact that there may be differences between these aggregated items. In other words, neither resources nor outputs are broken down into more specific categories; that occurs at a later stage.

The result of managerial iteration and changes to the aggregate plan is the organization's formal **production plan** for the planning horizon used by the organization (e.g., 1 year). Sometimes this plan is broken down (i.e., *disaggregated*) one level into major output groups (still aggregated)—for example, by models but not by colors. In either case, the production plan shows the resources required and changes in output over the future: requirements for hiring, limitations on capacity, relative increases and decreases in inventories of materials, and output rate of goods or services.

The driving force behind scheduling is the master schedule, also known in industry as the **master production schedule** (MPS). There are two reasons for this:

1. It is at this point that *actual* orders are incorporated into the scheduling system.

2. This is also the stage where aggregate planned outputs are broken down into individual scheduled items that customers actually want. These items are then checked for feasibility against lead time (time to produce or ship the items) and operational capacity (if there is enough equipment, labor, etc.).

The actual scheduling is usually iterative, with a preliminary schedule being drawn up, checked for problems, and then revised. After a schedule has been determined, the following points are checked:

- Does the schedule meet the production plan?
- Does the schedule meet the demand forecasts?
- Are there conflicts in the schedule involving capacity?
- Does the schedule violate any other constraints regarding equipment, lead times, supplies, facilities, and so forth?
- Does the schedule conform to organizational policy?
- Does the schedule violate any legal regulations or organizational or union rules?

Problems in any one of these areas may force a revision of the schedule and a repeat of the previous steps. The result is that the master schedule then specifies *what end items* are to be *produced in what periods* to *minimize costs* and gives some measure of assurance that such a plan is *feasible*. Clearly, such a document is of major importance to any organization—it is, in a sense, a blueprint for future operations.

As a part of checking the feasibility of the master schedule, a simple type of **rough-cut capacity planning** is conducted. One way of doing this, among many, is as follows. Historical ratios of workloads per unit of each type of product are used to determine the loads placed on the resources by all the products being made in any one period. Then the loads are assumed to fall on the resources in the same period as the demands; that is, the lead times are not used to offset the loads. If a resource's capacities are not overloaded (underloads are also checked), it is assumed that sufficient capacity exists to handle the master schedule, and it is accepted for production.

The term *priority planning* relates not to giving priorities to jobs (a topic included under *sequencing*), but rather to determining *what material* is needed *when*. For a master production schedule to be feasible, the proper raw materials, purchased materials, and manufactured or purchased subassemblies must be available when needed, with the top priority going to immediate needs. The key to production planning is the "needed" date. Years ago, scheduling concentrated on *launching orders*, that is, on when to *place* the order. Priority planning concentrates on when the order is actually needed and schedules *backward* from that date. For example, if an item is needed on June 18 and requires a 2-week lead time, then the order is released on June 4 and not before. Why store inventory needlessly?

The inventory control system and master schedule drive the **capacity requirements planning** (CRP) system. This system projects job orders and demands for materials into requirements for equipment, work force, and facility and finds the total required capacity of each over the planning horizon. That is, during a given week, how many nurses will be required, how many hours of a kidney machine, how many hours in operating rooms?

This may or may not exceed *available* capacity. If it is within the limits of capacity, then the master schedule is finalized, work orders are released according to schedule, orders for materials are released by the priority planning system, and *load reports* are sent to work centers, listing the work facing each area on the basis of the CRP system. Note that external lead times (often longer than internal lead times) from suppliers have already been checked at the stage of priority planning, so the master schedule can indeed now be finalized.

If the limits of capacity are exceeded, however, something must be changed. Some jobs must be delayed, or a less-demanding schedule must be devised, or extra capacity must be obtained elsewhere (e.g., by hiring more workers or using overtime). It is the task of production planning and control to solve this problem.

Loading means deciding which jobs to assign to which resources. Although the capacity planning system determines that sufficient gross capacity exists to meet the master schedule, *no actual* assignment of jobs to resources is made. Some equipment will generally be superior for certain jobs, and some equipment will be less heavily loaded than other equipment. Thus, there is often a "best" (fastest or least costly) assignment of jobs to resources.

Even after jobs have been assigned to resources, the *order* in which to process the jobs—their ***sequencing***—must still be determined. Unfortunately, even this seemingly small final step can have major repercussions on the organization's workload capacity and on whether or not jobs are completed on time. A number of priority rules have been researched, and some interesting results are available in the literature.

Once all this has been specified, detailed schedules itemizing specific jobs, times, materials, and workers can be drawn up. This is usually done only a few days in advance, however, since changes are always occurring and detailed schedules become outdated quickly. It is the responsibility of production planning and control to ensure that when a job is ready to be worked on, all the items, equipment, facilities, and information (blueprints, operations sheets, etc.) are available as scheduled.

All the previous activities constitute schedule *planning;* No production per se has taken place yet. ***Dispatching*** is the physical *release* of a work order from the production planning and control department to operations.

Once production planning and control has released a job to operations the department usually has no more responsibility for it, and it is the production manager's task to get the job done on time. This task is known as ***expediting***. When jobs fall behind schedule, managers have historically tended to use expediters to help push these "hot" jobs through the operations. Of course, expediting can be done more proactively by monitoring the progress of jobs to ensure that they stay on schedule.

Scheduling Services

In this section we consider the scheduling of pure services. Much of what was said previously applies to the scheduling of services as well as products, but here we consider some scheduling issues of particular relevance to services.

Up to now we have dealt primarily with situations where the jobs (or recipients) were the items to be loaded, sequenced, or scheduled. There are, however, many operations for which scheduling of the jobs themselves is either inappropriate or impossible, and it is necessary to concentrate instead on scheduling one or more of the input resources. Therefore, the staff, the materials, or the facilities are scheduled to correspond, as closely as possible, with the expected arrival of the jobs. Such situations are common in service systems such as supermarkets, hospitals, urban alarm services, colleges, restaurants, and airlines.

In the scheduling of jobs, we were primarily interested in minimizing the number of late jobs, minimizing the rejects, maximizing the throughput, and maximizing the utilization of available resources. In the scheduling of resources, however, there may be considerably more criteria of interest, especially when one of the resources being scheduled is staff. The desires of the staff regarding shifts, holidays, and work schedules become critically important when work schedules are variable and not all employees are on the same schedule. In these situations there usually exist schedules that will displease everyone and schedules that will satisfy most of the staff's more important priorities—and it is crucial that one of the latter be chosen rather than one of the former.

Approaches to Resource Scheduling

The primary approach to the scheduling of resources is to match availability to demand (e.g., 7 P.M.–12 A.M. is the high period for fire alarms). By so doing, we are not required to provide a continuing high level of resources that are poorly utilized the great majority of the time. However, this requires that a good forecast of demand be available for the proper scheduling of resources. If demand cannot be accurately predicted, the resulting service with variable resources might be worse than using a constant level of resources.

Methods of increasing resources for peak demand include using overtime and part-time help and leasing equipment and facilities. Also, if multiple areas within an organization tend to experience varying demand, it is often helpful to use *floating* workers or combine departments to minimize variability. On occasion, new technologies, such as 24-hour automated tellers, 24-hour order entry via the Web, and paying bills by telephone, can aid the organization.

As mentioned previously, the use of promotion and advertising to shift *demand* for resources is highly practical in many situations. Thus, we see *off-peak pricing* in the utilities and communication industries, summer sales of snowblowers in retailing, and cut rates for transportation and tours both in off-peak seasons (fall, winter) and at off-peak times (weekends, nights). Let us now consider how some specific service organizations approach their scheduling problems.

Hospitals   There are multiple needs for scheduling in hospitals. Although arrivals of patients (the jobs) are in part uncontrollable (e.g., emergencies), they are to some extent controllable through selective admissions for hernia operations, some maternity cases, in-hospital observation, and so on. With selective admissions, the hospital administrator can smooth the demand faced by the hospital and thereby improve service and increase the utilization of the hospital's limited resources.

Very specialized, expensive equipment such as a kidney machine is also carefully scheduled to allow other hospitals access to it, thus maximizing its utilization. By sharing such expensive equipment among a number of hospitals, more hospitals have access to modern technology for their patients at a reasonable level of investment.

Of all the scheduling in hospitals, the most crucial is probably the scheduling of nurses, as illustrated in the following example describing Harper Hospital (Filley 1983).

This is because (1) it is mandatory, given the nature of hospitals, that nurses always be available; (2) nursing resources are a large expense for a hospital; and (3) there are a number of constraints on the scheduling of nurses, such as number of days per week, hours per day, weeks per year, and hours during the day.

Like many other hospitals, Harper Hospital of Detroit was under heavy pressure from Blue Cross, Medicare, and Medicaid to provide more health care at less cost. In addition, it needed to achieve more economies of scale from a merger that had taken place some years before. It also desired to improve its patient care. One target to help achieve these goals was a better system for scheduling nurses.

Previously, nurses were scheduled on the basis of strict bed counts, problems with inadequate staffing during the prior day, and requests for extra help. What was developed was a *patient classification system* (PCS) that incorporated labor standards to determine what levels of nursing were needed. At the end of each shift, designated nurses evaluated each area's patients by their condition and assigned them to a "care level" ranging from minimal to intensive. An hour before the next shift begins, the patients' needs for care are added up—accounting for new admissions, checkouts, and returns from surgery—to determine the total levels of care required. Given the levels in each area, nursing labor standards are used to determine how many nurses are needed on the next shift.

As a result of the new system, both the quality of patient care and the nurses' satisfaction went up. Annual labor savings from the new system were estimated as exceeding $600,000. Harper has further fine-tuned the PCS system and now recalibrates its standards every 2 years.

Urban Alarm Services   In urban services that respond to alarms—such as police, fire, and rescue services—the jobs (alarms) appear randomly and must be quickly serviced with sufficient resources. Otherwise, extreme loss of life or property may result. In many ways this problem is similar to that of a hospital, since the cost of staffing personnel is a major expense, but floating fire companies and police SWAT units may be utilized where needed, and some services (such as fire inspection) can be scheduled to help *smooth* demand.

Sometimes a major difference vastly complicates some of these services (particularly fire): ***duty tours*** of extended duration, as opposed to regular shifts, run over multiple days. These tours vary from 24 to 48 hours in teams of two to four members. Common schedules for such services are "two (days) on and three off" and "one on and two off," with every fifth tour or so off as well (for a running time off, every three weeks, of perhaps 3 + 2 + 3 = 8 days). Because living and sleeping-in are considered part of the job requirements, the standard workweek is in excess of 40 hours—common values are 50 and 54 hours. Clearly, the scheduling of such duty tours is a complex problem, not only because of the unusual duration of the tours but also because of the implications concerning overtime, temptations of "moonlighting," and other such issues.

Educational Services   Colleges and universities have scheduling requirements for all types of transformations: intermittent (such as counseling), continuous (English 1), batch (field trips), and project (regional conferences). In some of these situations the jobs (students) are scheduled; in some the staff (faculty, administrators) are scheduled; and in others the facilities (classrooms, convention centers) are scheduled.

The primary problem, however, involves the scheduling of classes, assignment of students, and allocation of facilities and faculty resources to these classes. To obtain a manageable schedule, three difficult elements must be coordinated in this process:

1. Accurate forecast of students' demand for classes
2. Limitations on available classroom space
3. Multiple needs and desires of the faculty, such as
   - Number of "preparations"
   - Number of classes
   - Timing of classes
   - Level of classes
   - Leave requirements (sabbatical, maternity, etc.)
   - Release requirements (research, projects, administration)

Because of the number of objectives in such scheduling problems, a variety of multicriteria approaches have been used to aid in finding acceptable schedules, including simulation, goal programming, and interactive modeling.

In summary, the approach to scheduling services is usually to match resources and forecasted demand. Since demand cannot be controlled, it is impossible to build up inventory ahead of time, and backordering is usually not feasible. Careful scheduling of staff, facilities, and materials is done instead, with (limited) flexibility achieved through floating part-time and overtime labor and off-peak rates to encourage leveling of demand. The best schedule is often not the one that optimizes the use of resources or minimizes lateness for the expected demand, but rather the one that gives acceptable results under all likely operating conditions. As described later in this chapter, an important aspect of scheduling services is the queues that tend to build up if capacity is inadequate. Here, queuing theory and psychology concerning waiting can be profitably applied.

Yield/Revenue Management and Overbooking

Yield management, also called *revenue management*, is the attempt to allocate the fixed capacity of a service (although the process is now being used by retailers and manufacturers, also) to match the highest revenue demand in the marketplace. It appears that American Airlines was one of the first to develop this technique, but its use has spread to hotels, cruise lines, and other services who hold a fixed capacity for revenue-producing customers, jobs, items, and so on. As described by Kimes (1989), yield management is most appropriate under the following circumstances.

1. *Fixed capacity.* There is only a limited, indivisible number of capacity openings available for the period. There is no flexibility in either dividing up the capacity or in finding additional capacity.
2. *Perishable capacity.* Once the period passes, the capacity can no longer be used for that period. There is essentially no salvage value for the capacity.
3. *Segmentable market.* The demand for the capacity must be segmentable into different revenue/profit classes, such as business versus pleasure, Saturday night stayover or not, deluxe and budget, and so on.

4. ***Capacity sold in advance.*** The capacity is sold by reservation. Using yield management techniques, certain classes of capacity are held back for certain, more profitable classes of reservations or periods of the season. If the profitable classes fail to fill by a certain time point, some of the capacity is then released for the next lowest profit class. This procedure cascades down through both reservation classes and time points as the period in question approaches.

5. ***Uncertain demand.*** Although demand for each reservation class may be forecast, the actual demand experienced in each class for each time period is uncertain.

6. ***Low marginal sales cost, high marginal capacity addition cost.*** The cost to add a unit of capacity is extremely high, but the cost to sell (rent) a unit of it for the period in question is low.

The technique used to determine how to allocate capacity among the different classes is similar to that used for ***overbooking***. Overbooking is an attempt to reduce costs through better schedule management, as illustrated by Scandinavian Airlines (Alstrup et al. 1989). Scandinavian Airlines (SAS) operates a fleet of DC-9 aircraft with 110 seats each. If SAS accepts reservations for only these 110 seats, "no-shows" (passengers who fail to show up for a flight) will refuse to pay for their reservations and SAS can lose from 5 to 30 percent of the available seats. If there are 100 flights every day, these no-shows can cost the airline as much as $50 million a year. To avoid this loss, all airlines overbook flights by accepting a fixed percentage of reservations in excess of what is available.

The management of SAS decided to develop an automated overbooking system to include such factors as class, destination, days before departure, current reservations, and existing cancellations. The objective of the system was to determine an optimal overbooking policy for the different classes on each flight, considering the costs of ill will, alternative flight arrangements, empty seats, and upgrading or downgrading a passenger's reserved class.

A number of interesting findings were made in the process of conducting the study. For example, an early finding was that the probability that a reservation would be canceled was independent of the time the reservation was made. When the system was completed, it was tested against the heuristics used by experienced employees who had a good "feel" for what the overbooking rate should be. It was found that the automated system would increase SAS's net revenue by about $2 million a year.

To better understand the situation and demonstrate the solution approach, let us assume that the number of seats on a plane is fixed at 28. How many reservations should the airline accept, given the chances described in Table 8.6 of no-shows? For example, if 32 reservations are accepted, the probability that only 30 passengers show up is 35 percent.

Suppose that a profit of $50 is made for each passenger carried, but a cost is incurred if a passenger with a reservation has to be turned away. This cost could be a free ticket, ill will, passage on another airline, or whatever. If the cost is low—say, less than the profit—then it will be to the airline's advantage to overbook quite a bit (although possibly not all the way to 32, since there would then be a 90 percent chance of having an overbooking cost). On the other hand, suppose that the cost is

$\mathcal{T}$ABLE 8.6 • Demand for Flights

No. of No-Shows	Relative Frequency
4	0.10
3	0.20
2	0.35
1	0.25
0	0.10
	1.00

very high—much more than the profit. Then the airline would be very reluctant to overbook much at all, out of fear of having to pay one or more costs of overbooking. Table 8.7 gives the probabilities of demand for each set of overbookings accepted, as specified in the previous paragraph. Assume that turning a passenger away costs the airline $20, how many reservations should be accepted? Suppose the cost is $100.

Using the probabilities of no-shows (shown in Table 8.6), we can calculate the costs and profits according to Table 8.8. (There is no sense in accepting more than 32 reservations, because this will definitely fill the plane.) Here we see that the total profit is $1,359.

$\mathcal{T}$ABLE 8.7 • Demand Probabilities with Reservations (from Table 8.6)

Relative Frequency	Reservations				
	28	29	30	31	32
0.10	24	25	26	27	28
0.20	25	26	27	28	29
0.35	26	27	28	29	30
0.25	27	28	29	30	31
0.10	28	29	30	31	32
1.00					

$\mathcal{T}$ABLE 8.8 • Expected Profit with 32 Reservations

	Demand					
	28	29	30	31	32	Total
Probabilities	0.10	0.20	0.35	0.25	0.10	
Seats filled (S)	28	28	28	28	28	
Profit: $50 S	1400	1400	1400	1400	1400	
Turnaways (T)	0	1	2	3	4	
Cost: $20 T	0	20	40	60	80	
Net profit	1400	1380	1360	1340	1320	
Expected net profit	140	276	476	335	132	$1359

The process is repeated for 31 reservations, and the calculations are given in Table 8.9. Continuing with 30, 29, and 28 reservations (it makes no sense to accept fewer than 28 reservations), we get the values shown in Table 8.10. Clearly, the maximum profit is obtained with 31 reservations. The results of the turnaway rate raised to $100 are shown in Table 8.11. Now the highest profit is obtained with 29 reservations.

$\mathcal{T}_{ABLE}$ 8.9 • Expected Profit with 32 Reservations

	Demand					
	27	28	29	30	31	Total
Probabilities	0.10	0.20	0.35	0.25	0.10	
Seats filled (S)	27	28	28	28	28	
Profit: $50 S	1350	1400	1400	1400	1400	
Turnaways (T)	0	0	1	2	3	
Cost: $20 T	0	0	20	40	60	
Net profit	1350	1400	1380	1360	1340	
Expected net profit	135	280	483	340	134	$1372

$\mathcal{T}_{ABLE}$ 8.10 • Expected Profit at $20 Turnaway Cost

Reservations	Expected Profits
32	$1359
31	$1372 (best)
30	$1371
29	$1345.5
28	$1302.5

$\mathcal{T}_{ABLE}$ 8.11 • Expected Profit at $100 Turnaway Cost

Reservations	Expected Profits
32	$1195
31	$1280
30	$1335
29	$1337.5 (best)
28	$1302.5

$\mathcal{S}$HORT-TERM CAPACITY PLANNING

In the short term, capacity planning is primarily related to issues of scheduling, labor shifts, balancing of resource capacities, and other such issues instead of location decisions. We will look into a variety of such approaches in this section.

DILBERT: © Scott Adams/Dist. by United Feature Syndicate, Inc.

Process-Flow Analysis

Earlier, we discussed some factors that might limit the output of a production system, such as bottlenecks in the system and yield considerations like scrap and defects. Here we will introduce some other terms relating to the use of a production system. One capacity measure that is commonly used is **_utilization_**, which is simply the actual output relative to some expected, designed, or normal output rate. For example, if a machine runs 4 hours a day in an American plant and the maintenance and setup time are usually 2 hours a day, the utilization for that day might be reported as 4/6 = 67%, which is considered to be fairly high utilization for a machine in a job shop. However, if the machine was in a Japanese plant, the utilization would probably be reported as 4/24 = 17%, since the machine could, in theory, have been used for all 24 hours in the day!

Clearly, utilization figures do not mean much unless one knows what the "normal" or expected output rate is based on. (When labor utilization measures are used for wage payment plans, this "normal" definition is often a heated subject of union negotiations. For example, should mandated "breaks" be included in the base or not? Should sick time be included? Lunch? Inactivity due to lack of materials to work on? And so on.) An advantage of basing the utilization on 24 hours is that this shows how much more could be done with the resource if it were needed. On the other hand, most managers would not like hearing that their expensive machinery was only being 17 percent utilized!

Bottlenecks in a Sequential Process

Another, major concept in operations is that of _efficiency versus capacity_ (_output rate_). **_Efficiency_** is defined as output divided by input. Here we measure output as minutes of work embodied in the item being produced, and input as minutes of resource time spent overall in producing the item. It is important to understand what production situations are amenable to simple capacity improvements by adding capital resources and what production situations are not. Normally, we expect that the amount of productive capacity and the capital investment to gain this capacity will be about proportional. Suppose blood samples are being analyzed in a spectroscope run by one nurse (and both spectroscope and nurse are constantly busy with this task) at the rate of 10 per hour, and a capacity of 100 per hour is required. Then the resource investment translates directly—10 spectroscopes and 10 nurses will be needed.

However, if the production process is *sequential*, the resource investment may not translate so directly into the required output. Normally, many workers and machines are required to produce an output. In that case, the direct capacity-investment correspondence may not exist because of **bottlenecks** in the production process. Bottlenecks are places (there may be more than one) in the production process where production slows down because of a slow, or insufficient number of, machine(s), or perhaps because of a slow worker, or because the product needs to spend time drying. Fixing such bottlenecks usually only marginally improves the capacity of the system, however, because a new bottleneck arises somewhere else in the production process (this common problem is called "floating bottlenecks"). The following examples illustrate how this happens. For ease of understanding, we use a machine to illustrate the bottleneck, but any kind of service operation could also be a bottleneck, and often is in most services, but is less obvious.

Assume that King Sports Products produces a variety of tennis rackets *sequentially* on four machines, and the times required on each machine for one typical racket are as shown in Figure 8.8. Note in this figure that the work embodied in each finished tennis racket is 4 + 3 + 10 + 2 = 19 minutes, which is also the **throughput time** for a racket if there are no other rackets being made—that is, the system is not busy. However, during a busy production day, this throughput time will increase, as we will see next.

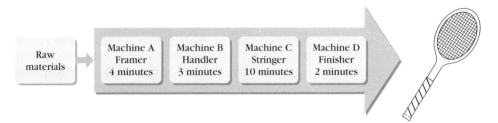

Figure 8.8 King Sports product process.

To minimize the cost of equipment, King could use one of each machine. The resulting capacity or output rate will then be based on the *slowest* machine's processing time of 10 minutes, resulting in 6 units per hour. That is, since every item must go through *each* of the machines, in order, every racket must wait for machine C, the bottleneck, to finish before it can proceed. During this wait, the first, second, and fourth machines will be idle 6, 7, and 8 minutes, respectively, out of every 10-minute cycle.

(Also, the throughput time during such a busy period now becomes 10 + 10 + 10 + 2 = 32 minutes. The racket need not wait at the last machine to exit but the machine must wait 8 minutes for the next racket.) Since the output in this process embodies 19 minutes of work, whereas the input consists of four machines that spend 10 minutes each during every cycle that produces an item (not all of which is necessarily productive), this gives an overall efficiency of only 47.5 percent:

$$\text{Efficiency} = \frac{\text{Output}}{\text{Input}} = \frac{4 + 3 + 10 + 2}{4(10)} = \frac{19}{40} = 47.5\%$$

Note that it does not matter whether the bottleneck is at the end of the sequence, at the beginning, or in the middle. The process is still slowed, on average, to the output rate of the slowest machine. The capacity of this process is thus six units per hour, and the **cycle time of the process** is 10 minutes, or 1/6 of an hour—the output rate and the cycle time are always reciprocals. The process cycle time can be visualized as the time between items coming off the end of the production line, whereas the throughput time can be visualized as the time you would spend in the production process if you attached yourself to the item being produced and rode along through the production process—there is often no relationship between them! And the final output work time is the productive time the item spends in the process.

If King is willing to invest in another, fifth machine, it should purchase another machine of type C, since that is the bottleneck. Then it could run machines C1 and C2 concurrently and put out two units every 10 minutes, obtaining an "effective" machine C processing time of 5 minutes for the machines by staggering their production. Note that machine C is still the bottleneck in the production process, so this effective 5-minute machine processing time is once again the cycle time for the system. The effect of this single investment would be to *double* the capacity/output rate to 12 units per hour (5-min cycle time) and increase the system efficiency to

$$\frac{4+3+10+2}{5(5)} = \frac{19}{25} = 76\%$$

Note in this efficiency calculation that the work output per racket is always 19 minutes, regardless of the number of machines; only the input changes. Now the input is five machines running at a 5-minute cycle time. Continuing in this manner results in the data shown in Table 8.12 and sketched in Figure 8.9. In developing Table 8.12, the next machine added was always the machine that currently had the longest machine time. For example, when there were six machines, machine A had the longest machine time. Thus, the seventh machine added was a machine A.

Note from the table and figure that efficiency of production does not always increase when machines are added, although the general trend is upward. This is because some systems are fairly well "balanced" to begin with. (For example, the cycles across the machines are quite even with seven machines, 2, 3, 3.33, 2; and

𝒯ABLE 8.12 • Return to King for Using More Machines

Number of Machines	Type of Next Machine	A	B	C	D	Cycle Time (min)	Total Hourly Output	Efficiency (%)
4	—	4	3	10	2	10	6	47.5
5	C	4	3	5	2	5	12	76.0
6	C	4	3	3.33	2	4	15	79.2
7	A	2	3	3.33	2	3.33	18	81.4
8	C	2	3	2.5	2	3	20	79.2
9	B	2	1.5	2.5	2	2.5	24	84.4
10	C	2	1.5	2	2	2	30	95.0
11	D	2	1.5	2	1	2	30	86.0
12	A	1.33	1.5	2	1	2	30	79.2
13	C	1.33	1.5	1.67	1	1.67	36	87.5
14	C	1.33	1.5	1.43	1	1.5	40	90.5

Machine Times (min)

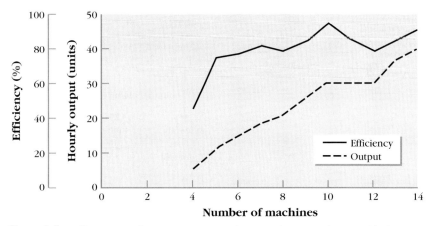

Figure 8.9   Efficiency and output increase when machines are being added.

even more-so at 10 machines. Also note that the addition of only one extra machine at such points does not pay for itself.) If points of high efficiency are reached "early" (as machines are added), these points will tend to be natural operating solutions. For example, a tremendous gain in efficiency (and in output percentage) is reaped by adding a fifth machine to the system. Further additions do not gain much. The next largest gain occurs when the tenth machine is added to the system.

Although this analysis describes the general tradeoffs of the system, no mention has been made of demand. Suppose that demand is 14 units per hour. Then, to minimize risk but still keep an efficient system, King might use five machines and either work overtime, undersupply the market, or use a number of other strategies, as will be discussed later. Similarly, for a demand of 25 to 35 per hour, the use of 10 machines would be appropriate.

Product and Service Flows

With the role of a bottleneck in a production process in mind, let us now consider the more general procedure of conducting a process-flow analysis, also known in service systems as "mapping" or "blueprinting." The purpose of conducting a process flow analysis is normally to identify bottlenecks, inventory buildup points, and time delays in a production process, crucially important in determining the capacity of the process. Standard nomenclature is to use rectangles for tasks/activities, triangles for storage or waiting points, diamonds for decision points, and arrows for flows. An activity changes the characteristics of a product or service, whereas a flow simply indicates the next step in the process, which may involve a change in position.

A simplified process-flow diagram for a manufactured unit composed of two purchased parts and one fabricated 25-pound component is shown in Figure 8.10. Demand is currently 120 units per 8-hour day or 15 units per hour, for an effective process cycle time of one unit every $60/15 = 4$ minutes. The inputs, on the left, consist of 1.5 tons (i.e., 3000 lbs) of raw materials delivered by a two-ton capacity truck once a day and 240 parts delivered by a 300-part capacity truck once a day, both of which immediately go into different storage facilities (with different capacities, as shown). The capacities of each stage in the production process are as labeled. Fabrication of the 15 hourly 25-pound components will require $15 \times 25 = 375$ pounds

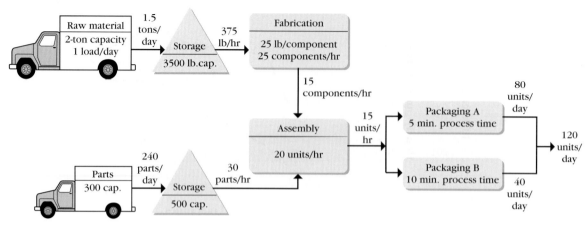

Figure 8.10   Process flow for manufactured unit.

per hour of raw material from the storage facility. The fabricated components will then flow into Assembly, along with 30 parts withdrawn per hour from the parts storage facility. Assembly then produces the 15 units per hour, which flow into two separate packaging lines with different processing times due to their age. New line A packages 10 units each hour while old line B packages 5 units an hour, for the required total demand. Although the output demand is currently 120 units a day, management anticipates an increase of perhaps as much as a third in the near future; their concern is whether the system can handle this increase in demand.

As we see from the diagram, there is currently excess capacity throughout the production system, but is there enough at each stage and process to handle the additional $0.333 \times 120 = 40$ units a day? Assembly, at 20 units per hour, could just handle the anticipated demand of $120 + 40 = 160$ units a day: $20 \times 8 = 160$. However, the raw material storage facility, which can only hold 3500 pounds (enough to produce only $3500/25 = 140$ units a day), is a bottleneck in the system, since we need 160×25 pounds/unit $= 4000$ pounds of storage (the limit of the delivery truck's capacity). Perhaps we could change our system to deliver a portion of the truckload directly to fabrication, or run out 500 pounds to fabrication as the raw material is unloaded from the truck so there is enough space for the full required 2-ton delivery. Note that any activity, resources or storage, could have been the bottleneck in the process. What's more, even if we increase the capacity of the storage facility, the bottleneck will shift to the packaging machines, being able to produce only 12 units per hour from A and another six per hour from B, for a total of 18 per hour, or 144 units a day. And if their capacity is increased, the bottleneck will shift to the 300-part truck delivery because we will need $160 \times 2 = 320$ parts delivered each day. As you can see, the bottleneck shifts around the facility as we solve one problem after another. However, the process-flow diagram allows us to *anticipate* such shifts and head them off before they become real problems.

In a similar manner, Figure 8.11 presents a flow diagram for a simple photocopy service. When used for a service process, the process flow diagram also typically illustrates potential failure points in the process and the *line of visibility* that divides those activities a customer perceives from those that are conducted out of the customer's sight (the "backroom," as in an auto repair shop, where operations can be conducted with efficiency). Since products are not usually produced in a service,

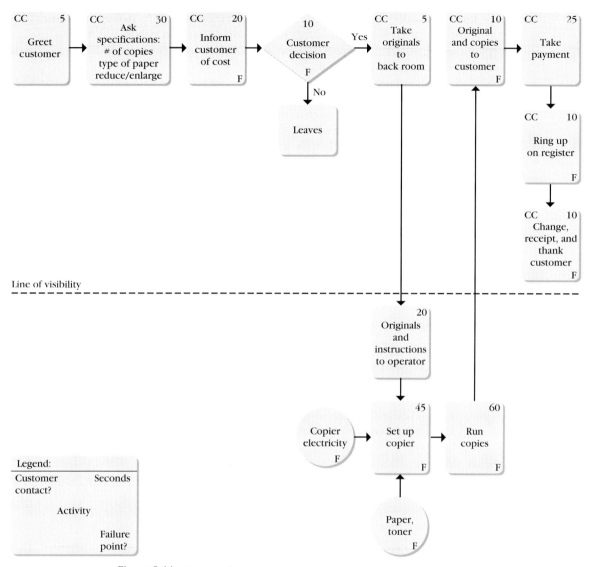

Figure 8.11   Process-flow map for a service.

the diagram is called a service "map" or "blueprint," as noted earlier, and shows the process times more prominently instead. Note the potential failure points in the photocopy service diagram, and the "line of visibility" that divides what the customer sees from the backroom operations. Although Figure 8.11 illustrates a simple service process for illustration purposes, service processes are frequently as complex as Figure 8.10, or even more so, and also involve bottlenecks and combined operations.

Short-term Capacity Alternatives

The problem of short-term capacity is to handle unexpected but imminent actual demand, either less than or more than expected, in an economic manner. It is known, of course, that the forecast will not be perfect; thus, managers of resources must plan what short-term capacity alternatives to use in either case. Such considerations are usually limited to, at most, the next 6 months, and usually much less, such as the next few days or hours.

Some alternatives for obtaining short-run capacity are categorized in Table 8.13. Each of the techniques in the table has advantages and disadvantages. The first set of alternatives concerns simply trying to increase the resource base. The use of overtime is expensive (time and a half), and productivity after 8 hours of work often declines. It is a simple and easily invoked approach, however, that does not require additional investment, so overtime is one of the most common alternatives. The use of extra shifts requires hiring but no extra facilities. However, productivity of second and third shifts is often lower than that of the first shift. Part-time hiring can be expensive and is usually feasible for only low or unskilled work. Floating workers are flexible and very useful, but of course also cost extra. Leasing facilities and workers is often a good approach, but the extra cost reduces the profit, and these external resources may not be available during the high-demand periods when they are most seriously needed. Subcontracting may require a long lead time, is considerable trouble to implement, and may leave little, if any, profit.

*T*ABLE 8.13 • Techniques for Increasing Short-run Capacity

I. Increase resources
 1. Use overtime
 2. Add shifts
 3. Employ part-time workers
 4. Use floating workers
 5. Lease workers and facilities
 6. Subcontract

II. Improve resource use
 7. Overlap or stagger shifts
 8. Cross-train the workers
 9. Create adjustable resources
 10. Share resources
 11. Schedule appointments/reservations
 12. Inventory output (if feasible) ahead of demand
 13. Backlog or queue demand

III. Modify the output
 14. Standardize the output
 15. Offer complimentary services
 16. Have the recipient do part of the work
 17. Transform service operations into inventoriable product operations
 18. Cut back on quality

IV. Modify the demand
 19. Partition the demand
 20. Change the price
 21. Change the promotion
 22. Initiate a yield/revenue management system

V. Do not meet demand
 23. Do not supply all the demand

The second set of techniques involves attempts to find ways to improve the utilization of existing resources. For daily demand peaks (seen especially in services, as discussed in the next section), shifts can be overlapped to provide extra capacity at peak times, or staggered to adjust to changes in demand loads. Cross-training the workers to substitute for each other can effectively increase labor flexibility. And there may be other ways to make labor and other resources adjustable also. A similar alternative is to simply share resources whenever possible. Especially for services, appointment and reservation systems, if feasible, can significantly smooth out daily demand peaks. If the output can be stocked ahead of time, as with a product, this is an excellent and very common approach to meeting capacity needs. If recipients are willing, the backlogging of demand to be met later during slack periods is an excellent strategy; a less-accurate forecast is needed, and investment in finished goods is nil. However, this may be an open invitation to competition.

Modifying the output is a creative approach. Doing less customization, allowing fewer variants, offering complimentary services, and encouraging recipients to do some assembly or finishing tasks themselves (as at self-service gasoline stations and check-out lines), perhaps with a small price incentive, are frequently employed and are excellent alternatives.

Attempting to alter the demand, partition it, or shift it to a different period is another creative approach. Running promotions or price differentials ("off-peak" pricing), or both, for slack periods is an excellent method for leveling demand, especially in utilities, telephones, and similar services. Prices are not easily increased above normal in high-demand periods, however. One formal method of partitioning both the demand and the resource supply is known as yield or revenue management, as discussed earlier. Last, the manager may simply decide not to meet the market demand—again, however, at the cost of inviting competition.

In actuality, many of these alternatives are not feasible except in certain types of organizations or in particular circumstances. For example, when demand is high, subcontractors are full, outside facilities and staff are already overbooked, second-shift workers are employed elsewhere, and marketing promotion is already low key. Thus, of the many possible alternatives, most firms tend to rely on only a few, such as overtime and, for product firms, stocking up ahead of demand.

So far we have primarily discussed increasing capacity in the short run, but firms also have a need to *decrease* short-run capacity. This is more difficult, however, and most such capacity simply goes unused. If the output involves a product, some inventory buildup may be allowed in order to make use of the available capacity; otherwise, system maintenance may be done (cleaning, fixing, preprocessing, and so on).

Capacity Planning for Services

Capacity planning is often much more difficult for pure service operations than for products, and with a service there is a clearer distinction between long- and short-run capacity planning. For services, the more difficult aspects of providing capacity occur in the short run, usually because the demand for a service is subject to daily peaks and valleys, and the output cannot be stored ahead of time to buffer this fluctuation. For example, doctors' offices see demand peaks at 9 A.M. and 1 P.M., and college classes see it at 10 A.M. Or there may be weekly peaks, monthly peaks, or yearly peaks, such as Friday's demand on banks to deposit (or cash) paychecks, and the first-of-the-month demand on restaurants when social security checks arrive in the mail. Some services, such as fire departments, experience multiple peaks, as illustrated in Figure 8.12*a*, which shows the regular *daily* cycle of fire alarms, with a peak from 3 to 7 P.M.; and Figure 8.12*b*, which shows the *yearly* cycle of fire alarms, with a peak in April.

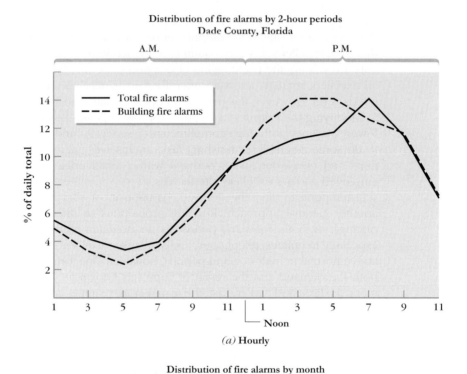

(a) Hourly

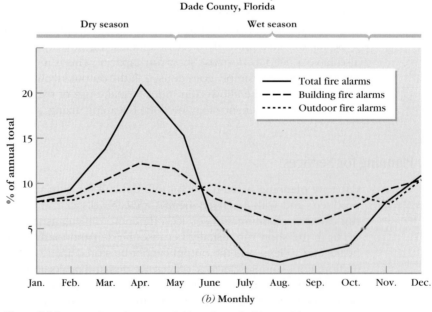

(b) Monthly

Figure 8.12   Fire alarm histories *(a)* hourly and *(b)* monthly.

As noted earlier with regard to products, frequently it is not clear whether a problem is a matter of scheduling or capacity; this is particularly true with services. The primary problem is matching availability of staff to demand in terms of timing and skills, both on a daily basis and over the longer term (such as weekly and monthly). As discussed earlier, service organizations have developed many novel approaches to this problem as just briefly described: split shifts, overlapping shifts, duty tours (e.g., 48 or 72 hrs for firefighters), part-time help, overbooking, appointment systems, and on-call staff. However, for services, a favorite alternative is to share capacity with neighboring units by pooling resources such as generators, police patrols, or hotel rooms. When one organization is temporarily overloaded, the neighbor absorbs the excess demand. Another favorite approach for some services that has even been too successful is that of shifting the demand to off-peak periods. When AT&T offered lower phone rates after 5 P.M., it found that it had to raise the Sunday night 5–11 P.M. rate owing to excessive shifted demand.

In many situations, it is almost impossible to measure an organization's capacity to produce a service, because the service is so abstract. Thus, a more common approach is to measure *inputs* rather than outputs, and assume (perhaps with regular checkups) that the production system is successful at transforming the inputs into acceptable services (outputs). For example, organizations that offer plays, art exhibits, and other such intangible services do not measure their patrons' pleasure or relaxation; rather, they measure number of performances, number of actors and actresses, and number of paintings (or painting days, since many exhibits have a rotating travel schedule). Even fire departments do not attempt to measure their capacity by the number of fires they can extinguish; instead, they use the number of engines or companies they can offer in response to a call, the service or response time, or the number of firefighters responding.

Clearly, this manner of measuring service capacity can leave a lot to be desired. Do more paintings give greater satisfaction? Do higher-quality paintings give greater satisfaction? Might there be other factors that are equally or more important, such as the crowd, the parking facilities, or the lighting on the paintings? Is a hospital where more deaths occur providing worse service? Is a hospital with more physicians on staff providing better service?

The Learning Curve

An extremely important aspect of capacity planning, and an important operations concept in and of itself, is the ***learning curve*** effect—the ability of humans to increase their productive capacity through "learning." This issue is particularly important in the short-term start-up of new and unfamiliar processes such as those involving new technologies (e.g., learning to use a new software program), and always occurs in the production ramp-up of new models of automobiles, planes, computers, etc. Thus, the characteristic of slow, possibly error-prone output initially, followed by better, faster production, should be of major concern to marketing and sales—which are often trying to market the output or have promised a certain volume to a customer by a set date; to accounting—which is checking productivity and yield rates in order to determine a fair cost for the output; and to finance—which is concerned with the timing of cash flows related to purchases, labor, and revenues.

The improvement with experience is not necessarily due to learning alone, however. Better tools, improvements in work methods, upgraded output designs, and other such factors also help increase productivity. Hence, such curves are also known as *improvement curves, production progress functions, performance curves,* and *experience curves.* The learning curve effect, from this viewpoint, also affects long-term capacity and should be factored into longer-term planning processes, another issue of interest to marketing and accounting, as well as finance. The Japanese, in particular, count on increasing the long-term capacity of a facility through the workers' development of better work methods and improvements in tools.

The derivation of the learning curve began in the airframe manufacturing industry during the 1930s, when it was found that the labor-hours needed to build each successive airplane decreased relatively smoothly. In particular, the learning curve law was found to be

Each time the output doubles, the labor hours decrease to a fixed percentage of their previous value.

In the case of plane production, this percentage was found to be 80 percent. Thus, when the first plane of a series required 100,000 labor-hours to produce, the second took 80,000 labor hours, the fourth took 80,000 × 0.80 = 64,000, the eighth 64,000 × 0.80 = 51,200, and so on. This type of mathematical relationship is described by the *negative exponential function*[1], illustrated for airplanes in Figure 8.13.

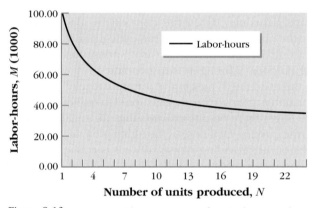

Figure 8.13   80 percent learning curve for airplane production.

---

[1]The function is as follows:

$$M = mN^r$$

where

M = labor-hours for the Nth unit
m = labor hours for first unit
N = number of units produced
r = exponent of curve corresponding to learning rate
  = log(learning rate)/0.693

Two forms of the learning curve relationship are used in the literature. In one form M corresponds to the cumulative average labor-hours of all N units, and in the other form M corresponds to the actual labor-hours to produce the Nth unit. The second interpretation is more useful for capacity planning and will be used here. For example, then, a learning rate of 90 percent would mean that each time production doubled from, say, N_1 to N_2, unit N_2 would require 90 percent of the labor hours that N_1 required. The log here is the "natural" log (the base e), and 0.693 is the natural log of 2.0. But base 10, or any other base, may be used if divided by the log of 2.0 to the same base. That is, r = log(learning rate)/log 2.0.

A number of factors affect the learning curve rate, but the most important are the complexity of the task and the percentage of human, compared with mechanical, input. The greatest learning—sometimes at a rate as much as 60 percent (lower rates meaning greater learning)—occurs for highly complex tasks consisting primarily of human inputs. A task that is highly machine-automated clearly leaves little opportunity for learning. (Thus, a rate close to 100 percent would apply, because only the human can learn.) In airframe manufacturing the proportion of human effort is about 75 percent, and an 80 percent learning rate applies. For similar work of the same complexity and ratio of human-to-machine input, approximately the same rate will apply.

But learning curves are not limited to manufacturing, or even to product-oriented organizations. These curves apply just as well to hairdressing, selling, finding a parking space, and preparing pizza. As indicated, they also apply to *groups* of individuals, and *systems* that include people and machines, as well as to individuals.

The primary question, of course, is what learning rate to apply. If previous experience is available, this may give some indication; if not, a close watch of the time it takes to produce the first few units should give a good indication. Let us illustrate the use of the learning curve, and some learning curve tables, with a simple example.

Learning Curve Tables

It is not usually necessary to solve the learning curve equation every time you run across a learning situation. First, the general law already stated will usually suffice for most purposes. Second, the solution to the equation for various learning rates, assuming that the first item took 1 time unit, has already been calculated and tabulated in Tables 8.14 and 8.15. These tables provide the percentage of time the Nth unit will require relative to what the first unit required (Table 8.14) and the cumulative amount of time that the first N units will take relative to what the first unit took (Table 8.15).

To use Tables 8.14 and 8.15, you multiply the values given in these tables by the labor-hours actually required for the first unit in your situation to get the time for the Nth unit, or the cumulative time for units 1 through N, respectively. Returning to our example—the 80 percent learning curve for airplanes—we see in Table 8.14 that unit 2 (left-hand column) under "80%" will require 0.8 of what unit 1 required (100,000 labor-hours), that unit 4 will require 0.64, that unit 8 will take 0.512, and so forth. In addition, we also see that unit 3 will take 0.7021 and unit 6, for example, 0.5617 (i.e., 0.5617 × 100,000 or 56,170 labor-hours). The *total* labor-hours to produce two, four, or eight planes can be found by adding the necessary values together, or by looking at Table 8.15, where this has already been done. Again, reading under "80%" for 2, 4, and 8 units, we get 1.8, 3.142, and 5.346 × 100,000, respectively, for 180,000, 314,200, and 534,600 labor-hours, cumulative. We next illustrate the use of the learning curve tables with a simple example, followed by a more complex example.

Following the engineering specifications for the assembly of a new motor, a production team was able to assemble the first (prototype) motor in 3.6 hours. After more practice on the second and third motors, the team was able to assemble the fourth motor in 1.76 hours. What is the team's learning rate, and how long will the next motor probably take?

Here the actual individual assembly times are given, so we can use Table 8.14, which tabulates *the ratio of what the N th unit took relative to the first unit.* First, we need to find the ratio from the given data and then locate that value somewhere in the table. Our ratio for the fourth motor would be: 1.76/3.6 = 0.49. Next, we turn to Table 8.14

$\mathcal{T}_{ABLE}$ 8.14 • Unit Values of the Learning Curve

Example: Unit 1 took 10 hours, 80% learning rate. What will unit 5 require? Solution: Unit 5 row, 80% column value = 0.5956. Thus, unit 5 will take 10 (0.5956) = 5.956 hours.

| | Improvement Ratios | | | | | | | |
Units	60%	65%	70%	75%	80%	85%	90%	95%
1	1.0000	1.0000	1.0000	1.0000	1.0000	1.0000	1.0000	1.0000
2	0.6000	0.6500	0.7000	0.7500	0.8000	0.8500	0.9000	0.9500
3	0.4450	0.5052	0.5682	0.6338	0.7021	0.7729	0.8462	0.9219
4	0.3600	0.4225	0.4900	0.5625	0.6400	0.7225	0.8100	0.9025
5	0.3054	0.3678	0.4368	0.5127	0.5956	0.6857	0.7830	0.8877
6	0.2670	0.3284	0.3977	0.4754	0.5617	0.6570	0.7616	0.8758
7	0.2383	0.2984	0.3674	0.4459	0.5345	0.6337	0.7439	0.8659
8	0.2160	0.2746	0.3430	0.4219	0.5120	0.6141	0.7290	0.8574
9	0.1980	0.2552	0.3228	0.4017	0.4930	0.5974	0.7161	0.8499
10	0.1832	0.2391	0.3058	0.3846	0.4765	0.5828	0.7047	0.8433
12	0.1602	0.2135	0.2784	0.3565	0.4493	0.5584	0.6854	0.8320
14	0.1430	0.1940	0.2572	0.3344	0.4276	0.5386	0.6696	0.8226
16	0.1296	0.1785	0.2401	0.3164	0.4096	0.5220	0.6561	0.8145
18	0.1188	0.1659	0.2260	0.3013	0.3944	0.5078	0.6445	0.8074
20	0.1099	0.1554	0.2141	0.2884	0.3812	0.4954	0.6342	0.8012
22	0.1025	0.1465	0.2038	0.2772	0.3697	0.4844	0.6251	0.7955
24	0.0961	0.1387	0.1949	0.2674	0.3595	0.4747	0.6169	0.7904
25	0.0933	0.1353	0.1908	0.2629	0.3548	0.4701	0.6131	0.7880
30	0.0815	0.1208	0.1737	0.2437	0.3346	0.4505	0.5963	0.7775
35	0.0728	0.1097	0.1605	0.2286	0.3184	0.4345	0.5825	0.7687
40	0.0660	0.1010	0.1498	0.2163	0.3050	0.4211	0.5708	0.7611
45	0.0605	0.0939	0.1410	0.2060	0.2936	0.4096	0.5607	0.7545
50	0.0560	0.0879	0.1336	0.1972	0.2838	0.3996	0.5518	0.7486
60	0.0489	0.0785	0.1216	0.1828	0.2676	0.3829	0.5367	0.7386
70	0.0437	0.0713	0.1123	0.1715	0.2547	0.3693	0.5243	0.7302
80	0.0396	0.0657	0.1049	0.1622	0.2440	0.3579	0.5137	0.7231
90	0.0363	0.0610	0.0987	0.1545	0.2349	0.3482	0.5046	0.7168
100	0.0336	0.0572	0.0935	0.1479	0.2271	0.3397	0.4966	0.7112
120	0.0294	0.0510	0.0851	0.1371	0.2141	0.3255	0.4830	0.7017
140	0.0262	0.0464	0.0786	0.1287	0.2038	0.3139	0.4718	0.6937
160	0.0237	0.0427	0.0734	0.1217	0.1952	0.3042	0.4623	0.6869
180	0.0218	0.0397	0.0691	0.1159	0.1879	0.2959	0.4541	0.6809
200	0.0201	0.0371	0.0655	0.1109	0.1816	0.2887	0.4469	0.6757
250	0.0171	0.0323	0.0584	0.1011	0.1691	0.2740	0.4320	0.6646
300	0.0149	0.0289	0.0531	0.0937	0.1594	0.2625	0.4202	0.6557
350	0.0133	0.0262	0.0491	0.0879	0.1517	0.2532	0.4105	0.6482
400	0.0121	0.0241	0.0458	0.0832	0.1453	0.2454	0.4022	0.6419
450	0.0111	0.0224	0.0431	0.0792	0.1399	0.2387	0.3951	0.6363
500	0.0103	0.0210	0.0408	0.0758	0.1352	0.2329	0.3888	0.6314

Source: Albert N. Schreiber, Richard A. Johnson, Robert C. Meier, William T. Newell, and Henry C. Fischer, *Cases in Manufacturing Management* (New York: McGraw-Hill, 1965), p. 464. Reprinted by permission of McGraw-Hill, © 1965.

$\mathscr{T}$ABLE 8.15 • Cumulative Values of the Learning Curve

Example: Unit 1 took 10 hours, 80% learning rate. What will be the total hours required to produce the first five units? Solution: Unit 5 row, 80% column: value = 3.738. Thus, the first five units will require 10 (3.738) = 37.38 hours.

	Improvement Ratios							
Units	60%	65%	70%	75%	80%	85%	90%	95%
1	1.000	1.000	1.000	1.000	1.000	1.000	1.000	1.000
2	1.600	1.650	1.700	1.750	1.800	1.850	1.900	1.950
3	2.045	2.155	2.268	2.384	2.502	2.623	2.746	2.872
4	2.405	2.578	2.758	2.946	3.142	3.345	3.556	3.774
5	2.710	2.946	3.195	3.459	3.738	4.031	4.339	4.662
6	2.977	3.274	3.593	3.934	4.299	4.688	5.101	5.538
7	3.216	3.572	3.960	4.380	4.834	5.322	5.845	6.404
8	3.432	3.847	4.303	4.802	5.346	5.936	6.574	7.261
9	3.630	4.102	4.626	5.204	5.839	6.533	7.290	8.111
10	3.813	4.341	4.931	5.589	6.315	7.116	7.994	8.955
12	4.144	4.780	5.501	6.315	7.227	8.244	9.374	10.62
14	4.438	5.177	6.026	6.994	8.092	9.331	10.72	12.27
16	4.704	5.541	6.514	7.635	8.920	10.38	12.04	13.91
18	4.946	5.879	6.972	8.245	9.716	11.41	13.33	15.52
20	5.171	6.195	7.407	8.828	10.48	12.40	14.61	17.13
22	5.379	6.492	7.819	9.388	11.23	13.38	15.86	18.72
24	5.574	6.773	8.213	9.928	11.95	14.33	17.10	20.31
25	5.668	6.909	8.404	10.19	12.31	14.80	17.71	21.10
30	6.097	7.540	9.305	11.45	14.02	17.09	20.73	25.00
35	6.478	8.109	10.13	12.72	15.64	19.29	23.67	28.86
40	6.821	8.631	10.90	13.72	17.19	21.43	26.54	32.68
45	7.134	9.114	11.62	14.77	18.68	23.50	29.37	36.47
50	7.422	9.565	12.31	15.78	20.12	25.51	32.14	40.22
60	7.941	10.39	13.57	17.67	22.87	29.41	37.57	47.65
70	8.401	11.13	14.74	19.43	25.47	33.17	42.87	54.99
80	8.814	11.82	15.82	21.09	27.96	36.80	48.05	62.25
90	9.191	12.45	16.83	22.67	30.35	40.32	53.14	69.45
100	9.539	13.03	17.79	24.18	32.65	43.75	58.14	76.59
120	10.16	14.11	19.57	27.02	37.05	50.39	67.93	90.71
140	10.72	15.08	21.20	29.67	41.22	56.78	77.46	104.7
160	11.21	15.97	22.72	32.17	45.20	62.95	86.80	118.5
180	11.67	16.79	24.14	34.54	49.03	68.95	95.96	132.1
200	12.09	17.55	25.48	36.80	52.72	74.79	105.0	145.7
250	13.01	19.28	28.56	42.08	61.47	88.83	126.9	179.2
300	13.81	20.81	31.34	46.94	69.66	102.2	148.2	212.2
350	14.51	22.18	33.89	51.48	77.43	115.1	169.0	244.8
400	15.14	23.44	36.26	55.75	84.85	127.6	189.3	277.0
450	15.72	24.60	38.48	59.80	91.97	139.7	209.2	309.0
500	16.26	25.68	40.58	63.68	98.851	151.5	228.8	340.6

Source: Albert N. Schreiber, Richard A. Johnson, Robert C. Meier, William T. Newell, and Henry C. Fischer, *Cases in Manufacturing Management* (New York: McGraw-Hill, 1965), p. 465. Reprinted by permission of McGraw-Hill, © 1965.

and scan across row "4" under the "Units" column. We find the value 0.49 under "70%," so this is our learning rate for the team (which is pretty good, by the way).

To find out how long the next (fifth) motor will take, we drop down the "70%" column to the next row that corresponds to the fifth unit. (*Note*: The rows are not always in increments of 1. For example, at 10 they jump by 2, and at 100 by 20.) At the fifth row the value is 0.4368, which, when multiplied by what the first unit took (3.6 hours), gives: $0.4368 \times 3.6 = 1.57$ hours. Remember: The tabulated values assume that the first unit took only 1 hour (or min., or day, or whatever the measure), so if the first unit took something other than "1," you need to multiply the table value by the actual time it took to produce the first unit.

Next, let us consider a more complex, real-life problem that also requires the use of the cumulative table, Table 8.15.

Spreadsheet, Inc.

Spreadsheet, Inc., has just entered the growing software training market with a contract from a financial organization to teach spreadsheet modeling techniques to the organization's 10 managers, for purposes of financial and pension planning. The lesson for the last manager has just ended, and the organization, considering the first 10 lessons highly successful, has engaged Spreadsheet to give the same lessons to its staff of 150 agents. The lesson for the first manager was highly experimental, requiring 100 hours in all, but careful analysis and refinement of the techniques have gradually decreased this time to the point where the average time for all 10 initial lessons was just under half that value, 49 hours each. To properly staff, schedule, plan, and cost out the work for the 150 lessons, Spreadsheet needs to know how many hours of lessons will be required.

To begin, we can use Table 8.15 to determine the learning rate: the average of 49 hours each, times 10 managers, gives 490 hours, cumulative. This is 4.9 times what the first manager required (490 hours/100 hours). Finding the value 4.9 in Table 8.15 for 10 units will then give the learning curve rate applying to these complex lessons. Reading across the 10-unit row, we find 4.931 (close enough) under the "70%" column. (On occasion, interpolation between columns may be necessary, or alternatively the exact quantities can be calculated directly using the formula. Spreadsheets can greatly facilitate the task of manually calculating time estimates based on the learning curve formula.)

Assuming that the lessons are continuous and the teaching techniques are not forgotten (an important assumption), we can look further down the "70%" column in Table 8.15 to find the value corresponding to the *total* number of lessons to be given: $10 + 150 = 160$. This value, 22.72, is then multiplied by the amount of time required for the first lesson (100 hours) to give a grand total of 2272 hours for the 160 lessons. Since the initial 10 managers required a total of 490 hours by themselves, the second group, consisting of the agents, will require $2272 - 490 = 1782$ hours. The time phasing of this 1782 hours is also available, if desired, from Table 8.14.

The learning curve is only a theoretical construct, of course, and therefore only approximates actual learning. A more realistic, and typical, learning pattern is illustrated in Figure 8.14. Initially, actual labor hours per unit vary around the theoretical curve until a "learning plateau" is reached at, perhaps, the tenth unit. At this plateau no significant learning appears to occur, until there is a breakthrough. Learning typically involves a number of such plateaus and breakthroughs. At about 30 units,

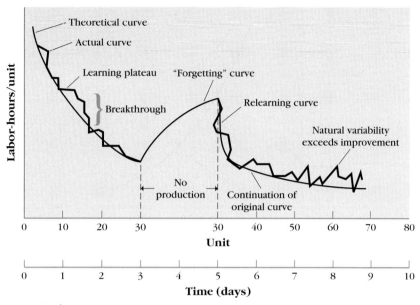

Figure 8.14 Typical pattern of learning and forgetting.

production is halted for a period of time and "forgetting" occurs, rapidly at first but then trailing off. When production is resumed, relearning occurs very quickly (as when someone relearns to ride a bicycle after 40 years) until the original efficiency is reached (at about 33 units). If the conditions are the same at this time as for the initial part of the curve, the original learning curve rate will then hold. After sufficient time passes, the improvement due to learning becomes trivial in comparison with natural variability in efficiency, and at that point we say learning has ceased.

Queuing and the Psychology of Waiting

An important element in evaluating the capacity of operations to produce either products or services concerns the waiting lines, backlogs, or *queues*, that tend to build up in front of the operations. Queuing theory provides a mechanism to determine several key performance measures of an operating system based on the rate of arrivals to the system and the system's capacity (specified as the system's service rate). With an unpaced production line, for example, buffer inventory between operations builds up at some times and disappears at other times, owing to natural variability in the difficulty of the operations. The Wiley website for this text (see Preface for URL) includes a discussion of the theory, equations, and some example calculations of queuing.

In the production of services, this variability is even greater because of both the amount of highly variable human *input* and the variable *requirements* for services. What is more, the "items" in queue are often people, who tend to complain and make trouble if kept waiting too long. Thus, it behooves the operations manager to provide adequate service to keep long queues from forming. This costs more money for service facilities and staffs. But long queues cost money also, in the form of in-process inventory, unfinished orders, lost sales, and ill will. Figure 8.15 conceptually

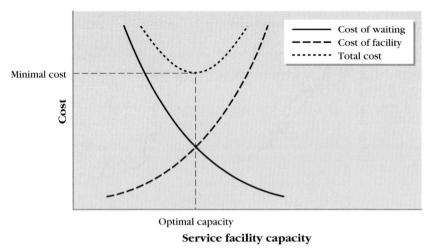

Figure 8.15   The relevant queuing costs.

illustrates, as a function of the capacity of the service facility, the tradeoffs in these two costs.

1. *Cost of waiting.* In-process inventory, ill will, lost sales. This cost decreases with service capacity.

2. *Cost of service facilities.* Equipment, supplies, and staff. This cost increases with service capacity.

At some point the total of the two costs in Figure 8.15 is minimized, and it is at this point that managers typically wish to operate. However, before investing resources in adding expensive service facilities, the manager may find it worthwhile trying to reduce the cost of waiting instead. Given that perceptions and expectations may have more to do with customer satisfaction than actual waiting time, David Maister (1984) has formulated eight insightful "principles" of waiting, which, if addressed carefully, may be more effective in reducing the overall cost of waiting to the organization than adding service facilities.

1. ***Unoccupied time feels longer than occupied time.*** Give customers something to do while waiting, hopefully something that will facilitate the service that is to come. An example is having customers key in their Social Security number while waiting on the phone so the representative will have their file on screen as they answer the call.

2. ***Pre-service waiting feels longer than in-service waiting.*** Using staging areas to complete portions of the service, such as taking a patient's temperature and blood pressure, communicates to them that the service has begun.

3. ***Anxiety makes waiting seem longer.*** Offer information to relieve anxiety, or distracters (even music, mirrors) to allay anxiety.

4. ***Uncertain waiting is longer than known, finite waiting.*** Provide cues, or direct announcements, to indicate how soon the service will be coming or finishing (especially in the case of a painful procedure).

5. ***Unexplained waiting is longer than explained waiting.*** Keep customers informed about why they are being delayed, and how long it will be before they can be serviced.

6. ***Unfair waiting is longer than fair waiting.*** Make sure that priority or express customers are handled in a manner transparent to other customers, and treated out of sight, if possible.

7. ***Solo waiting is longer than group waiting.*** In part this reflects principles 1 (someone else to talk to), 3 (seeing and talking to others can reduce anxiety), and 5 (other waiting customers may communicate reasons for the waiting), as well as the general principle that there is more security in groups.

8. ***The more valuable the service, the longer it is worth waiting for.*** The use of marketing and other means to increase the perception of the value of the service will reduce the impatience with waiting.

EXPAND YOUR UNDERSTANDING

1. What impact might the Internet, the World Wide Web, and intranets have on using the Delphi method?

2. Why might a decision maker choose a qualitative forecasting method when extensive historical demand data are available?

3. Frequently, simple models such as breakeven are much more appealing to management than more sophisticated models (such as linear programming). Why might this be so?

4. Exactly what decreases in unit cost occur with larger facilities as a result of economies of scale? Might any unit costs increase with the size of a facility?

5. Why has the concept of economies of scope never arisen before? List where the economies come from.

6. How ethical is it for airlines, hotels, and other service providers to overbook their limited-capacity facilities intentionally, knowing that at some point they will have to turn away a customer with a "guaranteed" reservation?

7. Describe how the concept of bottlenecks would apply to services as well as products. Give some examples from your experience.

8. What elements would be measured if a product firm were to measure its capacity by its inputs, as do some service firms?

9. Does the learning curve continue downward forever?

10. Which measures used to locate pure service organizations are direct measures of benefit and which are surrogate measures of benefit? Can you think of better direct measures? Why aren't they used?

11. Would the failure points, line of visibility, and processing times used in service maps be useful in process flow diagrams for products?

12. When might an organization not use all three stages of the location selection process described here?

13. Might the breakeven model be used for the national or site stage of location? Might the weighted score model be useful in the national or community stage of location? What factors would be used in these models at other stages?

14. Are the principles of waiting captured in the 23 capacity techniques of Table 8.13? Which ones?

15. Would a firm that simply expanded their current product line gain economies of scope? Might highly flexible and proficient labor also offer economies of scope?

16. Many services, such as airlines, conduct their scheduling in two stages. First, an overall macroschedule is constructed and optimized for costs and service to the customer. This schedule is then considered to be the baseline for detailed scheduling to attempt to achieve. The second, detailed stage is then a real-time schedule to adjust the macroschedule for any necessary changes, emergencies, and so on. Describe how this might work for airlines, hospitals, schools, and urban alarm services. What serious problems might arise with this approach?

17. Referring to the Revenue Management section, why might an early reservation be cancelled? A late reservation?

APPLY YOUR UNDERSTANDING

Bangalore Training Services (BTS)

BTS was an entrepreneurial startup developed by Deepa Anand and Monisha Patel, two recent MBA graduates from the United States who had served internships in the summer with a U. S. call center who was considering setting up operations in India but was unsure how to find suitable employees. Their plan was to offer training to Indian men and women in call center activities such as sales, service, and trouble-shooting for electronic goods of all sorts, and then match those employees to the needs of foreign firms looking to set up call centers. The training consisted of a dozen sessions covering culture, speaking fluency, electronic awareness, buying and service behaviors, and other such basic matters that all call centers required.

Questions

Discuss how the following topics from this chapter might be of relevance to Deepa and Monisha in setting up their new firm:
1. Capacity planning
2. Learning curve
3. Bottlenecks
4. Psychology of waiting
5. Scheduling
6. Service map/blueprint

Exit Manufacturing Company

The planning committee of Exit Manufacturing Company (made up of the vice presidents of marketing, finance, and production) was discussing the plans for a new factory to be located outside of Atlanta, Georgia, U.S.A. The factory would produce exterior doors consisting of prehung metal over Styrofoam insulation. The doors would be made in a standard format, with 15 different insert panels that could be added by retailers after manufacture. The standardization of construction was expected to create numerous production efficiencies over competitors' factories that produced multidimensional doors. Atlanta was felt to be an ideal site because of its location—in the heart of the sunbelt, with its growing construction industry. By locating close to these growing sunbelt states, Exit would minimize distribution costs.

The capital cost for the factory was expected to be $14 million. Annual maintenance expenses were projected to total 5 percent of capital. Fuel and utility costs were expected to be $500,000 per year. An analysis of the area's labor market indicated that a wage rate of $10 per hour could be expected. It was estimated that producing a door in the new facility would require 1.5 labor-hours. Fringe benefits paid to the operating labor were expected to equal 15 percent of direct labor costs. Supervisory, clerical, technical, and managerial salaries were forecast to total $350,000 per year. Taxes and insurance would cost $200,000 per year. Other miscellaneous expenses were expected to total $250,000 per year. Depreciation was based on a 30-year life with use of the straight-line method and a $4 million salvage value. Sheet metal, Styrofoam, adhesive for the doors, and frames were projected to cost $12 per door. Paint, hinges, doorknobs, and accessories were estimated to total $7.80 per door. Crating and shipping supplies were expected to cost $2.50 per door.

Exit's marketing manager prepared the following price-demand chart for the distribution area of the new plant. Through analysis of these data, the committee members felt that they could verify their expectation of an increase from 15 to 25 percent in the current market share, owing to the cost advantage of standardization.

Average Sales Price ($/door)	Area Sales (in units)
$90	40,000
$103	38,000
$115	31,000
$135	22,000

Questions

Develop a breakeven capacity analysis for Exit's new door and determine:

a. Best price, production rate, and profit.
b. Breakeven production rate with the price in a.
c. Breakeven price with the production rate in a.
d. Sensitivity of profits to variable cost, price, and production rate.

Stafford Chemical, Inc.

Stafford Chemical, Inc. is a privately held company that produces a range of specialty chemicals. Currently, its most important product line is paint pigments used by the automobile industry. Stafford Chemical was founded more than 60 years ago by Phillip Stafford in a small town north of Cincinnati, Ohio, U.S.A., and is currently run by Phillip's grandson, George Stafford. Stafford has more than 150 employees, and approximately three-quarters of them work on the shop floor. Stafford Chemical operates out of the same plant Phillip built when he founded the company; however, it has undergone several expansions over the years.

Recently, a Japanese competitor of Stafford Chemical by the name of Ozawa Industries announced plans to expand its operations to the United States. Ozawa, a subsidiary of a large industrial Japanese company, decided to locate a new facility in the United States to better serve some of its customers: Japanese automobile manufacturers who have built assembly plants in the U.S.A.

The governor of Ohio has been particularly aggressive in trying to persuade Ozawa Industries to locate in a new industrial park located about 30 miles from Stafford's current plant. She has expressed a willingness to negotiate special tax rates, to subsidize workers' training, and to expand the existing highway to meet Ozawa's needs. In a recent newspaper article, she was quoted as saying:

Making the concessions I have proposed to get Ozawa to locate within our state is a good business decision and a good investment in our state. The plant will provide high-paying jobs for 400 of our citizens. Furthermore, over the long run, the income taxes that these 400 individuals will pay will more than offset the concessions I have proposed. Since several other states have indicated a willingness to make similar concessions, it is unlikely that Ozawa would choose our state without them.

George Stafford was outraged after being shown the governor's comments. I can't believe this. Stafford Chemical has operated in this state for over 60 years. I am the third generation of Staffords to run this business. Many of our employees' parents and grandparents worked here. We have taken pride in being an exemplary corporate citizen. And now our governor wants to help one of our major competitors drive us out of business. How are we supposed to compete with such a large industrial giant? We should be the ones who are getting the tax break and help with workers' training. Doesn't 60 years of paying taxes and employing workers count for something? Where is the governor's loyalty? It seems to me that the state should be loyal to its long-term citizens, the ones who care about the state and community they operate in—not some large industrial giant looking to save a buck.

Questions

1. How valid is George Stafford's argument? How valid is the governor's argument? Is Stafford Chemical being punished because it was already located within the state?
2. How ethical is it for states and local governments to offer incentives to attract new businesses to their localities? Are federal laws needed to keep states from competing with one another?
3. Does the fact that Ozawa is a foreign company alter the ethical nature of the governor's actions? What about Ozawa's size?
4. What are George's options?

EXERCISES

1. Three professors are grading a combined final exam. Each is grading different questions on the test. One professor requires 3 minutes to finish her portion, a second takes 6 minutes, and the third takes 2 minutes. Assume there is no learning curve effect.

   a. What will be their hourly output?

   b. If there are 45 tests to grade, how long will the grading take?

   c. If each professor were to grade the exams separately in 18 minutes, how long would it take to grade the 45 tests? How long if another professor (who also required 18 min) joined them?

   d. If another professor pitches in just to help the second professor in the original arrangement, how long will it take the four of them to grade the tests?

   e. If a fifth professor offers to help, what might happen?

2. A toy firm produces drums sequentially on three machines A, B, and C with cycle times of 3, 4, and 6 minutes, respectively.

   a. Determine the optimum efficiency and output rates for adding one, two, . . . , six more machines.

   b. Assume now that two identical lines are operating, each with machines A, B, and C. If new machines can be shared between the lines, how should one, two, and then three new machines be added? What are the resulting efficiencies and outputs of the two lines? Is it always best to equally share extra machines between the two lines?

3. If the production system for a product has a utilization of 80 percent, and a yield of 75 percent, what capacity is needed to produce 1000 units a year?

4. If unit 1 requires 6 labor hours and unit 5 requires 1.8324, what is the learning rate? What will unit 6 require? What have the first five units required in total?

5. A production lot of 25 units required 103.6 hours of effort. Accounting records show that the first unit took 7 hours. What was the learning rate?

6. If unit 1 required 200 hours to produce and the labor records for an Air Force contract of 50 units indicate an average labor content of 63.1 hours per unit, what was the learning rate? What total additional number of labor-hours would be required for another Air Force contract of 50 units? What would be the average labor content of this second contract? Of both contracts combined? If labor costs the vendor $10 per hour on this Air Force contract and the price to the Air Force is fixed at $550 each, what can you say about the profitability of the first and second contracts, and hence the bidding process in general?

7. All the reports you wrote for one class had three sections: introduction, analysis, conclusion. The times required to complete these sections (including typing, etc.) are shown below in hours.

Report	Introduction	Analysis	Conclusion
1	1.	6	2
2	5	(lost data)	—
3	—	3	0.8

   The class requires five reports in all. You are now starting report 4 and, although you are working faster, you can afford to spend only 1 hour a day on these reports. Report 5 is due in one week (7 days). Will you be done in time?

8. Use the CVD model to evaluate the following three locations in terms of access to five destinations. Site I is located 313, 245, 188, 36, and 89 feet,

respectively, from the five destinations; site II, 221, 376, 92, 124, and 22 feet; and site III, 78, 102, 445, 123, and 208 feet.

9. Reevaluate exercise 8 if the number of trips to each of the destinations is, respectively, 15, 6, 12, 33, and 21.

10. The location subcommittee's final report to the board has focused on three acceptable communities. Table 15b in the appendix to the report indicates that the cost of locating in communities 1, 2, and 3 is approximately €400,000, €500,000, and €600,000 per year (respectively), mortgaged over 30 years. Paragraph 2 on page 39 of the report indicates that the variable cost per unit of product will increase 15 percent in community 1 but decrease 15 percent in community 3, owing to differences in labor rates. As plant manager, you know that variable costs to date have averaged about €3.05 per unit and sales for the next decade are expected to average 20 percent more than the last 10 years, during which annual sales varied between 40,000 and 80,000 units. Which location would you recommend?

11. Nina is trying to decide in which of four shopping centers to locate her new boutique. Some cater to a higher class of clientele than others, some are in an indoor mall, some have a much greater volume than others, and, of course, rent varies considerably. Because of the nature of her store, she has decided that the class of clientele is the most important consideration. Following this, however, she must pay attention to her expenses; and rent is a major item—probably 90 percent as important as clientele. An indoor, temperature-controlled mall is a big help, however, for stores such as hers, where 70 percent of sales are from passersby slowly strolling and window-shopping. Thus, she rates this as about 95 percent as important as rent. Last, a higher volume of shoppers means more potential sales; she thus rates this factor as 80 percent as important as rent. As an aid in visualizing her location alternatives, she has constructed the following table. "Good" is scored as 3, "fair" as 2, and "poor" as 1. Use a weighted score model to help Nina come to a decision.

	Location			
	1	2	3	4
Class of clientele	Fair	Good	Poor	Good
Rent	Good	Fair	Poor	Good
Indoor mall	Good	Poor	Good	Poor
Volume	Good	Fair	Good	Poor

12. What was the design capacity of a production system that produces 753 good units a year with a utilization of 90 percent and yield of 85 percent?

13. A defense contractor is bidding on a military contract for 100 radar units. The contractor employs 30 machine operators who work 165 hours a month each. The first radar unit required 1145 operator-hours, and the learning curve for this type of work is known to be 75 percent. It takes a month to order and receive raw material components, which cost $500 per radar unit. The material is then paid for in the month it is received. Fixed costs include a month to tool up, which costs $10,000, and then $5000 per month for every month of production. Direct labor and variable overhead are $8 per hour. The contractor can deliver only completed units and is paid the following month. Profit is set at 10 percent of the bid price. Find the bid price, derive the production schedule, and calculate the cash flow schedule.

14. Is Clarton or Uppingham the best location for a production volume of 600 services? The fixed costs of Clarton total £6000 (pounds, United Kingdom) per year, while those of Uppingham total only £4500. However, the variable costs of Clarton are £8, while those of Uppingham are £10.

15. The head of the Campus Computing Center is faced with locating a new centralized computer center at one of three possible locations on the campus. The decision is to be based on the number of users in each department and the distance of the various departments from each possible location. Which location should be chosen?

Department	Number of Users	Distance by Location		
		1	2	3
1	25	0	3	5
2	30	5	4	3
3	10	2	0	1
4	5	3	2	0
5	14	6	2	3

16. A new product involves the following costs associated with three possible locations. If demand is forecast to be 3900 units a year, which location should be selected?

	Location		
	A	B	C
Annual cost	$10,000	40,000	25,000
Unit variable cost	$10.00	2.50	6.30

17. A fancy Swiss restaurant has 30 tables. If it accepts N reservations, the probability that N will arrive is 0.1; $N-1$ is 0.2; $N-2$ is 0.3; and $N-3$ is 0.4. If each unfilled table costs F20 (Swiss francs) but a customer turned away costs F10, find how many reservations to accept. Solve again, assuming that a customer turned away costs F25.

18. The Arms Hotel in South Africa has only 56 rooms. An unfilled room represents R500 (rands) a night in lost profit, whereas every turnaway due to a filled room costs R300 in ill will. If N reservations are accepted, the probability of N, $N-1$, and $N-2$ guests actually showing up is 0.2, 0.5, 0.3, respectively. How many reservations should be accepted?

BIBLIOGRAPHY

Alstrup, J., S. E. Andersson, S. Boas, O. B. G. Madsen, and R. V. V. Vidal. "Booking Control Increases Profit at Scandinavian Airlines." *Interfaces* (July–August 1989): 10–19.

Armstrong, J. S. *Long Range Forecasting: From Crystal Ball to Computer.* New York: John Wiley and Sons, Inc., 1995.

Ballou, R. H. *Business Logistics Management,* 4th ed. Upper Saddle River, NJ: Prentice Hall, 1998.

Bartmess, A., and K. Cerny. "Building Competitive Advantage through a Global Network of Capabilities." *California Management Review,* 35 (1993): 78–103.

Belkaoui, A. *The Learning Curve.* Westport, CT: Quorum Books, 1986.

Blackstone, J. H. *Capacity Management.* Cincinnati, OH: South-Western, 1989.

Crandall, R. E., and R. E. Markland. "Demand Management—Today's Challenge for Service Industries." *Production and Operations Management,* 5 (Summer 1996): 106–120.

Drezner, Z. and H. Hamacher. *Facility Location: Applications and Theory.* Berlin: Springer Verlag, 2002.

Durrande-Moreau, A., and J.-C. Usunier. "Time Styles and the Waiting Experience: An Exploratory Study." *Journal of Service Research,* 2 (November 1999): 173–186.

Ferdows, K. "Making the Most of Foreign Factories." *Fortune* (March–April 1997): 73–88.

Filley, R. D. "Putting the 'Fast' in Fast Foods: Burger King." *Industrial Engineering* (January 1983): 44–47.

Fisher, M. L., J. H. Hammond, W. R. Obermeyer, and A. Raman. "Making Supply Meet Demand in an Uncertain World." *Harvard Business Review,* 72 (May–June 1994): 83–93.

Fitzsimmons, J. A., and M. J. Fitzsimmons. *Service Management: Operations, Strategy, and Information Technology,* 5th ed. New York: Irwin/McGraw-Hill, 2006.

Francis, R. L., L. F. McGinnis, Jr., and J. A. White. *Layout and Location: An Analytical Approach,* 2nd ed. Upper Saddle River, NJ: Prentice-Hall, 1998.

Goldratt, E. Y., and J. Cox. *The Goal: A Process of On-Going Improvement.* Croton-on-Hudson, NY: North River, 1984.

Hartvigsen, D. *SimQuick: Process Simulation with Excel.* 2nd ed. Upper Saddle River, NJ: Prentice-Hall, 2004.

Heskett, J. "Note on Service Mapping." Harvard Reprint No. 9-693-065, November 1992.

Hunt, V. D. *Process Mapping.* New York: John Wiley and Sons, Inc., 1996.

Kimes, S. E., and R. B. Chase. "The Strategic Levers of Yield Management." *Journal of Service Research,* 1 (November 1998): 156–166.

Kirchmier, B. and G. I. Plenert. *Finite Capacity Scheduling.* New York: John Wiley and Sons, Inc., 2002.

Klassen, K. J., and T. R. Rohleder. "Combining Operations and Marketing to Manage Capacity and Demand in Services." *The Service Industries Journal,* vol. 21, no. 2 (2001): 1–30.

Krajewski, L. J., and, L. P. Ritzman. "Shift Scheduling in Banking Operations: A Case Application." *Interfaces* (April 1980): 1–7.

Maister, D. H. "The Psychology of Waiting Lines." Harvard Reprint No. 9-684-064, May 1984.

Marshall, P. W. "A Note on Process Analysis (Abridged)." Harvard Reprint No. 9-689-032, September 1994.

Metters, R., and V. Vargus. "Yield Management for the Nonprofit Sector." *Journal of Service Research,* 1 (February 1999): 215–226.

Niebel, B., and A. Freivalds. *Methods, Standards, and Work Design,* 11th ed. New York: McGraw-Hill, 2002.

Port, O. "Huh? Chipmakers Copying Steelmakers?" *Business Week* (August 15, 1994): 97–98.

Price, W. L., and M. Turcotte. "Locating a Blood Bank." *Interfaces* (September–October 1986) 17–26.

Pullman, M. E., J. C. Goodale, and R. Verma. "Service Capacity Design with an Integrated Market Utility-Based Method." In J. A. Fitzsimmons and M J Fitzsimmons (eds.), *New Service Development*. Thousand Oaks, CA: Sage, 2000: 111–137.

Radas, S., and S. M. Shugan. "Managing Service Demand: Shifting and Bundling." *Journal of Service Research*, 1 (August 1998): 47–64.

Ramani, K. V. "Scheduling Doctors' Activities at a Large Teaching Hospital." *Production and Inventory Management Journal* (1st/2nd Qtr., 2002): 56–62.

Sanders, N. R., and L. P. Ritzman. "Bringing Judgment into Combination Forecasts." *Journal of Operations Management*. 13 (1995): 311–321.

Sanders, N. R., and K. B. Manrodt. "Forecasting Practices in U.S. Corporations: Survey Results." *Interfaces*, 24 (March–April 1994): 91–100.

Schmenner, R. W. "The Location Decisions of New Services." In J. A. Fitzsimmons and M. J. Fitzsimmons (eds.), *New Service Development*. Thousand Oaks, CA: Sage, 2000: 216–238.

Smith, B. C., J. F. Leimkuhler, and R. M. Darrow. "Yield Management at American Airlines." *Interfaces*, 22 (January–February 1992): 8–31.

Teplitz, C. J. *The Learning Curve Deskbook*. Westport, CT: Greenwood Publishing Group, 1991.

Trail, D. T. "Package Products Capitalizes on Data." *APICS—The Performance Advantage* (August 1996): 38–41.

Forecasting

FORECASTING PURPOSES AND METHODS

There is usually a close relationship between competing successfully and being able to predict key aspects of the future accurately. Clearly, it is not practical to try to plan without some prediction of the future. Even planning a simple party requires predicting how many people will show up, how much they will eat and drink, what kind of snacks and beverages they will enjoy, and how long they will stay. A business introducing a new service needs to predict the demand for the service, how prices and advertising will affect this demand, how competitors will respond, and so on.

Thus, we see that an accurate estimate of demand for the output is crucial to the efficient operation of the production system and, hence, to managing the organization's resources. For example, a supermarket chain that is contemplating the addition of a new store must have a reasonable estimate of demand in order to determine how big the store and the parking lot should be, what ancillary departments (such as a bakery, pharmacy, deli, and bank) should be included, and how many shopping carts and checkout lanes should be specified in the plans. Once the facility is constructed, a more specific, perhaps weekly, forecast of demand will be needed so that the manager will be able to schedule workers and order merchandise. The same is true for decisions about capacity, scheduling, and staffing in a product organization. Capacity (obtaining the proper level of resources) and scheduling (the timing of resource usage) both require forecasting, whether or not it be a formal procedure.

As an aside, it is worth noting that it is not only demand for the output that can be forecast. The tools of forecasting can also be used to predict the development of new technology, national and international economic conditions, and even many factors internal to the organization such as changes in lead time, scrap rates, cost trends, personnel growth, and departmental productivity. Here, however, we will restrict our discussion to the uses of forecasting for long- and short-term capacity planning.

Forecasts are used in organizations for four primary purposes, the first two of which are strategic and long range, and the last two of which are more tactical and short range.

1. To decide whether demand is sufficient to justify entering the market. If demand exists but at too low a price to cover the costs that an organization will incur in producing an output, then the organization should reject the opportunity.

2. To determine long-term (2- to 5-year) capacity needed, in order to design facilities. An overall projection of demand for a number of years in the future serves as the basis for decisions related to expanding, or contracting, capacity to meet the demand. Since there is competition, even in the not-for-profit sector, an organization is courting disaster if it produces inefficiently, because of excess idle capacity, or insufficiently to meet demand, because of too little capacity.

3. To determine midterm (3-month to 18-month) fluctuations in demand, in order to avoid shortsighted decisions that will hurt the company in the long run. To illustrate, if a company planned its staffing solely on the basis of its weekly forecast, each week it might adjust the level on the basis of a forecast for the coming week. Thus, in some weeks it might lay off workers only to rehire them in the following week. Such weekly adjustments would most likely lower morale and productivity. A better approach is to base staffing on a longer-term perspective.

4. To ascertain short-term (1-week to 3-month) fluctuations in demand for the purposes of production planning, work force scheduling, materials planning, and other such needs. These forecasts support a number of operational activities and can have a significant effect on organizational productivity, bottlenecks, master schedules, meeting promised delivery dates, and other such issues of concern to top management and to the organization as a whole.

Forecasting Methods

Forecasting methods can be grouped in several ways. One classification, illustrated in Figure 8S.1, distinguishes between formal forecasting techniques and informal approaches such as intuition, spur-of-the-moment guesses, and seat-of-the-pants predictions. Our attention here will obviously be directed to the formal methods.

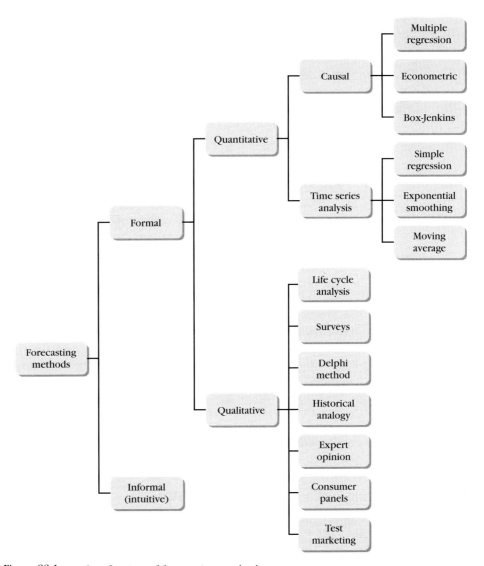

Figure 8S.1 A classification of forecasting methods.

In general, qualitative forecasting methods are often used for long-range forecasts, especially when external factors (e.g., an especially cold winter) may play a significant role. They are also of use when historical data are very limited or nonexistent, as in the introduction of a new product or service.

Some of the most significant decisions made by organizations, frequently strategic decisions, are made on the basis of *qualitative* forecasts. These often concern either a new product or service or long-range changes in the nature of the organization's outputs. In both cases, relevant historical data on demand are typically not available.

Qualitative forecasts are made using information such as telephone or mail surveys of consumers' attitudes and intentions, consumer panels, test marketing in limited areas, expert opinion and panels, and analyses of historical demand for similar products or services—a method known as *historical analogy*. One example of historical analogy would be the use of demand data for CD-ROMs to predict the demand curve for DVDs, or Broadway shows to predict the demand for movies.

A special type of expert panel uses what is called the *Delphi* method. The RAND Corporation developed the Delphi method as a group technique for forecasting the demand for new or contemplated products or services. The intent was to eliminate the undesirable effects of interaction between members of the group (such as loud and dominating individuals) while retaining the benefits of their broad experience and knowledge. The method begins by having each member provide individual written forecasts, along with any supporting arguments and assumptions. These forecasts are submitted to a Delphi researcher, who edits, clarifies, and summarizes the data. These data are then provided as feedback to the members, along with a second round of questions. This procedure continues, usually for about four rounds, when a consensus among panel members can often be reached on some of the issues.

Another qualitative device often used in forecasting is called *life-cycle analysis*. Experienced managers who have introduced several new products are often able to estimate how long a product will remain in each stage of its life cycle. This forecast, coupled with other market information, can produce reasonably accurate estimates of demand in the medium to long range.

Quantitative forecasting methods are generally divided between methods that simply project the past history or behavior of the variable into the future (*time series analysis*) and those that also include external data (*causal*). Time series analysis is the simpler of the two and ranges from just using an average of the past data to using regression analysis corrected for seasonality in the data. Simple projection techniques are obviously limited to, and primarily used for, very short-term forecasting. Such approaches often work well in a stable environment but cannot react to changing industry factors or changes in the national economy.

Causal methods, which are usually quite complex, include histories of external factors and employ sophisticated statistical techniques. In addition to using spreadsheets, many "canned" software packages are available for the quantitative techniques, both time series analysis and causal.

Factors Influencing the Choice of Forecasting Method

What method is chosen to prepare a demand forecast depends on a number of factors. First, long-range (2- to 5-year) forecasts typically require the least accuracy and are only for general (or aggregate) planning, whereas short-range forecasts require greater accuracy and are for detailed operations. Thus, the most accurate methods are usually used for short-term needs and, fortunately, the data in the near term is usually the most accurate.

Second, if the data are available, one of the quantitative forecasting methods can be used. Otherwise, nonquantitative techniques are required. Attempting to forecast without a demand history is almost as hard as using a crystal ball. The demand history need not be long or complete, but some historical data should be used if at all possible.

Third, the greater the limitation on time or money available for forecasting, the more likely it is that an unsophisticated method will have to be used. In general, management wants to use a forecasting method that minimizes not only the cost of making the forecast but also the cost of an *inaccurate* forecast; that is, management's goal is to minimize the total forecasting costs. Costs of inaccurate forecasting include the cost of over- or understocking an item, the costs of under- or overstaffing, and the intangible and opportunity costs associated with loss of goodwill because a demanded item is not available.

Fourth, with the advent of computers, the cost of statistical forecasts based on historical data and the time required to make such forecasts have been reduced significantly. It has therefore become more cost-effective for organizations to develop more sophisticated forecasts.

In the remainder of this supplement we briefly overview several of the quantitative forecasting methods. In the next section time series analysis is addressed. Then in the following section causal methods are discussed.

 IME SERIES ANALYSIS

A time series is simply a set of values of some variable measured either at regular points in time or over sequential intervals of time. We measure stock closing prices at specific points in time and quarterly sales over specific intervals of time. If, for example, we recorded the number of books sold each month of the previous year at Amazon.com and kept those data points in the order in which they were recorded, the 12 numbers would constitute a 12-period time series. Time series data can be collected over very short intervals (such as hourly sales at a fast-food restaurant) or very long intervals (such as the census data collected every 10 years).

Components of a Time Series

We analyze a time series because we believe that knowledge of its past behavior might help us understand (and therefore help us predict) its behavior in the future, normally just the next period. In some instances, such as the stock market, this assumption may be unjustified, but in planning many operational activities history does (to some extent, at least) repeat itself and past tendencies continue. Our goal is to find a forecasting model that is easy to compute and use, responsive to changes in the data, and accurate in its predictions. To begin our discussion of time series analysis, let us consider the component parts of any time series.

To analyze time series data, it is often helpful to think of it as being comprised of four components:

1. Trend, T.
2. Seasonal variation, S.
3. Cyclical variation, C.
4. Random variation, R.

The *trend* is the long-run direction of the time series, including any constant amount of demand in the data. Figure 8S.2 illustrates three fairly common trend lines showing changes in demand; a horizontal trend line would indicate a constant, unchanging level of demand.

A straight-line or linear trend (showing a constant amount of change, as in Panel A of Figure 8S.2) could be an accurate fit to the historical data over some limited range of time, even though it might provide a rather poor fit over an entire time series. Panel B in the figure illustrates the situation of a constant percentage change. Here, changes in a variable depend on the current size of the variable (rather than being constant each period as in Figure 8S.2A). The trend line shown in Panel C of Figure 8S.2 resembles the life cycle or "stretched-S" growth curve that describes the demand many products and services experience over time.

Seasonal fluctuations are fairly regular fluctuations that repeat within one year's time, or whatever period encompasses the full set of seasonals. Seasonal fluctuations result primarily from nature, but they are also brought about by human behavior. Sales of heart-shaped boxes of candy and pumpkins are brought about by events that are controlled by humans. Snow tires and antifreeze enjoy a brisk demand during the winter months, whereas sales of golf balls and bikinis peak in the spring and summer months. Of course, seasonal demand often leads or lags behind the actual season. For example, the production season for meeting retailers' demand for Christmas goods is August through September. Also, seasonal variation in events need not be related to the seasons of the year. For example, fire alarms in New York City reach a "seasonal" peak at 7 P.M. and a seasonal low at 7 A.M. every day. And restaurants reach three seasonal demand peaks every day at 7:00 A.M., 12:30 P.M., and 7 P.M.

The *cycle* or *cyclical component* is obvious only in time series that span several sets of seasonals or more. A cycle can be defined as a long-term oscillation, or a swing of the data points about the trend line over a period of at least three complete sets of seasonals. National economic cycles of booms as well as depressions and periods of war and peace are examples of such cycles.

Cycles, particularly business cycles, are often difficult to explain and economists have devoted considerable research and speculation to their causes. Identification of a cyclic pattern in a time series requires the analysis of a long period of data. For most decision-making situations, forecasting the cyclic component is not considered, since long-term data are typically unavailable to determine the cycle. In addition, cycles are not likely to repeat in similar amplitude and duration; hence, the assumption of repeating history does not hold.

Random variations are, as the name implies, without a specific assignable cause and without a pattern. Random variations are the fluctuations left in the time series after the trend, seasonality, and cyclical behaviors have been accounted for. Random fluctuations can sometimes be explained after the fact, such as an increase in the

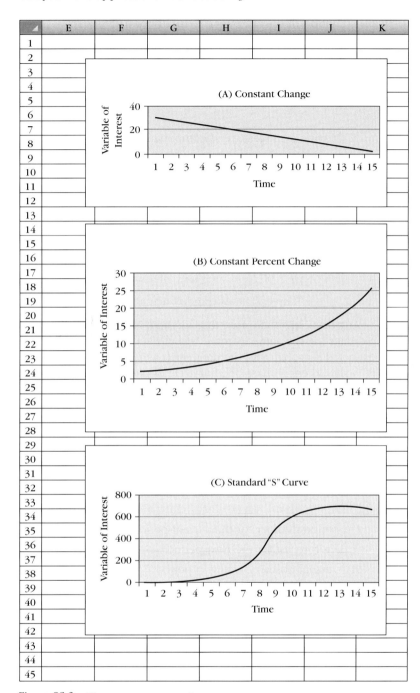

Figure 8S.2 Three common trend patterns.

consumption of energy owing to an abnormally harsh weather, but cannot be systematically predicted and, hence, are not included in time series models.

The objective of time series analysis is to determine the magnitude of one or more of these components and to use that knowledge for the purpose of forecasting the next period. In the remainder of this section we will consider three models of time series analysis:

1. Moving averages (trend component of the time series).
2. Exponential smoothing (trend component of the time series).
3. Linear trend, multiplicative model (trend and seasonal components).

Moving Averages

The *moving average* technique is one of the simplest ways to predict a trend. It generates the next period's forecast by averaging the actual demand for only the last n time periods (n is often in the range of 4 to 7). That is:

Forecast = Average of actual demand in past n periods

Any data older than n are thus ignored. Note also that the moving average weights old data just the same as more recent data. The value of n is usually based on the expected seasonality in the data, such as four quarters or 12 months in a year; that is, n should encompass one full cycle of data. If n must be chosen arbitrarily, then it should be based on experimentation; that is, the value selected for n should be the one that works best for the available historical data.

Mathematically, a forecast using the moving average method is computed as

$$F_{t+1} = \frac{1}{n} \sum_{i=(t-n+1)}^{t} A_i$$

where

t = period number for the current period

F_{t+1} = forecast for the next period

A_i = actual observed value in period i

n = number of periods of demand to be included in the moving average (known as the "order" of the moving average)

To illustrate the use of the moving average, data was collected on Intel's monthly stock closing price as shown in Figure 8S.3. In the spreadsheet shown, a four-period moving average was computed by entering the formula = AVERAGE(B2:B5) in cell C6 and copying it to cells C7:C26. The graph with the actual time series and moving average illustrates how a moving average smoothes out the fluctuations in the time series.

The plot also demonstrates one of the weaknesses associated with using moving averages. Specifically, whenever there is an upward or downward trend in the data, a forecast based on the moving average approach will always lag the time series. Therefore, the moving average approach is most appropriate for situations where the decision-maker would like to simply smooth out fluctuations around an assumed horizontal trend.

	A	B	C	D	E	F	G	H	I	J	K
1	Date	Closing Price	4 Period Moving Average								
2	May-07	21.18									
3	June-07	22.67									
4	Jul-07	22.56									
5	Aug-07	24.71									
6	Sep-07	24.81	22.78								
7	Oct-07	25.81	23.69								
8	Nov-07	25.13	24.47								
9	Dec-07	25.69	25.12								
10	Jan-08	20.33	25.36								
11	Feb-08	19.36	24.24								
12	Mar-08	20.53	22.63								
13	Apr-08	21.58	21.48								
14	May-08	22.60	20.45								
15	Jun-08	20.95	21.02								
16	Jul-08	21.64	21.42								
17	Aug-08	22.44	21.69								
18	Sep-08	18.38	21.91								
19	Oct-08	15.73	20.85								
20	Nov-08	13.66	19.55								
21	Dec-08	14.51	17.55								
22	Jan-09	12.77	15.57								
23	Feb-09	12.74	14.17								
24	Mar-09	15.03	13.42								
25	Apr-09	15.62	13.76								
26	Forecast		14.04								

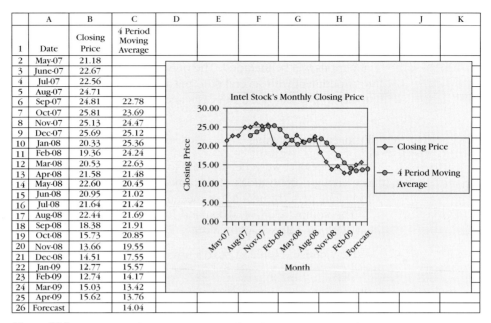

Figure 8S.3 Four-period moving average of Intel's monthly stock closing price.

A refinement of the moving average approach is to vary the weights assigned to the values included in the average. Such an approach is called a *weighted moving average* with the newer data typically weighted more heavily, rather than using equal weights. The reason for weighting the newer data more heavily is that since it is more current, it is often considered to be more representative of the future. Referring to Intel's closing stock price, a weighted moving average could be constructed by weighting the fourth oldest observation in the average by .1, the third oldest by .2, the second oldest by .3, and the most recent observation by .4. Of course any combination of weights that summed to one could be used. Likewise, any number of periods could be included in the weighted moving average.

Time series analysis involves two inherent difficulties, and a compromise solution that addresses both must be sought. The first problem is producing as good a forecast as is possible with the available data. Usually, this can be interpreted as using the most current data because those data are more representative of the present behavior of the time series. In this sense, we are looking for an approach that is responsive to recent changes in the data.

The second problem is to smooth the random behavior of the data. That is, we do not want a forecasting system that forecasts increases in demand simply because the last period's demand suddenly increased, nor do we want a system that indicates a downturn just because demand in the last period decreased. All time series data contain a certain amount of this erratic or random movement. It is impossible for a manager to predict this random movement of a time series, and it is folly to attempt it. The only reasonable conclusion is to avoid overreaction to a fluctuation that is simply random. The general interpretation of this objective is that several periods of data should be included in the forecast so as to "smooth" the random fluctuations that typically exist. Thus, we are also looking for an approach that is stable, even with erratic data.

Clearly, methods used to attain both responsiveness and stability will be somewhat contradictory. If we use the most recent data so as to be responsive, only a few periods will be included in the forecast; but if we want stability, large numbers of periods will be included. The only way to decide how many periods to include is to experiment with several different approaches and evaluate each on the basis of its ability to produce good forecasts and still smooth out random fluctuations.

Exponential Smoothing

As noted above, we generally want to use the most current data and, at the same time, use enough observations of the time series to smooth out random fluctuations. One technique perfectly adapted to meeting these two objectives is exponential smoothing.

The computation of a demand forecast using exponential smoothing is carried out with the following equation:

New demand forecast = (α)current actual demand + $(1 - \alpha)$previous demand forecast

or

$$F_{t+1} = \alpha A_t + (1 - \alpha)F_t$$

where α is a smoothing constant that must be between zero and one, F_t is the exponential forecast for period t, and A_t is the actual demand in period t.

The smoothing constant α can be interpreted as the weight assigned to the last (i.e., the current) data point. The remainder of the weight $(1 - \alpha)$ is applied to the last forecast. However, the last forecast was a function of the previous weighted data point and the forecast before that. To see this, note that the forecast in period t is calculated as

$$F_t = \alpha A_{t-1} + (1 - \alpha)F_{t-1}$$

Substituting the right-hand side in our original formula yields

$$F_{t+1} = \alpha A_t + (1 - \alpha)[\alpha A_{t-1} + (1 - \alpha) F_{t-1}]$$

Thus the data point A_{t-1} receives a weight of $(1 - \alpha)\alpha$, which, of course, is less than α. Since this process is iterative, we see that exponential smoothing automatically applies a set of diminishing weights to each of the previous data points and is therefore a form of weighted averages. Exponential smoothing derives its name from the fact that the weights decline exponentially as the data points get older and older. In general, the weight of the nth most recent data point can be computed as follows:

Weight of nth most recent data point in an exponential average = $\alpha(1 - \alpha)^{n-1}$

Using this formula, the most recent data point, A_t, has a weight of $\alpha(1 - \alpha)^{1-1}$ or simply α. Similarly, the second most recent data point, A_{t-1}, would have a weight of $\alpha(1 - \alpha)^{2-1}$ or simply $\alpha(1 - \alpha)$. As a final example, the third most recent data point, A_{t-2} would have a weight of $\alpha(1 - \alpha)^{3-1}$ or $\alpha(1 - \alpha)^2$.

The higher the weight assigned to the current demand, the greater the influence this point has on the forecast. For example, if α is equal to 1, the demand forecast for the next period will be equal to the value of the current demand. The closer the value of α is to 0, the closer the forecast will be to the previous period's forecast for the current period. (Check these results by using the equation.)

Rearranging the terms of the original formula provides additional insights into exponential smoothing, as follows:

$$F_{t+1} = \alpha A_t + (1 - \alpha)F_t$$
$$= \alpha A_t + F_t - \alpha F_t$$
$$= F_t + \alpha A_t - \alpha F_t$$
$$= F_t + \alpha(A_t - F_t)$$

In this formula $A_t - F_t$ represents the forecast error made in period t. Thus, the formula shows that the new forecast developed for period $t + 1$ is equal to the old forecast plus some percentage of the error (since α is between 0 and 1). Notice that when the forecast in period t exceeds the actual demand in period t, we have a negative error term for period t and the new forecast will be reduced. On the other hand, when the forecast in period t is less than the actual demand in period t, the error term in period t is positive and the new forecast will be adjusted higher.

Our objective in exponential forecasting is to choose the value of α that results in the best forecasts. Forecasts that tend always to be too high or too low are said to be biased—positively if too high and negatively if too low. The value of α is critical in producing good forecasts, and if a large value of α is selected, the forecast will be very sensitive to the current demand value. With a large α, exponential smoothing will produce forecasts that react quickly to fluctuations in demand. This, however, is irritating to those who have to constantly change plans and activities on the basis of the latest forecasts. Conversely, a small value of α weights historical data more heavily than current demand and therefore will produce forecasts that do not react as quickly to changes in the data; that is, the forecasting model will be somewhat insensitive to fluctuations in the current data.

Generally speaking, larger values of α are used in situations in which the data exhibit low variability and can therefore be plotted as a rather smooth curve. On the other hand, a lower value of α should be used for data that exhibit a high degree of variability. Using a high value of α in a situation where the data exhibit a high degree of variability would result in a forecast that constantly overreacted to changes in the most current demand.

As with n, the appropriate value of α is usually determined by trial and error; values typically lie in the range of 0.01 to 0.30. One method of selecting the best value is to try several values of α with the existing historical data (or a portion of the data) and choose the value of α that minimizes the average forecast errors. As you can probably imagine, spreadsheets can greatly speed the evaluation of potential smoothing constants and the determination of the best value of α. For example, in the spreadsheet shown in Figure 8S.4 that forecasts the monthly closing price of Intel's stock using exponential smoothing, various values of α can be easily investigated by simply changing the number entered in cell B1. Also note that when exponential smoothing is used, a forecast value is needed for the very first period. Since a forecast value for the first period is typically not available, it is common to simply set $F_1 = A_1$.

Thus, the forecasts proceed as follows:

$$F_1 = A_1 = 21.18$$
$$F_2 = .2(21.18) + .8(21.18) = 21.18$$
$$F_3 = .2(22.67) + .8(21.18) = 21.48$$

and so on as shown in Figure 8S.4.

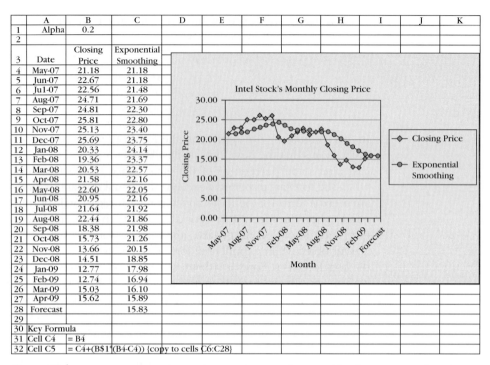

	A	B	C	D	E	F	G	H	I	J	K
1	Alpha	0.2									
2											
3	Date	Closing Price	Exponential Smoothing								
4	May-07	21.18	21.18								
5	Jun-07	22.67	21.18								
6	Jul-07	22.56	21.48								
7	Aug-07	24.71	21.69								
8	Sep-07	24.81	22.30								
9	Oct-07	25.81	22.80								
10	Nov-07	25.13	23.40								
11	Dec-07	25.69	23.75								
12	Jan-08	20.33	24.14								
13	Feb-08	19.36	23.37								
14	Mar-08	20.53	22.57								
15	Apr-08	21.58	22.16								
16	May-08	22.60	22.05								
17	Jun-08	20.95	22.16								
18	Jul-08	21.64	21.92								
19	Aug-08	22.44	21.86								
20	Sep-08	18.38	21.98								
21	Oct-08	15.73	21.26								
22	Nov-08	13.66	20.15								
23	Dec-08	14.51	18.85								
24	Jan-09	12.77	17.98								
25	Feb-09	12.74	16.94								
26	Mar-09	15.03	16.10								
27	Apr-09	15.62	15.89								
28	Forecast		15.83								
29											
30	Key Formula										
31	Cell C4	= B4									
32	Cell C5	= C4+(B$1*(B4-C4)) {copy to cells C6:C28}									

Figure 8S.4   Using exponential smoothing to forecast the monthly closing price of Intel's stock.

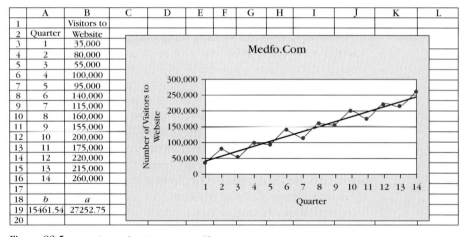

	A	B	C	D	E	F	G	H	I	J	K	L
1		Visitors to										
2	Quarter	Website										
3	1	35,000										
4	2	80,000										
5	3	55,000										
6	4	100,000										
7	5	95,000										
8	6	140,000										
9	7	115,000										
10	8	160,000										
11	9	155,000										
12	10	200,000										
13	11	175,000										
14	12	220,000										
15	13	215,000										
16	14	260,000										
17												
18	b	a										
19	15461.54	27252.75										
20												

Figure 8S.5   Number of visitors to Medfo.com.

Simple Regression: The Linear Trend Multiplicative Model

Figure 8S.5 presents the quarterly number of visitors to a fictitious website providing medical information (Medfo.com). Demand is seen to be generally increasing as is indicated by the linear trend line fit by Excel to the data. Given the apparent quality of the fit between quarter number and the number of visitors, the webmaster has decided to try a linear trend time series model. The model parameters for the regression model with quarter number as the independent variable and ridership volume as the dependent variable were calculated in cells A19 and B19 using Excel's LINEST function (discussed later). However, careful observation of the data reveals that the number of visitors is above average during the second and fourth quarters and below average during the first and third quarters, perhaps due to the weather related illnesses.

There are several versions of the linear trend time series model (for example, there are additive and multiplicative versions) and also many different approaches to determining the components of these forecasting models. We will present one method for determining the two demand components of a simple multiplicative model. Conceptually, the model is presented as

$$\text{Forecast} = \text{trend component (or } T) \times \text{seasonal component (or } S)$$

In order to develop this model, we must first analyze the available historical data and attempt to break down the original data into trend and seasonal components.

As indicated earlier, a trend is a long-run direction of a series of data. In our example the trend in the number of visitors to the website appears to follow a straight line—that is, to be a trend with respect to time. In order to project this linear trend into the future, we first estimate the parameters of the trend line in exactly the same fashion that was discussed earlier in the chapter. Referring to Figure 8S.5, we see that the trend line for the ridership volume is:

$$\text{Number of Visitors}_X = 27253 + 15462X$$

where X represents the quarter.

As was noted earlier, and made even clearer in Figure 8S.5, the data are above the trend line for all of the second and fourth quarters and below the trend line for all of the first and third quarters. Recognizing this distinct seasonal pattern in the data should allow us to estimate the amount of seasonal variation around the trend line (i.e., the seasonal component, S).

The trend line is the long-run direction of the data and does not include any seasonal variation. We can compute, for each available quarter of data, a measure of the "seasonality" in that quarter by dividing actual ridership by the computed value of the trend for that quarter. This method is known as the ratio-to-trend method. Using the notation developed thus far, we can write the seasonal component for any quarter X as

$$\frac{Y_X}{T_X}$$

where Y_X is the number of visitors to the website in quarter X and T_X is the trend estimate for quarter X. Excel's TREND function (discussed later) can be used to calculate the trend estimate for each quarter as shown in column C of Figure 8S.6.

Consider the second and third quarters of the first year. The computed trend value for each of these two quarters is

$$T_2 = 27252 + 15462(2) = 58176$$

and

$$T_3 = 27252 + 15462(3) = 73638$$

The actual volumes (in thousands) in quarters 2 and 3 were

$$Y_2 = 80,000$$
$$Y_3 = 55,000$$

Dividing Y_2 by T_2 and Y_3 by T_3 gives us an indication of the seasonal pattern in each of these quarters.

$$\frac{Y_2}{T_2} = \frac{80,000}{58,176} = 1.38$$

$$\frac{Y_3}{T_3} = \frac{55,000}{73,638} = 0.75$$

Similar indices were calculated for all quarters in the spreadsheet shown in Figure 8S.6.

In quarter 2 the actual number of visitors was 138 percent of the expected volume (i.e., the number of visitors predicted on the basis of a linear trend), but in quarter 3 the number of visitors was only 75 percent of that expected. Note that over the 14 periods of available data we have four observations of the number of visitors for first and second quarters and three observations of the number of visitors for third and fourth quarters. We can compute the average of each of these sets of quarterly data and use the averages as the seasonal components for our time series forecasting model as shown in Figure 8S.7.

	A	B	C	D
1				Seasonal
2		Visitors to		Factor
3	Quarter	Website	T_x	(Y/T)
4	1	35,000	42714.29	0.82
5	2	80,000	58175.82	1.38
6	3	55,000	73637.36	0.75
7	4	100,000	89098.90	1.12
8	5	95,000	104560.44	0.91
9	6	140,000	120021.98	1.17
10	7	115,000	135483.52	0.85
11	8	160,000	150945.05	1.06
12	9	155,000	166406.59	0.93
13	10	200,000	181868.13	1.10
14	11	175,000	197329.67	0.89
15	12	220,000	212791.21	1.03
16	13	215,000	228252.75	0.94
17	14	260,000	243714.29	1.07

Figure 8S.6 Calculation of quarterly seasonal factors.

	A	B	C	D	E
1	Year	Quarter 1	Quarter 2	Quarter 3	Quarter 4
2	1	0.82	1.38	0.75	1.12
3	2	0.91	1.17	0.85	1.06
4	3	0.93	1.1	0.89	1.03
5	4	0.94	1.07		
6	Average	0.90	1.18	0.83	1.07

Figure 8S.7 Calculating seasonal component (S) for Quarters 1 through 4.

Using both the trend component and the seasonal component, the webmaster now can forecast the number of visitors to the site for any quarter in the future. First, the trend value for the forecast quarter is computed and is, in turn, multiplied by the appropriate seasonal factor. For example, to forecast for the last quarter of the fourth year (quarter 16) and the first quarter of the fifth year (quarter 17), the webmaster would first compute the trend values.

$$T_{16} = 27252 + 15462(16) = 274,644$$
$$T_{17} = 27252 + 15462(17) = 290,106$$

Next, the forecast is computed by multiplying the trend value by the appropriate seasonal factor. For the fourth quarter S_4 is 1.07, so the forecast F is

$$F_{16} = 274,644 \times 1.07 = 293,869$$

The seasonal factor for the first quarter is 0.90; therefore, the forecast for quarter 17 is

$$F_{17} = 290,106 \times 0.90 = 261,095$$

These two forecasts correspond to the previous results for fourth and first quarters in that the fourth-quarter forecast is above the trend and the first-quarter forecast is below the trend. Seasonal indexes can be used in a similar way with exponential smoothing or moving averages. Again, simple ratios are calculated, averaged out, and then applied to the exponential smoothing or moving average forecasts.

$\mathcal{C}$AUSAL FORECASTING WITH REGRESSION

In this section we discuss causal forecasting with regression analysis. We begin the section with an overview of the simple linear regression model. We then expand our discussion to incorporating multiple variables in our model. The section is concluded with a discussion of suggested steps for developing regression models.

The Simple Linear Regression Model

Simple linear regression analysis involves using the values of a single independent variable to predict or explain the values of the dependent variable. If we wish to include more than one independent variable in our model, we have a *multiple regression model*, which will be discussed later in this section. Prior to using simple linear regression analysis, it is appropriate to plot the values of the independent and dependent variables to visually verify a key assumption that the variables are linearly related to one another. Figure 8S.8 illustrates three common ways two variables can be related to one another. If it is discovered that the variables are not linearly related to one another, it may be possible to "transform" one or both of the variables so that they are approximately linearly related. Frequently used transformations include taking the square root, inverse, or logarithm of the data. We will return to the topic of transforming the data later in the section.

The mathematical form of the simple linear regression model is as follows:

$$Y = \alpha + \beta X + \varepsilon$$

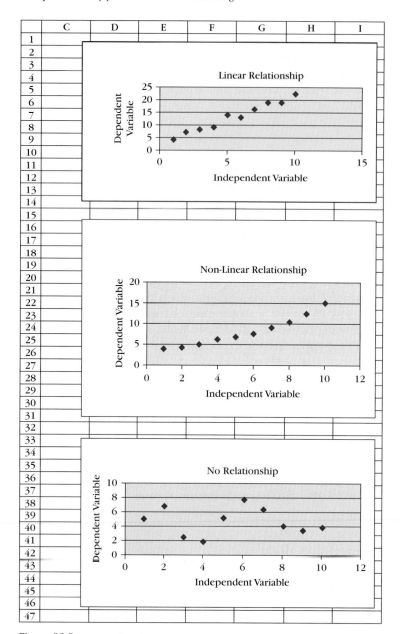

Figure 8S.8   Example relationships between variables.

where X corresponds to the independent variable, Y to the dependent variable, and α and β are the parameters of the model. According to this model, the value of the dependent variable Y is equal to the regression model constant α plus the model parameter β times the value of the independent variable X. Also notice that a *residual*, or error term, ε is included in the model to account for the fact that it is typically not possible to determine the exact value of the dependent variable based on just the two model parameters α and β and therefore there is likely to be a difference between the predicted value of the dependent variable and the actual value.

Because our regression models are typically based on sample data, the true parameters of the regression model are unknown. In cases where the regression model is based on sample data the model is written as:

$$Y = a + bX$$

where a and b are estimates based on sample data of the unknown population parameters α and β, respectively.

Earlier in your academic career, perhaps in an algebra class, you may have seen the equation of a line expressed as:

$$y = mx + b$$

where y represents the value on the vertical axis, x corresponds to the value on the horizontal axis, m represents the slope of the line (i.e., the amount the line rises for a unit change in x), and b corresponds to the y-intercept or the point where the line intersects the y-axis (which is also the point on the line where $x = 0$). The regression model presented earlier is completely analogous to this, the only differences being that a is used to represent the y-intercept (b in the standard equation of a line) and b is used in place of m to represent the slope of the line.

There are a wide variety of ways that a line could be fit to a set of data. One way would be to simply use a ruler and visually determine which line provides the best fit to a set of points plotted on a graph by adjusting the angle of the ruler. The best line could then be drawn and its equation determined. While this approach often yields good results, statisticians and decision-makers often favor the use of more formal, less subjective approaches. The approach most often used is based on minimizing the sum of the squared vertical distances between the data points and the regression line fit to the data points (that is, the *errors* from using the regression line to make a prediction). Because of this, it is often referred to as the *least squares regression* model.

To illustrate how the least squares approach works, consider the small data set consisting of four observations as shown in Figure 8S.9. In the figure, the vertical distance from each point to the line fit to the data is shown. These vertical distances can be thought of as errors, e_i, since they represent the difference between what the line predicts the value of Y will be for a given value of X and what Y actually is for the given value of X. The least squares approach fits the line to the data such that the sum of the squared errors, Σe_i^2, is minimized. In the example shown in Figure 8S.9 this means fitting a line to the data so that the sum $e_1^2 + e_2^2 + e_3^2 + e_4^2$ is minimized.

Fortunately, spreadsheets and other software programs have built-in functions that greatly facilitate the calculation of the regression model parameters. For example, Excel's LINEST function can be used to calculate the regression model parameters. The syntax of this function is:

LINEST(range of Y values, range of X values)

Note that the LINEST function is a special type of function called an *array function* because it is used to return multiple values (i.e., the parameters a and b) rather than a single value such as the average or standard deviation of a range of data. Because we are using the LINEST function as an array function, when the equation is entered into a cell we must press and hold down the Ctrl key and the Shift key as we press the Enter key. When using an array function in Excel, you must first highlight the cells where you want the results of the function displayed and then enter the formula in the usual way beginning with an equal (=) sign.

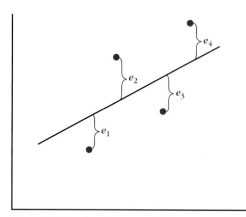

Figure 8S.9   Least squares approach to fitting line to set of data.

	A	B	C	D	E	F	G	H	I	J	K
1	Lot	House	House								
2	Number	Size (ft)	Price	TREND							
3	145	2,620	$266,500	$281,020							
4	144	2,635	$266,900	$283,927							
5	119	3,019	$364,500	$358,339							
6	136	3,049	$384,900	$364,152							
7	7	3,141	$389,900	$381,980							
8	114	3,141	$399,900	$381,980							
9	97	3,264	$439,000	$405,815							
10	90	3,319	$405,000	$416,473							
11	108	3,403	$414,500	$432,751							
12	200	3,578	$442,000	$466,663							
13											
14		*b*	*a*								
15		193.7816	-226.688	=TREND(C3:C12,B3:B12)							
16											
17											
18			=LINEST(C3:C12,B3:B12)								
19											

Chart (columns E–K, rows 2–16): House Price ($) vs House Size (square feet); $R^2 = 0.9006$. Y-axis from $200,000 to $500,000; X-axis from 2,500 to 3,700.

Figure 8S.10   Using Excel's LINEST and TREND functions.

Another useful Excel function is the TREND function. This function fits a straight line to a column of X and Y values and then returns the values that would appear on the trend line for each value of X. The syntax for the TREND function is as follows:

$$= \text{TREND(range of } Y \text{ values, range of } X \text{ values)}$$

Like the LINEST function, the TREND function returns multiple values and therefore the Ctrl and Shift keys must be held down while pressing the Enter key.

To illustrate the use of the LINEST and TREND functions, sample data for the square footage and price of homes in a particular neighborhood are shown in Figure 8S.10. The goal in developing the model is to be able to predict the price of a house based on its square footage.

In developing regression models, the analyst must often make judgments about how to handle outliers or extreme data points. In some cases, outliers may be the result of data entry errors and therefore should be corrected. At other times, outliers may be the result of unusual circumstances (e.g., a labor strike, a natural disaster, and so on) and in these cases they can perhaps be justifiably omitted or adjusted. In the remaining cases where no error or unusual circumstance can be discovered, it is difficult to justify eliminating or adjusting an outlier.

The issue of outliers is important because of the impact these data points can have on the regression model. As is illustrated in Figure 8S.11, an outlier is a data point that has an extreme value on the independent variable dimension, an extreme value on the dependent variable dimension, or on both dimensions. As shown in the top graph in Figure 8S.11, an outlier on the independent variable dimension can have a profound impact on the regression line fit to the data, altering both the slope of the line and its y-intercept. In contrast, an outlier on the dependent variable dimension primarily shifts the y-intercept of the regression line in the direction of the outlier, but generally has little impact on the slope of the line. Thus, the predicted change in the dependent variable for a unit change in the independent variable remains much the same in the case where the outlier is the result of an extreme value of the dependent variable. This is not the case when the outlier is the result of an extreme value of the independent variable, since the slope of the regression line also changes.

Having gone through the process of fitting a linear trend line to a set of data, it is next logical to consider how well the model fits the data. One way to assess the quality of the model is to simply plot the trend line and data on the same graph and visually evaluate the quality of the fit. Another, more objective, approach is to determine the proportion of variation in the dependent variable that can be explained by the

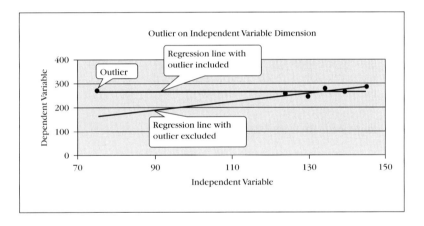

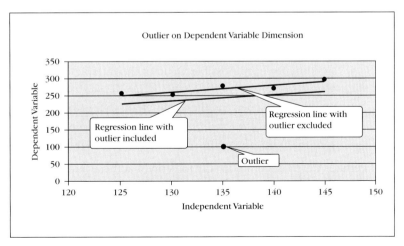

Figure 8S.11   Impact of outliers on regression line fit to set of data.

independent variable. This measure is called the *coefficient of determination* and is typically represented symbolically as R^2. Since R^2 corresponds to the proportion of variation in the dependent variable that is explained by the independent variable, it should not surprise you to learn that the R^2 will be between zero and one. An R^2 of one indicates that the independent variable completely accounts for the variation in the dependent variable, even though it may not *cause* it. (There could be a third factor causing both, or the direction of causation may be the reverse. For example, it has been observed that overweight people drink more diet soft drinks than others, but what causes which?) In this case, all data points will fall precisely on the trend line. Alternatively, an R^2 of zero indicates that there is no relationship between the independent and dependent variables.

The *correlation coefficient, R*, is another measure for assessing the extent to which two variables are related to one another. More specifically, the correlation coefficient measures the degree to which there is a linear relationship between two variables and is calculated by taking the square root of R^2 and appending a plus or minus sign, according to whether the slope is positive or negative. The correlation coefficient can thus range between -1 and $+1$. It is positive if Y tends to increase as X increases and negative if Y tends to increase when X decreases. Like the coefficient of determination, a correlation of zero suggests there is no linear relationship between X and Y, but a large value does not necessarily imply causation.

Both R^2 and R are typically provided as standard output of statistical packages including spreadsheets. Finally, we note that because R^2 provides precise information regarding the percent of Y's variation that can be explained by X, its interpretation is more meaningful than the correlation coefficient, and it is therefore the preferred measure of the two.

Regression Analysis Assumptions

In addition to the assumption that there is a linear relationship between the dependent and independent variables, regression analysis also assumes the following.

- *The residuals are normally distributed.* That is, for a particular value of the independent variable, a plot of all the errors around the regression line at this point would be normally distributed.

- *The expected value of the residuals is zero, $E(e_i) = 0$.* The plot of the errors would be centered about zero in terms of their mean value. This also implies that the expected value of the dependent variable falls directly on the regression line for each possible value of the independent variable.

- *The residuals are independent of one another.* The value of one error does not have any effect on the value of another error, either positive or negative.

- *The variance of the residuals is constant.* The spread of the errors about the regression line does not vary with the independent variable.

Perhaps the most common way to verify that these assumptions are met is to perform an analysis of the residuals (or errors). For a particular value of X, the residual is calculated by subtracting the trend line estimate of Y for that value of X from the actual Y value corresponding to that value of X. For example, referring to Figure 8S.10, the residual for the 2,620 ft² house is the actual price of the house minus what the trend line estimates a 2,620 ft² house would cost or $266,500 - \$281,020 = -\$14,520$.

Using the Regression Model

In addition to ensuring that the regression model assumptions are not violated, it is equally important to understand how to properly use the results of a regression analysis. Generally speaking, new users of regression analysis should be aware of three common pitfalls. The first pitfall or improper use of a regression model is to use it to make predictions outside the range of data that was used to develop the model. As an example, it would be improper to attempt to use the regression model fit to the data in 8S.10 to predict the price of a 4,500 ft² house. This would be improper since none of the observations in the data set is representative of a house of this size. Attempting to use a model to predict values that are not represented in the data set is called *extrapolation.*

A second pitfall to be aware of is attempting to overly *generalize* the results of a regression model. For example, the data shown in Figure 8S.10 were collected for the new homes built in a particular subdivision in North Carolina. It is not at all clear whether the regression model fit to this data could be used to predict the price of a new house in other subdivisions in the same city. And it is even less likely that the regression model could be used to predict the price of a new house in other parts of the state or regions of the country.

The problem of generalization may at first glance appear to be similar to the problem of extrapolation. There is, however, an important difference. In the case of extrapolation we are attempting to make a prediction beyond the values in our data set. Referring to our house price model, attempting to use the model to predict the price of a 4,500 ft² home in the subdivision of interest is an extrapolation of the model.

Alternatively, generalization occurs when we attempt to use the model fit to data collected from one population to predict values in another population. Again, referring to the house price model, we can think of each subdivision or region as a population. Clearly, house construction costs could vary from subdivision to subdivision based on a variety of factors including the cost of the land, quality of schools, distance to important destinations, available amenities, and so on. Thus, the problem of extrapolation occurs when we attempt to use a model to predict values for the population of interest that are not represented in our data set, while generalization occurs when we are attempting to use the model to make predictions for an entirely different population. Of course, it is possible to make both mistakes at the same time.

The final pitfall to be aware of is to improperly assume that the development of a regression model proves that there is a cause and effect relationship between the independent and dependent variables. Generally speaking, a regression model can be used to help validate that such a cause and effect relationship exists, but the actual existence of a cause and effect relationship must have its basis in some underlying theory. As a rather extreme example, suppose you collected monthly data for a number of years on ice cream sales and the number of drownings in the United States. If you were to develop a regression model with the number of drownings as the dependent variable and ice cream sales as the independent variable you would likely get a pretty high R^2. Of course, concluding that the use of ice cream causes drownings (or worse, vice-versa) on the basis of this regression model is a bit ludicrous. What is actually happening in this situation is that both variables are correlated with another variable—namely, weather. Thus, we remark that while regression analysis may be well suited to establishing the extent that two variables are correlated with one another, inferring causation between the variables is far more tenuous.

The Multiple Regression Model

Up to this point we have focused on the use of one independent variable to predict values of the dependent variable. As we demonstrate in this section, it is possible to extend this methodology and use multiple independent variables to predict the value of the dependent variable. Including more than one independent variable in the regression model is called *multiple regression*. Mathematically, the form of the multiple regression model is:

$$Y = \alpha + \beta_1 X_1 + \beta_2 X_2 + \cdots + \beta_n X_n + \varepsilon$$

where X_i corresponds to the ith independent variable for $i = 1, 2, \ldots, n$ and $\alpha, \beta_1, \beta_2, \ldots, \beta_n$ are the model parameters.

Like simple regression, when a multiple regression model is developed based on sample data the model is written as:

$$Y = a + b_1 X_1 + b_2 X_2 + \cdots + b_n X_n$$

The model parameters for a multiple regression model are calculated in a similar fashion as they are for a simple regression model. In both cases, the model parameters are chosen such that the summation of the squared errors (or residuals) over all observations in the data set are minimized. In the simple regression model, the error for a particular observation is calculated as:

$$e = Y_o - (a + bX)$$

where e is the error or residual for a given observation, Y_o is the actual observed Y value, and $(a + bX)$ is the predicted Y value for the observation based on the regression model. In English, the error for a given observation of the dependent variable is its observed or actual value minus the predicted value based on the regression model. Extending this, the error in a multiple regression model for a given observation can be calculated as:

$$e = Y_o - (a + b_1 X_1 + b_2 X_2 + \cdots + b_n X_n)$$

The least squares approach then selects the parameters of the regression model such that the sum of the squared errors or Σe_i^2 is minimized.

Calculating the parameters with a multiple regression model is typically done using spreadsheets or specialized statistical software packages. For example, the Excel LINEST and TREND functions previously discussed can be used to calculate the model parameters for a multiple regression model in a similar fashion to the way they were used to calculate the model parameters for a simple regression model. In fact, the only difference in using these functions to calculate the parameters for a multiple regression model is that the parameter corresponding to the range of X values will include more than one column of data.

As was the case with simple regression, one way to compare two or more regression models is to compare their R^2 (called the *multiple coefficient of determination* in the case of multiple regression) values. Adding additional variables to a regression model will help explain variation in the dependent variable to the extent that the independent variables are not correlated with one another. If two independent variables were perfectly correlated with one another, fitting a multiple regression model to the data with both variables would provide no better a fit than either of the variables alone.

This raises another important issue. Generally speaking, we can interpret b_i as the impact that any changes in the ith independent variable will have on the dependent variable while holding the other regression model parameters constant. However, the individual impact of each independent variable can get blurred when some of the independent variables are highly correlated with others. To check for this problem, the correlation coefficients between all pairs of independent variables can be calculated. As a rule of thumb, only include two independent variables in the regression model when the correlation coefficient between them is less than 0.80.

Developing Regression Models

Trying to remember all the issues related to proper regression model development can appear to be overwhelming at times. This challenge can be greatly diminished if the modeler breaks down the regression model development process into four logical and sequential steps. In the remainder of this section we overview this four-step process for regression model development.

Step 1: Identify Candidate Independent Variables to Include in the Model

Upon defining the dependent variable to be investigated, the first step in the development of a regression model is to identify candidate independent variables to include in the model. Of course, depending on the modeler's expertise with the dependent variable being studied, he or she may need to consult with managers and other people to identify the variables that may have an impact on the dependent variable. For example, suppose you were asked to develop a model for predicting the engine emissions of light-duty, diesel powered engines. Most likely, you would not know what variables impact engine emissions and therefore you would need to consult with one or more specialists such as engineers, mechanics, and scientists.

Once a candidate pool of potential independent variables has been identified, it is important to check the correlation among the independent variables. As was discussed previously, when two independent variables are highly correlated, the individual impact of each independent variable can get blurred if both variables are included in the multiple regression model. The easiest way to avoid this problem of *multicollinearity* is to calculate the correlation coefficients between all pairs of independent variables and not include in the model both independent variables if their correlation coefficient exceeds .80.

Step 2: Transform the Data

As was discussed earlier, prior to developing a regression model, it is prudent to plot the independent and dependent variables to verify that they are indeed linearly related. In the case of the multiple regression, a plot of each independent variable with the dependent variable should be developed to ensure that each independent variable is linearly related to the dependent variable. If one or more of these plots indicates that the variables are not linearly related, it may still be possible to transform the variables in order to obtain a linear relationship

To illustrate this, Figure 8S.12 depicts six possible relationships between the independent and dependent variable. In Panel A, there is a clear linear relationship

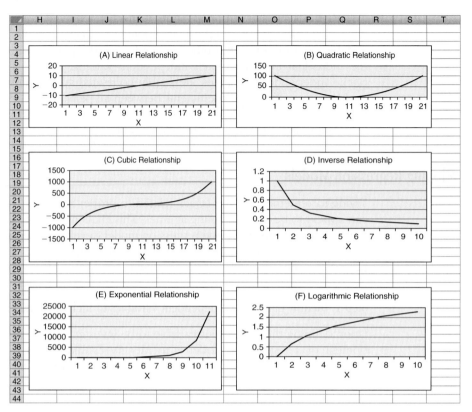

Figure 8S.12   Example relationships between the independent and dependent variables.

between X and Y and therefore no transformation is required. Panel B, however, indicates that there is a quadratic relationship between X and Y, such as $Y = X^2$. If this type of pattern is observed, a linear relationship between X and Y can be obtained by taking the square root of the X values. In other words, the regression model would be fit to the square root of the original X values.

Panel C is indicative of a cubic relationship of the form $Y = X^3$. In this case a linear relationship can be obtained by taking the cube root of the X values (i.e., $\sqrt[3]{X} = X^{\frac{1}{3}}$). Panel D suggests an inverse relationship between the variables of the form $Y = 1/X$. In this case, a linear relationship can be obtained by taking the inverse of the X values (i.e., dividing one by the X values).

Panel E depicts an exponential relationship of the form $Y = e^X$. A linear relationship can be obtained in this case by using Excel's LN function to take the natural log of the X values. Finally, a logarithmic relationship is suggested in Panel F. In this case a linear relationship can be obtained by raising the base e by the power of X (i.e., e^X). This can be easily accomplished using Excel's EXP function.

A couple of remarks are in order regarding transforming variables in a regression model. First, in addition to transforming the independent variables, it is also possible to transform the dependent variable. For example, if it is determined that several of the independent variables require the same transformation, the modeler may choose to simply transform the dependent variable rather than performing the same transformation on several of the independent variables. Second, note that the interpretation of the regression model is changed when the variables are transformed. To illustrate, suppose that in the house price example we have referred to throughout this chapter it was determined that there was a quadratic relationship between house price and house size. If the subsequent regression model fit house price to the square root of house size then the interpretation of the model parameter *b* would be altered. In this case, *b* would refer to the impact changes in the *square root* of house size would have on the price.

Step 3: Select the Variables to Include in the Model

Once the candidate independent variables have been specified, their correlations checked, and any necessary transformations performed, the next step is to determine specifically which variables to include in the regression model. Often computer packages use some type of *stepwise* procedure to determine which values to include in the final regression model. For example, with *backward elimination*, all independent variables are included in the model and the variables with the least predictive value are dropped one at a time with the model evaluated at each iteration. *Forward selection* works in exactly the opposite direction by selecting one new variable for inclusion at each iteration. One way that variables could be selected for inclusion is to determine which variable when added to the model will result in the greatest increase in R^2. Of course the opposite approach would be employed with backward elimination where the variable that resulted in the smallest decrease in R^2 would be removed from the model at each iteration.

Although it is theoretically possible for R^2 not to change as additional independent variables are added to the model, it is impossible for it to decrease as additional variables are added. Therefore, in general, including additional independent variables will tend to increase R^2. While the calculations are beyond our scope here, we note here that many analysts prefer to use a measure that adjusts R^2 for both the sample size and number of independent variables included in the model. This measure, called the ***adjusted R^2***, is used to help reduce the chances that R^2 is inflated as more variables are added, and is included in the output provided by statistical software packages including Excel's Regression Output Report.

Step 4: Analyze the Residuals

As was discussed previously in the section on simple linear regression, an analysis of the residuals is a useful way to validate that the assumptions of regression analysis are met. As noted earlier, two key assumptions are that the expected value of the error terms (residuals) equals zero and that they are normally distributed. Perhaps the easiest way to validate this assumption is to create a histogram for the residuals and in particular note if there tends to be a grouping around zero. Examination of the histogram can also provide an indication of the extent to which the data are skewed (unsymmetrical) and whether outliers (extreme values) are present.

To investigate whether the assumption of constant variance is met, it is common to plot the residuals against the predicted values of *Y*. Also, plots for each independent variable against the residual can be developed.

Finally, the assumption that the error terms are independent is important because if they are correlated with one another (called *autocorrelation*) the regression model fit to the data based on the least squares method will tend to underestimate the values of the error terms. This creates problems later when we attempt to construct confidence intervals for predictions made on the basis of the model. One common approach to test the hypothesis that the residuals are not correlated with one another and are therefore independent is with the Durbin-Watson test statistic (see Albright et al. 2006) for autocorrelation.

BIBLIOGRAPHY

Albright, S. C., W. L. Winston, and C. Zappe. *Data Analysis and Decision Making with Microsoft Excel*, 3rd ed., Cincinnati: South-Western, 2006.

Anderson, D. R., D. J. Sweeney, and T. A. Williams. *Statistics for Business and Economics*, 10th ed., Cincinnati: South-Western, 2007.

Georgoff, D. M. and R. G. Murdick. "Manager's Guide to Forecasting." *Harvard Business Review*, 64 (Jan.-Feb. 1986): 110–120.

Hildebrand, D. and R. L. Ott. *Statistical Thinking for Managers*, 5th ed., Cincinnati: South-Western, 2009.

Makridakis, S, S. C. Wheelwright, and R. J. Hyndman. Forecasting: Methods and Applications, 3rd ed. New York: Wiley, 1998.

Sanders, N. R. and K. B. Manrodt. "Forecasting Practices in U.S. Corporations: Survey Results." *Interfaces*, 24 (March–April 1994): 92–100.

PART IV

Cases

NEW LOOK

Competing Through the Design-Supply Chain Interface

The case examines the clothing retailer New Look's competitive position in a formidable retail environment which is increasingly competitive and facing difficult trading conditions. It examines the company's competitive strategy and the supply chain processes it has had to adopt to survive in a turbulent market. It leaves the reader to identify how New Look can maintain/improve its competitive position in the challenging retail climate of 2008.

New Look – Summary

New Look is the third largest women's wear retail brand in the UK behind M&S and Next. Its mission is selling value for-money fashionable clothing and accessories under its 'New Look' brand. Superior speed, flexibility and responsiveness in the supply chain are critical to staying ahead of the market and competitors. The company is a proponent of 'fast fashion': a term used to describe clothing collections based on the most recent trends on the catwalk but which are designed and manufactured quickly, are affordable and are aimed at mainstream consumers. New Look's success is based on its ability to respond quickly to changes in fashion trends. By virtue of its fashion sense and its skill in anticipating trends, New Look has achieved popularity among consumers, which has enabled the company to grow at a steady pace.

New Look has a keen understanding of its target market – which is the mid- to – high fashion end of the clothing sector and is in tune with what mainstream customers want. It enjoys a loyal customer base, mainly women of younger age groups, who make up the majority of its customers. By selling a broad range of fashionable collections including clothing, footwear and accessories, which are renewed frequently and with investment in new store layouts, fronts and window displays in prime city centre locations, New Look is ensuring a steady flow of customers in a volatile market and even at times when consumer spending is sluggish.

New Look's competitive position in the market place has been sustained in a formidable market place through internalising the product design capability and aligning it better with its supply chain. Underlying this approach, has been the constant need to speed up their global product development and supply chain process. Speed and flexibility in the supply chain has been achieved through direct global sourcing through its strategic partners in Turkey and China, through the growing use of information and communication technologies (ICT) in the supply chain and concurrent design. The concept of concurrent design involves a multi-functional design team, which is highly structured and with greater responsibility and authority for decision making. This means that the design function is broadening and that not only the product but also the supply chain processes related to product innovation are explicitly taken into account.

New Look's financial performance over the past five years has been impressive, thus enabling the company to pursue growth opportunities and to finance expansion which includes a new distribution centre in the UK, consolidation centres in Turkey and Singapore and a number of new stores across Europe. Growth has also provided the funds for heavy brand promotion, and for bold advertising in magazines and through their in-house magazine Biz in

This case was prepared by Omera Khan of Cranfield School of Management, Cranfield University *Bedford, United Kingdom.© Copyright Cranfield School of Management January 2008. All rights reserved. This case was made possible by the generous cooperation of New Look. The case is developed solely as the basis for class discussion and is not intended to serve as endorsements, sources of primary data or illustration of effective or ineffective management.*

which they promote the latest 'hot trends' and enlist high profile celebrities and/or designers to promote the latest fashion offerings and to reinforce the company's brand and image.

- **Company History**

Tom Singh founded the company in 1969. The original store was based in Taunton, UK and in 1988 the company expanded its operations into France, By 1990, the company had a total of 70 stores in operation in both the UK and France. By 1994, this figure had risen to 200. In 1995, the company opened its first store in Scotland. In the same year, it also launched its 915 brand of girl's casual wear. New Look had its first initial public offering in 1998 and was listed on the London Stock Exchange.

In 2000, the company sold its French stores to Mim in return for a 51% stake in the company. It also launched its Inspire range of clothes, which was intended for women size 16 and over. During 2003, New Look acquired the remaining 49% stake of French retailer Mim. In the same year it opened a flagship store in London, UK.

In March 2004, New Look announced that its share holders had backed a takeover of the company led by its founder, Tom Singh. The shareholders approved the takeover by Mr Singh's bid vehicle Trinitybrook, after recommending a £699 million offer, made the previous month, by Mr Singh and buyout-firms Permira and Apex Partners to take the company private.

- **Company Overview**

New Look Group (New Look) is a privately-owned fashion retailer. The company offers own brand clothing, accessories and footwear for women and men. It operates more than 600 stores with around 492 in the UK and 171 in France. In fact, what might be described as an independently family-owned, low cost, no frills operation has evolved into a successful chain of stores with **a turnover of nearly £10 million in 2005 and** over 12, 000 employees.

As well as its core products, New Look's product range includes: Inspire for sizes 16–24; 915 for teenage girls; footwear; lingerie; swimwear and accessories. These categories account for a third of the company's sales in the UK. The company's customers are fairly evenly divided between the under 20, 20–30 and over 30 age brackets, which account for 37%, 32% and 31% of customers respectively.

New Look positions itself as a value fashion retailer, its main competitor with the same market segment is H&M but other competitors include premium fashion retailers such as River Island, Miss Selfridge, Top Shop, M&S, Next, Zara and Warehouse as well as the low price discounters such as George (Asda), Peacocks, Dorothy Perkins, Primark, Matalan, Sainsbury's and Tesco (see Appendix 2).

The average customer age is 29 years and the average visitation is 34 times per year. 2007 was a good year for New Look, and the company has outperformed some of its competitors. Some of its product performance highlights from this year are below:

- The leading retailer for women's footwear within the 16–44 age group in terms of value and volume
- Largest teen wear (9–15 yrs old) retailer in the UK
- The leading retailer for accessories within the under 19 age group
- 2nd largest women's jeans retailer in the UK in terms of value and volume
- 3rd largest women's wear retailer in the UK

The company sees itself as a trend follower (see Appendix 1) which operates at the low priced end of the fashion retail industry with a broad range of products which fall into six main categories:

- Women's wear
- Men's wear
- Teenage wear
- Children's wear

- Footwear
- Accessories

The company aims to cater to as wide an audience as possible, but its brand is still widely perceived as one for 'young and trendy women' New Look's clothing range strikes a balance between fashion basics and high fashion.

New Look has adopted a fast and flexible approach to fashion and this is reflected in its ability to transform quickly the latest trends on the fashion catwalk into affordable clothing for the masses. New Look is able to transform a fashion idea into clothing in about 8 – 12 weeks, although there is the constant drive to shorten this even further. As the company is able to introduce new styles fast and at a low cost, it is able to keep its stock looking fresh and in tune with the times.

Fast fashion is increasingly becoming popular in Europe because it offers consumers the opportunity to buy high fashion clothes very cheaply. Furthermore it satisfies women's desire to change clothing quickly and often at a low budget. However, the rise of fast fashion has become a growing concern for environmentalists, who argue that fast fashion feeds a growing culture of disposable fashion. It encourages shoppers to buy large quantities of clothes which may be disposed of (often without wearing them once!) or when those clothes have gone out of fashion.

Going Global

Since he took over as chief executive in April 2004, Phil Wrigley has expanded New Look's women's wear market share from 3.9% to 4.5%, making the chain the third largest women's wear retailer in the UK behind Marks and Spencer and Next. But six months into his plans to revitalise the chain through introducing sleeker shop designs and better product, Mr Wrigley began to ponder a bigger adventure – taking New Look abroad.

After achieving a comfortable market position in the UK and a known brand image, New Look's mission to go global led them to open 6 stores in France, 3 in Belgium, 14 large franchised stores in the Middle East – in Saudi Arabia, Kuwait and Dubai. Holland, Singapore and Russia are also in the global plan to open 50 new stores in the next 3 years.

Globalising the New Look brand has presented a number of challenges to the company's sourcing and procurement process. The main challenge is to protect the range and brand integrity but at the same time factor in the tastes of the 'new' local market. New Look have gone through a painful learning curve in range development, they understand that if their global supply chain strategy is to be a success, New Look must design its supply chain according to the end market place and in essence be more demand-driven. This presents a number of challenges to the sourcing and procurement process which traditionally relied on production from either its Chinese or Turkish suppliers. This strategic relationship works well for New Look when sourcing for stores in the UK. Its Chinese supplier provides economies of scale for mainly the stable and basic range (lean supply chain), and the Turkish suppliers provide quick response for designs which are fashionable and require quicker replenishment lead times (agile supply chain). But in order to localise its products for different market places for example in Saudi Arabia, these suppliers are located far from the end market place and hence present a challenge for New Look to meet the tastes of an increasingly global market.

A number of strategies have been adopted to respond to these global challenges, of which one is to open 2 consolidation centres in Singapore and Turkey enabling New Look to distribute their products more effectively, and provides significant gains in transportation economies as well as reducing their carbon footprint. Instead of bringing everything back to the UK, pay import duty on it, process it and re-export it back out, New Look now raises two purchase orders which splits down the volume of their purchase into two destination points. So, the supplier will get two purchase orders and will make all the products in one batch, but then split them and send them to the consolidation centre in the specific region. Any localisation for the end markets can also be undertaken here. However, this is limited to packaging or labelling details and does not extend to the final configuration or tailoring and styling of products.

The consolidation centres have enabled New Look to reduce their mark-downs and optimise their supply chain. The cost differential from procuring products from the Far East through into UK, pick and pack in UK and then send it for processing in order for it to be ready for international export paperwork to be completed and the order to be packed, labelled and freighted out to the Middle East versus sending it to Shanghai to Singapore, consolidate and send direct to Middle East is about £1 per unit. Over the Next 5 years New Look is planning to sell 55 million units in to the Middle East, so by changing their global buying process New Look will save £55 million in operating costs as well as reducing product lead times by 3 weeks or more.

The Design-Supply Chain Interface

All New Look clothing collections are designed centrally in a design and buying department. New Look originally began with just two designers who scanned catwalk shows, used trend prediction agencies and created sketches based on their observations and worked with long lead times and were separate from buying and merchandising. Today New Look houses a team of 25 skilled designers who are responsible for developing over 50% of designs in-house at the same time as ensuring that the supply chain can make and deliver these designs in the most efficient manner. The designers endeavour to create fashion items which optimise the balance between the key components of the company's business concept – fashion, best price and quality. They carry out extensive field research and draw inspiration from trade fairs, exhibitions and foreign travel, among other sources. A major shift in their business process has been the interface between design and the supply chain, hence designers work closely with the company's buyers, pattern makers, merchandisers and often suppliers are incorporated into the team. The team use standard frameworks and processes which can quickly be communicated across the supply chain. This cross-functional team approach has been driven by the need to increase responsiveness in the supply chain this in turn reduces product lead time and supply chain risk.

A specially developed CAD system not only makes design transparent from designers in the UK to their suppliers offshore, but it has also improved the speed and quality of design samples. In addition New Look have invested in the Gerber system, which is a new CAD technology for pattern cutting, which enables designers or product developers to map out the individual parts for a garment on layers of fabric to minimise fabric waste and they link this technology with their suppliers so that they can share data and compress time from design to manufacture, hence, reducing lead times.

Previously, the time between design and what purchasing would choose to buy was a lengthy and frustrating process, often with many misunderstandings and miscommunications between design, purchasing and manufacture. This would cause delays in product development and of course add costs. A global strategy required better visibility in the supply chain, to manage supply chain risks. By closing the loop from design to manufacture through close collaboration between the functions now working more as a product development process, New Look have compressed time to market in their global supply chain. The points below highlight the main drivers for mitigating supply chain risk and enhancing agility:

- Move it quicker
- Reduce product development time
- Shorter planning lifecycles
- Design in-house
- Balanced portfolio of products
- Plan to be lean and agile

New Look analysed that transport time in their supply chain only represents 20% of the end-to end timeline – and that the biggest time saving opportunity is further back in the chain. This makes design a very critical function in maximising operational efficiency.

A Design-Centric Supply Chain

The importance of design and a better interface with the supply chain has been recognised at New Look over the years. The more New Look turned towards high fashion, the quicker response time they required from their supply chain and hence the more demands it placed on designers to constantly inject innovation within the supply chain. New Look's philosophy has changed from being just a value retailer to one which is based on designing and supplying its customers with newness.

> *"Design and the constant flow of new products is the life blood of this business" (Global Supply Chain Director).*

With a target of supplying 12% new SKUs each week, the success of New Look is based on how quickly the supply chain transforms designs into products. This requires a strong design input from the designers who must understand supply chain capabilities and/or constraints to avoid problems and a strong supply chain input which understands the designer's requirements and how efficiently and effectively it can translate the design into products. Of course designers must also consider the logistical implications of their designs and the supply chain must utilise the best mode of transport. Sourcing of raw materials and manufacture will also be of consideration at the design stage, but decisions will be made jointly by the cross functional team working on a particular range. By streamlining the processes from design to manufacture and with better co-ordination across the supply chain New Look reduce the mark down of products, because products are designed closer to season so are more closely linked to consumer demand and are replenished more frequently with new lines on a regular basis, so it limits old stock in the store which can make the stores look dull and dated.

A Marriage for Success

The company sources from many large independent suppliers mainly in Asia and Europe which are diverse in nature and hence, provide the company with immense flexibility. However, New Look relies heavily on a handful of strategic suppliers and over half of its clothing supplies are sourced from just two suppliers in Turkey and China.

> *"Success of New Look lies in its strong relationships with its suppliers" (Global Supply Chain Director).*

With strategic partners in Turkey and China, New Look has established a close network of suppliers dedicated to design collaboration (50% of design is managed in-house), sourcing and manufacturing. New Look has a joint venture with both its strategic partners but with China it is a non-financial arrangement although the offices are branded as New Look offices. New Look Turkey, New Look UK and Indo-chine (China) have established a very close relationship working together for mutual benefit. This provides New Look and their designers/buyers with great flexibility when range planning and they can optimise their supply chain to meet the requirements of its market.

Accessible Fashion – New Look is the New Vogue

Over recent years, the company has strived to lose the reputation of a throw away fashion retailer like Primark, by re-branding its clothing and its stores. The refreshed image is that 'New Look is always in trend, always in fashion and always in style'. The company has achieved this by replenishing its stores with new products and also by redesigning its store layouts and shop fronts to appeal to a more fashion conscious market.

In addition, New Look have only four continuity/seasonal continuity products; basic denim range, black trousers and black and white bras. These are the only products that customers will see year in year out, and often even these will have been modified in styling details. But the vast majority of product is fashionable or seasonable, it will come in and go out and will not be replaced again unless there is a hot trend which may run as a repeat product for a particular season. But basically the average lifecycle of a product is 6–8 weeks, after which it is not replaced

The company maintains a tight grip on its supply chain and has optimised communication flows by ensuring a constant exchange of information. In this way, it can respond quickly to changes in fashion trends, order the right products in the appropriate quantities, deliver these items to the correct destinations and then sell them at competitive prices. As far as logistics is concerned, products destined for New Look stores are transported from their country of production to the distribution centre or consolidation centre. Here they are checked before being dispatched, to the stores.

New Look has developed sophisticated IT systems to minimise the costs of carrying inventory and to facilitate rapid replenishment of stock in its distribution channels. The company's ability to respond quickly to demand for fast-changing fashion hinges on its skill to optimise lead times. Particularly to minimise the amount of time from when a product idea is conceived to when the finished product is available to customers. As a result of improvements to its design and buying process particularly the interface between design and the supply chain, New Look has been able to reduce its average lead times in recent years. In view of the fact that fashion cycles are constantly shortening, New Look aims to reduce its lead times even further with new investments in its supply chain processes especially in the case of high fashion items. Consequently, the production of such items is, to an increasing extent, undertaken in Europe rather than Asia.

New Look refreshes its product offerings often and replenishes the stock in its stores on a daily basis with deliveries to stores three times a week. Better management of the interface between design and the supply chain has enabled greater flexibility in production. For example, it is quick to order and stock new products or to make last minute changes to items which may not be selling well. As a result, the company can react quickly to changes in demand.

Cheaper is Chic

Primarily, the company aims to drive down costs and to move more volume from China, but moving into a more high fashion position which demands a fast fashion approach has meant that New Look has had to adapt its sourcing profile accordingly and increasingly source more from Turkey and because 50% of the design is in-house, it means that New Look can leverage their supply base by going direct to suppliers with designs, further speeding up the product development process.

As far as its purchasing strategy is concerned, the company makes regular purchases throughout the year rather than buying in bulk ahead of a season. This strategy provides a number of benefits.

- First it minimises the amount of capital which is tied up in stocked goods.
- Second, it reduces the risk of products being left unsold at the end of a season.
- Third, it minimises the need for retail markdowns which have a significant impact on profits.

Usually, when New Look develops designs for a particular range they will send them out to their Chinese and Turkish partners so that it is set up for manufacture in both facilities. But then based on production times and volume of production the appropriate decision is made from where to manufacture. Often the same style may be sampled in two different countries, so that the company can be both lean and agile. Design teams work closely with buyers and suppliers to achieve the ideal look from the most up to date international fashion trends at unbelievable prices

New Challenges

As 2007 drew to an end it was becoming apparent that the retail environment was becoming much tougher as fears of recession and declining consumer spending increased. Across much of the western world retailers were facing the prospect of lower sales and lower margins.

New Look was not immune from these trends and also recognised that competition was likely to become even more fierce as the struggle for survival was forcing many retailers to compete on price.

Question

How can New Look maintain/improve its competitive position in the challenging retail climate of 2008?

Appendix 1

𝒯ABLE 1 ● Major Players in the Fashion Industry

Price	innovators	trend setters	trend followers	late adopters
High	Prada, Gucci, Jean Paul Gaultier	Emporio Armani, Calvin Klein, DKNY	Ralph Lauren, Max Mara	Burberry, Aquascutum
Medium	Diesel, Kookai, Morgan	French Connection, Espirit, Mexx	Banana Republic, Benetton	Marks & Spencer, Pringle
Low		H&M, Zara	**New Look,** Gap	Supermarkets (George at Asda, Tesco, Sainsburys

Appendix 2

. . . Ideally Positioned to Capture Maximum Growth

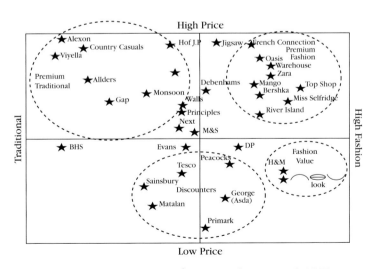

Source: Verdict, as at June 2006, (New Look as at March 2007, source: TNS)

SENSATIONAL FOODS (SF)

The year 2006 was just beginning and Mrs. Oluwole was contemplating how to move her fast food business to a higher level. The business was 12 years old. It started as a small business to keep her busy after retiring in good health from a fulfilling career in a manufacturing company. The growth of the business had been inspired, driven and managed by the founder in an entrepreneurial mode but with firm organizational structures, values and discipline.

SF maintained strong presence in Lagos and Kaduna where over 80 percent of the industry practitioners had outlets. While the other local fast food chains had focused largely on pastries and rice-chicken based dishes, SF had consistently cooked and served local Nigerian dishes with a hint of pastries found predominantly in its External Service Unit (ESU). Of late, the other fast food chains had responded to her dominant position in the market by offering Nigerian dishes as well.

However, like most businesses that involved retailing, the traditional cuisines and indeed the fast food industry were fragmented and competition varied regionally and locally. The fast food industry in Nigeria provided products and services that fulfilled an enduring human need for which no suitable substitute existed. The need was universal and had to be satisfied on a recurring basis. These were the characteristics of a huge and non cyclical market. It underscored an important point: that the basic restaurant product would never become obsolete. However, after attending a course at the Lagos Business School on "*improving fast food operations*", Mrs. Oluwole thought the business had a lot of loopholes and considering the increasing competition, she felt she had better make very good use of the opportunity the course offered.

Of late SF was developing an improved standard set of recipes for all the products in addition to considering the implementation of inventory management software which she hoped would link all the outlets (cafeterias) and enable her exert control over the escalating cost of operation. Recent techniques deployed to reduce the operating cost at the outlets had resulted in sub-standard quality of products and services. As the Head of Operations at SF put it:

> *"To improve performance we deployed a strategy that encouraged creativity among the different outlets to enable them reduce the outlet operating costs. But after a short while, we realized that some of the outlet managers were tampering with the quality in order to reduce cost. This is not acceptable! We are going back to the drawing board because we must ensure that anyone who moves into any SF outlet gets the same quality of service at all times. We cannot play with that. In fact we are in the process of standardizing all the operations of our outlets to ensure this company-wide uniformity ..."*

It would appear that part of the challenge to SF was to standardize the operational processes to ensure the achievement of acceptable and repetitive standard of service, while maintaining costs at a reasonable level.

The Birth of SF

SF started off in a rather unassuming way in 1993. It was a small eatery that catered for a rather small customer base with clean and hygienic environment. Satisfied with the quality of the food they got at this restaurant, some customers started requesting for Mrs. Oluwole to

Frank Ojadi prepared this case as the basis for class discussion rather than to illustrate either effective or ineffective handling of an administrative situation Support for development of the case was provided by the International Finance Corporation's Global Business School Network.
Copyright © Lagos Business School, 2007.

offer catering services for their social events. This grew little by little mainly by word of mouth marketing. At a time Mrs. Oluwole thought the external catering would require more attention. She devoted more time to this aspect of her business. With some funds raised from the outdoor catering Mrs. Oluwole was able to establish her first proper cafeteria in a popular street in Lagos. This turned out to be a real success.

Lagos the Nigerian commercial nerve centre was fast growing and the professional demands on the working population made it difficult for the usual traditional cooking. There was proliferation of eateries popularly known as '*bukas*' and '*food is ready*'. These were characterized by dirty and unhygienic conditions. Many people yearned to have our traditional cuisines in a clean and hygienic environment. SF bridged this gap. SF was actually among the first set of brand names in this kind of business. A couple of months later, SF developed two other outlets, one in Lekki phase I, and another in the Lagos Island. As more outlets were added the outdoor service unit blossomed since these outlets helped publicize the activities of the ESU.

ESU

The ESU operated as a quasi-business unit with its kitchen located at the head-office of the company. It operated on a contract basis with corporate and individual clients. The ESU had standard set of menu items from which clients could choose, and was more flexible and easily adaptable to clients' specific needs. For instance, the ESU catered for birthday ceremonies, wedding parties and corporate annual general meetings. At any particular time, the ESU was typically engaged in the provision of catering services to more than 4 clients at different locations within Lagos. ESU volume of service tended to peak during festive periods. It was generally believed that the ESU generated more volume sales and profitability than the cafeterias. Quite recently, ESU was considering acquiring equipment such as tables, seats, chairs, canopies to position its service as a one-stop shop. A distinguishing feature of the ESU was that it entered into contract to serve a group of people on behalf of any client during an event, while the cafeterias offered services directly to individual customers. The ESU planned for every contract on the basis of the number of client's guests and the agreed menu items and therefore, was better positioned than the cafeterias to take advantage of economies of scale and present a quotation that included current purchase prices of ingredients and materials. It would seem that it was not particularly feasible for the cafeterias to alter their tariff in line with frequent purchase price changes.

In the last three years SF had acquired and developed three new outlets in Kaduna state in the northern part of the country. Just last year SF also acquired and opened another outlet in a private University compound in Ogun state, the western part of Nigeria. Construction of another outlet was being completed in Ibadan, a city about 120 kilometres from Lagos. There were arrangements with some blue chip corporations in Lagos state to offer daily catering services. The growth of the company was moving at a very fast pace in spite of the challenges of reducing the high operating cost. In all, there were 12 outlets fully owned and operated by SF in February 2006.

Basic Operations at SF

The cafeterias operated as quasi-business units. They cooked and served the same menu items to customers and relied on the central stores to provide the ingredients including the packaging and take-away containers. The major operations carried out at SF head office included purchasing, stocking, processing, and the distribution of raw food and materials to cafeterias (outlets). Cooking and sales to customers was the primary responsibility of the outlets and the ESU.

Purchasing

SF operated 3 cycles of purchasing: direct daily and weekly purchases; and contract supplies from preferred vendors' list. The daily purchases which in a way represented the just-in-time model targeted perishables. Items purchased on a daily basis from the "Mile 12 market" included tomatoes, big fleshy red pepper, cabbage, carrot, shoko and ugu. Shoko and ugu were very popular local vegetables used for preparing assorted types of soup offered together with "semovita or eba" as a complete meal. Other items included fruits such as pawpaw, pineapples, and oranges. Weekly purchases were semi perishable items like onions, potatoes, green pepper, garlic, ginger, chilly pepper, coconut, brown beans, yams, garri (a cassava-based meal).

Items supplied by contractors included:

- printed and packaging materials, paper cups, plastic spoons and forks, wrapping nylons, etc.
- LPG gas, non-edible spirit and diesel.
- beef, rice, fresh fish, etc.

Altogether, there were over 50 key stock keeping units (SKUs) and about 35 suppliers. Most of the suppliers were wholesalers. The purchasing process was based on the stock level of items in the central store rather than sales forecast from the cafeterias and ESU. The cafeteria managers selected and purchased the beverages they sold. The bulk of the purchases at the cafeterias did not command a significant portion of the total purchases by the company. Incidents of multiple purchases of the same items by the cafeterias and central purchasing unit were low. The management of the company felt that by buying centrally it would take advantage of economies of scale, ensure wide uniformity in quality but some cafeteria managers complained about the high price of ingredients supplied them including the unresponsiveness of the central store. For instance, incidents of damaged and rejected items returned by the cafeterias were hardly accepted at the central store.

Stocking

The central store had very limited storage space for the food items and support materials needed for the company's operation. To aid control, stock in the central store was divided into dry and wet stock. Dry stock was made up of all the grains, and canned foodstuff. The wet stock included proteins such as chicken, cow leg, beef, fish, goat meat, etc. Vegetables were also part of the wet items. The central store operated on first in first out basis and was manned by a team of five people supervised by the store manager who reported to the head of Purchasing.

Processing

Some of the ingredients were processed prior to distribution to the outlets. They included beans and other grains, which were sieved to remove the chaff. It took an average of 2 days to completely sieve one bag of beans. The main processed items were proteins. The proteins were stored in the cold room but at the appropriate time sent to the butchery for processing into portions. Portioned proteins were stored in the freezers and issued to the outlets.

Distribution to outlets

Based on store requisitions the cafeterias and the ESU picked up their supplies from the central store. The cafeterias maintained mini stores which held about two-day supplies. To ensure effective operations of the cafeterias, pick-up vehicles were attached to every outlet.

Cooking and sales to customers

The cafeterias had about four units namely, a mini store, kitchen, sales counter and the dining space with tables and chairs. A room was reserved and used by the operating manager and account clerk. Supplies from the central store were received by the store man and account clerk, based on the requisitions issued by the outlet manager.

Based on the menu items planned for the day, raw food stuff was issued to the kitchen.

After cooking, the unit of measurement changed for all the menu items except protein (which was unitized and properly portioned and secured prior to cooking) and fried plantain. For example, raw rice was issued in kilogram and thereafter sold in portions (1 kg of raw rice was equivalent to 10 portions of rice measured with a portioning spoon). The kitchen staff supplied cooked products to the sales counter. Three waiters attended to the customers from different dishes positioned in an appealing manner along the counter rail, as the customers pointed out their requirements. Thereafter, the customer took possession of his order on a tray and proceeded to the cashier for payment. The cashier was positioned at the end of rail but on the same side with the waiters and dishes. The cashiers at the outlets prided themselves of possessing the capability of accurately determining the exact quantity and types of food items on the customer's plate, but quite often, had been observed "*giraffing*" unto the customer's dish in order to appropriately bill them. Essentially, "giraffing" is the act of striving to see by extending one's neck to get a full picture of the contents of a customers' plate without necessarily leaving your position.

The way forward

The Managing Director and the top managers of SF were worried about the increasing cost of operation, the varying quality of service at the outlets and the increasing competition. The management was of the view that they could not continue with outlet development and expansion until these problems were solved. In one of their top management meetings, a number of issues were raised:

- Continue with the present arrangement but negotiate with suppliers of key items to deliver directly to the outlets.
- Empower the outlet managers to procure, cook and serve customers with clear performance targets on cost of food and beverage and profitability.
- Centralize cooking at the head office and distribute to the outlets.

Should they go ahead and have the point of sale software installed in the belief that it would help control cost, or were there other internal operating processes they need to tackle to considerably reduce the cost of operation?

APPENDICES

List of Menu items cooked and served at the cafeterias

White rice	Jollof rice
Noodle rice	P/rice
Spaghetti	Exotic
Beans	Yam pottage
Plantain	Bush meat
Goat meat	Roasted chicken
S/chicken	Fish N ata
Cow leg	Beef
Stock fish	Gizzard
Snail	Cat fish
Ise ewu	Eba
Amala	Semovita
Egusi soup	Edikainyko
Moi-moi	Efo riro
Fruit salad	Vegetable salad

Tuna sandwich	Corn sandwich
Tea & coffee	Fried egg
Oat	Omelet
Chips	Bread
Ewedu soup	

Typical Recipe of Efo riro (a local soup served with semovita or pounded yam, or eda as a complete meal) for 10 persons

Shoko	2 kg (1 head = 400 grams)
Cray fish	0.02 gm (1 peak milk tin)
Stockfish head	100 gm
Dry fish	100 gm
Palm oil	¼ litre = 250 ml
Knorr cubes	4 sachets
Rodo	100 gm
Onions	300 gm
Iru	2 table spoons
Stock (beef)	1 kitchen spoon
Tatase	200 gm
Salt	to taste

Income statement for the past 12 months for the Lekki Outlet No 1 (in million Naira)

Account Name	Jan	Feb	Mar	Apr	May	Jun	Jul	Aug	Sept	Oct	Nov	Dec
Sales – food	8.9	8.6	7.9	8.1	7.8	8.5	8.1	8.0	8.5	7.6	8.2	9.7
Sales – beverage	1.3	1.4	1.3	1.4	1.3	1.3	1.1	1.1	1.1	1.0	1.2	1.4
Total revenue	10.2	10	9.2	9.5	9.1	9.8	9.1	9.1	9.4	8.6	9.4	11.1
Cost of food	4.7	3.6	5.1	4.4	3.2	4.5	4.2	3.8	4.6	3.8	3.6	4.8
Cost of beverage	0.6	0.7	0.8	0.6	0.7	0.9	0.7	0.4	0.6	0.5	0.4	0.8
Subtotal	5.3	4.3	5.9	5.0	3.9	5.4	4.9	4.2	5.2	4.3	4.0	5.6
Other exp	1.3	1.5	1.6	1.3	1.5	1.4	1.4	1.4	1.2	1.4	1.3	1.9
Total expense	6.6	5.8	7.5	6.3	5.4	6.8	6.3	5.6	6.4	5.7	5.3	7.5
Net income	3.6	4.2	1.7	3.2	3.7	3.0	2.8	3.5	3.0	2.9	4.1	3.6

Income statement for 12 months for Lagos Outlet
No 2 (in million Naira)

Account Name	Jan	Feb	Mar	Apr	May	Jun	Jul	Aug	Sept	Oct	Nov	Dec
Sales – food	6.4	7.1	6.3	7.3	7.3	7.5	7.9	7.7	7.3	6.9	7.2	7.8
Sales – beverage	1.2	1.3	1.2	1.7	1.5	1.6	1.4	1.4	1.1	1.2	1.4	1.4
Total revenue	7.6	8.4	7.5	9.0	8.8	9.1	9.1	9.0	8.3	8.0	8.5	8.9
Cost of food	3.3	4.0	3.7	4.5	3.4	3.7	4.1	4.3	3.4	3.5	3.4	4.0
Cost of beverage	0.5	0.6	0.4	1.1	0.4	0.7	0.6	0.5	0.6	0.5	0.7	0.8
Subtotal	3.8	4.6	4.1	5.6	3.8	4.4	4.7	4.8	4.0	4.0	4.1	4.8
Other exp.	2.3	1.9	1.5	1.5	2.0	2.3	1.7	1.7	1.8	1.7	1.8	1.6
Total expense	6.1	6.5	5.6	7.1	5.8	6.7	6.4	6.5	5.8	5.7	5.9	6.6
Net income	1.5	1.9	1.9	1.9	3.0	2.4	2.7	2.5	2.5	2.3	2.6	2.3

ZARA

Responsive, High Speed, Affordable Fashion

In 1975, the first Zara store was opened in La Coruña, in Northwest Spain. By 2005, Zara's 723 stores had a selling area of 811,100 m² and occupied "privileged locations of major cities" in 56 countries. With sales of €3.8 billion in financial year 2004, Zara had become Spain's best-known fashion brand and the flagship brand of €5.7 billion holding group Inditex. Inditex's stock market listing in 2001 had turned Amancio Ortega, its founder and a self-made man, into the world's 23 richest man, with a personal fortune that *Forbes* magazine estimated at $12.6 billion.

Zara strived to deliver fashion apparel, often knock-offs of famous designers, at reasonable costs to young, fashion-conscious city-dwellers. Zara used in-house designers to present new items of clothing to customers twice a week, in response to sales and fashion trends. Thus the merchandise of any particular store was fresh and limited. To produce at such short notice required that Zara maintain a vertically integrated supply chain that distributed the clothes through a single state-of-the-art distribution centre. Unlike its competitors, 70–80% of Zara garments were manufactured in Europe.

In 2005, Pablo Isla was appointed the new Inditex chief executive. With plans to double the number of its stores by 2009, the rapid pace of growth was necessitating changes. First, Zara had opened a second distribution centre to increase capacity. Second, expanding into more distant markets meant that the number of items carried had increased to 12,000. Would Zara's business model be able to scale up? Or would the resulting complexity compromise its speed advantage? Would Pablo Isla be able to maintain the focus that Zara had established?

THE RETAIL APPAREL INDUSTRY AND COMPETITORS

The apparel industry was one of the most globalised industries, with 23.6 million workers in over 20 countries. As labour costs in Western European countries had risen, labour-intensive manufacturing operations had become increasingly outsourced to less developed countries. Hourly wages in the textile industry could be as low as 60 cents in India and China, compared with $2 in North Africa, $3 in Eastern Europe, $8.50 in Spain, and around $15.00 in Italy.

The 1974 *Multi-Fibre Arrangement*, which placed import quotas on garments and textiles from developing countries to the industrialised world, had expired on 1 January 2005 for all members of the World Trade Organization. This was amplifying the relocation of textile and garment manufacture to countries with lower labour costs, especially China. For example, in 2004, 400 Spanish textile groups went out of business, due to competition from Asia, resulting in the loss of 15,000 jobs. The Spanish textile guild predicted a loss of another 72,000 jobs by 2009.[1]

The apparel retail channels had consolidated during the 1990s, with a few large players dominating most major markets. Competitors included department stores, mass merchandisers (e.g. discounters and supermarkets) and specialty stores. Department stores were usually national players, like Marks & Spencer in the United Kingdom or Federated in the USA. Typically, they had lost market share in recent years. Mass merchandisers such as Target, Tesco and Wal-Mart had increasingly added private label clothes to their mix over the years to become major players. There were many successful specialty chains like Benetton, C&A, Hennes & Mauritz (referred to as H&M), The Limited, Mango and Next.

The traditional apparel industry model worked on long lead times (see ***Exhibit 1***). The industry average was around nine months, around six months for design and three months for manufacturing. As a result, 45–60% of production was committed in the six-month pre-season period, with 80–100% committed by the start of the season. Only the remaining 0–20% was generally manufactured in-season in response to sales patterns. Excess inventory was marked down at the end of the season, and typically accounted for 30–40% of sales. Despite their best efforts, Zara's closest competitors, H&M and Gap, still took around five months to produce new clothing lines.

H&M

Swedish clothing chain H&M was founded in 1947. By 2005, it had close to 32,000 employees, just under 1,100 stores in 20 countries. In 2005, it planned to open 155 new stores in Europe and the US. Its 2004 sales were €6 billion, which yielded a profit of 1.24 billion. With close to 30% of its sales, Germany was H&M's largest market, while the US generated only 6.4% of its 2004 sales. It manufactured 60% of its clothes in Asia.

H&M's business concept was to offer fashion and quality at the best price. In order to offer the latest fashion, H&M had its own buying and design department. It claimed to achieve the best price by:

- Few middlemen
- Buying in large volumes
- Having a broad, in-depth knowledge of design, fashion, and textiles
- Buying the right products from the right market
- Being cost conscious at every stage
- Having efficient distribution

H&M's clothing lines in men's wear, women's wear and children's wear, as well as its cosmetics range, targeted cost-conscious shoppers. Within H&M women's wear were different sub-brands: Hennes (women aged 25–35), L.O.G.G. (casual sportswear), Impuls (young women's trends), BiB (plus-size line), Woman (classic), Clothes (current trends), MAMA (maternity) and Rocky (youth fashion). There were also different sub-brands within the men's and children's lines.

H&M stores generally had a somewhat chaotic, marketplace feel, with clothes packed tightly onto racks, frequent markdowns, and queues at the cash register. H&M devoted 5% of its revenues to advertising. Its high-profile ad campaigns featured celebrities, such as Claudia Schiffer, Johnny Depp, Naomi Campbell and Jerry Hall, wearing its low-cost clothes. Dedicated collections by star designers Karl Lagerfeld and Stella McCartney in 2004–5 continued to create buzz among its customers.

The Gap

Gap opened its first store in San Francisco in 1969, where it sold mainly Levis jeans. In 1991, Gap announced its decision to sell only private label brands. With around 3,000 stores and 152,000 employees worldwide, Gap positioned itself as a provider of high quality, basic items, such as jeans, khakis and t-shirts. In addition to Old Navy and Banana Republic, Gap's chains included GapBody, GapKids, and babyGap. Its 2004 sales were around €12.5 billion, with a profit of $1.4 billion. Nearly all of Gap's products were manufactured outside the US, with 18% of its collection made in China.

Gap's stores were spacious, with stock well spaced and neatly presented. There was an emphasis on service, with a call button in fitting rooms for customers requiring assistance with clothing sizes. Television advertisements featured hip music and dance sequences, with appearances by celebrities such as Madonna, Lenny Kravitz, Sarah Jessica Parker and Joss Stone.

INDITEX HISTORY

Spanish entrepreneur Amancio Ortega Gaona started a firm manufacturing lingerie and night-wear in 1963, after quitting his job as a runner for a shirtmaker in La Coruña. He founded Confecciones GOA in 1972, and opened the first Zara store in 1975, to sell stock after a customer cancelled a large order.

Ortega founded the Inditex group in 1985. After floating 26% of its shares on the Madrid stock exchange in 2001, he remained its majority shareholder, with 61% of the company's shares. Ortega retained a low profile, rarely making public appearances (apart from during the run-up to the IPO in 2000), and had never given an interview.

José María Castellano Ríos joined Inditex in 1985 and became its Chief Executive in 1997. Castellano had previously been IT manager of Aegon España SA, and had a doctorate in economics and business studies. In 2005, Inditex developed a five-year plan, which included a board restructure. As part of the restructure, Pablo Isla Álvarez de Tejera was appointed as Chief Executive in May 2005. Isla came from the Franco-Spanish tobacco group Altadis, where he had been co-chairman. Isla was chosen for his experience in international distribution. Ortega stayed on as the group's Chairman, and Castellano remained the Deputy Chairman.

Portfolio of Stores

Besides Zara, which was targeted at trendy city youngsters, Inditex grew its portfolio of apparel chains throughout the 1990s. Each chain was targeted at a specific segment (see **Exhibit 2**):

- Massimo Dutti – Young businessmen
- Pull & Bear – Elegant male clothing
- Berksha – Elegant fashion for young women
- Brettos – Trendy young suburban women
- Oysho – Lingerie
- Stradivarius – Youthful fashion
- Kiddy's Class – Trendy children

In 2003, Inditex opened a home furnishings chain called Zara Home. By 2005, Zara made up close to 70% of Inditex sales and led the group's international expansion (see **Exhibit 3**). While, as a group, Inditex had about twice the number of stores as H&M, Zara's 700 stores were fewer in number than H&M's. Inditex was aggressively expanding, and planned to increase its 2,000 stores to 4,000 by 2009, in Europe, Asia, and the U.S. (see **Exhibit 4**). In terms of profits, Inditex was performing well compared with its main competitor, H&M (see **Exhibit 5** and **Exhibit 6**).

THE ZARA STORE

91% of Zara stores were company-owned; the rest were franchises or joint ventures. Customers entering a Zara store on Regent Street in London, Rue Rivoli in Paris, Fifth Avenue in New York or Avenidas das Americas in Rio de Janeiro generally found themselves in the same environment: a predominantly white, modern and spacious store, well-lit and walled with mirror. The latest fashions hung from the store racks around them. A long line of people typically waited at the cash registers to pay for their purchases: a few select items.

In comparison with other clothing retailers, who spent 3–4% of sales on advertising, Zara spent just 0.3%. The little it did spend went to reinforce its identity as a clothing retailer that was low-cost but high fashion (see **Exhibit 7**). Instead Zara concentrated on creating compelling store windows and to the design of its shops, which had won awards. It relied on its shop windows, which were dramatically lit and used neutral backgrounds, to communicate its brand image. The shop windows of Zara stores were changed regularly, according to display designs sent by headquarters, and were critical for Zara to remain visible and entice customers. Store locations were carefully researched to determine that there was a sufficiently large customer base for Zara[2], and as such were generally busy, prestigious, city centre shopping streets.

Zara was a fashion imitator. It focussed its attention on understanding what fashion items its customers wanted and then delivering them, rather than on promoting predicted season's trends via fashion shows and similar channels of influence, that the fashion industry traditionally used. Its 200 in-house designers were trend-spotters who kept their finger on the fashion pulse, and translated trends into styles that were universally accessible. At Zara headquarters in La Coruña, store specialists (who were responsible for a number of stores in a region) worked closely with designers to develop styles that would work for different markets. Collections were renewed every year, with an average of 11,000 styles produced annually, compared with the more typical collections of 2,000–4,000 produced annually by rivals H&M and Gap.

Production and distribution of new clothing pieces was favoured over replenishing existing items, contributing to the perception of scarcity cultivated in Zara stores. Customers returned frequently to stores, to browse new items. The global average of 17 visits per customer per year for Zara was considerably higher than the three visits to its competitors.[3] Visitors were also more likely to purchase, as one senior executive explained:

> Zara's objective is not that consumers buy a lot but that they buy often and will find something new every time they enter the store.[4]

Comments by Luis Blanc, and Inditex director, illustrated how Zara stores fostered an environment of immediacy:

> We want our customers to understand that if they like something, they must buy it now, because it won't be in the shops the following week. It is all about creating a climate of scarcity and opportunity.[5]

Affordable prices helped to encourage purchases, and Zara's offering was often referred to as clothing to be worn six to ten times.

Zara's pricing differed across country markets. It set prices according to individual market conditions, rather than using cost plus margin as its basis (which was the formula used by most of its competitors). In Spain, Zara products were low-cost, while in the US, Japan and Mexico, they were priced as a luxury fashion item. Prices in France were somewhat higher than in Spain, since the average French consumer was willing to pay more for fashion than most other European consumers. For example, in 2003, the price of jeans in Zara stores in France was $34.58 compared with $24.87 in Spain and $54 in Japan.[6] Until 2002, Zara had used one price tag listing the price in different currencies, to simplify tagging of items. In 2002, however, it implemented a system of local pricing, using a bar code reader that printed the correct local price for items.

Compared with its competitors, Zara generally priced its products somewhat higher than C&A and H&M, but below Gap, Next and Kookai. For example, a similar shirt cost $26 at Zara, compared with a price of $29 at Gap and $9 at H&M.[7]

Store Management

Store managers were encouraged to run their store like a small business. Salespeople were well trained, and Zara promoted its people from within as much as possible. Store managers' remuneration was partially dependent on the accuracy of their sales forecasts and sales growth.[8] Each evening a handheld PDA displayed the newest designs sent by headquarters, which were available for order. Order deadlines were twice weekly, and were issued via the handhelds. Store managers who failed to order by the deadline received replenishment items only.

Store managers regularly spoke with store specialists, who also received real time sales data from stores, to discuss which items were selling well or if customers had requested specific items. This information was then fed back to the design process.[9] Deliveries arrived at stores twice per week from Zara headquarters, a few days after the order was made, and contained both replenishment items as well as new products. Headquarters also sometimes included products that had not been ordered, which stores expected to receive. If demand of an item exceeded supply, some stores did not receive the product they had ordered. Zara also tested some of its products in limited numbers in its test stores, before introducing them on a wider scale. Failure rates of Zara's new products were reported to be just 1%, considerably lower than the industry average of 10%.[10]

Technology was a key part of enabling communications and information flow. While information technology was fundamental to its business, its IT infrastructure was relatively simple (even dated by some standards), which meant that Zara's IT expenditure was significantly lower than its rivals (as much as five to ten times lower).[11] Deputy Chairman José María Castellano explained the key role played by technology:

> Technology in this company is important and will be more important in the future. The technology we use is mainly information technology and [enables] the communication between the shop managers and the design team here in headquarters.[12]

THE ZARA SUPPLY CHAIN

Around 50% of Zara's garments were sourced from third parties. Unlike its competitors, Zara's outsourced production came for the most part from Europe (60%), with just 27% coming from Asia, and another 10% from the rest of the world. The products sourced from Asia were basic collection items or wardrobe "staples," with minimum fashion content, such as T-shirts, lingerie and woollens, and where there was a clear cost advantage. Formal contracts were kept to a minimum, and Zara was generally a preferred customer due to its order volume and stability.[13] Externally manufactured items were shipped to Zara's distribution centre. Zara intended to source more of the collection from Asia in the future, as commented by Castellano: "In the next few years, we will source more basic items from China and Vietnam, but the high value added fashion items will continue to be made closer to home."[14]

The other 50% of Zara's garments, those that were more fashion-dependent, were manufactured in-house, in more than 20 Zara factories located in nearby Arteixo.[15] For its in-house manufacturing, it purchased fabric from Comditel, a subsidiary of Inditex. Half of this fabric was purchased grey (undyed) to enable Zara to respond to changes in colour trends during the season. Dye was purchased from Fibracolor, in which Inditex held a stake.

A team of 200 young, talented yet unknown designers were hired (often recent graduates of top design schools) to create designs, based on the latest fashions from the catwalk and other fashion hotspots, which were easily translatable to the mass market.[16] Working alongside the market specialists and production planners, designers for each of Zara's collections (Woman, Man, Child) kept in-touch with market developments, to create around 40,000 new designs per year, of which around one-quarter were manufactured.[17] The design and production working environment was consistent with Zara's flat hierarchical structure, in which prima donnas were not tolerated.[18]

Illustration: Fast Fashion

Zara was a master of picking up up-to-the-minute trends and churning them out to stores around the world in a matter of weeks.

- After Madonna's first concert data in Spain during a recent tour, he outfit was copied by Zara designers. By the time she performed her last concert in Spain, some members of the audience were wearing the same outfit.
- In 2003, when the Crown Prince of Spain announced his engagement to Letizia Ortiz Recasolano, she wore a white trouser-suit for the occasion (pictured left). In just a few weeks, the same white trouser-suit was hanging from Zara's clothes racks all over Europe, where it was snatched up by the ranks of the fashion-conscious.

Computers were used to guide the cutting tools, using patterns made from selected designs. Zara tried to keep its offering of any style simple, usually in three sizes and three colours only. The labour intensive sewing of the garments was outsourced to around 500 local subcontractors, who used seamstresses in cooperatives. Zara was usually their sole client, and they worked without any written contracts. Zara paid these subcontractors a flat fee per type of garment, (e.g., €5 for a pair of trousers and €15 per jacket) and they were expected to operate on short lead times and fast turnaround. Subcontractors picked up the prepared fabric pieces from Zara, and returned them to the 500,000 m² distribution centre.[19]

At the Zara distribution centre, optical reading devices were used to sort and distribute over 60,000 items per hour. The garments were then picked up and transported by truck to different destinations all over Europe (which made up about 75% of deliveries). Products for more distant destinations were transported by air (about 25%). Throughout the process, garments were tracked using bar codes. Shipments tended to have almost zero flaws, with 98.9% accuracy and under 0.5% shrinkage.[20]

Since Zara's garments were produced in-house, it was able to make a new line from start to finish in just three weeks (see ***Exhibit 8***). This varied somewhat depending on the type of garment: new garments took about five weeks from design to store delivery, while revamped existing items could take as little as two weeks. As a result Zara could be responsive to fashion items that were selling well during the season, and to discontinue those that were not. By constantly refreshing the collection, and manufacturing items in high-intensity, short-runs, Zara was able to prevent the accumulation of non-saleable inventories.

It was estimated that Zara committed just 15–25% of production before the season began, 50 to 60% at the start of the season, and the remainder manufactured in-season. Percentage of Zara sales consisting of markdowns was 15–20%. In some cases, stores ran out of stock. However, this was not viewed as a negative since it contributed to customers' perception of the uniqueness of their purchase: "Customers are actually satisfied to see items out of stock as they are then confident that there is little chance that many other customers will wear the same dress."[21]

Castellano explained the rationale for this departure from industry norms:

> We don't want to compete in the bottom end of the market. We offer fashion with a high design content.

> If I tried to source my collections in Asia, I would not be able to get them quickly enough to our stores. By manufacturing close to home, I can scrap collections when they are not selling. And without this rapid response, I would not be able to extract a good relation between quality, price and fashion which is what our customers have come to expect.[22]

A study in 2000 estimated that Zara managed to generate 14.7% operating margins as a percentage of sales, compared with 10.6% for Gap and 12.3% for H&M. Additionally, the same study put Zara's inventory turnover at 10.67 outpacing Gap at 7.18 and H&M at 6.84.[23]

THE FUTURE

Following Zara's success, competitors sought to reduce their own lead times. The competitive advantage achieved by Zara's vertical integration appeared to be eroding. With its highly centralised structure and its rapid growth, Zara was producing around 12,000 different items per year by 2005. As it opened stores in increasingly distant markets, would Zara be able to retain its flexibility in adjusting production to accommodate differences in local trends? Would the increase in complexity result in a need to create regional production facilities? How would this affect the advantage Zara gained from its centralization?

Might Chinese clothing manufacturers prove to be a competitive threat to Zara, with their high capacity and continuous improvements in quality? Castellano discounted this threat:

"Being a Zara or Gap is not just about designing fashionable clothes and manufacturing them cheaply. You must also make the transition to being a retailer. It is a big step from manufacturing to distribution. There is also the question of managing the location and presentation of stores, training staff and so on."[24]

The Zara model seemed to work better in markets where customers had an appetite for fashion (such as France, Italy, Japan and the UK). However, in countries such as France and Italy, Zara had received bad press for copying designs from couture labels, and the French Fashion Federation had called for limited access by reporters to fashion shows to minimize imitation by copycatters. In other markets, where consumers were less fashion-focussed (e.g. Germany and the U.S.A.) Zara seemed somewhat less successful. Would Zara be better served in the long run by increasing penetration in these fashion-sensitive markets, or by extending its global reach through increased presence in more markets?

EXHIBIT 1 • Traditional Season for a High Street Store

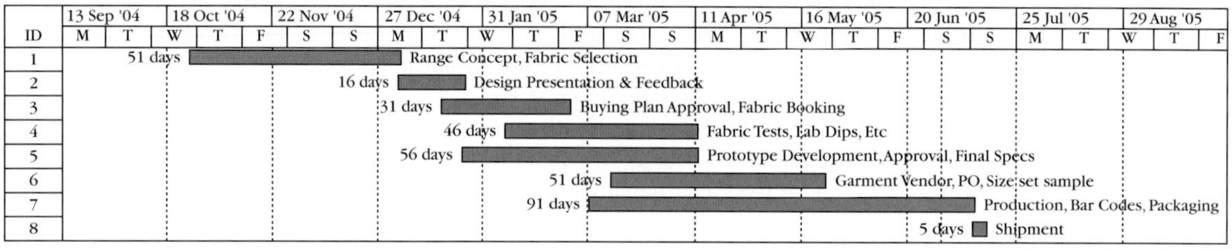

ID	Task	Duration	Description
1		51 days	Range Concept, Fabric Selection
2		16 days	Design Presentation & Feedback
3		31 days	Buying Plan Approval, Fabric Booking
4		46 days	Fabric Tests, Lab Dips, Etc
5		56 days	Prototype Development, Approval, Final Specs
6		51 days	Garment Vendor, PO, Size set sample
7		91 days	Production, Bar Codes, Packaging
8		5 days	Shipment

(Timeline columns: 13 Sep '04, 18 Oct '04, 22 Nov '04, 27 Dec '04, 31 Jan '05, 07 Mar '05, 11 Apr '05, 16 May '05, 20 Jun '05, 25 Jul '05, 29 Aug '05)

Adapted from Dutta, 2004[25]

EXHIBIT 2 • Inditex Stores and Sales

Sales, by Division (2004-5)

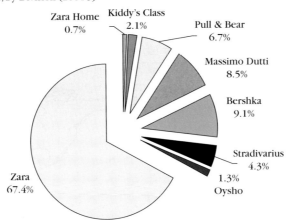

Zara Home
0.7%

Kiddy's Class
2.1%

Pull & Bear
6.7%

Massimo Dutti
8.5%

Bershka
9.1%

Stradivarius
4.3%

1.3%
Oysho

Zara
67.4%

Source: Handelsbank, 2005

Percentage of Stores (2005)

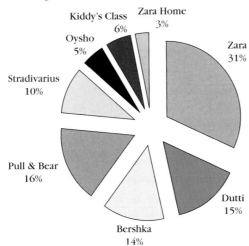

Kiddy's Class
6%

Zara Home
3%

Oysho
5%

Zara
31%

Stradivarius
10%

Pull & Bear
16%

Dutti
15%

Bershka
14%

Source: Financial Times, 2005

EXHIBIT 3 • Number of Zara Stores by Country (31 March 2005)

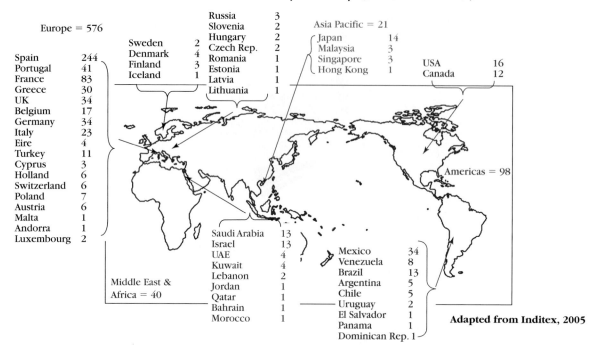

Europe = 576	
Spain	244
Portugal	41
France	83
Greece	30
UK	34
Belgium	17
Germany	34
Italy	23
Eire	4
Turkey	11
Cyprus	3
Holland	6
Switzerland	6
Poland	7
Austria	6
Malta	1
Andorra	1
Luxembourg	2

Sweden	2
Denmark	4
Finland	3
Iceland	1

Russia	3
Slovenia	2
Hungary	2
Czech Rep.	2
Romania	1
Estonia	1
Latvia	1
Lithuania	1

Asia Pacific = 21	
Japan	14
Malaysia	3
Singapore	3
Hong Kong	1

USA	16
Canada	12

Middle East & Africa = 40	
Saudi Arabia	13
Israel	13
UAE	4
Kuwait	4
Lebanon	2
Jordan	1
Qatar	1
Bahrain	1
Morocco	1

Americas = 98

Mexico	34
Venezuela	8
Brazil	13
Argentina	5
Chile	5
Uruguay	2
El Salvador	1
Panama	1
Dominican Rep.	1

Adapted from Inditex, 2005

EXHIBIT 4 • Inditex Store Formats

	Zara		Kiddy's Class		Pull & Bear		Massimo Dutti		Bershka		Stradivarius		Oysho		Zara Home	
	2004	2003	2004	2003	2004	2003	2004	2003	2004	2003	2004	2003	2004	2003	2004	2003
No of stores	723	626	129	103	371	350	327	297	302	253	227	191	104	76	62	26
Turnover*	3,820	3,220	121	90	379	288	481	389	516	395	242	162	72	45	40	11
Operating Income*	648	476	22	18.0	56	19	75	60	83	57	39	4	16	2	0.3	(0.5)
% international sales	65.8	63.5	12.8	13.4	30.5	31	41.9	40.9	35.7	33.8	15.4	16.6	31.5	35.1	12.7	8.5
% of Inditex	67.4	70	2.1	1.9	6.7	6.3	8.5	8.5	9.1	8.6	4.3	3.5	1.3	1	0.7	0.2
ROCE	38%	33%	61%	80%	44%	16%	50%	56%	52%	46%	43%	5%	52%	7%	2%	–

*in millions of Euros, rounded off.

Source: Inditex press dossier, 2005

EXHIBIT 5 • Key Indicators of Gap, H&M and Inditex
(Financial Years 2003 & 2004)

	Gap[i]		H&M		Inditex	
Reporting Date	*29 January 2005[ii]*	*29 January 2004[iii]*	*30 November 2004[iv]*	*30 November 2003[v]*	*31 January 2005*	*31 January 2004*
Sales (millions €)	12,470	12,696	6,029	5,330	5,670	4,599
Gross Profit (millions €)	4,892	4,780	3,449	2,994	3,034	2,306
Operating Profit (millions €)	1,598	1,522	1,198	1,019	925	627
Profit (millions €)	1,435	1,349	1,236	1,062	886	613
Profit after tax (millions €)	882	826	817	706	628	446
Total Assets (millions €)	7,703	8,579	3,159	2,847	4,209	3,510
Inventories (millions €)	1,390	1,365	577	558	514	486
Stores	2,994	3,022	1,068	945	2,244	1,922
Employees	152,000	150,000	31,701	28,409	47,046	39,760
Countries	5	6	20	18	56	48
Total square metres (thousands)	3,399	3,393	1,364[vi]	n/a	1,175	988

Source: Inditex, H&M and Gap, 2005

---

[i] Gap Inc's stores include Gap, Old Navy and Banana Republic. Gap's sales were €5.6 million, with 1643 stores, and 1.43 million square metres.
[ii] Exchange Rate of 29 January 2005 is used for all currency calculations: 0.76660 USD = 1€
[iii] Exchange Rate of 29 January 2004 is used for all currency calculations 0.80080 USD = €1
[iv] Exchange Rate of 30 November 2004 is used for all currency calculations 0.11230 SEK = 1€
[v] Exchange Rate of 30 November 2003 is used for all currency calculations 0.11050 SEK = 1€
[vi] Estimated (Adapted from Datamonitor, 2005).

EXHIBIT 6 • Iniditex vs. H&M (1998–2004)

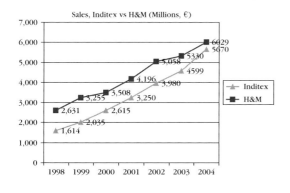

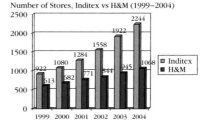

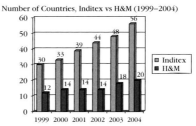

Adapted from Inditex and H&M, 2005

EXHIBIT 7 • A Zara advertisement

The Cheap
Frock coat (119)
White shirt (25) ZARA
Black necktie (65) HACKETT
Woollen Trousers (45) and
Black boots (55), both ZARA

The Expensive
Black cashmere frock coat (950)
White tuxedo shirt (190)
Black necktie (86) and
Woollen Trousers (380) both RALPH
LAUREN
Black boots (500) are by UNGARO

EXHIBIT 8 • Zara Season

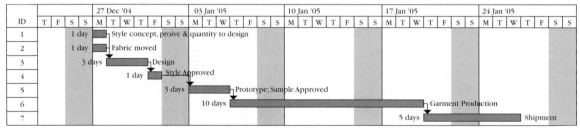

Adapted from Dutta, 2004

ENDNOTES

1. Crawford, L. (2005) "Inditex sizes up Europe in expansion drive," *Financial Times*, 1 February 2005, p. 30.
2. Ferdows, K.J., A.D. Machuca and M. Lewis (2003) "Zara," *CIBER Case Collection*, Indiana University.
3. D'Andrea, G. and D. Arnold (2003) "Zara," *Harvard Business School Case* 9-503-050, p.7.
4. "Zara, la déferlante de la mode espagnole," Interview with Stéphane Labelle, MD of Zara France, *Enjeux-Les Echos*, February 1996.
5. Crawford, L. (2000) "Inside Track: Putting on the style with rapid response," *Financial Times*, 26 February 2000.
6. D'Andrea, G. and D. Arnold (2003) "Zara," *Harvard Business School Case* 9-503-050, p.19.
7. D'Andrea, G. and D. Arnold (2003) "Zara," *Harvard Business School Case* 9-503-050, p.18
8. Ferdows, K.J., K.M. Lewis and J.A.D. Machuca (2003) "Zara," *Supply Chain Forum* 4(2): 62.
9. Ferdows, K.J., A.D. Machuca and M. Lewis (2003) "Zara," *CIBER Case Collection*, Indiana University, p.6.
10. Ghemawat, P. and J.L. Nueno (2003) "Zara: Fast Fashion," *Harvard Business School Case* 9-703-497, p.10.
11. "The Future of Fast Fashion," *The Economist*, 18 June 2005, p.63.
12. "Zara: A Retailer's Dream," from http://www.fashionunited.co.uk/news/archive/inditex1.htm <accessed 3 June 2005>
13. Ferdows, K.J., A.D. Machuca and M. Lewis (2003) "Zara," *CIBER Case Collection*, Indiana University, p.7.
14. Crawford, L. (2005) "Inditex sizes up Europe in expansion drive," *Financial Times*, 1 February 2005, p. 30.
15. Fraiman, N., M. Singh, L. Arrington and C. Paris (2002) "Zara," *Columbia Business School Case*, p. 5.
16. Ghemawat, P. and J.L. Nueno (2003) "Zara: Fast Fashion," *Harvard Business School Case* 9-703-497, p.10.
17. Fraiman, N., M. Singh, L. Arrington and C. Paris (2002) "Zara," *Columbia Business School Case*, p. 5.
18. Ferdows, K.J., A.D. Machuca and M. Lewis (2003) "Zara," *CIBER Case Collection*, Indiana University, p.6.
19. Fraiman, N., M. Singh, L. Arrington and C. Paris (2002) "Zara," *Columbia Business School Case*, p. 6.
20. Ferdows, K.J., A.D. Machuca and M. Lewis (2003) "Zara," *CIBER Case Collection*, Indiana University, p.8.
21. Interview with Anthony Pralle, Senior Vice President of Boston Consulting Group, Madrid, 13 July 1999, as quoted in Harle, N., M. Pich and L. Van der Heyden (2002) "Marks & Spencer and Zara: Process Competition in the Textile Apparel Industry," *INSEAD Case* 602-010-1.
22. Crawford, L. "Inditex sizes up Europe in expansion drive: Rapid design, manufacture and distribution keep pressure on rivals," *Financial Times*, 1 February 2005.
23. D'Andrea, G. and D. Arnold (2003) "Zara," *Harvard Business School Case* 9-503-050.
24. Crawford, L. (2005) "Inditex sizes up Europe in expansion drive," *Financial Times*, 1 February 2005, p. 30.
25. Dutta, D. (2004) "Brand Watch: Zara," *Images Fashion Forum Presentation*, New Delhi, 12 February 2004.

NOVO NORDISK ENGINEERING

Running for Fast-Track Project Execution

Novo Nordisk Engineering (NNE) had achieved the impossible! In July 2005 it finished building a new vaccine production facility in the record-breaking time of 11 months.

Six years earlier, in 1999, Hans Ole Voigt had taken over as CEO of NNE, a Danish company primarily involved in the construction of turnkey pharmaceutical facilities. Not an engineer himself, he was surprised to learn that it took 30 to 36 months to build a facility.

With the objective of differentiating NNE, Voigt got his management team together and introduced the idea of fast-track project execution. He set a challenging objective:

> Within five years we will have to be able to build a plant in less than 12 months!

The meeting room went silent. Those present thought it was not an achievable target. Considering themselves to be the engineering specialists, the employees were quite reluctant to be challenged by this "outsider."

Voigt needed to motivate NNE's employees and maintain their focus to achieve this goal without sacrificing quality. They would have to fundamentally reengineer many company processes.

Background

In 1991 Novo Nordisk A/S, a leading pharmaceutical company, spun off its engineering arm as NNE. The new company had considerable expertise in engineering projects for the pharmaceutical industry. For nearly ten years, it executed projects solely for customers in the Novo Nordisk "galaxy." By 1999, NNE had close to 1,000 employees and was active in Denmark, China, France, Sweden and the USA.

Setting the Challenge

When he joined the company, Voigt realized that its only customer was increasingly focusing on reducing the cost of engineering. Novo Nordisk would probably seek alternative suppliers for "commoditized" services. NNE's value proposition as a high-value-added pharma engineering specialist was not sustainable.

Also, relying on a single customer was risky. Yet, unlike other construction companies, NNE came from the highly regulated pharmaceutical industry. Few competitors in the world understood that industry as well as NNE.

Voigt looked for ways to appeal to other customers and set a challenge for the whole organization. He called it the Big Overarching Goal: To be able to build a complete plant in less than a year by 2005. Voigt explained:

> I wanted a vision to differentiate NNE and allow it to create a profile of its own.

The challenge was received with a great deal of skepticism. Coming from Novo Nordisk, where he was vice president of business support, Voigt had a good understanding of the

Research Associate François Jäger prepared this case under the supervision of Professors Carlos Cordon and Ralf Seifert as a basis for class discussion rather than to illustrate either effective or ineffective handling of a business situation.

pharmaceutical industry, but he was not an engineer. Some employees were willing to try, but the majority thought differently. As Klaus Illum, NNE's engineering director, recalled, the saying was:

> This guy is totally crazy! We are the experts, come on!

At the time, one year seemed like an impossible goal, since plant construction took 30 to 36 months on average. As Voigt put it:

> I was certain we could reduce the time – I wasn't sure about the one year goal!

Finding a Customer to Work With

Speed to market was decisive in the pharmaceutical industry. Patents protected drugs for 20 years. Yet, taking into account discovery, development and clinical trial time, the period of market exclusivity could go down to less than one year in some cases (*refer to **Exhibit 1***).

On the plus side, a blockbuster drug – one with a turnover of more than $1 billion per year – could make $1 million profit per day. Not all drugs required the construction of a new plant, but when necessary, gaining two years because of shorter construction time offered significant financial returns. Nevertheless, realizing such short construction time meant to overcome longstanding industry norms.

Building a pharmaceutical plant involved many long and interlocked processes that required extensive construction planning. In the US, the Food and Drug Administration (FDA) requirements were stringent and had to be closely followed. Just focusing on NNE's internal processes and organization would not be enough. The involvement of both suppliers and the client would also be necessary. Carsten Bech, VP of project management, explained:

> You can only optimize if clients and suppliers are involved. You need to have a common goal.
> You need to change processes also on their side, not just within NNE.

NNE had to find a company willing to invest in a fast-track project. There were substantial risks, since both NNE and its client would be moving into unknown territory. Most pharmaceutical companies had a lowest bidder approach to supplier selection. They were reluctant to engage in fast-track projects, assuming that speed would automatically increase costs. As John Frandsen, VP of sales, noted:

> With a lowest bidder approach, we cannot help a customer build a factory in 12 months.

There was significant risk. Although the project could go very well, it could also go really badly, which would mean costs up by 20% to 40% or delays in project delivery. NNE could not afford to bear all the risk, the client would have to share it. Frandsen explained:

> We are working against a [cost cutting] culture. We need to challenge the purchasing behavior of our clients. Their purchasing managers need to learn about risk management.

The First Step

In 1999 Novo Nordisk needed more insulin production capacity fast in order to supply growing market demand. Because of their long relationship, Novo Nordisk agreed to partner with NNE for the first-fast track project. Construction began in Denmark in June 2000.

A Modular Approach

Modular technology was used to simplify and speed up the project. By breaking a plant down into modules constructed in parallel and tested at the supplier's premises, NNE could be more efficient and get around some of the time- and space-related constraints arising at a construction site.

Modular design also helped measure the project's progress – when a module was installed and tested, a milestone was reached. All members of the team could visualize it. It was a fact. There was no target in terms of time reduction. As Bech explained:

> We tried to push the project managers and see what we could obtain.

Ensuring Consistency and Quality

To be consistent in all its projects, NNE had set up a project activity model (PAM) and a quality management system (QMS). PAM was based on three domains – project management, engineering disciplines and procurement (contract management) – and included documents and activities that were relevant for engineering purposes (*see figure below*).

Figure 1   Project Activity Model
Source: NNE

PAM described NNE's critical business processes associated with engineering activities. It provided all members and interested parties with a clear picture of each project and detailed guidance for its execution.

By combining PAM and modular design, engineers could reuse previous knowledge and thus reduce engineering time and cost. As Voigt put:

> Engineers have a tendency to engineer, to make inventions! Most of the time you can take 80% of a plant that has been made before.

Although speed was crucial, it was not to be achieved at the expense of quality. Every single project that NNE worked on had a quality activity plan, describing the quality goals agreed with the client, as well as the methods by which to achieve the goals. This allowed things to be standardized where possible, while still allowing flexibility.

NNE successfully completed the facility – the world's largest bulk insulin plant –in 24 months. People in the company started to change their mindset. Management was excited to see such a change.

The Second Step: Learn and Accelerate

While it was still engaged in the first fast-track project, NNE started a second one with Novo Nordisk: the Novo Seven facility. Resource conflicts emerged, and managers had to negotiate to find mutually acceptable solutions. Voigt explained:

> Managing resource conflicts is the most difficult part of running an engineering company.

New Approach to Human Resources

The need for speed left no time for politics, and NNE adjusted its HR strategy accordingly. Different project management teams (PMTs) managed each project within the fast-track process. Teams were cross-functional, with individuals coming from departments throughout the company. From the beginning, project managers had to identify employees who could make a difference. Then the company would start to identify individuals everyone could rely on to drive projects – the project managers themselves.

Top management made it clear that PMTs were a special entity. Project managers controlled the team from the start. Once on a project, employees belonged primarily to that team and functional hierarchy was far less important. All team members were based in the same building. Teams functioned in a holistic way; there was a sense of "we're in this together." If one person had a problem, the others would pitch in so the whole project would not be in delayed.

Each PMT included an HR person to challenge its way of working. This internal coach even led workshops to simulate critical situations. The focus was mainly on communications training so that people learned to communicate without insulting others and – occasionally – how to cope with being insulted. Michele Gundstrup coach for the Novo Seven PMT explained:

> A lot of time was spent on building a feedback culture. What was difficult was to make a difference between good and constructive feedback versus any old feedback.

The main idea was to keep all problems behind closed doors within the PMT. Once a decision had been taken, everyone would stick to it.

To reflect the importance of project management, the company created a project management career path, independent of other functional areas. Since NNE was the only company in Denmark that built such big pharmaceutical plants, hiring external project managers with the necessary competencies was almost impossible. Even experienced project managers with a construction background did not fit easily within NNE. The pharmaceutical industry had a culture of its own and a project manager would be poorly regarded by the client if he did not have what was deemed to be the necessary knowledge by industry standards. Hence NNE was looking for project managers with a good understanding of pharmaceutical processes and regulatory aspects rather than basic project management skills.

Changing the Client's Mindset

Fast-track projects meant a lot of pressure on the client, and some were just not ready to play. From the start, clients had to know what they wanted much earlier, and NNE would challenge a particular client's specifications in order to stick to its processes. It was a new way of doing business in a rather traditional industry, and the client had to adapt to these changes. It was not easy, since many clients associated changing the specifications with an increase in either cost or time. NNE's modular concept allowed for shorter construction time, even if set-up time was a bit longer. As a result, both costs and time remained under control.

Figure 2 From Specification-driven to Time-driven Project Management

Small companies with no internal engineering department were fast adopters. Large pharmaceutical companies with long industry experience were not ready for NNE's approach. Their usual reaction was:

> Don't come and tell us what to do!

To ensure fast decision making and client agreement on proposed solutions, the PMT included an executive from the client company. Whenever discussions at the PMT level did not lead to a mutually acceptable solution, the problem was elevated to an executive committee with representatives from both NNE and the client company.

From a risk management point of view, since 80% of the contract was specified and 20% was open, the challenge was to build trust between NNE and the customer. This would also make finding and implementing solutions quicker. As Frandsen noted:

> When you go this fast, you cannot do your specifications completely. It's truly about trust!

Purchasing departments were usually reluctant to sign an open contract, so NNE's sales force had to bypass procurement to reach the final customer within the client. NNE did not have to use such a strategy with Novo Nordisk since both companies trusted each other and worked in total cooperation. As Frandsen recalled:

> There was no contractual consequence on the first fast track project; Novo Nordisk was the only client so we were together on this.

NNE eventually completed the Novo Seven facility in just 18 months. Those who had still been skeptic after the first fast-track project were finally convinced. The challenge combined with the new processes and organization made total sense. A major milestone had been achieved.

The Last Dash

People within the company felt energized by these two major achievements. When Bavarian Nordic A/S, a small pharmaceutical company, approached NNE to build a vaccine production facility in 2004, everyone saw the opportunity to aim for the 12-month goal. With its proven track record, NNE started this project with a good idea of what worked and what did not.

Team Building

Before starting work with this new client, NNE organized a one-week team-building exercise for the PMT in the north of Sweden in winter. To kick off the week, the team was thrown out of a bus at night and had to walk 25 km in the snow. The rest of the time they did several outdoor exercises a day, with two hours' sleep if they were lucky. As Nielsen commented:

> After two days like that everything is broken down. There is no politics anymore. People find key value.

The exercise helped the PMT to create an identity of its own and to talk with one voice. Every employee knew that the voice of one PMT member was the voice of the entire team. But this effort was not limited to the NNE team.

Ole Broch Nielsen, the Bavarian Nordic project manager, sought the best craftsmen for the project and set about creating the best conditions on site to attract them. Craftsmen would find everything that they needed to provide first-class work.

To start with Nielsen organized a one-day seminar with engineers, foremen and craftsmen. They would all get to know each other personally so communication delays could be avoided later on. Then a subcontractor mentioned it would be easier and cheaper to build a temporary office for the engineers on the construction site. Nielsen liked the idea and implemented it. When problems occurred during the construction, craftsmen knew the engineers and it was easy for them to pop into the office and explain what the problem was. It was usually resolved quickly and the engineers would modify their plan then and there. Whenever a mile-stone was reached, small parties with coffee and cakes were held, and when employees reached one of the interim challenging targets set by Nielsen, he would offer gifts to keep morale high. Nielsen noted:

> It is all about giving people the right working conditions and the possibility to be productive.

Nielsen organized weekly meetings with offsite subcontractors. There were also monthly meetings with all the subcontractors, held either at the construction site or at one of the subcontractor's premises. These meetings fostered information sharing between all parties involved in the construction. They also helped to set common objectives and to give momen-tum to the project. Each time, the host organized a social event so people could form bonds with one another.

Rethinking Project Planning

Unlike the previous fast-track projects, construction took place in an existing building and modules could not be brought in from subcontractors. Bavarian Nordic wanted the project delivered within nine months. How could NNE deliver a fast-track project if it had to build everything on site, without using modules? What about other potential problems? The success of the project would rely on perfect project planning. Nielsen:

> Project planning is like the computer game Tetris – you never know which brick will come down next but you have to find a way to fit it.

Nielsen went back to Bavarian Nordic with a proposal for 11 months. He would do every-thing possible to reach the target but could not guarantee it.

Traditional project planning methods emphasized the need to identify all the tasks nec-essary to complete a project, as well as which ones depended on one another, and see what they added up to in terms of time. By using modular processes and documentation as well as PAM, and based on NNE's experience, Nielsen applied backward planning. He squeezed all the different tasks of the project into autonomous subprojects executed simul-taneously to fit the timeline. It was a top-down approach versus a traditional bottom-up approach.

While there was no time buffer, Nielsen knew he could devote additional resources to the project if necessary because of the open contract:

> That's why you have money in your wallet at the airport, to buy things you forgot to pack.

Nielsen also received full management support. For instance, Bech – who was part of the executive committee for the project – dedicated two days per week to customer management. Construction had its ups and downs, but NNE finally completed the project on time – in the record breaking space of 11 months.

Not long after this remarkable success, Novo Seven (*pictured below*) – the previous fast-track project – won the 2005 Facility of the Year award at the New York Interfex fair, a major pharmaceutical industry gathering. Bech commented:

> We had a stand at this fair and quite honestly it did not receive lots of attention. That is before we received the award. Right after, our stand was completely crowded with people who wanted to understand why we had won. It was surreal!

What Next?

NNE had finally achieved success after five years of continuous efforts. Now the company could rest at last. Or could it? While it had earned its new visibility and reputation by achieving what was previously thought impossible, the world was still moving fast and competitors were far from standing still. Voigt had to prove the sustainability of NNE's business model

Fast-track projects were certainly a good marketing tool, yet NNE still had many other projects that did not require the fast-track process. By the end of 2005 the company had enjoyed steady growth for more than a decade (*refer to **Exhibit 2***). It was managing a portfolio of more than a 1,000 projects ranging from simply changing a door in a lab to building an entire new plant. Most of these projects were monodisciplinary; about 80 were truly multidisciplinary, with a turnover of more than DKK 5 million each.[1] Of those, 30 critical projects managed by senior project manager under the direct scrutiny of top management generated about 80% of the company turnover. How sustainable was the current business model? What were its limitations?

New Challenges

Voigt needed to find more customers outside the Novo Nordisk galaxy, who, like Bavarian Nordic, were willing to undertake fast-track projects. This would be challenging but not impossible. NNE had achieved its fastest project to date with a customer outside Novo Nordisk. Since the facility of the year award, NNE had gained exposure in the pharmaceutical industry and many potential clients had seen opportunities for themselves. Yet, many customers were somewhat risk-averse, had incentive schemes that did not reward time savings or were simply using NNE as a benchmark to put pressure on their existing suppliers.

In addition, exporting the fast-track model outside Denmark would prove difficult, but was necessary if the model was to grow. By now NNE had a qualified and trusted supplier base in Denmark with experience in modular technology. Yet many of these suppliers would be too small to follow NNE internationally. NNE would probably have to go through a new learning curve with different partners. Culture was also a factor to take into account – successful strategy in Denmark could be difficult to replicate in other countries.

Finally, Voigt feared employees' motivation would be hard to sustain in the long run. Employees involved in the first fast-track project had already earned their stripes. The others would probably also be keen to achieve such a success, but it had already been done, and gaining a couple of months would not make such a big difference any more. NNE needed new energy to keep up the fast pace of the previous five years and maintain the teamgeist of the top teams.

Reflecting on how far they had come and how they had managed to overcome the employees' initial skepticism, Voigt commented:

> A lot of barriers in peoples' minds are just not real. Our job is to push those barriers.

---

[1] 1 Danish krone = US$0.15

EXHIBIT 1 • Pharmaceutical Research and Development Stages

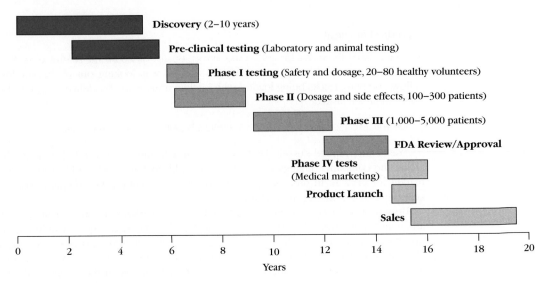

Sources: Scrip Magazine July/August 2003; PhRMA; Quintiles Transnational company presentation 2003.

EXHIBIT 2 • NNE Financial Profile

Unconsolidated data	31/12/2004 12 months DKK thousands	31/12/2003 12 months DKK thousands	31/12/2002 12 months DKK thousands	31/12/2001 12 months DKK thousands	31/12/2000 12 months DKK thousands	Average 5 years DKK thousands
Operating revenue/turnover	1,015,692	959,342	1,304,912	1,090,422	707,422	1,015,558
Profit (loss) before tax	56,408	4,201	91,330	53,953	23,379	45,854
P/L for Period [= Net Income]	39,184	4,105	52,605	37,454	15,004	29,670
Cash flow	51,262	11,421	58,017	43,204	18,594	36,500
Total assets	374,313	320,527	406,152	373,254	229,720	340,793
Shareholders funds	140,023	100,851	123,261	76,153	37,221	95,502
Current ratio (x)	1.56	1.33	1.35	1.25	1.21	1.34
Profit margin (%)	5.55	0.44	7	4.95	3.3	4.25
Return on shareholders funds (%)	40.28	4.17	74.09	70.85	62.81	50.44
Return on capital employed (%)	44.24	n.a.	89.22	62.82	59.53	63.95
Solvency ratio (%)	37.41	31.46	30.35	20.4	16.2	27.17
Employees	816	890	976	769	550	800

BRUYNZEEL KEUKENS

Mastering Complexity

NOVEMBER 2005, BRUYNZEEL KEUKENS HEADQUARTERS, BERGEN OP ZOOM, THE NETHERLANDS. A company board meeting was coming to an end. Jan Kessels was looking out of the window at the yellow company trucks being loaded with kitchen units ready for delivery. One of his fellow board members asked:

Are you actually suggesting we need to create a completely new supply chain?

"Yes, I am!" replied Kessels. He had been going through the myriad of strategic challenges facing the company. Strategically, Bruynzeel could no longer rely only on the construction market for growth. In order to grow and remain competitive, the company would have to adapt its kitchen cabinets to a different demand.

Bruynzeel's objectives were twofold: to double its market share in the Dutch retail market and maintain its leadership in the construction market. These two goals would require heavy investment in terms of both capacity and flexibility to fulfill the growing share of the retail channel in Bruynzeel's turnover. Retail customers were far more demanding than construction companies and increasingly requested custom solutions for the design of their kitchen. The mass production manufacturing set-up was no longer up to this task, it had to evolve.

Everyone on the board agreed with the idea of restructuring the supply chain. Bruynzeel was at a critical point in its history. The only remaining question was, how far should they go in the reorganization? Should they simply modify a few processes here and there or should they redefine the entire strategy from scratch? The discussion grew louder as every member of the board gave their opinion on what to do next.

Company Background

The Bruynzeel Company was created in the Netherlands in 1897 and specialized in carpentry, wooden floors and shipbuilding. In 1937 it also began to manufacture kitchens. In 1982, when it went bankrupt, Bruynzeel Keukens BV was created and began to compete in the low- and medium-range kitchen market in the Netherlands.

In 2004 sales reached nearly €108 million and were expected to grow by 12% (in value) for 2005. The company had almost 500 employees, 350 of which worked in production and order administration. Most of its turnover was made in business-to-business (construction market) and the remainder in retail.

Bruynzeel's success was based on three key factors: The first was excellent brand recognition in the Netherlands – 93% of Dutch customers were familiar with the brand; the second was the trust given by the construction industry – Bruynzeel was market leader in the Dutch construction market in 2004; and finally, a proven track record for the quality, reliability and performance of its kitchens.

Research Associate François Jäger prepared this case under the supervision of Professors Carlos Cordon and Corey Billington as a basis for class discussion rather than to illustrate either effective or ineffective handling of a business situation.

Dutch Kitchen Industry

After a period of consolidation in the Dutch kitchen market, by 2005 only three main national manufacturers remained. Bruynzeel was the market leader with a market share of 23% in volume and the second player was half its size. At the time, the Dutch kitchen industry was exporting €300 million to Germany and in turn, German manufacturers were exporting about the same volume to the Netherlands. With only 20 kitchen factories in the country, competition sourced some of its production from one of the 180 active German factories.

With about 2,000 stores, the Dutch kitchen market was saturated and Bruynzeel's management wanted to expand sales outside the Netherlands. Being the Dutch market leader was no longer sufficient; judging from the concentration of manufacturers in the European market, it was becoming apparent that the company's long-term survival and its independence relied upon its capacity to grow.

Bruynzeel's first attempt to go international was exporting just over the border to Belgium, less than 10 km from its plant. Belgium's market characteristics were different enough from those of the Netherlands to enable Bruynzeel to have a good first export experience. Unlike the Dutch market, the Belgium market was still very fragmented.

Market Strategy

The Construction Market

Over the years, Bruynzeel had earned a very good reputation and the trust of most construction companies in the Netherlands. By the end of 2005, it was the market leader in B2B in the Netherlands. Its market share was about 56% and rising. However, the company's management did not want to exceed 60% market share. The B2B channel was not part of its growth strategy.

The Dutch construction market was different from other countries. For example, houses were delivered "turnkey." Even for the rental market, houses and apartments had kitchens that were fully furnished at the landlord's expense. The tenant could even choose the kitchen within a certain price range. By 2005, the trend in the Dutch kitchen market was for the customer to ask for more and more extras. Generally, the landlord would agree to this as long as the tenant was willing to pay any additional costs out of his own pocket. He could then go to a Bruynzeel store and choose the kitchen and accessories he wanted.

The Retail Market

In 2005 Bruynzeel was making 31% in retail stores and 14% in wholesale. By October, the company owned 23 stores, 4 which had been created in 2004. Its market share in the retail channel was between 3% and 4% and the company's goal was to double this within five years. In 2000 the company launched a new store concept, different from a traditional kitchen store, which would enable the client to have a "fun" experience. The new layout had a big central kitchen with tables where clients could sit, relax and have a drink. Chefs were invited to present recipes and actually cook in this large kitchen. Around this central kitchen were different "universes," one for each line of kitchens. Every time a client entered the store, a hostess would come to him and direct him to a salesperson. The concept worked so well that 80% of the clients who sat with a salesperson would eventually buy a kitchen.

There were several reasons for expanding Bruynzeel's retail market. The first was strategic – the company was becoming ever more dependant on the construction market, if one or two of its bigger B2B customers were to move toward the competition, it could have a dramatic effect on the company's financial results. Furthermore, there was the profitability issue; selling kitchens in the retail market was far more profitable than selling them in the construction market. For instance, the average selling price of a fully equipped kitchen in the retail branch was 29 times higher than the standard white kitchen cabinets for the rental market (*refer to* **Figure 1** *below*).

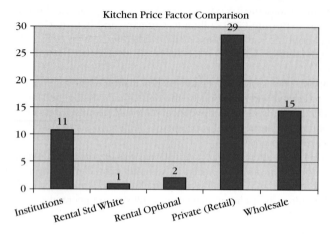

Figure 1   Kitchen Price Comparison per Type of Customer

Source: Bruynzeel Keukens

While Bruynzeel Keukens had traditionally seen itself as a kitchen manufacturer, the latest trends proved this vision wrong since the company was now in fact more of a kitchen seller. Such a transition in strategic vision did not come without issues and also meant making changes in the company's operations, from purchasing and manufacturing to logistics and distribution – everything would have to be restructured.

Operations

Strategic Change

Although Bruynzeel Keukens had been very successful at selling kitchens, this improvement in its commercial performance made it clear to the management that its operations had to improve dramatically to maintain those good results. When asked about the company's number one problem, the members of Bruynzeel's management team would reply unanimously, "Logistics!" The market dynamics had changed and so had the company's positioning.

Lead Time

One of the main problems for Bruynzeel was that synchronization between up- and downstream supply chains was poor. Customers were increasingly asking for better delivery performance but suppliers could not necessarily follow the trend. It was a difficult situation for the company. On average, the supplier lead time of four weeks was twice as long as what the customer required. Rush-in orders could also be entered into the system without prior notice from the sales department. This resulted in a logistical nightmare for the plant operations manager. With the ever-changing demand, keeping a sufficient level of the right stock keeping units (SKUs) was extremely difficult. The company had to serve two types of customers with different delivery requirements. Construction customers were easier to serve; the lead time to deliver to a house or an apartment was 20 weeks on average – there was plenty of room for rescheduling. Retail customers, however, were much more demanding and rescheduling was more difficult. To compensate for this uncertainty, production people tended to build up stocks.

Although this was a fairly acceptable short-term solution to fulfilling customer demand, it also involved several disadvantages. First, building stock cost money through inventory carrying costs. Second, the shorter product lifecycle resulted in raw materials and higher value semi-finished products rapidly becoming obsolete. By 2005, about 50% of the product offering was changing on a yearly basis. This led to another dilemma: On the one hand, the company had to lower its costs and face ever-faster product lifecycles and on the other, it had to make sure that it had enough SKUs available to support customer demand and 10 years' worth of product warranties. The complexity was increasing daily and the company had to do something about it –fast!

Variety

One of Bruynzeel's main competitive advantages was the extent of its offering. Each client could customize his kitchen the way he wanted, from the color of the cupboard to the style of the door handle – the possibilities were endless. For the basic kitchen line alone, there were more than 40 million different combinations. However, this advantage also had its drawbacks. The logistics necessary to handle such a complex manufacturing process were also becoming more difficult each day. As Kessels said:

> We should be able to make *our* problems our suppliers' problems.

A possible solution was to push the complexity upstream and let suppliers deal with it. Yet they were usually reluctant to insource complexity, and some were just not able deal with it. The purchasing department would have to find the right partners able to carry out this new mission.

Purchasing Strategy Implementation

By the end of 2005, following a new purchasing plan, the procurement team dealt directly with 300 suppliers out of 1,400, from an original pool of 1,800. It used ABC classification to rank the active suppliers: 26 were "A" suppliers with a spending of greater than €500,000 (the total "A" supplier spending represented 70% of the total spending); and 48 were "B" suppliers representing 20% of the spending. The spending per supplier was between €200,000 and €500,000.

The main criteria used to rate suppliers were logistics (on-time delivery), price and quality (number of defects). By this time, the purchasing department had been working on setting up partnerships with the top eight suppliers.

Kraljic Matrix

The other major tool used to classify suppliers was the Kraljic matrix (see below). The matrix was made of four quadrants and two axes (volume and risk). Each supplier fell in one of the quadrants.

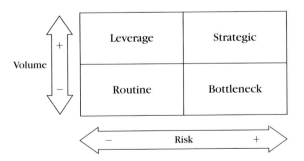

Figure 2 Kraljic Matrix

Strategic Quadrant

This quadrant included suppliers with high volume and high delivery risk. Most of the strategic suppliers were "A" suppliers with only a few "B" suppliers. These were very important to Bruynzeel and there was a clear need for close partnership with them.

Leverage Quadrant

Bruynzeel purchased a lot from leverage suppliers, yet the delivery risk was much lower than it was with strategic suppliers, therefore close monitoring was not needed. Leverage suppliers could be either "A" or "B."

Bottleneck Quadrant

This quadrant represented a problem to the purchasing department, since these were the suppliers with high delivery risk and low volume. Bruynzeel could not have a great impact on these suppliers since the volumes it purchased from them were small. Suppliers in this quadrant were best avoided.

Routine Quadrant

The suppliers in this quadrant had both a low turnover and a low delivery risk. The purchasing team would only look into this quadrant once in a while, unless the company was experiencing delivery problems.

Time for Change

The Bruynzeel management team had gone through a long process of identifying the key issues facing the company, listing possible solutions and implementation strategies. Supply chain management was undoubtedly on top of the list. The team needed to take important decisions fast; it could not afford to lose any more time in streamlining the supply chain. However, since Bruynzeel's supply chain was bigger than the company itself, it was possible that suppliers could help the company manage the necessary changes. Management simply needed to identify those suppliers and ensure that cooperation would follow. What exact processes and functions should be reorganized? More importantly, how far should Bruynzeel's management push the supply chain redesign? Would supplier involvement be absolutely necessary for success? If so, what would be the right approach?

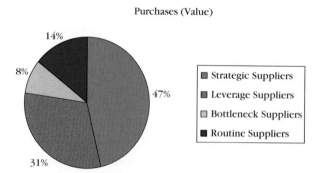

Figure 3   Spending per Type of Supplier

Source: Bruynzeel Keukens

EXHIBIT 1 • Bruynzeel Financial Results

Bruynzeel Keukens BV

Profit and loss account

(x € 1.000)	2004	2003	2002	2001
Sales	106.945	91.575	90.460	91.055
Added value	48.025	41.089	40.389	39.102
Business expenses	41.560	35.926	35.700	34.680
Results of operations	6.465	5.163	4.689	4.422
Financial expenses	27-	6-	59	236
	6.491	5.169	4.630	4.186
Company tax	2.271-	1.771-	1.584-	1.465-
	4.221	3.398	3.046	2.721
Extraordinary profits and losses	-	-	208	1.144-
	4.221	3.398	3.253	1.577
Results of paticipation	212	293-	720	703.-
Extraodinary Charges	843	843-		
Results after tax	5.276	2.262	3.973	874

	2004	2003	2002	2001
% Added value	44,91%	44,87%	44,65%	42,94%
% Results of operations	6,04%	5,64%	5,18%	4,86%
% Results after tax	4,93%	2,47%	4,39%	0,96%
Personnel (FTE)	489	477	497	517
Produced elements	670.004	638.256	642.009	595.000

Bruynzeel Keukens BV

Statement of assets and liabilities
(x € 1.000)

ASSETS	2004	2003	2002	2001
Fixed assets	18.415	19.460	19.531	20.806
Current assets	26.879	22.435	24.275	22.446
	45.294	41.896	43.806	43.252

LIABILITIES	2004	2003	2002	2001
Equity capital	32.555	28.296	27.910	24.145
Provision	763	875	885	1.963
Long-term liabilities	290	714	1.138	1.563
Short-term liabilities	11.686	12.011	13.873	15.582
	45.294	41.896	43.806	43.252
Investments fixed assets	1.967	4.117	2.673	2.274
Solvency	71,9%	67.5%	63,7%	55,8%

Source: Company information

Index

A

Activity, defined, 222
Activity durations, 222
  calculating, 226–228
Activity-on-arc (AOA), 223
Activity-on-node (AON), 223
Actual cost (AC), 236
Agco Corp., 40
Aggregate inventory value, average
  (AAIV), 255
Aggregate planning, 208, 317, 354,
  defined, 317
Aggregate project plan, 213–215
Air Canada, 127
Alaska Airlines, 113
Amazon, 273
American Airlines, 322
American Express, 113, 127
American Society for Quality, 163
American Standard, 127
ANOVA, 152, 164
Anticipation inventories,
  defined, 268
Anticyclic output, 302
Applied Materials, 247
Applied research, 16
As-is value stream map, 186, 189
Assembly line, 56
Assemble-to-order, 78
Assignable variation, 105
Auto Industry, 5, 6
Autodesk, 277
Available seat miles, 299

B

Backorders, 268
Balanced scorecard, 99–101
  benefits of, 99–100
  four major areas, 100
Bank of America, 125, 133
Barcoding and scanning, 274, 201
Batch size, 78
  and flow, 194
Beer game, 283–287
Benchmarking, 100–101, 137
Best Buy, 247, 257
Beta distribution, 227
Bias,

of forecast, 361
of measurement system, 152
Big Dig, 209
Binomial distribution, 112
Black and Decker, 38
Black belts, of six sigma, 162
Blue Cross, 321
Blueprinting, 329
Boeing, 38
Boston Consulting Group,124
Bottleneck resources, 416
Bottlenecks, 193, 195, 202,
  300, 329, 330
  defined, 327
  in a sequential process,
  326–329
Brainstorming, 153–155
Brainwriting, 154
Breakeven location model, 309
Breakthrough projects, 213
Buffer inventories, 268
Buffers, project and feeding,
  236–236
Bullwhip effect, 257–259
  business practices that contribute
  to, 258–259
Burger King, 77, 298
Business case, 217
Business model, 29–30
Business process design. See
  reengineering.
Business process outsourcing, 410
Business strategy, 29, 36, 37
  categories of, 31–32
  formulating, 27–30

C

c chart, 111–112
Campbell Soup, 272
Canon, 26–27, 38
Capacity
  defined, 298, 299,
  fixed, adding, 304
  and lean, 178, 192
  long-term planning, 299–304
  measures, 299
  planning, 15, 298
  for multiple outputs, 302–303

for services, 333–335
strategies, 300–304
and scheduling, 314, 352
short-run, techniques for
  increasing, 332
short-term alternatives, 331–333
short-term planning, 325–343
timing of increments, 304
Capacity requirements planning
  (CRP system), 318
Capital costs, 271
Carrying costs, 270
Cash conversion cycle, 255
Causal forecasting methods,
  365–376
Cause and effect diagrams, 126,
  136, 155–156, 160, 164, 202
Cellular production, 54, 69–76,
  179, 181
  advantages and disadvantages,
  71–73
  formation methods, 74–76
  layout, 73–74
  u-shaped cells, 179
Central Intelligence Agency, 29
Champions/sponsors, of six
  sigma, 163
Chance variation, 105
Channel assembly, 278
Chase, Richard, 82, 273
Chrysler, 5, 130, 297
Cisco Systems, 254, 262
Classification and coding, 76
Closed-loop supply chains,
  278–279
Closeness preferences, in job form
  layout, 65–66
CMI factory, 181
Coefficient of determination, 370
Columbia/HCA, 264
Commodities, 55
Community, location decision and,
  308–309
Competitiveness
  defined, 25
  global, 25–27
Continuous flow manufacturing,
  and value, 190–191

Continuous transformation process, 54, 55
Continuous process industries, 55
Contract manufacturers, 262, 307
Control, 104, 183
Control charts, 105–106, 136
    factors, 109
    for attributes, 111–112
    constructing, 108–112
    determining control limits, 108
    for variables, 107–108
Control limits, defined, 106
Control system,
    characteristics of, 104–105
Core capabilities, 29, 34, 37–41, 305
    strategically important parts
        of, 38
Core competencies, 29, 253, 262
Core process, 124
Corrective maintenance, 183
Correlation coefficient, 370
Cost
    and facility size, 301
    of goods, 272
    of inventory, 270–272
    minimization, 31–32
    reductions in, and
        responsiveness, 25
Cost-schedule reconciliation
        charts, 237
Cost-volume-distance model,
        66–69, 308
Cost-volume-profit model, 308
CPM (critical path method)
    defined, 220
    and project scheduling, 221–226
Creativity
    enhancing team, 154–155
    threats to, 154
Credit Crisis, 5, 26
Creeping breakeven, 41
Critical activities, 222, 224
Critical chain, 231–236
    defined, 235
    task-resource dependency, 235
Critical path, 224–235
    defined, 222
    project completion and, 223–225
Critical to quality trees, 126
Crosby, Phillip B., 19
Cross-docking, 33, 278
Cross-training, 333
CRP, 318

Cummins, 127
Cumulative capabilities
        model. See
    Sand Cone Model
Customer performance, 100
Customer relationship management
        (CRM), 273, 275
Customer requirements, 138
Customer satisfaction, 6, 12
    surveys, 113
Customer service, 12, 129
    See also responsiveness
Customization,
    continuum of, 21
    defined, 21
    See also mass customization
CVD model, 66–69, 308
Cyclical component, 356
Cycle inventories, defined, 269
Cycle time, 60, 188, 191, 328

D
D&H Manufacturing
        Company, 247
Dana Corporation, 34
Days of supply, 256
Decision support system
        (DDS), 132
Decoupling inventories, 268–269
Deere & Co., 40
Defects per million opportunities
        (DPMO), 125, 126, 136,
        143–147
Defects per opportunity, 145
Defects per unit, 145
Delayed differentiation, 278
Dell Computer, 6, 255,
        262, 278,
Delphi method, 354
Demand
    chain, 251
    forecast, 317
Deming Prize, 20
Deming, W. Edwards, 20
Dependability, competitiveness
        and, 24
Dependent variable, 365
Derivative projects, 213
Design capacity, 300
Design for assembly (DFA), 178
Design for manufacturability
        (DFM), 178
Design for Six Sigma, 128

Design of experiments,
        159–161, 202
    considerations of, 160–161
Detailed scheduling, 319
Development, 16
Direct Sales Model, 6
Dispatching, 319
Division of labor, 128
DMAIC improvement process,
        132–136, 202
Dover Corp., 197
Downstream, in supply chain, 249
DPMO, and process levels, 148
Drop shipping, 278
Drum-buffer-rope (DBR), 192
Dun and Bradstreet, 274
Dupont de Nemours, 17
Duty tours, 321

E
Early adopters, 15
Early finish times, 223
Early start times, 223
Early supplier involvement, 64
Earned value, 236–237
    of projects, control and,
        236–237
    variances, 236–237
Earned value chart, 237
eBay, 273
E-business, 273
E-commerce, 274
Economic order quantity (EOQ)
    assumptions, 290
    cautions regarding, 293–294
    defined, 290
    for inventory management,
        289–294
    and lean, 181, 184, 193
    model, 289–294
Economies of scale, 296
    defined, 301
Economies of scope, defined, 301
Educational services, resource
        scheduling, 321–322
    stages of operational, 98–99
Efficiency, 11, 22
    defined, 326–327
    formula, 61
Electronic data interchange
        (EDI), 273
Electronics industry, 247
Embassy Suite Hotels, 113

Enterprise resource planning (ERP), 250, 273, 275–277
Environment, 8, 97
EOQ model. *See* Economic order quantity (EOQ) model
Ericsson, 254
Event, 222
Exchange rates, 26
Expected completion time, 227
Expediting, 65, 319
Experience curves, 336
Exponential smoothing, 360–362
External setup time, 181
Extranets, 275

F
Facebook, 13
Facilitating good, 11, 12
Facility
  layout, 15
  location, 15
  size, planning, 300–301
Fail safing, and service guarantees, 85–87
Failure Mode and Effect Analysis (FMEA), 103–104, 202
Federal Express, 274
Feeding buffer, 235
Fender Guitars, 52–53
Finish times, and project completion, 223–225
Finished goods inventory, 270
Finite capacity scheduling, 298
Finite loading, 314
Fire alarm distributions, 334
First-to-market, 31
Fishbone diagrams. *See* Cause and effect diagrams
5S, 199
Flexibility, 22, 35
  defined, 21
  competitive advantages of, 21
Flextronics, 262, 307
Float, 225
Floating bottlenecks, 327
Floating workers, 320
Flow analysis, for products and services, 329–331
Flow shops, 54, 55, 56–62, 73
  advantages and disadvantages, 56–58
  defined, 56
  layout of, 58–62

Focus, 34–36, 80, 301
  areas of, 35
  defined, 34
  reasons for loss of, 36
Focused factory, 53
Focused organization, 54
Ford, 5, 130
Forecasting
  causal methods, 365–376
  demand, 317, 352
  error, 361, 366, 367
  exponential smoothing, 360–362
  method and influencing factors, 354–355
  moving averages, 358–360
  outliers, 368–369
  purposes and methods, 352–355
  qualitative, 354
  quantitative, 354
  relationship between variables, 366
  residual, 366
  seasonal component, 363
  trend component, 363
  weighted moving average, 359
  with regression model, 362–365
Forward buying, 258
Fraction-defective (p) charts, 111–112
Fujitsu Microelectronics, 277
Functional organizations, 53, 190
Functionality, 18

G
Gage R&R, 151
Gantt chart, 220, 232, 298, 314
Garbage in, garbage out (GIGO), 293
GATT, 261
General Electric (GE), 34, 130, 125, 126, 133, 274
General Motors (GM), 5, 130, 181
Geographic information system, 297
Global sourcing, 261–267
Global trends, 25–27
Goldratt, Eliyahu, 154, 192, 208, 231–236
Gravity method, and location, 313
Green belts, of six sigma, 162
Group technology, 69

H
Hammer, Michael, 33, 37, 129, 130
Harley-Davidson, 34, 177

Harper Hospital, scheduling at, 321
Hayes, Bob, 78
Hewlett-Packard (HP), 23, 34, 142, 177, 197, 208, 278
Hill, Terry, 35
Historical analogy, 354
Holding costs, 270
Hollowed out, 262
  defined, 39
Home Depot, 278
Honeywell, 125, 173–174,
Honda, 5, 38
Hospitals, resource scheduling, 320–321
House of quality, 138, 140–142
Hybrid shop, 77
Hybrid stage, in cellular production, 74

I
IBM, 34, 52, 53, 130–132, 262, 274, 248, 277, 308
Idle time, 60
Imitation, 17
Immelt, Jeffrey, 126
Improvement curves, 336
Improvement trajectories, 33–34
Independent variable, 365
Infinite loading, 314
Information outputs, economics of, 13
Information technology
  in supply chains, 272–277
Innovation, defined, 31
  product-process, 81
Innovativeness, 15–17
In-process inventories, 65
Inputs
  into transformation system, 9
Inspection for variables, 105
Inspection of attributes, 105
Intel, 358–359
Intensiva HealthCare, 34
Internal setup time, 181
International operations, location decision and, 306–308
International Organization for Standardization, 101
Internet, 274
Intranets, 275

Inventory
  annual costs graph, 292
  considerations, 267–272
  control, 4
  costs, 270–272
  forms of, 269–270
  functions of, 268–269
  and lean, 180–181
  problems with holding, 293–294
  turnover, 256
Inventory management, 15, 250,
      267–272
  decisions in, 272
ISO 9000, 101–102, 267
ISO 14000, 102

J
Jabil Circuit, 262, 307
Japan
  and lean, 176
  quality emphasis, 20
JC Penney, 33
JD Power and Associates, 113
Jeep, 297
JetBlue, 113
JIT. *See* Just-in-time
Job shop, 54, 55, 63–69,
      71, 73, 179
  advantages and disadvantages,
      64–65
  layout, 65–69
Jobbers, 54
Johnson Controls, 94, 256
Just-in-case, defined, 178
Just-in-time (JIT) systems, 176, 258
  in services, 198
  See also Lean
JVC, 32

K
Kaizen blitz, 199
Kanban, 197–198
  in services, 198
  See also Pull systems
Kmart, 4, 34
Kodak (Eastman), 40

L
Land's End, 4
Late-to-market, 31
Latest finish time, 224
Latest start time, 224
Layout analysis, purposes of, 54

Layout, and lean, 179
Layout, service operations, 54
Lead time
  defined, 318
Lean
  benefits of, 201–202
  compared with traditional
      systems, 177–184
  defined, 175
  history and philosophy of,
      175–177
  principles, 175
Lean management, 6, 15
Lean manufacturing, 250, 253
Lean organization, tools for
      perfection, 198–201
Lean production, 6, 175, 250
Lean Six Sigma, 173, 202
Learning curve, 335–341
  cumulative values, 339
  defined, 335
  factors that affect learning
      rate, 337
  tables, 338–339
  typical learning-forgetting
      pattern, 341
  unit values, 338
Lewis, Ken, 125
LG Electronics, 5
Life-cycle, 30, 35, 356
  analysis, 354
  of anticyclic outputs, 303
  curve, 30
  multiple outputs, 303
  product/process, 79–81
  of projects, 215–216
  and selection of transformation
      system, 80
Line balancing, 59–62, 188
Line of visibility, 330
Linearity, of measurement system,
      152, 202
LINEST Excel function, 367
Litton Industries, 60
Liz Claiborne, 246
LL Bean, 137
Load
  matrix, 68
  reports, 319
Loading, 319
Location
  and developing capabilities,
      305–306

  and logistics, 260–261
  long-term planning, 299–304
  modeling, 306–312
  planning strategies, 305–312
  of services, 312–313
Logical cell, 72
Logistics, 256–261
  defined, 256
Lot-size inventories, 269
Lot sizing rules, 190
Lou Dobbs, 261
Lower control limit (LCL), 106
Lucent, 254
Luen Thai Holdings Ltd., 246

M
Machine-part matrix, 75
Made-to-order customization, 21
Maintenance, and lean, 183–184
Maintenance, repair, and operating
      (MRO) supplies, 269
Make-to-order items, 77–78, 79, 192
Make-to-stock items, 77–78, 79
Malcolm Baldridge National Quality
      Award, 133
Management by exception, 106
Mapping, 329
Market evolution, 26–27
Market segmentation, 32
Martin Marietta, 53
Mass customization, 22–23
  Hewlett-Packard example, 23
  strategies, 22–23
Master black belts, of six sigma, 162
Master production schedule (MPS),
      317–318,
Master scheduling, 317–318
Matrix organizations, 216
Matsushita Electronics, 6
Mazak, 27
McDonalds, 7, 77, 86, 113
McKinsey and Company, 34
Measurement systems analysis, 136,
      149–152
  Repeatability, 151
  Reproducibility, 151
Medicaid, 321
Medicare, 321
Mercedes-Benz, 296, 306
Merrill Lynch, 127
Metcalfe's law, 273
Microsoft, 273, 274
Microsoft Project, 231–234

Milestone points, 220
Minimill, 296
Miniplant, 72
Mission, 100
Mission statements, 28–29
Mississippi Power, 208
Mixed-model assembly, and flow, 191–192
Model shops, 54
Modular design, 23
Monitoring and control, 13, 96 –97
Monster.com, 126
Moore's law, 273
Most likely time, 226
Motorola, 17, 125, 132, 133, 143, 149, 163
Moving averages, 358–360
MPS. *See* Master production schedule
Muda, 184
Multiple sourcing, 182
MySap modules, 276

N
NAFTA, 261
National Science Foundation, 24
Network, 222
New Balance, 40
Nike, 27, 262
Nominal cell, 72
Nominal Group Technique, 154
Normal distribution, 105
North Shore – Long Island Jewish Health System, 95
Northshore University Hospital, 135
Number-of-defects (c) charts, 111–112
Nynex, 124, 129

O
Off-diagonal transformation process, 79
Off-peak pricing, 320
Offshoring, 39–41, 254, 307
One factor at a time (OFAT), 159
Operation splitting, 315
Operational effectiveness, 98–99
    measures of, 99
Operational innovation, 7, 33, 37
Operations
    activities, 13–14

defined, 7
    major subject areas, 15
Opportunity costs, 271–272
Optimistic time, 226
Optimized production technology, 192
Order qualifier, 35
Order winner, 35
Ordering costs, 270
Osborn, Alex, 153
Outliers, 368–369
Output, 10–13
    See also Product
Outsourcing, 39–41, 249, 252, 253, 261, 262, 307
    and global sourcing, 261–267
Overall equipment effectiveness, 200–201
Overbooking, 322–325
Overlapping, 56
Owens Corning, 277

P
p chart, 111–112
Paced line, 58, 269
Package Products, 297
Palm Inc., 246, 278
Pareto analysis, 126, 164
Parts,
    organization into families, 69–71
Path, defined, 222
Path slack, 225
Performance frontier, 32–34
PERT (program evaluation and review technique)
    chart, 233
    defined, 220
    and project scheduling, 221–230
Pessimistic time, 226
Pilot cell, 74
Pipeline inventories, defined, 268
Planned value (PV), 236
Planning
    and control, and lean, 182–183
    horizon, 317
    See also Aggregate planning
Platform projects, 213
Point-of-sale (POS), 274
Poisson distribution, 112
Poka yoke, 200
Population, 106
Postponement, 23, 278
Precedence graph, 59

Precedence relationships, 222
Preemption, 315
Preventive maintenance, 183
Priority planning, 318
Process batch, 193
Process capability
    analysis, 156–159
    index, 157–159
    one-sided index, 159
Process centered organization, 130
Process control, 104–112
Process distributions, changes in, 108
Process flow analysis, 329
Process improvement, 15
    approaches for, 127–128
Process industries, defined, 54
Process map, 136, 174, 202
Process mapping, 126, 164,
Process monitoring, 97–104
Process owners, 163
Process performance measures, 142–143
Process shift, 143–144
Process sigma, 126, 147 149
    and DPMO, 148
    drivers of, 149
Process-flow analysis, 326–331
Procter and Gamble, 34
Procurement, defined, 263
Product
    characteristics, 11
    development process, 94
    development strategies, 31–32
    flows, 329–331
    ideas, generating new, 15–17
    life cycle, 30–31, 35–36
    and process life cycle, 31, 79–80
Production flow analysis (PFA), 74–75
Production line, 56
    balancing, 59–62
Production plan, defined, 317
Production system, 7–8, 97
    components of, 8, 14
Productivity, 306
Product-process matrix, 78–79
Product/Service design, and lean, 178
Project
    categories of, 213–214
    charter, 217
    and critical paths, 222–225, 227

Project (continued)
  defining a, 76, 211, 210–212
  examples of, 211
  life cycle, 215–216
  location of, 261
  operations, 54, 76–77
  plans, 217–221
  probabilities of completion,
    228–229
  as a process, 210
  schedule, 218
  scheduling, 221
  scheduling, PERT and CPM,
    221–230
  simulating, 229–231
  team organizing, 216–217
Project buffer, 235
Project management, 15
  defined, 210
  objectives, 219
  reasons for growth, 211–212
  software capabilities, 231–234
Project master schedule, 220
Project planning, 212–221, 221
  known activity times, 222–226
  outputs, 222
  unknown activity times, 226–231
Project portfolio, 50–51, 213–215
Project scope, 210
Psychology of waiting, 341–343
Pull systems defined, 251, 195–196
  See also Kanban; Just-in-time
    systems
Purchase strategy, 17
Purchasing/procurement, 13,
    263–265
  effective practices, 264–265
Pure research, 16
Pure services, 11, 12

Q
QFD, 137–142, 185
  overview, 138–140
Quality
  benefits and costs, 19
  competitiveness and, 19
  control, 15
  costs, categories of, 19
  defined, 18–19
  defining and measuring, 18–19
  Japanese approaches to, 20–21
  and lean, 183
  in services, 112–114

statistical control of, 105–112
Quality function deployment.
    See QFD
Quebec City, relocating the blood
    bank, 312
Queue
  formation process, 341
  psychology of waiting,
    341–343
Queuing theory, 54, 341

R
RACI matrix, 218–219, 221
RAND Corporation, 354
R&D. See Research and
    development.
Rational subgrouping, 106
Random variation, 356
Raw materials, 9, 269
Red Cross,7, 312
Reengineering, 124, 128–132
  concept keywords, 130
  defined, 130
Region, location decision and,
    306–308
Regression analysis
  Adjusted R^2, 375
  assumptions, 370
  backward selection, 375
  coefficient of determination, 370
  developing regression models,
    373–376
  extrapolation, 371
  forward selection, 375
  linear trend multiplicative
    model, 362–365
  multicollinearity, 373
  multiple coefficient of
    determination, 372
  multiple regression model, 365,
    372–373
  relationship between
    variables, 366
  simple regression, 362–365,
    365–370
  transforming data, 373–375
  using regression model, 371
Reliability
  and maintenance, 15
Remainder cell, 71, 74
Remanufacturing, 263
Repeatability, 151
Reproducibility, 151

Research
  applied, 16
  and development (R&D), 15–17
  mortality curve of, 16–17
  product, 17
  projects, 214
  pure, 16
Resources, scheduling in services,
    320–322
Responsiveness, 24–25
Revenue management, 300,
    322–325
Reverse auctions, 264
Reverse engineering, 38
Reverse logistics, 263, 278–279
RFID (radio frequency identifi-
    cation), 248, 274, 201
Rich Products, 248
Rickard Associates, 53
Right-to-work laws, 306
Risk cost, 271
Risk management, 209
Roberts, Paul Craig, 261
Robotics, 7, 301
Rough-cut capacity planning, 318
Routing problem, 259
Royal Philips Electronics, 5

S
Safety stocks, 268
Safeway, 23
Samsung, 6, 247
Sand cone model, 36–37, 53, 298
SAP, 275–276
Sara Lee Corp., 43
Scandinavian Airlines, overbooking,
    323–325
Scanning and barcoding, 274
Schedule planning, 15
Schedule management, 316–325
Scheduling
  capacity and, 314, 353
  projects, with PERT/CPM, 220,
    221–230
  sequence of activities, 316–319
Schonberger, Richard J., 18
SCI Systems, 262
Scope change, 209
ScottishPower, 164
Sears, 4, 34
Seasonality, 302, 356
Second-to-market, 31
Selectron, 307

Sequencing
  defined, 319
  and flow, 191–192
Sequential process, defined, 327
Sequential production system, 196
Service, 12
  blueprint, 82, 331
  capacity planning for, 333–335
  characteristics, 11
  controlling quality, 112–114
  defections, 113–114
  defined, 11
  flows, 329–331
  gaps, 84–85
  guarantees & fail safing, 85–86
  kanban/JIT in, 198
  life cycle, 30–32
  pure, 11, 12
  scheduling, 319–325
Service level agreements, 86
Service matrix, 83–84
Service organizations
  layout, 54
  locating, 312–313
  process design in, 81–87
Setup costs, 270
7-Eleven, 23
Sharp, 6
Shewhart, Walter A., 105
Shingo, Shigeo, 181
Single-sourcing, 182
Site, and location decision, 309–310
Six Sigma, 6
  becoming certified, 163
  common tools, 135
  customizing programs, 164
  defined, 133
  and DMAIC, 132–135
  example project, 135–136
  financial benefits, 127
  history, 132–133
  and lean, 175
  phases
    analyze, 152–159
    control, 162
    define, 136–142
    improve, 159–162
    measure, 142–152
  in practice, 127, 162–164
  process compared with 3 sigma,
    148
  process shift assumption,
    143–144

roles, 162–163
  training, 127
  tools and methodologies, 135
Slack time, 225–226
SMED, 181
Smith, Adam, 128
Smith, Bill, 132
Sole-sourcing, 266
Sony, 6, 32, 38
Southside Hospital, 125–126,
    147, 160
Spaghetti chart, 179
Speed. See Responsiveness
Sport Obermeyer, 278, 297
Spreadsheet analysis: simulating
    project completion times,
    229–231
Stability, of measurement system,
    152
Stakeholder, 211
Stakeholder analysis, 126, 164
Standard deviation, 106
Stanton, Steven, 130
Start times, and project completion,
    223–224
Station task assignments, 62
Statistical quality (process) control,
    21, 105–112
Stockless purchasing, 266
Stockout costs, 271
Stockouts, 268
Storage costs, 271
Strategy, 9, 100, 298
  formulation, 27–30
  frameworks, 30–37
  maps, 101–102
  of mass customization, 22
  purchase, 17
  second-to-market, 31
Stretch goals, 137
Stretched-S curve, 30, 215
Student syndrome, 233
Suboptimization, 9, 27–30
Sun Microsystems, 127
Sunk costs, 293
Super Valu, 297
Supplier
  Audits, 267
  certification and audits,
    266–267, 182
  characteristics of good, 265
  and lean, 182
  management, 265–267

relationships, 266
  selection, 265–266
Supply chain,
  closed-loop supply chains,
    278–279
  defined, 249
  design, 256–261
  partnerships, 246
  performance, measures,
    254–256
  simplified, 257
  strategy, 252–256
Supplies, 9
Supply chain management
    (SCM), 13, 176,
    249–252, 300,
  benefits, 254
  defined, 259
  factors driving need for, 254
  goal, 251
  information technology,
    272–277
  strategic need for, 253–254
  success, 277–279
Suzuki, 181
Synchronous manufacturing,
    175, 192
System, 7
  See also Production system
System flow times, 63
Systems perspective, 8–9

T
Taguchi Methods, 161–162
Takt time, 60, 191
Tasks, critical/slack, 221
Taiwan Semiconductor
    Manufacturing Company, 247
Teams, and cellular
    layout, 71
Texas Instruments, 94
Theory of constraints,
    192–195, 231
  ten guidelines, 192–195
Third-party logistics (3PL), 252
Thompson, Leigh, 154–155
3M, 38, 126
Throughput time, 327
Time series analysis, 354,
    355–365
  components of, 355–358
To-be value stream map, 189
Toshiba, 247

Total productive maintenance (TPM), 184, 200–201
Total quality management (TQM), 21, 130, 253
Toyota Motor Company, 5, 142, 250, 267, 172, 175
    kanban at, 197
Toyota Production System, 174, 175–176, 181, 250
TQC. *See* Total quality management (TQM)
Trade deficit, 26
Trade-offs, transportation vs. location, 260–261
Trade promotions, 258–259
Transfer batch, 193
Transformation system, 8–9
    defining basic forms, 54
    design considerations, 54
    forms of, 55–77
    selection of, 77–81
    volume/variety considerations, 77–79
Transit inventories, defined, 268
Transportation, 259–260
    decision factors, 260
    location trade-offs, 260
    modes of, 259
Traveling salesman problem, 259
Trend, 356
    Excel function, 368
TRW, 126, 147
Turns, 256
Tyco International, 127

U
Upper control limit (UCL), 106
Upstream, in supply chain, 249
Upton, David, 21

Urban alarm services, resource scheduling, 321
Utilization, 11, 326

V
Valley Baptist Hospital, 174
Value, 6, 12, 37, 184
    defined, 14
Value, adding, 7, 10, 186, 202
Value analysis, of purchases, 264
Value chain, 251
Value, defining, 184–185
Value, flow of, 190–195
Value stream,
    identifying, 185–190
    map, 185–190
        symbols, 187–188
    and pull systems, 195–198
Variables, control charts for, 107–108
Vendor analysis, 265–266
Vendor-managed inventory, 248, 259
Venture, 262
ViewStar Corporation, 94
Virginia Mason Medical Center, 172, 175, 184
Virtual cell, 72, 73
Virtual organization, 53
Vision statements, 28–29
Visual factory, 199
Vizio, 6
Voice of the customer, 126, 136, 138, 140, 185
Voice-over IP, 138

W
Wagoner Jr., Richard, 5
Waiting line theory, 54

Waiting, principles of, 342–343
Wal-Mart, 4, 6, 23, 33, 34, 248, 274, 278
Waste, 184
    categories of, 184–185
Web. *See* World Wide Web
Weighted moving average, 359
Weighted score location model, 310–312
Welch, Jack, 126
West Babylon school district, 155–160
Wheelwright, Steve, 78
White elephant, 80
Work breakdown structure (WBS), 218–219
Workforce, and lean, 177, 179
Work-in-process, 57, 58
    inventory, 269
World Trade Organization (WTO), 26
World Wide Web (WWW), 7, 82, 274
World-class suppliers, 267

X
Xerox, 137, 173, 202

Y
Yellow belts, of six sigma, 163
Yield, 200, 300
Yield management, 300, 322–325

Z
Zero defects, 83
Zoran Corp, 247

Area Under the Normal Distribution

Example: the area to the left of $Z = 1.34$ is found by following the left Z column down to 1.3 and moving right to the 0.04 column. At the intersection read 0.9099. The area to the right of $Z = 1.34$ is $1 - 0.9099 = 0.0901$. The area between the mean (dashed line) and $Z = 1.34 = 0.9099 - 0.5 = 0.4099$.

Z	0.00	0.01	0.02	0.03	0.04	0.05	0.06	0.07	0.08	0.09
0.0	0.5000	0,5040	0.5080	0.5120	0.5160	0.5199	0.5239	0.5279	0.5319	0.5359
0.1	0.5398	0.5438	0.5478	0.5517	0.5557	0.5596	0.5639	0.5675	0.5714	0.5753
0.2	0.5793	0.5832	0.5871	0.5910	0.5948	0.5987	0.6026	0.6064	0.6103	0.6141
0.3	0.6179	0.6217	0.6255	0.6293	0.6331	0.6368	0.6406	0.6443	0.6480	0.6517
0.4	0.6554	0.6591	0.6628	0.6664	0.6700	0.6736	0.6772	0.6808	0.6844	0.6879
0.5	0.6915	0.6950	0.6985	0.7019	0.7054	0.7088	0.7123	0.7157	0.7190	0.7224
0.6	0.7257	0.7291	0.7324	0.7357	0.7389	0.7422	0.7454	0.7486	0.7517	0.7549
0.7	0.7580	0.7611	0.7642	0.7673	0.7704	0.7734	0.7764	0.7794	0.7823	0.7852
0.8	0.7881	0.7910	0.7939	0.7967	0.7995	0.8023	0.8051	0.8078	0.8106	0.8133
0.9	0.8159	0.8186	0.8212	0.8238	0.8264	0.8289	0.8315	0.8340	0.8365	0.8389
1.0	0.8413	0.8438	0.8461	0.8485	0.8508	0.8531	0.8554	0.8577	0.8599	0.8621
1.1	0.8643	0.8665	0.8686	0.8708	0.8729	0.8749	0.8770	0.8790	0.8810	0.8830
1.2	0.8849	0.8869	0.8888	0.8907	0.8925	0.8944	0.8962	0.8980	0.8997	0.9015
1.3	0.9032	0.9049	0.9066	0.9082	0.9099	0.9115	0.9131	0.9147	0.9162	0.9177
1.4	0.9192	0.9207	0.9222	0.9236	0.9251	0.9265	0.9279	0.9292	0.9306	0.9319
1.5	0.9332	0.9345	0.9357	0.9370	0.9382	0.9394	0.9406	0.9418	0.9329	0.9441
1.6	0.9452	0.9463	0.9474	0.9484	0.9495	0.9505	0.9515	0.9525	0.9535	0.9549
1.7	0.9554	0.9564	0.9573	0.9582	0.9591	0.9599	0.9608	0.9616	0.9625	0.9633
1.8	0.9641	0.9649	0.9656	0.9664	0.9671	0.9678	0.9686	0.9693	0.9696	0.9706
1.9	0.9713	0.9719	0.9726	0.9732	0.9738	0.9744	0.9750	0.9756	0.9761	0.9767
2.0	0.9772	0.9778	0.9783	0.9788	0.9793	0.9798	0.9803	0.9808	0.9812	0.9817
2.1	0.9821	0.9826	0.9830	0.9834	0.9838	0.9842	0.9846	0.9850	0.9854	0.9857
2.2	0.9861	0.9864	0.9868	0.9871	0.9875	0.9878	0.9881	0.9884	0.9887	0.9890
2.3	0.9893	0.9896	0.9898	0.9901	0.9904	0.9906	0.9909	0.9911	0.9913	0.9916
2.4	0.9918	0.9920	0.9922	0.9925	0.9927	0.9929	0.9931	0.9932	0.9934	0.9936
2.5	0.9938	0.9940	0.9941	0.9943	0.9945	0.9946	0.9948	0.9949	0.9951	0.9952
2.6	0.9953	0.9955	0.9956	0.9957	0.9959	0.9960	0.9961	0.9962	0.9963	0.9964
2.7	0.9965	0.9966	0.9967	0.9968	0.9969	0.9970	0.9971	0.9972	0.9973	0.9974
2.8	0.9974	0.9975	0.9976	0.9977	0.9977	0.9978	0.9979	0.9979	0.9980	0.9981
2.9	0.9981	0.9982	0.9982	0.9983	0.9984	0.9984	0.9985	0.9985	0.9986	0.9986
3.0	0.9987	0.9987	0.9987	0.9988	0.9988	0.9989	0.9989	0.9989	0.9990	0.9990
3.1	0.9990	0.9991	0.9991	0.9991	0.9992	0.9992	0.9992	0.9992	0.9993	0.9993
3.2	0.9993	0.9993	0.9994	0.9994	0.9994	0.9994	0.9994	0.9995	0.9995	0.9995
3.3	0.9995	0.9995	0.9995	0.9996	0.9996	0.9996	0.9996	0.9996	0.9996	0.9997
3.4	0.9997	0.9997	0.9997	0.9997	0.9997	0.9997	0.9997	0.9997	0.9997	0.9998